Dvorak's Guide to DOS and PC Performance

Dvorak's Guide to DOS and PC Performance

John C. Dvorak
Nick Anis

Osborne **McGraw-Hill**
Berkeley   New York   St. Louis   San Francisco
Auckland Bogotá   Hamburg   London   Madrid
Mexico City   Milan   Montreal   New Delhi   Panama City
Paris   São Paulo   Singapore   Sydney
Tokyo   Toronto

Osborne **McGraw-Hill**
2600 Tenth Street
Berkeley, California 94710
U.S.A.

Osborne **McGraw-Hill** offers software for sale. For information on software, translations, or book distributors outside of the U.S.A., please write to Osborne **McGraw-Hill** at the above address.

Dvorak's Guide to DOS and PC Performance

4567890 DOC 9987654321

ISBN 0-07-881658-0

For information about our audio products, write us at:
Newbridge Book Clubs, 3000 Cindel Drive, Delran, NJ 08370

To Parents Everywhere

CONTENTS

I'm going to have to explain this to my wife, and my children, maybe even my mother. Why would I write a foreword to a book about DOS? Why would a staid, middle-aged guy like me call attention to a book by a gonzo columnist like John C. Dvorak? What could a wannabe farmer/rancher in the mountains of Montana have to say about a book born and bred in the high-tech, fast-lane world of Silicon Valley?

If you read *Dvorak's Guide to PC Telecommunications*, like this book — a collaboration by John C. Dvorak and Nick Anis — you should have a clue. That work gave a whole new meaning to the *magnum* in *magnum opus*, covering the field of telecommunications for personal computers like nothing before or since. This weighty tome follows suit, and well it might. If you want to give your readers, in John's own words, "more than you wanted to know about DOS," the *opus* better be *magnum*.

Magnum it might be, but this is more than just another big book; it's the most thorough coverage of DOS and DOS-related topics that I've ever seen between two covers. You might be able to pick up most of the information by getting every back issue of *PC Magazine*, but you'd need a boxcar to store them, and looking up something could be an all-day job. Those of you who have become telecommunications mavens (thanks to the aforementioned *Dvorak's Guide to PC Telecommunications*, of course) could download all the DOS-related forums and threads and SIGs from CompuServe and BIX and PC MagNet, but you'd be out a few big ones for telephone bills and connect charges, you'd need a monster disk to store it all, and it would still be a Herculean task to find a particular item. You'd still have to download dozens of programs and their documentation, to equal the software that comes with this book.

But all those nuggets are here, neatly packaged and organized. If you're new to computers, this book won't teach you how to use DOS — there are other books for that (ahem). But if you've learned your way around the C> prompt, this book can help you get the most out of DOS and your computer.

If you absorb the information in *Dvorak's Guide to DOS* and use just a few of the programs included with it, you should find yourself getting more work done every day without adding any hardware or software to your system. Some call that increased productivity; I call it a good investment.

—Van Wolverton
Alberton, Montana
Author of *Running MS-DOS*

ACKNOWLEDGMENTS

This book, like most books in the Dvorak series, is not simply the work of Dvorak and Anis. From the start, our goal was to have both very detailed and very broad coverage of DOS performance tools, techniques, and commands, as well as some detailed coverage of other operating systems. Without numerous and substantial research from many of the top minds in the PC world, such an encyclopedic reference could not have been completed. Because of this, our acknowledgments of the many able minds who provided us technical advice and assistance serve as a virtual "Who's Who" in the industry and may well be one of the more valuable listings in the book.

We received technical material and comments from as many as ten different experts on some chapters, and all chapters underwent technical editing and review from yet other veterans of the PC wars. The entire process was managed by the coauthors, Nick Anis and John Dvorak, and expertly edited by Bob Wanetick and the crack staff at Osborne/McGraw-Hill, overseen by editor in chief Jeff Pepper.

Our profound thanks to the staff of Osborne/McGraw-Hill's production department who put in The Big OT necessary to bring such a monster to press by deadline. Special thanks to Deborah Wilson, Judy Wohlfrom, Stefany Otis, Lance Ravella, Marcela Hancik, Linda Streeter, and our technical editor, Jeff Nelson.

We would never have made it without Madhu Prasher's and Erica Spaberg's incredible efforts in organizing the book's production. Special thanks to Jill Pisoni, Emily Rader, Lisa Kissinger, Ann Kameoka, and Kendal Anderson for their efforts on the book.

And a fond thank you to Ann Pharr, who always answers Osborne's phone with a smile and who helped us track down our editor, Jeff Pepper, on at least 30,000 different occasions.

Our wives endured a special hell reserved especially for them. Aside from the usual project terror, Mimi Dvorak was given the chore of prepping and editing some of the most complicated chapters. Patty Anis helped keep Nick on his diet so that he could lose 40 pounds and 5 inches. . . .

John Bean whipped the installation files and software into shape with no small degree of agony. It is largely owing to his uncanny talents that this book's installation program is the best yet.

Father-and-son team Bud and Alex Aaron provided research assistance in a number of areas of this book, including sections on understanding DOS and how it works, upgrading PCs, OS/2, BASIC, and DR-DOS and Concurrent DOS. Bud and Alex served as our resident DOS experts and were a great help with the DOS command reference as well.

Our thanks to Craig Menefee, as well as Chuck Guzis, of Sydex Software, whose research was also crucial to our chapter on understanding DOS and how it works.

On the subject of menu programs, Mark Perkel of Computer Tyme, author of Mark's Menu, and Delta Technology and Fifth Generation Systems, publishers of Direct Access, provided expert insight into the intricacies of menu programs.

DCA/Crosstalk's documentation expert, Maria Forrest, did an outstanding job helping us explain the leading DOS shells, on which we also received help from Mike Ceranski, of Athena Software, and King Lee, Bob Kimball, Henry Hernandez, Rick James, and Todd Walker, of XTree Systems.

Tom Anderson helped us prepare the chapter on DOS utility programs, and we received tons of cooperation from Doug Marento, of Fifth Generation Systems; Anna Shannon, Kraig Lane, Bob Chappelear, and Peter Norton, of Peter Norton Computing/Symantec; and Ellen Pfeifer, of Central Point Software. As publishers of absolutely the pinnacle titles in the field, what these people don't know about DOS utilities hasn't been developed yet.

Being coauthor of the superb DOS-extension shareware program 4DOS, Tom Rawson probably knows the innards of DOS as well as anyone walking. We tapped him for information in the system startup and environment chapter—and rather successfully, we think. Thanks, Tom.

Alfred Glossbrenner, Mimi Dvorak, and Tom Anderson ganged up to research the particularly thorny issues of multitasking and task switching.

Author Lenny Bailes worked with Teresa Meyers and Stanton Kay of DESQview publisher Quarterdeck Office Systems, to unwind the tangles in our memory-management section as well as in our chapter section on DESQview itself.

Jack Rickard, publisher of the BBS publication *Boardwatch Magazine*, teamed up with Colorado Memory Systems to treat the subject of backup software, hardware, and strategies—an increasingly crucial area for operators of on-line services and LAN managers and for the increasing number of individuals whose data value exceeds their hardware investment.

Craig Menefee, Tom Anderson, and *Boardwatch Magazine* columnist Dave Hakala all worked on keying us to some of the gaps in our section on data security.

Tom Sheldon, author of *Windows: The Complete Reference* and *Windows Made Easy,* along with Maria Forrest, of DCA/Crosstalk, and Ed Meadows, of Asymetrix, were all part of our Windows review team.

Authors Bud Aaron and Robert LaFore helped us explain OS/2, which was changing faster than we could write about it.

Author and Bostonian Werner Feibel was our UNIX guru. Werner did an outstanding job helping us whip our UNIX section into shape. No Steve's Ice Cream this time, Werner—Nick's on a diet.

The gang at Digital Equipment Corporation, including Steve O'Brien, Rick Spitz, Judy Finman, and Linda Giragosian, helped us sort through mountains of VMS operating system material to put it into a presentable summary form. Additionally, Digital Press and authors James F. Peters III and Patrick J. Holmay even offered us the use of their command reference from their book, *The VMS User's Guide.*

Mary Lorram, of Digital Research, provided valuable assistance in our coverage of their DR-DOS and Concurrent DOS products.

For our section on networks, we again turned to Mark Perkel, of Computer Tyme, publishers of Mark's Menu. Artisoft, developer of the LANtastic local area network, was a big help with information in this area, as well.

Writing about diagnostics and benchmarks was made easy with help from TouchStone Software's (CheckIt!), Rob Whittle and Shannon Jenkins as well as from Dariana Technology's (System Sleuth) Paul Bauman and Steven Leno.

Deborah Buurman and Bruce Shafer had all the answers to our questions on disk caching, RAM disks, defragmenters, and optimizers.

Dave Hakala served as our resident text editor expert, as one who uses them, along with Sammy Mitchell, of SemWare, publisher of QEdit, one of the most popular programmer's text editor shareware packages, as one who creates them. Special thanks also to Eric Meyer, author of VDE, an extremely fast and compact word processor, for his insight and for making the program available to our readers.

Coverage of the DOS DEBUG program is one of the best things in this book. Best-selling author Jim Turley and Chuck Guzis were our sources of inside information in this area.

Batch files is another subject we wanted to cover well in this book, and it took a talented gang of coaches to do it. No one knows batch files better than Lee Pelletier, of Wenham Software, publisher of BAT.COM, and Tom Campbell of Hyperkinetix, Inc., publisher of Builder—with the notable exception, perhaps, of Craig Menefee, who helped as well. Even Tom Anderson pitched in along with Tom Rawson, of JP Software, and Mike Callahan (Dr. File Finder) with tips on how to make magic with batch files.

For device drivers and command processors, we turned to Dave Hakala; Hector Santos, of Sentronics Software; Tom Campbell; Chuck Guzis; Eric Cockrell, of Thumper Technologies; Mark Epley, of Traveling Software; and Charlie Burman.

We also got lots of help from the folks at Northgate Computer Systems, who provided us with an evaluation system for testing. Special thanks to Northgate's Stan Kalisher and Craig Keefner. Thanks in this department also goes to Bob Gilogowski and the people at Grid Systems Corporation, and to the folks at Packard Bell.

Thanks to Iomega Corporation, makers of the fabulous Bernoulli box storage system.

Special thanks to Ronald J. Bandy for his support and to Karen Novak and the people at U.S. Robotics, who were always there to answer our questions.

Our thanks to Alfred Glossbrenner for advice, counsel, friendship, and assistance in making sense of some of the user guides in Appendix D.

Also, thanks to Doug Hay and Phil Katz, of PKware, developer of the PKZIP compression utilities; Paul Masters of Freemont Communications, our fax-board man; and Tanya Van Dam, of Microsoft, for all the support, encouragement, and attention.

We also owe thanks to Logitec, Delta Technology, and Craig and Sammy Menefee, who helped us more times than we can count.

Thanks to Applied Micro Systems Technology, publishers of Point & Shoot Backup/Restore, for rushing a special version of their program with data compression just for this book.

Special thanks to Brian Miller and Tess Heder, of Channel One BBS. We want also to thank our friend Dr. File Finder, aka Mike Callahan, who helped us countless times in accumulating files and sorting through material.

And, of course, we thank the authors of the bound programs included with this book. Their efforts are what made this book possible. Some of the programs are the result of a team of authors. Among those we owe our sincere thanks to are Phil Katz, Henry Hernandez, Eric Cockrell, Paul

Mace, Chuck Guzis, Mark Epley, G. Allen Morris III, Eric Meyer, Steve Grant, Andrew Rossmann, Kim Kokkonen, and Bruce Shafer.

And, finally, special thanks to Martha Pepper, who lent us her husband evenings and weekends, and to Joey Anis, age 3, who promised not to press Nick's computer's reset button again until the book was finished.

November 1990

John C. Dvorak—Albany, California
Nick Anis, Jr.—Diamond Bar, California

Let's be frank: This book is a killer. Besides telling you more than you ever wanted to know about DOS and how to use it to make your machine run faster and more efficiently, we throw in some of the most important software you can own. The software is worth many times the price of the book. You get disk-caching software, the original XTree program (the world's greatest disk organizer) and over 70 other programs.

This book shows you how to wring the maximum performance from the hardware you already own without spending additional thousands of dollars to upgrade to the next IBM PC-compatible "power" platform. It's designed to provide a clear, practical guide to using inexpensive software utilities, little-known standard DOS features, and some simple insider tips and usage techniques to increase performance by 15 to 20 percent or more—on the cheap. You don't have to be a programmer, technician, or rocket scientist to read, enjoy, and benefit hugely from this book. It is specifically designed to give nontechnical users a more effective understanding of DOS while answering, in English, some of the recurring questions many would love to ask—if they knew how and whom to ask.

For the technical reader disenchanted with the DOS reference manual, this book provides the most complete DOS command reference available and provides extremely thorough coverage of DEBUG, EDLIN, and DOS batch file programming. It serves as an excellent reference resource, covering a number of areas virtually ignored elsewhere in print.

During the past decade, wave after wave of new PC models, each offering increased speed, increased capacity, increased everything, have been introduced. Unfortunately, few users maximize the power of their existing systems before buying into the next upgrade. And, often, just putting off that upgrade purchase by a few months can make a difference of *thousands* of dollars in the prices they eventually pay: Just a few months after the initial premium introductory prices, the cost of the next platform always falls dramatically. If you can tune up the old VW model to Porsche performance, it makes dollars and sense to do so.

Getting the most out of a system isn't a trend or fad—it's just plain good sense. But these days, it's more difficult than ever. The IBM PC platform has matured. Thousands of products push the traditional 640KB memory constraint, disk access, and available processor speed to the limit. Getting a number of these applications to work well together is no longer a trivial task. As a result, using the typical system as it comes "right out of the box," with no tweaking, tuning, or adjustment, could be a big mistake. In the long run, it could cost you hundreds of hours of wasted time and untold amounts of wasted money.

For example, every day tens of millions of hard disk users force their disks to strain mightily to satisfy their needs. No one ever told them that an inexpensive—or even free—disk-caching program could not only deliver superior performance but save wear and tear on the disk drive mechanism, as well.

Or consider the problem of memory management. Managing available memory is just as important to getting the most out of a system. DOS's 640KB memory barrier is being strained to its limits by a growing number of high-powered, RAM-hungry applications. Meanwhile, memory-resident background (or TSR, for terminate-and-stay-resident) programs compete for what's left—and there are hundreds of them to choose from.

To make everything work efficiently together, today's PC user needs a memory-management package. This kind of software is almost essential in today's computing environment. Yet most users have only begun to learn the necessary techniques. Memory managers can give your applications all the expanded memory they need by relocating TSR programs, device drivers, and other background programs from DOS's conventional memory to "high memory," also known as UMBs (upper memory blocks). The results can be astonishing.

HIGH-POWER TIPS

These are only a few of the most obvious ways to get the most out of any system. There is much more ground to cover to bring yourself fully "up to speed." This book was designed to show you how to do it.

Whether you're a power user or a technophobe, we'll guide you gently along the winding road to top-flight DOS and PC performance. We'll do it in an organized way so that you don't have to thumb through 10 or 20 index references to find the information you need.

If you're not sure what a disk cache is or why you should have one, you'll discover the answer—and much, much more—between these covers. For those who want more technical detail, this book will help you keep up with the latest PC trends without buying a pocket-protector pen holder and a set of crooked-frame glasses.

You don't have to devote your life to system tweaking and power performance. All you need is a bit of information and the proper tools. Even the more technical chapters are written so that an amateur can understand them. Each chapter offers useful analogies, examples, and actual reproductions of what you'll see on your own screen when using these techniques.

You'll also find a bit of background and history. Not only is this interesting, but it also helps explain why things are the way they are. You'll enjoy the anecdotes and insider observations. You'll also find detailed discussions of pertinent products and some tips on what to look for in the immediate future.

Throughout the book, we discuss real products, offer practical examples and hands-on tips, and alert you to little-known user traps. You may find just skimming through the book's READ.ME sections to be an interesting education.

WHAT YOU'LL FIND IN THIS BOOK

There are 900-plus pages in this book offering the broadest coverage of MS/PC-DOS and systems that operate under DOS, as well as information on other advanced operating systems running on the IBM PC platform. Coverage in the book includes:

- A detailed history of DOS and an explanation of how DOS works.

- A complete DOS command reference covering all versions of MS-DOS, from the original to the latest, as well as Digital Research's DR-DOS 5.0.

- A comprehensive discussion of DOS menu programs, complete with detailed screen shots covering all of the leading commercial and shareware menu systems.

- A thorough explanation of leading DOS shells and DOS utility and data-recovery programs.

- A full explanation of the step-by-step system start-up process, including the POST (power-on self-test), the CONFIG.SYS and AUTO-EXEC.BAT files, and the DOS environment.

- An insightful look at multitasking and task switching under DOS, including DOS hardware and software interrupts.

- Detailed descriptions of leading memory-management software, including explanations of conventional, extended, and expanded memory, plus techniques for increasing conventional DOS memory.

- Common-sense, easy-to-use backup strategies and useful explanations of backup hardware and software.

- A thorough examination of data security, including practical, effective methods for protecting your data from system failure, user error, and rogue software.

- Insightful guides to leading operating environments under DOS, including DESQview, Windows, Concurrent DOS, and DR-DOS.

- Specially prepared overviews of advanced operating environments, such as OS/2, UNIX, and VMS, that highlight the similarities and differences with DOS.

- An informative introduction to PC networks of all sizes, including how to link computers for efficient file transfers.

- Detailed explanations, diagnostics, and benchmarks, including their origin and purpose. Bound with the book is INFOPLUS, which provides a whopping 17 screens of system information.

To this broad coverage, we add chapters covering the intricacies of disk caching, RAM disks, disk defragmenters, screen accelerators, and keyboard and print buffers. The coverage of DOS text editors is extensive, and includes the VDE program bound with the book, the DOS 5.0 EDIT program, and even a comprehensive guide to DOS EDLIN.

Extensive coverage of DOS DEBUG covers all of DEBUG's commands, from examining system memory to creating, modifying, and assembling programs.

A massive section on programming DOS batch files includes sample programs and techniques for using the Dvorak batch file utilities included with the book. Native DOS batch commands, tricks, and traps are included, too.

There's no shortage on coverage of DOS device drivers. The book describes in detail DRIVER.SYS, VDISK.SYS, and others. There's a detailed section on COMMAND.COM substitutes, like the highly regarded program 4DOS. And there's a massive guide to ANSI.SYS and ANSI.SYS substitutes, complete with examples and tips for using the ANSI utilities included with the book.

There is coverage of upgrading your system to enhance its performance without the expense of a new system.

And as if all this isn't enough, *Dvorak's Guide to DOS and PC Performance* describes DOS 5's new features, commands, and programs in detail.

Software Included

Like most books under the Dvorak•Osborne/McGraw-Hill label, this book comes complete with two 360KB, 5.25-inch disks of useful utilities and programs to make life in the fast lane a bit easier. These disks do not have the DOS system files required for start-up disks; so, you won't be able to boot up your system from them. The programs themselves are in a compressed format and must be installed before you can use them.

Before installing these disks, start up your system with your normal DOS start-up disk or (more likely) from your hard drive.

To install the more than 70 programs on the two disks that come with this book, you'll need either a dual-floppy system and three formatted disks or a hard disk system with at least 1MB of available disk space. If you are installing these on a network, consult with your network administrator prior to adding any programs to your system. INSTALL also supports high-capacity floppies. If you need the programs on a set of 3.5-inch disks or a set of three uncompressed disks, follow the instructions in Appendix C to order them.

Disk Contents

Disk #1:

Filename	Size (KB)	Contents
INSTALL.EXE	20356	Menu-driven installation program
DV1A.EXE	55078	Self-extracting archives with programs
DV2.EXE	214971	Self-extracting archives with programs
DV3A.EXE	60321	Self-extracting archives with programs
README.TXT	9777	Supplemental instructions

Disk #2:

Filename	Size (KB)	Contents
DV1B.EXE	161989	Self-extracting archives with programs
DV3B.EXE	198734	Self-extracting archives with programs

If your disks are bad for whatever reason, call Osborne/McGraw-Hill at 800-227-0900 for a replacement.

Programs Included with this Book

The programs included with this book are a special collection of user-supported software, custom-written utilities, and special versions of commercial programs. The more than 70 programs include:

- One of the leading DOS shells, XTree, which offers advanced file-and-directory management.

- DeskConnect, from Traveling Software (makers of Laplink), which links two PCs together for transparent file exchange and drive sharing.

- DOG, DiskOrGanizer, a lightning-fast disk defragmenter that offers advanced options, such as directory squeezing, and really speeds up the operation of your disks. (Large partition sizes or third-party partition software may not be compatible with this program.)

- A special edition of the Mace Utilities, with data recovery, disk-speed enhancement, and tools to prevent data loss.
  Note: This is a special edition that does not include all of the programs that come with the commercial program.)

- The Dvorak Utilities, a collection of 12 general-purpose assembly language utilities that expand the capabilities of DOS's batch file commands.

- The TSR Utilities, a collection of programs that manage your system's terminate-and-stay-resident programs.

- InfoPlus diagnostic program, which offers 17 screens full of system information.

- DOSCACHE, from Multisoft (makers of the PC-KWIK cache) which dramatically speeds up disk reads and writes.

- PKZIP and PKLITE data-compression utilities from PKware, the compression leader.

- VDE, a tiny text editor with advanced word processing capabilities, compatible with both WordPerfect and WordStar files.

- Many other utilities that simplify working with ANSI.SYS, park hard disks, move files and directories, aid batch file creation, find files, and write-protect your disks.

Appendix C lists all the programs on these disks and gives detailed instructions on how to install the software. If you're no stranger to menu-driven programs, you can skip the instructions. Simply enter

```
A:install
```

and follow the prompts.

Appendix D contains the manuals you'll need to run the programs. If you use any of the shareware programs on an ongoing basis, please remember to register them, using the forms at the back of the book. If you have problems with the disks, refer to the instructions in Appendix C.

Warning: If you have trouble running XTree, type **XTREE***path* to reconfigure the program for your drive and directory.

In short, *Dvorak's Guide to DOS and PC Performance* provides not only the most complete independent reference to IBM/Microsoft's disk operating system, but also a thorough overview of *all* the available utility programs, tips, and techniques you will need to get the most from your investment in the IBM PC-compatible computer platform.

We hope you'll catch the same "kid in a candy store" feeling from this book and software selection that we had in putting it together.

PART ONE

DOS Basics

CHAPTER ONE

Introduction

Where the radio buff might have been a fan of Buck Rogers, the computer generation watched "Star Trek" on television. The Altair, the early microcomputer kit, was named after an episode. The original name for dBASE, the database program, was Vulcan—after Spock, the pointy-eared logician.

Back in 1975 and 1976, personal computers were gadgets for hobbyists—toys for techies. A generation earlier, these people would have been tinkering with homemade radio receivers.

It's not uncommon to find some history in personal computer and MS/PC-DOS books. What isn't common knowledge is the true origin of MS/PC-DOS. DOS is a natural child of *CP/M*. CP/M was the most popular operating system for the old 8-bit computers that dominated the world until the IBM PC came along. It all stemmed from work done much earlier.

In the 1960s, Digital decided to standardize user interfaces and created DCL (digital command language). Many operating systems have since adopted this standard; in fact, most MS/PC-DOS commands conform to it. For example, DIRECTORY, COPY, and DELETE are commands for TOPS, RT11, VMS, CP/M, and MS/PC-DOS.

3

The early Digital operating system was called TOPS and ran on the PDP-11. TOPS evolved into RT11, used on the DEC models 10 and 20. The roots of TOPS can be traced to BBN (Bolt Berneck and Newman), a research facility in Cambridge, Massachusetts, where Digital's operating system research was done. TOPS was a multiuser, time-sharing system. The TOPS and RT11 systems were common in universities, where many people became familiar with them. In 1975, Digital developed a new operating system, called VMS, which replaced TOPS and RT11. In other words, DOS, as we know it on the PC, has deep roots.

THE FAMILY TREE

Altair, the First Personal Computer

While there were actually a few companies trying to market personal computers, it's generally accepted by the old-timers that the Altair is the progenitor—if not the absolute first machine—of the modern desktop computer revolution.

The Altair's heart was an 8080 microprocessor chip, an early ancestor of the 80386. The Altair had 256 bytes (that's *bytes*, not kilobytes) of memory, no permanent storage, and no keyboard. Input was done in straight binary with manual switches at the front of the panel. (You almost had to be a computer to operate this computer!) The Altair was sold as a kit made by a small New Mexico company, MITS. For a while, a string of Altair computer stores dubbed "Kit Computers" cropped up around the country.

Enter Bill Gates and Paul Allen

Bill Gates first began with computers as a youngster. One of his first ventures was a company called Traf-O-Data, a traffic-measurement business. Along with a friend, Paul Allen, he built a device to gauge automobile traffic flow. This device used an Intel microprocessor that read when cars passed over a rubber hose stretched across the street. It wasn't a bad try, but the business folded.

Paul Allen read about the Altair in the January 1975 issue of *Popular Electronics*. He was an employee of Honeywell in Boston, and Gates was a student at Harvard University. At Paul's suggestion, Bill developed a BASIC program for the new computer— in six weeks. Allen flew to New

Mexico to demonstrate the language for MITS, to be used by the Altair. Microsoft was born, and the BASIC licensed to MITS was the first product.

The early BASIC was loaded from paper tape, with a sequential keying with switches on the front panel of the Altair. In February 1976, Bill Gates wrote a disk version of BASIC. (Now things were *really* rolling.)

Gary Kildall and CP/M

At about the same time, an Intel programmer named Gary Kildall developed a small computer-operating system, CP/M (Control Program for Microcomputers). This was a scaled-down version of the PL/1 mainframe-programming language that could interpret operator commands with less than 4KB of memory. It was quite a feat, but Intel didn't see much future in it for their minicomputers. They turned over all the rights to Kildall. With CP/M, he founded Digital Research.

Enter IBM

In about 1980, in response to a growing market for desktop computers, IBM decided to get involved. "Big Blue" wanted a piece of the action, despite their not expecting microcomputers to become the wave of the future. (They probably didn't even expect the dinky computers to cut into their typewriter business, for that matter.) They designed a personal computer with off-the-shelf parts—in nine months, which is still some kind of record.

But there were two problems: It had no operating system, and full BASIC could not be handled by the machine. So, IBM approached Digital Research for a workable operating system and Microsoft for a microsized BASIC interpreter.

During this period, Tim Patterson of Seattle Microcomputer Products worked on a 16-bit operating system for the Intel 8088 and 8086 chip family. Everything else did 8-bit operations, but Patterson figured 16-bit processing, with twice the data throughput, would be better.

The result of Patterson's work was QDOS, which later evolved into SCP-DOS. It was a true 16-bit operating system modeled after CP/M. Over at Microsoft, they fully agreed with Patterson. In fact, they agreed so much, they offered Patterson's firm $50,000 for the new system—a wise purchase. It was during this time that IBM decided not to use the then-popular Z-80 microprocessor and instead go with the Intel 8088.

This is one of the most interesting aspects of the story. IBM's decision was based on one fact: At the time, Zilog was wholly owned by Exxon, which was making a lot of noise about office automation and how it would take on IBM. This made IBM uneasy. Rather than rely on a processor from a potential competitor, it looked to Intel and decided to use the 8088. This meant it could not use CP/M but had to use either the SCP-DOS or CP/M-86, which wasn't fully debugged. Gates talked them into the SCP-DOS, agreeing to modify it for the PC as necessary and release it as MS-DOS.

In November 1980, IBM and Microsoft agreed that DOS would be included with the new IBM personal computer. The stage was set. In August 1981, IBM finally announced the IBM PC. It used a new operating system that IBM called PC-DOS. IBM said it would be compatible with a multitude of operating systems and programs. They meant the then-dominant CP/M operating system of Digital Research. In fact, various add-in cards were quickly produced to interface IBM PCs with CP/M systems. Because there was a huge base of CP/M software, a dual operating system was an attractive alternative.

By 1983, CP/M-86 was out. It tried to rival MS-DOS, but it was too late. With only 4 percent of the market, it couldn't last for long. These "alternative systems" quickly fell by the wayside, leaving the field clear for Microsoft.

NEW DOS VERSIONS

The initial DOS release, version 1.0, with all its bugs and problems, had an experimental air about it. By June 1982, version 1.1 had replaced it. Version 1.1 supported IBM's new double-sided floppy disk drives and had fewer bugs. This was the first step in what was to become a steady march toward power and flexibility. The double-sided, double-density (DSDD) format doubled the storage capacity of DOS 1.0 floppy disk systems. This time Microsoft released a generic version of DOS (for IBM-compatible systems) called MS-DOS (Microsoft DOS) 1.25.

Version 2.0, the next major release, emerged in March 1983. Like 1.1, version 2.0 added support for a new IBM option, the fixed disk drive (now called the hard disk). DOS 2.0 introduced the directory tree and supported various peripheral devices with the use of a CONFIG.SYS file. There were new enhancements: new commands built into the COMMAND.COM command processor, file handles, volume labels for floppy disks, a printer spooler, and environment variables. Version 2.0 further increased floppy disk storage, with the number of sectors increased from 8 to 9 per track.

READ.ME

Microsoft DOS

The original Microsoft DOS, released in August 1981 as DOS 1.0, was the offspring of Tim Patterson's 86-DOS system. In fact, IBM considered the effect this would have on sales with a CP/M compatibility for their new operating system. At the time, few microcomputer software packages existed. Those that weren't written for the Apple II were written for CP/M. The conversion of programs from CP/M to PC-DOS was given high priority.

There are many similarities between the 8-bit systems—CP/M and early PC-DOS and MS-DOS. They use a single program-command processor and two input/output-data-handler files. The main difference between the two was memory requirements: DOS 1.0 used 10KB.

The common heritage of DOS and CP/M is apparent. Features designed to drive users and programmers crazy are hand-me-downs from Gary Kildall's original CP/M system, from which Tim Patterson grew the 86-DOS 16-bit system. Parallel features include:

- Eight-character filenames

- Three-character file extensions

- The A> prompt

- No progress reports from commands such as DEL

- Use of file control blocks (FCBs)

- Program segment prefixes (PSPs)

DOS did change some of CP/M's quirks. File lengths were reported precisely instead of rounded off. Commands used a syntax turned around to the logical format of source to destination. And DOS was the first operating system to employ a file allocation table, or FAT, which tracks where all the pieces of a file are stored. Even at this early stage, the DOS evolution was proceeding in the right direction.

All these innovations made a maintenance release inevitable. In March 1984, DOS 2.1 was released. (Incidentally, DOS 2.1 supported the new "Peanut" IBM PCjr. Oddly enough, DOS 2.1 was noticeably slower than DOS 2.0—they slowed down the system to accommodate the slow PCjr drives!) Microsoft produced several generic versions of 2.1, including 2.05, 2.11, 2.2, and 2.25.

The Upgrade Track

Newer DOS versions are more complex. More features are added with each revision. It comes in approximately 70 different languages (as well as Japanese Kanji characters). Here are the flavors of DOS, followed by the IBM machines they support:

Version	Year	Purpose
1.0	1981	Original Disk Operating System
1.1	1982	Support for double-sided disks
2.0	1983	Support for subdirectories
2.01	1983	Support for international symbols
2.25	1983	Bug fixes
3.0	1984	Extended character set; support for larger hard disks
3.1	1984	Support for PC networks; bug fixes
3.2	1986	Support for 3.5-inch disks (micro-floppies)
3.3	1987	Support for PS/2 computers
4.0	1988	Support for large partitions
4.01	1989	Bug fixes
5.0	1990	New shell, new editor, smaller kernel, new memory management

PROGRAMS AND COMMANDS TO USE WITH CARE

Everyone loses his or her way, at some time, when working at the DOS prompt level. These things happen. Occasionally, you can expect the following computer nightmares:

- Files are altered or erased.

- Program settings mysteriously change from one session to the next.

- A utility program that promised to increase efficiency only causes multiple disk-error messages.

- A handy memory-resident program creates monitor havoc (too scary to depict).

READ.ME

The Operating System

In many ways, operating systems are all alike. They manage disk storage, program execution, and system resources. The difference between DOS and UNIX, VMS, OS/2, or any other operating system is the way the resources are managed—that is, the organization of the file system.

DOS has four main functions:

- It organizes disk storage into a system with files and directories.
- It has a facility to load and execute programs.
- It manages other system resources, such as memory and peripheral devices (keyboards, displays, and printers).
- It has a command processor, or shell.

The command processor is the part of DOS that waits for commands. Acceptable commands are either the name of an executable program within the path or an internal command of the command processor in use. For instance DIR, DEL, and COPY, are internal, as they are part of DOS's standard command processor, COMMAND.COM.

If the command at the command line is the name of an executable program, DOS reads the file into memory and gives control of the system to that program. (The DOS command processor is clearly an executable program, with a distinction: It is the first program to be loaded after the system is booted.) While the program operates, DOS provides various support services (such as file-access and peripheral- and resource-management services). When the program concludes, the command processor regains control.

The DOS files necessary for a readable disk include the following:

PC-DOS	**MS DOS**
IBMBIO.COM	IO.SYS
IBMDOS.COM	MSDOS.SYS
COMMAND.COM	COMMAND.COM

The first two system files are "hidden." They include the directory listing and locations of files on the disk itself. The files IBMBIO.COM and IO.SYS require contiguous sectors of the disk. The two hidden files and the command processor make up what is called the DOS *kernel.* The DOS kernel controls services offered by DOS to application programs running under DOS.

The Operating System (*continued*)

When a program requests a DOS service, the program is said to be making a DOS *function call*. There are close to 100 DOS services in the current version of DOS.

IBM-compatible systems have a program that interacts with DOS to provide device support. This program is called the BIOS (basic input/output system). It is stored electronically in a ROM chip (or chips). The BIOS is not actually part of DOS.

A small program in the BIOS reads the first sector of a hard or floppy disk into a specific area of all IBM-compatible machines. This code is executed when the BIOS control is transferred to the 512 bytes of code read in from the first sector of the disk. The 512 bytes in turn read in the rest of the system.

If you have an experimental nature, you'll run into hairy events more often than the fainthearted. If you bought this book to explore the DOS cosmos, you're probably in search of these thrills.

When Things Go Wrong . . . Go Wrong . . . Go Wrong . . .

If you—or your Aunt Hildegard or Ralph, the computer-techie-wizard—hit the ENTER key at the wrong moment, you can really screw up. Reformatting a disk already full of information is one way.

The best preventive medicine is to get to know your programs. Know where the manuals are kept so that you can get out of unexpected trouble. If your best efforts don't solve your problem, *don't hit keys at random*. After all, you're not a reincarnation of Liberace. Of course, we all do it. I have a tendency to pop the ESC key if I get lost.

Programmers sophisticated in DOS have made much progress toward safer data. Their customers demanded it. These data safety nets are everywhere, but, just as in life, sometimes you miss the net. You are your own best judge of expertise, and if a problem goes beyond yours, don't be shy about it. Get help.

Seeds of Disaster

If a programming bungle doesn't cause you dementia, a misunderstood DOS command might. Something as simple as a negligent COPY command can cause devastation. A power cable across the traffic lane can give the two-pronged horror of a power crash *and* a lawsuit. *Anything* using a "wildcard" can have wholly unexpected results.

The point is that there are many ways to get nailed by a system as powerful and flexible as DOS. To most of us, the power is worth an occasional system freeze-up. Nothing will ever make computing completely safe so long as a simple COPY command will let us copy a file over another file and accidentally destroy essential data. There ought to be a bumper-sticker: "Computers don't kill files—users do."

Automobiles have been around for a while, and they aren't so safe, either. Even the vacuum cleaner is in almost every household in the country, yet there's still an occasional accident.

Luckily, you can minimize your potential woes. Follow the golden rules of hunting, adapted for computers: Be careful, and acquaint yourself with a program before you load and use it.

The remainder of this chapter will discuss the other important rules: Be prudent. Don't shoot your foot just because it moves. Plan your actions with common sense and reason.

Take Reasonable Care

Being an "old hand" is no guarantee of smooth sailing (far from it: There are many one-handed sailors). But most experienced users discover that they need to *pay attention.* Caution won't always keep you out of trouble, but carelessness is guaranteed to cause problems.

OK, so it pays to be careful. But what if you're really, simply, and utterly a board-certified ignoramus and don't have a clue to what you're doing? (We dearly hope that you're not the new-hire "computer guru.") Well, it *is* hard to acquire a new art without making mistakes. That's how we learn. And, when you come right down to it, it's not all that easy to damage your computer physically—short of actual abuse (for example, a fall from a '60 DeSoto station wagon on the freeway at 60 mph).

So, the admonishment "Be careful, pay attention" means more than just don't take chances. It means don't spill coffee on the keyboard, don't put knives into the floppy disk drive, don't let the kids pound on the keyboard, don't use the computer as a plant holder, and don't think that just because your sister finds a program easy, it will be a snap to figure out. Keep your sense of humor when dealing with computers. They don't act or think like humans.

Avoiding Trouble

Here are some things you should do to avoid trouble:

Read the Documentation   Nine times out of ten, the answer is in the manual. Manuals may be difficult to fathom or written in "manualeze." If you lack the patience or inclination to go over the whole manual, at least browse through the warnings and command reference sections.

Scrutinize the Manual's Compatibility Section   If your new program has a section labeled "Compatibility," read it. These are the program author's attempt to warn you if, say, your XT clone manufactured in Albania before 1986 isn't supported by the program. It can also alert you to your machine's specific incompatibilities with a thoroughbred IBM machine.

Heed the warnings. If a program warns you, "Do not run with any TSR programs," and you forget to disable or remove a cache program (for example, you leave SideKick installed) you could blow your hard disk partition. Or, less onerous, your system could lose its setup information.

By the same token, make sure you have the correct version of DOS. Many programs require DOS 3.X to run properly. Other programs designed for DOS 2.1 may do things the author never intended in DOS 3.X. Often, especially in the early days, programmers used accesses to DOS that IBM seems to have forgotten about. Then, in the next upgrade, lo and behold: DOS claimed the "forgotten" interrupt for some basic service, such as writing to a hard disk. (Most knowledgeable programmers no longer assume an unused DOS function is free and forgotten.) It's safest to stick with programs that specifically state they'll work with your version of DOS.

Other likely areas for compatibility problems depend upon the program. If it's a graphics-display program, check for compatibility with your type of graphics display—monochrome, CGA, EGA, VGA, LCD, or other. If it's a disk-oriented program, such as a disk organizer, check whether it's designed for your type of hard disk. If you're not sure what type of hard disk you have—MFM, RLL, ESDI, or SCSI—take the trouble to find out.

Study the Minimum Memory Requirements Most program documentation will tell you the minimum amount of memory required to run the program. If you have a machine with only 256KB of memory, many, many of the new programs cannot run.

Find the Contact Numbers An important item to locate in the manual is the number of a help line, the program manufacturer's "technical support" number. If you run into problems, or have questions that you cannot locate the answer to in the manual, call! If the manual is really an unintelligible, jumbled mess, complain!

Problem-Causing Features

Some program features that may cause problems include:

Memory-Resident-Program Loading Order Utility programs are designed to be loaded into memory. They then sit and wait for you to call (activate) them by use of a "hot key." Some terminate-and-stay-resident (TSR) programs behave better than others. If you try out a TSR, be sure not to load it into memory after you've loaded another program that insists upon being the absolute last one loaded.

Memory-resident programs are touchy. If you violate their specific loading order, they will show their spite. Your computer may freeze up, and you'll end up wondering what happened.

Screen-Mode Manipulation Programs that alter your screen's operating modes are able to provoke problems. For example, some programs sense an EGA monitor and assume there's an autoswitching graphics card or a "multisync" display. The program will attempt to force the screen to a higher mode. This can result in an unnatural screen presentation.

If you have a choice, pay a little more for an autoswitching video card. Try to use programs that permit the user to select the video mode — most good programs do.

Multitasking Programs   "Window"-type programs let you keep different application programs in different areas of memory. They can "hang" your machine for subtle reasons, all unique but not necessarily entertaining. Identifying the problem can be a major frustration. How can anyone sanely determine what's wrong when your machine freezes up for no apparent reason every, say, 10 minutes or so?

Sometimes such problems "heal themselves," disappearing as mysteriously as they appeared. This may leave you scratching your head to ponder divine intervention. The cause — and cure — may have been a trivial utility program you replaced. You may never figure it out.

Multitasking programs (such as DESQview and Windows 3) have evolved over a period of years, and are "safe." Like all good programs, they must be installed correctly — one mistake in the parameter setting and you'll wallow in a sea of trouble, for no obvious reason.

Expanded Memory Programs   With expanded memory, everyone was going to break that 640KB DOS barrier. The microcomputer giants — Lotus, Intel, and Microsoft — gathered together to bring forth a standard, the LIM 4.0 extended-memory standard (EMS).

Unfortunately, expanded memory requires a manager, and not all programs are compatible with the same managers. This has improved as the market has settled down, but programs designed to work outside the normal 640KB limit are still likely problem zones.

Conflicting Interrupts   TSR programs, device drivers, utilities, and other programs (and even new hardware) can develop interrupt conflicts. When two sets of software (or two different cards) try to use the same DOS interrupts (functions) at once, the results may be bizarre.

Several programs can help you identify interrupt conflicts. MAPMEM comes with MARK and RELEASE as part of the classic memory-management program TSRCOM; such commercial programs as Quarterdeck's MANIFEST and Golden Bow Systems' VTSR produce similar reports. These can help you interpret problems. Interrupt problems can be troublesome, though — if it's too technical, call in the dragoons.

Remember: DOS is the master system of computer operations—memory, storage, keyboard, monitor, and printer. It is the central control panel for the entire system, used by almost all other application programs.

DOS lets all the components of your system work together. But it goes deeper than that: DOS lets you, the user, control the system's functions. At the DOS level—the DOS prompt—you perform all basic file- and disk-management chores. You can copy disks and files, create a system start-up disk, and even list and print out text files.

If you have a handle on hardware and software compatibility, you—and your applications—can use DOS without much trouble. But some of the DOS commands can be troublemakers. (Learn about these commands from other people's mistakes, not your own!)

Troublesome DOS Commands

Let's not forget that the most powerful program on an MS-DOS machine is the operating system (MS-DOS itself).

If you're not DOS adept, one very good option for you is the purchase of a shell to mediate between you and the operating system. Or you may want to switch to a different command processor, such as 4DOS, with its greater concern for the user (see Chapter 6). In any case, if you use DOS, here are some specific commands that can cause trouble. (They aren't the obvious ones, either.)

RECOVER   This DOS utility program merits special caution. It is one of the poorest general-consumption utility programs ever put out. (It comes with DOS.)

RECOVER is intended to recover damaged files. If you use it on a hard drive and, in error, fail to specify a filename, the darn thing will attempt a recovery of everything on the disk. It handles only the first 512 files, however. The program considers subdirectories to be files; so, it moves the first 512 of your files and subdirectories (and all the files *they* contain) into your root directory. Then it labels them with generic names, starting with FILE0000.REC. The worst thing is that it does all this in memory—so you don't even get a drive light to warn you that something is going on (not that you could do anything, anyway).

When it's all done, you have a jumbled mess that can never be put right—at least not easily. (The Norton Disk Doctor program has an option, "Recover from DOS's Recover," that may solve some of the problem.) Another good defense is an up-to-date backup. But the best idea is to get rid of this ill-conceived program. Delete it from your disk!

COPY and XCOPY These commands—the first an internal function of COMMAND.COM and the second an external utility program—carry out needed functions. XCOPY is a fine utility, with options to use archive flags, dates, and other variables to determine what to copy. It will prompt you before a copy.

Use the copy commands conscientiously. COPY and XCOPY do not automatically ask if you want to replace a file copied to a target device. Copying over the wrong file has caused more lost data than any other command except DELETE.

Here are some things that can go wrong with the COPY command:

- Copy one file on top of another that has the same name but different contents (oops).

- You mix binary files with ASCII files accidentally when you add one file to another with the COPY *file1 + file2 file3* form of the command.

- You misspell a path directory. For example, if you say COPY *.* \DOSS instead of COPY *.* \DOS, you'll get a huge file named DOSS in the root directory. DOS is flat-out stupid about such things.

- If you copy a file without enough room in the destination to hold it, you're likely to wind up with an unintended 0-byte file instead. If you erase the original, you might find out much too late that you never actually made the copy you thought you made!

- If you type a semicolon instead of a colon, you can have strange results. For example, the command:

```
COPY C:\COMMAND.COM A;
```

will copy COMMAND.COM into a file named A in the current default directory.

REPLACE This command, like XCOPY, has built-in flexibility. But it can copy over the wrong files if you're not careful.

DELETE or DEL   This is a classic mischief maker. For some reason, Microsoft never added a pause or a warning message, except for when you attempt to delete everything (as in DEL *.*). People usually don't learn this error until it's too late. If you tell DOS to delete a filename, and if that filename happens to be a directory name, DOS does what it thinks you asked—delete every file in that directory. So if you get that odd message "Are you sure? (Y/N)" when you don't expect it—especially if you just used the DEL command—*don't* automatically answer "Y." Go over it again.

FORMAT   Another potential troublemaker is the FORMAT command. Once you begin to format, you cannot back out (it's like leaping off a bridge.) There are now some utilities to help you recover most of your files—if the disk isn't too fragmented.

It's easier than you might think to reformat your hard disk in error: Enter FORMAT instead of FORMAT A: or FORMAT B: and—at least with DOS 2.1—you're done for. (Later versions of DOS will ask for confirmation if the hard disk is in peril.)

READ.ME

Heal Deleted Files

When you delete a file, you don't actually write over all the data the file contained. Rather, you replace the first letter of the file's name with the delete character, a lowercase Greek omega character (σ). Because the contents of the file are not erased, you can use certain programs to retrieve a file when you accidentally erase it. The success depends upon which version of DOS you use—it's harder with DOS 2.1 than with DOS 3.X—and how fragmented the file was.

Fragmented files are stored in separate little pieces here and there on the disk. Unfragmented files are stored in a single place on the disk. Highly fragmented files have the tendency to lose pieces when you try to retrieve them after an accidental erasure. If you've written to disk between the delete and the attempted retrieval, it's doubtful that you'll have any luck: Once you erase a file, DOS considers its space empty and may use it for new data.

If you accidentally erase a file, use an unerase utility (like the Mace UnDelete program included with this book) to get it back right away!

Your best bet is an alternative to DOS FORMAT, such as John Newlin's Format Master program. These DOS alternatives are safer, faster, and more flexible than the DOS utility.

ASSIGN, JOIN, and SUBST   These programs perform some sophisticated stunts that fool DOS into assuming it's dealing with a different disk drive. Used wisely, they are handy. They can also be trouble: You've redirected DOS; so, DOS gives you misinformation. If you must use these commands, use them from a batch file, not on the fly at the DOS prompt. That way, you'll be less likely to make careless errors.

DEBUG   This program writes directly to your hard disk to modify COM and EXE files. It can mess up CMOS and directly address board-mounted memory. Unless you know what you're doing, stay away from DEBUG. Instead, use one of the many menu-driven track-and-sector editors that ask for user confirmation before they write directly to the disk.

CHKDSK   This diagnostic program is the tool used when someone has a disk or file problem. That's fine—the program was intended for that. But when CHKDSK reports a problem, many people run it again right away with the /F parameter. That tells CHKDSK to "fix" the problem it found. They end up with no lost clusters and no major problems, but with some (usually useless) new files in the root directory.

Sometimes what was really needed was a reboot. If the computer's internal memory tables took a hit from a stray cosmic ray or something, what CHKDSK reports is not necessarily correct—it's just a sign of some sort of trouble.

Always reboot your system before the use of CHKDSK to check any file, cluster, or lost-chain manipulations on your disk!

Redirection Symbols   Misuse of the redirection symbols (< and >) can trash files or create files that are 0 bytes. Sometimes, long or complex batch files use 0-byte files to track their progress, and there are other uses. For example, the command

```
REM > QUIT.BAT
```

creates a 0-byte batch file that lets you quit in the middle of a long batch file procedure without a hunt for an exit label.

Too many users find out about redirection symbols only when use of a >
sign accidentally writes a 22-byte error message over a 97KB data file.

OTHER "SAFE COMPUTING" PRACTICES

To round out this chapter, here are some recommended practices for using
both software and hardware:

- *Don't experiment with original program copies*   Vendors *always*
  have a notice: "Copy these files onto another disk and store the
  original in a safe place." There's a simple reason. The only disks that
  ever get erased or damaged are the ones you have only one copy of.
  Make a backup and a working copy, and use the working copy. If the
  disk gets ruined, make another working copy, and try again.

- *Make the right connections*   Don't plug your computer and peripherals into a "spaghetti factory" of four-way plugs or power strips
  plugged into power strips. If your wall outlets are faulty or the power
  cords come loose for no reason, replace the outlets immediately. If
  you see spitzen and sparken when you plug a power cord into an
  outlet, call in an electrician.

    Keep your power cords off the floor and out of the way of dogs,
  vacuum cleaners, and people's feet. Use a separate power circuit if
  possible, preferably with its own 15-amp breaker. In an area plagued
  with brownouts (voltage fluctuations), surges, spikes, or power failures, it pays to invest in a reliable uninterruptable power supply.

- *Don't be abusive*   Never remove or add printed circuit cards with
  the power on. It can cause sparks or even short out other cards, and
  it will void your warranty—service centers can easily spot "toasted"
  (burned) components. Be gentle with your equipment. Avoid moving
  your computer with hard disks grinding: It may interfere with a thing
  called centripetal motion.

- *Take care with floppy disks*   Floppy disks are extremely vulnerable
  to problems. Don't open your drive door when the light is still on:
  You could interrupt a DOS operation and lose your data. If a disk is
  badly deformed or looks dirty, don't put it in your drive: Dirt could be
  transferred to your disk drive heads and cause problems. Don't
  reformat your disks to densities they're not designed for. (Some

careless practitioners try to get more storage by formatting double-density disks in high-density drives.) Aside from having to listen to the disk drive make a racket while it grinds away at unreadable sectors, you're almost guaranteed to lose data. Marginal sectors may be readable one time but unreadable the next.

Nothing will eliminate all problems with a system as complex as your computer. But a small amount of thought will go far in the elimination of the headache of lost or ruined — but vital — files.

CHAPTER TWO

Introduction to DOS

The Disk Operating System (DOS) controls your computer's operation. It is a "layer" of software between the user and the actual hardware (the CPU, memory, disk drives, keyboard, display, and so on). Its purpose is to control the movement of information in the computer and present a uniform interface that allows you to "command" the hardware to do specific tasks. You could compare DOS to a traffic signal at a busy intersection. DOS controls the way the computer uses programs, games, and other applications in much the same way.

DOS version 1.0 was the first release. It was both "buggy" and limited in capability. Within a year, in June 1982, version 1.1 replaced it. Version 1.1 fixed many of the bugs and also supported IBM's new double-sided floppy disk drives. Microsoft also released a generic version of DOS this time, called MS-DOS 1.25.

Version 2.0 was released in March 1983. Like 1.1, it added support for a new IBM option, the hard disk drive. DOS 2.0 also introduced the directory tree and supported various peripheral devices through a CONFIG.SYS file. It threw in many enhancements, including new commands built into the

COMMAND.COM command processor. It used file handles, it could label disks, and it had a printer spooler. It used environment variables and further increased floppy disk storage by increasing the number of sectors from eight per track to nine.

All these innovations, replete with bugs, made a maintenance release inevitable. It appeared in March 1984 as DOS 2.1 and supported the new IBM PCjr. DOS 2.1 was noticeably slower than DOS 2.0—it had to slow down the system to accommodate the slower PCjr disk drive!

Microsoft produced several generic versions of 2.1, including 2.05, 2.11, 2.2, and 2.25. If you have an older version of DOS, especially DOS 2.1, you'll enjoy significantly better performance if you upgrade to a more recent version (3.30, 4.01, or 5.0). DOS now comes in nearly 70 different languages, including Japanese Kanji characters. The following table gives more information on the various versions of DOS:

No.	Year	Purpose
1.0	1981	Original Disk Operating System
1.1	1982	Support for double-sided disks
2.0	1983	Support for subdirectories
2.01	1983	Support for international symbols
2.25	1983	Bug fixes, more international language support (didn't carry over to version 3)
3.0	1984	Extended character set; support for larger hard disks
3.1	1984	Support for PC networks; bug fixes
3.2	1986	Support for 3.5-inch disks (microfloppies)
3.3	1987	Support for PS/2 computers
4.0	1988	Support for large partitions
4.01	1989	Bug fixes
5.0	1990	New shell, new editor, smaller kernel, new memory management

In this chapter, you will be introduced to DOS. The chapter includes a detailed command reference and ends with a quick reference.

FLOPPY DISK DRIVES, FLOPPY DISKS, TRACKS, SECTORS, AND BYTES

Information is written on floppy disks in concentric circles called *tracks*. The read/write head of the disk drive moves from one track to another as the disk turns at about 300 revolutions per minute. A stepper motor accurately controls the location of each track on the surface of the disk. There are either 40 or 80 tracks on a floppy disk. Each track is split into *sectors*. As the read/write head moves, it finds data to read or locates places on the disk to write. Space on a disk is measured in *bytes*. One byte is equivalent to one character.

The number of tracks, sectors, and bytes on a disk depends on the type of disk. The following sections describe the types of disks and disk drives.

Types of Floppy Disk Drives

The following table shows the types of disk drives your computer can have:

5.25-inch	Single-sided	160KB/180KB
5.25-inch	Double-sided	320KB/360KB
5.25-inch	High-capacity	1.2MB
3.5-inch	Double-sided	720KB
3.5-inch	Double-sided	1.44MB
5.25-inch	High-capacity	2.88MB

- A 5.25-inch single-sided floppy disk (160/180KB) has 40 tracks, 8 or 9 sectors per track, and 512 bytes per sector.

- A 5.25-inch double-sided floppy disk (320/360KB) has 40 tracks on each side, 8 or 9 sectors per track, and 512 bytes per sector.

- A high-capacity floppy disk (1.2MB) is a double-sided disk that has 80 tracks per side, 15 sectors per track, and 512 bytes per sector.

- A 3.5-inch double-sided floppy disk (720KB) has 80 tracks per side, 9 sectors per track, and 512 bytes per sector.

- A 3.5-inch double-sided floppy disk (1.44MB) has 80 tracks per side, 18 sectors per track, and 512 bytes per sector.

- A 5.25-inch double-sided high-capacity floppy disk (2.88MB) has 80 tracks per side, 36 sectors per track, and 512 bytes per sector.

Floppy Disks and Drive Compatibility

Various floppy disks can be read on various drives. Some combinations for reading and writing between different disk and drive types are not allowed.

- A 160/180KB single-sided drive (5.25-inch) can read and write to 160/180KB single-sided, double-density disks.

- A 320/360KB double-sided drive (5.25-inch) can read and write to 160/180KB single-sided, double-density disks and 320/360KB double-sided, double-density disks.

- A 1.2MB high-capacity drive (5.25-inch) can read and write to 160/180KB single-sided, double-density disks, 320/360KB double-sided, double-density disks, and 1.2MB high-capacity, double-density disks.

Note: If you write on either of these floppy disk types using a 1.2MB high-capacity drive, you may not be able to read the floppy disks in a 160/180KB or 320/360KB drive.

- A 720KB double-sided drive (3.5-inch) can read and write to 720KB double-sided floppy disks.

- A 1.44MB double-sided drive (3.5-inch) can read and write to 720KB double-sided floppy disks and 1.44MB double-sided floppy disks.

Note: When you use the DISKCOPY or DISKCOMP command, the floppy disk types must be identical.

Formatting Your Floppy Disks

You must format each new or blank floppy disk before it can be used by DOS. Do not use the FORMAT command every time you want to put information on a floppy disk. Use it only on new floppy disks. For more information about formatting floppy disks, refer to a later section of this chapter.

Write-Protected Floppy Disks

It is possible to format a floppy disk unintentionally, causing important data to be lost. For this reason, floppy disks can be write-protected. You can read data from write-protected floppy disks, but you cannot write data to them or format them.

5.25-Inch Floppy Disks   Most 5.25-inch floppy disks have a notch called a *write-protect notch.* If the notch is covered with an adhesive tab, the floppy disk is write-protected. To write-protect a 160/180KB, 320/360KB, or 1.2MB floppy disk, cover the notch with a write-protect tab that came with the box of disks. You can also use a piece of tape, but do not use transparent tape, as the notch is sometimes optically sensed.

Some 5.25-inch floppy disks do not have a notch. This means that the floppy disks are permanently write-protected. Information cannot be written on them.

3.5-Inch Floppy Disks   On the back of a 3.5-inch 720KB or 1.44MB floppy disk, in the lower right corner, is a *write-protect "window"* with a plastic tab. When you slide the plastic tab so that the window is open, the floppy disk is write-protected. When the window is closed, data can be written on the floppy disk. Some 3.5-inch floppy disks have a write-protect window but no plastic tab. This means that the floppy disks are permanently write-protected. Information cannot be written on them.

Information on Floppy Disks

Programs and information have to be stored in some way. Early computers used (and some still use) punched cards for long-term storage of programs and information. Magnetic tape and large hard disk drives and drums are commonly used now. Early microcomputers used ordinary cassette recorders and tape to store programs and data. In fact, the first IBM PC could record programs and data on cassette tape as well as on floppy disks. The storage media of choice has become the floppy disk. If you do not have a hard disk in your computer, you will be making very extensive use of floppy disks.

Floppy disks are sturdy enough to be used and reused many times, but they do not tolerate abuse. Unlike a phonograph record, a floppy disk cannot accumulate a few scratches and still work. One scratch can destroy part of the data stored on a floppy disk and render the whole disk useless. Fingerprints, liquid spills, and dust will also cause problems.

It is important to handle your floppy disks properly to keep your data secure. The following guidelines tell you how to take care of your floppy disks. By observing these guidelines, you will greatly reduce your chances of losing computer data because of floppy disk failure.

READ.ME

Floppy Disk Do's and Don'ts

Keep the work area clean. Floppy disks are designed for use in a normal office or home. Do not use them in a place that is unusually dirty or dusty.

Protect floppy disks when they are not in use. Keep each floppy disk in its paper envelope whenever it is not in the floppy disk drive. Store floppy disks in closed boxes or other containers. Never leave them out where dust can accumulate on them.

Protect floppy disks from pressure. Excessive pressure can grind particles of dirt into the recording surface. Store your floppy disk boxes on end (not flat) and leave some loose space in each one. Never place a book or other heavy object on top of a floppy disk.

Write on a floppy disk's label only with a felt-tip pen. A pencil or ballpoint pen can exert great pressure on a small area.

Do not touch a floppy disk's recording surface with your fingers, a cleaning tool, or anything else. Even the softest, cleanest object may leave scratches or dirt on a floppy disk.

Avoid extremes of temperature and humidity. Do not leave a floppy disk in direct sunlight, on a radiator, or near any other source of heat. See your floppy disk manufacturer's instructions for specific advice.

Protect floppy disks from strong magnetic fields such as stereo speakers, which may erase the information stored on them.

Back up everything with COPY or DISKCOPY or a backup program. Never, under any circumstances, assume that you are safe without a backup.

Whenever you add or change information on a floppy disk, back up that floppy disk before the end of the day. Devise a routine for creating and filing backup floppy disks, and stick to it!

Remember that dirt or other abrasive material on floppy disk media surfaces can also damage your drive's recording heads. It's bad enough risking the loss of data, but even worse risking a damaged drive.

STARTING YOUR COMPUTER

To start your computer, or *boot* it, turn on the power. Be sure your monitor and printer are also turned on. You will hear the fan start and, if your computer has a hard disk, you will hear that start. A cursor will appear on the monitor, and the floppy disk drive will make sounds. The monitor may display information about the computer and ROM-BIOS. The computer will beep when all self-checks are complete and the computer is ready for use.

If you have no hard disk drive, turn your system on, then insert the DOS floppy disk in drive A (usually the upper drive) after removing it from the paper envelope. Be careful not to touch the recording surface with your fingers or let it come in contact with any object. Hold the floppy disk so that the side with the preprinted label is facing up and the write-protect notch (the small, square cutout on the left side of the disk) is on the left. Open the latch on the drive and insert the floppy disk. Carefully close the drive latch.

On systems without a hard disk, if you did not insert the floppy disk soon enough, don't panic. You will see a message on the screen asking you to insert the floppy disk. Simply follow the screen instructions. If all else fails, leave the DOS floppy disk in the drive, hold down the CTRL and ALT keys, press the DEL key, and release all keys.

If your system is equipped with a hard disk, besides starting it with a floppy disk you can also start it with the hard disk. This is done by leaving open the latch of each of your floppy drive doors. During the power on sequence, the system will check these drives, pass by them, and load the DOS start-up files it finds on your hard disk. Once the system check out is complete and your system has read DOS into RAM, and if your system doesn't have a built-in battery backed-up clock or a clock or multifunction card, you will see the following display:

```
Current date is Tue 1-01-1980     (This is the date systems will
                                   default to on computers that
Enter new date:                    don't have a clock card.)
```

The flashing bar after "Enter new date:" on the screen is the *cursor*. The cursor marks the place where the next character you type will appear on the display.

At this point, DOS is requesting a date entry. If the date displayed by DOS is correct, you can tell DOS to use it by pressing ENTER. Otherwise, enter the date numerically in the format DOS displays: month, day, and year, with hyphens in between. Do not enter the day of the week—DOS computes that itself. For example, if today were April 13, 1991, you would enter the following (note the hyphens):

```
4-13-1991
```

If you make a mistake, you can erase it by pressing the BACKSPACE key. If the date is correct, press ENTER to cause DOS to accept it.

Next, DOS displays its idea of the current time:

```
Current time is 0:00:43.55
Enter new time:
```

Again, if DOS's time is correct, you can accept it simply by pressing ENTER. Otherwise, enter the correct time in the same format that DOS used. To simplify data entry, you should omit the seconds and fractions of a second. For example, if the time were 9:30 A.M., you would enter

```
9:30
```

and press the ENTER key. Use 24-hour notation to enter times later than 12:59 P.M. For example, enter 13:00 for 1:00 P.M. and 21:30 for 9:30 P.M.

After you enter the time, DOS displays its version number and a copyright notice. You have now turned on your computer and started DOS.

Rebooting Without Turning Off Your Computer

Occasionally, a hardware or software problem makes it necessary to *reboot* your system, that is, start it again. Your computer will reboot automatically if you turn it off and then turn it on again. The preferred way to reboot is to hold down the CTRL and ALT keys and press the DEL key. You might try rebooting your computer now by pressing this combination of keys.

In some cases the CTRL-ALT-DEL combination does not work. If this happens to you, turn your computer off, wait a few seconds, and turn it on again.

Note: Try not to turn your computer's power off unless the DOS prompt is displayed on the screen and the drive access lights on the disk drive are off. If you turn the computer off while a program is running or the drive light is on, any work you have been doing might be lost.

The Prompt

The A> display is called the *DOS prompt.* A *prompt* is simply a message inviting you to enter some command. The letter A appears in the prompt if you booted from disk drive A. If you booted from the hard disk (which is usually drive C), DOS prompts you with C>.

Whenever you see the DOS prompt, you may enter a line of input. Since this input instructs DOS to perform some action, it is called a *command.*

Booting from a Hard Disk

To boot from the hard disk, do not put a floppy disk into drive A before turning on your computer or pressing CTRL-ALT-DEL. The computer will try to boot from drive A, but when it finds no floppy disk there, it will boot from the hard disk instead.

When you boot from the hard disk, DOS automatically designates drive C (the hard disk) as the default drive. Since drive C customarily contains copies of all the standard DOS command files and data files, you do not need a DOS floppy disk in drive A.

There are a few systems that can only be started from their floppy drives. These systems will have a hard disk and controller that are not fully supported by their computer's BIOS (basic input and output system). When you start your computer from a floppy, drive A becomes the default drive and the comspec is set to A:\COMMAND.COM. if you have a hard disk, type \C: at the A prompt and press ENTER. C:\ will appear on your screen. At the C prompt, type **set comspec=C:\COMMAND.COM**. These two commands will eliminate the need to keep a disk in drive A while running your system.

DIR AND CHKDSK

DIR stands for "directory" and is used to list the contents of floppy or hard disks. CHKDSK stands for "check disk" and is used to check various conditions relating to floppy and hard disks.

The DIR Command

The DIR command lists a floppy disk or hard disk directory. The directory is a part of the floppy or hard disk that tells you what information is stored on the disk, much as a directory in an office building tells you what businesses are in the building.

Just type **DIR** or **dir**. (DOS commands may be entered in uppercase or lowercase.) These characters will be *echoed*; that is, they will appear on the display. Press the ENTER key to indicate that the command is ready for execution. Note that the ENTER key is sometimes labeled the RETURN key.

Execution of a DOS command is always signaled by a press of the ENTER key. In the rest of this chapter, assume that any time you are instructed to enter text on the command line, you need to press the ENTER key to execute the command. The ENTER key on your keyboard may be marked with a hooked, left-pointing arrow, or it may be labeled "Enter" or "Execute"—all signify that a command line is finished and should be executed.

In this case, we have given a command to list the contents of the floppy disk directory so that we can see what is stored on that floppy disk. When you press ENTER, the computer reads the floppy disk and then displays something like the following:

```
Volume in drive A has no label
Directory of A:\
COMMAND   COM  17664    3-08-83   12:00p
ANSI      SYS  1664     3-08-83   12:00p
FORMAT    COM  6016     3-08-83   12:00p
          .
          .
          .
MORE      COM  384      3-08-83   12:00p
PRINT     COM  4608     3-08-83   12:00p
TREE      COM  1513     3-08-83   12:00p
23 File(s)
31232 bytes free
A>
```

The first part of the display may disappear off the top of the screen (*scroll*) before the last part appears. You will learn how to prevent that.

Each line in the DIR command's output represents one *file*. A file is an area on a disk containing a collection of data or a program. The first two columns in the line are the file's name and extension. The third column shows the size of the file in bytes. The last two columns show the date and time when the file was created or last changed. This is called the *date-and-time stamp.*

The CHKDSK Command

CHKDSK is another DOS command. As its name indicates, it checks the condition of a floppy disk. Try entering it now: Type **chkdsk** and press ENTER. The command and the computer's resulting output will vary from version to version but should look something like this:

```
A>chkdsk
362496 bytes total disk space
22528  bytes in 2 hidden files
329728 bytes in 43 user files
10240  bytes available on disk
262144 bytes total memory
235920 bytes free
A>
```

Halting Your Computer in the Middle of a Command

Sometimes you may want to halt the computer in the middle of a command to examine what is on the display. For example, you may have wanted to do this when you entered the DIR command and the first part of its output disappeared from the screen before you could read it.

To make the system halt in the middle of a command, hold down the CTRL key and press the S key, or press the PAUSE key. Press any key to make the computer continue. Run DIR again and try this.

Correcting Mistakes and Discarding Commands

If you press the wrong key while entering a DOS command, it is not serious: You can erase your mistake by pressing the BACKSPACE key. For example, type the following at the A> prompt: **dur.** That is an error; you should have typed **dir.** Press BACKSPACE twice to erase as far back as the incorrect character, and type the correct characters: **dir.**

DOS also allows you to discard an entire command line at any point before you press ENTER. To discard a command line, press the ESC key. For example, type **dir** and press ESC. DOS displays a \, discards the command you have just entered, and moves the cursor to the next line. Now you can enter any other command you choose.

If you enter an erroneous DOS command and press ENTER, will something terrible happen? Certainly not! Try entering a misspelled command or a line of complete nonsense to see how your computer responds.

If you enter a command that you decide you should not have entered, you can abort the command in most cases by holding down CTRL and pressing either C, the SCROLL-LOCK, or the BREAK key. (Of course, CTRL-BREAK cannot undo anything the command has already done.)

Many application programs have special commands for ending the program and returning to DOS. You should always use a program's "end," "quit," or "exit" command, if one exists, instead of CTRL-BREAK. This will ensure that the program ends in an orderly way and that the data the program was operating on is left in a usable state. Reserve CTRL-BREAK for ending DOS commands and other programs that have no end command of their own and for emergencies when a program's end command does not seem to work.

Some application programs actually disable CTRL-BREAK or change its function. When you run such a program, you must use that program's end command to return to DOS (or reboot the computer). Always check an application program to find out how to stop it before you start it.

Only rarely will you cause damage to a program or data by using the CTRL-C or CTRL-ALT-DEL or ESC key to quit. The most critical time is disk writes or updates to the file allocation table. The most likely result of interupting a write will be that a data file will not be saved, and recent entries will not have been recorded.

DISKCOPY

This command is used to make exact duplicates of disks. It makes a track-by-track copy of a source floppy to a destination floppy. The two floppy disks *must* be the same type; in other words, the source and destination disks must have the same number of sides, tracks, and sectors. Trying to use DISKCOPY on dissimilar media will result in an error.

Using DISKCOPY to Back Up the DOS Floppy Disk

Because floppy disks can be damaged, it is important to make a backup copy of every floppy disk you use. If the original floppy disk is damaged, you will be able to recover the data from the backup.

Backing Up a System with Two or More Disk Drives

Make sure the DOS floppy disk is in drive A, usually the upper drive or the drive on the left, and enter the following command:

```
diskcopy a: b:
```

This command line contains something new: the "a:" and "b:" after the name of the command. These are *parameters*. They tell the DISKCOPY command what you want it to do.

The first parameter, a:, tells DISKCOPY to copy *from* the floppy disk in drive A. The second parameter, b:, tells DISKCOPY to copy *to* the floppy disk in drive B. With DOS command lines and programs, you must always refer to a disk drive in this way, that is, with a letter followed by a colon.

DISKCOPY asks you to insert the *source* floppy disk (the one to copy from) in drive A, and the *target* floppy disk (the one to copy to) in drive B. (If the two drives are not the same size, then this command does not work and should not be used.) Here's how your screen looks:

```
A>diskcopy a: b:
Insert source diskette in drive A:
Insert target diskette in drive B:
Strike any key when ready
```

You need not act on the first instruction in this case: You want to copy the DOS floppy disk, and it is already in drive A. Insert a blank, formatted floppy disk in drive B, and press any typing key.

DISKCOPY reads from the floppy disk in drive A and writes to the floppy disk in drive B, a process that may take some time. When it is done, DOS asks you if you want to copy another disk:

```
Copy another(Y/N)?
```

You are not going to copy another floppy disk right now; press the N key to end DISKCOPY. To copy another floppy disk (or make another copy of the same one), you would press the Y key. DISKCOPY would return to the "Insert source disk" prompt and go through the procedure again.

Backing Up a System with One Disk Drive and a Hard Disk

Enter the DISKCOPY command just as you would on a system with two floppy disk drives:

```
diskcopy a: b:
```

Since you have only one floppy disk drive, DOS uses that drive when you refer to drive A or drive B. DISKCOPY does not copy the DOS floppy disk onto itself, though. Instead, it lets you switch floppy disks between operations on the source floppy disk and the target floppy disk. In this way, you can process two floppy disks even though you have only one floppy disk drive.

DISKCOPY prompts you to insert the source floppy disk in the drive and reads part of it. Next, it prompts you to insert the target floppy disk in the drive and writes what it just read. Then, it prompts you to insert the source floppy disk again, and so on, until it has copied everything. Be sure to wait for the disk drive light to go off before you open the drive door to change floppy disks.

READ.ME

DISKCOPY Traps

- **Your computer displays the message "Not Ready Error Reading Drive A. Correct, then strike any key."** DISKCOPY is trying to read the floppy disk in drive A, but the drive is not ready for use. Make sure the floppy disk is properly inserted and the drive door is closed, and then press any standard typing key.

- **Your computer displays the message "Bad command or filename."** You may have misspelled the DISKCOPY command. If you did not misspell DISKCOPY, then DISKCOPY must be missing from your DOS floppy disk or else it's on a different path.

- **Your computer takes more than several minutes to copy a floppy disk, or the floppy disk drive makes rattling sounds.** Either your target floppy disk is defective, or your floppy disk drive is not working. Reboot the computer by holding down CTRL and ALT and pressing DEL. Try backing up the DOS floppy disk to a different target floppy disk. If your second attempt fails in the same way, and a third attempt with yet another floppy disk also fails, you can be virtually certain that one of the drives is defective. Have it checked.

- **Your computer displays a message beginning "Unrecoverable write error on target drive."** You may be using the wrong kind of floppy disk. If you are using the right kind of floppy disk, the floppy disk is probably defective.

DISKCOPY Traps *(continued)*

- **Your computer displays the message "Target disk write-protected."** Your target floppy disk's write-protect notch (the square notch on the edge) is covered. This prevents the computer from writing anything on the floppy disk. If the floppy disk is not one you want to protect, uncover the notch; otherwise, use another floppy disk. You will also get this message if you insert the floppy diskette upside down or if it either doesn't have a notch at all or the notch is not aligned correctly.

- **Your computer displays the message "Invalid drive specification."** You entered the drive name of a nonexistent drive or omitted the colon or used a semicolon by mistake after the drive letter. Try again by re-entering the drive commands.

When the Copy Is Done

Write something like "DOS backup" on an adhesive floppy disk label, and firmly press the label onto the backup floppy disk. Put the floppy disk in a safe place. You might need it some day.

If your original DOS floppy disk is the one supplied by your computer dealer, put it away in a safe place. Let the backup you just made be your working copy. To be especially safe, you may want to make a second copy and put that in a safe place too.

By the way, never write on a label that is already attached to a disk with anything but a felt-tip pen. The pressure created by the point of a ballpoint pen or a pencil can damage a floppy disk's recording surface.

What Drive Names Does Your Computer Accept?

In many of the following sections, you will work with files that are on various disk drives. The drive names you use in these lessons will depend on which drives your computer has and whether DOS commands and data are stored on a floppy disk or a hard disk.

Here is a summary of the rules for determining what drive names your computer accepts and which drive holds DOS:

- If your computer has two floppy disk drives, usually the first drive is drive A, and the second drive is drive B. If you have three or four floppy drives, the additional drives are C and D. DOS must be on a floppy disk in drive A.

- If your computer has one floppy disk drive and a hard disk, the floppy disk drive is drive A, and the hard disk is drive C. If you have a second hard disk, it is drive D. If you have a second floppy disk drive, it is drive B. DOS may be on a floppy disk in drive A or on the hard disk in drive C. (IOMEGA and other firms have developed hard drives that can be configured as A or B, but this configuration is rarely used.)

- If your computer has a nonstandard hard disk, you must experiment to find out what drive letters are assigned to each disk. Place a formatted disk in each floppy disk drive and run CHKDSK with different drive names (such as B, C, and D) until it displays information about the hard disk. You may find that two or more drive names address different parts of the hard disk, as though the hard disk were divided into several smaller disks. If you enter a drive name that DOS does not recognize as valid for your computer, DOS will simply display the message "Invalid drive specification." You can access any physical drives such as your floppy disk drive A or B, or C if you have a hard drive. In some cases you may be able to access a logical drive. A logical drive is created from DOS's FDISK partitioning, which divides a single hard disk into multiple drives. DOS will not recognize non-DOS hard disk partitions.

Rather than give several sets of instructions, we are going to proceed as if you had a computer with two floppy disk drives. We will use the drive name A to represent the drive holding the DOS floppy disk and the drive name B to represent "any other drive." If you have a computer with a hard disk, just translate these drive names to the names appropriate for your own computer.

Changing the Default Drive

Most commands do not insist that you enter all the parameters they expect. If you omit a parameter, they will perform as if you had entered a default value.

When a command such as DIR expects a parameter giving a drive name, the parameter's default value is the name of the current drive. DOS displays the current drive name before the > in its command prompt. When DOS's command prompt is A>, for example, the default drive is drive A. Thus, when you enter DIR with no parameter, DIR assumes you want a listing of the disk in drive A.

When you perform many operations on a certain disk drive, it is convenient to make that drive the default drive. That way, you do not have to enter its name every time you type a command. You make a drive the default drive by entering its drive name followed by a colon as a command. For example, the following command would make drive B the default drive:

```
b:
```

DOS commands would now address drive B whenever you omitted a drive name in a parameter.

Change your computer's default drive to your second floppy disk drive (B) or your hard disk (C), and enter **dir** with no parameter. DIR lists the files on the new default drive.

You can always override the default drive by using a drive name in a parameter. For example, when drive B is the default drive, you can list files on drive A by entering

```
dir a:
```

When you are finished experimenting with the default drive, reset it to drive A with the following command:

```
a:
```

You should reset the default drive because many DOS commands are retrieved from the DOS disk when you run them. If you make drive B the default drive and the DOS commands are not on the disk in that drive, you will get the following message when you try to run a DOS command:

```
Bad command or filename
```

In this case, you must tell DOS that the command is on disk A (the DOS disk), not on the current default disk. Put A: before the command name; for example:

```
a:chkdsk
```

Of the commands you have seen so far, all except DIR are retrieved from disk when you run them. DOS's DIR command, which is resident, is kept in RAM all the time DOS is running; you do not need the prefix A: to run it.

INTRODUCING FILES

Disks are your computer's primary media for storing information. They can store DOS and DOS commands, such as CHKDSK and DISKCOPY; other computer programs, such as word processors, accounting systems, and games; and data, such as business records, budget plans, and correspondence.

The basic unit of disk storage is the *file*. A file is a collection of data, somewhat like the contents of a paper file folder. You might use a file to hold a computer program, your business's accounts receivable, or a letter you are writing to a friend.

Using DIR with a File Specification

You have used the DIR command to become familiar with the process of entering DOS commands. Now, you will use it to learn how DOS uses files to store information.

Enter the DIR command, and look at the information it displays. Each line in DIR's output describes one file. Look at the contents of any of the lines in DIR's output, such as the following:

```
TREE     COM 1513  3-08-83   12:00p
```

The first two words, TREE and COM, are the file's *filename* and *extension*, respectively. The purpose of the filename is to identify the file. The purpose of the extension is often to describe the type of data that the file contains.

When you type a filename and an extension, you must separate them with a period:

```
TREE.COM
```

The filename and the extension, taken together, make up the *file specification* ("spec" for short). This example is read "TREE dot COM."

Many DOS commands, including DIR, allow you to use file specifications as parameters. Try entering DIR with TREE.COM: as a parameter, as follows:

```
dir tree.com
```

DIR displays the same information as before, but only for the file TREE-.COM rather than for every file on the default disk.

You can combine a drive name with a filename in a command, if you wish. To make DIR display information about a file named TREE.COM on the disk in drive B, you would enter

```
dir b:tree.com
```

The parameter b:tree.com is a complete file specification. It tells the file's filename and extension and the drive it is currently mounted on. You should read it as "B colon TREE dot COM." Since "file specification" is an awkward term, we often speak instead of a file's "name" when we mean its specification.

Rules for Creating a File Specification

List the whole contents of your DOS disk with DIR again. Notice that none of the filenames is longer than eight characters, and none of the filename extensions is longer than three characters. Those are the maximum lengths allowed for the filename and the extension.

In addition to these limitations, certain rules also govern the use of characters in a file's specification, primarily because certain symbols have special meaning when used in or with a file spec.

It is important to choose filenames that will help you remember what is in your files. For example, you might use the filename PAYR8905 for a file containing payroll records from May 1989. In addition, you should choose file extensions that will help you remember what kind of information is in your files. For example, you might use extension LTR for letters and RPT for reports.

READ.ME

Characters in a File Specification

The following characters can be used in a file spec:

- ! @ # $ % & ( ) - _ { } ' ` ~
- Any alphabetic character
- Any numeral

The following characters may not be used in a file spec:
^ * + = [ ] ; : " \ , . / ? < >

- And spaces

READ.ME

Traps

Certain file extensions have fixed, conventional meanings. For example, BAS represents a computer program written in the programming language BASIC. You should avoid using these extensions except in their intended ways; otherwise, you are likely to confuse anyone who tries to interpret the names of your files—including yourself.

A list of standard file extensions and their accepted meanings follows. Notice the extensions marked with asterisks. It is particularly important to avoid using these because they have special meaning to DOS itself.

For example, if DOS finds a file named AUTOEXEC.BAT on the DOS disk when it is booted, it will assume that the file contains a list of commands. It will try to execute those commands before letting you type anything at the keyboard. For this reason you should not use, for example, the name AUTO-EXEC.BAT for a file that contains a letter to the president of a company that sells car batteries.

$$$ Temporary file, used within a program and then discarded. A file with this extension may be erased by any program at any time.

ASM   Assembly language program source listing.

READ.ME

Traps (*continued*)

BAK Backup file, the next-oldest copy of a modified file.

BAS BASIC program.

BAT* Batch file, containing DOS commands that can be executed as though they were typed at the keyboard.

COB COBOL source code.

COM* Command file, a program that will be run when the filename is entered as a DOS command.

DAT Data file.

EXE* Executable file, similar to COM.

LIB Compiler library file.

LST Listing of compilation or assembly.

MAP Memory map for linker.

OBJ Object code compiled programs prior to linking.

OVR Program overlay module.

PAS Pascal source code.

PRN Print file, output from a program that would normally have been sent to a printer.

SYS* System file, information used by DOS to control some aspect of DOS's operation.

TMP Temporary file. Some programs use files with this extension for temporary storage.

*Avoid creating files with this extension; it has a special meaning to DOS.

* Reserved on DOS

Wildcard Filename Characters ? and *

You can type out a full file specification each time you want to make your computer operate on a file. However, there will be times when you want to act on a group of files at the same time. In these cases, a "shorthand" system lets you operate on DOS files that have related specifications.

This shorthand system lets you use *wildcard characters* to write a file specification that refers to a group of files rather than to a single file. There are two wildcard characters: ? and *.

The first wildcard character, ?, replaces a single character in a file spec and matches any single character. To use it, try entering the following command with the DOS floppy disk in the default drive.

```
dir disk????.com
```

It should list two files: DISKCOPY.COM and DISKCOMP.COM.

When you use one or more ?s at the end of a filename or extension, each one means, "Any character may be in this position." Thus, the file specification DISK????.COM matches any file specification that has a filename of eight characters beginning with the characters DISK and a file extension of COM.

When you use one or more ?s within a filename or extension, each must match exactly one character. Thus, the file specification T???EE.COM would match TEEPEE.COM but not TREE.COM.

The second wildcard is *, which you may use only at the end of (or in place of) a filename or extension. It means, "Any number of characters, or no characters, may be in this position."

Thus, the following command lists all files with a filename beginning with BASIC and the extension COM:

```
dir basic*.com
```

The following command lists all files with a filename beginning with F and any extension:

```
dir f*.*
```

Global filename characters can be most useful if you name your files consistently to create useful patterns. For example, if you have a set of files containing profit-and-loss statements for the 12 months of 1989, you might name them PNL8901.DAT, PNL8902.DAT, . . . PNL8912.DAT. Then, you could display the status of those files—and only those files—by entering

```
DIR PNL89??.DAT
```

When You May Use Global Filename Characters

You may use global filename characters with any DOS command that can act on a group of files. Global filename characters cannot be used with certain commands, however, because they would have no meaning.

If you try to use global filename characters with a program that does not access them, the program will do one of three things:

- The program may use the first filename it finds that matches the specification.

- The program may tell you that a file specification containing these characters is invalid.

- The program may lack error trapping and interpret ? and * as ordinary characters, creating a file that you cannot name in the parameters of most DOS commands.

Special Filename Rule for DIR

DIR interprets its parameters somewhat differently from all other commands. DIR accepts the standard global filename characters, but it also accepts another type of global filename notation that other commands do not accept.

DIR allows you to specify *every* filename simply by omitting the filename from the parameter and *every* extension by omitting the extension. Thus, both of the following commands produce a directory listing of all files with the filename extension COM:

```
dir *.com
```

```
dir .com
```

If you omit both the filename and the extension from DIR's parameter, DIR produces a directory listing of *all* the files on a disk. This is the simplest form of DIR.

The following command produces a directory listing that includes only a file named EXAMPLE:

```
dir example.
```

Because the dot is present, DIR considers the filename to have a null filename extension (one that is zero characters long), rather than no extension at all.

COM, EXE, and BAT Files

Look again at the DIR listing of your DOS disk. Notice that the disk contains files named CHKDSK.COM, FORMAT.COM, and DISKCOPY-.COM. These files contain programs that DOS runs when you enter the commands CHKDSK, FORMAT, and DISKCOPY, respectively. (You can list all such COM files by entering the command DIR *.COM.) Files with the filename extension EXE also contain programs that DOS runs.

When you enter a command, DOS searches the default disk for a file with the command as its filename and the extension COM. If it cannot find such a file, is searches for the same filename with the extension EXE. It then searches for the filename with the extension BAT. If it cannot find that file either, it displays the error message "Bad command or file name."

Files with the extensions COM and EXE contain *external commands*, which are commands that reside on a disk (usually, the hard disk). When you tell DOS to run an external command, it must read the command from the disk to run it.

Some commands are built into DOS so that they are in RAM all the time that DOS is running. These commands are called *internal commands.* Unlike external commands, they have no COM or EXE files. DIR is an internal command; notice that there is no DIR.COM or DIR.EXE file on your DOS disk. DOS has several internal commands besides DIR. We will encounter some of them, including COPY, RENAME, and ERASE, later in this book.

As we noted previously, you can tell DOS to run a command from a disk other than the default disk by prefixing the disk's name to the command. With the A>prompt on your screen and your DOS disk in drive B, enter the following command:

```
b:chkdsk
```

Notice that running a command in this way does not change the default drive. CHKDSK still checks the disk in drive A unless you specify another drive in a parameter. Thus, to run CHKDSK from drive B and make it check the disk in drive B, you would have to enter

```
b:chkdsk b:
```

The disk from which DOS runs a command has no effect on what the command does.

You could also run CHKDSK from the disk in drive B by making drive B: the default drive. Your screen would look like this:

```
A>b:
B>chkdsk
```

This time, CHKDSK would check the disk in drive B, since CHKDSK always operates on the default drive when no parameter is given.

Formatting a Floppy Disk

Before you can store files on a new floppy disk, you must prepare the floppy disk for use by *formatting* it. Formatting a floppy disk consists of recording a special pattern of data over the floppy disk's entire surface (all tracks and sectors).

The DISKCOPY command automatically formats the target floppy disk if that floppy disk is not already formatted. That was the meaning of the "Formatting while copying" message that DISKCOPY displayed when you ran it.

If you plan to use a brand-new floppy disk for a purpose other than backing up another floppy disk with DISKCOPY, you must first format the floppy disk yourself. You do this with a command called FORMAT.

FORMAT expects one parameter: the name of the drive on which the floppy disk is to be formatted.

```
A>format a: (if your computer has one floppy disk drive) or

A>format b: (if you are formatting in drive B)
```

The first example works on single and dual floppy disk systems. The second example is recommended for dual floppy systems because it saves the time and trouble it takes to swap diskettes and helps reduce the chances of accidentally erasing the wrong disk. It is not uncommon to have an original program disk or your DOS disk in drive A. Pressing the ENTER key at the wrong time would be a serious mistake in this instance. For that reason, drive B, if available, is safer to use for formatting.

FORMAT prompts you to insert a floppy disk in drive A or B. Insert an unused floppy disk in the appropriate drive, and press any key. FORMAT proceeds to format the floppy disk. You can hear the drive hum as its read/write head moves over the floppy disk's recording surface. Note that FORMAT will by default try to format for the highest capacity that the drive supports. If you try to format a 360KB diskette in a 1.2MB drive, your computer will try to format to 1.2MB despite the diskette's lack of capacity.

If you have only one floppy disk drive, remove the DOS floppy disk from the drive to insert the new floppy disk only when the red light is not on.

When FORMAT is done, remove the formatted floppy disk from the drive. If you have only one floppy disk drive, reinsert the DOS floppy disk. Write some identification on an adhesive label and stick the label firmly on the front of the newly formatted floppy disk.

If you want to format more floppy disks, respond to the "Format another disk?" prompt by pressing Y. FORMAT will prompt you to insert the next floppy disk. When you are finished formatting floppy disks, respond to the "Format another disk?" prompt by pressing N.

Options or Switches

An option consists of a \ followed by one other character. It may be used after a command name or after a parameter. In most commands, the position of an option does not matter, but it is customarily placed after the last parameter. For instance, the directory command DIR has two options. The \w option is used to specify a five-column wide directory listing. The \p option is used to specify that DOS pause every 23 lines. Different commands access different sets of options and interpret them in different ways.

Using the VOL Command (DOS 2.0 and Later Versions)

Besides one of the drive designators (A through Z), each drive can have a volume label of up to 11 characters. Volume labels are not required, but they are recommended. They can help you quickly identify the disk at which you are looking. The two most common ways of creating a volume label are the DOS LABEL command, which you can run at any time providing you have the command file LABEL.COM, or the volume option /V of the FORMAT command. The alternative method is to use the /V option when you format the disk with the DOS format command. There is now an assortment of utilities available that allow you to add, change, or delete volume labels and enter them in mixed case, including spaces, and so on. Regular DOS, however, is less flexible. It limits you to uppercase and no spaces.

Once you have formatted a disk and given it a volume label, you can display the volume label at any time with the VOL command.

For example, to display the volume label of the disk in drive B, enter

```
vol b:
```

Another way to display the volume label of a disk is to run the DIR command.

Using Commands with a Drive Name

Just as DISKCOPY accepts two parameters naming the drives to copy from and to, most commands accept a parameter naming the drive you want to use. For example, to run CHKDSK on a floppy disk in drive B, you would enter

```
chkdsk b:
```

To get a directory listing of a floppy disk in drive B, you would enter

```
dir b:
```

If your computer has a hard disk, you may check on the status of this disk by entering the following command with the DOS floppy disk in drive A:

```
C>:chkdsk c:
```

The drive name C normally refers to the hard disk. If the hard disk has been properly formatted, CHKDSK displays information about it.

READ.ME

Traps

If DOS displays

```
disk error reading drive x
```

```
Abort, Retry, Ignore?
```

the floppy disk in drive *x* has not been formatted for use with DOS, nor it is damaged. (The *x* in the actual message would be replaced by the letter of the disk drive you were trying to use.) Press the R key (for Retry). The error may not happen again. If it does, press the A key (for Abort) to stop the operation you were trying to perform. This message also appears if *x* is a single-sided drive and you are trying to read a double-sided floppy disk. If the hard disk has not yet been formatted, you will receive a message such as "Invalid drive specification."

Using the COPY Command

The COPY command is used to make a copy of a file. COPY expects two parameters. The first parameter describes the file to copy from; the second describes the file to copy to.

Make drive A the default drive. With the DOS floppy disk in drive A, put one of your formatted floppy disks into drive B, and enter the following command:

```
copy chkdsk.com b:xyzq.com
```

This command says, "Copy file CHKDSK.COM on the disk in drive A to file XYZQ.COM on the disk in drive B." Display the files on disk B with DIR. Notice that there is now an XYZQ.COM file there.

Try running XYZQ.COM with the following command:

```
b:xyzq
```

XYZQ does the same thing as CHKDSK, since it is a copy of CHKDSK. It even has the same date-and-time stamp. DOS does not consider a copy of a file to be a newly created or modified file. So, a copy has the same date-and-time stamp as the original.

Now let's try something else. Enter

```
copy chkdsk.com b:
```

There are two parameters here, but the second one is not a complete file specification; rather, it is just a drive name. In this case, COPY makes the new file's name the same as the original file's name. If you run DIR on the disk in drive B, you should now find that CHKDSK.COM is listed.

What happens if you omit the second parameter completely, like this:

```
copy b:xyzq.com
```

COPY makes the new file's name the same as the original file's name and puts the new file on the disk in the default drive. If you check the directory of drive A, you will see that XYZQ.COM is now listed.

READ.ME

Traps

If you tell COPY to write a file on a certain disk and there is already a file with that name on that disk, the copy completely replaces the original file. Be careful of this, as it is easy to wipe out important data by copying other data over it—particularly when you use COPY with global file specification characters.

If you back up your disks conscientiously, you can often recover lost data after you make this mistake.

Using COPY with Global Filename Characters

Just as you can use COPY to copy a single file, you can also use COPY with global file spec characters to copy more than one file at a time. For example, with A as the default drive, the following command:

```
copy *.com b:
```

would copy every file on the disk in drive A with the extension COM to the disk in drive B.

By using global characters with the COPY command, you can copy a whole group of files to a new group of files with different names. For instance, the following command:

```
copy b:july.* b:august.*
```

would make a copy on the disk in drive B of every file on that disk that has the filename JULY and any extension, giving the copies the filename AUGUST and the appropriate extensions.

COPY can do many more things. After you have become comfortable with DOS, you may wish to learn more about COPY from the Disk Operating System manual.

READ.ME

Traps

1. COPY displays the following message

```
Write-protect error writing drive x
Abort, Retry, Ignore?
```

You are trying to copy a file to a floppy disk whose write-protect notch is covered. Press the A key to abort the command. If you are certain that the material on the disk does not need to be protected, uncover the write-protect notch, and enter the command again.

    If the write-protect notch is not covered, this message may indicate that the floppy disk is improperly seated in the drive or that the drive's write-protection sensor is stuck. To seat the floppy disk properly or unstick the write-protection sensor, open the drive's door and gently wiggle the floppy disk. If this does not work, have the drive repaired.

2. COPY displays the following message:

```
File cannot be copied onto itself
```

You tried to copy a file to an identically named file on the same disk. This is a meaningless operation, and therefore COPY refuses to do it.

    This situation can arise if the second parameter of COPY has the same drive name as the first parameter and no filename. It can also arise if the first parameter refers to a file on the default drive and the second is omitted.

Renaming Files

RENAME (or REN) is another internal command. It changes the specification of a file on a disk. Like COPY, RENAME takes two parameters. The first is the "from" name and the second is the "to" name. For example, the following command would change a file specification from CHKDSK.COM to CHEKDISK.COM (provided the DOS floppy disk is not write-protected):

```
rename chkdsk.com chekdisk.com
```

If you change the name of a command such as CHKDSK, you should use
RENAME again to restore its original name:

```
rename chekdisk.com chkdsk.com
```

When you rename a file on a disk other than the default disk, enter the
drive name with the first parameter only, as follows:

```
rename b:xyzq.com abcd.com
```

Since it makes little sense to rename a file to a different drive, DOS does
not expect a drive name with the second parameter.

You may use global filename characters to rename a group of files:

```
rename *.com *.moc
```

This command would change every COM file on the default drive to a MOC
file. If you make this change, undo it immediately, or you may not be able to
execute any of those commands. Use the following format:

```
rename *.moc *.com
```

Using the ERASE Command

ERASE (or DEL) is another internal command. You use ERASE to remove
a file from a disk, freeing the space it occupied for use by other files.
ERASE expects one parameter, the name of the file to be erased:

```
erase b:abcd.com
```

ERASE, like COPY and RENAME, allows you to use global file spec
characters. When you use the global file specification *.* to erase all the
files on a disk, DOS will ask you if you are sure before proceeding.

READ.ME

Traps

Once you have erased a file, it is gone. The only sure way to get an erased file back is to restore it from a backup disk. Practice the use of ERASE by erasing all the strangely named files you created with COPY and RENAME. Be careful to include the correct disk drive parameter, as you do not want to erase important files on your DOS floppy disk.

ABOUT SUBDIRECTORIES

Until now, each of your disks has had one directory that contained pointers to all the files on the disk. This arrangement is perfectly adequate for a disk that contains only a few files. As you learned, however, there is a limit to the number of files that a floppy disk will hold in its main directory. In addition, directories are difficult to read when they become too long.

Versions 2.0 and 3.X of DOS let you deal with these problems by defining several directories on a disk. One directory (the one you have been using up to now) is the *root directory*. The root directory may hold both data files and subdirectories. There is no limit to the number of files you can store in a subdirectory, nor to the number of subdirectories you can define on a disk.

Whenever you are using a disk, one of the disk's directories is its current directory. For most purposes, the files in the current directory are the only ones on the disk that you can work with.

You can change the current directory with the CHDIR (or CD) command, described later. Once you change the directory, it remains set until you change it again, reboot, or put a new disk in the disk drive. (When DOS detects the new disk, it makes the disk's root directory the current directory. DOS remembers the last CHDIR done on each drive, so that there is a current directory for each drive.)

Subdirectories may contain files with the same names as other directories and subdirectories. This does not create a conflict, any more than having files with the same name on several different disks would create a conflict. In fact, giving two files in different subdirectories the same name can be a very useful way of emphasizing a connection between them.

Using Paths to Refer to Subdirectories and Files

Every subdirectory has a name, just as every file has a name. A subdirectory's name follows the same rules as a file's name: It may be one to eight characters long, followed by an optional dot and an extension of one to three characters.

There are two ways you can refer to a subdirectory or a file in a subdirectory. First, you can identify each subdirectory between the root directory and the subdirectory or file that you want—for instance, C:\wp\DOCS\memo.wp. Second, you can name each subdirectory between the current directory and the subdirectory or file you want—for instance, DOCS\memo.wp. The second way is shorter, as long as the file you want is part of the same "branch" as the current directory. However, the first way lets you refer to any subdirectory or file on a disk, no matter what directory is current.

Some Examples of Paths

DOS uses path names to refer to files and subdirectories. A path name may consist of one or more of the following: the drive designator, which is a letter and a colon; the path, which is the subdirectory or subdirectories; and the filename. The subdirectories must be separated by a backslash. No spaces are allowed in a path name. A backslash is required after the drive designator and before each subdirectory name. Do not include the backslash, however, after the filename.

Here are some examples of how paths may be used in command lines.

The following command refers to subdirectory NOTICE2, relative to the root directory of the disk in the default drive. (This command's function is to make that subdirectory the current directory.)

```
chdir\overdue\dunning\notice2
```

The following command types file SMITH.DAT in subdirectory NOTICE2:

```
type\overdue\dunning\notice2\smith.dat
```

The following command is the same, but it refers to the file on disk b:

```
type b:\overdue\dunning\notice2\smith.dat
```

The following command is the same, but it refers to the file relative to the current subdirectory when the current subdirectory is NOTICE2:

```
type b:smith.dat
```

Observe how the path name reduces to only the file spec when the file is in the current directory.

Creating Subdirectories and Subdirectory Files

Just as you must create a file before you can tell a program to read the file, you must create a subdirectory before you can tell DOS to put a file into that subdirectory. You create subdirectories, one at a time, with the MKDIR (or MD) command.

Using MKDIR to Create Subdirectories

Start with an empty, formatted floppy disk. Insert the floppy disk in drive B (or whatever drive is free on your computer).

First, use the MKDIR command to create the three subdirectories that reside in the root directory. MKDIR expects one parameter: the path to the subdirectory being made.

To make the subdirectories INVENTRY, RECVABLE, and OVERDUE in the root directory, enter the following commands:

```
md b:inventry
md b:recvable
md b:overdue
```

Now make the subdirectory DUNNING in the subdirectory OVERDUE, like this:

```
md b:overdue\dunning
```

Notice that you typed this path with no leading \. That was just to save yourself the trouble of pressing the extra key. When the root directory is the current directory, it does not matter whether you enter the leading \ or not.

Next, make three more subdirectories in DUNNING. You could do it by entering three MKDIR commands with parameters as, for example, OVERDUE\DUNNING\NOTICE. But if you make DUNNING the current directory, you can save yourself most of that typing.

Use the CD (change directory) command to make the subdirectory DUNNING the current directory:

```
cd b:overdue\dunning
```

Now you can create the three subdirectories NOTICE1 through NOTICE3 like this:

```
md b:notice1
md b:notice2
md b:notice3
```

At this point, you would *not* get the same result if you entered a \ at the beginning of the path. The command

```
MD B:\NOTICE1
```

would make a NOTICE1 subdirectory in the root directory, not in DUN-NING.

Creating Files in Subdirectories

Now you can create files in each subdirectory. Now that the directory structure is complete, it does not matter in what order you define the files. To keep things orderly, however, we will return to the root directory and go through each of the subdirectories one level at a time.

To designate the root directory on the disk in drive B as the current directory, enter the CHDIR command like this:

```
chdir b:\
```

or like this:

```
cd b:\
```

This is the first type of reference to a directory, reduced to its simplest form: a leading \, meaning "Start at the root directory," followed by no subdirectory name.

Create the files BILLING.DAT and SHIPPING.DAT by any convenient means. For example:

```
copy chkdsk.com b:billing.dat

copy chkdsk.com b:shipping.dat
```

Now, create the files JONES.DAT and SMITH.DAT in the subdirectory INVENTRY. You can do it like this:

```
copy chkdsk.com b:inventry\jones.dat

copy chkdsk.com b:inventry\smith.dat
```

Now, you create JONES.DAT and SMITH.DAT in the subdirectory RECVABLE. Instead of copying the files the way you copied them into INVENTRY, you can save some keystrokes by making RECVABLE the current directory:

```
cd b:\recvable

copy chkdsk.com b:jones.dat

copy chkdsk.com b:smith.dat
```

Notice that you entered CHKDSK.COM, not \CHKDSK.COM, even though the current directory is RECVABLE and you were copying from the root directory. This is because you were copying from disk A, and the root directory is still current on disk A. Every disk on your system has its own current directory, independent of every other disk.

Next, make OVERDUE the current directory. Then copy SMITH.DAT
to it from the subdirectory INVENTRY:

```
cd b:\overdue
copy b:\inventry\smith.dat b:smith.dat
```

Here you have used a path in COPY's first parameter to refer to a file
that is not in drive B's current directory nor in its root directory. You need
no path in the second parameter, because you are copying to drive B's
current directory, which you just set to OVERDUE.

The exercises you have just performed should have familiarized you
enough with paths that you can finish up on your own. Make NOTICE2 the
current directory, and create a SMITH.DAT file in it.

CHDIR, DIR, AND TREE

Now that you can create subdirectories and create files in them, you need to
know how to display information about subdirectories. You can do this with
the CHDIR and DIR commands.

Using CHDIR and DIR

You can display the path to a disk's current directory by entering CHDIR
(or CD) with no parameter or with only a drive name in the parameter:

```
cd b:
```

When you enter DIR with no parameter or with no path in the parameter, it
displays information about the current directory.

On a disk with subdirectories, DIR's output contains some things that
you have not encountered yet. Enter the following commands to see an
example:

```
cd b:\overdue
dir b:
```

The result you see will be similar to the following:

```
Volume in drive B has no label
Directory of B:\OVERDUE

   .         <DIR> 9-08-83 3:47p
   ..        <DIR> 9-08-83 3:44p
SMITH   DAT 6061 3-08-81 12:00p
DUNNING     <DIR> 9-08-81 3:50p
```

The second line of DIR's display shows the current directory's path. Looking back at earlier DIR displays, you now can see the reason for the puzzling "Directory of B:\" line: It displayed the path of the root directory.

In the directory listing, each subdirectory is listed with the notation "<DIR>" after its name. It has no size value. Each subdirectory contains two special directory entries: "." contains information about the subdirectory itself; ".." contains a pointer to the subdirectory's parent directory. The parent directory of OVERDUE is the root directory. The parent directory of the subdirectory DUNNING is OVERDUE.

You can use DIR to display a directory other than the current directory by including a path in the parameter. For example, to display the contents of subdirectory NOTICE2 in subdirectory DUNNING, you would enter

```
dir b:\dunning\notice2
```

You can also use global file spec characters with paths if you want to display only a certain group of files in a subdirectory. For instance, you could use the following command to display files with the extension DAT in the subdirectory INVENTRY in the root directory:

```
dir b:inventry\*.dat
```

Using the TREE Command

While the DIR command will list the contents of one directory at a time, you may want to scan *all* the directories and subdirectories on a disk. The TREE command lets you do this by displaying a complete picture of the directory structure of a disk. The TREE command expects one parameter, identifying the disk you want to display:

```
tree b:
```

TREE displays the path to each subdirectory on the disk and the names of any subdirectories defined in the subdirectory. If you use the /F (files) option, it also displays the names of files in each subdirectory.

REMOVING A SUBDIRECTORY WITH RMDIR (OR RD)

You learned how to create subdirectories earlier in this chapter. You may also want to remove a subdirectory from a disk. The RMDIR, or RD, (remove directory), command accomplishes this. RMDIR expects one parameter: the path to the directory to be removed. For example, to remove the subdirectory NOTICE3 from the disk, you would enter one of the following commands:

```
rmdir b:\notice3
```

```
rd b:\notice3
```

You cannot remove a subdirectory that contains any files or any subdirectories of its own. If you want to remove such a subdirectory, you must first erase all the files and remove all the subdirectories that are in it. Also, you cannot remove a subdirectory while it is the current directory.

Referring to a Parent Directory

You can use a double dot (..) in a path to represent the parent directory of a subdirectory. For example, if DUNNING were the current directory, you could make OVERDUE the current directory by using the following command:

```
cd b:..
```

Traps

Do not try to remove a subdirectory with ERASE. If you do, DOS will delete every file in the subdirectory. In addition, do not try to rename a subdirectory. To accomplish the equivalent of renaming a subdirectory, you must

1. Create a new subdirectory

2. Copy all the files in the old subdirectory to the new one

3. Delete all the files in the old subdirectory

4. Remove the old subdirectory

If NOTICE2 were the current directory, you could make NOTICE1 the current directory with the following command:

```
chdir b:..\notice1
```

And if NOTICE1 were the current directory, you could type the file SMITH.DAT in the OVERDUE subdirectory with the following command:

```
type b:..\..\smith.dat
```

(If you created SMITH.DAT by copying CHKDSK.COM, of course, displaying it would be pointless. TYPE is used for displaying text files, and a COM file is not a text file.)

Double-dot notation is useful mainly with a disk whose directory structure is rather complex but very regular.

Backing Up Disks with Subdirectories

Backing up a floppy disk with subdirectories is simple. The DISKCOPY command copies the entire disk—subdirectories and all.

Backing up a hard disk is a little more complex. You must take into account that a hard disk has subdirectories if you want to back up the disk properly.

The BACKUP Command

BACKUP normally backs up only one directory, the current directory if you specify no path in BACKUP's first parameter. Use the /S (subdirectory) option to make BACKUP back up all the files in the specified directory and in subdirectories below it in the directory tree. For example, to back up subdirectory OVERDUE and all subdirectories whose paths go through OVERDUE, you could enter

```
backup c:\overdue a:/s
```

To back up an entire hard disk, you back up the root directory and its subdirectories with the following command:

```
backup c: a:/s
```

The RESTORE Command

Ordinarily, the RESTORE command restores files that were backed up from the directory that you specify in the second parameter (or from the current directory if no directory is specified). In every case, RESTORE will restore a file only to the directory that held it when it was backed up.

For example, let's suppose the disk structure you just created is defined on a hard disk. You back up the entire hard disk by running BACKUP on the root directory with the /S option, and then restore to OVERDUE. Your command lines should be as follows:

```
backup c:\ a:/s

restore a: c:\overdue
```

Only the files in OVERDUE will be restored, because you named OVER-DUE in RESTORE's second parameter. The RESTORE command restores files only to the directory from which they were originally saved.

If you back up the files in INVENTRY and try to restore them to OVERDUE, like this:

```
backup c:\inventry a:

restore a: c:\overdue
```

no files will be restored. None of the files on the backup floppy disk came from OVERDUE.

You can make RESTORE restore files to a directory and all its subdirectories by running RESTORE with the /S option. Thus, if you ran the following RESTORE command on a backup of the whole hard disk:

```
restore a: c:\overdue/s
```

it would restore everything in and below OVERDUE in the directory tree (a total of two files and four subdirectories).

To restore all the files on the backup floppy disk, restore to the root directory with /S:

```
restore a: c:\/s
```

When you run RESTORE with /S, it restores each file to the directory it was backed up from. If the necessary directory does not exist, RESTORE creates it and any other subdirectories on the path to it.

When you run RESTORE without /S, it does not create subdirectories. If you want to restore files to a particular subdirectory, you must first create that subdirectory with MKDIR if it does not already exist.

SEARCHING FOR COMMAND FILES WITH PATH

Subdirectories are helpful for running internal commands, such as COPY and TYPE. But what if you want to run external commands and application programs? Suppose, for example, you are using a word processing program on text files stored in many different subdirectories. Must you keep a copy of the program in every subdirectory?

One way to avoid having to do that would be to make the directory containing all your programs the current directory, and refer to your data files with their path names. This is a nuisance, however, especially if you build a directory structure in which many subdirectories are nested within other subdirectories. And many application programs can't operate on files that aren't in the current directory.

Another way to solve the problem is to keep all of your programs on one disk and all of your data on another. If your computer has two floppy disk drives, for example, you can keep programs and command files in the root directory on disk A and data files in various directories on disk B. No matter what directory is current on disk B, DOS will retrieve programs and command files from disk A.

If you have one hard disk, however, that solution is unsatisfactory. You want to keep both the programs and the data on the hard disk because of its speed and capacity. But you cannot have two different current directories on the same disk at the same time.

The PATH command solves this problem by letting you define a search path—that is, a path to a directory that DOS uses to search for programs and command files that it cannot find in the current directory.

For example, suppose your computer has a hard disk, drive C. The drive's root directory contains DOS commands and other programs, including a word processing program called WP. The root directory also contains a subdirectory named CLIENTS. This subdirectory has its own subdirectory, LETTERS, which contains your correspondence with clients.

Using the PATH Command

To make LETTERS the current directory on the hard disk and tell DOS to search the root directory on the hard disk for any programs not found in LETTERS, enter

```
C:
chdir \clients\letters
path \
```

Now you can enter a command such as WP or CHKDSK without concern that the necessary program files are in the root directory rather than the current directory.

When DOS fails to find a program in the current directory, it automatically searches the directory defined by PATH. PATH is an internal command; you need not enter it with a path or keep a copy of it in each of your directories.

To replace the current search path with a new one, simply run PATH again. To cancel the current search path without defining a new one, run PATH with a null parameter:

```
path ,
```

The solitary comma tells DOS that there is a null parameter. To display the current search path, execute PATH with no parameters:

```
path
```

ABOUT DOS DEVICES

Some devices that you can use with your computer are displays, floppy disk drives, hard disk drives, and printers. DOS refers to these devices by a DOS device name. You may need to know the DOS device names for the devices you have attached to your computer.

The following table lists some devices and their DOS device names. For a complete list of DOS device names, refer to the DOS manual.

Device	DOS Device Name
Printer	LPT1 or PRN
Display or console	CON
Drives (floppy disk or hard disk)	The letters A through Z

What System Do You Have?

Your computer can have floppy disk drives, hard disk drives, or a combination of both. DOS refers to floppy disk and hard disk drives with the letters A through Z. DOS assigns drive letters to all the floppy disk drives attached to your computer, beginning with the letter A. Then DOS assigns drive letters to any hard disks attached to your computer, usually starting with the letter C.

One Floppy Disk Drive

If your computer has one floppy disk drive, DOS refers to it as both drive A and B. Instead of A and B representing physical drives, the letters represent floppy disks. When you use a DOS command such as COPY with one floppy disk drive, DOS displays a message on your screen telling you when to switch floppy disks.

Two Floppy Disk Drives
If your computer has two floppy disk drives, the first floppy disk drive is referred to as drive A, and the second floppy disk drive is referred to as drive B. You can have floppy disks in both drive A and drive B at the same time. DOS does not have to tell you to switch floppy disks if you have two floppy disk drives.

One Floppy Disk Drive and a Hard Disk Drive
If your computer has one floppy disk drive and one hard disk drive, the floppy disk drive is referred to as both drive A and drive B. The hard disk drive is called drive C.

DOS Functions and Keys
Your computer keyboard has keys that initiate particular tasks or functions. The following information applies to most keyboards.

For the following functions, the SHIFT, CTRL, and ALT keys work much like the shift key on a typewriter—they change the "meaning" of regularly typed keys. When a combination such as CTRL-BREAK is specified, hold down the first key or keys in the combination, press the last key, and release all the keys. Notice that you can press and hold down the CTRL, ALT, or SHIFT key with no results. Nothing happens until you press the final key in the combination.

Function	Keys
Break	CTRL-BREAK or CTRL-C or CTRL-SCROLL-LOCK
Pause Screen	CTRL-S or PAUSE
Print Screen	PRTSC or SHIFT-PRTSC
Printer Echo	CTRL-PRTSC or CTRL-P
System Reset	CTRL-ALT-DEL or RESET

Entering a Command (Enter)   Use the ENTER key when you have finished typing an entire command line. It tells DOS to interpret the line you typed and act on it.

Canceling a Command (Break)   CTRL-BREAK stops a command from finishing its job normally. This is sometimes called *terminating* a program.

Correcting a Typing Mistake (Backspace)   Each press of the BACKSPACE key (the left-pointing-arrow key above the ENTER key) moves the cursor back one space to erase a typing mistake.

Stopping the Screen (Pause Screen)   CTRL-S or PAUSE cause the screen to pause when information is scrolling on the screen too fast for you to read.

Printing the Screen (Print Screen)   This prints all the information currently on the screen. The printer must be on before you press the PRINT SCREEN key.

Printing What You Type (Printer Echo)   This allows you to prints one line at a time as it appears on the screen. With Printer Echo on, each time you press the ENTER key or the computer displays a line, the line is printed, or *echoed*, on the printer. To stop echoing to the printer, press the Printer Echo key combination again.

Restarting DOS (System Reset)   CTRL-ALT-DEL reboots the computer. This is sometimes referred to as *loading*, or starting, DOS.

DOS Editing Keys

When you type a line and press ENTER, DOS puts a copy of the line in an input *buffer*, a temporary storage place. This allows you to change it or use the line again. This saves you time, because you do not have to type the whole line over.

The following DOS editing keys are used to edit the line that is put in the input buffer:

INS   Allows you to insert characters within a line.

DEL   Deletes one character in the input buffer. The character in the buffer is not displayed, and the cursor does not move.

ESC   Cancels the line currently being displayed. The buffer remains unchanged.

F1 or RIGHT ARROW   Displays one character from the buffer each time it is pressed.

F2   Displays all characters up to a specified character.

F3   Displays all characters in the buffer.

F4   Deletes all characters up to, but not including, the specified character. F4 is the opposite of F2.

F5   Accepts the line you edited as the current buffer line.

BATCH FILES

A *batch file* is a file that contains DOS commands. You can make DOS run the commands in a batch file by entering a single command through the keyboard. Batch files have many uses, including:

- Entering a sequence of many commands that must be run the same way many times

- Entering one or more commands with long, complex parameters

- Entering a sequence of long-running commands while you attend to other tasks

- "Packaging" a sequence of commands so that an inexperienced person can run them by typing one command line

A batch file specification must have the extension BAT. You run the batch file by entering its filename through the keyboard, just as if it were a command.

A batch file may have any filename that is not the same as the name of a command in the same directory. If a batch file and a command have the same filename, entering the filename makes DOS run the command. You cannot run the batch file until you change its name. Chapter 26 offers complete coverage of batch files. We encourage you to take advantage of this as an excellent boost to your productivity.

The AUTOEXEC.BAT File

Many users have a series of commands that they run each time they boot. If you have a serial-interface printer, for example, you must run two MODE commands before you can print anything. If you have a battery-powered clock card in your computer, you may run a program provided with the card to set the DOS date and time from the card.

If you use such a series of commands, you have probably realized that you can run them more conveniently by putting them in a batch file. In fact, you can do even better: You can make DOS run the batch file automatically whenever you boot. To accomplish this, all you need to do is store the batch file in the root directory of your DOS disk and name it AUTOEXEC.BAT. When DOS is booted, it checks the root directory of the DOS disk for an AUTOEXEC.BAT file. If it finds such a file, it runs it.

When DOS finds an AUTOEXEC.BAT file, it does not prompt you for the date and time as it otherwise would. This is so you will not be bothered by DOS's date and time prompts if AUTOEXEC.BAT sets the date and time from a clock card. If you want to get the usual date and time prompts with an AUTOEXEC.BAT file, you must include the DATE and TIME commands in the file.

DOS COMMAND REFERENCE

This section contains a reference for all DOS versions. Each entry includes the command's full form, the command's parameters, a description, and an example if appropriate.

Note: Not all options are supported by all versions. Where possible, we will note supported versions. Most DR-DOS commands support the /H option, which brings up help information for that command. Most MS-DOS 5.0 commands support a help option. Digital Research's DR-DOS also has an /H option for command help.

DOS Command Line Commands

APPEND
MS/PC-DOS 3.2 DR-DOS

External

The first version of the command tells DOS to look in the drive and path indicated for data files. The second version of the command tells DOS to use an application's Search First, Find First, and Exec functions.

Note: Use this option with care, as it can cause problems with certain application programs.

The third version of the command is used to cancel the APPEND command.

Syntax: append *drive:path*[;[*drive*:][*path*]...]

append [/X]

append [;]

Examples: append c:\letters;c:\memos

append /X

append;

ASSIGN
MS/PC-DOS 2.0 and later and DR-DOS

External

Causes commands that access a certain drive to access a different drive. To cancel ASSIGN, type **assign** with no drive letters.

Syntax: assign [*drive1*]=[*drive2*]

Examples: assign a=c

Causes a program to access drive C as if it were drive A.

assign

Resets the drive letters to what they were originally.

ATTRIB
MS/PC-DOS 3.0 and later and DR-DOS (+a and −a are 3.2 and later)

External

Sets the file attributes. You can use this command to prevent accidental erasure of files.

Syntax: attrib [/ H][+ | −a][+ | −r][+ | −s][*path*][*filename*][/ P][/S]

Options: / H

Displays help information (DR-DOS only).

+a

Sets the file's archive flag.

−a

Removes the archive flag.

+r

Makes the file read-only (cannot be changed or erased).

−r

Allows the file to be written to or erased.

+s

Sets the file's system flag (DR-DOS only).

−s

Removes the system flag (DR-DOS only).

/P

Pauses after each screen (DR-DOS only).

/S

Sets the attributes in the subdirectories associated with the chosen directory.

Example: attrib +r needed.txt

Sets the file to read-only.

BACKUP
MS/PC-DOS 2.0 and later and DR-DOS

External

Normally used to make backup copies of files from a hard disk to floppies or streaming tape.

Syntax: backup [/H][*source*][*path*][*filename*] *destination* [*options*]

Options: / H

Displays help information (DR-DOS only).

/S

Backs up all subdirectories.

/ M

Backs up only those files modified since last backup.

/A

Adds files to destination disk (does not erase destination).

/D:*date*

Backs up only those files modified after *date*.

/L:*filename*

Makes a log file named *filename* in the root directory.

/T:*time*

Backs up only those files modified after *time*.

Example: backup c: a:/s

This command will back up all files, including those in subdirectories, in the C: drive to the A: drive. You should have enough formatted floppy disks and labels to number them. DOS will prompt you to insert the floppy disks by number as backup progresses. Numbering is essential for the RESTORE command to work correctly.

BREAK
MS/PC-DOS 2.0 and later and DR-DOS

Internal

Tells DOS how often to check for CTRL-C or CTRL-BREAK. Default is BREAK OFF. Some programs do not tolerate BREAK ON.

Syntax: break [on|off]

Examples: break on

break off

CACHE
DR-DOS

External

A disk cache program that speeds up access to the hard drive.

Syntax: cache [/ H] [/S=*nnnn*] [/X] [/ E]

Options: / H

Calls up help.

/S=*nnnn*

The buffer size in KB.

/ X

Sets up the cache in expanded memory.

/ E

Sets up the cache in extended memory.

Example: cache /s=256 /e

CHCP
MS/PC-DOS 3.3 and later and DR-DOS

Internal

Allows you to display and change the current code page for the command processor.

Syntax: chcp [*nnn*]

Option: *nnn*

The number of the code page, which is one of the following:

Number	Code Page
437	United States
850	Multilingual
860	Portuguese
863	Canadian-French
865	Nordic

Examples: chcp

chcp 850

CHDIR or CD
MS/PC-DOS 2.0 and later and DR-DOS

Internal

Allows you to switch between directories. Practice with this command. It allows you to move through directories smoothly if used properly. The full form of the command (from UNIX) is CHDIR, but DOS allows CD, which saves typing.

The DOS directory structure was adopted from UNIX. Originally, in the CP/M operating system, one of DOS's predecessors, the directory was kept on one or two tracks of the floppy disk and could hold some restricted number of entries (for example, 32, 64, or 112). If your system contained many small files, you could, under the old system, run out of filename slots before you ran out of disk space. This was particularly true for hard disks with 10 or more MB of storage capacity.

The root directory of a disk is still restricted in this way. But each subdirectory can hold an unlimited number of filenames. So if you have many filenames, subdirectories are the answer. You can still stick with the root directory and forget subdirectories if you have a small number of filenames. But properly used subdirectories, like a properly arranged filing cabinet, can save you time and headaches.

Syntax: chdir [*drive*:][*path*][/A]

cd [*drive*:][*path*][/A]

Option: /A

Lists the current directory path for all the current drives (DR-DOS only).

Examples: cd

Tells you where you are.

cd \

Changes to the root directory.

cd *newdir*

Changes to a new directory (from the root directory).

cd *newdir*

Changes from *any* directory to a directory in the root.

cd..

Changes to one directory level up (the two dots indicate one level closer to the parent directory).

CHKDSK
MS/PC-DOS 1.0 and later and DR-DOS

External

Checks a disk for any problems, and reports the amount of space used and available.

Syntax: chkdsk [*drive:*][*options*]

Options: /A

Shows memory totals (DR-DOS only).

/B

Marks bad blocks (DR-DOS only).

/C

Prints cluster numbers of all bad files (DR-DOS only).

/D

Locates directories (DR-DOS only).

/F

Finds lost clusters.

/L

Rebuilds cluster links (DR-DOS only).

/M

Maps bad blocks (DR-DOS only).

/P

Displays parent blocks for all directories (DR-DOS only).

/R

Recovers root directory (DR-DOS only).

/S

Shows actual file space (DR-DOS only).

/V

Displays files and directories as checked.

Example: chkdsk /f

Responds with message "Convert lost clusters to files?" You may as well respond by typing **y** for yes, since lost clusters are not recoverable any other way. When finished, you will find one or more files (if there were lost clusters) with the names FILE0000.CHK, FILE0001.CHK, and so on. You can try TYPEing them to see what they contain. Then ERASE them to free up disk space.

CLS
MS/PC-DOS 2.0 and later and DR-DOS

Internal

Clears the screen and places the prompt (and cursor) in the upper left corner of the screen.

Syntax: cls

COMMAND
MS/PC-DOS 1.0 and later and DR-DOS

External

Starts a new command processor.

Syntax: command [d:][*path*][ctty=*device*][/e:*nnnnn*][/p][/c *string*]

Options: ctty = device

Allows you to specify where input and output goes.

/e:*nnnnn*

Specifies the amount of environment space to allocate.

/p

Keeps the second command processor in memory.

/c string

Tells the command processor to perform the commands that are in *string* and return to the first command processor.

Examples: command c:\bin ctty=com2 /e:1024

command c:\bin /e:1024 /c myprogrm

command c:\bin ctty=com1 /c modemwrk

COMP
PC-DOS, MS-DOS 3.3, DR-DOS

External

Compares two files and reports differences.

Syntax:
  comp [/H][*drive:*][*path*]*filename1* [*drive:*][*path*]*filename2* [/A][/M:*n*]

Options: /H

Displays help information (DR-DOS only).

/A

Displays the reported matches in ASCII format (DR-DOS only). The default is to display them in hexadecimal format.

/M:*n*

Specifies the maximum number of mismatches before COMP terminates automatically (DR-DOS only). 0 allows an unlimited number of mismatches.

Examples: comp new.doc old.doc

comp mywork.txt yourwork.doc

comp newfile.txt oldfile.txt /A /M:0

COPY
MS/PC-DOS 1.0 and later and DR-DOS

Internal

Combines two or more source files into one target file. It creates the target file if it does not exist. It can also concatenate one or more source files onto the first source file in the list. The source files are connected by "+". If a target file is not specified, the files are concatenated into the first source file.

Syntax: copy [*d:*][*path*]*source*[*/option*] [*d:*][*path*]*target*[*/option*]

Options: /A

Copies ASCII files.

/ B

Copies binary files.

/ V

Provides read-after-write verify.

/S

Copies SYS and hidden files (DR-DOS only).

/C

Confirms before copying each file. (DR-DOS only).

COPY can be used to copy the output of a device to another device or to a file. Terminate input by pressing F6 or CTRL-Z to indicate the end of the file.

Example: copy con prn

Copies input from the console to the printer.

copy con my.txt

Copies console input to MY.TXT file.

COPY can copy a file to a device.

Example: copy my.txt prn

Copies file MY.TXT to the printer.

COPY can also copy a file to a file. This is the most used option.

Examples: copy my.txt your.txt

Copies MY.TXT to YOUR.TXT.

copy *.doc + finished.doc

Copies all DOC files to one file.

CTTY
MS/PC-DOS 2.0 and later and DR-DOS

Internal

Changes where DOS looks for input and sends its output.

Syntax: ctty *device*

Example: ctty com2

CURSOR
DR-DOS

External

Lets you set the cursor blink rate.

Syntax: cursor [/ H] [/S*nn*] [/C] [OFF]

Options: / H

Calls up help.

/S*nn* Sets the flash interval, in 1/20th-of-a-second increments; the default is 4.

/C

Enables CGA compatibility.

OFF

Returns the cursor to the hardware cursor.

Example: cursor /s8

DATE
MS/PC-DOS 1.0 and later and DR-DOS

Internal

Can be used to display the date or to set the date.

Syntax: date [*month-day-year*]

Example: date 6-17-90

DEBUG
MS/PC-DOS 1.0 and later

External

Allows you to test and change EXE and COM files.

Syntax: debug [*path*][*filename*]

Examples: debug

debug myprog.exe

DEL
MS/PC-DOS 1.0 and later and DR-DOS

Internal

Same as ERASE.

Syntax: del [*drive:*][*path*]*filename*

Example: del myfile.txt

DELQ
DR-DOS

Internal

Same as DEL, except that it asks if you want to delete the file.

Syntax: delq [drive:][*path*]*filename*

Example: delq *.txt

Prompts before deleting each TXT file to confirm that you want to erase it.

DIR
MS/PC-DOS 1.0 and later and DR-DOS

Internal

Displays the contents of a directory.

Syntax: dir [*drive:*][*path*][*filename*][*options*]

Options: / D

Displays files with DIR attribute (DR-DOS only).

/S

Displays files with SYS attribute (DR-DOS only).

/A

Displays all files (DR-DOS only).

/W

Displays a wide directory listing file specifications only.

/L

Includes file date, time, and size (DR-DOS only); the default.

/P

Displays one page at a time.

/N

Eliminates paging (default) (DR-DOS only).

/R

Remembers options (DR-DOS only).

/C

Changes options. (DR-DOS only).

DISKCOMP
MS/PC-DOS 3.2 and DR-DOS

External

Compares two floppy disks of the same type and reports if differences exist.

Syntax: diskcomp [/H] [*drive1*:] [*drive2*:][/1][/8][/V]

Options: /H

Calls up help (DR-DOS only).

/1

Compares only the first side of the floppy disks, even if the floppy disks are double-sided.

/8

Compares only eight sectors per track, even if the first floppy disk contains more.

/V

Verifies that the disk can be read (DR-DOS only).

DISKCOPY
MS/PC-DOS 1.0 and later and DR-DOS

External

Copies a disk of one format to another disk of the same format. DOS formats the second disk as it makes the copy.

Syntax: diskcopy [/H][*drive1:*] [*drive2:*][/1]

Options: /H

Displays help information (DR-DOS only).

/1

Copies only side 1 of a double-sided disk.

Example: diskcopy a: b:

DOSKEY
MS-DOS 5.0

External

A terminate-and-stay-resident (TSR) program that allows you to recall and edit previous command line commands. DOSKEY also allows you to create macros of commands normally run.

Syntax:
doskey [/reinstall] [/bufsize] [/dmacs] [/dhist] [*macroname = command*]

Options: /reinstall

Reloads DOSKEY even if it is already loaded.

/bufsize

Specifies the buffer size for DOSKEY; the default is 1024 bytes.

/dmacs

Lists the DOSKEY macros available.

/dhist

Lists the command line in the buffer.

macroname = commands

Specifies the macro name and command.

Examples: doskey

doskey /dmacs > prn

doskey wdir = dir /w

EDITOR
DR-DOS

External

The DR-DOS full-screen text editor.

Syntax: editor [*filename*]

Example: editor

EDLIN
MS/PC-DOS 1.0 and later

External

The MS/PC-DOS text-editing program.

Syntax: edlin [*filename*]

Example: edlin

EMM386
MS-DOS 5.0

External

Enables or disables EMM386 Expanded Memory, and enables or disables Weitek coprocessor support.

Syntax: emm386 [onlofflauto] [w = onlw = off]

Options: onlofflauto

Enables or disables the expanded memory portion of the EMM386.EXE device driver or sets it to auto.

w = onlw = off

Turns the Weitek coprocessor support on or off.

Examples: emm386 emm386 on w=on

emm386 auto

ERAQ
DR-DOS

Internal

Same as ERASE, except that it asks if you want to delete the file.

Syntax: eraq [*drive*:][*path*]*filename*

Example: eraq *.txt

Prompts before deleting each TXT file to confirm that you want to erase it.

ERASE or ERA
MS/PC-DOS 1.0 and later and DR-DOS

Internal

Erases files or the entire contents of directories. Use with care: If you have
a directory named MYTXT and are trying to erase file MY.TXT, you could
erase the entire contents of your MYTXT directory if you neglect to type
the period.

Syntax: erase [*drive*:][*path*][*filename*]

EXE2BIN
MS/PC-DOS 2.0 and later DR-DOS (not included in PC-DOS 4.0)

External

Converts an EXE file into a binary-format COM file.

Syntax: exe2bin *filename1 filename2*

Examples: exe2bin myfile.exe myfile.com

exe2bin calcint.exe calcltr.com

EXIT
MS/PC-DOS 2.0 and later and DR-DOS

Internal

Returns you to a running program. Some programs allow you to go to DOS temporarily. Type **exit** to return to where you were in the program.

Syntax: exit

FASTOPEN
MS/PC-DOS 3.3 and later and DR-DOS

External

Speeds up access to files and directories by recording file locations.

Syntax: fastopen [/H][*d*:[= *numfile*]] /x

fastopen [*d*:[= (*numfile,fileext*)]] /x

fastopen [*d*:[= ([*numfile*],*fileext*)]] /x

Options: /H

Displays help (DR-DOS only).

numfile Number of files FASTOPEN will work with; the range is 10 to 999.

fileext

Number of file extents; the range is 1 to 9999.

/x

Sets the FASTOPEN cache into LIM expanded memory.

Examples: fastopen c:=100

fastopen c:=50,10

fastopen c:=100 /x

FC
MS-DOS 2.0 and later

External

Compares two files or sets of files and reports differences.

Syntax: fc [*/options*] [*d:*][*path*]*filename1* [*d:*][path]*filename2*

Options: /a

Shortens the output of the ASCII comparison to the first and last lines of any differences.

/b

Forces a binary comparison.

/c

Ignores the case of the letters.

/ L

Compares files in ASCII mode.

/ Lb *n*

Sets the line buffer to *n* lines.

/*n*

Displays line numbers.

/t

Does not expand tabs to spaces.

/w

Compresses white space.

/*nnnnn*

Specifies the number of lines that must match after a difference.

Example: fc /a myfile.txt yourfile.txt

FDISK
MS/PC-DOS 3.2 and DR-DOS

External

No network

The hard disk partitioning program.
   Note: Use this command with caution. Improper use could cause a disaster, such as the loss of your hard disk files!

Syntax: fdisk

FILELINK
DR-DOS

External

Allows you to transfer files between computers.

Syntax: filelink [/ H]

Example: filelink / h

FIND
MS/PC-DOS 2.0 and later and DR-DOS

External

Searches for a text string in a group of files and displays the lines contain-ing the text string.

Syntax: find [/ H][/ B][/ C][/ N][/ S][/ U][/ V] *"string"* [*filename*]

Options: / H

Displays help information (DR-DOS only).

/ B

Changes display format (DR-DOS only).

/C

Shows only the number of lines containing *"string"*.

/ N

Displays line numbers.

/S

Searches subdirectories (DR-DOS only).

/ U

Sets case sensitivity (DR-DOS only).

/V

Displays the lines not containing *"string"*.

Example: find "INVOICE" billing.doc

FORMAT
MS/PC-DOS 1.0 and later DR-DOS (not included in PC-DOS 4.0)

External

No network

Formats floppy disks according to the options selected or the default format for the drive.

Syntax: format [/ H][*drive:*][*options*]

Options: / H

Displays help information (DR-DOS only).

/S

Copies the system files to the formatted floppy disk.

/V

Allows setting of the volume name.

/1

Forces single-sided format.

/4

Forces 360KB-format on a 1.2MB drive.

/8

Formats 9 sectors but uses only 8.

/ T:80

Sets number of tracks to 80.

/ T:40

Sets number of tracks to 40.

/ N:9

Sets number of sectors to 9.

/ N:8

Sets number of sectors to 8.

/ B

Formats 9 sectors but uses only 8. Reserves space for system files.

Example: format a:

GRAFTABL
MS/PC-DOS 3.0 and later and DR-DOS

External

Enables DOS to display graphics characters.

Syntax: graftabl [/H][*nnn*][/STATUS]

Options: / H

Displays help information (DR-DOS only).

nnn

The number of the character set, which is one of the following:

Number	Character Set
437	USA (default)
850	Multilingual
865	Norway
860	Portugal
863	French Canada

/STATUS

Displays the currently selected country code page.

GRAPHICS
MS/PC-DOS 3.2 and DR-DOS

External

Enables DOS to print graphics to printers of some types.

Syntax: graphics [color][/ R]

Options: color

Allows graphics to produce color output on a color printer.

/ R

Prints black and white exactly as they appear on the screen. The default is to print what is white on the screen as black on the printer.

HILOAD
DR-DOS

External

Loads a program, device driver, or TSR program into high memory. You can load the following DR-DOS programs:

CURSOR.EXE
KEYB.COM
NLSFUNC.EXE
GRAPHICS.COM
GRAFTABL.COM
JOIN.EXE
SHARE.EXE

Syntax: hiload *filename*

Example: hiload cursor.exe

JOIN
MS/PC-DOS 3.0 and later and DR-DOS

External

No network

Allows you to join a disk drive to a path.

Syntax: join [*d: d:path*] [/d]

Option: /d

Turns off JOIN.

Examples: join a: c:\work\acct
join a: /d

KEYB
MS/PC-DOS 3.2 and DR-DOS

External

Allows the keyboard to be used with other languages.

Syntax: keyb *xx*[+]

Options: *xx*

The following abbreviations are used in place of *xx*:

Abbreviation	Language
US	U.S. English (default)
DV	Dvorak (MS-DOS only)
DK	Danish
FR	French
GR	German
IT	Italian
NO	Norwegian
SP	Spanish
SV	Scandinavian (Swedish and Finnish)
UK	United Kingdom English

+

Identifies enhanced keyboards.

LABEL
MS/PC-DOS 3.1 and later and DR-DOS

External

No network

Allows you to assign, change, or delete volume labels on floppy disks and hard disks.

Syntax: label [*drive:*][*label*]

Example: label a:save disk

MEM
MS/PC-DOS 4.01 and DR-DOS

External

Displays memory usage.

Syntax: mem [*options*]

Options: / H

Displays help (DR-DOS only).

/ B

Displays memory used by the operating system (DR-DOS only).

/ D

Displays memory used by device drivers (DR-DOS only).

/S

Displays the disk buffers (DR-DOS only).

/ P

Pauses at each screenful of information (DR-DOS only).

/ M

Displays RAM, ROM, and EMS memory (DR-DOS only).

/A

Combines all the switches above (DR-DOS only).

/ PROGRAM

Displays programs loaded into memory (MS/PC-DOS only).

/DEBUG

Displays programming information (MS/PC-DOS only).

Example: mem

MKDIR or MD
MS/PC-DOS 2.0 and later and DR-DOS

Internal

Makes new directories as required. Experiment with this and RD to get a feel for the commands.

Syntax: mkdir [*drive:*][*path*]*directory*

md [*drive:*][*path*]*directory*

Example: md newdir

MODE
MS/PC-DOS 1.0 and DR-DOS

External

Allows you to configure your printer, configure your serial ports, redirect printer output, and set the video type.

Mode: Configure Printer mode LPT*n*[:][*chars*][,[*lines*][,p]]

Examples: mode lptl:132,8,p

132 columns, 8 lines per inch, continual retry if printer busy.

mode lptl:80,6,

80 columns, 6 lines per inch, report printer busy.

Mode: Configure Serial Ports mode COM*n*[:]*baud*[,*parity*[,*databits*[,*stopbits*[,p]]]]

Options: com: COM1, COM2, and possibly COM3

baud: 110, 300, 600, 1200, and so on.

parity: n = none; o = odd; e = even

databits: 7 or 8

stopbits: 1 or 2

p: same as printer

Examples: mode coml:1200,o,7,2,p

mode coml:300,n,,,p

Mode: Redirect Printer   mode LPTn[:] = COMn[:]

Example: mode lptl: = coml:

Mode: Select Display   mode [*display options*]

Options: mono: monochrome (black and white)

40: any color display, 40 columns, same colors

80: any color display, 80 columns, same colors

bw40: color display, 40 columns, no color

bw80: color display, 80 columns, no color

co40: color, 40 columns

co80: color, 80 columns

Example: mode co80

Color display, 80 columns, color enabled.

MORE
MS/PC-DOS 2.0 and later and DR-DOS

External

Takes input from a standard device and prints it a screen at a time on the display.

Syntax: more

Examples: type my.txt | more

Displays MY.TXT 23 lines at a time.

dir | more

Displays directory 23 lines at a time.

NLSFUNC
MS/PC-DOS 3.3 and later and DR-DOS

External

Provides support for extended country information.

Syntax: nlsfunc [/H][*path*][*filename*]

Options: /H

Displays help information (DR-DOS only).

filename

The name of the file that contains the extended country information.

Example: nlsfunc

PASSWORD
DR-DOS

External

Assigns a password to a file or path. The password can be up to eight characters long.

Syntax: password [/H] [*path*][*filename*] [/R] [/W] [/D] [/P] [/G]:*password* [/N] [/NP] [/NG] [/S]

Options: /R:*password*

Sets a password required for reading, copying, writing, deleting, or renaming the file.

/W:*password*

Sets a password required for copying, deleting, or renaming the file.

/D:*password*

Sets a password required for deleting or renaming the file.

/P:*password*

Sets a password to operate on a path rather than a file. Each time you try to access the path, you will be asked for the password.

/G:*password*

Sets a global default password.

/N

Removes all password protection.

/NP

Removes password protection from a directory.

/NG

Removes the global password.

/S

Sets a password to operate on files and subdirectories associated with the
current directory.

Example: password secret.doc /r:*password*

PATH
MS/PC-DOS 2.0 and later and DR-DOS

Internal

Establishes a search path for programs.

Syntax: path [[*drive*:][*path*][;[*drive*:][*path*]. . .]]

Examples: path

Displays search path currently in effect.

path c:\mywork;d:\yourwork\wstar

PRINT
MS/PC-DOS 2.0 and later and DR-DOS

External

Sets up a printer queue, and prints files.

Syntax: print [*path*][*filename*][*options*]

Options: /D:*device*

Sets up a device, PRN for example. Other valid devices are LPT1, LPT2,
LPT3, AUX, COM1, and COM2.

/B:bufsize

Sets buffer size from 1 to 32,767 bytes; the default is 512.

/U:busytick

Sets the number of time ticks (1 to 255) the printer will wait before it gives up its processor time slice; the default is 1.

/M:maxtick

Sets the number of time ticks the printer will retain control during each of its time slices.

/S:timeslice

Sets the number of time slices (1 to 255) per second during which the printer will be given control of the system; the default is 8.

/Q:size

Tells DOS the number of files it can queue (4 to 32); the default is 10.

/T

Stops all printing.

/C

Removes a path or filename from print queue.

/P

Adds a path or filename to print queue.

Examples: print mytext.txt

print mytextl.txt mytext2.txt

PROMPT
MS/PC-DOS 2.0 and later and DR-DOS

Internal

Lets you set the prompt (ordinarily C>, for example) to anything you like.

Syntax: prompt [*options*][*string*]

Options: $$

Displays the $ character.

$T

Displays the current system-clock time.

$D

Displays the current system-clock date.

$P

Displays the current drive and directory.

$V

Displays the DOS version number.

$N

Displays the current drive.

$G

Displays the ">" character.

$L

Displays the "<" character.

$B

Displays the "|" character.

$Q

Displays the "=" character.

$H

Effects a backspace, erasing the preceding character.

$E

Displays the escape character.

$_

Begins a new line on the display.

Examples: prompt pg

prompt Your Wish $_ Is My Command.

RECOVER
MS/PC-DOS 2.0 and later and DR-DOS

External

No network

Allows you to recover files that have been corrupted.

Syntax: recover [/H][*drive:*][*path*][*filename*]

Options: /H

Displays help information (DR-DOS only).

Examples: recover a:

recover c:\letters\myletter.txt

RENAME or REN
MS/PC-DOS 1.0 and later and DR-DOS

Internal

Renames a file or files.

Syntax: rename [*drive:*][*path*]*oldname newname*

ren [*drive:*][*path*]*oldname newname*

Examples: ren *.doc *.wp

Renames all files with DOC extensions to the same filenames but with WP extensions.

ren a:my.txt your.txt

Changes the filename from my.txt to your.txt.

REPLACE
MS/PC-DOS 3.2 and DR-DOS

External

Selectively adds or replaces files on the destination disk.

Syntax: replace [/ H][*drive:*][*path*]*filename* [*path*]*filename*[*options*]

Options: / H

Displays help information. Must be the first command line parameter (DR-DOS only).

/A

Transfers only files that do not exist on the destination disk.

/H

Instructs REPLACE not to ignore system or hidden files (DR-DOS only).

/M

Merges changed files on the source floppy disk with unchanged files on the destination floppy disk (DR-DOS only).

/P

Prompts before copying each file (DR-DOS only).

/R

Allows destination files marked read-only to be overwritten.

/S

Searches all subdirectories of the destination directory.

/W

Causes a wait for keypress before copy.

RESTORE
MS/PC-DOS 2.0 and later and DR-DOS

External

Restores files saved with the BACKUP command.

Syntax: restore [/H] *source destination* [*path*][*filename*] [*options*]

Options: /H

Displays help information (DR-DOS only).

/S

Restores subdirectories.

/P

Prompts to restore system or hidden files.

/A:*mm-dd-yy*

Restores all files that have been altered on or after the specified date.

/B:*mm-dd-yy*

Restores all files that have been altered on or before the specified date.

/E:*hh:mm:ss*

Restores all files that have been altered at or before the specified time.

/L:*hh:mm:ss*

Restores all files that have been altered at or after the specified time.

/M

Restores all files that have been altered or deleted on the original disk since the backup was done.

/N

Restores files not on the destination drive.

/R

Displays what files would be restored but does not restore any files (DR-DOS only).

Examples: restore a: c:\ /s

restore a: c:\work\letters*.doc

RMDIR or RD
MS/PC-DOS 2.0 and later and DR-DOS

Internal

Removes a directory. This command will *not* remove the files or subdirectories in a directory—only the directory itself, which must be empty.

Syntax: rmdir [*drive:*]*path*

rd [*drive:*]*path*

Examples: rmdir work

rd work\letters

SELECT
PC-DOS

External

Sets up the configuration by creating an AUTOEXEC.BAT file and a CONFIG.SYS file.

Syntax: select

SET
MS/PC-DOS 2.0 and later and DR-DOS

Internal

Sets the command processor's environment space.

Syntax: set [*envname* = [*param*]]

Examples: set

Displays the current environment.

set temp = c:\temp

SETUP
DR-DOS

External

Brings up a menu-driven program that allows you to configure your system.

Syntax: setup

SETVER
MS/PC-DOS 5.0

External

Sets up, modifies, and displays a version table of what DOS versions are required by various applications.

Syntax: setver *d*: [*filename*] [*n.nn*] [/delete]

Options: d:

Indentifies the drive that contains MSDOS.SYS.

filename

Names the EXE file that is to be used with this version of DOS.

n.nn

Gives the DOS version number.

/delete

Removes the entry from the version table.

Examples: setver c: myapp.exe 3.3

setver c: wordapp.exe /delete

SHARE
MS/PC-DOS 3.0 and later and DR-DOS

External

Sets up file sharing and locking. Since the ability to share files is built into DR-DOS, you do not need to load SHARE to perform file-sharing operations.

   SHARE is included with DOS for compatibility with packages that load or require SHARE. In PC/MS DOS 4.0, you must load SHARE with disk partitions larger than 32MB. This version of SHARE does not perform any functions.

Syntax: share

SID
DR-DOS

Internal

The Symbolic Instruction Debugger. This allows you to debug and test programs.

Syntax: sid

SORT
MS/PC-DOS 2.0 and later and DR-DOS

External

Takes data from the standard input device, sorts the data, and sends it to the standard output device.

Syntax: sort [/R][/+n]

Options: /R

Sorts in reverse order.

/+n

Starts sorting with column n.

Examples: dir | sort > sortdir.txt

dir | sort /r > revsort.txt

SUBST
MS/PC-DOS 3.1 and later and DR-DOS

External

No network

SUBST allows you to substitute a drive letter for a drive-and-path combination.

Syntax: subst [*drive: path*]

subst *drive:* /D

Options: /D

Removes drive assignment from specified drive.

Examples: subst g: c:\work\letters\may

subst g: /d

SYSTEM or SYS
MS/PC-DOS 1.0 and later and DR-DOS

External

No network

Transfers system files to blank formatted disk.

Syntax: sys *drive*:

Example: sys a:

TIME
MS/PC-DOS 1.0 and later and DR-DOS

Internal

Sets or displays the time.

Syntax: time [*hh:mm*[:*ss*[.*xx*]]]

Examples: time

Displays the time.

time 10:30:00

Sets the time to 10:30 A.M.

TOUCH
DR-DOS

External

Changes the date-and-time stamp of a file or group of files.

Syntax: touch [/ H] [*path*][*filename*] [*options*]

Options: / H

Displays help information.

/ T:*hh:mm:ss*

Designates the time to set.

/ D:*date*

Designates the date to set.

/ P

Prompts before touching each file.

/ R

Includes read-only files.

/S

Includes subdirectories associated with the current directory.

Examples: touch *.doc /d:Ol-Ol-90 /s

touch *.txt /t:08:00:00 /p

TREE
MS/PC-DOS 3.2 and DR-DOS

External

Displays a tree listing of directories and files.

Syntax: tree [/ H][*drive*:][/ F][/ P]

Options: / H

Displays help information (DR-DOS only).

/ F

Displays all the files in the subdirectories.

/ P

Pauses after each screen (DR-DOS only).

Examples: tree c:

tree a: /f

TYPE
MS/PC-DOS 1.0 and later and DR-DOS

Internal

Displays the contents of a text file on the display screen.

Syntax: type [*drive:*] [*path*][*filename*] [/P]

Options: /P

Pauses after each screenful (DR-DOS only).

Example: type myletter.txt /p

UNFORMAT
MS-DOS 5.0

External

Restores a hard drive to its initial state after an accidental FORMAT is done to it.
   Note: If the /U switch was used with FORMAT, UNFORMAT will not be able to restore the hard drive.

Syntax: unformat *d:*

Example: unformat c:

VER
MS/PC-DOS 2.0 and later and DR-DOS

Internal

Displays the DOS version number.

Syntax: ver

VERIFY
MS/PC-DOS 2.0 and later and DR-DOS

Internal

Turns the disk write verification on or off.

Syntax: verify [on|off]

Example: verify on

verify off

VOL
MS/PC-DOS 2.0 and later and DR-DOS

Internal

Displays the volume name.

Syntax: vol [*drive:*]

Example: vol a:

XCOPY
MS/PC-DOS 3.2 and DR-DOS

External

The extended copy command. It allows you to specify additional information for the copy parameters.

Syntax: xcopy [/ H] [@]*path*]*filename1* [*path*]*filename2* [*options*]

Options: / H

Displays help information (DR-DOS only). Must be the first command line switch.

@

Specifies that the source file is a list of files to copy (DR-DOS only).

/A

Copies only files with archive bit set.

/ D:*date*

Copies only files whose date is the same or later than the specified date.

/ E

Creates subdirectories on the destination, even if subdirectories are empty.

/ H

Includes system and hidden files in the copy process (DR-DOS only).

/ M

Copies files that have the archive bit set, and resets the archive bit on the source file.

/ P or /C

Prompts for each file.

/R

Overwrites read-only files (DR-DOS only).

/S

Copies subdirectories also.

/V

Verifies data written.

/W

Waits for disk change.

Examples: xcopy *.doc a: /s

xcopy a: /s

XDEL
DR-DOS

External

Extended delete function for files and subdirectories.

Syntax: xdel [/ H] [*path*][*filename*] [*options*]

Options: / H

Displays help information.

/ D

Removes empty subdirectories.

/N

Deletes all specified files without prompting.

/P

Prompts before each delete.

/S

Deletes files in subdirectories.

Examples: xdel *.bak /s

xdel c:\work\letters*.bak /p

XDIR
DR-DOS

External

Extended directory command.

Syntax: xdir [+|−ADHRS] [*path*][*filename*] [*options*]

Options: +|− [A] [D] [H] [R] [S]

Includes (+) or excludes (−) files with certain attributes.

/B

Uses the brief directory-display format.

/C

Computes hash code for each file and display.

/L

Uses the long directory-display format; the default.

/P

Pauses after each screen.

/R

Reverses the sort order.

/S

Displays subdirectories.

/T

Sorts by date and time.

/W

Uses the wide directory-display format.

/Z

Sorts by file size.

Examples: xdir *.* /z

xdir a: *.* /s /p

Batch File Commands

The following commands are primarily used in batch files.

CALL
Loads and runs a second batch file.

ECHO
Allows or inhibits the screen display of DR-DOS commands.

EXIT
Allows you to end a batch file before reaching the end.

FOR
Allows you to execute a command multiple times.

GOTO
Goes to the line label specified.

IF
Allows checking to see if a condition is true or false.

PAUSE
Pauses the execution of a batch file.

REM
Indicates a remark line for a batch file.

SHIFT
Increases the number of control line variables you can have in a batch file.

CONFIG.SYS Commands
The following commands are used in creating or modifying the CONFIG-.SYS file for a computer.

BREAK
Indicates when to check for break sequence.

BUFFERS
Sets the number of buffers.

COUNTRY
Sets the country codes.

DEVICE
Loads device drivers. Device drivers included with DOS 3.3 are:

ANSI.SYS
EMM386.SYS
EMMXMA.SYS
DRIVER.SYS
VDISK.SYS

DRIVPARM
Sets the parameters for a drive.

ENVSIZE
Sets the environment size.

FASTOPEN
Sets the number of file entries in an indexing scheme.

FILES
Sets the number of files that can be open at one time.

HISTORY
Allows you to recall command lines that you typed in.

LASTDRIVE
Allows you to set the last drive.

REM
Indicates a remark line.

SHELL
Allows programmers to write their own command processor and use it instead of COMMAND.COM.

DOS QUICK REFERENCE

The following is a quick reference to DOS commands.

Command	Ext	Int	DOS 1.0	DOS 1.1	DOS 2.0	DOS 2.01	DOS 2.25	DOS 3.0	DOS 3.1	DOS 3.2	DOS 3.3	DOS 4.0	DOS 4.01	DOS 5.0	DR DOS 5.0	CDOS 386	Switches	Help
APPEND	X									X					X	X	Y	1
ASSIGN	X							X							X		N	1
ATTRIB	X							X							X	X	Y	1
BACKUP	X				X										X	X	Y	1
BREAK		X			X										X	X	N	1
CACHE	X														X		Y	1
CHCP		X			X										X		N	1
CHDIR or CD		X			X										X	X	N	1
CHKDSK	X		X												X	X	Y	1
CLS		X			X										X	X	N	1
COMMAND	X		X												X		Y	1
COMP	X				X										X		N	1
COPY		X	X												X	X	Y	1
CTTY		X			X										X		N	1
CURSOR	X														X		Y	1
DATE		X	X												X	X	N	1
DEBUG	X		X														N	1
DEL		X	X												X	X	Y	1
DELQ		X													X	X	Y	1
DIR		X	X												X	X	Y	1
DISKCOMP	X							X							X	X	Y	1
DISKCOPY	X				X										X	X	Y	1
DOSKEY	X														X		Y	1
EDIT	X														X		Y	1

Command														
EDITOR	X										X		N	1
EDLIN	X		X										N	1
EMM386	X									X			N	1
ERAQ		X									X	X	Y	1
ERASE or ERA		X	X								X	X	Y	1
EXE2BIN	X			X							X		N	1
EXIT		X		X							X		N	1
FASTOPEN	X			X							X		Y	1
FC	X			X									Y	1
FDISK	X						X				X	X	N	1
FILELINK	X										X		Y	1
FIND	X			X							X	X	Y	1
FORMAT	X		X								X	X	Y	1
GRAFTABL	X				X						X		Y	1
GRAPHICS	X						X				X		Y	1
HILOAD	X										X		N	1
JOIN	X				X						X		Y	1
KEYB	X				X		X				X		Y	1
LABEL	X					X					X	X	N	1
MEM	X								X		X		Y	1
MKDIR or MD		X		X							X	X	N	1
MODE	X						X				X		Y	1
MORE	X			X							X	X	N	1
NLSFUNC	X			X							X		N	1
PASSWORD	X										X	X	Y	1
PATH		X		X							X	X	N	1
PRINT	X			X							X		Y	1
PROMPT		X		X							X	X	N	1
RECOVER	X			X							X		N	1
RENAME or REN		X	X								X	X	N	1
REPLACE	X						X				X	X	Y	1
RESTORE	X			X							X		Y	1
RMDIR or RD		X		X							X	X	N	1
SELECT	X							X					N	1
SET		X		X							X	X	N	1
SETUP	X										X	X	N	1
SETVER	X									X			Y	1
SHARE	X				X						X		Y	1
SID	X										X		N	1

SORT	X			X						X		Y	1
SUBST	X					X				X	X	Y	1
SYSTEM or SYS	X		X							X		N	1
TIME		X	X							X	X	N	1
TOUCH	X									X	X	Y	1
TREE	X						X			X	X	Y	1
TYPE		X	X							X	X	Y	1
UNFORMAT	X								X			N	1
VER		X		X						X	X	N	1
VERIFY		X		X						X	X	N	1
VOL		X		X						X	X	N	1
XCOPY	X						X			X	X	Y	1
XDEL	X									X	X	Y	1
XDIR	X									X	X	Y	1
CALL		X		X				X		X	X	N	
ECHO		X		X						X	X	N	
EXIT		X		X						X	X	N	
FOR		X		X						X	X	N	
GOTO		X		X						X	X	N	
IF		X		X						X	X	N	
PAUSE		X	X							X	X	N	
REM		X	X							X	X	N	
SHIFT		X		X						X	X	N	
BREAK		X		X						X		N	
BUFFERS		X		X						X		N	
COUNTRY		X			X					X		N	
DEVICE		X		X						X		N	
ANSI.SYS	X			X						X		N	
EMM386.SYS	X							X		X		Y	
EMMXMA.SYS	X							X		X		Y	
DRIVER.SYS	X			X						X		Y	
VDISK.SYS	X			X						X		Y	
DRIVPARM		X					X						
ENVSIZE		X						X		X		N	
FASTOPEN		X						X		X		N	
FILES		X		X						X		N	
HISTORY		X								X		N	
LASTDRIVE		X				X				X		N	
REM		X		X						X		N	
SHELL		X		X						X		Y	

Command Line Commands

APPEND
Specifies a search path for data and overlays.

ASSIGN
Reassigns a drive letter to a different drive.

ATTRIB
Displays and modifies a file's attributes.

BACKUP
Makes backup copies of hard disks and floppy disks.

BREAK (Built-in)
Allows you to break out of programs.

CACHE (DR-DOS only)
Disk cache program.

CHCP (Built-in)
Changes the code page.

CHDIR or CD (Built-in)
Changes the current directory path or displays the current subdirectory.

CHKDSK
Checks the integrity of data on disks, and restores corrupted disks.

CLS (Built-in)
Clears the screen.

COMMAND
Loads a copy of the command processor.

COMP
Compares files character by character.

COPY (Built-in)
Copies files between directories and to devices.

CTTY (Built-in)
Redirects input and output.

CURSOR (DR-DOS only)
Lets you change the cursor attributes.

DATE (Built-in)
Displays and changes the date.

DEBUG
Debugging program.

DEL (Built-in)
Deletes a file or group of files.

DELQ (DR-DOS, Built-in)
File delete with query.

DIR (Built-in)
Displays the files in a directory.

DISKCOMP
Compares two disks of the same format.

DISKCOPY
Copies an entire disk to another of the same format.

DOSKEY (MS-DOS 5.0 only)
TSR that recalls DOS commands, edits the command line, and creates macros.

EDITOR (DR-DOS only)
Text-editing program.

EDLIN (MS/PC-DOS only)
Text-editing program.

EMM386 (MS-DOS 5.0 only)
Enables and disables EMM386 expanded memory and Weitek coprocessor support.

ERAQ (DR-DOS, Built-in)
File delete with query.

ERASE or ERA (Built-in)
Erases files.

EXE2BIN
Converts an EXE file to a binary file.

EXIT (Built-in)
Returns you to a running application.

FASTOPEN
Speeds up access to disk files.

FC
File-compare program.

FDISK
Sets and changes partitions on a hard disk.

FILELINK (DR-DOS only)
Transfers files over a serial cable.

FIND
Locates a string of characters in a file.

FORMAT
Formats floppy disks.

GRAFTABL
Displays extra characters on a color graphics display.

GRAPHICS
Allows you to print graphics with the PRINT SCREEN key.

HILOAD (DR-DOS only)
Loads programs, device drivers, and TSRs into high memory.

JOIN
Joins a disk drive to an empty subdirectory.

KEYB
Allows use of non-USA keyboards.

LABEL
Sets the volume label on a floppy disk.

MEM
Displays amount of memory and usage.

MKDIR or MD (Built-in)
Makes a directory.

MODE
Sets COM port parameters, printer type, and monitor type.

MORE
Causes output to screen to be displayed one screen at a time.

NLSFUNC
Provides extended country information, and allows the CHCP command to be used.

PASSWORD (DR-DOS only)
Sets password protection to files or paths.

PATH (Built-in)
Sets or displays path information.

PRINT
Enables print spooling.

PROMPT (Built-in)
Sets the command prompt.

RECOVER
Recovers files from a corrupted disk.

RENAME or REN (Built-in)
Renames files.

REPLACE
Selectively copies files.

RESTORE
Restores files that were backed up using the BACKUP command.

RMDIR or RD (Built-in)
Removes subdirectories.

SELECT (MS/PC-DOS only)
Configuration program.

SET (Built-in)
Inserts strings into the command processor's environment.

SETUP (DR-DOS only)
Configuration program.

SETVER (MS-DOS 5.0 only)
Sets the DOS version number to be used with executable files.

SHARE
Enables file sharing and locking.

SID (DR-DOS only)
Symbolic debugger program.

SORT
Takes standard input, sorts it, and sends it to the standard output.

SUBST
Allows you to replace a path with a drive.

SYSTEM or SYS
Copies the system files.

TIME (Built-in)
Displays and changes the system time.

TOUCH (DR-DOS only)
Sets the date-and-time stamp on groups of files.

TREE
Displays the path of directories and subdirectories.

TYPE (Built-in)
Displays the contents of a text file.

UNFORMAT
Restores a hard disk drive to its condition prior to the running of the FORMAT program.

VER (Built-in)
Displays the version number.

VERIFY (Built-in)
Verifies that the data has been written correctly to disk.

VOL (Built-in)
Displays the volume label.

XCOPY
Selectively copies groups of files.

XDEL (DR-DOS only)
Selectively deletes groups of files.

XDIR (DR-DOS only)
Displays an extended directory list.

CHAPTER THREE

Menu Programs

Many people without any background or interest in the technical side of computing use computers for specific business tasks. For those users, the vagaries of DOS are of no interest or value. Menu programs allow these people to use specific applications without dealing directly with DOS. In actual practice, millions of users boot their systems and are immediately presented with an applications menu rather than the DOS command line. They do this with the help of a menu system.

THE MENU SYSTEM

Simply put, a menu system is a specialized software program that sets up a screen listing all the applications you normally run. You, the user, simply touch a button and the program is executed. When you are through, the menu program returns to the screen. The menu program takes care of the

135

housekeeping chores by jumping to appropriate subdirectories and maintaining necessary paths so the user has few responsibilities. Most menu programs also create a log of usage so that work can be traced.

Single-Purpose Systems

A significant number of the 40-plus million PCs in operation are used for a few basic automated office tasks. It's not uncommon for a system used in an office environment to boot up and execute a program such as WordPerfect from AUTOEXEC.BAT. A batch file may be left by a programmer to start another application in the event the user needs to deviate from the normal single-application routine.

However, technical support can be a problem with single-application configurations. The problem surfaces when new versions of software or companion products appear. A company decides to upgrade its computer— add spreadsheet capability, maintain the company inventory, or even implement an accounting system. Any of these changes means additional support time and expense. Inexperienced users won't know how to make this system work without a lot of training. Here's where menus come in handy.

Standardizing The Workplace

Menus are important to businesses because of their need to standardize paperwork and reduce support requirements. The importance of menus has grown in recent years with larger capacity hard disks and a growing number of computer applications.

When you read through a publication today you'll see a lot more references to multiple hard drive partitions and high capacity drives. The DOS prompt was a lot less forbidding when everything was on the root directory of a 360K diskette. A user with a 330MB SCSI hard disk with 10 partitions, drive C: through L:, will have a tough time finding applications even with today's advanced Shells. A good menu will save even an experienced user the memory and time it takes a DOS Shell program to sift through thousands of files.

Navigation through native DOS can be frustrating for anyone. DOS users can find themselves lost in a maze of directories, subdirectories, and files. Of course, experience helps but there's no substitute for quick and painless alternatives that make the whole process convenient and enjoyable. For the die-hard command-liner, menu programs even have an option to temporarily shell to the DOS command line when the mood strikes.

Shells for Navigating and Menus for Executing

DOS shells are most useful as a DOS navigational tool. You can use a DOS shell to locate and execute programs. Menu systems are a more effective way to catogorize your applications and execute them with the least number of keystrokes.

Traditionally, DOS shells have been viewed as a tool for both advanced and novice users while menus have been seen as something that more advanced users set up for novices. But menus can be for advanced users as well. As hard disks have grown from a standard of 10MB to disks that often have more than 80MB of memory, the sheer volume of program and data files on disk can delay or confound even the experienced user.

History of Menus

Menus are an outgrowth of DOS batch files. Menu systems include Progressive Computer Services' ez Menu, Marshall McGee's Automenu, Fifth Generation's Direct Access, and Fixed Disk Organizer (FDO) from IBM.

Menu systems began to take hold when hard disk drives did in 1983 with the announcement of the PC/XT just as PCs began to become business productivity tools.

In the past eight years the number of menu systems available for DOS has grown from a handful to hundreds.

Benefits of Menus

- Simplified software installation and maintenance
- Insulating the user from the complexities of DOS
- Controlling access to programs and files
- Maintaining a record of program and file access for billing and security
- Organizing applications
- Increased productivity
- Reduced training
- Standardization

Most stand-alone menus cost less than $150. In fact, there is a strong shareware tradition in the menu field making some menus available for the cost of a phone call to a local bulletin board.

Network menus usually cost less than $500. When you factor in the number of workstations served by the menu and the added functions that network management provides, you'll find that this is a great value.

Advanced Features

Advanced features found in many menus include custom applications, timed applications, usage tracking, and virus protection. Some programs, of course, take things several steps further. They include such features as TSR management, compatibility with keyboard-enhancement and RAM-resident programs, and encryption of menu files. These special features can mislead you, wowing you with intricacies and completely masking how the program works.

We'll first look at the three main tasks of a menu, and then review some of the more advanced features. Then, we'll take a look at how these features are implemented in some of the most popular menu packages.

Installation

Many of today's menus offer automatic installation, with data bases of popular software programs to build the user menu. Unless you opt to forgo automatic installation when you add the menu to your hard drive, you won't need to know DOS-sensitive words such as *drive, directory,* and *file*; it's all handled for you.

Using a Menu

In general, all menus offer single-keystroke access to software options. The language is easy to understand, and DOS interaction is very limited. Selecting menu options is as easy as using the cursor, typing a letter, using a mnemonic, or clicking a mouse.

Maintenance

Maintenance may be the most difficult part of menus. You may have to tell
the menu system how to find and start your applications. Generally, you will
be required to indicate drive and directory information as well as the name
of your executable files.

Figure 3-1 shows the set-up process in PowerMenu. While the set-up
and modification procedures will vary from menu to menu, this example is
representative. It should give you a sense of the type of information you will
be required to supply.

Getting Help

As you add and delete software programs, you will inevitably have to meet
the intricacies of DOS head-on at some point or another. The easier the

Figure 3-1

PowerMenu set-up process

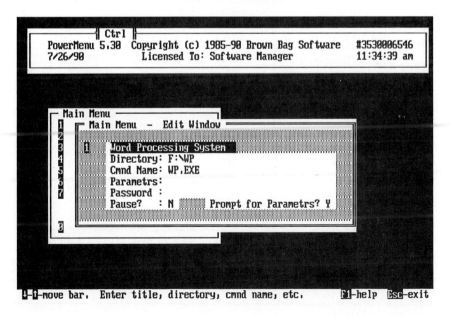

modification process, the better. Tutorials, help screens, and the tree function make the job of modification much easier. Menuworks offers two tutorials. One walks you through the menu-building process; the other shows you how to use finished menus. Automenu has on-line help that is accessed at the touch of a key.

The tree feature available in some menus eliminates the need to remember the locations, numerous program names, and executable files necessary to add programs to a menu. Figure 3-2 shows how the tree is used to add a word processing program to a submenu in Direct Access.

Going Deeper

As you become more familiar with a menu, you may want to change its basic features. For some users, one level of submenus just isn't enough to

Figure 3-2

Direct Access submenu directory tree

```
       C R E A T E / M O D I F Y    S U B - M E N U S
  ┌──────────────────────┬────────────────────────┬──────────────────┐
  │   The Title Of This Su│ Directory Of Drive H:  │      Files       │
  ├──────────────────────┼────────────────────────┼──────────────────┤
  │  Program Description  │ ├─LOG                  │ CONVERT   EXE    │
  │ ─────────────────────│ │ └─B4RESTOR           │ CURSOR    COM    │
  │ A)»Word Perfect 5.1   │ ├─MERGE                │ DIR       BAT    │
  │ B)                    │ ├─MISCELL              │ FIXBIOS   COM    │
  │ C)                    │ ├─PERSONAL             │ GRAB      COM    │
  │ D)                    │ ├─POLPRO               │ GRAPHCNV  EXE    │
  │ E)                    │ ├─PRESS                │ INSTALL   EXE    │
  │ F)                    │ ├─PRODUCT              │ MACROCNV  EXE    │
  │ G)                    │ ├─REPORTS              │ PTR       EXE    │
  │ H)                    │ ├─SALE                 │ SPELL     EXE    │
  │ I)                    │ ├─TECHCALL             │ WP        EXE    │
  │ J)                    │ │ └─MACROS             │ WPINFO    EXE    │
  │ K)                    │ ├─TRADE                │                  │
  │ L)                    │ └─UPGRADE              │                  │
  │ M)                    │»├─WP51                 │                  │
  ├──────────────────────┼────────────────────────┴──────────────────┤
  │                       │ F1 Drive    F2 Find Next File    Esc Exit │
  └──────────────────────┴────────────────────────────────────────────┘
                           H:\WP51
```

accommodate all necessary functions. For example, you may use several word processing programs and have your files separated into business and personal sections. It would be nice to have the main menu display the word processing option, have a submenu display the program names, and have another submenu indicate options.

The later versions of DOS allow this type of logical organization of a hard disk. Menu programs have taken full advantage of it. For example, PowerMenu has four menu levels, and Direct Access has six.

In menus that allow you multiple levels, there may be a distinction between the main menu and submenu levels: The main menu organizes and names your applications, whereas the submenus are where you actually launch the programs. Figures 3-3 and 3-4 illustrate this. Both are from the maintenance facility of Direct Access. Figure 3-3 illustrates the setup of main menus. You simply type the menu description. Figure 3-4 illustrates

Figure 3-3

Main menu set-up process

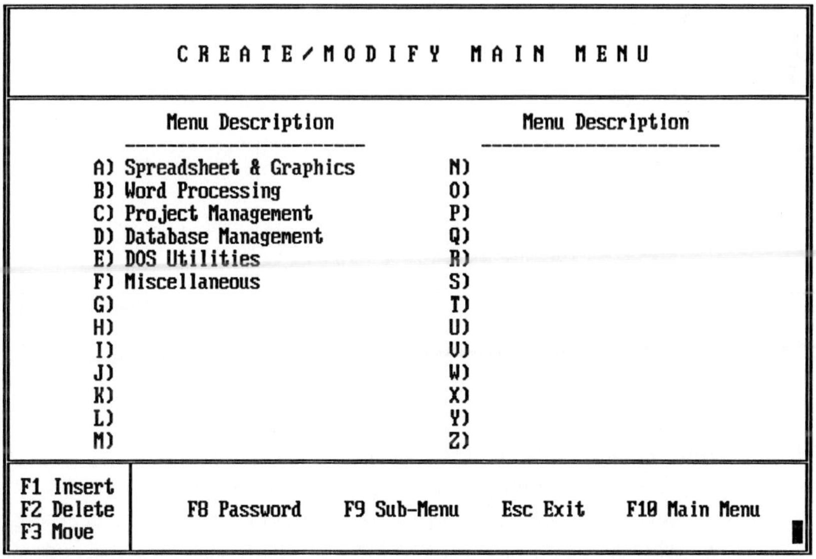

```
             C R E A T E / M O D I F Y   M A I N   M E N U

            Menu Description                    Menu Description
        ----------------------            ----------------------
     A) Spreadsheet & Graphics         N)
     B) Word Processing                O)
     C) Project Management             P)
     D) Database Management            Q)
     E) DOS Utilities                  R)
     F) Miscellaneous                  S)
     G)                                T)
     H)                                U)
     I)                                V)
     J)                                W)
     K)                                X)
     L)                                Y)
     M)                                Z)

 F1 Insert
 F2 Delete      F8 Password    F9 Sub-Menu    Esc Exit    F10 Main Menu
 F3 Move
```

Figure 3-4

Submenu set-up process

```
┌────────────────────────────────────────────────────────────────────┐
│              C R E A T E ⁄ M O D I F Y   S U B - M E N U S            │
│        The Title Of This Sub-Menu Is 'Word Processing'.   (2nd Level) │
├────────────────────────────────────────────────────────────────────┤
│      Program Description  Drive   Directory        Filename          │
│     ──────────────────── ───── ───────────────    ──────────        │
│ A) Word Perfect 5.1        C \WP51               WP              ▓   │
│ B)                                                                   │
│ C)                                                                   │
│ D)                                                                   │
│ E)                                                                   │
│ F)                                                                   │
│ G)                                                                   │
│ H)                                                                   │
│ I)                                                                   │
│ J)                                                                   │
│ K)                                                                   │
│ L)                                                              ▓   │
│ M)                                                                   │
├────────────────────────────────────────────────────────────────────┤
│ F1 Ins                                                               │
│ F2 Del  F5 Custom  F7 Tree  F8 Options  F9 Sub-Menu  Esc Exit  F10 Main │
│ F3 Mov                                                             ▓ │
└────────────────────────────────────────────────────────────────────┘
```

---

submenu setup. Here you are required to give drive, directory, and executable—filenames that will actually launch your applications.

WHAT ABOUT NETWORKS?

If you have set up a network, you can imagine how menus can help waylay some of the fears involved in such a major system. Think about it for a minute: You are the network supervisor for a company that has just networked its 100 workstations. You must set up access rights to the 320MB hard drive and keep new users from accessing DOS directly.

Menus will help with such network maintenance. A supervisor can set up a networkwide system and distribute menus and passwords throughout. Any modification of menu groups is simple: Tag the users in question, modify their menus, and redistribute the format throughout the system.

POPULAR PROGRAMS

We've seen what menus can do in a general sense; now let's examine some of the more popular menu programs.

As noted earlier, there are three primary tasks a menu program must address in order to be effective: installation, use, and maintenance. Below are five popular menus that address these three tasks.

These menus were selected because they have all recently appeared on one or more lists of best-selling software. In addition to these five packages, we will also take a look at how to create a menu with DOS batch files.

Automenu, Version 4.7, by Magee Enterprises, Inc.
Registration: $50
P.O. Box 1587
Norcross, GA 30091
404-446-6611
404-368-0710 (24 hour fax)
404-446-6650 (24 hour BBS)

PowerMenu, Version 5.3, by Brown Bag Software
Registration: $89.95
2155 S. Bascom Ave., #114
Campbell, CA 95008
408-559-4545

Direct Access, Version 5.0, by Fifth Generation Systems
Registration: $99
10049 N. Reiger Rd.
Baton Rouge, LA 70809
800-873-4384
504-291-7921

ez-MENU, by Progressive Computer Services
Registration #1: $35 includes documentation on disk
Registration #2: $50 includes documentation in a full color, 3 ring binder
P.O. Box 8721
New Orleans, LA 70182
504-831-9717

Point and Shoot, Version 2.2, by Vartcok
Registration: $49.95
3 Regent St.
Livingston, NJ 07039
201-740-1750

This is by no means a complete list—there may be 50 or 60 such menu programs. It's hard to recommend any one in particular. We recommend you obtain the specifications for each program and decide which best suits your needs.

DOS BATCH FILES:
DO-IT-YOURSELF MENUS

To create a batch file menu, you need three elements:

- A screen that identifies the available choices
- A batch file to display this opening screen
- A set of batch files that let you execute menu choices

Opening Screen (MENU. ANS)

The opening menu display, which we will name MENU.ANS for clarity, can be created with any program that can create an ASCII text file. ANSI-DRAW, for example, lets you tap into the abilities of the ANSI.SYS device driver. This lets you create a menu screen that utilizes different screen colors or flashing displays in your design. ANSIDRAW, a public domain program, is available as ANSIDR.ARC in Library 1 of the IBM Applications Forum on CompuServe.

If you would like to keep it simple, any text file that lists the choices will do. Name the menu batch file MENU.BAT. Add the following two lines to the end of your current AUTOEXEC.BAT file to activate your menu when the computer is started:

```
CD\MENU
MENU
```

The first command changes to the directory in which you keep the menu file. The second executes the batch file called MENU.BAT.

Batch File for Opening Screen

MENU.BAT is the batch file we identified as the second necessary item for your homemade menu. It displays the menu text file you created and prompts you to make a selection. It looks like this:

```
ECHO OFF
CLS
TYPE MENU.ANS
PROMPT Please Select An Item And Press Enter:
```

The first three lines clear the screen and display the menu text file. The prompt at the bottom is not part of the MENU.ANS file but is part of the DOS PROMPT command.

Batch Files for Menu Choices

In our example, you could select menu choices (A, B, C, and so on) to stand for the actual names of the batch files that run the applications listed. For example, A.BAT may look like this:

```
ECHO OFF
CLS
CD \123
123
CD \MENU
MENU
```

The name of the directory in line three and the application name in line four reflect the directory and filename of the application you plan to use.

Menus that contain too many choices can be confusing. You can elect to make some of the selections in the main menu lead to submenus, from which you make the final selection. There will be times when you don't want to run any program or you select a submenu by mistake; so, it's a good idea to include the option to return to the main menu in your submenus.

As the last item on your main menu, include "Exit To DOS" (a misnomer, really, since you have been in DOS all along). This selection merely puts you temporarily into a normal DOS environment. It restores the conventional DOS prompt and displays a message that reminds you how to get back to the menu system. Here's the batch file:

```
CLS
CD \
PROMPT Enter MENU to return to the main menu $_ $P$G
```

The prompt command creates a two-line prompt that looks like this:

```
Enter MENU to return to the main menu
C:\>
```

DOS batch files are not without their disadvantages. Creating and maintaining a multitude of batch files is labor-intensive. Often, only one individual in the entire organization knows how the system works. Most organizations will find it more cost-effective to purchase one of the commercially available packages. These often contain security, virus detection, usage tracking, and a host of other features.

CONCLUSION

A menu system helps simplify navigating with DOS. A menu system is essential with new users who are often bewildered by the DOS prompts. Businesses can standardize their PCs and simplify their use with menu systems as well as control access to sensitive files and programs. A power user's access to multiple hard drives or hundreds of applications is only a keystroke or two away with the use of a menu. In short, every PC user can benefit from a menu system.

There are alternatives to menu systems—DOS shells, for example. A DOS shell can have a separate application module and may also have point-and-shoot program execution.

DOS batch files are another alternative to menu systems. In fact, there are a number of menu systems that rely on DOS batch files and all menu systems support their use. While the learning curve for menu systems is relatively short, mastering DOS batch files can take a little longer.

Point-and-shoot program execution is no longer an advanced feature. Users are beginning to rely on the speed and convenience offered by menu systems. New releases of DOS now support a shell with these features and both Windows' and OS/2's support point-and-shoot program execution as well.

New features are turning up in menu systems all the time—hot keys, scroll bars, pop-up windows, usage tracking, context sensitive help, security and virus control, and more. These colorful programs become ever more useful to users as they are steadily refined. Even with all the alternatives, menu systems are still the most effective way to get quick and painless access to programs.

CHAPTER FOUR

Classic DOS Shells

The terms "shell" and "menu system" are often used to refer to the same thing, but they are really two different types of utilities. Today's DOS shells are programs that function as disk and file managers, let you perform DOS-type operations without having to use the DOS command line, and usually add capabilities not found in DOS. A shell provides a "front end" for DOS. You can start using a shell program right after it's installed. It doesn't require programming or customizing beyond any personal preferences you might have for its selection of display colors and options.

DOS SHELLS

DOS shells give you the ability to navigate your system's disk and perform DOS and DOS-like functions on files, directories, and disks. They provide a PC user with an alternative to using DOS directly, and they add functions not normally found in DOS. The latter is of particular importance, since DOS itself does not have everything required to effectively manage files and subdirectories.

Even if you feel comfortable wandering around your hard disk on your own, there are many benefits to be gained from using a shell. For example, because most shells let you view your files and directories as a "tree," you can easily examine your directory hierarchy. Other options let you see all files on the disk at once, spot duplicate files, and perform general cleanup and organization.

Two powerful shell features are sorting, and pruning and grafting of directories. As the name suggests, the prune-and-graft option allows you to remove (prune) a directory from one location and place (graft) it elsewhere.

A shell can also take the place of—and often surpass—the utility of many smaller programs you may now be using. With a shell, you can move files from one directory to another, rename or move directories, and look for files. Using separate utility programs to perform all these operations will work, but it requires learning each program and its particular idiosyncrasies. A DOS shell provides you with a single, consistent interface for all such tasks.

The DOS shell market is extremely competitive. As a result, some programs have added features that go beyond the basic requirements for a DOS shell. The first and foremost purpose of all DOS shells is to provide the user with insulation from the complexities of the native operating system. Another major aspect of most DOS shells is to make up for inadequacies within the operating system itself.

USING SHELLS

Any DOS shell program should let you

- Visually check your location

- Change your location

- View a directory's files and tag them

- Perform operations (copying, deleting, and so on) on files

- Run other programs

The following sections provide a closer look at these five basic requirements.

The Tree

Most DOS shells include a "tree" display of your system's hard disk. This function goes far beyond what DOS's TREE program provides you. As mentioned earlier, a shell's tree display is a graphical representation of your system's directories that enables you to view how they are interrelated. See Figure 4-1 for an example.

Changing from one directory to another is usually accomplished by moving the bounce bar with either the cursor keys or the mouse. This makes the operation very quick, especially if you have several subdirectory

Figure 4-1

Picture of a directory tree

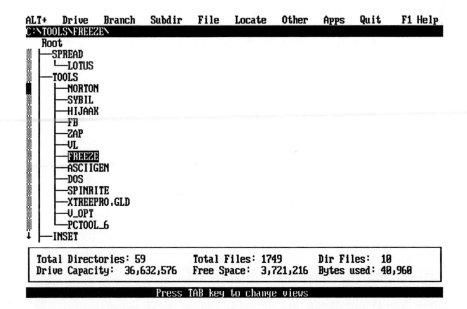

levels. It also eliminates the need to enter a CHDIR (or CD) command, with its sometimes long path argument, to indicate your destination. The shell provides a simpler and much more convenient "point-and-shoot" approach.

Most shells show the directory tree in one window while displaying the selected directory's contents in another. The contents of the file window change as you change directories in the tree window. Changing from one window to another is usually accomplished with a single keypress (or by a click of the mouse button while the pointer is in the desired window).

The Bounce Bar and Tagging

If you change to the file window, you can then use the bounce bar to select files or to view directory files if they don't all fit in the window. Often the SPACEBAR lets you tag files for group operations, such as COPY, MOVE, or DELETE. Tagging is a very important part of a shell, for it lets you manipulate a dissimilar group of files. Unlike DOS, which requries some kind of similar characteristic to define a group (for example, all EXE files or all files that begin with "K"), shells allow any combination of files to be tagged.

Once files have been marked, you can perform some type of operation on them. A good shell offers the basics, such as COPY, RENAME, and DE-LETE, but goes further and includes such others as BROWSE, MOVE, COMMENT, and WIPE (overwrite the file with nulls and then erase).

Point and Shoot

The final basic function is execution of other programs or applications. This is similar to what menu programs provide (hence the common confusion between shells and menus). Some shells allow you to point to the name of the program you want to execute and then issue a command or click the mouse button. This causes the application to run just as if you'd started it from DOS. Before running an application, most shells "shrink" to use only a small amount of memory and leave the rest available for the application. When you exit the program, you automatically return to the shell.

This approach to starting applications requires the user to know which program file (for example, WP.EXE) to use to start it. Some shells can "auto-launch" an application when the user selects any one of the application's data files. For example, in the case of a word processor, the user can select a document file rather than the word processor program to have the shell start the application. Yet another approach involves the use of an "application menu" from within the shell. Setting this up requires some knowledge of DOS and the disk setup (location of applications and their files).

Help

All good shell programs provide on-line help, using the standard F1 key. Help is usually context sensitive. Most programs have both a command index and a structured list of items through which you can read for general information. On-line help is not meant to be a substitute for a good manual, but it's an excellent and convenient source of information. Some programs even make reference to a manual page number while displaying help, letting you know where to go for more details on the subject.

The more advanced bells and whistles are data backup and recovery, file transfer (between a PC and a laptop), automatic startup of applications, file commenting, and file viewers. The latter allows you to view files from any of several applications without having to load the application. For example, you can view a Lotus 1-2-3 spreadsheet from within the DOS shell program without having to run Lotus. Because most applications' data files are anything but text, it takes more than just a text-file browser to view them. The shell accomplishes this task by interpreting the information in the data file so that it can be displayed on screen as it would appear in its native environment. Many shells include file viewers for popular spreadsheet, word processing, and data base programs.

FIVE SHELL PROGRAMS

In the remainder of this chapter, we'll look at the following DOS shell programs: Disc Director, from Athena Software; DOS Toolbox, from Computer Tyme; Norton Commander, from Peter Norton Computing; PC Tools Deluxe, from Central Point Software; and XTreePro Gold, from Executive Systems. Most of these programs provide the functions just discussed. The following sections discuss some specifics of each program and point out features that are outstanding or unique to them. We also hope you'll use the program provided with this book, XTREE. This is the original disk-organizing program and still one of the best.

Disc Director 2.0

Athena Software
4915 Twin Lakes Road, #19
Boulder, CO 80303
303-530-0693
List Price: $79
Disk space required: 463K
Documentation: Installation and operation manual, 86 pages

Disc Director represents a new trend in hard disk management. Disc Director (referred to as DD for brevity's sake) treats directories and subdirectories much like it treats files. In other words, discrete functions that can be done to files (such as copy, move, and delete) can also be performed on single directories or even a branch of subdirectories in one simple step. Disc Director is well designed for the intermediate and advanced user but is still intuitive enough for the novice.

Disc Director provides all the basic functions expected in a good shell and goes on to add much more. One of the more interesting features is the ability to attach a descriptive comment onto a file or directory. A comment may be 78 characters long. It can be used to provide more information about the contents of a file than DOS's eight-character file and directory names. A typical comment might be something like this:

```
INSURANC.CLM--Letter to insurance co. explaining recent storm
damage to car.
```

Comments may also be attached to directories. Comments can be used to tell who owns a directory, describe what the directory contains, or remind a user when the directory was last backed up. Here's an example:

```
<WORD>  Last backed up 7-25-90. Critical Directory!
```

Comments can be searched for specific keywords or strings. By doing this, you can quickly locate any file or directory anywhere on the hard disk. You can also view comments in real-time mode as you scroll through the directories or files.

In addition to having such handy features as date-and-time-stamp editing, attribute editing, and file tagging, Disc Director allows users to search for data by a variety of powerful methods. A text search will look for a specific word or string in every file in the defined scope, including EXE and COM files. Other methods let a user search by a date range, by a byte range, or by an attribute pattern. However, the most interesting search is the duplicate search. This search finds all files that have either the same filename or the same filename and byte size. This helps eliminate wasteful duplicates and recover precious hard disk space.

Another powerful feature, rarely found in DOS shells, is the "Phantom directory." Whenever a search is completed, the matching filenames are loaded into a phantom directory. From inside the phantom, it is possible to perform any of Disc Director's file operations as though the files were actually in one common directory. This saves an enormous amount of time and nicely complements the host of searches found in DD.

Disc Director takes an intuitive visual approach to such directory operations as pruning and grafting, as shown in Figure 4-2. This "cut-and-paste"

Figure 4-2

The Disc Director screen

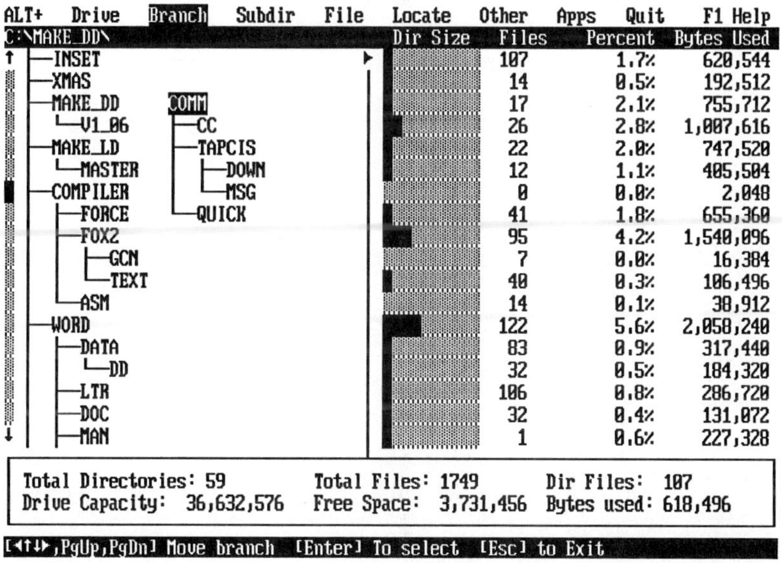

```
ALT+   Drive  Branch  Subdir  File  Locate  Other  Apps  Quit   F1 Help
C:\MAKE_DD\                               Dir Size  Files   Percent  Bytes Used
↑  ┌─INSET                         ►              107     1.7%     620,544
   ├─XMAS                                          14     0.5%     192,512
   ├─MAKE_DD   ┌COMM                               17     2.1%     755,712
   │  └─V1_06  ┌─CC                                26     2.8%   1,007,616
   ├─MAKE_LD   ┌─TAPCIS                            22     2.0%     747,520
   │  └─MASTER ├─DOWN                              12     1.1%     405,504
   ├─COMPILER  └─MSG                                0     0.0%       2,048
   │  ├─FORCE  └QUICK                              41     1.8%     655,360
   │  ├─FOX2                                       95     4.2%   1,540,096
   │  │ ┌─GCN                                       7     0.0%      16,384
   │  │ └─TEXT                                     40     0.3%     106,496
   │  └─ASM                                        14     0.1%      30,912
   ├─WORD                                         122     5.6%   2,050,240
   │  ├─DATA                                       83     0.9%     317,440
   │  │ └─DD                                       32     0.5%     184,320
   │  ├─LTR                                       106     0.8%     286,720
   │  ├─DOC                                        32     0.4%     131,072
↓  │  ├─MAN                                         1     0.6%     227,328
```

| Total Directories: 59 | Total Files: 1749 | Dir Files: 107 |
| Drive Capacity: 36,632,576 | Free Space: 3,731,456 | Bytes used: 618,496 |

`[◄↑↓►,PgUp,PgDn] Move branch  [Enter] To select  [Esc] to Exit`

method of directory and branch management makes tree reorganization so simple and safe that even novices will enjoy reorganizing their trees into a more logical and streamlined structure.

Disc Director is designed for complete hard disk management. This is reflected in another unique concept, the "view." Views show different information about the directories themselves, including their size, amount of cluster slack (unused space because of poor file-to-cluster sizing), files in the directory, and attached comments. With this information, it is easy to see which directories are grossly oversized, underused, inefficient, or poorly utilized.

Disc Director's interface is very easy to use, and its on-line help is context-sensitive and complete. Disc Director also has very interesting graphics and screen effects that make using it enjoyable. On a CGA, EGA, or VGA monitor, a fireworks display comes up after a certain amount of inactivity has occurred. On other monitors, a text string of the user's choosing appears. The user may define the timeout delay period, that is, the amount of time before this feature is activated.

Disc Director has a wide variety of other features, including file launching and program execution, user-definable application and utility menus, expanded and extended memory support, and more. All but 5.5K of RAM is released to an application. Disc Director supports a mouse and has 43-line EGA-mode and 50-line VGA-mode support. The documentation is complemented with numerous screen illustrations and an extensive index.

XTreePro Gold

XTreePro Gold, version 1.31
XTREE Company, A division of Executive Systems, Inc.
4330 Santa Fe Road
San Luis Obispo, CA 93401
805-541-0604 or 800-551-5353
List price: $129
Disk space required: 872K
Documentation: "Start-Up Manual," 11 pages; "Operations Manual", 167 pages; and "1Word Manual" (a reference booklet on the use of the XTreePro Gold text editor), 39 pages

XTreePro Gold has been around and quite popular for some time. Although the program is aimed at more experienced users, it's used by intermediate users, too. XTreePro Gold provides all the basic DOS shell features in an enjoyable form (see Figure 4-3).

The configuration program runs from DOS or from the program menu. It can perform directory grafting and pruning, support a mouse, show a split file window, and provide file date-and-time stamping. You can run applications from within XTreePro Gold or use the command shell to access DOS. XTreePro Gold can reduce its memory requirement to 7K, leaving plenty of room for applications to run.

XTreePro Gold can view files in a number of formats. The ASCII format, for example, displays files in ASCII text format. Dump format displays files without formatting, showing all displayable characters. Hex format displays the file in a format similar to that of DOS's DEBUG program and supports

Figure 4-3

The XTreePro Gold screen

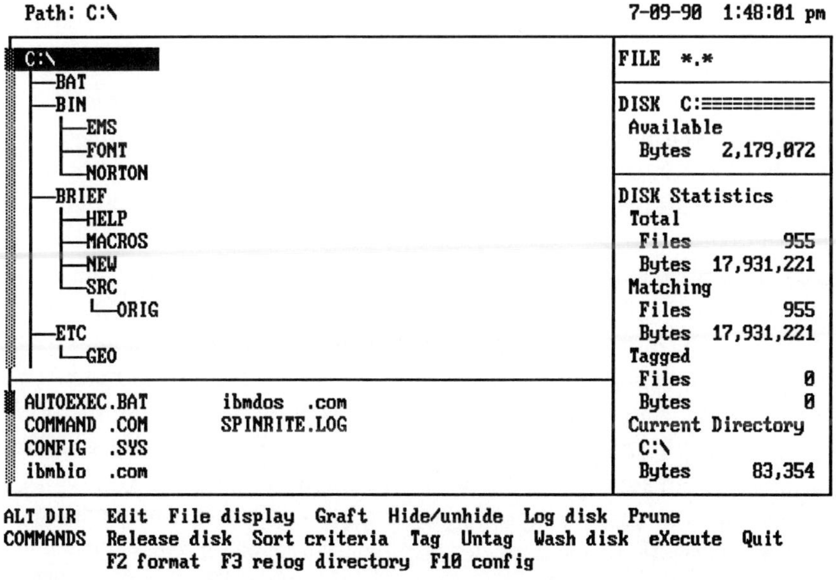

```
Path: C:\                                        7-09-90  1:48:01 pm

C:\                                    | FILE  *.*
 —BAT                                  |
 —BIN                                  | DISK  C:===========
   |—EMS                               | Available
   |—FONT                              |   Bytes    2,179,072
   |—NORTON                            |
 —BRIEF                                | DISK Statistics
   |—HELP                              | Total
   |—MACROS                            |   Files          955
   |—NEW                               |   Bytes   17,931,221
   |—SRC                               | Matching
      |—ORIG                           |   Files          955
 —ETC                                  |   Bytes   17,931,221
   |—GEO                               | Tagged
                                       |   Files            0
 AUTOEXEC.BAT    ibmdos  .com          |   Bytes            0
 COMMAND .COM    SPINRITE.LOG          | Current Directory
 CONFIG  .SYS                          | C:\
 ibmbio  .com                          |   Bytes       83,354

ALT DIR    Edit  File display  Graft  Hide/unhide  Log disk  Prune
COMMANDS   Release disk  Sort criteria  Tag  Untag  Wash disk  eXecute  Quit
           F2 format  F3 relog directory  F10 config
```

editing. The formatted-display option views files directly from Lotus 1-2-3, dBASE, and popular word processing programs. You can mark data in a file you're viewing and then write that data into another file. This is very useful for extracting data from files of different formats.

The built-in 1Word text editor can be used to modify or create text files. You invoke it with the Edit command from the File menu. 1Word uses WordStar commands and key sequences, but it can be reprogrammed to fit user preference. You can also define an external editor of your own choosing if you don't want to use 1Word.

Norton Commander

The Norton Commander
Symantec Corporation
10201 Torre Avenue
Cupertino, CA 95014
408-253-9600
List price: $149
Disk space required: 800K, although this can be reduced by removing non-essential file viewers
Documentation: "The Norton Commander," 201 pages

The Norton Commander is a well-designed DOS shell that is part of the family of products that includes the Norton Utilities.

The main display screen shows the directory tree, through which you navigate with the arrow keys or a mouse (see Figure 4-4). You can also press the first letter of a directory name to skip directly to it. If there's more than one directory starting with the same letter, pressing it again will take you to the next one.

The Norton Commander file viewer allows you to view many files from more than 20 native formats without leaving the Norton Commander. Many file formats are supported, including spreadsheets, such as Lotus 1-2-3, Microsoft Excel, and Quattro; data base files, such as those from FoxBASE, R:base, dBASE, and Clipper; and word processing files from Microsoft Word and WordPerfect. The Norton Commander will also display graphics from any program supporting the PCX file format.

If you launch another application from the Norton Commander, it shrinks itself to 13K of memory, leaving enough room for most operations you need to perform. The Norton Commander automatically reloads itself after you exit the application.

Figure 4-4

The Norton Commander screen

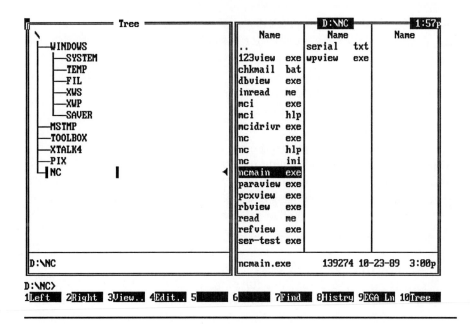

Commander Mail sends and receives files, electronic mail, and faxes over MCI Mail. A free MCI Mail subscription offer is included with the package. Commander Link transfers files between two PC systems and is most useful for moving data from a desktop PC to a laptop. You need a cable to use this feature; Peter Norton Computing will supply one if you send in $29 with the order form included in the package. The cable should work with any PC setup, as it comes with both 9- and 25-pin connectors at each end. This is a pretty good deal if you need this function.

Laptop computer users will also appreciate a chapter in the manual dedicated to laptops. This chapter explains how to conserve disk space by removing files you don't need from your Norton Commander directory or disk, and covers the use of the Commander Link program in depth.

PC Tools

PC Tools Deluxe, Version 6.0
Central Point Software, Inc.

15220 N.W. Greenbrier Parkway, #200
Beaverton, OR 97006
503-690-8090
800-690-8088
Retail Price: $149   Upgrade: $40
Disk space required: About 2.6MB for the entire package, 1.2MB for the PC Shell alone
Documentation: "Data Recovery/DOS Shell," 403 pages; "Hard Disk Back-up," 183 pages; and "Desktop Manager," 411 pages

PC Tools Deluxe 6.0 is probably the most feature-rich product in the DOS-shell category. It's becoming one of the most popular packages available. Not only does PC Tools include a usable DOS shell, but you get data backup and recovery, a disk cache, a disk optimizer that defragments files, and password protection for files. Its Desktop Manager offers support for fax boards; a telecommunication module that can be used to access MCI Mail, CompuServe, and other services; and even an emulator of the Hewlett-Packard HP11-C calculator.

The portion of PC Tools that functions as the DOS shell is called PC Shell. The PC Shell interface consists of a text-based windowing setup with pull-down menus accessed from a menu bar located at the top of the screen. A message bar at the bottom of the screen lists other options that can be selected by pressing a function key or by pointing to the function with the mouse and clicking the mouse button (see Figure 4-5).

PC Tools can be used with the keyboard, but its mouse support makes its operation much smoother. The mouse can be used to pull down menus and execute commands or to select the active window. You can also zoom in on either window to allow the window's information to fill the entire screen, change a window's size, and move the windows.

PC Shell has three user levels (Advanced, Intermediate, and Beginner), which allow you to set the program at a level with which you feel comfortable. For a novice, the Beginner mode has fewer choices and is much less intimidating. Intermediate and Advanced modes offer more choices along with access to more complex and lower-level functions.

The PC Shell can optionally be used as a TSR (memory-resident) program. In this mode, it uses only about 10K of memory when it's not active. When you need to use PC Shell, just press a hot key. Running the program in this mode allows you to bring up PC Shell and make use of it at any time, even if you're in the middle of running another application.

Figure 1-5

The PC Shell screen

```
PC Shell V6  File  Disk  Options  Applications  Special  Help        | 3:59pm
Drive A  B  C  D  E                                            Beginner Mode
═════════ID = CERANSKI═════════╪■════════════════C:\PBRUSH\*.*═══════════════╪
   ┌FOX2                    ↑    PBRUSH   EXE   BIT16X16 FNT   P3228    ICO  ↑
   │ ┌GCN                        FRIEZE   COM   BIT8X16  FNT   P6448    ICO
   │ └TEXT                       HBIOS    COM   BIT16X14 FNT   PBSETUP  MSG
   └ASM                          PBRUSH   OVL   BIT5X8   FNT   PBSETUP  SCR
 ┌WORD                           PBRUSH1  OVL   BIT9X14  FNT   PBSETUP  EXE
 ├DATA                           PBRUSH2  OVL   COMPUTER FNT   PRINTERS DAT
 │ └DD                           MSCVERT  OVL   EURO     FNT   CARDS    DAT
 ├LTR                            MSCVERT1 OVL   GREEK    FNT   DRIVE1
 ├DOC                            MSCVERT2 OVL   LTROMAN  FNT   DRIVE2
 ├MAN                            GRAY16   PAL   OENGLISH FNT   DRIVE8
 ├CONTRACT                       DEF2     PAL   SANSERIF FNT   ATT      DEV
 ├PROTEC                         DEF4     PAL   SCRIPT   FNT   EGA      DEV
 ├TXT                            DEF16    PAL   P644     ICO   HER      DEV
 ├LD                             DEF256   PAL   P643     ICO   IBM      DEV
 ├FAX                            BIT8X8   FNT   P642     ICO   TWO      DEV
 └NMR                            ROMAN    FNT   P723     ICO   CN1      DEV
 ┌PBRUSH               ↓         BIT8X14  FNT   P322     ICO   CN8      DEV  ↓
├──────────────────────────────┼────────────────────────────────────────────┤
│    3,731,456 Bytes Free      ║     101 Listed =      753,084 bytes          │

C:\PBRUSH>
1Help  2View  3Exit  4Unsel  5Copy  6Display 7Locate 8Zoom  9Select 10Menu
```

Menu commands let you check memory usage, view the current equipment configuration, and examine system performance. You can also use menu commands to change the type of information displayed in the windows. For example, you can look at multiple drives and subdirectories simultaneously.

The DOS command line is always close by when you're using PC Shell. A simple command lets you invoke DOS commands directly, without leaving PC Shell. If you like, you can even hide the windows while showing the DOS command line. This makes things look more like DOS, although PC Shell still displays its own function key commands at the bottom of the screen. One of the function keys provides access to PC Shell menus.

PC Tools provides file viewers for more than 30 applications. You can view data files without having to load the applications associated with them. PC Tools includes LapLink, a utility used to copy files, directories, or entire disks from one system to another. Its most common use is to transfer data from a desktop PC to a laptop, and vice versa, through the serial port on the systems. Central Point Software will sell you cables for $39.95 each (plus $6 for shipping and handling) to connect systems with either 9- or 25-pin serial port connectors. You can use an included order form to get the cable or order it by calling a toll-free number.

DOS Toolbox

Computer Tyme
216 S. Glenstone
Springfield, MO 65802
417-866-1222
List price: $59.95
Disk space required: 346K
Documentation: "DOS Toolbox Reference Manual," 61 pages

Computer Tyme's DOS Toolbox contains numerous utilities that replace standard DOS utilities. Installation is simple. Although the documentation recommends placing all the files in the root directory, the best approach is to create a directory for the Toolbox files and copy the files from the diskette into that directory. You can then include this directory name in your regular DOS path so that you can access the utilities from anywhere on your hard disk.

Among the utilities found in this package are D, a directory-listing program that lists files in multicolumn format and has many options. Among the options are Move, used to move files from one location to another; WhereIs, used to locate files anywhere on the disk; Sort, a faster version of DOS's SORT program that is not limited to 64K; PD, used to quickly go from one directory to another; and Park, a disk-head-parking utility.

Another very useful utility, called DoList, provides DOS command line editing and recalls the last few directories you've been in. Previous DOS commands can be retrieved with the up and down arrow keys and edited using standard keypad keys and WordStar editing commands. DoList also provides a way to program function keys to execute DOS commands. Function key definitions are predefined and stored in a standard ASCII text file. You can edit the text file to change definitions or create new ones.

Figure 4-6

The Directory Master main menu

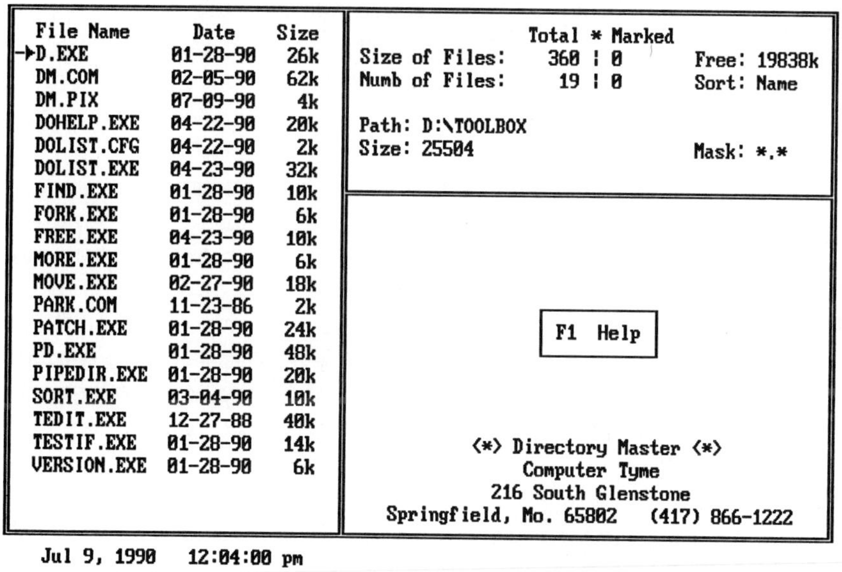

```
┌─────────────────────────────────┬──────────────────────────────────────┐
│ File Name    Date     Size      │          Total * Marked               │
│→D.EXE        01-28-90   26k     │ Size of Files:   360 ┆ 0    Free: 19838k│
│ DM.COM       02-05-90   62k     │ Numb of Files:    19 ┆ 0    Sort: Name  │
│ DM.PIX       07-09-90    4k     │                                        │
│ DOHELP.EXE   04-22-90   20k     │ Path: D:\TOOLBOX                        │
│ DOLIST.CFG   04-22-90    2k     │ Size: 25504                 Mask: *.*   │
│ DOLIST.EXE   04-23-90   32k     │                                        │
│ FIND.EXE     01-28-90   10k     ├────────────────────────────────────────┤
│ FORK.EXE     01-28-90    6k     │                                        │
│ FREE.EXE     04-23-90   10k     │                                        │
│ MORE.EXE     01-28-90    6k     │                                        │
│ MOVE.EXE     02-27-90   18k     │                                        │
│ PARK.COM     11-23-86    2k     │                                        │
│ PATCH.EXE    01-28-90   24k     │            ┌──────────┐                │
│ PD.EXE       01-28-90   48k     │            │ F1  Help │                │
│ PIPEDIR.EXE  01-28-90   20k     │            └──────────┘                │
│ SORT.EXE     03-04-90   10k     │                                        │
│ TEDIT.EXE    12-27-88   40k     │                                        │
│ TESTIF.EXE   01-28-90   14k     │        (*) Directory Master (*)        │
│ VERSION.EXE  01-28-90    6k     │           Computer Tyme                │
│                                 │          216 South Glenstone          │
│                                 │  Springfield, Mo. 65802   (417) 866-1222│
└─────────────────────────────────┴──────────────────────────────────────┘
  Jul 9, 1990   12:04:00 pm
```

DM (Directory Master) is a utility program that provides the basic features of a DOS shell. At startup, the DM display consists of two windows: the file window and the status window (see Figure 4-6). The file window lists files in the current directory, with date and file-size information (rounded off to the nearest 1024 bytes). Status window information includes DM's current location on your hard disk, the file mask, file attributes, and the selected sort. Basic shell functions supported in DM include file copy, deletion, moving, editing, viewing, renaming, and attribute changing.

DM allows you to mark files upon which to perform an operation and supports the use of wildcards to mark files (you can select all *.BAT files, for example). All files can be marked or unmarked with a single keystroke, and special ALT keystrokes copy, move, delete, or change attributes on all marked files.

The file-viewing option displays the selected file in ASCII text format. Like other DOS shells, the DM utility lets you view applications' files. Instead of interpreting the files in their native format, however, DM loads the application, from which you can then select the file you want to view. This is not so fast as viewing the file from within the shell, but it does get the job done. Application program files (EXE, COM, or BAT) are launched from within DM by pressing F3 when the file is highlighted. When you finish using the application and viewing the file, you are automatically returned to DM.

DM commands are not listed on the screen, but you can recall them at any time by pressing the F1 key for help. Up to 30 function keys may be programmed to execute a particular utility. A full eight pages of documentation detail this procedure.

This package doesn't require much disk space, and since you can delete the utilities you don't use, it's a good choice where disk space is a concern. Documentation is pretty good, although parts of it may be a little difficult for novices to understand.

CONCLUSION

The DOS shells discussed are commercial products and, as such, have very good technical-support departments backing them. In addition, new versions are always being developed and released, ensuring that the features and power are always improved and strengthened. This is by no means a complete listing of shells.

If you are not using a DOS shell on your computer, you should consider the benefits. Whether you are a beginner, a work-a-day user, or a power user, you'll find that a good DOS shell increases your productivity while decreasing any latent computer anxiety. A good shell helps you find, organize, manipulate, and understand files and directories far better than DOS. And, in this age of ever-increasing hard disk size, that is increasingly important.

CHAPTER FIVE

Data Protection and Recovery

So far, we have described the DOS interface, DOS commands, and various third-party menu and shell programs. In this chapter, we cover the three most popular DOS data-protection-and-recovery programs: Mace Utilities 1990, Norton Utilities 5.0, and PC Tools Deluxe 6.0.

These programs are designed to keep your data in tip-top shape. Just as you wouldn't drive a car without regular tune-ups, you shouldn't use your computer without running "tune-up programs." And, just as you wouldn't drive your car without insurance, you shouldn't use your PC without the insurance these programs offer.

Using a PC without a data-protection-and-recovery program just doesn't make sense. They are so important, some would say they should be inherent features of the operating system—something that MS-DOS just happens to lack. We would tend to agree.

Although the backbone of these programs is data recovery and data protection, they do much more. All can boost your PC's disk performance, and all have extended DOS utilities. PC Tools even comes with productivity software, such as an appointment scheduler, a telecommunications program, and a mini word processor.

This chapter does not describe how to use these utilities (there are already several books written on how to use each program). But it does tell you what they do and help you decide which is right for you. (Notice we didn't say, "If one is right for you." You *need* one of these programs.)

We hope you aren't reading this chapter because you've just formatted your hard disk or run into some other problem. If we make no other point so clear, *prevention is the key to safe computing.* If you purchase one of these programs before you lose any data, you will find that recovering data is relatively easy. Attempting to recover lost data while just learning about the concept can be a nightmare.

THE MACE UTILITIES

The original Mace Utilities was one of the first data-recovery programs of its kind. Mace's original claim to fame—being the first package capable of restoring a formatted hard disk—helped sell thousands of copies. Named after its creator, Paul Mace, Mace Utilities has come a long way since its introduction in 1984.

Still, with all the advancements and new versions, Mace Utilities remains purist. Except for a few programs to improve disk performance, Mace is strictly a data-protection-and-recovery program. Thus, Mace has one simple manual. It is probably the easiest to get started with, as it doesn't overwhelm you with "unnecessary" utilities and extra reading.

The current version of Mace Utilities, 1990, comes in an attractive package containing six 5.25-inch disks. The disk included with this book contains the Mace Utilities Special Edition (SE), a scaled-down version of the program containing fewer features than the regular commercial version.

The files on the Mace disk are standard format. Because they aren't compressed or copy protected, you can DISKCOPY the original disks or COPY the files to your hard disk. (Although the manual recommends that you install Mace on a hard disk, the programs can be used from floppies.) Mace also includes a special Install program that instructs your computer to run certain Mace Utilities every time you reboot your system.

Install also allows you to choose passwords for the three Mace user levels: Universal, Intermediate, and Advanced, as shown in Figure 5-1. To access Advanced, the user must know the Advanced password. If the user

Figure 5-1

The Mace Utilities Customize User Levels

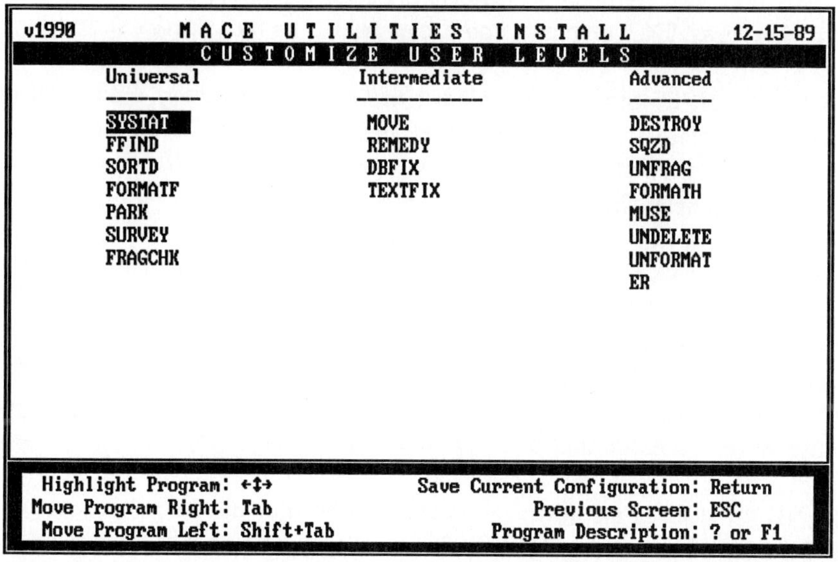

```
 v1990          M A C E   U T I L I T I E S   I N S T A L L          12-15-89
               C U S T O M I Z E   U S E R   L E V E L S
          Universal              Intermediate            Advanced
          ---------              ------------            --------
          SYSTAT                 MOVE                    DESTROY
          FFIND                  REMEDY                  SQZD
          SORTD                  DBFIX                   UNFRAG
          FORMATF                TEXTFIX                 FORMATH
          PARK                                           MUSE
          SURVEY                                         UNDELETE
          FRAGCHK                                        UNFORMAT
                                                         ER




          Highlight Program: ←↕→         Save Current Configuration: Return
          Move Program Right: Tab                    Previous Screen: ESC
          Move Program Left: Shift+Tab         Program Description: ? or F1
```

knows no password, he or she must use the program at the Universal level.
This feature is extremely useful in an office environment or any place where
a computer containing Mace Utilities will be accessible to overzealous joes
and would-be hackers.

The Mace documentation does an excellent job of guiding the panic-
stricken user who ran out and bought Mace to fix some immediate problem.
However, take note: With all data-protection-and-recovery programs, prevention is the key. If your system is running fine now, be thankful, and
purchase one of these programs before anything does happen.

Once Mace is installed, you can choose to use the program either from
the DOS command line or from Mace's menu system. The command line
programs are useful for those who are familiar with DOS or know exactly
what they want to do with the utilities. These users can bypass the menu
system and go directly to the utilities they need. The Mace menu system is
truly user friendly. Mace's features are organized logically with descriptions

that clarify their purpose. The menu system even offers access to the DOS command line and special extended-DOS commands.

Each of Mace's command line programs has a corresponding menu item. All features available from the menu are available from the command line, and vice versa. The command line programs (or menu selections) are:

DBFIX DBFIX uses its knowledge of the most common data base file formats to locate and repair data base files that have been lost, corrupted, or partially overwritten. DBFIX can repair dBASE II, dBASE III, Fox-Base, and Clipper files.

TEXTFIX TEXTFIX uses its knowledge of the most common word processor file formats to locate and repair word processing files that have been lost, corrupted, or partially overwritten. TEXTFIX can repair files saved from DisplayWrite, WordStar, WordStar Professional (but not WordStar 2000), MultiMate Advantage II, Microsoft Word, WordPerfect, and any other word processor that uses EBCDIC or ASCII coding.

MUSE MUSE is an advanced sector editor that allows you to examine and modify boot sectors, FAT tables, directory entries, system areas, and file contents. MUSE works with logical disks (floppy disks and hard disk partitions). It cannot edit hard disk partition tables.

PARK PARK is a disk-parking utility. This is a protection device that makes sure your hard disk's head "parks" in a safe "landing zone," where there is no possibility of data loss.

POP POP stands for Power-Out Protector. POP is a memory-resident program that protects you from accidental data loss. POP saves a copy of your computer's memory at regular intervals. If the computer should lock up or crash, you can reboot the system and restore your memory from the last save.

REMEDY REMEDY is an excellent utility for finding and locking out disk errors and bad sectors. REMEDY performs both read and write tests, increasing its chances of finding bad sectors before they cause data loss.

RXBAK RXBAK is used to save recovery information (boot sector, FAT table, and root directory) in case of a disk failure. The INSTALL program can automatically place a command to load RXBAK in your AUTOEXEC-.BAT. This will cause RXBAK to save your system information each time you turn on or reboot your computer. If you have a disk failure, the data saved by RXBAK will help Mace recover lost data.

SQZD   SQZD reduces the size of a directory by removing all references to deleted files. This should be used only when you are sure you want to delete a file. (Mace cannot easily recover files whose directory entries have been SQZD.)

SYSTAT   SYSTAT determines and reports technical information about your computer system. Included are the number and types of ports and disk drives, the amount of conventional, extended, and expanded memory, the BIOS date, the display type, and other information.

FRAGCHK   FRAGCHK locates and displays the names of fragmented files. A fragmented file is one whose contents have been spread out over the disk. This is undesirable, as it slows disk access and reduces the chances for easy data recovery.

UNFRAG   UNFRAG defragments drives, thereby increasing performance. When running UNFRAG, Mace first runs FRAGCHK. If no files are fragmented, no defragmenting is attempted.

UNDELETE   UNDELETE recovers deleted files. If Mace was already installed, you can easily undelete a file. If Mace was not installed and the file is fragmented, things get a little more difficult, but recovery is still possible.

UNFORMAT   UNFORMAT recovers formatted hard disks. If Mace was already installed, this process is simple and almost guaranteed. Without Mace, your chances are still good. Mace can also restore some data on floppy disks that were partially formatted (meaning you aborted midway through the format by removing the disk or hitting CTRL-BREAK).

VACCINE   VACCINE is a memory-resident program that protects your system from alteration and destruction. VACCINE monitors your system while you use it, stepping in to question whether you really want to perform operations that result in data loss. VACCINE is also useful in combating viruses. If a program you run attempts to format, erase, or write to a disk, VACCINE lets you know about it and stop it, if necessary.

MCACHE MCACHE is a disk-caching program. It sets up an area of cache memory to hold the most recent hard disk data reads and writes. In many cases, disk reads are for data that was previously read. Thus, MCACHE boosts disk performance by allowing the computer to read from the cache rather than accessing the disk again and again for the same data.

MKEYRATE MKEYRATE is used to set the repeat rate (how fast characters are repeated while a key is pressed) and delay speed (how long it takes to start repeating after pressing a key) for AT and PS/2 keyboards.

MOVE MOVE allows you to move a file or group of files quickly and easily from one directory to another. Normally, utilities like this can be found in a DOS shell.

DESTROY DESTROY irrevocably erases a file. Using DESTROY to erase a file ensures that the file is actually gone and cannot be restored by any recovery program—not even Mace. DESTROY is useful if you have sensitive data that you need to dispose of.

ER ER stands for Emergency Room. ER automatically corrects problems with hard disks and diskettes without risk. It has a feature that allows you to "undo" any changes ER makes. ER is similar to Norton's Disk Doctor and PC Tools Deluxe's DiskFix.

FFIND FFIND is useful in locating misplaced files. FFIND searches all directories on the specified drive, looking for a match for the filename you specify. It displays each match it finds, including the path.

FORMATH FORMATH is a safe hard disk formatter. Unlike some hard disk formatters, FORMATH erases only the partition's file allocation table (FAT) and root directory. This makes it much easier to recover data if you change your mind.

FORMATF FORMATF is used to replace DOS's FORMAT program.

Mace is a good value. It has several features that neither Norton nor PC Tools has, including TEXTFIX, POP, and SQZD. Mace has some features that PC Tools has and Norton doesn't and others that Norton has and PC Tools doesn't. You really have to consider what features are important to you.

Currently, Mace's purpose is strictly data protection and recovery. Fifth Generation has indicated that they wish to expand their market by redesigning their user interface to appeal to a wider group. We feel they are doing pretty well right now.

Mace Utilities, 1990
$149
Fifth Generation Systems, Inc.
10049 N. Reiger Road
Baton Rouge, LA 70809-4559
Orders: 800-873-4384

NORTON UTILITIES

The original Norton Utilities was conceived and designed by one of the most authoritative figures in the PC industry—Peter Norton. You know the guy. Peter Norton is known as the father of UnErase. The current version of Norton Utilities 5.0, as with previous releases, is excellent.

The package contains six 5.25″ disks and three 3.5″ disks. The disks contain several programs that can be divided into four categories:

- Data Protection/Recovery
- Speed/Performance Enhancement
- Data Security
- Tools/Utilities

The Install program copies the files to the disk you specify, replaces the destructive DOS FORMAT program with Norton's Safe Format, modifies CONFIG.SYS and AUTOEXEC.BAT so that you can run Norton programs at startup, and lets you password-protect the dangerous program files as shown in Figure 5-2.

Each of the Norton Utilities can be started from the command line or from the main menu program: NORTON.EXE. The main menu program is very flexible and lets you add your own choices to the menu. For example, you could add a menu option to run Lotus 1-2-3, dBASE, and Crosstalk from your Norton program. The menu program also offers on-line help for each utility along with advice for CHKDSK, disk, and DOS errors.

Figure 5-2

Set Password Protection on Norton Utilities

```
╔════════════════════════════════════════════════════════╗
║                                                          ║
║         ══════ Set Password Protection ══════            ║
║                                                          ║
║      Select programs which require a password to run     ║
║                                                          ║
║      [ ] Calibrate            [ ] Safe Format            ║
║      [ ] Disk Editor          [ ] Speed Disk             ║
║      [ ] Disk Monitor         [ ] UnErase                ║
║      [ ] Disk Tools           [ ] UnFormat               ║
║      [ ] FileFix              [ ] WipeInfo               ║
║      [ ] Norton Disk Doctor II                           ║
║                                                          ║
║     ┌──────────┐    ┌──────────┐    ┌──────────┐        ║
║     │ Continue │    │ Go Back  │    │  Abort   │        ║
║     └──────────┘    └──────────┘    └──────────┘        ║
║                                                          ║
║                                              ┌─────────┐ ║
║                                              │ Install │ ║
╚══════════════════════════════════════════════╧═════════╝
```

The user-interface is a well done graphical interface, with mouse support and user-configurable settings. The menu program lets you set your preferences for the interface. Once set, all of the utilities adhere to those preferences. The programs include network support.

The programs included with Norton Utilities are described next.

Data Protection/Recovery

Norton Disk Doctor II   Norton Disk Doctor II automatically diagnoses and repairs more disk-related problems than any other program of its kind. NDD's Test routines examine and repair boot records, file allocation tables, directory and file structures, the disk surface, lost clusters, partition tables, and cross-linked files. NDD also has an UNDO feature that allows for risk-free repair.

Disk Editor   Disk Editor lets you view and edit the entire contents of a diskette or hard disk. Disk Editor is the most powerful and flexible disk sector editor available. It features split-screen, cut-and-paste editing, data links that connect related areas and disk viewers for repairing boot records, FAT areas, and directories.

Disk Tools   Disk Tools performs six functions: it makes a disk bootable, recovers from a DOS RECOVER, revives a defective diskette, marks a sector as bad, saves a disk's crucial data, and restores a disk's crucial data.

FileFix   FileFix repairs damaged Lotus 1-2-3, dBASE, and Symphony data files.

FileSave   FileSave intelligently manages the erased file space on a disk. It relocates erased files to an unused portion of the disk where the files are less likely to be overwritten by new files. On Novell networks, FileSave works in conjunction with Norton's UnErase utility to recover erased files located anywhere on the network.

Image   Image takes a "snapshot" of your system and saves the information (boot record, FAT table, and root directory) in a special file. If you erase a file or format your hard disk by accident, the Image snapshot file can be used by UnFormat or UnErase to ease recovery.

UnFormat   UnFormat recovers an accidentally formatted hard disk.

UnErase   UnErase can recover accidentally deleted files and directories. UnErase is easy to use, offering easy access to files that have been previously deleted. The program also works with networks, and can unerase partially over-written files. See Figure 5-3.

Speed/Performance Enhancement

Calibrate   Calibrate tests the "interleave" of your hard disk to ensure that data are read and written as quickly as possible. Calibrate also performs read and write tests to locate and lock-out bad sectors on your disk surface.

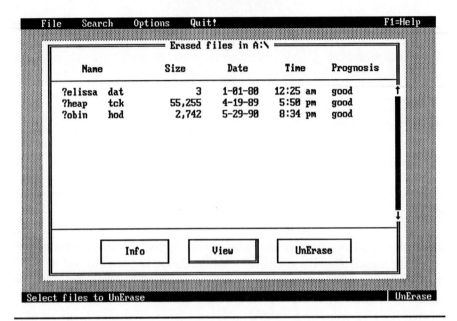

Figure 5-3

Norton Utilities UnErase

Speed Disk   Speed Disk enables you to rearrange the logical structure of your hard disk for optimal speed and performance. It can also defragment files, which also dramatically increases performance.

Norton Cache   Norton Cache speeds disk/system operation by storing the most frequently accessed disk data in memory.

Data Security

Disk Monitor   Disk Monitor performs three functions: Protect, Light, and Monitor. Protect monitors all attempts to read and write to disk drives (including network drives) to prevent disk damage from unauthorized access. Light provides an on-screen substitute for the disk indicator light (useful on networks, when the user cannot see the physical disk light).

Park Park is a utility that parks a hard disk head on the landing zone of the hard disk (the safe area set aside for the disk head).

Wipeinfo Wipeinfo permanently erases sensitive information with no chance of recovery. The utility is intelligent and searches the disk for all occurrences of the data you wish to delete.

Diskreet Diskreet encrypts files or disks you specify. Unlike less sophisticated security packages, Diskreet works while running in the background.

Tools/Utilities

System Information System Information displays twenty screens of information including AUTOEXEC.BAT, CONFIG.SYS, technical data on hardware interrupts, available ports, CMOS status, memory usage (expanded, extended, conventional), installed disk drives, loaded TSRs, CPU benchmarks, and additional information for network environments.

Norton Change Directory Norton Change Directory lets you bypass standard DOS conventions and easily navigate subdirectories.

Batch Enhancer Batch Enhancer is a utility that increases the flexibility of standard DOS batch files. The program lets you create interactive batch files, display windows and graphics characters, change screen and text colors, and incorporate sounds.

Norton Control Center Norton Control Center is used to configure your system's hardware settings.

FileFind FileFind can locate lost files or directories buried deep within your hard disk.

In addition, FileFind can print the directory tree of an entire disk, display the total size of a group of files or an entire directory, attach descriptive comments to files and directories, view files, print a list of found files, or alter a file's attribute or time/date stamp. FileFind is the most advanced search program available.

Safe Format Safe Format is a non-destructive alternative to the DOS FORMAT program.

The Norton Utilities are an excellent group of programs. They comprise perhaps the most sophisticated data recovery tools available. The programs can both boost your PC's performance, and offer insurance against data loss.

The Norton Utilities 5.0
$179 Upgrades: $49
Peter Norton Computing Product Group
10201 Torre Avenue
Cupertino, CA 95014
For more information: 800-441-7234
In California call: 800-626-8847

PC TOOLS

PC Tools comes in an attractive package containing three manuals and program disks for both 5.25-inch and 3.5-inch drives. The installation procedure is easy enough on its own, but PC Tools comes with a small installation guide. This is a package that makes you feel good before you run the program! Heck, they even have a sticker for your PC that reads, "This computer is backed up by PC Tools 6.0."

Installing the program on a hard disk is very easy. The system allows you to selectively install only the programs you want. You can also configure the programs from the installation menu. As with Mace, the installation program can modify AUTOEXEC.BAT to run programs that record system information every time the computer is turned on or rebooted. You may also want to run certain PC Tools Desktop Manager programs at startup.

If you do not have a hard disk, you may run into problems in copying the PC Tools files to floppy disks. Most applications (except those used for Disk Recovery) come compressed on the PC Tools disks. To uncompress them, you'll need to install the program on a system with a hard disk, or, if you have the memory, set up a large RAM disk.

Most PC Tools applications are completely menu driven; others can be run as command line options. All programs have context-sensitive help and mouse support. The program can be used from one of three user levels: Beginner, Intermediate, and Advanced. Its main features are data recovery, a DOS shell, hard disk backup, and a desktop manager.

Data Recovery and Disk Utilities

PC Tools offers several disk-recovery, data-protection and disk-perfor-mance-enhancing utilities:

DiskFix   Like Mace's Emergency Room and Norton's Disk Doctor, Disk-Fix quickly and automatically diagnoses and repairs file allocation errors, corrupt directory or partition information, and lost or cross-linked files or directories. See Figure 5-4.

Compress   Compress unfragments disks and files to speed disk access. Unfragmenting disks also increases the chance of problem-free file recovery.

Mirror/Rebuild   Mirror saves information about your system, and Rebuild restores it in case of accidental data loss. Central Point suggests placing

Figure 5-1

PC Tools DiskFix

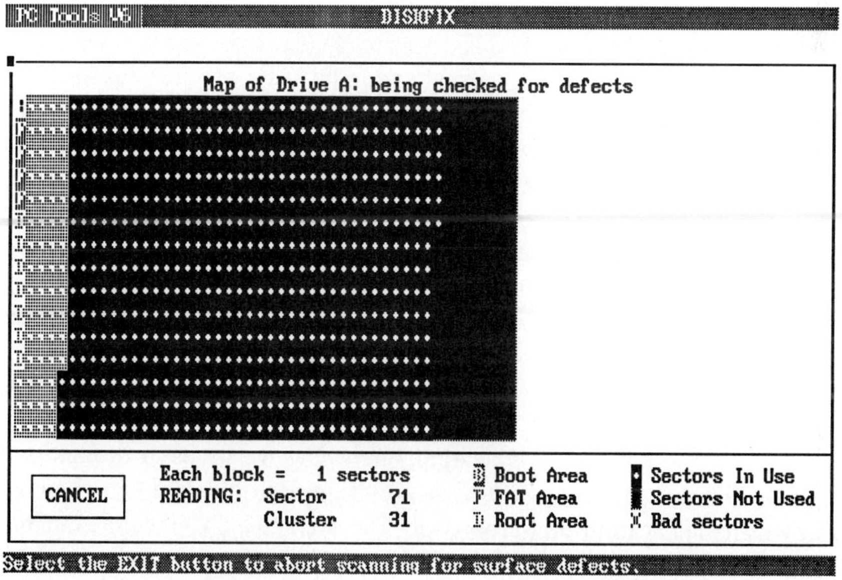

Mirror in your AUTOEXEC.BAT to save a snapshot of your system each time you boot.

Undelete   Undelete recovers deleted files and subdirectories.

PC Format   PC Format is designed to replace the standard DOS FOR-MAT program. It formats both hard and floppy disks in a manner that allows easy recovery of inadvertently erased information.

PC Cache   PC Cache speeds up hard disk access by storing the most frequently used information in your computer's memory.

PC Secure   PC Secure enables you to password-protect data files and programs. It encrypts data with Department of Defense (DES) standards. (See Chapter 11 for more on DES encryption.)

DOS Shell

The PC Tools DOS shell (fully described in Chapter 4) lets you perform basic and advanced DOS functions in a user-friendly environment. The DOS shell is divided into three windows: tree, directory, and view. The directory window shows the standard DOS directory, the tree window shows the directory in a graphical tree format, and the view window shows Larry Bostwick playing baseball with his kids.

Most DOS commands are available with a single keystroke. Other features are:

File Viewers   A file viewer allows you to view data files in their native format—that is, as they would appear in the programs that created them. The DOS shell has more than 30 file viewers, including 1-2-3, Excel, Works, Quattro, WordPerfect, Word, WordStar, XyWrite, dBASE, Paradox, and R:base.

Application Launching   Application Launching works hand in hand with the File Viewers. If you are viewing a certain data file, you can choose to "launch" the application that created it. For example, if you were examining a Lotus 1-2-3 file, you could launch Lotus 1-2-3. The program would be loaded with the file you were examining, and you could begin to use it.

Locate Locate lets you find files by name or by content. You can then view the files with a file viewer or launch an application.

File Transfer File Transfer lets you transfer files to and from a laptop computer. You need a serial cable and LapLink from Traveling Software.

Programmable Function Keys You can customize PC Shell's function keys for quick access to your most-often-used commands.

Sort, Move, Prune and Graft These commands allow you to move and reorganize files with ease. The DOS shell makes it easy to copy files or groups of files by allowing you to create user-defined lists; use multiple filenames, paths, and wildcards; or tag multiple files.

DOS Command Line This gives you instant access to the DOS command line from PC Shell.

Network Support PC Tools supports Novell and IBM PC local area networks.

Memory Resident The DOS shell can be run in normal mode or memory-resident mode. The DOS shell uses 10K of RAM while in memory-resident mode.

Hard Disk Backup

PC Tools' backup features are fully discussed in Chapter 8. PC Backup is fast, easy to use, and sophisticated. You can store backups in standard DOS format or in a special file-saving format. You can also protect your backups with passwords. If a file should go bad, PC Tools can tell you which disk it is on in your backup set. If your backup disk goes bad, PC Tools can try and reconstruct it. It even comes with a set of stickers to label your disks PC Tools Backup Disk #1, #2, and so on.

PC Backup features include:

Tape Drive Support You can back up your disks to QIC-40, QIC-80, and Irwin tape drives from IBM, Compaq, Mountain, Colorado Memory, and Archive (QIC-80). PC Backup records up to 250MB on one tape.

DOS Device Support   You can back up to any DOS device—floppy or hard drives, Bernoulli cartridges, and so on.

Fast, Reliable Backup   You can back up disks at up to 2.5MB per minute, with complete bit-for-bit verification of all data.

Adaptive Data Compression   This feature reduces disk usage by up to 60 percent without increasing backup time.

Easy File Selection   PC Backup displays a tree for simplified file or directory selection. You can easily pick and choose which files or directories you wish to back up.

Scheduled Backups   PC Backup can automatically back up your system at scheduled intervals without user intervention.

Named Backup Options   Backup options can be saved to use with scheduled backups and when you don't want to reenter backup commands.

Advanced Error Correction   If one of the backup disks goes bad, PC Backup attempts to reconstruct missing data.

Compare Feature   PC Backup can tell you which files have been altered by comparing your system's current status to the last backup.

Incremental/Append Backups   Full and incremental backups can be retained in a single set of disks or tapes. If you wish, you may back up only files that have changed.

Disk/Tape/Time Estimate   PC Backup dynamically estimates the amount of disk or tape space you will use and the length of time the entire process will require.

Desktop Manager

The PC Tools Desktop Manager is a set of useful utilities that can increase your productivity. It runs resident (that is, you can pop it up without getting out of the application you are working on) and allows you to cut and paste data between modules, create macros, and use an autodialer. Features include:

Fax Support You can use a fax board (Intel, Spectra, or Gamma Fax) to send or receive faxes at any time. Desktop Manager also supports networks.

Telecommunications Desktop Manager's telecommunications module features XMODEM/ASCII transfers, ANSI and VT emulation, scripting, a dialing directory, and the basic features of any telecommunications program.

Appointment Scheduler The Appointment Scheduler displays a daily calendar, a monthly calendar, and a to-do list. The program has a strong interface and is as powerful as most stand-alone appointment schedulers. It can also be used to schedule program execution (such as PC Backup or fax or electronic-mail transmissions).

Notepad The Notepad is a mini word processor, complete with spelling checker, block moves, search and replace, and other standard word processing features.

Calculators PC Tools includes an HP-11C scientific calculator, an HP-12C financial calculator, an HP-16C programmer's calculator, and a standard algebraic calculator.

Data Base Desktop Manager lets you create and maintain data bases. Features include dBASE compatibility, indexing, append and transfer functions, field editing, and a browse mode. It can easily be used with mailing lists and form letters.

Outliner The Outliner helps you organize your thoughts and structure documents. It takes care of the format, letting you concentrate on your data.

If you are looking for an all-in-one utility, PC Tools is definitely the answer. But it may not be the all-in-one answer for disk utilities. Although PC Tools has a number of useful features, both Norton and Mace are stronger as disk utilities. For instance, PC Tools does not have batch enhancements, virus protection, a sector editor, or small utilities such as those that change the time-and-date stamp or volume labels.

If you decide PC Tools doesn't have enough disk utilities to suit your current needs, you may want to purchase it for everything else it has to offer. Every one of its utilities rivals those of stand-alone programs. Overall, PC Tools is definitely one of the best bargains available today.

SO WHICH ONE IS FOR ME?

You may have jumped directly to this section in hopes that you would read, "Buy this; forget this." To make a statement like that would be unfair — all of the programs are useful. Each has features and capabilities that the others do not. All three utilities are priced the same, all are dependable, non-copy-protected, and well documented. All programs are capable of basic and advanced data recovery.

Which utility is better is unclear. We could stand three people in front of you, and each would tell you the other programs just can't do what his or her program can. No one program overshadows the others.

The choice comes down to you and what you want. You must look at each program's features and decide which program is right for you. If you already have telecommunications and data base packages, and would prefer more disk utilities, look at Mace and Norton. Which of these two programs has the disk utilities you would like? If you want the all-in-one software bargain and don't care about DOS command line technicalities, PC Tools is probably the answer.

We have found, however, that most people can't settle for one program. All of them are good. The advantage to buying more than one (or all of them) is increased capabilities. You can use features from each program, mixing and matching those you like best. In the case of data recovery, if one program can't help you, you'll be able to try the other.

CHAPTER SIX

Starting Your Computer

You've probably noticed that once they've been turned on, most PCs end up at a C> prompt (or an A> prompt, if there's no hard disk). You may also have noticed that some systems *don't* end up there. Maybe they display a menu or start a multitasking program, such as DESQview. Some jump into Microsoft Windows.

If you watch the screen, you'll also see that every system seems to have a slightly different route for getting where it's going when it starts up. Between the time you get up in the morning and the time you start work, you do a lot of things to get ready. Everyone does them a little differently, but the beginning and end of the process don't look so different for many of us. Starting your PC works the same way.

This chapter will explain the details of that process: how you get from a blank screen and a cold system to a functioning computer with all the software bells and whistles you want. If you want to go into more depth and more technical detail, you'll find that information in Chapter 27.

Here's a summary of the start-up process:

1. The power is turned on.

2. The microprocessor tests and initializes itself, the memory, and the attached devices (keyboard, display, and so on).

3. The core portion of DOS is read into memory from the floppy disk or hard disk.

4. The CONFIG.SYS file is processed to configure DOS for your particular system.

5. The command processor is loaded into memory.

6. AUTOEXEC.BAT is executed.

7. The DOS prompt is displayed, or—if specified in AUTOEXEC.BAT— a menu or shell program is run.

Let's look at each of these steps in some detail. In this chapter, you will be introduced to CONFIG.SYS commands and shown some samples designed for systems of varying complexity. In the next chapter, we'll explain how to set up the CONFIG.SYS and AUTOEXEC.BAT files, which are the primary tools you have for controlling the start-up process.

Of course, what happens first is that someone turns on the computer's power switch.

POWER ON

When the power goes on, circuitry on the system board sends a signal to the microprocessor. When the engineers draw the wire for this signal on their circuit diagrams, they label it RESET—and that's what it does: It resets the microprocessor and all the other devices in your system that are plugged into the system board to a known, stable state. (Without such a signal, electronic chips start off in a random state and may not work correctly.)

The RESET signal is usually held on for a second or two after the system starts. Once it goes off, the microprocessor can begin its work. This delay gives the memory and devices time to settle down from the impact of having the power applied before the microprocessor actually starts trying to do anything.

If you have a computer with a RESET button on the case—one that reboots the computer without your having to turn it off and back on—this button manually performs the same function as the power-on circuitry on the system board. It sends an electrical RESET signal to the microprocessor and other devices inside the system, restarting them as if the power had just been turned on.

Once the RESET signal has been applied and then removed, the microprocessor, by design, starts running a program at a specific location in memory. The circuitry to do this is built into the microprocessor. Without it, the processor would start in an uncontrolled fashion, and you could never get it to do what you wanted. (Well, almost never. A typical PC microprocessor might start up right once in a million or more tries!)

The place where the microprocessor looks for this start-up program is specified by the company that makes the microprocessor, Intel. When the original 8086 and 8088 chips were designed, Intel decided that when a RESET occurred, the microprocessor would look for a start-up program at the very end of memory, location FFFF:0 in hexadecimal. (For those of you who are checking, this location is actually 16 bytes below the end of memory—there has to be a few bytes to put the start-up program in!) This location is at the end of the 1MB of memory that the 8086 and 8088 can address. In 286, 386, and 486 processors, which can address much more memory, the "end of memory" is in a different place. But for compatibility reasons, these processors effectively begin executing at address FFFF:0, as well.

When IBM designed their first PC, they decided to use Intel's 8088 microprocessor. One of the consequences of that decision was that they had to build a permanent program into the PC's hardware at address FFFF:0 so that the microprocessor would have something to do when it was turned on.

At the same time, IBM decided to build some other programs into the PC. These programs provide very low level control of basic hardware devices, such as floppy disks, the keyboard, and the display. Collectively, the start-up program and the low-level hardware-control programs are called the *basic input/output system,* or *BIOS.* It's stored in permanent memory chips (ROMs, BIOS ROMs, or ROM BIOS) on the system board.

The Power-On Self-Test

The description here of how the BIOS's start-up program works is based on the BIOS used by IBM in the PC. Different PC-compatible systems have BIOS chips from a variety of manufacturers. The three most common are

Terminology Blizzard

The terminology used to describe these BIOS chips can sound like a blizzard of acronyms, but it's really pretty simple. The chips are called ROMs. ROM stands for "read-only memory," the electrical engineers' term for this type of device. "Read-only" means that the computer can only read information from the chips. It can't store anything there or erase anything there. The information in the chips is permanent—it doesn't go away when the power is turned off.

Some chips are also designated PROMs (programmable read-only memory) or EPROMs (erasable programmable read-only memory). "Programmable" means that information can be stored in the chips after they're manufactured, using a device designed for the purpose (a "PROM burner"). "Erasable" means that the chips can be deliberately exposed to strong ultraviolet light to enable the information in them to be destroyed. EPROM chips can be reprogrammed, if necessary.

Phoenix, Award, and AMI. All these flavors of BIOS work in pretty much the same way that IBM's does, and the description covers them as well.

When the microprocessor runs the start-up program in the BIOS, the first thing that program does is check over your PC for any troubles. This part of the BIOS is called the *power-on self-test* or *POST.*

The first thing the POST does is test the microprocessor itself. You're probably asking, "How can the microprocessor test itself, especially if it might not be working?" That's a good question. The basic idea is that the program in the BIOS tries some very simple operations and tests the results for consistency. For example, it may add 2 and 2 and see if the result is 4. Or it may set an internal register (a storage area on the microprocessor chip) to 0 and then test whether it really is 0.

If any of these tests fails, the processor does its best to indicate the error by beeping or by turning on lights on the system board that a technician can see. It can't do much more than that, because anything more (say, displaying a message on the screen) would require most of the microprocessor to be working. In most cases, if your microprocessor chip fails, it will fail completely, and the POST will never get started. But it's still worth it for manufacturers to use up the few instructions included in this part of the POST to detect any residual failures in the microprocessor.

If you have an AT, 386, or 486 system, the next thing the POST does is read the information stored in a semipermanent memory chip on the system board, called the *CMOS RAM*.

READ.ME

CMOS

The CMOS RAM chip was added to PC systems with the introduction of IBM's PC-AT. It is powered by a small battery that lasts one to three years. This chip stores information about your system that shouldn't disappear when the power is turned off—things like the amount of memory you have and the number and types of your disk drives. It also has a built-in clock that keeps track of the current date and time; so, you don't have to enter that information each time you start your system.

PC and XT systems, which don't come with this chip, obtain information about your system from switches that you must set on the system board. They may have a battery-powered clock on an add-on board to keep track of the date and time when the power is off. The introduction of the CMOS RAM on the AT allowed PC users to set hardware-configuration variables with software rather than with the bewildering array of switches that would have been necessary for an advanced system like the AT.

On most systems, you change the information stored in the CMOS RAM using a SETUP utility. This is accessed by using the SETUP command at the DOS prompt, by pressing certain keys, or both. For example, most 386 system boards manufactured by American Megatrends Inc. (AMI) come with a SETUP utility that lets you adjust the CMOS RAM parameters but also allows you to adjust these parameters by pressing the DEL key during the system start-up process.

CMOS stands for "complementary metallic-oxide semiconductor" and refers to the methods used to manufacture the chip for random access memory. CMOS chips use very little power and therefore are often considered the best technology to use for battery-powered storage.

Next, the POST goes on to test your system's memory. The test is very simple: The POST tries to read and write every single byte of memory in your system. (Remember, you've just turned the power on, and so there's nothing useful stored in memory at this point.) The amount of memory tested depends on the amount specified in the system-board switches (on PC and XT systems) or the CMOS RAM (on AT/386/486 systems).

In many cases, the POST program tries a variety of data patterns in each byte to detect common memory failures. (The art of determining the data patterns needed to test a particular memory design could take several chapters to explain.) The progress of the memory test is indicated by the familiar "nnnnK" message on the screen. If any errors are detected, they are displayed to allow you or a repair technician to change the offending memory chip or otherwise repair the problem.

Next, the POST tries to communicate with every device it can find in your system: disk drives, the keyboard, the display, and so on. Again, any errors are displayed on the screen.

If you'd like to see how the POST handles an error, here's a small, safe experiment you can do:

1. Be sure your system is at the DOS prompt and no applications are running.

2. Turn off the system and wait a few seconds.

3. Unplug the keyboard from the system.

4. Turn the system back on and watch the screen. In a little while, on most systems, you'll see error code 301, which means the keyboard isn't working; generally, you'll hear a beep as well. On some systems you'll get the message "Press F1 to continue," which of course you can't do if the keyboard is not working!

5. Turn off the system, reconnect the keyboard, and turn it back on.

When the POST is complete, the next thing the start-up program does is initialize as much of the hardware as it can. Serial and parallel ports are set to an inactive state, and the interrupt vector table is initialized. (This table is stored at the very beginning of memory and is used when external devices or programs interrupt normal system operation to communicate with DOS, the BIOS, or a user program.) The direct memory access (DMA) controller, used for high-speed data transfer between memory and such storage devices as disk drives, is also initialized at this time.

Loading DOS

The final job the BIOS has is to go looking for a disk drive from which to load DOS. (Actually, the BIOS doesn't care that what it's loading is DOS—it just loads whatever it finds.) First, it checks floppy drive A. If there's a disk there and it can read it, it does so. If there's nothing in the A drive, it goes looking for a hard disk (drive C on most systems) and tries to read from it. On some systems, there may be additional devices the BIOS will try to read (for example, a Bernoulli box or bootable tape drive).

When the start-up program finds a disk drive or other device that it can read, it reads the very first block of data on the device. This block is generally one sector, or 512 bytes. If it's able to read the first sector successfully, it assumes that there's a program there and passes control to that program. At this point, the start-up program built into the BIOS has completed its work, and the program that's just been read takes over.

READ.ME

Does This Computer Seem Dopey?

You may wonder why the system bothers to try the floppy drive first even when it has a hard disk. If you reboot very often, you've probably noticed—and maybe been frustrated by—the time spent with the light on the A drive glowing, waiting to see if there's a disk there. But there's a simple and very important reason for this approach.

Suppose the start-up program checked your hard drive first. Now, suppose that it can read the hard drive but what it finds there is gibberish. The BIOS, which has no way of knowing better, will dutifully assume that the gibberish is a program and try to execute it. At that point, the system will stop cold. Ah, you say, we'll go back and boot from a floppy disk. But of course you can't, because the start-up program will again check the hard disk first! At that point you'd be stuck, and the only way out would be to open up the system and disconnect the hard disk.

You may find the read-drive-A delay frustrating, but it's a crucial safeguard in allowing you to get the system up and running even if there's a problem with your hard disk.

The program in the first sector of your disk is put there by the DOS FORMAT command when you format the disk. Its purpose has to be limited: A sector is only 512 bytes long, and a 512-byte program can't do much.

One of two events happens at this point in the startup:

1. If the disk was formatted with a plain FORMAT command and does not have DOS installed on it, the program displays some variation on the message

   ```
   Non-system disk or disk error, press any key to reboot
   ```

   It waits for you to press a key and then restarts the BIOS start-up program, telling it not to bother with the memory tests. The BIOS goes through the sequence described above all over again and (you hope) this time finds a disk that has been formatted with the system on it.

2. If the disk was formatted with FORMAT /S or had the system installed later with the SYS command, the program in the first sector uses some other information from that sector to find the root directory of the disk and from there the very first file on the disk (stored physically immediately following the root directory). It assumes this file is MSDOS.SYS, which contains the kernel (core portion) of DOS. (This file is named IBMDOS.SYS if you have PC-DOS. See Chapter 1, for a further discussion of the MS-DOS files.) The loader reads MSDOS.SYS into memory and passes control to it.

Once MSDOS.SYS has been loaded, it in turn loads the second file, IO.SYS (IBMBIO.SYS if you have PC-DOS), into memory and begins the DOS-initialization process.

Note that at this point three programs have been involved in the process of loading DOS into memory: (1) the ROM BIOS read in the first sector of the disk; (2) the program there read in MSDOS.SYS; and (3) MSDOS.SYS read in the rest of DOS. This process is called *bootstrapping*, or *booting* for short, because the system "pulls itself up by its bootstraps," with each program reading in another level of program to do the next piece of work.

Bootstrapping allows each part of the system to be progressively more complex than the last part. It makes it easy to change software by keeping the fixed part of the program, stored in the ROM BIOS chips, very simple. This idea is not new with the PC. Similar methods have been in use for many years on mainframes and minicomputers.

Once MSDOS.SYS and IO.SYS have been read into memory, they must initialize the system before it can do any real work. Most of the initialization software is part of IO.SYS. It performs the following functions:

- It relocates all portions of DOS to their proper place in memory.

- It initializes the device drivers built into DOS to control operation of standard devices, such as the keyboard, display, and communication ports.

- It initializes the portion of DOS that controls the allocation of memory for other programs.

- It reads and processes the CONFIG.SYS file to load additional device drivers and other configuration information.

- It loads the command processor and passes control to it.

Once its job is done, this part of IO.SYS is removed from memory.

CONFIGURING YOUR SYSTEM WITH CONFIG.SYS

If you've read through the first part of this chapter, you can see that the system does a lot of work before it gets around to doing anything with DOS. (And you wondered why the system boot took so long!) Pretty much all of this process is designed into the hardware, the BIOS chips, and DOS itself. You have almost no control over what it does.

The first point at which you do have some control is in the processing of your CONFIG.SYS file. The remainder of this chapter discusses CONFIG-.SYS and some commands you may wish to use with it.

CONFIG.SYS is a text file stored in the root directory of the disk from which your system boots. You can edit it with any text editor or any word processing program that can create plain ASCII files. If CONFIG.SYS isn't there, DOS will start anyway; it will just use default values for the parameters that could have been specified in CONFIG.SYS.

CONFIG.SYS has three functions:

- It allows you to set certain parameters for DOS, such as the maximum number of files that can be in use by programs in your system at any one time and the number of file buffers.

- It allows you to load device drivers to control physical devices connected to your computer (such as a mouse or a network board) or perform other functions not provided by DOS itself.

- It allows you to specify the command processor once DOS initialization is complete.

We'll explain each function and then look at some annotated examples of CONFIG.SYS files.

Because CONFIG.SYS is processed only when the system starts, changes you make to it will take effect only after you reboot the system.

The basic form of entries in CONFIG.SYS is

```
name=value
```

Name must begin in the first column of the line. Here's an example of a typical CONFIG.SYS line:

```
FILES=20
```

This command sets the FILES parameter to 20.

If you specify an invalid directive, DOS will report the error message "Unrecognized command in CONFIG.SYS" and continue normal processing of the rest of the file. This allows you to temporarily deactivate a directive in CONFIG.SYS by prefacing it with a character that makes it invalid (for example, a period or an asterisk).

Beginning with DOS 4.0, you can insert comments in CONFIG.SYS by beginning the line with REM, as in the following example:

```
REM   Set the number of files to 20
```

The entries in CONFIG.SYS are not necessarily processed in the order they appear. DOS has its own sequence for processing CONFIG.SYS directives while initializing your system, and it processes them in that order regardless of the order in which you placed the directives in the file. For example, SHELL is always processed last, regardless of where it appears in the file. The partial exception to this rule is the DEVICE directive, which can appear multiple times. DOS processes the group of DEVICE directives in its own sequence like other directives, but within the group, it does process them in the order it finds them in the file.

DOS Parameters

CONFIG.SYS lets you set certain parameters for DOS. The parameters you can specify are listed alphabetically in the remainder of this section. These parameters are available in all versions of DOS from 2.0 on unless otherwise noted.

BREAK=ON
BREAK=OFF

BREAK sets extended CTRL-BREAK checking on or off. If BREAK is on, DOS will check for a CTRL-C or CTRL-BREAK keypress every time it is called by a program for any purpose (which is quite often in most programs). If BREAK is off (which is the default), DOS makes this check only while performing input or output to a character device, such as the screen, keyboard, communications port, or printer. Setting BREAK on slows DOS down slightly, but it makes it easier to stop the operation of programs that don't do much character I/O or don't use DOS to do it. On most systems, you will find that the increased control you get from setting BREAK on is well worth the infinitesimal performance degradation it causes.

You can also turn BREAK on and off in a batch file or at the command prompt, using the DOS BREAK command:

```
BREAK=ON
```

There is no particular advantage or disadvantage to setting BREAK on in CONFIG.SYS versus in AUTOEXEC.BAT or elsewhere.

BUFFERS=*nn*

BUFFERS specifies the number of one-sector (512-byte) buffers that DOS should set up. A *buffer* is simply an area of memory that DOS uses when a program transfers information to and from the disk. The allowed range is from 1 to 99 buffers; the default is 2 for PC and XT systems and 3 for AT, 386, and 486 systems. If you have more than 512KB of RAM and a more recent version of DOS, the buffers will default to 15 for any system unless you override the setting with a BUFFERS=nn line in your CONFIG.SYS file, such as the following:

```
BUFFERS=20
```

Device drivers for certain hard disks (such as SCSI drives with large DOS partitions) may increase the buffer size. Increased buffer size reduces the amount of memory available for other purposes, such as running programs. You'll find a disk cache a better alternative for these situations.

To understand what buffers are for, consider the following scenario. Your spreadsheet program needs to read 10 bytes from your worksheet file, beginning at byte number 230. But the disk is divided into 512-byte sectors, and the disk hardware can transfer only 512 bytes at a time. So, DOS has to read in the entire first sector of the file to retrieve those 10 bytes and make them available to the spreadsheet program. It uses a buffer to do so.

When accessing the disk, DOS checks all the buffers first to see if the information needed is already in memory. If not, the information in the least recently used buffer is written to disk, if necessary, and the buffer is used. (This common method of buffer allocation is typically called LRU, for the "least recently used" buffer, which is allocated to fill a new request.)

Increasing the number of buffers makes it more likely that the information you need from the disk will already be in a buffer. This can speed program operation significantly. It takes only microseconds to access data from memory; finding data on the disk can take anywhere from several milliseconds on a hard disk to a couple of seconds on a floppy. On the other hand, each buffer uses 512 bytes of memory. So, using too many of them can boost DOS's memory usage very quickly, reducing memory available for your applications. If the number gets high enough, the overhead of managing the buffers can actually cost more time than it would take to get data from the disk.

If you have a PC with only a floppy disk drive, and less than 512KB of memory, the default of 2 buffers (3 on AT and 386 systems) will be sufficient. Later versions of DOS will give you more automatically if you have more than 512KB of memory. If you have a hard disk, you need more; how many more depends on the programs you're running. In most cases, 10 or

20 will be sufficient. If you increase the number of files (discussed later in this section) above 20, increase the number of buffers accordingly—it shouldn't be too much less than the number of files.

The best way to find a good number of buffers is to try running your system for a while with 5 or so. (Test your system by using programs that access the disk a lot and that also use a large number of files simultaneously.) Then, increase the number to 10 and run the system some more. Then try it with 15, and so on. Assuming you can spare the memory, the number to use is the number above which there's no significant performance improvement.

Programs that access data sequentially (such a word processor, which usually reads in long sections of a document at once) will benefit less from additional buffers than those that access data at random (like a data base). The process of sequentially reading the data will often fill up all the buffers, perhaps several times over, before there is a second request for a sector that was read earlier. By the time the second request occurs, the required sector isn't in a buffer any more. On the other hand, programs like data base managers, which go back and forth frequently between index and data files, are very likely to require repeated access to the same sector; so, additional buffers can be very helpful.

If you're using a disk-caching program that supports floppies and hard disks, such as Super PC-KWIK, SMARTDRIVE, PC-Cache, or Vcache, you need to think about buffers a little differently. DOS buffers constitute a very crude cache; that is, they save data in (fast) memory to reduce (slow) disk accesses. If you have another caching-program active, you'll have two programs performing the same function. This will waste processing time and, more important, will waste memory, as the same data will be kept in two places—the DOS buffers and the cache.

With a cache active, you should reduce the number of DOS buffers to 2 or 3 to reduce this wasted memory to the absolute minimum. If your disk cache doesn't support floppies, you should set your buffers higher to speed up floppy disk operations. Using disks without buffering or caching can be a real bottleneck. Most cache manufacturers recommend this practice. (Of course, if your cache comes with a different recommendation, you should follow it.) Don't go below 2 or 3 buffers though, or DOS can be very slow at the work it has to do before the cache is loaded!

COUNTRY = *nnn*
COUNTRY is used to set the country code for DOS to use. It is supported in MS-DOS version 2.1 and later and in PC-DOS version 3.0 and later.

READ.ME

A Buffers Substitute?

Lately, a new twist has appeared in buffer allocation. The auxiliary program BUFFERS.COM, supplied with Quarterdeck's QEMM 5.0 and QRAM memory managers, has the ability to load buffers in high DOS memory (above 640KB), giving you the advantage of additional buffers without the cost in low-memory usage. You still have to allocate a couple of buffers in CONFIG-.SYS but BUFFERS.COM is run from AUTOEXEC.BAT and adds to that number with additional buffers in high memory. Other memory managers, such as Qualitas's 386 MAX and MOVE'EM, may include this capability in the future. BUFFERS.COM doesn't always buy you much: Any system sophisticated enough to be using these memory-management products is likely to be using a cache; so, the number of buffers required will be small in any case and, therefore, so will the savings from loading buffers into high memory.

The country code determines the way DOS handles date, time, and currency symbols to meet national conventions. For example, in many European countries, the date is written as *dd.mm.yy*; in the United States, the standard form is *mm/dd/yy*; and in Japan, it is *yy/mm/dd*. The variable *nnn* is the international telephone dialing code for the country for which you want to set up your system and *ppp* is the code page for that country. Dialing codes are listed in the appendix of many DOS manuals (and in most telephone books). The optional code page number specifies the display and keyboard character set; these numbers are also generally listed in the DOS-manual appendixes.

The optional *filename,* which may include a drive and path, is the name of a country-information file, generally COUNTRY.SYS.

If the COUNTRY command is not included, DOS will use the default USA values: country code 001, code page 437, and no country-information file. To set the country code for Germany without changing the code page or country-information file, you would use the following command:

COUNTRY=049

DRIVPARM = *parameters*

DRIVPARM is a short-lived directive that was used only in DOS 3.2 to set parameters for disk drives. Its primary use is to specify different parameters for floppy disk drives than those assumed by DOS. The main reason for doing so is to set up additional floppy drives beyond the first two or to set up a nonstandard drive. We will not go into the details of using DRIVPARM, because it existed in only the one DOS version. In many cases, external device drivers (such as DRIVER.SYS from DOS 3.3) provide a better solution for accessing nonstandard floppy disk drives.

FCBS = *n,p*

FCBS tells DOS how to configure access to files using file control blocks (FCBs) when running on a network or with file-sharing support (SHARE.EXE) loaded. It is supported in DOS 3.0 and later.

File control blocks were introduced in DOS 1.0, but since the release of DOS 2.0, Microsoft has recommended that programs use the newer file-handle method for accessing files. Nevertheless, a number of programs (including DOS itself) continue to use the old FCB file-access methods.

The *n* parameter sets the maximum number of files that can be open at any one time using FCBs; the default is 4. The *p* parameter sets the number of these files that are protected against automatic closure by MS-DOS; the default is 0. In general, you will find that these defaults are sufficient. If you receive an "FCB unavailable" or similar error message when running a program, try increasing the value of *n* in the FCBS statement. The FCBS values are used only when SHARE.EXE or a network is loaded and are meaningless in other situations.

To set the number of FCBs for use under SHARE or a network to 8, with 4 protected from automatic closure, type

```
FCBS=8,4
```

FILES = *n*

FILES is probably the most commonly used parameter in CONFIG.SYS. It sets the maximum number of files that can be open at any time using file handles. (File handles are the newer and recommended method of opening files and the one used by most programs; the older method is file control blocks.) The number can be anywhere between 8 and 255. Here's an example:

```
FILES=32
```

The reason this directive is used so often is that the default value is 8. For most PC users, this is much too small: These days, even relatively simple programs may use more than 8 files at a time. It has become common for programs to require a minimum FILES setting of 20, and some, especially data base programs or those with data base capability built in, require many more. In virtually all cases, you should set FILES=20 or more. The default of 8 will often slow down the system and sometimes halt the program.

The effect of setting the number of files is to adjust the size of an internal table kept by DOS to keep track of all open files. This table uses about 50 bytes of memory per file; so, for every 20 files specified, about 1KB of additional memory will be taken for the file table. This gives you an incentive to keep the number reasonably low.

In most cases, you can find the appropriate value for FILES by examining the recommendations that come with the software you use. Just use the highest value recommended by any of your software packages. If you receive "Out of file handles" or similar error messages, try increasing the value of FILES to solve the problem.

As with BUFFERS, an auxiliary program, FILES.COM, supplied with Quarterdeck's QEMM 5.0 and QRAM memory managers, has the ability to load part of the file-handle table in high-DOS memory (above 640KB). This gives you the advantage of additional files without the cost in low-memory usage. You must allocate at least 5 files in CONFIG.SYS for DOS to get started properly. FILES.COM is run from AUTOEXEC.BAT and adds to that number by making room for additional file-table entries in high memory. Other memory managers, such as Qualitas's 386 Max and MOVE'EM, may include this capability in the future. FILES.COM doesn't save a huge amount of memory, since each file-table entry takes only 50 bytes, but it can still save you a couple of KB or more if you are using a lot of files.

LASTDRIVE $= x$

LASTDRIVE, supported in DOS 3.0 and later, sets the highest disk drive letter DOS will recognize. x must be a single letter, from A to Z.

READ.ME

System-File Handles and Process-File Handles

The FILES directive sets the number of files that can be open at any time using file handles. This is also called the number of system-file handles. It specifies the size of the DOS system-file-handle table, which contains one entry for every file that is open in your system.

When any program is started by DOS, it gets its own process-file-handle table. This table is stored in memory belonging to the program and exists only while that program is loaded. It is used by DOS to establish a correspondence between file handles used within the program and the entries in the system-file-handle table. It contains 20 entries, and the only way to expand it is for the program to do so through its own methods or (in DOS 3.3 or later) through a DOS function call. The size of this table is not affected by the FILES setting in CONFIG.SYS.

If you shell to DOS from inside an application or run a multitasker such as DESQview, you may have several programs running at once. Each program in use has its own process-file-handle table and can open up to 20 files (more if the program expands its table). In this case, you may find that DOS runs out of space in the system-file-handle table before your program has all its files open. When this happens, you'll probably receive an "Out of file handles" or similar error message. You can resolve this simply by increasing the FILES value in CONFIG.SYS.

In other circumstances, the reverse can be true: Your program can run out of file handles before DOS does. This condition will also give you an "Out of file handles" error message, but adjusting the FILES setting in CONFIG-.SYS won't solve the problem. What's happening is that the program doesn't have enough file handles in its own internal table—regardless of how you set FILES in CONFIG.SYS. The only solution to this is to check with the program's publisher to determine whether there is a way to tell the program to allocate more file handles internally.

Occasionally, a program may exhibit the behavior described in the preceding paragraph, but only when it is run from inside another program (say, from a menu). This occurs because the "parent" program isn't closing all of its files before starting your program. In this case, the files can be "inherited" by the "child" program, taking up unnecessary space in its process-file-handle table and leading to "Out of file handles" errors. In such a case, your recourse is to contact the manufacturer, run the program directly from the DOS prompt, or get another menu program.

If you load device drivers in CONFIG.SYS to set up additional drives (for example, a third floppy drive accessed with DRIVER.SYS or a RAM disk established with VDISK.SYS), DOS will allocate letters to those drives automatically. But if you allocate drive letters after CONFIG.SYS is processed (for example, with DOS's SUBST command or a RAM disk loaded in AUTOEXEC.BAT), you'll need to "make room" for the additional drive letters to be used by setting LASTDRIVE.

We recommend setting LASTDRIVE to the highest drive letter you normally use, plus one. This gives a little room to maneuver without taking up space for unnecessary drive information. If you set LASTDRIVE to a value less than the highest drive letter already in use, it will be ignored.

You can set the last drive letter to M using

```
LASTDRIVE=M
```

STACKS = n,s

STACKS tells DOS how many stacks to allocate for interrupt processing. It is supported in DOS 3.2 and later.

Your PC's operation depends on external signals from various pieces of hardware (for example, disk drives or your system's timer chip). These signals are called *interrupts*. They stop the normal flow of processing and temporarily transfer control of the microprocessor to a special program called an *interrupt handler*, which addresses whatever external condition caused the interrupt.

All programs in the PC use an area of memory called a *stack* to hold temporary data and keep track of where to return to when a subprogram (such as one of the interrupt handlers) has finished its work. Under conditions where many interrupts are occurring, quite a bit of space can be needed to avoid running out of room on the stack. Because some programs don't have enough room on the stack to meet these needs, DOS maintains a pool of stacks, which it assigns for use by interrupt handlers. The STACKS directive in CONFIG.SYS sets the size of this pool.

The n parameter sets the number of stacks, from 8 to 64; the default is 9. The s parameter sets the size of each stack in bytes, from 32 to 512; the default is 128. If you receive "Internal stack error" messages when your system is busy, try increasing the value of n.

The stacks allocated by this directive can take up quite a lot of memory. For example, if you use

```
STACKS=32,256
```

you will use 32 * 256, or 8KB, of memory. In many cases, program stacks are big enough to accommodate the interrupt handlers in your system; so, you can save memory by disabling DOS's stacks with the following command:

```
STACKS=0,0
```

Device Drivers

A *device driver* is simply a program that allows DOS to communicate with a particular physical device, such as a network, mouse, memory board, or RAM disk. Device drivers are loaded into memory when the system starts, via the DEVICE directive in CONFIG.SYS, and remain there until the system is rebooted.

Device drivers were introduced in DOS 2.0 to allow manufacturers to write their own software for add-on products for the PC and to make DOS more flexible. As PC software has matured, software developers have realized that device drivers can be used for other purposes beyond controlling physical devices. For example, two popular 386 memory managers, 386 Max (Qualitas) and QEMM (Quarterdeck) are both implemented as device drivers. Yet they control a "device"—memory—that is integral to the system, not an add-on.

The syntax for the DEVICE directive is:

```
DEVICE=filename parameters
```

Filename is the name of the file containing the device driver, including drive and path if necessary. (The default drive and path is the root directory of the boot disk.) Most drivers have the extension SYS. The optional *parameters* part of the line specifies any additional information needed by the driver; its format varies and can be found in the documentation for the driver.

We recommend that you store device drivers somewhere other than in the root directory of your boot disk. Typically, PC users spend a lot of time in the root directory, making it easy to inadvertently delete or destroy a crucial driver file—and you won't notice it until the next time you boot the system. Since DOS allows you to specify a path in the DEVICE statement, there's no reason not to keep driver files with the software they came with or in a directory all their own.

DOS comes with a number of device drivers, which you may install if you want to take advantage of their capabilities. The following standard drivers are included with most versions of DOS:

ANSI.SYS

ANSI.SYS provides improved screen and color control. For more details, see Chapter 27, which discusses ANSI drivers in some detail.

DRIVER.SYS

DRIVER.SYS provides control for external floppy disk drives and additional disk formats for existing floppy drives. DRIVER.SYS is distributed with DOS 3.3 and above and was also available in some versions of DOS 3.2. The parameters for DRIVER.SYS are:

/D:n n is the drive number (0 = A, 1 = B, and so on). This switch must be the first one on the line.

/C   This indicates that the device provides "disk changed" status information to the system.

/F:n   This is the device type (form factor). The options are as follows (the default is 2):

```
0 = 320KB or 360KB, 5.25"
1 = 1.2MB, 5.25"
2 = 720KB, 3.5"
3 = 8" single-density
4 = 8" double-density
5 = hard disk
6 = tape drive
7 = 1.44MB, 3.5", or other
```

/H:n n is the number of heads.

/N   This indicates that the disk is not removable.

/S:n n is the number of sectors per track.

/T:*n* *n* is the number of tracks on each side of the disk.

You can load DRIVER.SYS if you have an external floppy drive to control. You can also load it to provide better control over an existing drive, especially in the case where you have an older PC whose BIOS cannot recognize the capabilities of a newer drive.

For example, suppose you have a 3.5-inch, 1.44MB floppy drive installed as drive B but your system's BIOS can handle only the older, 3.5-inch, 720KB drives. Let's assume you have a hard disk partitioned into two logical drives, C and D. You can install DRIVER.SYS to create a new drive, E, which will allow you to access the full capacity of your 1.44MB drive. The command to do so is

```
DEVICE=C:\DRIVER.SYS /D:1 /C /F:7
```

With DRIVER.SYS installed in this way, the drive would be accessible as a 720KB drive under the letter B and as a 1.44MB drive under the letter E. Since 1.44MB drives can read and write 720KB diskettes, you could refer to the drive as E for all operations. The DOS FORMAT command would now default to 1.44MB. You can use command line options to specify 720KB or just use the drive B designator instead. When DRIVER.SYS, it uses the next available drive letter (in this example, drive E).

VDISK.SYS

This driver provides the capability to create a RAM disk. VDISK is included with IBM's PC-DOS. Other versions of DOS may include RAMDRIVE.SYS.

A RAM disk is an area of memory that appears to DOS and your programs to be a very fast disk drive. It can provide a convenient place to store frequently used programs or temporary files. There are a wide variety of RAM disk drivers available; VDISK is only one of them. Many others are more sophisticated and provide greater flexibility and control, but if all you need is a basic RAM disk in main or extended memory, VDISK should do the trick. (VDISK cannot access expanded or EMS memory.)

The basic VDISK command syntax (assuming VDISK.SYS is in directory C:\) is

```
DEVICE=C:\VDISK.SYS disksize secsize dirsize /E:n
```

Disksize is the RAM disk size in KB. The range is 1 to the amount of memory available; the default is 64KB. If the RAM disk is in main memory, VDISK will always leave at least 64KB free after the disk is created, regardless of the size you specify.

Secsize is the sector size in bytes. The allowable values are 128, 256, and 512. The sector size should normally be set to 512 bytes (the PC standard), rather than the default of 128 bytes.

Dirsize is the number of entries (files) that can be stored in the RAM disk's root directory. The range is 2 to 512. The default of 64 should be sufficient unless you plan to place a large number of files in the root directory.

The optional parameter /E tells VDISK to use a RAM disk in extended memory. In most cases, a RAM disk won't be large enough to be useful if you have to squeeze it into main memory; so, you'll probably use this parameter most of the times you have occasion to use VDISK.

/E can be followed by a number (/E:n) to limit the number of sectors VDISK will transfer to extended memory at one time. This capability is available only in PC-DOS 3.1 and later. The n must be between 1 and 8; the default is 8. The value of n should be reduced to less than 8 only if you have trouble with I/O devices while using VDISK (for example, characters lost by a printer or communications port). Reducing n limits the amount of time VDISK will disable processing of interrupts from these devices while it is transferring data to and from extended memory.

In addition to these standard drivers, your system may use others. In some cases, you will need drivers because your hardware requires them; the most common cases are the use of network interfaces and mice. In other cases, drivers will be used to provide utility functions, such as memory management. The following chapter discusses the wide variety of drivers available and what they can do for you.

One tip for solving compatibility problems with device drivers is to try rearranging the DEVICE statements to load the drivers in a different order. Sometimes, drivers that appear to conflict with each other will get along fine when a different load order is used. Unfortunately, the number of possible combinations of drivers is so large that the only tip we can give you is to try for yourself and see what works. It isn't hard to do so long as you are systematic and thorough and you change only one thing at a time.

If you do have compatibility problems (drivers that don't work or don't work correctly), it's often best to remove all the drivers you can and reload them one by one until the problem occurs. That approach can often identify the culprit much faster than random rearrangements or guesswork.

Recent software improvements have added a new capability for device drivers: the "loadhi" option. This allows drivers to be loaded into the area between 640KB and 1MB, conserving precious low-memory resources. The major programs that provide this capability are Qualitas's 386 Max (for 386s) and MOVE'EM (for other systems) and Quarterdeck's corresponding QEMM and QRAM.

Loading drivers high requires a line like the following:

```
DEVICE=D:\QEMM\LOADHI.SYS filename parameters
```

In this case, as far as DOS can tell, the driver being loaded is LOADHI-.SYS. But what this driver does is load the real driver, whose name is specified in the *filename* and whose parameters are in *parameters*, and store it in high memory.

Loading drivers into high memory is a bit of an art. Some drivers require considerably more memory to load than they do to run, and some won't work at all if loaded high. Couple that with the need to load drivers in the right order and the characteristics of a typical system where "high memory" is really two or more pieces of non-contiguous memory space, and it can be quite tricky to find a load order that meets everyone's needs.

Quarterdeck's new OPTIMIZE program for use with QEMM attempts to automate the load-high process and determine the best loading order. Qualitas is reported to be preparing a similar program for use with 386 Max. But these software approaches aren't perfect. If you want the benefits of loading drivers into high memory, you should plan to spend some time getting it done right.

The Command Processor

There's one more directive you can use in CONFIG.SYS: SHELL. SHELL specifies the name of the command processor to be loaded when DOS is started and any parameters for the command processor. If you don't specify a command processor, DOS looks for its default command processor, COMMAND.COM, in the root directory of the boot drive.

The syntax for SHELL is just like that for DEVICE:

```
SHELL=filename parameters
```

where *filename* is the name of the file containing the command processor, including drive and path if necessary (the default drive and path is the root

directory of the boot disk), and *parameters* specifies any additional information needed by the command processor.

If invoking COMMAND.COM as the command processor, SHELL can
be used to access COMMAND.COM when it is not in the root directory of
the boot disk (a good practice, for the same reason as for drivers) and to set
the environment size. In this case the syntax is

```
SHELL=[d:][path]\COMMAND.COM /E:n /P
```

where [*d:*][*path*] is the drive and path where COMMAND.COM is stored; *n*
is the size of the DOS environment in bytes from 160 to 32768 (DOS 3.2 and
above) or in 16-byte paragraphs (DOS 3.1); and /P signifies that this is the
primary command processor and that AUTOEXEC.BAT should be executed. The default if the /E:*n* is omitted is 160 bytes, or 10 paragraphs. If
the /P switch is missing, AUTOEXEC.BAT will not be executed.

The ability to select a command processor was introduced in DOS 2.0.
However, until DOS 3.0 was released, COMMAND.COM included some
undocumented but necessary functions that could not easily be duplicated
by programmers writing alternative command processors. As a result, while
it is theoretically possible to completely replace COMMAND.COM under
DOS 2, it is only practical under DOS 3.0 and above. Alternate command
processors can generally run under DOS 2, but they must be loaded after
COMMAND.COM rather than as a replacement for it.

A program that replaces COMMAND.COM must provide certain features required by all programs running under DOS, such as critical error
and CTRL-BREAK handling. Beyond these basic features, the replacement command processor can implement any set of commands the author chooses;
the resulting system need not look like DOS at all. In fact, until recently,
the primary programs that took advantage of the ability to install an
alternate command processor were shells (another term for command processors) designed to make DOS look and work like UNIX.

Recently, many PC users have begun using a shareware replacement for
COMMAND.COM: 4DOS, from J.P. Software. 4DOS provides the same
basic commands as COMMAND.COM plus a variety of new commands and
enhancements. (It is discussed in more detail later in the book.) As an
example of the use of SHELL, here is a typical SHELL command for
loading 4DOS as the command processor:

```
SHELL=C:\4DOS.COM /E:2048 /A:2048 /U /P
```

One special note regarding the SHELL directive: A bug in all versions of DOS from 2.0 through 4.01 limits the length of the parameters portion of the line. The length of the entire line is immaterial; it is only the parameters portion that matters. If the parameters (including any leading and trailing spaces) take more than 32 bytes, the system will not boot properly. Symptoms will include garbage in the DOS environment and perhaps incorrect behavior on the part of the command processor. This bug is not a problem with COMMAND.COM, because the longest useful parameter string is /E:*nnnnn* /P, which is less than 32 characters. However, it may easily affect replacement command processors, which must provide a mechanism for dealing with it.

Note: For those interested, the bug is that DOS has only a 29-byte buffer for the parameters portion of the SHELL directive, and it does not check whether the parameters have exceeded this length. The first 3 bytes beyond the buffer can be overwritten without causing trouble; hence the 32-byte limit. The limit may be slightly longer than 32 bytes in some versions of DOS.

CONFIG.SYS Examples

This section will give you three sample CONFIG.SYS files, which we've labeled "beginner," "intermediate," and "advanced." (We take another approach and do this again with more details later in the book). The terms refer, not to the level of knowledge required to use the systems these files are on, but to the level of experience and familiarity with the information above that you'll need to create the file.

Beginner

This version of CONFIG.SYS is pretty simple. Our hypothetical user needs to expand the FILES and BUFFERS settings, and—per our recommendations—load a single device driver, ANSI.SYS, and load COMMAND-.COM from the DOS directory, not the root directory.

```
FILES=20
BUFFERS=16
DEVICE=C:\DOS\ANSI.SYS
SHELL=C:\DOS\COMMAND.COM /P
```

Intermediate

This user has a slightly more complex setup. The system has an expanded memory board, which requires an EMS driver. It also has a mouse, which requires a mouse driver. This system can have a lot of files open at once, but a cache is in use; so, the number of buffers has been reduced. Also, the environment size is expanded beyond the default 160 bytes to 1KB (1024 bytes). We assume this user is running DOS 3.3; so, the environment size is stated in bytes. This user has a large hard disk partitioned into two drives, with most software stored on the D drive. Drive F is defined as an alternative drive letter for the second disk drive, a 3.5-inch floppy, to allow access to it as a 1.44MB drive.

```
FILES=64
BUFFERS=3
STACKS=0,0
DEVICE=D:\EMS\MEMM40.SYS
DEVICE=D:\MOUSE\MOUSE.SYS
DEVICE=D:\DOS\ANSI.SYS
DEVICE=D:\DOS\DRIVER.SYS /D:1 /C /F:7
DEVICE=C:\DOS\VDISK.SYS 384 512 64 /E
SHELL=D:\DOS\COMMAND.COM /E:1024 /P
```

Advanced

This user has a 386 with a number of device drivers, most of which are loaded high. The system uses 4DOS as the command processor. Because of the complexity of this file, we have commented each line or group of lines with indented comments marked with asterisks.

```
lastdrive=j
buffers=2
files=8
```

This sets up the last drive as J, 2 buffers, and 8 files. (More buffers and files will be loaded later with QEMM's BUFFERS.COM and FILES.COM.)

```
device=e:\qemm\qemm.sys ram=b000-b7ff ram=cc00-dfff
```

This loads Quarterdeck's QEMM memory manager, specifying two areas of high memory to use for loading drivers and TSRs high.

```
device=e:\qemm\loadhi.sys c:\xdrive.sys /d:2 /f:1 /u
```

This loads a floppy disk driver similar to DRIVER.SYS into high memory.

```
device=e:\qemm\loadhi.sys c:\keystack.sys
```

This loads the 4DOS KEYSTACK.SYS driver into high memory.

```
device=e:\qemm\loadhi.sys e:\pckwik\pckramd.sys /s:512 /d:128
```

This loads Multisoft's Super PC-KWIK RAM disk program into high memory, setting the sector size to 512 bytes and the number of directory entries to 128.

```
device=e:\qemm\loadhi.sys e:\util\burndev.sys
```

This loads Chris Dunford's freeware screen blanker BURNDEV, which blanks the screen to avoid "burning in" an image when the PC is inactive, into high memory.

```
device=e:\pkii\kybd.buf /b64/n1
```

This loads the shareware PowerKit II keyboard-buffer program.

```
.device=f:\peri\sysload.sys /p=f:\peri\ps.com
```

This loads the Periscope debugger, which this user wants loaded only occasionally. If you start the line with a period (.), the "." keeps the line in place, so that it doesn't have to be recreated, but keeps it from being executed; a harmless error message will be displayed instead.

```
shell=d:\4dos\4dos.com /l:d:\4dos /e:u /a:5120u /u /p
```

This loads 4DOS as the command processor, specifies a 5KB alias buffer, and loads the master environment and the command processor itself into high memory.

We hope this helps you feel more comfortable with your start-up environment. If you take advantage of some of the items mentioned in this chapter, you may see a significant boost in performance.

WHAT IS AUTOEXEC.BAT?

After CONFIG.SYS has configured your system, the command processor named by the SHELL directive (or COMMAND.COM if none was named) is executed. The command processor's first job is to check for the existence of the AUTOEXEC.BAT file.

AUTOEXEC.BAT is simply a batch file, very much like any other batch file. In other words, it's a file of DOS commands to be executed by the command processor. The name comes from AUTOEXEC's one special characteristic: When stored in the root directory of the boot disk, it is AUTOmatically EXECuted by the command processor when your system boots.

If AUTOEXEC.BAT does not exist in the root directory of the boot disk, the command processor will start without it. For example, if you're using COMMAND.COM and AUTOEXEC.BAT isn't there, COMMAND-.COM will prompt you for the current date and time, then display the prompt.

AUTOEXEC gives you the ability to do almost anything you'd like when the system is started. In most cases you'll want to use it to do at least three things:

- Load any memory-resident (TSR) programs you need on your system

- Set the PATH and, if necessary, the PROMPT and COMSPEC

- Set any environment variables used by the programs you typically use

In some cases, you may want to do some other things in AUTOEXEC as well, for example:

- Run programs that you wish to execute only when the system boots

- Issue commands to log on to a network

- Start a multitasker, task switcher, menu program, or visual shell if you use one of these programs and want it loaded every time you boot

In this chapter we are concerned only with the environment variables. The discussion of the environment variables will be useful to you to gain an understanding of the bootup process. Other capabilities of AUTOEXEC-.BAT and batch files are described throughout the book.

The DOS "Environment"

The so-called environment is another area that has some mystery surrounding it, but is really quite simple. The environment is a user-specified portion of memory set aside to hold data for use by programs and DOS. There are three environment variables (COMSPEC, PATH, and PROMPT) defined implicitly by DOS or by the corresponding DOS commands. Other environment variables must be defined by you, using the DOS SET command (programs can also modify the master environment directly, but most programs do not do so).

SET
SET can add variables to the master environment, remove them, or modify existing variables. You can view the contents of the master environment by entering the SET command with no arguments, such as:

```
SET
```

The amount of memory set aside for the master environment is determined by the /E:*nnnn* switch on the SHELL line in CONFIG.SYS. For example, the following SHELL line starts DOS 3.3's COMMAND.COM with a 1024-byte master environment:

```
SHELL=C:\DOS\COMMAND.COM /E:1024 /P
```

The following line loads 4DOS as the command processor, with a 2048-byte master environment:

```
SHELL=C:\4DOS\4DOS.COM /E:2048 /P
```

We recommend that you start your system out with 512 bytes of environment space, and add more if you run out.

Every time DOS starts a program it makes a copy of the master environment. Because this copy is "passed" to the program it is sometimes called the "passed environment".

Once a program has started, it can look into this passed copy of the environment and find the value of any variables it needs. The variables may be used to tell the program where to find its files, how to perform an operation, or anything else the designer wants.

For example, the popular shareware directory manager, DX, uses a command:

```
SET DX0=/ca:1/h+/s+
```

that specifies that DX should automatically invoke the options /ca:1 (display in lower case), /h+ (include hidden files), and /s+ (include system files) every time it is run.

Typically, options which are modified every time the program is run wouldn't be used with an environment variable, because this would require you to execute several commands to run the program: First one or more SETs to set up the environment variable(s), then the command to run the program itself. Where environment variables are really useful is to define options that may not be the default for the program, but that you want to use all the time on your system.

Since there's no "central registration bureau" for environment variable names, you can easily run into name conflicts. If you run into one, you'll have to run each of the conflicting programs from a batch file that sets the environment variable appropriately.

The three variables defined by DOS for its own use are PATH, PROMPT, and COMSPEC.

PATH
PATH tells the command processor what directories to look in when it is searching for a program you've asked it to run. It is created when you issue a PATH command. If you don't define the path, or remove the path with a "PATH ;" command the PATH variable will not be present in the environment. You can also modify the PATH variable with a SET command, but beware: The PATH command converts the path you enter to uppercase, but SET does not. Some programs—notably Novell's NetWare—will not work properly if the path is stored in lowercase.

PROMPT
PROMPT tells the command processor how to display the DOS prompt on your screen. It is created when you issue a PROMPT command. If you don't

define the prompt, or remove it with an empty PROMPT command, the PROMPT variable will not be present in the environment. You can also modify the PROMPT variable with a SET command; SET PROMPT [prompt-string] will do the exact same thing as PROMPT [prompt-string].

COMSPEC

COMSPEC tells COMMAND.COM where to find itself when it must be reloaded (see the discussion of the command processor's resident and transient portions below). It also tells other programs where to find the command processor when "shelling to DOS" (starting a secondary copy of the command processor to allow you to perform some DOS commands, then return to your application). Our experience is that if you have trouble shelling to DOS or running one program from inside another, there's an excellent chance that the COMSPEC isn't set correctly.

COMSPEC is set automatically to point to the root directory of the boot drive (for example, on a normal hard disk-based system COMMAND.COM will set the COMSPEC to C:\COMMAND.COM). You can override this setting with a SET command in CONFIG.SYS. For example, if COM-MAND.COM is stored in the D:\USR\BIN directory on your system, then you'd need to use the following SET command in AUTOEXEC.BAT:

```
set comspec=d:\usr\bin\command.com
```

Once you've taken care of DOS's variables and the ones needed for your programs, there's one other use that you can make of environment variables, and that's in batch files.

COMMAND.COM's environment variable handling functions are primitive, but they do provide some important and necessary functions for use in your batch files.

AUTOEXEC.BAT Samples

This section will give you three sample AUTOEXEC.BAT files, similar to the examples given earlier for CONFIG.SYS. Like the CONFIG.SYS examples, we've labeled these "beginner," "intermediate," and "advanced." The terms refer not to the level of knowledge required to use the systems these files are on, but to the level of experience and familiarity with DOS that you'll need to create the file.

READ.ME

Problems with TSRs

If you load a series of memory-resident programs in AUTOEXEC.BAT, sometimes they'll conflict with each other. You may notice the conflict when they're loaded, in the form of odd error messages or a complete system freeze. Or you may notice it later when you try to use the TSRs or other parts of your system.

One good technique in such situations is to first unload all drivers and TSRs except those required for basic operation of your system. Then put them back one at a time until the problem reappears. Once that happens, you know that either the problem is with the program you just put back, or that program is interacting with one of the others. At this point you may also wish to change the order in which the TSRs are loaded in AUTOEXEC.BAT. Some TSRs that work quite happily together when program B is loaded before program A will go completely to pieces if A is loaded first. This is an unfortunate fact of life with the PC: There are no standards or rules for TSR programming (Microsoft didn't even have a TSR capability built in to the original versions of DOS), so almost anything goes, and as a result there are conflicts.

Beginner

This version of AUTOEXEC is simple. Our hypothetical user only wants to set the date and time (this must be an old PC), load the DOS PRINT command from the A drive, set the prompt to show drive and directory, and clear the screen:

```
date
time
a:\print.com
prompt $p$g
cls
```

Intermediate

This user has a slightly larger file. It reduces the environment size and loads several TSRs, then sets up the environment. It also runs Golden Bow

Systems' VOPT to defragment the hard disk, which must be done before any TSRs are loaded:

```
set comspec
c:\gbow\vopt
c:\util\mouse.com
c:\pckwik\superpck /a
c:\uv\uv
path c:\batch;c:\util;c:\arc;c:\word
set pktmp=d:\
set timer=off
set sys_id=AA2745
```

Advanced

This user has a 386, and wants to load TSRs into high DOS memory using Quarterdeck's LOADHI program. A number of environment variables must be set, but these are in a separate batch file, not shown, called SETENV-.BAT (SETENV simply consists of a long group of SET commands). Similarly, the path is set with SETPATH.BAT. This user also has a complex prompt, which uses the capabilities of ANSI.COM (one of the TSRs installed, a substitute for the DOS ANSI.SYS driver) to display the date, time, and current directory in bright white with a magenta background across the top row of the screen, then return the color to the user's standard bright cyan on blue and return to the original cursor position for the regular prompt display. The prompt is shown here on two lines, but would be entered on a single line in the file. The TOGGLE program invoked at the end is a small utility that turns off the NUM LOCK light, which is left on on enhanced keyboards by most BIOS startup programs in order to emulate IBM's decision to start enhanced keyboards in NUM LOCK mode.

Note: If you find your AUTOEXEC getting long and complex, and you are using DOS 3.3 or later (or 4DOS), you can make it easier to maintain your system by breaking up AUTOEXEC into smaller files and then invoking each file with the CALL command.

```
@echo off
break on
echo ------------------------------------------------
echo !              Start AUTOEXEC              !
echo ------------------------------------------------
rem
rem  Defragment the disk (DEFRAG.BAT, not shown)
```

```
rem
call defrag
echo .
echo . Setting up TSRs

echo .
e:\qemm\loadhi.com e:\pckwik\superpck /t:8/r:512
e:\qemm\loadhi.com e:\mouse\mouse
e:\qemm\loadhi.com e:\uv\uv.com
e:\qemm\loadhi.com c:\ansi.com
rem
rem  Activate UltraVision
rem
e:\uv\uv /L
echo .
echo . Setting up environment and command
aliases
echo .
call setpath
call setenv
prompt $e[s$e[1;1f$e[0;45;37m$e[K$d $t $p $e[u$e[0;44;36$p$g
toggle n
cls
echo --------------------------------------------------
echo !                  AUTOEXEC Complete                  !
echo --------------------------------------------------
```

Now that you have completed reading this chapter you're ready to examine your system's DOS environment and make adjustments to your COMSPEC, PROMPT, and PATH.

PART TWO

Multitasking and Memory Management

CHAPTER SEVEN

Multitasking, Task Switching, and Background Processing

Have you ever discovered that you needed some information from your spreadsheet while you were involved in a document on your word processor? Have you ever become frustrated while you waited for your computer to complete some lengthy task, such as printing? Would you like to jump from one application to another whenever you wanted to? This isn't a Ginsu Knife commercial—it's an introduction to multitasking, task switching, and background processing.

A PC right out-of-the-box is usually a single-tasking system. In this type of system, one chore dominates the machine. When something must be done, the machine does it; when something isn't ready, the machine waits.

When your Lotus 1-2-3 program reads in a spreadsheet from disk, the program instructions are to read a sector on a disk. DOS requests the sector from the disk. The disk drive says, "I'm not ready—wait." DOS says, "Okay, okay, I'll wait." (Note that this is a translation.) Then, DOS finally receives the information and passes it to Lotus 1-2-3. "Here you go," DOS says. Lotus 1-2-3 becomes the foreground task, while DOS sits around and waits for another command.

The following three methods can be used to increase your system's task modes:

- Multitasking

- Task switching

- Background processing

MULTITASKING

Multitasking is the most complex of the three. It is a front-end system—an adjunct to the operating system—that allows you to run several processes at the same time. Multitasking makes it possible to process concurrently more than one job and to dynamically switch between background and foreground tasks. (A background task is one that takes place "off screen." The foreground task dominates the screen and your attention.) The background can interrupt the foreground as well as switch into the foreground.

DOS wasn't designed with multitasking in mind. To get *true* multitasking on your PC, you'll have to use an operating system other than DOS. Many multitasking operating systems are available, including UNIX/ XENIX, VMS, and OS/2. Multitasking is not possible on the slower, 8088 processors.

A multitasking system can be added to a DOS-based system. It isn't the same as true multitasking, but it offers many of the same features. These systems include Windows and DESQview (which are covered in detail in other chapters of this book). One advantage of using a DOS "multitasking" system is that you can continue to use the DOS programs you're familiar with.

If you opt for a DOS-based system, there are some trade-offs. DOS-based multitasking takes longer to run and execute commands than other systems. With each additional simultaneous task, the system will slow a little more. Each application task takes a portion of the computer's cycle of 18 clock ticks. (Even with your tasks running slower, however, you will save time with the concurrent run.)

TASK SWITCHING

A task switcher is a limited version of a multitasking system. Task switching permits you to freeze one action and run another. It's a simple approach to a complex problem. Task switching can suspend the foreground and switch it to a chunk of RAM or disk storage. Then, another program can be moved to the foreground from disk or summoned from suspension in RAM or disk storage. Restoring a suspended program is faster than reloading it from scratch.

Multiple suspended programs can be a time saver if you need to switch among them frequently. When one of these applications is run, it will get all of the processor's computing power except during the minimal time needed for a keyboard-interrupt scan. (The keyboard interrupt signals a task swap.)

When the task switcher receives a signal from the keyboard to swap a program, it will wait for DOS to come to a point where DOS can be safely interrupted. The switcher freezes and moves the foreground task, reads the new task from RAM or disk, and brings it to the foreground. DOS then takes over the new task.

Applications that use some of the extended video modes are a management burden for task switchers and multitaskers. It is difficult for these programs to accurately track the applications, identify them, and reproduce them faithfully. One of the difficulties arises with a video card that is initialized in an unconventional way. When control is returned to a program that requires the use of the video card, the initialization must be restored along with the task. If it's not, the system will crash, or the video card will hang.

In systems with limited RAM, multitaskers can be set to operate like a task switcher to transfer tasks to the disk. (On a system with enough RAM, it makes little sense to task switch.) Even when running a single task with a multitasker, there is a significant reduction in program-execution speed compared with a single-task system or task switcher. It's better to use these programs for the purpose they were designed for.

Task switchers may have interrupt conflicts with TSRs, some graphics applications, or marginal memory chips. This is especially apt to occur when these programs make use of a system's upper memory.

The top four task switchers are Software Carousel; Switch-It; DESQview; and OmniVision. Some task switchers have been adapted for use as true multitaskers on the 386 chip; DESQview is an example (see the chapter dedicated to DESQview).

Each program allows you a division of tasks or partitions. In each partition, you may run a separate program. At any time, you may press a hot key to start a new partition or call up a menu of available partitions. When a new partition is requested, the current partition (memory and the screen image) is saved in the swap area. The swap area can be disk space, expanded memory, extended memory, or a combination of the three. The partition you request is copied out of the swap area into conventional memory.

There are six considerations in the choice of a task switcher:

- Ease of use and installation
- Task-switch speed
- Memory usage
- Number of possible partitions
- Reliability (Does it crash? Does it work?)
- Cost

Background Processing

Background processing is a limited form of multitasking known as *terminate-and-stay-resident* (TSR). It lacks the medley of features that a multitasking system has to offer, and background tasks cannot be switched from foreground to background.

Printer spooling is a common background task (and one that requires little in the way of computing resources). Print spoolers are controlled by the physical activity of the printer. If the printer isn't ready to accept new characters, the print spooler won't have anything to do.

A background process doesn't have to be a print job. It can encompass a disk formatter (for example, Sydex's Concurrent Format) or a background telecommunications program (such as DIRAC System's BFT, Background File Transfer). The DOS commands PRINT and GRAPHICS are a form of background process. These programs characteristically have a *hook interrupt,* which is a way to connect into the process chain of sequence interrupts. Normally, a background processor or multitasker relies on the timer interrupt INT 0 to let it share the CPU with other tasks. Even if other interrupts are used, the timer interrupt will still be necessary.

All background programs are TSRs, but not all TSRs are background programs. Some of these TSR programs take control of the system when they receive an interrupt request (such as a keypress or a call to a device) and suspend other chores. These programs are not background processors or multitaskers. A TSR can remain inactive and wait for its hot key to be pressed. One example of a TSR program that is not a background program is SideKick.

PRODUCTS

Multitasking Systems

The VMos/3 PC-MOS and VM/386 systems are designed to take advantage of the advanced features of the 386 microprocessor. These programs run tasks separately in multiple sessions called "virtual 86." The virtual-86 mode has many advantages, including improved compatibility and program stability. These improvements are possible because the virtual-86 mode isolates each application. It is less likely to be affected by misbehaving programs, system lockups, and crashes.

One option for true multitasking is OS/2, although few applications run under this operating system. To use true multitasking with OS/2, an 80286- or 80386-based computer with at least 2MB of memory is required. The newest version of Microsoft Windows also performs multiple tasks (see the chapter dedicated to Windows).

VM/386 is priced at $245.

Intelligent Graphics Corp. (IGC)
1740 Technology Dr.
San Jose, CA 95110
800-458-9108; 408-441-0366
Fax: 408-441-0390

Software Carousel

A popular task switcher is Software Carousel. Software Carousel can be started from an AUTOEXEC.BAT file. It loads programs that you specify to set up all your tasks and lets you create your own hot-key combos to switch partitions. Software Carousel allows you to load all your programs once; throughout the day, you can jump back and forth between them. It is excellent when you have enough RAM to hold all the applications you wish to work with. If your system does not have enough RAM, programs can be swapped to disk in less than 12 seconds.

Each partition uses about 35KB and includes a copy of the transient portion of COMMAND.COM for programs that require it. You can cut the 35KB bytes overhead down to about 15KB by caching parts of the program in expanded or extended memory.

Software Carousel has its own memory manager. It can swap to LIM EMS 4.0 or 3.2 expanded memory, extended memory, disk, conventional memory, or a combination. Software Carousel can even change the swap area—from expanded memory to extended memory to disk—automatically as each area fills up. The amount stored in each area is user designated.

Software Carousel has a "Print'n'Run" module to allow background printing while the foreground task is running. Graphics programs require VGA. MCGA is supported, and the program is compatible with NetBIOS and IEEE 802.2 network protocols.

Software Carousel's list price is $89.95. Available add-on functions are OLE (Open Link Extender), a background telecommunications program; Magic Mirror, which gives you the ability to pass data between your task's partitions; and the Print'n'Run module. SoftLogic also offers low-cost upgrades.

SoftLogic Solutions, Inc.
One Perimeter Road
Manchester, NH 03103
800-272-9900
New Hampshire residents call 603-627-9900

OmniView

OmniView is a program with cult followers; some rave about it. OmniView is similar to Software Carousel, but it can perform multiple tasks, as well. OmniView runs full-screen tasks easily. Windows-designed programs cannot run on OmniView.

Setting up OmniView is easy. You can specify which tasks should be run in the background. Like Carousel, OmniView allows partitions and a toggle between applications. You can specify whether the information will be swapped to disk or to memory. The documentation has sample option sets for 50 or so popular applications. Applications not listed can still be tried; you may need to experiment.

OmniView's multitasking capabilities allow new partitions to be generated for background operations (copy files or print, for example). Software

Carousel lacks this capability, but it can mimic the feature by use of a background-process program, such as DOS's PRINT program or Softlogic's own OLE program.

Multitasking with more than 640KB requires an EEMS board or LIM 4.0 memory to swap above the 640KB boundary. An 80386-based computer with 386 or QEMM-386 will give you this LIM 4.0 capability with specific OmniView support. (The support includes virtual screens and bleed-through of one application to another.)

The price of OmniView is $80.

Sunny Hill Software
10121 Evergreen Way, Suite 259
Everett, WA 98204
800-367-0651; 206-367-0650

Switch-It

Switch-It is a convenient tool, but it is short on graphics support. Switch-It users are able to cut and paste data among applications files. A feature of Switch-It is that it remembers the last 30 DOS commands entered.

Switch-It enables users to load TSR programs from DOS's 640KB conventional-memory address space to extended or expanded memory as well as to a hard disk. This memory management frees up more RAM for application tasks.

Extended memory isn't directly supported, but applications can be swapped to a virtual disk in extended memory. The program uses about 28KB for each partition. Unlike similar products, Switch-It doesn't load COMMAND.COM into each partition. This saves some memory, but programs cannot run until COMMAND.COM is loaded.

Switch-It lists for $79.95. It requires an IBM PC-compatible system with a minimum of 512KB of RAM.

Better Software
55 New York Ave.
Framingham, MA 01701
800-848-0286; 508-879-0744
Fax: 508-872-1734

PROCESS MODES

The various microprocessors operate in what are called *modes*. Multitaskers can use any mode. Multitaskers exist even for 8088 machines, which have only one mode (although the robust use virtual-86 mode).

Real Mode

Real mode, which is the mode supported by the 8088, offers no protection from badly behaving programs. If a program execution locks up, the whole machine will lock up, and the user will have to reboot the computer.

Protected Mode

Protected mode puts a layer of hardware between the foreground task and any background tasks. Protected mode allows programmers to set limits and control the privileges of programs executed. If a program steps outside of these limits, the system generates an exception to the control program (which is usually the multitasker).

Virtual-86 Mode

Virtual-86 mode takes the protected mode even a step further. Considerable hardware is involved. Virtual-86 also creates the illusion of separate 8086 machines, complete with the full address space, interrupts, and I/O.

READ.ME

The Interrupt

What is an *interrupt*? Early microcomputers did not have interrupt capabilities. They performed input /output activities to print and receive data. Overall, this approach isn't bad.

Then, some clever people decided there was a better way. Why sit around and wait for an I/O device? Why not give the devices the capability to tell the machine that they are ready — no matter what other processes are in the foreground? This was accomplished by means of an instruction to the microprocessor execution-instruction stream. These instructions are predefined in the 8086 family.

The Interrupt *(continued)*

The designations 8088, 8086, 80286, 80386 and 80486 refer to the interrupt number—the location of the interrupt call. Each of these interrupt numbers was given a device to "service." A device can be a printer, a keyboard, a program, a mouse, and so on.

The interrupt control chip on the 8088 can service up to eight devices. These interrupts can be arranged in order of importance of the devices. For instance, when a key is pressed on the keyboard, it can interrupt any activity occurring on the floppy disk—a less critical device, from the computer's perspective. In the logic of this interrupt, computers can't go back to the keyboard to have the user rekey, but the floppy driver can be reinitiated.

An interrupt executes the *call instruction* of the specific device connected and places the information into the instruction stream of the processor. The processor immediately intrudes on the instruction stream to execute the call instruction. This is a *device service routine.* Once the routine is executed, the service routine returns to the event in progress before the intervention.

Some operations are more time critical than others. The 80259 interrupt-controller chips can order up to eight interrupts on the 8088/8086 (plain PC and XT machines). On 80286, 80386, and 80486 machines, there are two 80259 interrupt-controller chips. This interrupt-support logic is built into the motherboard by means of the 80259 chip.

One of the interrupts contains the day/clock timer, which measures 55-millisecond intervals (18.2 ticks per second). This is the date and stamp for files. When the timer hits 55 milliseconds, a service routine bumps a counter to compute the time and day.

After the timer, the next instruction set is put into motion. This continues down the chain of instructions. When the end of the instruction chain is reached, control is returned to the program that was in control before the timer interrupt occurred. This is why the number of background tasks has an impact on system performance.

Hardware interrupts initiate from the device itself. They call the 80258 interrupt chip, which works with the processor. Software interrupts are not device dependent, can be included as instructions in a program, and also call the 80258 interrupt chip. All IBM-compatible systems support hardware and software interrupts.

In addition to interrupts generated by hardware and software, there are also some generated by the processor and its associated memory. These are the first eight interrupts in the chain (0, 1, 2, 3, 4, 5, 6, 7). There are no IRQs associated with these—they are system generated.

This is a good place to explain the distinction between an IRQ and an interrupt. An *IRQ* is an abbreviation for "interrupt request." The number of

──────────── **READ.ME** ─────────

The Interrupt *(continued)*

interrupts on the chip totals 250. They begin with 0. The time-of-day clock is IRQ 0, the keyboard is IRQ 1, and network adapters are normally IRQ 2.

IACK is an abbreviation for "interrupt acknowledge." After an IRQ, the response is IACK. When a device issues an interrupt request, the chip responds.

There are a limited number of IRQs. Because of this, there are instances when an IRQ is shared by devices. The program that services this interrupt must ask each device if it initiated the interrupt request. (All programs manage the problem of shared interrupts.)

In DOS, IRQ 0 results in the execution of interrupt 8. This is the range in which the 80259 is mapped. IRQ 1 results in interrupt 9; IRQ 2, in interrupt 10; and so on.

When Intel designed the 8086's instruction set (8088 to the 486), they decided to give the interrupt instruction 256 (0-255) possibilities. The interrupt instruction calls a table of addresses that has 256 entries. This system works, although the PC/XT limit of eight interrupts and the AT's limit of 15 are far from the 256-interrupt-instruction possibility. (This is on account of the limited capability of the 80259 interrupt chip.)

In DOS, the interrupt-instruction numbers are from 8 through 15. OS/2 and other PC-based operating systems use other sets. These groups are changeable through software, but it's not done. The default group remains unchanged.

The instruction set, 2 bytes long, is a convenient way for software to communicate with the rest of the system. In this sense, the DOS call—INT 33—is not an interrupt in the true sense. It is a clever convention that can use 2 bytes to call DOS instead of 5 bytes.

Routines in the BIOS (for the time of day or to output characters to the screen) can also be called with interrupt instructions. It is easier to refer to the interrupt instructions than to reload the entire instruction.

By convention, each of the BIOS services is assigned an interrupt number. Software interrupts tend to be the most compatible from one system to another. The locations of DOS services and BIOS services can differ, but the interrupts are consistent throughout all 256 of them.

A physical event is required to cause the processor to switch from the foreground to the background task. In the case of a spooler, this will take place at the 55-millisecond clock interrupt 0. In fact, all background processing requires the timer interrupt, but it may also involve other interrupts.

The following is a list of the AT's default group of 15, which starts at 08 and runs through 015 HEX.

READ.ME

The Interrupt *(continued)*

Here is the first group of eight hardware interrupts:

INT No.	Instruction	Address	Usual Value
INT 08	System timer	FFFE:F468	
INT 09	Keyboard event	FFFE:6E8D	
INT 0A:	IRQ 2	F000:1916	System ROM
INT 0B	IRQ 3	F000:18C0	System ROM
INT 0C	IRQ 4	F000:18C0	System ROM
INT 0D	IRQ 5	F000:18C0	System ROM
INT 0E	Diskette event	F000:EF57	System ROM
INT 0F	IRQ 7	0070:0481	IBMBIO

Here is the second group of seven interrupts for 286, 386 and 486 machines:

INT No.	Instruction	Address	Usual Value
INT 70	Real-time clock	F000:D2A6	System ROM
INT 71	IRQ2 Redirect	F000:1906	System ROM
INT 72	IRQ 10	F000:18C0	System ROM
INT 73	IRQ 11	F000:21A8	System ROM
INT 74	IBM mouse event	F000:18C0	System ROM
INT 75	Coprocessor error	F000:1922	System ROM
INT 76	Hard disk event	F000:327F	System ROM
INT 77	IRQ 15	F000:18C0	System ROM

The first eight interrupts are reserved for system use:

INT No.	Instruction	Address	Usual Value
INT 00	Divide by 0	B43E:11A8	
INT 01	Single step	0070:0481	IBMBIO
INT 02	NMI	F000:DD50	System ROM
INT 03	Breakpoint	F000:18C0	System ROM
INT 04	Overflow	0070:0481	IBMBIO
INT 05	Print screen	FFFE:AECE	
INT 06	Invalid opcode	F000:18C0	System ROM
INT 07	Reserved	F000:18C0	System ROM

READ.ME

The Interrupt (*continued*)

The following are the remainder of the 256 interrupts:

INT No.	Instruction	Address	Usual Value
INT 10	Video	FFFE:AE28	
INT 11	Equipment	F000:F84D	System ROM
INT 12	Memory size	F000:F841	System ROM
INT 13	Disk request	B774:0048	
INT 14	Communications	FFFE:00ED	
INT 15	System services	FFFE:1C3B	
INT 16	Keyboard request	FFFE:7327	
INT 17	Printer request	F000:EFD2	System ROM
INT 18	IBM basic	0070:0018	IBMBIO
INT 19	Bootstrap	B7C0:0033	
INT 1A	System timer	F000:FE6E	System ROM
INT 1B	Keyboard ^break	B43E:27C9	
INT 1C	User timer tick	FFFE:F699	
INT 1D	Video parameters	F000:F0A4	System ROM
INT 1E	Diskette parameters	0000:0570	System Data
INT 1F	Graphics characters	C000:3560	Video ROM
INT 20	Program terminate	B43E:11C7	
INT 21	DOS request	B43E:1358	
INT 22	Terminate address	211B:012F	COMMAND
INT 23	DOS ^break	211B:013C	COMMAND
INT 24	Critical error	FFFE:EC24	
INT 25	Absolute disk read	B43E:1415	
INT 26	Absolute disk write	B43E:1450	
INT 27	Terminate/resident	B43E:11BA	
INT 28	DOS idle	FFFE:2028	
INT 29	DOS TTY	B43E:20C5	
INT 2A	MS net	FFFE:1FBF	
INT 2B	DOS internal	033B:1445	IBMDOS
INT 2C	DOS internal	033B:1445	IBMDOS
INT 2D	DOS internal	033B:1445	IBMDOS
INT 2E	Batch EXEC	0B85:0281	COMMAND
INT 2F	Multiplex	FFFE:1FD2	

READ.ME

The Interrupt *(continued)*

INT No.	Instruction	Address	Usual Value
INT 30	CPM jump (part 1)	B43E:0859	
INT 31	CPM jump (part 2)		
INT 32	Reserved	033B:1445	IBMDOS
INT 33	MS mouse	033B:1445	IBMDOS
INT 34	Reserved	033B:1445	IBMDOS
INT 35	Reserved	033B:1445	IBMDOS
INT 36	Reserved	033B:1445	IBMDOS
INT 37	Reserved	033B:1445	IBMDOS
INT 38	Reserved	033B:1445	IBMDOS
INT 39	Reserved	033B:1445	IBMDOS
INT 3A	Reserved	033B:1445	IBMDOS
INT 3B	Reserved	033B:1445	IBMDOS
INT 3C	Reserved	033B:1445	IBMDOS
INT 3D	Reserved	033B:1445	IBMDOS
INT 3E	Reserved	033B:1445	IBMDOS
INT 3F	Reserved	033B:1445	IBMDOS
INT 40	Diskette request	F000:EC59	System ROM
INT 41	Fixed Disk 1 params	F000:04CF	System ROM
INT 42	Reserved	F000:F065	System ROM
INT 43	EGA graphics chars	C000:3160	Video ROM
INT 44	Reserved	F000:18C0	System ROM
INT 45	Reserved	F000:18C0	System ROM
INT 46	Fixed disk 2 params	F000:E401	System ROM
INT 47	Reserved	F000:18C0	System ROM
INT 48	Reserved	F000:18C0	System ROM
INT 49	Reserved	F000:18C0	System ROM
INT 4A	User alarm	F000:18C0	System ROM
INT 4B	Reserved	F000:18C0	System ROM
INT 4C	Reserved	F000:18C0	System ROM
INT 4D	Reserved	F000:18C0	System ROM
INT 4E	Reserved	F000:18C0	System ROM
INT 4F	Reserved	F000:18C0	System ROM
INT 50	Reserved	FFFE:F53E	
INT 51	Reserved	FFFE:6EAE	

READ.ME

The Interrupt *(continued)*

INT No.	Instruction	Address	Usual Value
INT 52	Reserved	FFFE:F277	
INT 53	Reserved	FFFE:F27D	
INT 54	Reserved	FFFE:F2A9	
INT 55	Reserved	FFFE:F260	
INT 56	Reserved	FFFE:F26B	
INT 57	Reserved	FFFE:F271	
INT 58	Reserved	8000:18C0	[Available]
INT 59	Reserved	F000:18C0	System ROM
INT 5A	Reserved	F000:18C0	System ROM
INT 5B	Reserved	F000:18C0	System ROM
INT 5C	Reserved	FFFE:F68C	
INT 5D	Reserved	F000:18C0	System ROM
INT 5E	Reserved	F000:18C0	System ROM
INT 5F	Reserved	F000:18C0	System ROM
INT 60	Program use	0000:0000	None
INT 61	Program use	0000:0000	None
INT 62	Program use	0000:0000	None
INT 63	Program use	0000:0000	None
INT 64	Program use	0000:0000	None
INT 65	Program use	0000:0000	None
INT 66	Program use	0000:0000	None
INT 67	EMS Request	1516:096D	
INT 68	Reserved	F000:D2A6	System ROM
INT 69	Reserved	FFFE:F283	
INT 6A	Reserved	F000:18C0	System ROM
INT 6B	Reserved	F000:21A8	System ROM
INT 6C	Reserved	F000:18C0	System ROM
INT 6D	Reserved	F000:1922	System ROM
INT 6E	Reserved	FFFE:F25A	
INT 6F	Reserved	F000:18C0	System ROM
INT 70	Real-time clock	F000:D2A6	System ROM
INT 71	IRQ2 Redirect	F000:1906	System ROM
INT 72	IRQ 10	F000:18C0	System ROM

The Interrupt *(continued)*

INT No.	Instruction	Address	Usual Value
INT 73	IRQ 11	F000:21A8	System ROM
INT 74	IBM mouse event	F000:18C0	System ROM
INT 75	Coprocessor error	F000:1922	System ROM
INT 76	Hard disk event	F000:327F	System ROM
INT 77	IRQ 15	F000:18C0	System ROM
INT 78	Reserved	0000:0000	None
INT 79	Reserved	0000:0000	None
INT 7A	Reserved	0000:0000	None
INT 7B	Reserved	0000:0000	None
INT 7C	Reserved	0000:0000	None
INT 7D	Reserved	0000:0000	None
INT 7E	Reserved	0000:0000	None
INT 7F	Reserved	0000:0000	None
INT 80	Reserved for BASIC	0000:0000	None
INT 81	Reserved for BASIC	0000:0000	None
INT 82	Reserved for BASIC	0000:0000	None
INT 83	Reserved for BASIC	0000:0000	None
INT 84	Reserved for BASIC	0000:0000	None
INT 85	Reserved for BASIC	0000:0000	None
INT 86	Used by BASIC	0000:0000	None
INT 87	Used by BASIC	0000:0000	None
INT 88	Used by BASIC	0000:0000	None
INT 89	Used by BASIC	0000:0000	None
INT 8A	Used by BASIC	0000:0000	None
INT 8B	Used by BASIC	0000:0000	None
INT 8C	Used by BASIC	0000:0000	None
INT 8D	Used by BASIC	0000:0000	None
INT 8E	Used by BASIC	0000:0000	None
INT 8F	Used by BASIC	0000:0000	None
INT 90	Used by BASIC	0000:0000	None
INT 91	Used by BASIC	0000:0000	None
INT 92	Used by BASIC	0000:0000	None
INT 93	Used by BASIC	0000:0000	None
INT 94	Used by BASIC	0000:0000	None

READ.ME

The Interrupt *(continued)*

INT No.	Instruction	Address	Usual Value
INT 95	Used by BASIC	0000:0000	None
INT 96	Used by BASIC	0000:0000	None
INT 97	Used by BASIC	0000:0000	None
INT 98	Used by BASIC	0000:0000	None
INT 99	Used by BASIC	0000:0000	None
INT 9A	Used by BASIC	0000:0000	None
INT 9B	Used by BASIC	0000:0000	None
INT 9C	Used by BASIC	0000:0000	None
INT 9D	Used by BASIC	0000:0000	None
INT 9E	Used by BASIC	0000:0000	None
INT 9F	Used by BASIC	0000:0000	None
INT A0	Used by BASIC	0000:0000	None
INT A1	Used by BASIC	0000:0000	None
INT A2	Used by BASIC	0000:0000	None
INT A3	Used by BASIC	0000:0000	None
INT A4	Used by BASIC	0000:0000	None
INT A5	Used by BASIC	0000:0000	None
INT A6	Used by BASIC	0000:0000	None
INT A7	Used by BASIC	0000:0000	None
INT A8	Used by BASIC	0000:0000	None
INT A9	Used by BASIC	0000:0000	None
INT AA	Used by BASIC	0000:0000	None
INT AB	Used by BASIC	0000:0000	None
INT AC	Used by BASIC	0000:0000	None
INT AD	Used by BASIC	0000:0000	None
INT AE	Used by BASIC	0000:0000	None
INT AF	Used by BASIC	0000:0000	None
INT B0	Used by BASIC	0000:0000	None
INT B1	Used by BASIC	0000:0000	None
INT B2	Used by BASIC	0000:0000	None
INT B3	Used by BASIC	0000:0000	None
INT B4	Used by BASIC	0000:0000	None
INT B5	Used by BASIC	0000:0000	None

The Interrupt *(continued)*

INT No.	Instruction	Address	Usual Value
INT B6	Used by BASIC	0000:0000	None
INT B7	Used by BASIC	0000:0000	None
INT B8	Used by BASIC	0000:0000	None
INT B9	Used by BASIC	0000:0000	None
INT BA	Used by BASIC	0000:0000	None
INT BB	Used by BASIC	0000:0000	None
INT BC	Used by BASIC	0000:0000	None
INT BD	Used by BASIC	0000:0000	None
INT BE	Used by BASIC	0000:0000	None
INT BF	Used by BASIC	0000:0000	None
INT C0	Used by BASIC	0000:0000	
INT C1	Used by BASIC	0000:0000	
INT C2	Used by BASIC	0000:0000	
INT C3	Used by BASIC	0000:0000	
INT C4	Used by BASIC	0000:0000	
INT C5	Used by BASIC	0000:0000	
INT C6	Used by BASIC	0000:0000	
INT C7	Used by BASIC	0000:0000	
INT C8	Used by BASIC	0000:0000	
INT C9	Used by BASIC	0000:0000	
INT CA	Used by BASIC	0000:0000	
INT CB	Used by BASIC	0000:0000	
INT CC	Used by BASIC	0000:0000	
INT CD	Used by BASIC	0000:0000	
INT CE	Used by BASIC	0000:0000	
INT CF	Used by BASIC	0000:0000	
INT D0	Used by BASIC	0000:0000	
INT D1	Used by BASIC	0000:0000	
INT D2	Used by BASIC	0000:0000	
INT D3	Used by BASIC	0000:0000	
INT D4	Used by BASIC	0000:0000	
INT D5	Used by BASIC	0000:0000	
INT D6	Used by BASIC	0000:0000	
INT D7	Used by BASIC	0000:0000	

The Interrupt *(continued)*

INT No.	Instruction	Address	Usual Value
INT D8	Used by BASIC	0000:0000	
INT D9	Used by BASIC	0000:0000	
INT DA	Used by BASIC	0000:0000	
INT DB	Used by BASIC	0000:0000	
INT DC	Used by BASIC	0000:0000	
INT DD	Used by BASIC	0000:0000	
INT DE	Used by BASIC	0000:0000	
INT DF	Used by BASIC	0000:0000	
INT E0	Used by BASIC	0000:0000	
INT E1	Used by BASIC	0000:0000	
INT E2	Used by BASIC	0000:0000	
INT E3	Used by BASIC	0000:0000	
INT E4	Used by BASIC	0000:0000	
INT E5	Used by BASIC	0000:0000	
INT E6	Used by BASIC	0000:0000	
INT E7	Used by BASIC	0000:0000	
INT E8	Used by BASIC	0000:0000	
INT E9	Used by BASIC	0000:0000	
INT EA	Used by BASIC	0000:0000	
INT EB	Used by BASIC	0000:0000	
INT EC	Used by BASIC	0000:0000	
INT ED	Used by BASIC	0000:0000	
INT EE	Used by BASIC	0000:0000	
INT EF	Used by BASIC	0000:0000	
INT F0	Used by BASIC	0000:0000	
INT F1	Program use	0000:0000	
INT F2	Program use	0000:0000	
INT F3	Program use	0000:0000	
INT F4	Program use	0000:0000	
INT F5	Program use	0000:0000	
INT F6	Program use	0000:0000	
INT F7	Program use	0000:0000	
INT F8	Program use	0000:0000	

READ.ME

The Interrupt (*continued*)

INT No.	Instruction	Address	Usual Value
INT F9	Program use	0000:0000	
INT FA	Program use	0000:0000	
INT FB	Program use	0000:0000	
INT FC	Program use	0000:0000	
INT FD	Program use	0000:0000	
INT FE	Program use	0000:0000	
INT FF	Program use	35AC:0000	

CHAPTER EIGHT

PC Memory Management

The biggest complaint people have about DOS is its nasty old 640KB barrier. Back in the days of 8-bit computing, it was amazing how much people could cram into a mere 64KB work space. Code was tight and efficient. Now, everyone moans about the limitations of 640KB.

When introduced by IBM, the PC was expected to run with 64KB of RAM, as the older CP/M systems did. Microsoft and IBM assumed that ten times that amount would be more memory than anyone would ever need.

Today, of course, all members of the PC family can use multiple megabytes of memory for multitasking and data storage. Individual applications break the 640KB barrier by use of DOS-extender technology. In the last several years, IBM and Microsoft have attempted to lure the user base to OS/2 with promises of more desktop power and true multitasking. Microsoft has only recently begun to recognize that users won't give up their huge installed base of MS-DOS applications. The release and instant success of Microsoft's new Windows product proves this.

As long ago as 1983, pressures were exerted on the marketplace to give users more for their money with MS-DOS. PC-Memory Shift and Multi-Channel were among the first programming attempts to allow users to run multiple programs without having to quit one to start another. These early attempts were the basis of what we now call "task-switching" software. They divided the 640KB of usable DOS memory into partitions, each with its own functioning copy of COMMAND.COM. The user could switch back and forth between two applications by hitting a *hot key*. While one application was active, the other was "frozen" in the background.

A small company in Santa Monica produced a product called DESQ. Not only could DESQ load two applications at the same time, but both would continue to operate! IBM was so impressed by this concept that in 1984, they decided to produce their own multitasking product, called TopView. TopView was a menu-driven program that allowed users to pick and choose from a list of specially written applications and cycle between them, all still within the limit of 640KB. The authors of DESQ did not want to be left behind by this development. They translated their product from its original AI-based programming language to 8088 assembly language. The "view" suffix was annexed, and DESQview was born.

TASK SWITCHING VERSUS MULTITASKING

Task switching is partitioning available RAM to allow an either/or choice of applications. This is naturally an easier programming chore than multitasking. Just as some programs let you "escape" to DOS without terminating, task-switching software allows multiple DOS shells to be created from the command line. Such programs as Software Carousel allow the user to start up a series of different programs and cycle between them by pressing a hot key. As control is passed from one program to the next, the background applications remain frozen. Only the application currently displayed on the screen is active.

The more challenging idea is to allow the background programs to continue to run; this is what is usually referred to as *multitasking*. For example, a user can tell Lotus 1-2-3 to calculate spreadsheet values off screen while typing in an independent word processor on the screen.

MS-DOS was actually never designed to "multitask" in this fashion. DOS can't really run two sets of instructions through the CPU chip at the same time. A useful work-around solution was discovered, though, in the concept of CPU time sharing. The CPU uses a certain number of clock ticks every minute for executing assembly language instructions. If those clock ticks are parceled out between two or more processes, DOS appears to multitask by switching very rapidly between competing programs. This CPU time sharing is what allows DESQview and Microsoft Windows to appear to run multiple applications concurrently. (We discuss this in more detail in the chapters about multitasking and task switching.)

BREAKING THE 640KB BARRIER

As PC programming became more complex, user perceptions of PC memory requirements began to change. Memory-hungry spreadsheet and data base applications demonstrated that the huge base of 640KB was not going to be enough for "power users."

Lotus and Intel, two companies whose fortunes were made by the PC's initial success, teamed up with Microsoft in 1985. Together, they devised a way to "cheat" on DOS's memory limitations. The LIM 3.2 Expanded Memory Standard (EMS) was the result. What the three partners came up with was the concept of a 64KB "expanded memory window" inside of DOS's permitted 640KB.

Imagine a virtual warehouse of data stored off to the side of your motherboard's 640KB in a separate silo of chips. These chips are mounted on an add-in card. Now, imagine the 64KB window in DOS is a dumbwaiter that can be sent on trips to fetch information to and from the silo. The dumbwaiter can dump the information into a specified 64KB range within DOS. That was how LIM 3.2 expanded memory worked. Applications like 1-2-3 and dBASE III could ferry a virtual mountain of data out of DOS's range to the RAM mounted on the add-in card, carrying it 64KB at a time.

Why 64KB? Memory on PC systems is counted in multiples of 64 because of the basic structure of the 8088 processor chip: 8 bits make 1 byte; 2 bytes make one 16-bit 8088 word. One word stores 2 to the 16th power—65,536—possible bit combinations. 1 kilobyte equals 2 to the 10th—1024—bytes; 65,536 bytes equals 64 kilobytes (65,536 divided by 1024 equals 64).

EXTENDED VERSUS EXPANDED MEMORY

IBM's adoption of the Intel 80286 chip in 1985 gave the new IBM AT family of computers a significant increase in hardware processing power. The 80286 chip was capable of addressing 16MB of memory, while the 8088 could address only 1MB. At first, this wasn't much good to users of MS-DOS/8088 software. DOS could address only 640KB of conventional memory plus 384KB reserved for ROM BIOS and peripherals. The additional memory above 1MB, called *extended memory*, couldn't be used by DOS to run programs. At that time, there were no dumbwaiters to run back and forth between extended memory and DOS, as provided by expanded memory. The best use anyone could come up with for extended memory was as electronic disk space and print spoolers.

Expanded memory (LIM 3.2) was more useful than extended memory. It permitted spreadsheet, data base, and graphics programs to store large data arrays interactively in a RAM area, off to the side, that neither DOS nor the 80286 chip specifically addressed.

To understand the next developments in PC memory management, it's helpful to look at the structure of memory as seen by MS-DOS. This will clarify how DOS uses conventional, expanded, and high RAM with third-party memory-management software.

Structure of the First Megabyte

DOS is written to address a total of 1MB of memory, divided into sixteen 64KB segments. The first ten of these segments (numbered 0 to 9 in hexadecimal notation) comprise *conventional memory*. 10 times 64KB equals 640KB.

The next six segments (designated A to F in hexadecimal notation) make up what is commonly called *high memory*. High memory is used by the ROM BIOS and various hardware peripherals to talk to DOS. It is divided into the following address ranges:

0000-9000   DOS loads COMMAND.COM into this area at boot time. The remainder is used to execute device drivers and application programs.

A000-Afff (640KB-704KB)   EGA and VGA graphics cards use this address range to page graphic data in and out of the RAM on your video card. (If you have a CGA or a Hercules card, this area is unused.) It may be assigned as an expanded-memory page frame or annexed to conventional memory to allow a total of 704KB.

B000-Bfff (704KB-768KB) This block is used for video memory. B000-B7ff is reserved for monochrome text or Hercules graphics. B800-Bfff is reserved for CGA, EGA, and VGA text.

C000-Cfff (768KB-832KB) This block is typically used by EGA and VGA video cards (C000-C7ff) and disk controller cards (C800-Cfff). If no card is using the memory, it can be assigned as an EMS page frame or used as "loadhi" space for RAM-resident TSRs.

D000-Dfff (832KB-896KB) This block is generally empty unless used for special hardware adaptors (such as network cards and cartridges on the PCjr). The D block is commonly used as an EMS page frame on IBM PS/2 systems and can be used as "loadhi" space.

E000-Efff (896KB-960KB) This block is used as a shadow-RAM area for the ROM BIOS on some systems (particularly PS/2s). It's a good area for the EMS page frame on other systems.

F000-Ffff (960KB-1024KB) This block contains the ROM BIOS. On ISA (AT Bus) systems, the area from F000 to F7ff is often empty and can be used as "loadhi" space. On some systems, it can contain part of the EMS page frame.

Your 286 or 386 machine may have additional memory on the motherboard above the first megabyte (you can see the computer count it at bootup). By default, this is *extended memory*. Extended memory is not recognized by MS-DOS, but it is assigned a hardware address by the 80286 or 80386 processor. Extended memory's address range begins in the 17th segment, at 10000:0000. (This is the first segment of the second megabyte.)

If you have an expanded-memory card mounted on your computer's bus, you will not see its memory counted until a special device driver is run in the CONFIG.SYS file. Expanded memory is not assigned a specific address either by DOS or by the CPU. Like the RAM on your video card, expanded memory exists in a kind of limbo. DOS makes use of expanded memory only when an EMS device driver assigns it a specific address range between 0KB and 1MB. The EMS memory manager establishes a 64KB area within the first megabyte to unload its rotating EMS dumbwaiter. This 64KB block is called the EMS page frame. The page frame receives and ships data back to the unassigned RAM on the EMS card (the silo off to the side).

READ.ME

Examining Contents of High Memory

If you are at all curious, it is easy to examine the contents of high memory to see what is actually being stored there. CORELOOK is a public domain utility that lets you type in an address and displays the contents of that address in hexadecimal on the screen. DOS's DEBUG utility does the same thing. If you would like to see the contents of your AT class system's E block of memory, type the following:

```
DEBUG
```

At the − prompt, type

```
-d E000:0000
```

You will see the contents of this memory area in both hexadecimal on the left and in ASCII on the right, as shown here:

```
C:\>debug
-d e000:0000
E000:0000  4D 09 E0 07 00 00 00 00-00 00 00 00 00 00 00 00   M...............
E000:0010  43 4F 4D 53 50 45 43 3D-43 3A 5C 43 4F 4D 4D 41   COMSPEC=C:\COMMA
E000:0020  4E 44 2E 43 4F 4D 00 50-41 54 48 3D 43 3A 5C 44   ND.COM.PATH=C:\D
E000:0030  4F 53 3B 43 3A 5C 55 54-49 4C 3B 43 3A 5C 42 41   OS;C:\UTIL;C:\BA
E000:0040  54 3B 43 3A 5C 55 54 49-4C 5C 46 4F 4E 54 3B 45   T;C:\UTIL\FONT;E
E000:0050  3A 5C 57 49 4E 48 3B 45-3A 5C 50 4D 00 00 01 00   :\WINH;E:\PM....
E000:0060  43 3A 5C 44 4F 53 5C 4D-4F 55 53 45 2E 43 4F 4D   C:\DOS\MOUSE.COM
E000:0070  00 00 00 00 00 00 00 00-00 00 00 00 00 00 00 00   ................
```

What you are actually looking at here is a copy of the DOS environment loaded into high memory by the QEMM memory manager.

```
                    READ.ME
```

Examining Contents of High Memory (*continued*)

Let's try location F800. The Phoenix BIOS I'm using on my 286 machine has its starting address at F800 which happens to be the copyright notice. To display it, I type the following:

```
C:\>debug
-d f800:0000
```

The display looks like this:

```
F800:0000  43 43 6F 6F 70 70 79 79-72 72 69 69 67 67 68 68   CCooppyyrriigghh
F800:0010  74 74 20 20 31 31 39 39-38 38 35 35 2C 2C 31 31   tt  11998855,,11
F800:0020  39 39 38 38 36 36 20 20-50 50 68 68 6F 6F 65 65   998866  PPhhooee
F800:0030  6E 6E 69 69 78 78 20 20-54 54 65 65 63 63 68 68   nniixx  TTeecchh
F800:0040  6E 6E 6F 6F 6C 6C 6F 6F-67 67 69 69 65 65 73 73   nnoollooggiieess
F800:0050  20 20 4C 4C 74 74 64 64-2E 2E E6 80 EB 01 90 2E     LLttdd........
F800:0060  8A 3E D3 FF 8A F0 B0 0C-C0 C6 02 B3 03 C0 C6 02   .>..............
F800:0070  8A D6 80 E2 03 FE C2 BE-2C 01 34 02 E6 61 8A CF   .........,.4..a..
```

The reason you will see duplicate characters is a legal one. Since there are two ROM chips that store the BIOS in a 286-based system. Each must contain the full copyright notice. One ROM contains all of the even numbered address bytes, the other has all the odd. It gets even sillier with 386 systems that have 4 ROMs.

EEMS and LIM 4.0

If you own an EMS 3.2 memory board, you may have noticed that it works fine for applications like 1-2-3, dBASE, and FRAMEWORK. But if you run DESQview and open a Memory Status window, you learn that there is no expanded memory available for running additional programs. This is because with EMS 3.2, your PC can still "see" only one 64KB chunk of memory at any one time. Although this is enough RAM to carry data, it is not enough to run most DOS programs.

In 1986, AST Research Corporation, QUADRAM Corporation, and Ashton-Tate improved upon the Lotus-Intel-Microsoft standard for expanded memory. These companies devised a hardware board that allowed

DOS to page more than one 64KB chunk at a time through their EMS window. They called their new product Enhanced Expanded Memory.

Under Enhanced Expanded Memory Specification, Standard DESQview became capable of running entire programs (larger than 64KB) from EEMS memory cards. Programs in EEMS could be run concurrently with programs in conventional DOS memory.

With EEMS, you can type text into a word processor while your spreadsheet recalculates values in the background. With EEMS, you can do file maintenance while your communications program dials into a bulletin board. You can copy files, draw a picture, or type a report while files are automatically uploaded or downloaded in the background.

The Lotus-Intel-Microsoft people recognized a good thing when they saw it. They collaborated with AST in 1987 to define the current LIM 4.0 standard. LIM 4.0 became a superset of EEMS. It added the hardware upgrade of EEMS to an improved software standard. LIM 4.0 addressed 32MB of expanded memory instead of only 8.

The LIM 4.0 standard supported all of the older LIM 3.2 memory functions. Like EEMS, it allowed multitasking by mapping large sections of expanded memory into the conventional address range.

Both EEMS and LIM 4.0 require special hardware in order to allow multitasking.

Hardware Limitations

As outlined in the preceding section, the EEMS/LIM 4.0 hardware uses what are referred to as "alternate mapping registers" to substitute or map RAM into the conventional area on your motherboard. *If your older LIM 3.2 EMS card has been upgraded only with LIM 4.0 software, this won't work.* With LIM 3.2 boards, DESQview still reports 0KB available to run programs in expanded memory. To allow multitasking, a memory board must be EEMS/LIM 4.0 "hardware compatible."

More on Memory Mapping

Memory mapping is the trick that allows EMS multitasking to work. A map of the data stored in "extra" RAM is transferred to the conventional address area on the motherboard.

Owners of 80386 machines don't need to worry about the mechanics of this process. A 386 automatically allows all motherboard RAM to be used as LIM 4.0 memory with the addition of a software memory manager.

READ.ME

Testing for LIM 4.0 Hardware Compatibility

How can you tell whether your motherboard or memory card is LIM 4.0 Hardware Compatible?

Both Quarterdeck and Qualitas post utilities on their BBS systems to test your EMS hardware. These programs are available to anyone. Quarterdeck's Manifest utility will also tell you whether your expanded memory can be used to run programs.

EEMRAM is a shareware utility available on most public bulletin board systems that examines your system and provides similar information. The key items to look for are support for alternate map registers and mapping of more than the 64KB page frame. If your EMS hardware supports alternate map registers, it probably supports multitasking.

Most 8088 and 80286 motherboards do not support alternate map registers (the AST Premium 286 is a notable exception). To take advantage of EEMS/LIM 4.0 on these reluctant systems, you need to pull several banks of RAM chips out of the motherboard. Designated banks on the EEMS hardware card are substituted to bring conventional memory back up to 640KB. This is known as *backfilling* memory to the motherboard.

The DESQview manual includes a large section devoted to the concept of backfilling on 8088 and 80286 machines. The more conventional memory you borrow from the EMS card, the more expanded memory can be mapped to a window. Equal amounts of "pageable memory" must be available in EMS and below 640KB.

Older PCs and XTs will let you backfill up to 384KB (leaving 256KB on the motherboard). With these machines, DESQview can run one conventional window of 450KB to 550KB. DESQview can open as many extra 384KB windows as you like, if chips are mounted for them on the EMS board. Programs in these windows will run concurrently. (On CGA and Hercules systems, the secondary window size can sometimes be stretched to 442KB by annexing the A000 block to conventional memory. This is the same process that allows some systems to have 704KB on bootup.)

Many 80286 clones require that 512KB remain installed on the motherboard. These systems will allow the EMS board to backfill 128KB for DOS.

On these machines, DESQview can open one conventional window of 450KB to 550KB. Successive concurrent windows are limited in size to 128KB each. (On CGA and Hercules systems, this can sometimes be stretched to 192KB, by annexing the A000 block to conventional memory.)

Dealing with Limitations

Clearly, this is not an optimum state of affairs for users who want to run WordPerfect, Ventura Publisher, and Lotus 1-2-3 simultaneously. What can they do about this?

Task Switching   Some people don't need to have all of these applications up and running concurrently. It may be enough to load the word processor, save a file, and switch to the desktop publisher. For editing graphics, you can toggle back and forth between page-layout and graphic-design programs. This is called *task switching*.

With a task switcher, you can open as many applications as you want, even if your memory is limited. When your conventional memory is exhausted, the task switcher reclaims it by swapping the prior applications to temporary files. The files are stored in expanded memory or on your hard disk. When you want to go back to a program, the task switcher scrapes it off the hard disk, and you resume where you left off.

Tip: If you have no expanded memory but your 80286 motherboard is loaded with extended memory, DESQview can be used effectively as a task switcher. Just configure as much extended memory as you want to a RAM disk. Run the DESQview setup program, and specify the RAM disk as DESQview's swap drive. This will let DESQview swap between large applications almost instantaneously.

MMUs

If you aren't ready to upgrade to an 80386, you have another alternative for running large applications concurrently on a 286. A memory management unit (MMU) is a small piece of hardware that gives an 80286 the memory-paging capability of an 80386 with no additional EMS hardware card.

Two companies, ALL Computers, Inc., of Toronto, Canada, and SOTA, Inc., of California, currently make these cards. The MMU is placed on the motherboard in the socket that formerly housed the 80286 CPU chip. The CPU chip is placed in a socket mounted on the MMU card.

With an included device driver, the MMU automatically converts the conventional and extended memory in the system to LIM 4.0 EMS. All of this memory can be used by DESQview to run programs, and you can open multiple application windows of 640KB or more. You can program the device driver to allocate part of your memory as extended and part as expanded and even load TSR utilities into the upper memory block area, as on an 80386.

EMS Emulators

It's possible on a 286 to emulate many of the LIM 3.2 functions in software. A subset of LIM 4.0 functions can be emulated, as well. If you want to run stand-alone programs that require EMS memory on an 8088 or 286, you may be interested in testing a software EMS emulator. These software emulators do not support multitasking under DESQview. EMS emulators range from simple public domain programs to commercial products that integrate extended memory and spare hard disk space.

One simple EMS emulator was written by Charles Petzold as a *PC Magazine* utility. It is available on most public bulletin board systems. This program will allow applications like 1-2-3 and dBASE III to use extended memory as expanded memory. (It will crash almost immediately if you try to use it with DESQview.)

EMS emulators usually run at a much slower speed than real expanded memory, particularly when the emulation is being created from hard disk space. They're useful for situations where an "Ace bandage" is needed. Some programs flat out refuse to run unless they see some kind of EMS installed. Ventura Professional Extension requires expanded memory for its dictionary hyphenation modules. Some bit-map paint programs require EMS to let you pan around in a drawing larger than 640 by 480 pixels.

Above Disk and Turbo EMS are commercial software products that can solve these problems. These packages provide software drivers that can convert extended memory or hard disk space into a limited form of expanded memory. Turbo EMS can coexist with true LIM 4.0 memory boards and other EMS managers. However, the multitasking ability of "true" LIM 4.0 is canceled when Turbo EMS is providing the additional memory.

EXPANDED MEMORY ON A 386

The 80386 CPU permits a superset of the instructions available to 286 programmers. For MS-DOS users, the important improvements are that

(1) all motherboard memory can be paged by software and mapped to any address, and (2) 80386 memory can be split into several "virtual" 8086 machines that perform independently of one another.

The consequences of these differences are the following:

1. The LIM 4.0 memory standard can be emulated perfectly in software. You can get LIM 4.0 memory on a 386 without adding any third-party EMS boards or MMU cards.

2. Multitasking software can allow programs to presumptively take over hardware functions without conflict. Independent graphics processes may be displayed on the screen simultaneously. For DESQview and Microsoft Windows, this means that incompatible programs can be run together, each displayed in a separate, small window.

386 Memory Managers

386 memory managers have evolved to perform several distinct housekeeping chores. All RAM on the system is assigned for potential use as LIM 4.0 memory, extended memory, or shadow RAM caches to speed hardware performance.

Some of the address space between 640KB and 1MB is unclaimed by hardware peripherals and ROM BIOS. A good 386 memory manager allows DOS to run programs in this space. This is a logical combination of the concepts of shadow RAM and expanded memory. A portion of motherboard RAM configured as LIM 4.0 memory is remapped to specified address ranges in the upper-memory-block area of DOS.

The "Loadhi" Area

The DOS memory range from 640KB to 1MB achieved sudden fame in 1990. Although it was always there, many software companies first recognized the "loadhi" potential at that time. The upper DOS region is now known by several names.

Quarterdeck first coined the term "high RAM" to complement their "Loadhi" program for QEMM in 1987. Microsoft decided that the term "high memory area" should refer to something entirely different! So, Microsoft refers to the 640KB to 1MB block as upper memory blocks (UMBs). Qualitas Software, Inc., temporizes and refers to "high DOS memory." They call 0 to 640KB "low DOS memory" instead of conventional memory.

READ.ME

What Is Shadow RAM?

Video cards, disk controllers, and BIOS chips include hard-coded ROM, which is often slower than motherboard RAM. When DOS is told to read a video or BIOS address, it can be diverted from the ROM to a copy of the instructions stored in the faster motherboard memory. This memory is mapped to the address space between 640KB and 1MB formerly used by the slow ROM chips. The remapped RAM is referred to as *shadow RAM*.

The motherboard and BIOS assign the specific shadow addresses to the extra 384KB. This is wasteful, as you might guess, since only 64KB to 96KB of the upper DOS memory area is actually occupied by ROM devices.

If the shadow RAM option is turned off in the BIOS, the extra 384KB is usually reassigned a new address range above 1MB. The physical RAM on the motherboard is then recognized by the system as extended memory.

Since Microsoft is the biggest company, their UMB terminology will probably win out, eventually. We will refer to the 640KB to 1MB region in this way throughout this chapter so that our readers can get used to it.

A Common Mistake

Remember, the UMB area is *not* part of extended memory. Clone operating manuals are sometimes confused on this point.

As we've seen, the extra 384KB on a typical 386 system can be set up either as shadow RAM (within the UMB area) or as extended memory (1024KB to 1408K). To make the situation more confusing, some 386 systems are poorly designed, and the memory may get "stuck" in one category or the other. (If you're on the verge of buying a system, you may want to check the BIOS options to make sure your memory can be switched freely.)

DOS Extenders

During the last year, more than 150 DOS programs have been written to run code in extended memory using the 80286/386 protected-mode functions. This is a newer wrinkle than expanded memory. The current versions of Lotus 1-2-3, TOPS Network, and AutoCAD 386 are loaded from DOS but

READ.ME

How to Enable or Disable Shadow RAM on a 386

Most new 386 systems have a setup program built into the BIOS. When you start up your computer, right after the memory count you see a message such as "Press del to run setup." (If your setup program isn't built in, it should be supplied separately on a disk or located in a directory on your hard disk.) The setup program may be further divided into basic and advanced options. Find the option for shadow RAM in the setup. There are usually separate categories for ROM shadowing and video shadowing. To enable or disable shadowing, toggle the appropriate boxes from on to off or vice versa.

Some setup programs have a further option that says, "Relocate Shadow RAM to Address 10000:0000." In the Chips and Technologies chip set, this is one of a series of options that are toggled by columns of 0s and 1s. You may have to page through all of the options until you get to it.

If you have to go into the advanced setup to find this option, be careful. *You may want to record all of the settings with pencil and paper before you change anything!* Change only the option for relocating shadow RAM. Exit the setup program, and let the system reboot. On some systems, you may be asked to run the simple setup once more. It will now show you that the 384KB is recognized as extended memory.

---

make use of special, protected-mode extender software. The DOS extender allows each program to independently access more than 640KB. Extended memory is used without any LIM 4.0 emulation. DOS-extender technology was developed by Rational Systems, Inc., and Phar Lap, Inc., in 1988. Sixteen-bit DOS extenders for the 80286 allow individual programs to access 16 megabytes of extended memory. Thirty-two-bit DOS extenders for the 80386 allow the use of 4GB! This system was developed by people who were impatient with the long wait for a usable version of OS/2.

DOS extenders and LIM 4.0 memory are able to coexist under a memory standard known as *virtual control program interface* (VCPI). This standard was developed jointly by Phar Lap, Inc., and Quarterdeck Office Systems.

In the past year, Microsoft has popularized its own concept of extended memory management (XMS) to define how RAM above 1MB is allocated to Microsoft applications. Prior to the release of Windows version 3, memory managers like QEMM, from Quarterdeck, and 386-to-the-Max, from Qualitas, coordinated with Microsoft's XMS specification under VCPI.

Since the release of Windows 3, XMS management is in a state of flux. With Windows 3, Microsoft introduced a new memory standard, called *DOS protected-mode interface* (DPMI). DPMI gave Windows the power to run megabytes of concurrent Windows applications at the expense of compatibility with the previous VCPI standard. QEMM and 386-to-the-Max could not cooperate with Windows 3 in its "standard" and "386-enhanced" modes. Programs like 1-2-3 or TOPS, which use the Rational Systems DOS extender, are also incompatible with Microsoft's new standard.

As of this writing, both Quarterdeck and Qualitas are at work on new versions of their products to accommodate Microsoft Windows and DPMI. They will probably have been released by the time you read this.

Using Memory Management

The LIM/EMS 4.0 standard is still widely used by PC applications. QEMM and 386-to-the-Max are leading products because of the fine control they provide for 386 memory usage. Key features these managers offer include:

- Specific allocation of all motherboard RAM as XMS (extended), LIM 4.0 (expanded), or Reserved (excluded, shadow RAM, or "loadhi") memory

- User-designated page frame for LIM 4.0

- Swapping of slow and fast RAM to optimize performance

- EMS shadowing of ROM areas

- Graphic display of all memory addresses on the system, with maps of DOS usage for individual programs

- Automatic memory testing to load TSR programs and device drivers into "upper-DOS" RAM (640KB to 1MB)

The "Loadhi" Feature

The 5.0 versions of QEMM and 386-to-the-Max both automatically check for hardware peripherals that use the 640KB to 1MB area of DOS. Any unclaimed address space can be reserved as "loadhi" area. Your AUTOEXEC-.BAT and CONFIG.SYS are checked for device drivers and TSR utilities.

Optimize, from Quarterdeck, and Maximize, from Qualitas, will reboot your computer several times. Any programs or TSRs that will fit are loaded above 640KB.

With 386-to-the-Max, all usable memory between 640KB and 1MB is automatically reserved to load high. With QEMM, you enable this option by including the parameter "RAM."

Since 64KB of the upper-DOS area is usually reserved as an EMS page frame, most systems yield from 80KB to 120KB as loadhi memory. If you don't run programs that require the EMS page frame, you can disable it and add an extra 64KB to the loadhi area.

Tip: DESQview will use LIM 4.0 memory without requiring an EMS page frame. If you want to multitask a series of applications that don't individually require expanded memory, the EMS page frame can be disabled. This will provide an extra 64KB to loadhi, or increase the size of your program windows under DESQview.

Owners of 286 machines should be aware that Quarterdeck and Qualitas also market 286-specific loadhi utilities. These run in conjunction with the third-party EMS managers provided with 286-expanded memory boards. The 286 utilities are slightly less versatile, since the 80286 UMB area must be controlled in 16KB segments rather than 4KB.

Expanded Versus Extended Memory

Both QEMM and 386-to-the-Max allow the user to configure 386 motherboard memory to be used as extended or expanded. They are memory managers for both the LIM 4.0 and XMS standards.

ROM Shadowing

Both memory managers optionally replace the built-in BIOS shadowing system by mapping expanded memory as shadow RAM. To take advantage of this feature, you should first disable your system's internal shadow RAM. EMS ROM Shadowing is generally more economical than using the system's built in shadow RAM.

Excluding UMB Areas

Remember that there are video cards and disk controllers that also want to use address ranges A000-Ffff. (A000-Ffff is 640KB to 1MB in hexadecimal notation. It's a good idea to be familiar with both notations—hexadecimal is often used in place of decimal to describe memory usage above 640KB.)

The 386 memory manager will automatically exclude most addresses used by hardware peripherals. If you experience operating difficulty, you can also exclude these addresses manually by adding a parameter. For instance, many VGA cards use the range C000-C800. To enter this information in your CONFIG.SYS file, type

```
Device=QEMM.SYS X=C000-C800
```

or

```
Device=386MAX.SYS RAM=C000-C800
```

With 386-to-the-Max, the word RAM means the opposite of what it means to QEMM!

High Memory Area (HMA) Usage

This is the confusing term that Microsoft invented to cover usage of the first 64KB of extended memory (10000-11000 hex). Microsoft Windows, Xerox Ventura Publisher, 4DOS, DESQview, and other programs are written to take advantage of this area when extended-memory management is present. The HMA parameter controls how much extended memory (from 0KB to 64KB) will be allocated to these programs. Both QEMM and 386-to-the-Max default to 64KB.

If you're going to be running DESQview, there is a slight advantage to using Quarterdeck's QEMM as your memory manager. For 386-to-the-Max to give DESQview its extra 64KB, an additional device driver supplied with the DESQview program must also be loaded. This driver, QEXT.SYS, consumes additional system memory. If QEXT.SYS is used in conjunction with 386-to-the-Max, it disables the HMA feature for programs other than DESQview.

Summary of Comparisons

The Quarterdeck and Qualitas 386 products are fairly similar, although they vary in their usage of command line parameters. Both offer VCPI support for DOS extenders. Both allow the user to create EMS ROM shadowing, turn LIM 4.0 management on or off, and relocate BIOS addresses of recalcitrant hardware.

Note: Compaq and PS/2 systems sometimes tie up address ranges, which results in a smaller loadhi area. Sometimes the addresses used by hardware can be remapped to increase the loadhi area.

Quarterdeck's utilities provide more system information for resolving memory conflicts. QEMM has a watchdog feature that monitors all memory-read and -write activity on the system after installation. QEMM advises on which addresses should be included or excluded from its control.

Qualitas allows slightly more control of the loadhi process. Qualitas's Maximize shows a step-by-step display of how programs are placed in upper DOS memory. You can choose whether to load each program in your CONFIG.SYS and AUTOEXEC.BAT into conventional or upper DOS memory. Maximize also reads nested batch files called from the AUTOEXEC-.BAT.

Other 386 Memory Managers

VM/386 is a multitasking, 386 control program similar to DESQview. In general, it offers more independence for its "virtual 8086 windows" and less interprogram coordination.

DR-DOS, from Digital Research, is an entire alternate operating system to Microsoft's MS-DOS. Version 5 of DR-DOS includes expanded memory and loadhi support similar to that provided by Quarterdeck and Qualitas for MS-DOS.

When the operating system itself is loaded above 640KB, there is a distinct advantage: Even more conventional memory is made available for applications. Microsoft is expected to incorporate this feature in its MS-DOS version 5.

Microsoft Windows and EMS Management

Microsoft Windows release 3 includes its own set of memory-management utilities. These are partially incompatible with other 386 memory managers.

Windows has three modes of operation: real, standard, and enhanced. Windows in real mode can be used in conjunction with any LIM 4.0 memory managers and all version-2 releases of DESQview.

Windows in standard mode takes advantage of 286/386 extended memory to multitask applications specifically written for the Windows environment. DOS applications can be run one at a time and swapped in and out of memory. Windows in standard mode is incompatible with the 5.0 versions of QEMM and 386-to-the-Max. Quarterdeck's QEMM 5.1 will support Microsoft Windows in either standard or enhanced mode. It is expected that the 5.1 version of 386-to-the-Max will also offer support for Windows.

Microsoft includes its own limited LIM 4.0 manager with Windows 3. Their 386EMM.SYS will convert a user-designated amount of extended memory for LIM 4.0 use. Microsoft's driver does not include loadhi or ROM-shadowing functions, but it will permit DOS applications to use LIM 4.0 separately or running under Windows.

Windows in 386/enhanced mode automatically converts extended memory to LIM 4.0 for its own use or for DOS applications. This memory is available only while running under Windows. Windows will multitask DOS applications on a 386 and provide additional memory by converting unused hard disk space. All memory management for Windows in enhanced mode is done with Microsoft's newest HIMEM.SYS device driver.

PART THREE

Backup and Security

CHAPTER NINE

Software Backup

Today's PC is a remarkably reliable device (if it doesn't fail in the first 30 days or so). The electronic circuitry will probably run long after newer technology has made it obsolete. Electronic equipment seldom fails.

This is not true of mechanical devices—they break down all the time. (When was the last time your car was in the shop?) Some people are surprised to learn that hard disk drive units are almost entirely mechanical, not electronic. A hard disk drive is a stack of aluminum platters spinning at 3600 rpm (the cruising speed of an automobile engine). It has a pair of tweezers poised about a rat's hair from the surface, raking back and forth.

Although fairly reliable, hard disks are the number-one failure component on a PC. In fact, more hard disk failures occur than all other component failures combined.

The real danger is that they will operate remarkably well day in and day out for months or even years, lulling you into a warm, pleasant feeling of security—and then fail with little, if any, warning. Oh, there may be a few days where only a few files are damaged. (A tune-up program, such as

Norton Speed Disk, OPtune, or Vopt, may indicate you've lost a few clusters.) Then suddenly, the disk drive grinds to a stop. Often, it stops without notice. If you're lucky, you get a high-pitched screech like a cat with its tail caught in the screen door, and then silence. Or you boot up the machine to find a cheery message that drive C wasn't found—and your data is a historical footnote.

There lies the moment of truth. Once it is a dead drive, there are two possibilities: You made a backup, or you didn't. Generally, all the powers of heaven and earth can't return you to the point where you can remake the decision that would determine that result.

If you backed up your files before the drive died, the replacement of the drive is a minor inconvenience (often covered under warranty). If you didn't, your work is completely gone, and you must start over from scratch. If you operate a business with all your customer lists, accounts receivable, and inventory on your hard disk, you are all but out of business.

How often and how devoutly you should back up can't really be determined by a formula. That's a personal decision for you. You may use your system primarily to play games. Or you may have it act as an expensive calculator, clock, or other nonstorage device. If that's the case, backup won't matter. You can reload the games from the original program disks and begin again to record those high scores.

If you use applications that you have spent considerable time installing, but use only occasionally (for example, to write letters, to track investments, or to maintain a personal appointment calendar), the recovery process will be a little longer.

If you operate a business with a computer, backups are crucial. The question is how often should you back up. The answer is brutally simple: Never have more data on your hard disk without a backup record than you can afford to lose—*forever.* (This same rule applies to how frequently you save to disk a file that you are working on.)

In this section, we'll explain:

- General backup principles

- Components of successful recovery

- Conventional backup strategies

- DOS backup functions

- Archive utilities

- Dedicated floppy-backup software

While this chapter focuses on backup strategies and software to back up to floppy disks, Chapter 10 goes into further detail on hardware devices specifically designed to make the backup process easier.

COMPONENTS OF SUCCESSFUL RECOVERY

Backup strategies should be simple. The technology to perform backup has developed in fits and starts. "Typical" user backup requirements vary widely. As a result, there are software programs to back up to floppy disk, hardware/software combinations to back up to tape, specialized removable-media disk devices (such as Bernoulli drives), and write-once-read-many (WORM) drives.

All of these devices attempt to provide unique features. They must also adapt to the widest possible number of machine mutations. As a result, the instruction manuals describe how to operate each system specifically. They cannot provide all the information necessary for you to protect your system completely.

An overall backup strategy must be directed at recovery. Conjure up the image of your office gutted by fire. *Everything* is lost—not a usable paper clip remains. There's a bright side, an ace in the hole: You made a complete backup just the other day (part of your weekly routine), and your assistant ran it over to the bank and put it in the safety deposit box. Now you can buy a new machine and a few paper clips and relocate. You'll be back in business instantly!

Now, imagine what would have happened if you didn't have the foresight to have a safety deposit box, or gave up the "backup habit" months ago, or never, ever got around to making a backup. (That soup line down on Fourth Street serves at 4:00 P.M. Better get down there.)

Here's what's in the safety deposit box:

- Disaster-recovery disk
- Full-system backup
- Crucial data files
- Hardware-configuration record

Disaster-Recovery Disk

The first item we find in our box is a "disaster-recovery," or "oops," disk. When your machine was new, there were DOS and a few device drivers to load onto the disk. Then came device driver files, an AUTOEXEC.BAT file, a CONFIG.SYS. file, and program software. This is what should be on your disaster-recovery disk: the information to reconfigure your machine's basic organization.

This particular disk should be able to boot up a machine, load your tape- or floppy-backup software, and begin the process to restore from your backup.

On newer IBM-compatible systems, disk drives of 1.2MB or 1.44MB are common. It is easy to create an initial-state-recovery set on a sole floppy disk. (Even with 360KB drives, two disks will usually do the trick.) When you create this disk, formulate a bootable disk with the system files on it. This disk will allow you to start up on *any* MS-DOS machine.

To create a bootable floppy, load a blank disk into drive A and enter the following command:

```
FORMAT A: /S
```

This formats the disk and transfers the two hidden DOS files from your hard drive to the floppy.

If you want to make sure the floppy is bootable, try the following command:

```
SYS A:
```

If you get an error message like "Drive not ready," you need to reformat the disk. If you get the error message "No room for system," then you need to reformat the disk with the /S option.

If the SYS command is successful, you'll eventually need to reboot with this disk to be sure it works right. Don't do that just yet. First get the other files you'll need.

Now survey your hard drive for the following items:

- AUTOEXEC.BAT
- CONFIG.SYS
- Any other device drivers (These normally have the extension SYS or BIN.)
- COMMAND.COM

- Other DOS files (for your version of DOS)
- Your backup-program files

AUTOEXEC.BAT
The AUTOEXEC.BAT file is a batch file in your root directory that is automatically executed on power-up. (This is further described in Chapter 6.) Many programs alter the AUTOEXEC.BAT file during installation to add path data, external variables, and other information required for the programs to run. Additionally, you may have added commands to display the current directory, set colors, or vary your display in some other way.

CONFIG.SYS
The CONFIG.SYS is also automatically loaded on power-up. Normally, it will contain commands to load all the various device drivers to run your peripheral equipment. Many of these device drivers include option-switch statements for the expanded memory card to use certain addresses, RAM disks to use areas of expanded memory, or scanners to use assigned addresses.

It could have taken 30 minutes or an hour to install a device when you first added it (not to mention the hours spent with the user's manuals, trying to figure out what you should do). Over time, you may have made changes, some minor alterations, as you discovered conflicts. This is information you will likely remember. A reconstruction from scratch would require you, again, to endure the installation instructions for every piece of add-on equipment.

Device Drivers
The device drivers are loaded by CONFIG.SYS to operate various pieces of equipment. Good policy: Unless you're confident you won't need one, add all files that have extension SYS or BIN to your disaster-recovery disk.

COMMAND.COM
This is the DOS command processor. It allows the entry of commands from the keyboard.

Other DOS Files
Ideally, you want all the external files for your version of DOS. Realistically, there are a number of these that aren't essential, such as DEBUG.COM,

EDLIN.COM, and GWBASIC. However, you may need FDISK.COM, DE-BUG.COM, or EDLIN.COM to get your hard disk back on line; think twice before you delete these files. If in doubt, copy *all* the DOS files.

Back Up Your Software

The primary mistake people make in backup is putting the backup copy of the program needed to restore the system onto the backup floppy or tape. This becomes a classic "chicken and egg" riddle. If you have the software to make the tape or floppy backup on the backup, how do you restore it?

In some cases, companies that have faithfully backed up data to tape cartridge have gone for years without a disaster. Then, on "D-day," they couldn't find the disks with the tape backup software. No other tape-drive manufacturer's software would read the tapes; in some cases, the manufacturer was no longer in business. They have their system on tape, but they can't get it back out easily. (They *could* send it to a service bureau somewhere for weeks of expensive analysis.)

It is absolutely crucial that copies of all floppy backup programs, tape backup programs, or specialized backup-hardware-operating software are included on your disaster-recovery disk.

Finally, there is one more item to include. Today's AT-class machines save a portion of their setup in CMOS RAM. *CMOS* is an acronym for complimentary metal oxide semiconductor, which is a technique used to manufacture chips. The device has low power requirements, which makes it an excellent candidate for battery-powered applications.

CMOS RAM is actually a small section of battery-backed RAM that remains powered even with the machine off. The crucial item contained in it is the setup table for a hard disk, which includes data on bad clusters, number of platters and heads, and other information. If you replace the disk or the entire machine, this may not be vital, since a new setup will have to be performed anyway. But if your disk lost some data or was erased, a copy of your CMOS can enable you to get running again quickly.

To copy your CMOS RAM onto your disaster-survival disk, you can use the program CMOSMGR by G. Allen Morris III. Put a copy of the program on the disaster-recovery disk as well, to allow you to copy the file back into CMOS RAM when you recover.

Some machines have the SETUP function in ROM. Others must use a disk-based program to tell the system what type of hard drive is installed. If your machine uses the disk program, put it on your survival disk.

CONVENTIONAL BACKUP STRATEGIES

Once you've used your disaster-recovery disk to get the machine back up, you can use the backup software to start the recovery process.

This is where the full system backup comes into play. This backup might be on tape, floppy, WORM disk, or removable hard disk. The important thing is that it has a full backup of all subdirectories and files on the original system. (Normally, it's advisable to do a full system backup at least once a week, but this can vary with your particular situation.)

Once you have restored the system from the full backup, you have recovered to the point of the last full system backup. It would be nice if there was also a disk with the most current customer lists, inventory, accounts receivable and payable, and other pertinent business data. If you have this, a restoration of all current data is possible.

Data files may be incremental or differential update backups (actual data base or word processing files or archived/compressed data files). There are several types of backup processes, including the following:

- Full backup

- Incremental backup

- Differential backup

- Selective or partial backup

- Rotation and off-site storage

Full Backup

Full backup refers to putting a complete copy of everything on your hard disk drive onto the backup media—usually tape or floppy disk. Use your disaster-recovery disk and your full backup to restore your entire system to the date the full backup was made.

The full backup also has a function related to the overall backup strategy: It forms a baseline system from which you can back up changed files.

DOS keeps track of all files in a directory in a special area called the *directory area*. There is a directory area in the root directory and another in each subdirectory. The directory area contains a 32-byte entry for each

---

READ.ME

An Extra Precaution

The process of backing up requires the hard drive to locate and transfer every file on the disk. This is a workout for your hard drive. It doesn't shorten the life of the drive, but if there are problems, they will be brought to light in the process. As a result, disk failure is not uncommon. If you are in the process of the backup and the disk goes down, you may have ruined your backup copy and destroyed your chance for recovery.

Consider the practice of alternating two backup copies: If you perform a full system backup on a weekly basis, use one set of backup media one week and another the next. Should disaster strike in the backup process, you have the previous week's copy to fall back on.

---

file contained in that directory. File title, extension, date and time of creation, and size are all contained in an entry. You can list this information with the DOS DIR command.

Two elements are *not* indicated by DIR: the *start cluster* and the *attribute byte*. The start cluster is the physical location of the first element of the file. The file attributes are contained in an 8-bit byte. Each bit of a file's attribute byte represents an attribute of the file (read only, hidden, system, and so on). One bit marks a disk's volume label.

Bit 5 of the attribute byte serves as the archive bit. When you make a full backup, the archive bit of each file on the disk is reset to 0. Subsequently, each time you alter a file or create a new one, its archive bit is set to 1. (All backup software takes advantage of this DOS feature to determine what to backup.) In this way, a usable record of all files changed since the last backup can be maintained. This concept is key to the way incremental and differential backup processes work.

The archive bit is DOS's automatic way of keeping track of what has been backed up and what has not. You can alter the archive bit at the DOS prompt for any or all files with the DOS ATTRIB command.

Use the following command to set an archive bit to indicate that the file has been changed and should be backed up:

```
ATTRIB +A D:\FILENAME.EXT
```

Use the following command to reset one file archive bit to show that the file should not be backed up:

```
ATTRIB -A D:\FILENAME.EXT
```

Use the following command to set the archive bits for *all* files on a disk:

```
ATTRIB +A D:\*.* /S
```

The /S switch indicates that the operation should be performed on all files in all subdirectories beneath the current one. Changing the +A to −A will reset the archive bit for all files on the drive. This is actually a common use of this command for backup. Subsequent incremental or differential backups will be based on any changes to files after this command.

Incremental Backup

An incremental backup looks through each directory area and backs up all files for which the archive bit is set to 1 (changed or new files). A copy of each file is made, and its archive bit is reset to 0. In this way, incremental backups copy all files that haven't been backed up by the full-backup procedure or another incremental backup.

In operation, you would make first a full backup, and then, each day, an incremental backup. For example, you make a full backup on Sunday. On Monday, you make an incremental backup. This creates a backup disk of all files that changed from Sunday to Monday and resets the archive bits. On Tuesday, you make another incremental backup. It makes a copy of those files that changed from Monday to Tuesday and again resets all archive bits.

Since few files change each day, an incremental backup can be the quickest and easiest to perform. The problem comes when you want to restore: You must restore first from your full backup and then from each incremental backup in the proper order. This requires a written record of the order of backup disks or tapes. Failure to keep an accurate record can cause problems in a restoration.

Differential Backup

Differential backup works like incremental backup in that all files with the archive bit set are copied. Differential backup differs, however, in that it does *not* reset the archive bit. Each differential backup contains a copy of all files that changed since the last full or incremental backup.

For example, you might make a full backup on Sunday. On Monday, like the incremental backup, the differential backup copies all files that changed between Sunday and Monday. Unlike the incremental backup, on Tuesday, a differential backup copies all files changed from Sunday to Tuesday. On Wednesday, it copies all files on the hard disk that differ from those on the full backup made Sunday.

Since the archive bit is not reset, the differential backup allows DOS to maintain a record of what was backed up in the full backup process. Each differential backup then represents the total difference in the data set from the full backup to the time of the differential backup.

In a restoration, you will need the original full backup and the *last* available differential backup to bring the system back on line.

Selective Backup

Selective backup, sometimes referred to as "partial" backup, doesn't use the archive bit. It is a manual backup process.

The DOS COPY command is a selective-backup process. Backup software will offer an option to back up files manually selected. In each of these, the archive bit is not modified.

Selective backup can be performed without interference with your regular backup schedule. You might use the selective backup when you have entered data into a data base file throughout the day and can't afford to lose any of the entries.

Rotation and Off-Site Storage

One final matter that bears discussion is off-site storage. Disasters happen. Fires, theft, hurricanes, tornadoes, floods, and earthquakes can be insured against. But the insurance company cannot replace your data or assign a monetary value to it.

Numerous companies now offer secure, fireproof storage facilities. You can rent space in one for a few dollars a month. Bank safety deposit boxes are also good protection.

If nothing else, keep a backup copy in your own home. Or send backed-up data to the home office of your company. Or to Aunt Hildegarde. A second backup may complicate the backup process, but it makes the data safe and accessible in the event of a catastrophe.

Even for individuals, to have a copy of your home system ditched in a second location (at work, at Mom's, and so on) is not a bad idea. While you may not depend on this data, it certainly has some importance to you.

DOS BACKUP FUNCTIONS

DOS also has commands for backup purposes. DOS supports the concept of backup through the archive bit 5 of the attribute byte of each file in the directory area.

BACKUP and RESTORE

First introduced in version 2.0 of DOS, these commands were designed to back up hard disk drives onto floppy disks. At the time, 10MB hard disks were common, and about 30 floppy disks were needed for the backup.

The BACKUP C:\ A:\ command copies each file that has its archive bit set from your hard disk drive, C to the floppy in drive A. Each file has header information appended to it to identify its directory location. As each disk is filled, you are prompted to insert a new one and press a key to continue the backup process. As each file is copied, its archive bit is reset to 0.

The RESTORE command performs the opposite function. Each file on the floppy is read, its header information is noted, and it is placed on the hard drive in the proper directory.

In DOS versions 3.3 and later, the files aren't simply copied to the floppy disk; they are compiled into a disk file. This increases the operating speed and decreases the number of disks required to make a backup.

The drawbacks to the available DOS backup functions are

- You cannot individually access files backed up with BACKUP without the RESTORE function

- There are no provisions for error correction. (If you have a bad bit on the backup set, it won't restore properly, and there will be no indication of an error until you try to restore it)

In full swing, this utility sounds remarkably like a World War II tank division in hot pursuit across the desert. The drives yowl, clank, and grind loudly and seemingly interminably as they rake back and forth to first copy a file, then update a directory, and then move on to the next file.

The result is that the DOS backup functions themselves are unreliable and the slowest, least efficient of the available options. However, by including these functions within DOS, Microsoft and IBM provided the foundation for programmers to develop some excellent backup software.

XCOPY

The XCOPY function was first introduced in DOS version 3.2; the first useful version appeared in DOS 3.3. Like the DOS command COPY, the XCOPY command copies files from one area to another—but en masse. The command will copy individual files or entire directories and subdirectories. It makes excellent use of the archive bit and has a verification function for rudimentary error checking.

It still requires numerous floppies, and it takes longer than a snail slithering across a driveway. However, one of the cheapest and most effective lazy person's backup strategies makes excellent use of XCOPY.

Hard drives fail often. Two hard drives fail less often. And two hard drives on two different machines fail less often still. In many of today's installations, more than one machine may be available. There may even be two or three PCs linked in a local area network (LAN).

Suppose you have a vital data set on drive C. Drive F is across a small LAN on your boss's machine across the room. She doesn't use it much and will never notice the loss in drive space anyway. Use the following command to back up your C drive to her F drive:

```
XCOPY C:*.* F:\ /S /M /V
```

The /S switch directs DOS to copy all files in all subdirectories of the root directory. The /M switch restricts this to only files that have the archive bit set, indicating that the file needs backing up. It also resets the archive bit on all files it copies.

This corresponds to an incremental backup. You could use the /A switch instead to make it a differential backup—in this instance, it doesn't really matter. Your full backup is on drive F and your incremental or differential backup is to the same drive and, in fact, the same subdirectories. So, changed files are simply copied over the previous versions. Drive F contains a full backup all the time.

The /V switch ensures that a verify operation will be performed to make certain each file made it to drive F intact.

When you use this ploy the first time, you may want to omit the /M switch so that all the files will be copied. Subsequently, the /M switch will ensure that only the changed files (with archive bit set) are copied. If you put this command in some sort of batch file that runs automatically at night, you in effect set up a "mirrored" disk on another machine. It updates once daily with the DOS XCOPY command across a LAN or even to another drive on the same system.

This scheme won't help you much in case of a real disaster. But for a simple disk drive malfunction or some accidentally damaged files, it's quick and effective.

On a small office LAN, this ploy can have another application. For example, the drive you want to back up is on a busy machine crucial to your operation. The XCOPY function from one hard drive to another is relatively quick and painless. You can XCOPY your drive to a secondary drive on an old, tired XT machine across the room and continue working on that crucial but behind-schedule proposal on the fancy 33 MHz 80386 machine. Someone else can then make a proper backup from the old XT to disk or tape without tying up the main machine.

ARCHIVE UTILITIES

Floppy capacities have increased modestly compared with the size of today's application programs. The original IBM PC stored 160KB per floppy disk. That rose to 360KB and eventually to 1.2MB on the 5.25-inch format. The 3.5-inch disks now hold 1.44MB.

But what if your data base grows beyond 1.44MB? It would still be nice to put 2MB on a disk and take it with you. Commonly available utility programs called *archive/compression utilities* or "split-and-gather" utilities make this possible.

Archive/compression utilities were developed in the on-line communications world to solve a real problem. IBM programs are made up of series of executable, configuration, and data files. Many programs actually require

20 or more files to operate. To transfer a program by modem, each file had to be transferred from one machine to another by telephone.

Early in the development of the on-line telecommunications culture, someone developed the concept of *library files*. These files combined the component files of a program into an individual file entity that could be transferred. At the destination machine, the original files could be *extracted* from the library.

Much of the on-line/BBS world involved long-distance transfers. Budget-minded hobbyists were paying the freight for long-distance telephone calls to move these files. Anything that could increase the speed of the transfer was embraced.

As a result, modem speeds have inexorably increased. Further, a number of talented individuals have enhanced the library function to include extremely facile compression algorithms. These algorithms compress data with a statistical reduction of repetitive bit patterns to expressions that require less space. These shorthand expressions are then translated to re-create the original bit patterns.

Here's a simple analogy of this: A text file contains a line with 32 consecutive spaces. The 32 spaces require 32 bytes. If you used a specific symbol to bracket spaces, say, the # symbol, you could reduce this to #32#, requiring four bytes. Later, you could reconstruct the original data file using the same rule in reverse.

The actual techniques used by compression utilities are considerably more advanced than our example. The result: A 50-file subdirectory totaling 700KB can be stored as one file on one disk. Your 2MB data base can easily be stored on a 1.2MB disk. In fact, the archive/compression utilities average about a 2:1 compression on all files.

But all files are not created equal. EXE and COM program files are difficult to compress, because their bit patterns are inherently random. Data files such as those found in data bases and word processing text files, on the other hand, are compressible to as little as 20 percent of their original size. Often, a 5MB data base can be carried away on a 1.2MB floppy disk.

There are at least 20 such utilities in existence. Three have come into common use:

- ARC

- LHARC

- PKZIP

ARC was the earliest of the three. PKZIP offered many improvements in speed and compression over ARC. LHARC, a free utility from Japan, was introduced in March 1989. Although slower, LHARC offered better compression. This spurred new releases by the other two. Right now, compression, not speed, seems to be the main consideration.

It is of interest to note that the command line interfaces for the programs are almost identical. The compression schemes are different; therefore, they are not interchangeable.

ARC

ARC was developed by Thom Henderson of System Enhancement Associates in Wayne, New Jersey. The program became enormously popular in the on-line world and for a while reigned as the favorite. The program can archive an almost unlimited number of files into one file while compressing it dramatically. The latest version is 7.0, and the title is now ARC+PLUS.

ARC Version 7.0 provides good overall compression, although it does so at the sacrifice of speed. The program features an easy to use point-and-shoot interface through an included utility, EZ-ARC.

ARC offers compression to multiple disks. The -V command line switch allows you to archive a file or files across multiple disks or, alternatively, to create a series of archives on your hard disk, each limited to a certain specified file size. In this way, you can take a 10MB data base file, for example, and easily archive it to two floppy disks. Files compressed with ARC or ARC+PLUS are denoted by the ARC extension.

To create an archive of all files with the DBF extension within a certain subdirectory, use the following command:

```
ARC A MYFILE C:\SUBDIR\*.DBF
```

This results in a single file, titled MYFILE.ARC, containing all DBF files from the C:\SUBDIR subdirectory. To extract the original files, use the following command:

```
ARC E MYFILE C:\SUBDIR
```

This reconstructs all the original files from the MYFILE.ARC file and stores them in the C:\SUBDIR subdirectory.

ARC+PLUS is not shareware—it is a commercial software product, available at a list price of $89.95.

System Enhancement Associates
925 Clifton Avenue
Clifton, NJ 07013
201-473-5153
800-899-4732

LHARC

LHARC was developed by a team of Japanese hobbyists led by Haruyasu Yoshizaki. The program offers competitive compression but lacks some of the advanced features available in ARC and PKZIP. The program, while it carries a copyright notice, is distributed free of charge, without registration or solicitations for contribution. In fact, source code for the technology in LHARC was released into the public domain.

LHARC is commonly available on local BBS and commercial on-line services in the file LHARC113.EXE. Files compressed with LHARC are tagged by the LZH extension.

To create an archive to contain all files with the TXT extenxion within a certain subdirectory, use the following command:

```
LHARC A MYFILE C:\SUBDIR\*.TXT
```

This results in a file, titled MYFILE.LZH, containing all TXT files from the C:\SUBDIR subdirectory. To extract the original files, use the following command:

```
LHARC E MYFILE C:\SUBDIR
```

This reconstructs all the original files from the MYFILE.LZH file and stores them in the C:\SUBDIR subdirectory.

PKZIP

PKZIP was developed by Phil Katz of PKWARE, Inc. of Glendale, Wisconsin. PKZIP started life as a clone of ARC titled PKARC. It was originally file and command compatible with ARC—with significantly faster operation and better compression. After some legal disagreements between the companies, PKWARE issued their PKZIP product. The files are no longer compatible with ARC, but the programs use like commands.

PKZIP is the fastest of the available compression utilities. The current release of PKZIP offers tighter compression than LHARC. SCA's soon-to-be released ARC+ PLUS version 7.1 can compress files even smaller. PKZIP has consistently offered dramatic speed improvements and excellent compression with each release. It also provides a rich set of features: a facile use of the archive bit to compress changed files, some security functions to prevent tampering with zipped files, and the ability to add comments to the file. Files compressed by PKZIP all have the extension ZIP.

To create an archive that contains all files with the DOC extension, within a certain subdirectory, use the following command:

```
PKZIP MYFILE C:\SUBDIR\*.DOC
```

This results in a file, titled MYFILE.ZIP, containing all DOC files from the C:\SUBDIR subdirectory. To extract the original files, use the following command:

```
PKUNZIP MYFILE C:\SUBDIR
```

This reconstructs all the original files from the MYFILE.ZIP file and stores them in the C:\SUBDIR subdirectory.

PKZIP is distributed as shareware with a $25 registration fee. Disk and documentation are available directly from the company at $47.

PKWARE, Inc.
7545 North Port Washington Road
Glendale, WI 53217
414-352-3670

Dedicated Floppy Disk Backup Software

Despite the number of hardware backup options—tapes, optical drives, and removable-media hard disks—many people continue to back up to floppy disk. Floppies are cheap, portable, and universal. Once data is on a floppy, almost any IBM-compatible machine can be used to read the data. You can go to the library and access your data on their public-use machines. This low-cost and simple backup system leads many to rely on floppy disk backup (probably past the point where they become candidates for a dedicated backup hardware device).

Fortunately, a number of vendors have developed advanced utility software to ease the backup chore. These provide an elegant interface to allow you to select the type of backup you want to perform. They all have the following features: data compression to require fewer floppy disks; advanced error-correction functions to recover data from damaged disks; disk formatting; and advanced direct memory access (DMA) techniques to improve operational speed.

The DOS COPY, XCOPY, and BACKUP commands read a certain amount of data from one device and then write it to another. The cycle is repeated until all data have been transferred. The modern backup utilities read from one device and simultaneously write to the other. The result is a fast copy operation.

There are now nearly a dozen such backup utilities on the market, at prices ranging from $50 to $200. We'll briefly describe three of the popular contenders, which provide adequate and comparable features.

Fastback Plus

Fastback Plus was developed by Fifth Generation Systems. It is the oldest established backup program on the market—and the most expensive, at $189.

The program performs full, incremental, differential, and selective backups. The program uses DMA techniques to speed transfer and stores files in a proprietary format that can be listed but not accessed by DOS.

The program provides an excellent on-line help function, and almost all processes can be customized. The degree of data compression and error correction can be specified. The program will estimate the number of disks required to back up a particular hard drive. It will also format the disks. Fastback Plus also supports backup to streaming tape drives. (This is a better software interface than the software provided with the drives themselves, in most cases.)

Fifth Generation Systems, Inc.
10049 N. Reiger Road
Baton Rouge, LA 70809
504-291-7221
800-873-4384

Norton Backup

Peter Norton Computing made a name with a series of hard disk utilities. Norton Commander has furthered their reputation with an excellent DOS-shell interface. More recently, they've introduced a backup product called Norton Backup, priced at $149.

Norton Backup is the newest of the three programs discussed here. Version 1.0 had some recovery anomalies that could cause the program to certify a restored file error-free when it did in fact contain errors; this has been corrected in Version 1.1.

The current version of Norton Backup is limited to floppy disk backup. It will not address streaming tape drives, although the company has announced plans to do so in future versions. Further, it is not designed for use with 360KB floppy drives—a consideration if you use an older PC or XT machine. To protect users from a DOS compatibility anomaly, 48TPI disks (DSDD) cannot be used with 80 track drives that ordinarily use 1.2MB floppy disks (DSHD).

The strong end of Norton Backup revolves around speed and the user interface. The program is undoubtedly the fastest backup program available. In its proprietary mode, it is fast. You can also have it store files in a format directly readable by DOS. Even in the slower DOS mode, Norton Backup's speed exceeds the other two products. The program actually tests both drive and processor speed before making a backup and automatically selects the optimum compression level for your system. These options can be overridden manually.

The mouse-driven, windowed interface is advanced in the backup-software field. It has a remarkably Windows-like feel. (This was no accident: The company has worked on a version specifically to run under Windows 3.0.) The on-line help function is a hypertext user's manual.

Symantec
10201 Torre Avenue
Cupertino, CA 95014
408-253-9600
800-626-8847 (inside CA)
800-441-7234 (outside CA)

PC Backup

Central Point Software markets a set of DOS utilities, titled PC Tools Deluxe. PC Tools has sold over 750,000 copies as of this writing. The current deluxe version, 6.0, includes a desktop program, a DOS shell, a disk cache utility, communications functions, fax support, Traveling Software's LapLink utility (to link laptop computers to a desktop unit), file defragmentation, and a host of other functions—all for about $149 retail price, with a street price of $90 to $100 and upgrades of about $40.

Among the numerous utility programs included in PC Tools is a full-featured backup utility, titled PC Backup. The program comes with a 160-page manual and features a reasonably usable, windowed, mouse-driven interface. It will perform full, incremental, differential, and selective backup of files to all floppy disk formats as well as to several different tape backup devices.

The program provides features comparable to those of Norton Backup and Fastback Plus, with DMA transfer, compression, error correction, and an array of user-configurable options.

Central Point Software
15220 N.W. Greenbrier Parkway
Beaverton, OR 97006
503-690-8090
800-690-8088

CONCLUSION

As today's business and professional applications come to depend on personal computers, the value of the data they contain increases. An effective backup strategy is crucial to the successful use of PCs. For many applications, floppy disk backup offers an inexpensive and simple solution. Because DOS backup functions are rudimentary, the use of a dedicated backup software utility is recommended.

For active offices where crucial daily-transaction records carry the life-blood of the business, use of a dedicated hardware backup device to simplify the backup process should be considered.

CHAPTER TEN

Backup – The Hardware Solution

Backup software has advanced from the original DOS Backup and Restore functions. The new programs are generally reliable and inexpensive. Their job, to off-load data from a hard disk drive to floppy disks, is mainly suited to backing up small data bases. But, as a daily work tool, floppy disk backup may not meet the requirements of a professional environment. The reason for this has nothing to do with the software or the reliability of floppy media.

Almost everyone starts out to back up data to floppy disks. But, the task is both redundant and dull. (It can take an hour or more with some of the hard disk capacities available.) As a result, while the floppy routine is theoretically effective, in practice you won't use it. You'll make one backup, perhaps a second, and that will be it.

The solution is a dedicated hardware backup device. This might be difficult to sell to the boss. Dedicated hardware backup devices can cost several hundred dollars or more. It doesn't make the machine run any faster, allow you to run more software, or add a byte to your current on-line storage capacity (in most cases). It is used to make copies of data that you hope never to use.

But the dedicated backup hardware device is the only option for serious personal computer applications where a daily backup is necessary. It reduces the process to three steps:

1. Start the program

2. Put in a tape

3. Wait

In most cases, this hardware backup can be maximized to run unattended on an automated nightly schedule. Then, you can start the workday by taking the storage media out and storing the previous night's archive. If a system failure occurs, you can recover by restoring the data from tape.

READ.ME

Hardware Selection Criteria

There are seven basic criteria to use in selecting hardware for your backups:

- Standards and interoperability
- Data security
- Speed
- Capacity
- Ease of use
- Physical installation
- Price

STANDARDS AND INTEROPERABILITY

Hardware approaches to backup are constantly evolving. The newer technologies (such as high-capacity floppies, optical disks, and other removable media) are less reliable and generally priced at a premium. The older, streaming-tape technologies are more economical and have an established record of sound operation.

The floppy backup system has a standard, universally recognized device configuration. It should be no problem to hook a backup system to your computer. The problem is in the individual device-to-device compatibility of the data. There are many different systems.

Numerous devices come and go quickly. They disappear from the market, replaced by newer, more capable devices. Some are technically elegant but cost too much (there is a very limited market for $12,000 PC backup devices, no matter how well they perform).

Vendor stability is an important factor in choosing a backup device. (After a fire is *not* the time to learn that the manufacturer of your backup device is out of business and the device is not compatible with anything on this planet.) If your hard disk drive proves to be a lemon and the maker goes under, you can plug a new one into your system. Keyboards, motherboards and monitors are, likewise, interchangeable. But your data backup *must* have a compatible hardware device before you can retrieve the data.

The more widely used and popular your selected system is, the more successful you'll be in the event of some catastrophic event. You should be in a position to carry a pocket-size tape or optical disk into a computer store, hand it to the dealer and say, "Build me a computer around this tape and try to deliver it by tomorrow morning." Ideally, you want the dealer to be able to use an off-the-shelf device to read that data and then build up a system around it with minimum time lost in a search and the wait for a long-distance delivery.

The variety of available devices gives rise to a chaos of data "standards." Since there are so many standards, there are effectively none. As a result, carefully consider the selection of a device based on its popularity. If you are one field office of an organization with 200 other such offices, it might pay to become familiar with what the other offices use. If they all use QIC-40 quarter-inch tape devices, your Bernoulli hard drive cartridge system would prove to be a black sheep in your organization.

Data Security

For many applications, data security is an issue. If your data set contains data that is classified as confidential or secret by the Department of Defense, you may be required to "lock it up" at night. If it is on a permanently installed disk drive, you must have provisions to secure the entire computer in an approved safe. Removable-media hard drives and Bernoulli cartridges can be completely removed from the computer and locked away in a safe. (Some TEMPEST class installations absolutely require this.) With the data set locked up, the computer is just another piece of office equipment. Reinstall the data set the next morning, and you're back in business.

More commonly, it is an attractive feature to be able to lock up private information to avoid worries about who might try to get a peek at it.

The bottom line on standards and interoperability is that you want the system with the widest-possible installed base of users that will perform the functions you desire.

Speed

Speed is relative. You can't get something that operates *too* fast. And, no matter how fast the selected device is, that speed will become the minimum acceptable speed for you. In other words, once you are accustomed to a certain level of performance, anything less becomes unbearable.

Speed in backup devices is not crucial. The ideal backup situation is having the device operating unattended. Typically, this is done when you're not even in the same room. The advantage of the hardware solution is that it relieves you of the active role in the backup process. It's best when the backup doesn't tie up your hardware for hours when you could be using it for something else.

But there are exceptions. If the nature of your business is such that you need hourly backups or can't afford to lose *any* data, you probably need a mirrored disk or hard-disk-to-hard-disk backup. By copying one hard disk to another of similar size, you can safeguard your data against the most common disaster, a hard disk crash. While this offers no safeguards against destructive software programs, fire, and sabotage, it does provide very fast backup.

Removable-media hard disks, Bernoulli drives, and optical disks copy data at very high speeds to a backup. They have the added ability to produce a portable backup archive that can be stored safely.

Tape units are, by contrast, slow. The differences between tape drive data-transfer rates are, for the most part, inconsequential. The difference from one tape unit to another is a few minutes and probably not a consideration in the choice of one over another.

Capacity

Disk drive magnitude is increasing each year. The original IBM XT computer had a 10MB hard drive, and that was a big deal! Within a year, 20MB drives became common. The current popular size is the 40MB drive, although its popularity is waning. The 80BM and 100MB sizes are now offered as standard by several manufacturers.

How big is your drive? Its size is most likely a reflection of the current market price and what you can afford. As prices continue to fall, more people opt for increased disk drive capacity. (It's like closet space: you can never have enough.)

Your choice of backup hardware should reflect a farsighted vision of this trend toward ever-larger disk sizes. If you select a 20MB tape backup and within 18 months find 100MB (or even 330MB) hard drives available, you'll be right back in the "media-swap game." This time, instead of a floppy swap, it will be tapes.

Fortunately, backup hardware capacities are also growing. With the compression technologies and slightly enhanced tape cartridges, some manufacturers are now squeezing 120MB onto a single quarter-inch QIC-40 tape cartridge.

For most tape-backup installations, a backup media capacity of 1.5 times the largest physical disk size allows for some future expansion. An 80MB hard drive coupled with a 120MB backup capacity is a good match. You may have the 80MB partitioned into three 27MB partitions and back each up separately. You can get by with a 40MB backup device, but it will prove less flexible if you decide to repartition later. Further, you will not be able to back up your entire system if you're not around to swap the media.

The economics of removable hard disk media make the 1.5-to-1 ratio impractical. A 44MB Bernoulli drive is now common and larger sizes are all but unavailable. You may need to swap media in this instance. But it will take less time to copy 44MB to the removable hard drive media than to back up the same amount of data to tape. Likewise, optical media provide large backup capacities—substantially more than the hard disk equipment they back up.

Ease of Use

The value of a backup system is often more a function of the software that drives the device than of device performance. Almost all backup hardware devices require the use of an associated software program. The person who does the backup will often perform a foreign task (although it will not involve the same continuous hands-on interaction as a spreadsheet, data base, or word processor program). The software should be simple to operate, reliable, and intuitive. Floppy backup products are more advanced in this area than tape and optical-disk backup software.

There are two basic methods offered by almost all backup hardware: disk imaging and file-by-file backup.

A disk-image backup can be likened to a camera taking a "data snapshot" of your hard disk drive. Each disk sector is transcribed precisely from the hard disk to the backup media. This is easy and straightforward. The system reads the disk sector by sector and track by track, and transfers the information to the backup device. With advanced Direct Memory Access (DMA) techniques, the machine can read the data from the disk and write to the backup media simultaneously. The result is a quick and faithful reproduction of the precise disk arrangement at the moment the "snapshot" is taken.

The down side is that hard disk drives do not store files as single entities. DOS, which manages the disk, sometimes stores single files in various areas on the disk surface. This is called *fragmentation.* This inefficiency gradually slows operation and is faithfully reproduced on the disk-image backup. Completely recreating a system from a disk-image backup presents one other problem: When you copy data from the backup media to the disk, it destroys any other data placed on the disk since the backup.

File-by-file backup, in contrast, copies files logically from the disk to the backup media one file at a time. This has become the backup mode of choice for most applications, as it offers much greater flexibility. A single file or group of files may be restored from the backup. This can include the files that have been modified since the last backup or all files, as need dictates. If a single file is lost or damaged, you can easily call it up from the backup device and bring it back onto your hard drive.

Further, on a newly formatted hard drive, the file-by-file method places the files on the hard disk media in logical, contiguous order. This provides dramatically improved disk efficiency over restoration from a disk image that contained fragmented files.

Another element of ease of use involves unattended backup. To realize the maximum potential of your hardware investment, backup systems should allow for unattended operation. The software that comes with many tape devices often includes a small terminate-and-stay-resident (TSR) utility for unattended operation.

To use a TSR utility, you set up and schedule the operation you would like performed. You should be able to set the device to perform a nightly backup of all files that have changed during the day. When the system clock indicates the scheduled time, the TSR activates the system to copy all modified files from the specified drives to the tape-backup unit.

While many of the removable-disk devices do not offer this feature, most tape-backup units do. If you consider purchasing a tape-backup unit, demand this feature. It is effective and useful.

Physical Installation

Over the years, we have come to what is recognized as a standard architecture, which we call "PC compatible." But installation of specific peripherals can still vary from machine to machine, and backup peripherals are notoriously machine dependent. The problem is that PC compatibles range widely in installed equipment, microprocessors, Basic Input Output System (BIOS), and more.

If you have more than one machine in an office or organization, there is an advantage in using the same type of backup device on each machine. In this way, you can exchange data between machines with the backup media. In the event of a system failure, you can also restore from backup to a second machine and get back in operation.

Unfortunately, not all devices can be installed in all machines. Some tape units, for example, will work on an 80286 AT-class machine but not on an 8088 XT-class machine. Backup devices designed for Macintosh computers do not necessarily work on PC models; on the other hand, some do. Some tape units will work off of existing floppy controller cards, but others require their own controller cards.

Manufacturers make a difference. Don't be swayed into believing that two tape units that feature the same size cartridge and even the same cartridge standard will deal with backups interchangeably. They may not be compatible. Check the operability of your proposed backup device with *all* machines in your group before you put down the cash.

A word on networks: Most LAN managers are all-too-familiar with LAN compatibility problems. But for novices to this area, we offer this advice: You cannot assume *any* peripheral device is compatible with your LAN setup without a specific statement to that effect from the peripheral vendor. Even then, the setup and installation will usually vary slightly when the device is installed to a LAN network.

Internal devices require an empty drive bay in your machine. They might require a slot on your motherboard, or they may operate from an existing disk-controller card. IBM-compatible computers have a limited number of interrupt request lines (IRQs) and Direct Memory Access (DMA) channels. If the proposed device does not use regular drive-controller cards, make sure the IRQ/DMA requirements for the device match the available IRQ/DMA resources of your machine.

External devices usually require a dedicated controller card. This is more expensive, but offers some flexibility. One unit is capable of servicing more than one machine. If each machine in your office is equipped with the right interface card, the external drive unit can be connected to any machine as needed.

Price

There is a wide range of hardware backup-device prices. Reliable, useful units to back up as much as 120MB are available for as low as $250. There is no upper limit on prices. Newer optical storage media cost $8000 or more.

Larger capacities, higher speeds, and newer technologies all cost more. The established technologies that offer slower backup speeds can be a good solution. In some ways, the demonstrated technologies can offer some attractive price-performance trade-offs. As a result, they offer an advantage of widespread availability and a wider information base. (This is an important criterion of backup-hardware selection. The lone experimenter treading new ground with a glitzy device can cost you time and money.)

HARDWARE TYPES

Backup hardware falls into the following categories:

- Mirrored disk drives
- Removable-media disk drives

- Optical drives
- Tape backup units

Mirrored Disk Drives

Disk mirroring is not a new concept. It has been commonplace in mainframe and minicomputer applications for years. In such on-line services as interactive trading and sales, airline reservations, emergency 911 services, and poison control, you can't afford downtime from hard drive problems.

The economics are such that the financial traffic a system handles exceeds the cost of disk storage devices. To stop to change disk drives and restore from tape is tantamount to halting the General Motors assembly line because the line supervisor's ballpoint pen ran dry.

Disk mirroring is like using Siamese-twin disk drives. Each byte of data on one drive is duplicated on a second. When data is read, it can be read from either disk. If a byte of data is written, it is written to both disks. It doesn't matter how many transactions are processed. Each drive contains a real-time record of the complete system.

If one of the drives goes down, the system operation continues from the twin drive. Later, during an off-peak period, the damaged drive can be repaired or replaced. Then the data can be restored from the twin. In such an operation, disk mirroring is not really a backup; instead, it is considered a part of "fault tolerance."

Until recently, PC applications have not been so crucial. The climax has been the LAN, which depends on ever-larger and faster 80486 servers with massive disk drive units. On-line data base services are turning to PCs to serve 20, 30, or even 100 telephone-line hookups.

DPT   One mirroring system offered specifically for PC use is made by Distributed Processing Technologies, of Maitland, Florida. The system is a model PM 3011 caching controller and the SmartCache Disk Mirroring Module. The caching controller provides 512KB of RAM cache (expandable to 16MB) and is available for MFM, RLL, and ESDI drives. An SCSI model will be available soon. The cache speeds disk-access times. The mirroring module allows two disk drives to run from the cache controller. Anything written to one disk drive will be written to the other.

The system operates entirely at the hardware level and is transparent to the operating system. If one drive goes down, the system sounds an audible alarm while the operation continues to run normally from the twin drive. The caching/mirroring system sells for around $2000 (not including the cost of two disk drives). Unlike other non-hardware disk/mirroring systems, the OPT system has no speed degradation and both drives are independently bootable and functional.

Unfortunately, this system cannot protect you from a complete disaster, such as fire, flood, or theft. For these catastrophes, you will still need to use a removable-media backup in tandem.

Distributed Processing Technologies
132 Candace Drive
Maitland, FL 32751
407-830-5522

Nonstop Networks   On the software side, an innovative mirroring solution is provided by Nonstop Networks, of New York City. This is a 20KB terminate-and-stay-resident (TSR) software program that intercepts all DOS interrupt 21 requests.

Any hard disk read or write operation is intercepted and repeated to a second drive. This is an effective way to mirror two drives without additional hardware. The product also includes utilities to compare the primary and secondary drives. With this, you are able to resynchronize the drives if one has been replaced. This ensures that both contain the same information.

This system operates at the DOS interrupt level. It will work with almost any LAN and has been tested with Novell Netware, 3COM, TOPS, and 10Net. The only drawback is that Nonstop Network increases the load on the workstation by 5 to 7 percent (a small price to pay for an economical disk-mirroring solution if you need one). The LAN version also supports a full duplicate server to allow continuous processing. Single-station versions are available for $495; a LAN version costs $1295.

Nonstop Networks
20 Waterside
New York, NY 10010
212-481-8488

Vortex Systems   A more exotic system that solves the problem of removable-media backup *and* offers disk mirroring is Retrochron, by Vortex Systems, of Pittsburgh, Pennsylvania.

Retrochron is actually a hard drive controller card with three control ports. Port one operates the primary hard drive device for the system. Port two operates a dedicated 40MB control drive used exclusively by Retrochron to buffer data. Port three can be connected to a write-once-read-many (WORM) optical drive, an erasable optical drive, or a backup hard disk.

This system is an ultimate real-time backup device. Each byte of data written to the primary drive is also written to the backup media. The buffer/control drive on the second port buffers the speed difference between the primary drive and the optical backup media on the third port. If the primary drive fails, the system continues from the backup hard drive. If optical drives are used for backup with Retrochron, operation is uninterrupted but is slowed by the longer access times of optical media.

Retrochron is fully compatible and designed for use with Novell and 3COM LAN servers (where downtime is not an option). The controller card is priced at $4995 for a NetWare 286 or DOS-based server and $5995 for NetWare 386-based servers. This does not include any of the media devices. What you get is both the up-to-the-second backup of disk mirroring and, when used with optical backup media, the removable-archive backup capabilities necessary for surviving a major calamity.

The product has an additional feature: It keeps a dynamic chronological record of the data set. From this data set, you can limit backup to files that have been modified to a specific date and time.

Vortex System's newest product, the TC376, is a storage management system for local area networks and multiuser computers. Besides the TC376's dynamic data management, it also offers infallible data protection. The system provides continuous backup, backs up open files and incompatible file system structures, prevents downtime due to disk failure, isolates the storage devices from the host system, accurately and quickly re-creates "lost data," displays real-time information on devices attached to the system, and co-exists with traditional backup, archiving, and fault-tolerant systems.

The TC376 system is compatible with all major LAN and multiuser computer hardware architectures that support SCSI, and will be available for most hardware architecture/operating system combinations. TC376 supports ISA, EISA and MCA busses and is compatible with NetWare 286 and 386.

Vortex Systems
800 Vinial Street
Pittsburgh, PA 15212
412-322-7820
800-842-2186

For on-line reliability and up-to-the-minute backup, disk mirroring is an effective means to keep the system up. Mirroring operates without attention and without data loss. It is, however, an expensive solution, especially when coupled with the protection of a removable-media backup device.

Removable-Media Disk Drives

Since hard drives first appeared for personal computers, their one drawback has been the inability to remove the media. Indeed, early on they were referred to as "fixed" disk drives. They offered larger capacities and faster access than the more convenient, removable floppy disks, and so they came to dominate the personal computer primary-storage field.

Some manufacturers have continued to work on the concept of a removable-media hard disk. One manufacturer has carved out a niche making floppy disks with storage capacity and access speed comparable to a conventional hard drive. Today, a handful of vendors hang on in this small market to serve a small group of users who need the removable-media feature while retaining the speed and capacity of a hard drive.

First among these users are the large corporations that desire to "lock up the data" at night. With the use of a removable-media hard disk, the data stored on the PC can be removed at the end of the workday and secured in a locked safe. This can be an advantage with classified or private company data.

This removable disk also can be an asset when several employees share a machine. If their software and data environments are on removable cartridges, they can carry the essence of "their" machines to any of several desktop computers, plug it in, and work. When they're through, they can remove their media and take it back to their desks. In this way, a group of 20 employees might share five or six desktop PCs with a minimum of stress and confusion.

There are *no* standards for removable-media hard drives. Each manufacturer produces its own cartridge, which works only in its "docking unit." This results in relatively high prices.

Iomega   Iomega has been successful in this market with the Bernoulli drives. The original units used an 8-inch floppy disk housed in a special plastic cartridge case. The cartridge, which became available in 1981, held 10MB of data.

The device spins at 3600 rpm. The drive head hangs above the floppy material. As the disk spins, airflow around the media causes the media to rise to just below the drive head and "hang" there at a precise distance. This takes advantage of a principle of fluid dynamics termed the *Bernoulli effect*, after the 18th-century Swiss mathematician Daniel Bernoulli, who first described it.

The Bernoulli technique effectively eliminates head crashes. If anything disturbs the drive, the Bernoulli effect is broken and the floppy media immediately falls away from the aerodynamically designed drive head.

The specialized cartridges typically cost $80 to $100, and the curious who peek inside would feel "had." Inside the cartridge is what looks like just another floppy disk. But actually, the media is much more durable than an ordinary floppy media. It uses a proprietary barium ferrite coating that can last up to 20 times longer and support higher storage density than ordinary floppy disks.

Iomega has developed a good niche market for their devices. Their current popular configuration is the Bernoulli Box II 44. It employs a cartridge with two 5.25-inch floppies for a total cartridge capacity of 44.5MB. The drive unit costs $2599 and requires a PC adapter card priced at $265. The cartridges list for about $140.

Iomega Corporation
1821 West 4000 South
Roy, UT 84067
800-456-5522

Tandon   Tandon took a different approach. Their Personal Data Pac is a 40MB full-height disk drive that contains both the standard hard disk drive platters, read/write heads, and control circuitry in the removable cartridge itself. The docking unit in the PC provides a mechanical home and electrical connections to what is, in effect, a completely removable hard disk drive. The Add Pack consists of the receptacle, controller card, cables, and software and has a unit cost of $580. Each Personal Data Pack lists for $539.

Tandon
609 Science Drive
Moorpark, CA 93021
805-523-0340
800-800-8850

Plus Development   Plus Development Corporation has recently followed Tandon into removable hard drives with their Passport removable hard drive unit. The Passport is a half-height hard disk that is not quite so bulky as the Tandon. It features a 40MB capacity. The unit consists of an external chassis ($399), a PC interface kit ($659), and 40MB cartridges ($795 each), making this a fairly expensive hard drive solution.

Plus Development Corporation
1778 McCarthy Boulevard
Milpitas, CA 95035
408-434-6900

Optical Drives

Optical-drive technologies are the best hope for the future of backup hardware devices. Their rugged removable media is relatively impervious to damage from dust, magnetic erasure, mishandling, and the gradual degradation of magnetic media by age. You literally could smear peanut butter over one of these small platters, pour root beer on it, place your coffee cup on top of the mess, rinse it off in the sink, dry it with a paper towel—and then use the optical drive platter, no worse for wear.

The drives are more rugged than other devices. To increase recording densities, magnetic devices must position the read/write head close to the media surface. The result is a disk spinning at 3600 rpm with a sharp spur floating a few thousandths of an inch from the surface, raking back and forth in a furious search for data.

Optical devices use lasers to read and write data. The lasers can be focused precisely from any distance. As a result, the platter can be spun at any rate, with the heads safely removed from the media. Additionally, the media can be covered with a transparent protective coating. Optical drives don't have head crashes.

Since the devices use light rather than magnetic fields, data can be recorded at much higher densities. The result is devices that can put as much as 650MB on a single platter smaller than a standard floppy diskette. With the use of an automatic disk changer, archival storage is unlimited. Hundreds of gigabytes can be available on line.

The magnetic areas associated with tape and other magnetic backup media can "wander" over time. Gradually, they lose their charge; over a period of years, the data fades. With optical media, the data is burned onto metal, and decades can pass with no degradation. Optical devices are ideal for long-term archival applications.

Like the magnetic disk drives and unlike sequential-access tape devices, optical units read and write data in a random-access fashion. This allows quick access to backup data. In some cases, optical drive access speeds approach hard disk access rates, with average times on some advanced units below 30 milliseconds.

The shortcomings of optical media are a relatively high cost (approximately $8000 per device) and the lack of standards among manufacturers.

There are three primary optical device types:

- Compact disk read-only memory (CD-ROM)

- Write-once-read-many (WORM) optical drives

- Erasable optical drives

CD-ROM

Optical drive technology is based on light rather than magnetic fields. The basic drive operates mechanically like a regular magnetic hard drive. The media rotates like a phonograph record, with the read/write head positioned over the rotating media. To record data, a laser beam burns a small charred spot on a reflective media or simply raises a bubble in the reflective media. The effect is the same either way: Data bits are represented by reflective spots on the media that alternate with nonreflective spots.

The earliest optical data devices were Compact disk read-only memory (CD-ROM), based on the popular compact disk audio technology. Powerful argon lasers are used to burn tiny pits in the media. The alternating pits and nonburned areas represent data. This master disk is used to produce injection-molded duplicates that mirror the deformities in the master. The duplicates then are covered with a transparent, protective, polycarbonate plastic sheath. In this way, alternating deformed areas and flat reflective areas represent the 1s and 0s of digital data. The result is a small (4.75-inch) platter that is nearly indestructible and can be mass produced.

The access drives are read-only and don't use much of a laser. A small infrared light bulb is focused on the media at an angle. An infrared phototransistor is the pickup device, or "read" head, positioned at a complementary but opposite angle. Flat and reflective areas of the disk mirror the light from the infrared transmitter to the phototransistor, which produces an electrical pulse each time light strikes it. Deformed areas of the media

reflect light in various directions. Too little light is focused on the phototransistor to trigger the electrical output. In this way, nothing actually
touches the spinning platter but a low-power beam of light.

While the actual recording is performed with powerful and expensive
lasers, playback is more like shining a flashlight on the result. In this way,
the CD-ROM drives can be made inexpensively. The media is tough and
does not degrade with time or with repeated use.

The problem with CD-ROM is that it is read-only. While it does provide
a reasonably usable means of "publishing" data bases and large, unchanging
data sets, CD-ROM is largely unusable as a daily backup device. A number
of service bureaus will archive existing historical data on CD-ROM. This
remains expensive. Additionally, CD-ROM access times are slow, at 300 to
500 milliseconds.

READ.ME

CD-ROM Drive Vendors

Pioneer Communications of America, Inc.
600 East Crescent Avenue
Upper Saddle River, NJ 07458
201-327-6400
800-527-3766

Hitachi Sales Corporation of America
401 West Artesia Boulevard
Compton, CA 90220
213-537-8383
800-369-0422

Toshiba America, Inc.
Disk Products Division
9740 Irvine Boulevard
Irvine, CA 92718
714-583-3000

The CD-ROM has evolved into a publishing medium. Thousands of large data bases are available on everything from the complete works of Shakespeare and the adventures of Sherlock Holmes to a complete series of medical reference books.

Write-Once-Read-Many (WORM) Optical Drives

Write-once-read-many (WORM) devices operate like CD-ROMs, but the device *does* contain a write laser. The write laser can write a data bit by pulsing to burn a deformity into the blank disk. The lasers are not so powerful as those used to master CD-ROMs, and the media is easier to write to.

The actual media varies by manufacturer. Some use the laser to burn through a thin, nonreflective coating to expose a reflective substrate beneath. Others raise a tiny blister in a semimetallic substance, such as tellurium, that deforms easily in the presence of heat.

The disks are typically a half-inch larger than CD-ROMs and can hold more data, up to a gigabyte. The access times are much better, at 35 milliseconds—comparable to hard disk drives. The disks typically hold 500MB or more of data. For many applications, you can operate for some time on one disk. The media itself is often expensive—as much as $100 per disk—and there are almost no standards among WORM drive manufacturers.

The critical thing about WORM drives is that they can write data to any area of the media only one time. Data cannot be overwritten. Because the media can contain immense amounts of data, if a data file is changed, the entire file is simply written to the disk again. Software keeps track of the physical location of the latest version of any file. WORM drives can be used as a backup device in this way. The drawback is that when one disk is filled, another must be inserted.

One advantage that is unique to WORM drives is that data written to the disk is permanent. Each and every version of a data file can be reviewed. Every version of the data file is written on the WORM disk and stored in an unalterable form, in unalterable order. This audit trail is useful in a number of business situations.

Given the large data capacities of WORM cartridges, they can be used as backup media. The access time is good. While there are few standards, IBM markets a WORM drive for PCs, which lends some credibility to the technology.

WORM Drive Units

Corel 940
940MB capacity, 90-millisecond access time
Cost: $4,865

Corel Systems
1600 Carling Avenue
Ottawa, Ontario K1Z8R7
CANADA
613-728-8200

Laser Drive 4100
5.6GB capacity, 130-millisecond access time
Cost: $12,000

Laser Magnetic Storage
4425 Arrows West Drive
Colorado Springs, CO 80907
800-777-5674

Filepower
940MB capacity, 123-millisecond access time
Cost: $3,299

Optika Imaging Systems
980 Enchanted Way
Simi Valley, CA 93065
805-527-9060

DD-S5001
654MB capacity, 77-millisecond access time
Cost: $3,100

Pioneer Communications
600 East Crescent Avenue
Upper Saddle River, NJ 07458
800-527-3766
201-327-6400

READ.ME

WORM Drive Units (*continued*)

RF5010
940MB capacity, 90-millisecond access time
Cost: $3,299

Reflection Systems
99 West Tasman Drive
San Jose, CA 95134
408-879-0300

LANStor LNW
940MB capacity, 90-millisecond access time
Cost: $3,640

Storage Dimensions
2145 Hamilton Avenue
San Jose, CA 95125
408-879-0300

Erasable Optical Drives

The optical technology is called erasable optics (EO). Several vendors have developed a solution to the biggest optical problem: the inability to erase or write over information on the optical disk. In the process, some vendors have lowered the average access time to the point where erasable optical drives could conceivably be used as a primary storage device. The technology remains expensive and mostly unstandardized but hopeful.

Erasable optical drives use both lasers and magnetic technologies to record data. A laser beam heats a tiny area of substrate to a temperature at which a magnetic sector can be easily aligned. A magnetic write head then adjusts the sector to magnetize the area.

When the spot cools, this magnetic alignment becomes stable. When a laser is aimed at the spot, the reflection will exhibit a detectable polar rotation based on the polarity of the magnetic media. (This takes advantage of an anomaly of physics termed the Kerr Effect.) To erase the spot, a laser reheats it without writing to it. This resets, or demagnetizes, the zone. The vendors claim this erase/write cycle can be performed up to a million times before the area begins to wear.

Erasable optical drives don't genuinely read and write individual data bytes per se. To write over an area, an entire 512-byte disk sector is first erased with heat from the laser and is then written over with the laser and magnetic head. A third pass to verify the data is usually performed. As a result, these drives are noticeably slower in writing data than they are in reading it, limiting their usefulness as a primary data-storage device.

The International Standards Organization (ISO) has defined WORM drives as erasable cartridges. The standard calls for a 650MB disk storing 325MB per side. The drives are characteristically single-sided (you must flip the disk to access the second side).

The disks cost approximately $250 each. Given the substantial storage capacity and reusable nature of the media, it is, in a sense, a bargain at about 40 cents per MB. To the PC, the erasable optical drives look and act like any hard disk drive.

Storage Dimensions   One of the leaders in this field is Storage Dimensions, a subsidiary of hard disk drive manufacturer Maxtor. The LaserStor erasable drive offers the standard ISO 650MB capacity as well as a 928MB capacity using proprietary Maxtor cartridges. The disk spins at 2200 rpm and features an average access time of 35 milliseconds (comparable to today's hard disk drive access times of 22 to 28 milliseconds). Units are available for the PC or Macintosh as well as Novell file servers. A dual drive unit is available. The units are expensive, with a single-drive-unit cost of about $8000.

Erasable optical drives offer the highest performance, best durability, and permanence. They are an ideal back up medium and a viable solution for large LAN networks. Their pricing is well beyond the reach of individual backup applications, however.

Tape Backup

Tape backup undoubtedly provides the biggest bang for the buck in backup technologies. It is slow, however, and the media itself is fragile.

Data is stored on tape in a sequential, linear fashion. Almost all other backup technologies operate much like the disk drive technologies in that

READ.ME

Erasable Optical Drives

DISCUS Drive
650MB capacity, 62-millisecond access time
Cost: $6,310 for the kit, which includes the drive, the controller, the
software, and the media.

Advanced Graphic Applications
653 Eleventh Avenue, Eleventh Floor
New York, NY 10036
800-DISCUS-1 (347-2821)
212-265-0655

Inspire Drive
650MB capacity, 83-millisecond access time
Cost: $7,200 for the kit, which includes the drive, the controller, and the
software. $250 extra for the cartridge.

Alphatronix
2300 Englert Drive, Suite C
P.O. Box 13687
Research Triangle Park, NC 27709-3687
919-544-0001

Optical Disk Drive
650MB capacity, 78-millisecond access time
Cost: $5,990

Asuka Technologies
17145 Von Karman Avenue, Suite 110
Irvine, CA 92714
714-757-1212

RS600 Drive
595MB capacity, 61-millisecond access time
Cost: $3,995 for the kit, which includes the drive, the controller, the
software, and the media.

Consan
14625 Martin Drive
Eden Prairie, MN 55344
612-949-0053

READ.ME

Erasable Optical Drives (*continued*)

REO-6500 Drive
6GB capacity, 65-millisecond access time
Cost: $9,995

Pinnacle Micro
15265 Alton Parkway
Irvine, CA 92718
800-553-7070
714-727-3300

Cosmos 600
590MB capacity, 50-millisecond access time
Cost: $5,095

Racet Computers
3150 East Birch Street
Brea, CA 92621
714-579-1725

LANStor LNE
880MB capacity, 35-millisecond access time
Cost: $8,495

Storage Dimensions
2145 Hamilton Avenue
San Jose, CA 95125
408-879-0300

they provide a random-access storage medium where any file or block of data can be located quickly. Tape units must wind through the data serially until the desired file or block is found.

The tape backup is a mature technology, the least expensive of all backup hardware, and common. Nine-track, half-inch, reel-to-reel tapes have been used on mainframe computers as storage for decades—they even predate hard disk drives. In fact, the first generation of home computers (including the early Sinclair ZX-81/Timex 1000, Atari, Commodore, TRS-80, and even the early IBM PC) used ordinary audio cassette tapes for their primary storage. The first IBM PC was a 64KB machine with cassette-tape storage.

Magnetic tape is ideal for applications that require storage of massive amounts of data on a single media unit and is the classic prerequisite for unattended backup of hard disk drives in today's capacities. The amount of data a tape can store is a function of the recording density and the physical length of the tape itself (theoretically unlimited). As a result, backing up a hard drive on tape can be as simple as slam-dunking a formatted tape into the drive and starting the software. At that point, you're off to get coffee. When you return in half an hour, a backup of your entire hard drive is complete. There is now software to allow you to run unattended backup. You place the tape in when you leave for the night and return the next morning to a completed backup.

Popular tape drive formats include:

- Half-inch magnetic tape

- Quarter-inch magnetic tape cartridge

- Four-millimeter digital audio tape cartridge

Half-Inch Magnetic Tape

Half-inch, open-reel, magnetic tape drives are perhaps the oldest tape drive storage devices available. Developed for mainframe applications in the 1950s, these tapes made numerous appearances in grade-B science fiction movies. They became almost a symbol for "computer" in television and movies. You may remember them as refrigerator-size boxes with a glass door over the top half and huge spools of tape racing back and forth.

The media is a half-inch-wide ribbon of plastic film coated with iron oxide. They typically come in 2400- or 3600-foot lengths wound on 7-inch- or 10.5-inch-diameter hard plastic spools. The spools are posted on capstans, and the tape is directed through a series of tension rollers. The tapes can be removed and placed in a round plastic storage box, which is labeled, dated, and archived for a month or two—or forever. Some insurance companies have archives of as many as 50,000 such tape spools.

Data is written to the tape in nine parallel data tracks. In this way, each byte of data is written sequentially to the tape, one bit per track, with a ninth parity-check bit for error checking. These nine bits are referred to as a *frame*, with a number of sequential frames comprising a *block*. Blocks are separated by *interrecord gaps (IRGs)*, and files are separated by interfile gaps called *tape marks*.

Longitudinally, data is recorded at one of several densities, including 800, 1600, or 6250 bits per inch. A 2400-foot tape recorded at 1600 bits per inch usually holds 40MB of data—not much by today's PC standards.

The tape drive units themselves feature spring-loaded tension rollers that allow dramatic differences in the speeds of the take-up and supply reels. The tape between the reels is routed through a sensing device that monitors tape tension and regulates reel drive speed.

It is easy to assume that nine-track magnetic tape is an obsolete technology, and it is true that it has not assumed any significant role in PC backup strategies. However, it has developed into a medium of exchange between computer systems. Often, mainframe computer services, including many mailing-list companies and governmental entities, still use this tape format for exchanging large quantities of data. The IRS, for example, has experimented with electronic tax filing. The filing sequence is typically from a PC to a service bureau by modem, and from the bureau to the IRS by nine-track tape.

Likewise, the U.S. Department of Commerce provides census data primarily on nine-track tape, although the Department is now moving into CD-ROM and floppy disk distribution.

As a result, you may find the nine-track format to be the only one available for the specific information exchange you require. Or you may find a need to provide information to a company or governmental entity that specifies nine-track tape format. In this respect, nine-track tape has taken on some aspects of a common exchange format, particularly for extremely large data sets.

There are several service bureaus that will convert data to or from nine-track formats. If you need frequent or regular transfers, nine-track tape units are available for PCs. They work just fine for backup purposes, as well. However, they are not inexpensive (typically $2000 to $5000), and compared with PC technologies, they are a bit large and awkward. But they do have a proven track record. They fill a substantial need for bridging large data bases between mainframes and PCs. For some applications, nine-track tape may be just the ticket.

```
READ.ME
```

Vendors of Nine-Track Drives and Software for IBM-Compatible PC Equipment

AKSystems Inc.
20741 Marila Street
Chatsworth, CA 91311
818-709-8100

Contech Computer Corp.
P.O. Box 570397
Tarzana, CA 91357
818-343-2700

Qualstar
9621 Irondale Avenue
Chatsworth, CA 91311
818-882-5822

TDX Peripherals, Inc.
80 Davids Drive
Hauppauge, NY 11788
800-842-0708
516-273-5900

Quarter-Inch Tape Cartridge Devices

Quarter-inch tape cartridges were patented in 1971 by Robert von Behren of 3M Corporation. These cartridges are probably the medium of choice for tape backup of PC systems today.

Magnetic tape is an inherently fragile medium. A long strip of plastic film is coated with ferrous oxide for magnetically recording data. It must be notably thin to be able to store any quantity of tape in a useful size. The problem is that the tape itself can stretch in the process of spooling through a reading device. This can damage the stored data.

Common audio cassettes use a capstan drive that turns the cogged center of the tape spools. The problem is that as more tape is wound on a spool, the same axial rotation speed at this hub tends to increase the linear speed of the tape as the outer diameter of the take-up spool increases. In data applications, it is necessary to hold the relative speed of the tape constant. It is also important for the tape media not to be stretched unduly. A fairly complex drive mechanism is required to manage this dilemma.

The 3M data cartridge ingeniously solves this by driving the outer diameter of the spool rather than the inner hub. The speed of the tape is constant, regardless of the amount of tape on either side of the spool. The difference between the inner drive hub and the outer diameter is eliminated. In fact, there is no hub-drive mechanism at all.

The 3M cartridge has a drive belt that makes contact with a drive wheel in the tape unit. Within the cartridge is a belt assembly routed around the tape spools. When the drive wheel is turned, the belt drives both spools at the same speed and tension. The drive unit is able to detect the end of a tape because there are holes punched in it.

The 3M cartridge is more expensive than a regular tape ($20 to $30), since the drive mechanism is contained in the cartridge. The drive unit, however, is relatively simple and lower in cost than other designs.

Quarter-Inch Tape

The 3M quarter-inch cartridge was originally developed for data logging in long-term collection of seismological or telemetry data. It is very good for tape backup—so good that 3M has licensed two other vendors, Sony Corporation and DEI, to produce a quarter-inch tape under their patent. In general, these tape brands can be used interchangeably (although drive manufacturers will certify only one brand of cartridge with their units).

Quarter-inch tape is readily available. Almost all computer stores and mail-order computer-supply houses carry a selection in a variety of dimensions and tape lengths.

One factor in tape selection is termed *coercivity* (measured in *oersteds*). Data is recorded by exposing it to a positive or negative magnetic field. This causes magnetic particles (*domains*) in the metal-oxide coating to align in the direction of the field (positive or negative). This field is modulated to encode data on the tape as it passes.

There is some resistance to this alignment of magnetic particles. The lower the coercivity, the more resistance. To overcome the resistance, either the strength of the magnetic field or the amount of time the material is

same tape speed and length, more data can be stored on higher-coercivity tapes by some higher-capacity drives.

Besides the basic drive design, there are two sets of standards that have emerged in regard to the quarter-inch tape design. One standard is the actual physical properties of the cartridge—external dimensions and length of tape. The other standard addresses the actual method of encoding data onto the tape and the interface to the PC.

Cartridge Sizes

Several quarter-inch tape cartridge sizes have been introduced. By convention, cartridge names begin with the acronym DC, for data cartridge, followed by a numeric designation that seems to have no explanation. (The DC600 cartridge contains 600 feet of tape. One would think, then, that the DC1000 would offer 1000 feet of tape; actually, it contains 185. Oh, well.) This standard, which was originally proposed by 3M, has been adopted by the American National Standards Institute (ANSI).

Available tape formats include the following:

- DC600
- DC1000
- DC2000
- DC2000XL

DC600   The DC600 cartridge is approximately 4 inches wide and 6 inches long. The cartridges cost about $30 and hold 600 feet of tape. This is the largest capacity commonly available in DC tape. It was subject to design experimentation before the Quarter-Inch Cartridge Drive Standards Organization was formed. As a result, the DC600 is probably the least standardized cartridge format, which is a drawback.

Unfortunately, the DC600 is the media of choice of the tape drive units on the market. The 600-foot length of the tape is attractive for large-capacity units. Tecmar, of Solon, Ohio, has a DC600 drive model, QT-525es. It features a Small Computer Systems Interface (SCSI), a 525MB capacity, and a high data-transfer rate of 14MB per minute. Combined with data compression, the Tecmar device can contain over 1GB of data. The list price is $3495. For systems that require capacities in excess of 150MB, the DC600 cartridge drive may be a good choice.

An innovation in DC600 cartridges is the TAPEXCHANGE Model 60TX. This model is a more modest, 60MB capacity unit. (The company is working on a 150MB model.) The 60TX plugs into the standard parallel printer port in the back of the computer. The unit costs $1295. It can serve as a backup for several computers, using ordinary parallel AB data switches to connect the unit to each PC.

It is also possible to plug one of these units into any parallel port and copy whatever data set. Both the tape and the drive can move to a second PC to transfer data to the hard drive in that unit. This does not require the installation of an interface device in either PC.

DC1000   The DC1000 was the first of the "mini" cartridges. It measures 2.5 inches wide and 3 inches long. The cartridge contains 185 feet of tape. One company, Irwin Magnetics, uses the tape in a 10MB capacity, although it has not proven to be popular. They do not work in any drive units made by any other manufacturers.

DC2000 and DC2000XL   This is a popular quarter-inch-tape cartridge in a successful format in regard to standardization. The DC2000 and DC2000XL

READ.ME

DC600 Tape Subsystems

Tecmar
6225 Cochran Road
Solon, OH 44139
800-344-4463
216-349-0600

Interpreter Corporation
11455 W. 48th Avenue
Wheat Ridge, CO 80033
800-232-4687
303-431-8991

Colorado Memory Systems, Inc.
800 South Taft Avenue
Loveland, CO 80537
800-432-5858
303-669-8000

share the mini-cartridge dimensions of 2.5 by 3 inches. The DC2000 contains 205 feet of tape and is priced at $19 to $23. It can provide a formatted capacity of 40MB. The DC2000XL contains 300 feet of tape and provides a standard formatted capacity of 60MB for a cost of $25 to $27.

Drives that use this format are economical and readily available. Colorado Memory Systems offers a highly regarded drive that uses the DC2000/DC2000XL cartridge. Their JUMBO model employs software compression to squeeze as much data as possible on a single DC2000 (up to 80MB) or DC2000XL (as much as 120MB). The cost of the unit is under $400.

QIC Standards

The Quarter-Inch Cartridge Drive Standards Organization was formed in 1982 as a cooperative committee by streaming-tape-drive manufacturers. The committee has published 36 Quarter-Inch Cartridge (QIC, pronounced "quick") standards.

After a universal cartridge size and tape length were established, the work in standardization had just begun. Actually recording data from PC equipment to a tape involves a number of factors. These include recording-head properties, error-correction codes, data-compression algorithms, recording densities, and a common electrical interface to the PC-industry-standard-architecture machine.

These "floppy tape" standards use a floppy controller card. The computer is fooled into thinking that the tape drive is a huge floppy drive. It's less expensive than a custom controller card, and it can save slots. On the other hand, it is limited to floppy data-transfer rates (500K bps for the AT and 250K bps for the XT), and usually prevents use of the B floppy drive.

The emerging leaders are titled QIC-40 (which is dominant) and QIC-80. QIC-40 specifies a 40MB formatted capacity with interface to an ordinary floppy disk controller. QIC-80 features the same floppy-controller-card interface in an 80MB capacity. It's likely the QIC-80 will become the technology leader.

Quarter-Inch Cartridge Drive Standards Committee
311 East Cabrillo Street
Santa Barbara, CA 93101

Format   Data is written to the tape in similar ways to floppy and hard disks except the sector size is 1024 bytes or 1KB. The sectors written linearly on the tape are mapped to the tracks, sectors, and sides of an imaginary floppy disk. The tape even has a directory corresponding to the file allocation table (FAT) on a disk. And like a disk, the tape must be formatted before you can store data on it. Formatting 40MB tape can take as long as 30 minutes.

A nine-track tape has each of nine bits written across the tape surface in parallel, with bytes following one another along the length of the tape. On a "floppy tape," data is written serially bit by bit on one track from the beginning of the tape to the end. At one end of the tape, the read/write head is dropped to the next track, and the tape drive reverses direction. The data is then written, again serially, on track two. When the beginning of the tape is reached, the head is dropped to track three and data is again written serially from beginning to end. This continues through all 20 tracks. This "snaking" of data back and forth serially across the length of the tape is termed a "serpentine" record.

Each track is divided into 68 blocks, with each block containing 29 sectors. Each sector contains 1KB of data. In this way, each track holds roughly 2MB, for a total formatted capacity of 40MB.

The tape media is a bit more fragile than diskette media, owing to the thinner metal-oxide coating and underlying structural material. In addition to the normal cyclic redundancy check performed by the floppy disk controller, a software algorithm named Reed-Solomon is provided to further reduce the possibility of error. Some manufacturers advertise unrecoverable-data-error rates as low as one occurrence in 300,000 tapes.

Compression   The QIC committee recently established a registry of data-algorithm identifiers that can be written to the tape to indicate the data-compression scheme used. A tape-backup unit can then read this "label" and select the correct compression algorithm to retrieve the data—if it knows the algorithm.

The QIC committee selected a compression method, QIC-122, that uses a chip hardware device developed by Stac Electronics, of Pasadena, California. The device uses a modified Ziv-Lempel algorithm (much like that used in PKZIP and many modem compression schemes) to achieve 2:1 data-compression ratios with an average throughput of 750KB per second. This is faster than the data-transfer rate of many of the tape drives. This hardware compression device should begin to appear in tape backup systems by late 1990.

Some manufacturers have extended the capacity of the QIC-40 standard by use of proprietary compression schemes. Two modes of operation exist: the 40MB standard QIC-40 and the manufacturers' proprietary mode. The tapes remain formatted for 40MB. The data is compressed with a software algorithm before it's recorded on the formatted tape, providing effective capacities as high as 80MB.

Another QIC-40 standard tape drive is technically able to read the data stored on the tape but cannot uncompresses it. This makes it almost useless.

READ.ME

QIC-40 Manufacturers

Pericomp, a Massachusetts-based independent testing laboratory has certified QIC-40 drives from three manufacturers as compatible in all respects to QIC-40:

Archive Corporation
1650 Sunflower Avenue
Costa Mesa, CA 92626
800-227-6296
714-641-0279

Maynard Electronics
A Division of Archive Corporation
460 East Semoran Boulevard
Casselberrg, FL 32707
800-227-6296
407-263-3500

Colorado Memory Systems, Inc.
800 South Taft Avenue
Loveland, CO 80537
800-432-5858
303-669-8000

Mountain Computer
240 Hacienda Avenue
Campbell, CA 95008
800-458-0300
408-379-4300

Digital Audio Tape

Digital audio tape (DAT) was developed by Sony Corporation as an audio recording technique that delivers higher fidelity than conventional audio cassettes.

DAT digitizes the audio data. Since the data is stored digitally, any noise or hiss caused by oxide-media anomalies is eliminated. The digital nature of the data is much less sensitive to variable tape speeds. As a result, the quality of the sound on the tape is almost solely a function of how accurately it was digitized in the first place. The tape media itself has little effect.

The Recording Industries Association has successfully blocked the importation of DAT recording devices. Their fear is that the ability of this tape recorder to copy compact disk recordings accurately will result in an escalation of copyrighted music piracy.

The DAT industry and the RIA negotiated a settlement. The DAT-player manufacturers would install a chip that would allow you to record anything you liked directly but would encode a signal on the tape to prevent copying it to another DAT tape cartridge. This would limit copyright crime to a single "generation." Unfortunately, even after the compromise, the RIA filed suit against the vendors to again delay entry of the audio devices.

For data backup, DAT devices offer the advantage of a large data capacity. The drive units can back up over a gigabyte of data on a cartridge that is three-fifths of the size of a standard audio cassette tape, at speeds of up to 10MB per minute. Their price is in the $6000 range.

There are two DAT sizes: eight millimeter and four millimeter. The eight-millimeter cartridge is identical to a standard VHS video cassette. While it can store as much as 2.2GB, the eight-millimeter devices are not popular. The four-millimeter cartridge is priced at around $18.

Both DAT sizes use a type of recording termed *helical scan*. This was first developed for video tape recorders. The tape travels around the partial circumference (usually about 90 degrees) of a drum spinning at about 2000 rpm. The drum is mounted at an angle to the tape (5 to 6 degrees). As a result, as the drum spins, the data is recorded in long diagonal stripes across the tape as it passes, to create sections of a spiral helix of data on the tape surface.

The spinning drum contains two read and two write heads. In this way, two tracks can be laid simultaneously. To reduce "crossover" between tracks, the heads are actually angled on the spinning drum differently. Each track has a different azimuth angle. The two tracks comprise a "frame" of 8KB of data. The result is an efficient use of the tape surface—about 60KB per inch with substantial data storage capacities. There are two primary four-millimeter data formats in use: Digital data storage (DDS) and Data/ DAT.

DAT technology is still young. There are some standardization problems and a hefty price tag. It is effective for installations that require exceptional backup capacities in excess of a gigabyte. As the technology matures and prices drop, it will become a viable alternative for tape backup.

CONCLUSION

Hardware backup systems offer easy and reliable solutions to a tedious task. There are a number of different choices, each with their own faults and features. Price alone should not be the sole consideration, but instead, your individual need. This overview should give you the basic information necessary to begin to explore your requirements.

CHAPTER ELEVEN

Security, Viruses, and You

Computer security has been an ongoing concern since the start of the "Information Age," more than 40 years ago. Traditionally, security was an all-or-nothing issue: Either you needed it or you didn't. If you needed security, you dealt with it with secret keys, passwords, user IDs, and arcane recognition signals. But you were wary. It all seemed like something out of a James Bond movie.

At a time when most Americans left their doors unlocked, the attitude was: If the computer people were that neurotic to think they needed the security, let them live with the inconvenience. By the mid 1960s, however, data processing departments really *did* need extra security. As anti-Vietnam War activists and others began to associate computers with the government, it became necessary to enforce security procedures more strictly. In the early stages of computer security, access to entire computer facilities was restricted. This "fortress mentality" was imposed through the use of distinctive double doors, sophisticated locks, and specially trained security guards.

In the late 1960s, IBM came up with a more sensible approach to computer security: Secure the computer from the inside. IBM's model 360 mainframe was one of the first computers to use a special password-security system as standard equipment. With security built in, it didn't matter who sat down at the computer—only those privileged with the authorization code could gain access. By today's standards, these systems were easy to crack. But in the 1960s, few people knew how to operate a computer, much less foil a security system. (Of course, many companies continued with the double doors and fortress-like rooms, as well as the password system.)

The 1970s marked the arrival of such microcomputers as the Altair, Cromemco, Osborne, and Apple II. As the popularity of micros increased in the early 1980s, users came to appreciate the need for a confidential personal computer system.

With the wave of computer awareness, people also began to appreciate the need for privacy in their daily affairs. Resulting laws govern access to private information, limit how long data is active in computer records, and establish the individual's right to know and respond to negative reports.

In the 1990s, so many of us work with desktop computers that security has become demystified. Anyone who writes a letter or other private document with a PC will understand how vulnerable we are to snooping. It is no secret that users with the least bit of computer savvy can browse through an unprotected hard disk, read this file, and copy that one to a floppy disk. This could happen without a trace that the intrusion ever occurred. It doesn't take CIA training to do it (to unglue and reseal an envelope requires more talent). *That* can make us nervous.

A QUESTION OF BALANCE

A majority of people accept that computer security is necessary. But where do you fit in? The cost and extent of computer security is really a question of balance. How much time, effort, and money you put into security for your system depends on a number of factors:

- How important or private is your data?
- How easy is it for someone to get to your data?
- How likely is it that someone would try to get to your data?

Let's answer these questions.

Data Sensitivity

The first thing to determine is the "sensitivity" of your data. If your PC is used for daily Tetris tournaments and an occasional letter to Aunt Frannie, there's not much to lose in the way of an unsecured, or open, system (except maybe those high Tetris scores). If you are a government-employed management-information system (MIS) manager whose PC is used to manipulate classified data, you have a lot to lose.

If you don't fall into either of these extremes, ask yourself several questions:

- How do I feel about the privacy of my data?
- If my computer contains data used by my company, what security precautions are required?
- Does my computer contain sensitive information about my clients?
- Do state laws require me to secure such data?

Many types of business records hold sensitive information. A few that come to mind are personnel evaluations, attendance records, medical information, business plans, and customer records. These matters are confidential. Lawyers, doctors, counselors, brokers, and other professionals risk serious legal and financial liability if they neglect to ensure confidentiality.

If your PC is for personal use, you may think that there is little or no sensitive information. You may prepare your taxes on your computer, use a home banking service, or manage a spreadsheet to calculate a budget or balance a checkbook. You may wish to keep this kind of information private. Is it worth securing your computer to do so?

This may depend on who you are. You can bet Donald Trump would like to keep his PC private from "inquiring minds." Does your occupation or lifestyle invite the possibility of such an intrusion? Even if you aren't a public figure, some minimal security is useful. It is nice to restrict access to keep out the kids, the housecleaner, or whomever.

Data Accessibility

The accessibility of data is an important factor to consider in the decision to secure your system. If your home computer has the only copy of the company's new business plan, the odds of someone breaking and entering just to get a look at it are pretty remote. The odds change if the PC is in an unsecured, open-to-the-general-public office. In one instance, in a small business, the resident PC hobbyist entered the payroll manager's office and, with the use of a $59, off-the-shelf DOS shell program, looked through the payroll records of every member of the staff, from the CEO to the janitor.

Protections, common in more robust operating systems, are not available on PCs. DOS was designed as an open system. Log-ins and passwords aren't required as they are on mainframes, and on some minisystems.

The popularity of the hard disk makes office security more difficult. The hard disk centralizes information. An intruder enjoys the same benefits you do: Everything's in one place, making it fast and easy to access.

A networked PC is even harder to secure. Any terminal connected to the PC can access data, and *anyone*, anywhere, can tap into the network cables (including those in the building's telephone closet). If your office uses a LAN, your computer may be open to mischief and possibly some serious damage.

LEVELS OF DATA SECURITY

The yardstick for deciding what level of security is right for you is sensitivity and accessibility of your data. At the lowest level are simple programs that require a password upon startup. At the other end of the spectrum are add-in boards that provide automatic "check-in, check-out" encryption with complex algorithms.

Don't forget to secure your backup disks. You can install password protection, encrypt the hard disk, bolt the machine to the desk, and lock away the keyboard, but it's all useless if someone makes off with the backup disks.

Security Levels

Level 0—No Security   With no security and sensitive data, the "it can't happen to me" attitude is probably at work. Level-0 security is for those with no data or programs worth safeguarding.

Level 1—Keyboard/Disk Lock   The round key provided with each AT machine fits into a keyhole in the front panel. When locked, the machine cannot receive input from the keyboard. Although it provides a low security level (an intruder could simply plug another keyboard in), it's good to use when you step away from your PC in an open office environment.

Level 2—User Log-on or Password   This level of security requires the entering of either an approved log-on ID or a secret password before the computer will finish booting up.

One program that provides this security is FastLock, by Rupp Corporation. The program allows three password attempts before sounding a loud alarm. It also changes your system's boot track and file allocation table. The hard disk remains unreadable until FastLock is installed with the correct password.

Other systems, such as PC-Lock (a shareware program), place a device driver in the CONFIG.SYS file to require a password at bootup. PC-Lock directs the computer to look for drive C in drive D. This renders the hard disk unusable until the correct password is entered.

Note: Some password programs can be bypassed by booting the system from a floppy disk. Check all potential purchases for this flaw.

Level 3—User Log-on and Password   Users must provide both a user ID and a password. The better systems record all log-ins, both accepted and unsuccessful, as well as a time stamp (as reported by the system clock).

Level 4—User Log-on, Password, and Audit Trail   This system is more secure than Level 3—and more expensive. A Level-4 system will keep an audit trail (a record) of user actions, such as time of log-on, files opened, attempted entry to files, total time on system, and time of log-off.

A distinctive feature of this type of system is contolled access based on the user's account. Each user is allowed entry to defined files and functions. The audit trail will identify user attempts to enter unauthorized files.

Level 5—Data Encryption   Data encryption is one of the best security levels available. Encrypted data is data that has been coded through a series of mathematical operations. This data becomes unreadable without the decryption code. It's a secret code. Mainframe systems use encryption to send information through their networks. Without the encryption, anyone could tap in and read the data flowing over the lines.

The encryption and decryption is activated by a series of keys, which may be, for example, a sequence of numbers or a password. If your security requirements are stringent enough to require encryption, take the necessary precautions to ensure that you don't get stranded without the keys.

Keep a copy of the key sequence in some secure place, such as a bank deposit vault. For that matter, keep an unencrypted copy of data there, too: If the keys are lost or something malfunctions, you won't be stranded with unusable data. (It's not as if you can call a locksmith to fix it if you lose the keys.)

The best systems in the United States use the Data Encryption Standard, or DES. The DES is so secure that to export it to other countries is illegal except under tightly controlled conditions. There are other methods of encryption, and some may be faster than a DES program or involve fewer calculations. In general, however, if you must encrypt, use the DES instead of the alternatives. It is well proven and widely available.

Before encrypting everything on your hard disk, spend some time considering potential consequences. The whole point of encryption, with DES or otherwise, is to make your data completely unusable by anyone who doesn't know the key. Let's face it, password keys can be forgotten or misplaced. With an encryption system, if the key is lost, so is the file.

Level 6—Hardware-Based Systems   Hardware-based access-control systems are add-on boards. They offer a range of choices, from log-on and password audits to multiple access levels, individual file encryption, and full disk encryption. The hardware-based system is fast. It also offers more flexibility in recovering files if the password is lost.

Several encryption boards are available. The newer ones are secure against intruders and transparent to the user—that is, after completing the initial sign-on, the user may not be aware that encryption is occurring. The system decodes the material while reading it off the disk and reencodes it when writing.

What Should You Do?

First, develop a security policy and follow it. A well-defined security policy is essential for protecting your system. Once you determine it, use it.

Second, no system will ever be 100 percent safe from attack. So, keep a "fallback position": Make sure you have insurance coverage that will cover the loss or damage of your computer equipment and make sure you have an unencrypted backup copy of critical data in a secure location, for instance, an offsite fireproof vault.

Third, the creation of your security policy should mix security techniques to form multiple lines of defense. Individual security plans may be vulnerable on their own but strengthened in conjunction with others.

Password Selection

The right choice of a password is important. The password will make the difference in the integrity of your system. Those who illegally access computers know the most common types of passwords people choose. To foil them, **DON'T USE:**

- Your name

- Your spouse's, child's, or dog's name

- Your birthday

- Your street

- 386, if you have a 386-based system

- Your telephone number or extension

- Anything about your company

- The word *secret* (probably the worst of all)

- Love (a common choice of ex-hippies)

- Anything spelled backward

The best passwords are those that have little or no meaning for you. Pick a word out of the air. Choose your mother's maiden name, or your father's middle name, or your long-dead Aunt Hildegard's pet name for you as a child, or a word that describes your secret fetish.

No matter how you safeguard your system with passwords and other security methods, you are not guarded against theft of the system itself. A seized machine is one way to lose all data. Thousands of dollars spent to keep data secure from snoops and spies won't do you any good if thieves waltz in during the night.

The best deterrent against thieves is a well-protected building. If your building lacks security guards or an effective monitor, you might consider a lock box for your computer and a well-labeled alarm for the office.

On a different track, there are alarm cards available that emit a loud shriek if your computer is moved from a horizontal position when the power is off.

VIRUSES, WORMS, AND OTHER ROGUE PROGRAMS

One of the most widely heralded threats is the dreaded computer virus. This menace can travel from program to program and machine to machine, bent on mayhem to disfigure data in its wake. Right?

Let's be clear from the start: Viruses do exist. However, taking reasonable precautions, a single user with a stand-alone PC will rarely, if ever, catch a computer virus. The probability of having all your data wiped out by a virus is extremely low. It happens occasionally, and everybody talks about it when it does. If you stick to some simple rules, you can safeguard your system from almost every virus discovered so far.

That said, let's remember that viruses *are* out there and are not always benign. The Computer Virus Industry Association, in Santa Clara, California, estimates that more than one million PCs are, or have been, infected by some strain of computer virus (176,000 authenticated virus hits were reported in 1989 alone). David Stang, director of research for the National Computer Security Association, cites evidence that as much as one percent of all PCs in the United States are infected.

The statistics are alarming, and they account for the reaction from the national press. Actual numbers are hard to come by. Some of this may be hearsay, and some may be pure speculation. There is no computer equivalent for the Centers for Disease Control.

Viruses

Small parcels of program code, called *viruses*, have garnered most of the press in recent years. They are fiendishly clever programs. The notion that they can spread from computer to computer (like Dutch elm disease) to infect our systems and kill programs captures the imagination.

A virus is a piece of code that "propagates." It can move from program to program and then wait for a set of circumstances to "trigger" it. The action may be benign, and some viruses are downright comical. The trend, however, is away from amiable or funny.

A recently discovered virus called the 123NHALF does what its name implies: It targets Lotus 1-2-3 data bases and cuts them in half. Other contemporary viruses are designed to spread for years before being triggered at a specific date and time.

Trojan Horses

A *Trojan horse* is considered, by some experts, to be a virus that doesn't spread. A Trojan horse looks like a benign program, but hidden inside is havoc in the form of code.

Trojan-horse programs are particularly common in "hacked" versions of commercial programs (programs with their copy-protection routines removed). Some rumors say that companies have put out their own Trojan-horse versions, always clearly labeled "Hacked." This seems dubious, at best.

It is difficult to determine the number of actual Trojan horses there are. They are indistinguishable from program "glitches" unless clearly labeled (like the infamous "Arf Arf! Gotcha!" message).

Avoid Trojan horses by keeping away from hacked software and shareware programs that sound too good to be true ("Amazing program gives VGA capabilities to your monochrome monitor!").

Logic Bombs

The destructive code contained within a virus or Trojan horse—the part that does the actual damage—is sometimes referred to as a *logic bomb*. The logic bomb "explodes" (performs some sort of destructive action) after a required set of conditions occurs.

Worms

The term *worm program* does not have a definition that everyone agrees upon. Worms are uncommon at the PC level; they target mainframes, minicomputers, packet switchers, and other fully networked systems.

Worms are more sophisticated than viruses, Trojan horses, and logic bombs. They serve a more unique and explicit purpose, with limitless capabilities.

Most worm programs are written by hackers as experiments. By its nature, a worm program can seriously cripple a computer system or extract or modify data—without any visible trace. Worms are stand-alone programs. Unlike viruses, they don't attach themselves to other programs. Once a worm is running, it goes into memory and then searches for another location.

The famous Internet worm, for example, searched for passwords and then traveled down communication wires to a second system, where it installed itself in memory and repeated the process. It managed to clog up the entire international system. To a PC user, the threat of worm programs ranks somewhere up there with mildew.

Recommended Products

Don't let an excitable press throw you into a panic about viruses, Trojan horses, or other computer mischief. Society has always suffered from antisocial elements and always will. It is wise to guard against them as best we can and go on to enjoy life as it is. Here are the some of the leading antivirus products:

CHECKUP Virus Detection System

Program registration for Rich Levin's CHECKUP Virus Detection System is $20 for personal use and $40 for business use; site licenses are available. Rich is the author of *The Computer Virus Handbook*, published by Osborne/McGraw-Hill.

Richard B. Levin
Levin & Associates
9405 Bustleton Avenue
P.O. Box 14546
Philadelphia, PA 19115
Lab: 215-333-8274
BBS: 215-333-8275

READ.ME

Safe Computing Practices

- Backup your programs frequently.

- Save your work often. Keep track of the sizes of your work files so that you may be aware of any sudden, unaccountable alterations.

- Use write-protect tabs on any floppy disk to which you're not actively copying data. It's both prophylactic and diagnostic: If you get a sudden, inappropriate "Write protect error" message, you know something suspicious is going on.

- If you use bulletin boards, avoid downloading new files that the system operator hasn't had a chance to test. For that matter, avoid downloading files from boards that do not state clearly that they test every file they keep posted.

- Never boot from a floppy disk unless you know its origin. Most virus infections spread by floppy disk—not by bulletin board, as some mistakenly believe.

- Stay away from pirated software. Many virus infections come about because of informal but illegal passing around of programs.

- Don't loan out program disks: They may become infected.

- Don't let others use your machine, especially with their own program disks. If you do, make a complete backup of your system first.

- Consider a security system, such as a hardware-based system, to keep others from booting your machine. (Software drivers cannot stop a virus from infecting your hard disk at bootup.)

- Use a good virus-prevention program, such as Richard B. Levin's CHECKUP. CHECKUP provides a sanitary floppy disk with a batch file method to detect any virus change to your files. A sanitary floppy disk has only the MS or PC DOS files necessary to start your system. These files include the hidden DOS files and the DOS command processor. In some cases, you may also need a CONFIG.SYS file, which includes the special device driver for your hard disk. A clean disk that normally excludes AUTO.EXE, CONFIG.SYS, and associated files gives you a vanilla DOS system. CHECKUP is available on BBSs.

Safe Computing Practices (*continued*)

- Use one of the several good antivirus programs available to detect and remove virus infections after they occur. SCAN, by John McAfee, searches for all known viruses and will tell you if it finds any. SCAN is available on BBSs and is updated to search for new viruses within days of their discovery.

- Every week or so, compare your write-protected DOS disk's version of COMMAND.COM with the one on your hard disk. If they are not identical, you'll know something's fishy.

- Use the DOS diskette's SYS command to reinstall the system files on your hard disk. This just takes a moment and overwrites any viruses lurking in the boot sectors.

- Consider installing a hardware device that looks for viral activity and warns you against it. The ViroCrypt board stops virus infections that originate on a floppy disk on bootup.

- Keep an eye on how long it takes programs to load. An infected program is likely to take longer. It looks at other programs on your disk, seeking clean files to infect.

- Make all your executable files (those ending in COM, EXE, or SYS) read-only files. A number of good programs are available for this, including a huge assortment of shareware file-management programs. Similar programs are commercially available with the Norton Utilities, Mace Utilities, Golden Bow TOOLS collection, PC Tools, and just about every commercial shell program.

McAfee Associates Programs

Program registration is $25 for personal use and $25 for business use; add $9 if you want disks mailed. Site licenses are available. The programs are

SCAN, VSHIELD, and CLEAN.

McAfee Associates/Interpath
4423 Cheeney Street
Santa Clara, CA 95054

Voice: 408-988-3832
BBS: 408-988-4004
Fax (best for upgrades): 408-970-9227

Flushot

One of the classic antiviral programs is Flushot, available from Ross Greenberg. Its shareware price is $25.

Ross M. Greenberg Software Concepts Design
594 Third Avenue
New York, NY 10016
212-889-6438

PART FOUR

Windows and Other Operating Environments

CHAPTER TWELVE

Microsoft Windows

Microsoft Windows is a program that provides information in a format called a *graphical user interface (GUI)*. This is a term used for environments that mix text and graphics or that use graphics as a major part of their design. Using a graphical interface is somewhat like working with pictures on the screen. Some of its major benefits are that it can be fun, easily understood, and customized to suit individual tastes.

Microsoft Windows is presently the most widely used graphical user interface for IBM PC systems and compatibles. Its main competition is the older GEM program, from Digital Research, and a new program called GeoDOS, from Geoworks, in Berkeley, California.

The Windows interface provides an alternative to the rather impersonal DOS command line interface. A significant advantage Windows has over DOS is that in the Windows environment, all programs have the same fundamental look and feel, just like they do on a Macintosh. This kind of environment smooths out the learning curve for all applications: A user will often know how to operate much of a new application simply because he or she already knows the basic concepts used.

Microsoft Windows is also a multitasking environment. Windows does not multitask in the traditional sense, but it manages to simulate the process. The technique works well enough in most cases, but it may cause degradation in performance when applications in the "background" process hardware interrupts from device drivers such as the Windows communications driver. An operational mode available for running on a 386 system (described later) gives the best performance in this area.

Windows 3 offers three operational modes that determine how Windows manages memory: Real mode is used for low-end machines, such as 8088-based systems. Standard mode, which requires at least a 286 system, allows access to the protected mode of the 286 and 386. Enhanced mode is designed specifically for 386 systems. These modes are described later in this chapter.

Windows was created by Microsoft Corporation, of Redmond, Washington. The objective of Windows was to offer computer users a system that would present all applications in a consistent manner. To get things going after the release of Windows, Microsoft developed several applications specifically for the environment, among them the very successful Microsoft Excel.

The original Microsoft Windows, version 1.03, was released in the fall of 1985. In retrospect—and in comparison with the expectations of today's users—this first release of Windows was immature. It used adjacent, "tiled" windows rather than overlapping windows, and it needed work in the area of memory management.

UNIQUE WINDOWS FEATURES

Applications in the Windows environment are presented in *windows,* boxes that have a number of unique qualities. A window can take up the entire display area when it's maximized; it can also be reduced in size, or minimized, to form an icon unique to the application. Because the Windows environment allows minimized applications to continue to run, you can have one or more applications running while using another application in the foreground.

Applications windows may also be sized, allowing display of applications in an almost infinite variety of ways. Sizing of windows allows great flexibility, letting the Windows user organize information in the manner that best suits him or her. The ability to size Windows is especially useful when you are running more than one application. It allows you to simultaneously view the applications to monitor what's happening or to have information from one application visible while you work on another.

A simple keystroke allows you to switch applications. This switching ability allows you to go from one application to another without having to exit the first application before starting the next.

Window operations, such as maximizing, minimizing, and sizing, can be performed using each window's control menu, by pressing a function key, or by using the mouse. Mouse operation is supported by all Windows applications, and its operation is consistent. A pointer moves about on the screen as the mouse is moved on the desk. Mouse buttons are used to make selections or execute a command that the pointer points to on the screen.

While a mouse isn't required by Windows, it is an extremely useful addition. In word processing or desktop publishing applications, for example, a mouse allows you to select areas of a document very quickly or mark and "drag" information from one location to another. This also works between applications: You can cut or copy data from one application and paste it into another.

Windows applications present a *dialog box* when more information is required for a particular operation. For example, more information is often required when you execute commands or when you make changes to the configuration of a program. A dialog box can contain any combination of input devices, such as text and list boxes, option and command buttons, and check boxes. Each of these items has a distinct purpose in a dialog box, and the type of item identifies its operation. For example, a check box is an on/off switch. When a check box appears in a dialog, any user already familiar with Windows knows how it works and what it means when it's checked and when it's not.

Another interesting and unique Windows feature is *dynamic data exchange (DDE)*. DDE is a protocol used by applications to exchange information directly, usually in an automated fashion. Most applications that use DDE also support a scripting or programming language. It's possible, for example, to link together a spreadsheet and a word processor to have the text document use figures from the spreadsheet. If the figures change in the spreadsheet, they also automatically change in the document.

DDE links are often used to link applications with no communications ability with those that are dedicated communications programs. For example, you can link a spreadsheet to a communications program that dials an on-line service, retrieves the latest stock quotes, and plugs them into the appropriate places in the spreadsheet.

People want to use Windows because it's attractive and fun. There are many things you can do in Windows that simply cannot be done under a

DOS character-based system. Part of this limitation is based on the type of display used in a character-based system: Because characters are of equal size, the number of characters that can be displayed on the screen at any time is limited.

Compared to character-based applications, one might think of any Windows application as having high resolution. The lettering style (font) and size of characters in Windows applications is flexible. This gives the Windows user a much wider range of options and capabilities.

Another reason to pursue Windows is that it's multitasking. It's quite convenient for running applications between which you want to exchange data. Using a communications program, for example, a user could connect to another system to view information. That information could be cut from the communications program and placed in the clipboard or into another application, such as a word processor or spreadsheet.

Advances in hardware technology have also influenced the use of Windows. Improvements in display technology make Windows look better, and make its applications even more useful. The latest VGA drivers give Windows a truly polished look.

Most Windows applications provide WYSIWYG (What You See Is What You Get) display. In word processing or desktop publishing applications, pictures are often used to represent concepts, and it's possible to mix fonts to see what your work will look like right on the screen.

NEW FEATURES FOR WINDOWS 3

If you have been using earlier versions of Windows, you will be interested in learning about the new features in version 3. The most significant additions are the Program Manager, the File Manager, and Task List.

Program Manager

The Program Manager is the first window displayed when you start Windows. It is used to organize your applications, utilities, and files into meaningful groups, making access to them easier. Figure 12-1 shows a Program Manager screen in which all windows are reduced to icons. Note that loaded or running programs are reduced to icons and placed on the desktop below

Slow, Steady Improvements

Perhaps the most important change to Microsoft Windows version 2.0 was its improved interface. The tiled window style was replaced by overlapping windows, allowing an application's window to partially or completely cover other windows. A mechanism was devised to allow the user to "flip" though the windows until the desired one was displayed. Version 2.0 also added support for more printers and video-display types.

Windows 3's differences from its preceding versions are evident from the very beginning. Installation is started from DOS, but it soon takes you into a graphical Windows 3-style program that completes the process. If you haven't previously used Windows, you start to get a feel for the environment right away. If you've been a Windows user, you immediately feel familiar with the process. Windows 3 will also optionally modify your system's start-up files (AUTOEXEC.BAT and CONFIG.SYS) as part of the installation process. Even if you're not installing Windows for the first time, it's best to let Windows do this for you. There are few reasons to make these changes manually.

The release of Windows 3 introduced many refinements that make the package truly polished. For example, many aspects of the screen have taken on a three-dimensional effect; for example, when you "push" a button, it actually appears to be depressed into the screen. The interface is perhaps Windows 3's most obvious improvement, but there are many other changes that are not quite so visible.

the Program Manager window. On an 80386 or 80486 system, the Terminal program could be running its communications processes in the background while you open and close other windows.

File Manager

The File Manager is one of the most practical additions to Windows. It allows you to use the mouse to work with files and directories in a whole

---
READ.ME

Using Windows 3

The operating modes supported by Windows 3 allow it to function optimally in almost any environment. Windows can be forced to operate in a particular mode by using a command line argument, for example, /E for enhanced or /S for standard.

The standard and 386-enhanced modes allow Windows access to protected-mode memory (memory that is beyond 1MB and that exists on a 286 or better machine). This translates into better and more efficient memory management under Windows and better performance from your applications.

Windows 3 supports the use of "virtual machines," whereby an application is allowed to run under Windows as if it were running on its own 8086. The virtual machine is essentially an 8086 emulator. This feature provides good protection against collision among applications; it's even possible for one application to crash while another keeps running. Windows 3 also supports three operating modes, which allow it to be at its best for the environment under which it is being used.

Right now, this is the hot ticket in computing. If you think you need a program like this, you should take a look at Windows 3.

---

new way. The File Manager is illustrated in Figure 12-2. Inside its window, on the left, is the Directory Tree window, which shows a graphic representation of your hard drive filing system. On the right is a directory window, which shows the files in a directory (in this case, the WINDOWS directory). With File Manager, new methods of file manipulation are possible. For example, copying a file from one directory to another or from the hard drive to the floppy drive is a matter of clicking on the file and dragging it to the appropriate directory or drive icon.

Task List

The Task List is a useful tool for moving from one window to another, especially when a lot of windows are on the desktop. You can open the Task

READ.ME

Programs that Come with Windows

Windows offers several accessories and utilities you'll want to use every day. These are located in the Accessories Group window. During your normal Windows sessions, you may want to keep any of these utilities loaded on the desktop for easy access.

Windows Write Write is a utility you can use to write, edit, format, and print documents. Although Write is not a full-featured word processor like Microsoft Word, you will no doubt find it useful for memos, letters, reports, and other everyday documents.

Windows Paint Paint is a convenient, easy-to-use drawing program. You can use it to create simple or complex drawings to be included in your Write documents or in documents created with any Windows application.

Windows Terminal Terminal is the Windows communications program of interest to readers of this book. It is used with a modem to connect to other computer systems or on-line data services over the phone line.

Windows Notepad Notepad allows you to create, store, and retrieve notes and memos quickly during your Windows sessions.

Windows Recorder Recorder allows you to save keystrokes and mouse movements so that they can be repeated at any time. Recorder is useful for establishing procedures for novice users or for replaying keystrokes and mouse sequences that you perform on a regular basis.

Windows Cardfile Cardfile is an electronic card-filing system with many of the sorting and searching features of advanced data base systems.

Windows Calendar Calendar is an appointment-scheduling utility, with day and month views, alarms, and other features.

Windows Calculator Calculator is a desktop calculator with two modes: standard and scientific.

Windows Clock Clock produces an analog or digital time display you can place on the screen during idle computer time.

PIF Editor The Program Information File (PIF) Editor is used to create and alter files used by Windows to run non-Windows applications.

Figure 12-1

Program Manager screen with all Windows icons

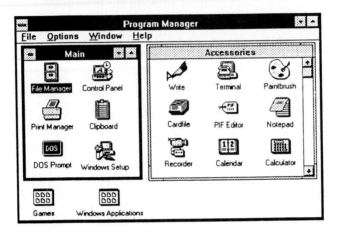

Figure 12-2

The File Manager

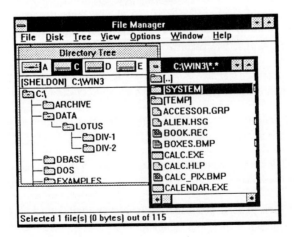

List at any time by double-clicking on the desktop. A number of applications are listed in the Task List, each representing an application in an open window or icon. To switch quickly to any application, simply click on its name. The Task List is also used to rearrange the windows and icons on the desktop.

Network Support

Windows now recognizes network connections and allows you to display and work with files on network drives and to use network printers. Popular networks such as Novell NetWare, Microsoft LAN Manager, and Banyan VINES are supported.

Additional New Features

Windows presents a whole new appearance that is the result of enhanced colors, proportionally spaced fonts, and interesting graphics icons. Along with this new interface are the following features:

- Easy installation (Windows determines how it should be installed and searches your hard drive for applications that can be run under Windows. It then creates start-up icons for the applications.)

- Full, on-line help facilities

- An enhanced Print Manager, which now supports network printing

- A utility called Recorder, which allows you to save keystrokes and mouse movements to be repeated at any time

- An enhanced Terminal communications program

- Expanded printer support

- New, expanded symbol fonts

- An enhanced 386 mode, which provides even more compatibility with non-Windows applications

- Solitaire, a new game

WINDOWS OPERATING MODES

Windows will operate in three different modes, depending on the type of hardware you have. When Windows is first started, it automatically determines which mode to use. However, you can choose to run Windows in a particular mode if the software you are attempting to run will not operate in the mode Windows selects. This may be the case with older Windows applications or non-Windows applications.

Real Mode

Windows automatically runs in real mode if your system has less than 1MB of memory or if it uses an Intel 8086 or 8088 microprocessor. Real mode is the slowest and least desirable running mode for Windows. In addition, it does not take advantage of extended memory, which means that Windows will have less memory available to run multiple applications; it may not be able to do so at all in some cases. However, real mode is often the only way to run applications written for earlier versions of Windows. If you have such applications, you can activate real mode by starting Windows with the /R option.

Standard Mode

Windows automatically runs in standard mode if your system has 1MB or more of memory and if it has an Intel 80286 microprocessor. Running in standard mode, Windows can access extended memory and allow you to switch among non-Windows applications. Multitasking is not possible in standard mode; however, a speed enhancement may be realized on some 80386 machines when operating in standard mode rather than 386 enhanced mode, owing to the lack of overhead in handling multitasking.

386 Enhanced Mode

Windows loads in 386 enhanced mode if your system has an Intel 80386/80486 microprocessor and at least 2MB of memory. Multitasking of both Windows-specific and non-Windows applications is possible in this mode.

When windows runs in 386 enhanced mode, it uses a special operating mode of the 80386/80486 microprocessor known as the "virtual 86" mode. In this mode, the 80386 or 80486 processors will act like separate 8086 microprocessors, each handling an application running in a separate window. Each virtual 8086 machine runs in its own protected environment. If a program crashes in a virtual 8086 window, the entire system is not brought down.

HARDWARE REQUIREMENTS FOR WINDOWS 3

Windows will operate on most DOS-based computers, including personal computers with Intel 8088 and 8086 processors (although the performance on these systems will not be spectacular). Windows runs best on AT-type systems with Intel 80286 microprocessors or advanced systems with Intel 80386 or 80486 microprocessors.

In general, the hardware you use should be 100-percent compatible with the tested hardware list published by Microsoft. If you have problems running Windows, you may need to obtain special software upgrades or drivers from the hardware manufacturer to make your system compatible with Windows.

The minimum software and hardware requirements are as follows:

- PC-DOS or MS-DOS 3.1 or higher
- A personal computer based on the Intel family of 8088/8086 microprocessors (this family includes the 80286, 80386, and 80486)
- A hard disk drive, with at least 8MB of free space
- A graphics monitor
- A mouse (Although a mouse is not required, operating Windows without a mouse is too difficult. This book is written with the assumption that you have a mouse.)
- A Hayes-compatible modem (if you intend to use the Windows Terminal communications software)

Other Considerations

There are a few things you may need to take into consideration before you install Windows. These have to do mainly with the type of system you intend to use and the mode it will be operating in.

Memory

Windows may use expanded or extended memory, depending on the run mode. Expanded memory is used only in the real mode; if you have an application that requires expanded memory, you may need to run your system in this mode. Standard mode and 386 mode use extended memory, which is faster and more efficient than expanded memory. If you have an 80386 system and you need to run applications that require expanded memory, you can install a special expanded-memory simulator supplied with Windows.

The expanded memory used in real mode must conform to version 4.0 of the Lotus-Intel-Microsoft Expanded Memory Specification (LIM EMS). Because extended memory is preferable to expanded memory, you should use whatever method is available to take advantage of it. While this is not possible on systems based on the 8088 and 8086 microprocessors, 80286 systems with installed memory boards like the AST RAMpage! or the Intel Above Board/AT should be installed with those boards set for extended memory. You should then run Windows in the standard mode whenever possible.

The memory requirements for the three types of systems vary.

8088/8086   Systems in this class can run only in real mode and can use only expanded memory. Set your memory-expansion boards for expanded memory. You will need 640KB of conventional memory and as much expanded memory as possible to conform to the LIM EMS 4.0 specification.

80286   Systems in this class can run in the standard mode. 1MB of memory is required, but 2MB or more is recommended.

80386/80486   Systems in this class will run Windows in 386 enhanced mode. 2MB of memory is required, but more is recommended.

Older Windows Applications

If you have applications that were written for older versions of Windows, you may not be able to run them in Standard or 386 enhanced mode. You will need to start Windows in the real mode to use these programs until you can get an update from the software manufacturer.

Memory-Resident Software

Memory-resident software remains in memory after you start it, even if you start another application. This type of software may pose problems for

Windows. Most applications that are simply loaded and then have no further interaction with the user can be loaded in the normal way before starting Windows. So-called "pop-up" programs that interact with users may need to be loaded after Windows is started.

Disk-Caching Programs

Windows uses its own disk-caching program, called SMARTDrive, to improve access to your hard drive. In most cases, you should replace your existing disk-caching program with SMARTDrive. SMARTDrive increases the efficiency of your system by keeping previously read hard disk information in memory in case you need it again. Because most computer systems typically read the same blocks of information from a disk system on a regular basis, programs like SMARTDrive offer a dramatic improvement in overall speed. This is especially true if you are running several applications at once.

SMARTDrive requires at least 512KB of extended memory or 256KB of expanded memory. The utility is installed automatically by the Windows SETUP program.

CHAPTER THIRTEEN

Operating System/2

OS/2 hit the pavement in April 1987 with 300 man-years of development effort already in place. There are those who would contend that it hit the pavement on its face, but we're talking about an operating system that is orders of magnitude more complex than DOS.

The initial release, Version 1.0, which did not include Presentation Manager (PM), was publicly released in the fall of 1987.

Presentation Manager was introduced with Version 1.1 in 1988. It might be compared to a simultaneous release of DOS and Windows, since it contained both a standard command line interface and a graphical user interface (GUI). Version 1.2 was released in 1989. Presentation Manager had a considerable facelift, but this release still suffered from a lack of functional printer drivers. Version 1.21 is the latest version available. Its most striking improvement is a wide range of new printer drivers that are much easier to install.

Version 2.0, which will take full advantage of the 80386 and newer Intel 32-bit computers, has been announced and should be available in the very near future.

READ.ME

OS/2 History

1.0	1987	This version can run in 1.5MB of RAM, but more is highly recommended. A phenomenon known as "thrashing" occurs when the operating system runs low on RAM space and must swap out to disk more frequently. Although some packages of Version 1.0 may be on dealers' shelves, this is not a recommended purchase.
1.1	1988	This was the first PM version. It should be noted that this is a little like introducing DOS and Windows simultaneously. This version needs at least 2 to 3MB of RAM. Again, more is recommended, and if you find a copy on a dealer's shelf, it is not a recommended purchase.
1.2	1989	This version introduced the new High Performance File System, extended attributes, a much improved PM, and a number of other goodies. Recommended minimum memory is 4MB. The required disk space of 8 to 20MB will depend on what facilities you install and what drivers you use. This is the only version you should buy if you are installing OS/2 yourself. You should also insist on it if you are buying your system with OS/2 installed.
2.0	1990	OS/2 Version 2.0. This version will make full use of the 80386 32-bit address capability. It will also run up to 16 virtual DOS machines, each with 600 to 620KB of available memory and access to EMS and XMS memory! You'll be able to run almost any existing DOS application. Six MB of RAM and 20MB of available disk space will be adequate, but more is highly recommended.

WHAT IS OPERATING SYSTEM/2?

Operating System/2 is a preemptive, time-slice, multitasking operating system that runs in protected mode on computers that use the Intel 80286 or

READ.ME

Virtual Memory and Protected Mode

In the early days of computers, when core memory was very expensive, computer designers hit on the idea of storing program fragments on hard disk when a particular part of a program was not being used. The idea was called *virtual memory*. The idea is great; implementation is a different story. Many applications swap data to disk, but making an operating system that can successfully swap program parts to disk presents a whole new problem.

To get such a system to work requires a special CPU and some special coding techniques. Intel's 80286, 80386, and 80486 CPUs have these capabilities, called *protected mode*. These machines will also run in what Intel calls *real mode*. In real mode, these CPUs act like fast 8086s (8088s). DOS is a real-mode operating system.

80386. When you start OS/2 Version 1.1 or 1.2, you will be running on a "desktop" similar to that of Microsoft Windows 3. From the desktop, you can start Presentation Manager applications, full-screen or windowed character-based sessions, or the DOS session.

All sessions (except the DOS session) continue to run once started. You can "detach" programs, which then run in the background like DOS terminate-and-stay-resident applications, but without the attendant side effects that tend to make TSRs unruly. You can activate detached programs with a hot key, as you might activate a TSR under DOS. All sessions and running applications make use of virtual memory.

Operating System/2 was designed to ultimately supplant DOS and take advantage of the 80286 and beyond. Most existing operating systems, including UNIX, started on mainframes and used early technology. These systems have undergone massive rewrites to keep up with the newer CPUs, but the underlying technology was simply not designed for some of the new computers.

OS/2 introduced many new techniques and concepts that take maximum advantage of the new computers. In fact, the newest version (2.0) is designed to be portable to platforms other than the Intel processors. It would be possible, for example, to port OS/2 to the Macintosh. Although OS/2 was born, so to speak, on microcomputers, it has the ability to be the operating system of the future on many computers.

OS/2, like UNIX, is based on the C language, and the first applications-development environments are designed for use with C. Other languages are available. In fact, a version of Microsoft BASIC (Version 7.0) has an add-on kit available from Microsoft that allows the development of OS/2 Presentation Manager applications. FORTRAN, COBOL, and assembly language are available, as is a Software Development Kit for Presentation Manager applications under C.

WHY USE OS/2?

OS/2 gives you a lot of options. You can have Microsoft Windows or another program running in a DOS session, several Presentation Manager and OS/2 windowed sessions running on the desktop, and several OS/2 full-screen sessions working all at the same time. The ALT-ESC key combination will bring up the Task Manager window, where you can switch to any running session or start new sessions. Although Windows 3 has some of these functions, it's not quite the same.

Key Benefits

First, you will never run out of memory. Those dread messages advising that one program or another is out of memory are a thing of the past under OS/2. And you will find it next to impossible to lock up your system. It can happen in the DOS session, but under OS/2 the offending session is simply terminated. An application may not run, but it won't clobber your system.

You have access to the functions of DOS. The OS/2 command line and Presentation Manager are under one operating environment, with a simple system of moving from session to session. If you need to make a drawing under AutoCAD while running Ventura Publisher, you simply press CTRL-ESC to get to the Task Manager, go to the group containing AutoCAD, and start AutoCAD to do your drawing. If you convert the drawing to a Ventura-compatible format, you can then go back to Ventura, exactly where you left it, and import the drawing.

If you add OS/2 LAN Manager to the mix, you have a multitasking system and a multiuser system that give you most of the advantages of a mainframe environment generally better than an "equivalent" UNIX system.

WHY MIGHT DOS BE BETTER?

With the release of MS-DOS 5.0 and Windows 3, many of the advantages of OS/2 have been provided under DOS. Many software developers have re-tooled to provide Windows 3 ports of their software, somewhat at the expense of OS/2 development. If you use a large number of DOS applications, a switch to OS/2 may be counterproductive.

There is no question that OS/2 will be around for a long time, but it's also obvious that OS/2 is still in its infancy. OS/2 will probably never eliminate DOS: There are simply too many machines in the world that still rely heavily on DOS and the capabilities it provides.

The route to OS/2 may well be through Windows 3. Microsoft is already providing a Software Migration Kit that allows Windows 3 applications to be recompiled (without rewriting) to run under OS/2 Presentation Manager.

SIMILARITIES BETWEEN DOS AND OS/2

If you are a DOS command line user and run in an OS/2 full-screen session, you will find that the DOS commands you are familiar with behave almost exactly the same under OS/2. In the DOS session, you may not be able to tell you're in OS/2 except for the help line across the top of the screen. Put simply, you will not have to relearn most of what you already know. And in case of difficulty, you can always refer to the on-line Command Reference available under OS/2.

If you use Microsoft Windows 3 (or an earlier version, for that matter) you will be very comfortable with Presentation Manager. Since it provides much the same environment as Windows, you should have little trouble understanding PM.

INSTALLING OS/2

Insert the disk labeled "Install," and reboot your computer. It really is that simple. OS/2 will load a basic version of itself, check the hardware you have installed in your computer, and prompt you for disk changes and other information as it proceeds. Screens of text will tell you what is happening as the package is installed and prompt you to accept or change various options. Help is available on screen for virtually every option.

You should be aware that to install the "dual-boot" capability under OS/2 Version 1.2, you should have DOS installed and have a DOS AUTOEXEC.BAT and CONFIG.SYS file in the root directory when you begin installation. With this requirement satisfied, OS/2 will automatically install the dual-boot feature. When installation is complete, you will be asked to remove the disk from the A drive and reboot your computer. This reboot will take from 30 seconds to a minute.

If you activate the File Manager and look in the OS2 directory, you will find a program named BOOT.COM. If you look in the OS2\SYSTEM directory you will find COMMAND.DOS, AUTOEXEC.DOS, and CONFIG.DOS. These files are used when you boot DOS. To boot DOS, go to a full-screen or windowed session and type **boot /dos** at the prompt. You will be prompted to confirm your intentions. A Yes answer will cause the system to move some files around and reboot your regular DOS. If you again take a look at the files in OS2\SYSTEM, you'll find COMMAND.OS2, AUTOEXEC.OS2, and CONFIG.OS2.

OS/2 system files are, by default, installed in an OS2 directory. It is good practice to have a DOS or BIN directory for your DOS files. Don't mix them up, and don't put the OS2 directory in your path for DOS. BOOT.COM is a "bound" program that will run in either DOS or OS/2. Make a second copy of BOOT.COM in your DOS or BIN directory. That way, you can type **boot /os2** from the root directory to reboot the system in OS/2.

OS/2 CONFIG.SYS

The OS/2 CONFIG.SYS file is far more extensive than the DOS equivalent. In the first place, it serves as both CONFIG.SYS and AUTOEXEC.BAT for OS/2 operation. Yes, I know there's an AUTOEXEC.BAT—it's used for the DOS box or DOS session under OS/2. The first time you double-click the DOS icon in the lower left corner of the screen (or select it from the Task Manager), AUTOEXEC.BAT is executed. After that, double-clicking simply switches you to the DOS box. Here is a typical OS/2 CONFIG.SYS:

```
PROTSHELL=C:\OS2\PMSHELL.EXE C:\OS2\OS2.INI
C:\OS2\OS2SYS.INI C:\OS2\CMD.EXE
SET COMSPEC=C:\OS2\CMD.EXE
LIBPATH=C:\OS2\DLL;C:\;
SET PATH=C:\OS2;C:\OS2\SYSTEM;C:\OS2\INSTALL;C:\BINP\IPF;C:\BIN
```

```
P\DTL;C:\BINP;C:\BINB;C:\ACAD;C:\ALDUS;C:\WORD;C:\;
SET DPATH=C:\OS2;C:\OS2\SYSTEM;C:\OS2\INSTALL;C:\BINP\IPF;C:\BI
NP\DTL;C:\;
SET PROMPT=$i[$p]
SET HELP=C:\OS2\HELP
SET BOOKSHELF=C:\OS2\BOOK
SET TMP=C:\OS2\TMP
SET TEMP=C:\OS2\TMP
IOPL=YES
BUFFERS=30
DISKCACHE=128
MAXWAIT=3
MEMMAN=SWAP,MOVE
PROTECTONLY=NO
SWAPPATH=C:\OS2\SYSTEM 1024
THREADS=128
SHELL=C:\OS2\COMMAND.COM /P
BREAK=OFF
FCBS=40,10
RMSIZE=640
DEVICE=C:\OS2\DOS.SYS
COUNTRY=001,C:\OS2\SYSTEM\COUNTRY.SYS
DEVINFO=SCR,VGA,C:\OS2\VIOTBL.DCP
SET VIDEO_DEVICES=VIO_IBMVGA
SET VIO_IBMVGA=DEVICE(BVHVGA)
DEVICE=C:\OS2\POINTDD.SYS
DEVICE=C:\OS2\MSSER01.SYS MODEL=199
DEVICE=C:\OS2\MOUSE.SYS TYPE=MSSER$
DEVICE=C:\OS2\PMDD.SYS
DEVICE=C:\OS2\EGA.SYS
SET KEYS=ON
DEVICE=C:\OS2\COM01.SYS
```

The CONFIG.SYS file is established when you install OS/2. It probably won't look exactly like this one, but if you've used DOS CONFIG.SYS, you will understand a lot about this one.

From the top, the PROTSHELL= statement is like the SHELL= statement in a DOS CONFIG.SYS. It establishes PMSHELL as the Presentation Manager SHELL and CMD.EXE as the character-based shell (equivalent to COMMAND.COM in DOS). It also indicates the INI files (somewhat like WIN.INI in Windows) that will be used. The SET COMSPEC= statement is normally included in AUTOEXEC.BAT for DOS, but we put it here for the OS/2 DOS session.

Most of OS/2 runs from dynamic link libraries (DLLs). You will probably find close to 100 DLL files, some DRV files and a couple of FON files in your OS2\DLL directory. The LIBPATH= statement tells OS/2 where to find these. You can add to this path as you would any other, or you can simply copy *all* DLL files to this directory.

SET PATH= is identical to the DOS command. SET DPATH= is an addition that lets you point to DATA files. SET PROMPT= sets the prompt for OS/2 full-screen and windowed sessions. The remaining SET statements are like those in DOS in that they point to resources or temp-file locations.

IOPL (Input/Output Privilege Level) can be set to YES or NO. If set to YES, it allows DOS- and OS/2-session programs to directly access COM, LPT, and other ports. IOPL needs to be set to YES if you intend to run communications programs from the DOS session. Buffers= is identical to that command in DOS and applies to the DOS session. DISKCACHE= establishes a disk cache for OS/2 operations.

We've already said that OS/2 is a preemptive, time-slice, multitasking operating system. If we start a very long spreadsheet calculation, we may want to work on something else at the same time. In a true multitasking system, we must expect that if we next start a C program compilation, each running program will get a fair share of time on the processor. For this reason, OS/2 implements a priority system that ensures that no running program is starved for processor time.

Part of the kernel is a program that simply monitors running programs and their priority and switches between them as required. If a thread is waiting for processor time and doesn't get any, the kernel will boost its priority after the number of seconds specified by MAXWAIT=. There are also TIMESLICE and PRIORITY settings that could be made, but in the CONFIG.SYS file shown, we choose the chicken's way out and take the defaults.

MEMMAN= has to do with virtual-memory operations. The selections can be SWAP or NOSWAP and MOVE or NOMOVE. SWAP means that program segments can be swapped out to disk if required. MOVE means that OS/2 is allowed to compact memory by moving segments around if required.

PROTECTONLY= can be either YES or NO. If YES, the DOS session is disabled. SWAPPATH= establishes the path and size of the swap file used for virtual-memory operations. The THREADS= statement specifies the maximum number of threads that can be running simultaneously.

The remainder of the entries involve the DOS session, the display, and the mouse. The very last entry loads a COM driver for communication ports in the DOS session, which must be present for DOS-session communications.

We've left out a lot, but this should get you past some of the rough spots. More information is available in your OS/2 system documentation.

START.CMD

When OS/2 starts, you will have the Desktop Manager, Print Manager, Group-Main, and the DOS-session icon available on the PM Desktop. You can establish additional groups from the Group menu selection in the Desktop Manager. You can set up additional programs to run from these groups using the Program menu selection in the Group window.

You may also want to start other programs that will reside on the Desktop so that they can be more easily selected. The File Manager will take some time to initialize, depending on the size of your hard disk, since it reads, sorts, and displays a directory tree. You may want to set up a group of programs in a file named STARTUP.CMD or INIT.CMD. The following are some suggestions for inclusion:

```
mode com2:9600,n,8,1
START "File Manager" /PM /I C:\OS2\PMFILE.EXE
START "Process Status" /PM /I C:\PROFILER\PS.EXE
START "Clock" /PM /I C:\OS2\DIGCLOCK.EXE
detach qh -120 -m50 -q
```

This file first runs MODE to set COM port 2 for serial communication. Each START entry has a name in double quotes that will appear with the icon on the Desktop. The /PM tells START that this is a Presentation Manager application; /I indicates that it is to start as an icon. The final part is the path and program name of the program to start. The last entry starts Quick Help (QH.EXE) as a background program. Like a DOS TSR, it shows itself only when the appropriate hot key is pressed.

If you name the file STARTUP.CMD, you can add it to Group-Main or another group of your choice and activate it once the system is started. If, for example, your serial printer is attached to COM2, this is an excellent way to ensure that it's properly initialized.

AUTOEXEC.BAT

This file applies to the DOS session only and is run once the first time you activate the DOS session. You can do many of the things you do in DOS, as you can see from the listing:

```
PATH C:\OS2;C:\OS2\SYSTEM;C:\BIN;C:\WORD;C:\WINDOWS
APPEND C:\OS2;C:\OS2\SYSTEM
SET COMSPEC=C:\OS2\COMMAND.COM
CALL HELP ON
COPY C:\OS2\COMMAND.COM C:\ >NUL
setcom40 com2=on
mode com2:9600,n,8,1,p
```

The first three entries should be familiar. CALL HELP ON is part of the OS/2 Help system and puts a Help message bar across the top of the DOS screen. The COPY command copies OS/2 COMMAND.COM (the DOS session shell) to the root directory, redirecting any messages to never-never-land (NUL).

The last two entries are required to establish serial communication in the DOS session. SETCOM40 COM2=ON simply turns on com2 capabilities for the DOS session. MODE sets the parameters for the COM port. (Yes, you just set it in OS/2. But, believe me, you must do it again for the DOS session. They are separate drivers and must be initialized.)

In both cases, the ports have been set for a serial printer running at 9600 baud. If you are running a communication program that sets communication parameters, you will need to use only the SETCOM40 entry to activate the port for DOS.

WORKING WITH OS/2

When OS/2 Version 1.2 starts you will see a gray Desktop with several items on it. It has the flavor of Microsoft Windows in that items on screen have such things as a title bar, a menu bar, scroll bars, and the like. The Desktop Manager can be identified by its appearance and by its title bar. Shown in Figure 13-1, the Desktop Manager is your point of focus for all operations in OS/2. From it, you can manage Groups and other systemwide things, such as "Shut down" and "Close all."

Figure 13-1

The OS/2 Desktop Manager

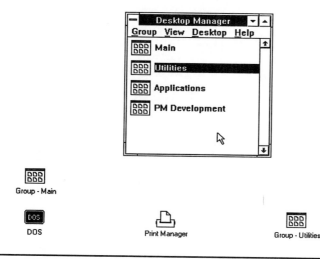

Figure 13-2 shows the Task List. You can access the Task List by pressing CTRL-ESC. You can then switch to any listed task by selecting it and clicking the "Switch to" button or by simply double-clicking on your selection.

Figure 13-3 shows the Group menu selected (in the Desktop Manager window). From this menu you can open a group. New... allows you to make a new group. Delete... will delete an existing group, and Rename... will allow you to rename a selected group.

If you select OS/2 Full Screen in Group-Main, then select Program, and from the Program menu select Properties, you will get the screen shown in Figure 13-4. This screen allows you to set the various properties of programs you want to run from the Group box. You can always get Help by selecting an item and pressing F1.

Figure 13-5 shows the System Editor screen. This editor will allow you to edit files but you not print them.

Figure 13-6 shows the Command Reference. This is your on-line documentation that provides detailed Help on much of OS/2. Again, you can best

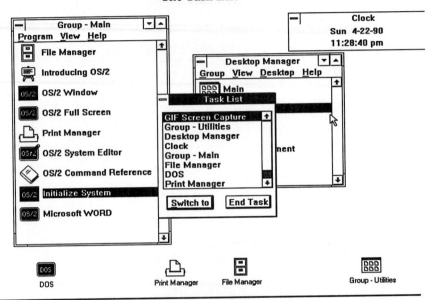

Figure 13-2

The Task List

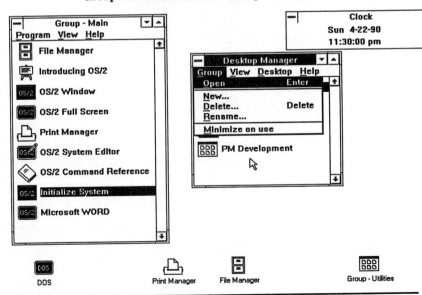

Figure 13-3

Group menu selected in Desktop Manager

Figure 13-4

The Properties dialog box

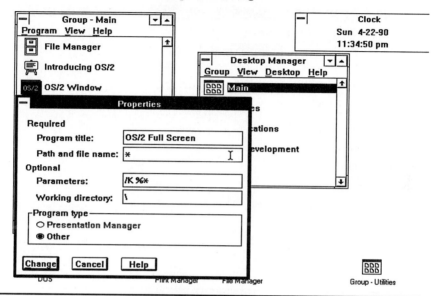

Figure 13-5

The System Editor screen

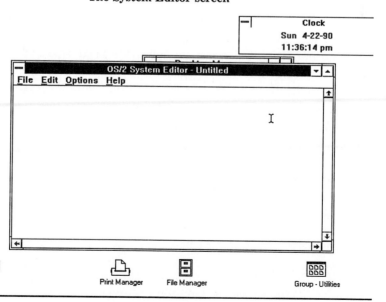

Figure 13-6

The Command Reference

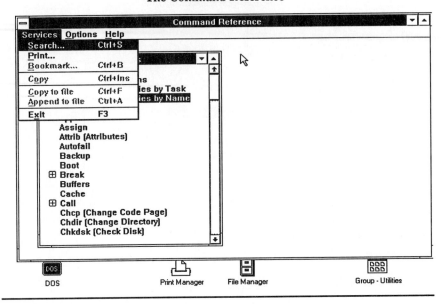

learn how to use the Command Reference by selecting various items and using the built-in Help facilities.

The OS/2 File Manager (like the Windows 3 File Manager) is a very powerful way to manage your disk space. It presents the disk space as a directory tree, from which you can move and make selections. (A complete discussion would take more pages than we have available.) Figure 13-7 shows the File Manager screen. Figure 13-8 shows the same screen with the contents of one directory displayed as icons and the File menu pulled down. A look at this menu will give you some idea of the richness of File Manager.

OS/2 AND DOS SESSION COMMANDS

The following commands are either OS/2 specific or have significant differences from their DOS counterparts. There are many other commands, but they are, for the most part, identical to those in DOS.

autofail=yes|no
Turns hard error messages on or off.

Figure 13-7

The File Manager screen

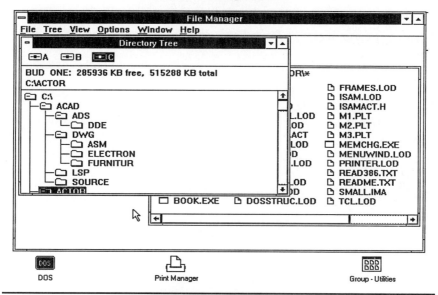

Figure 13-8

Another look at File Manager

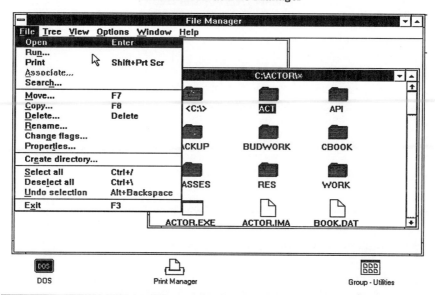

yes   Turns on the AUTOFAIL mechanism, preventing OS/2 from displaying a full-screen error message.

no   Turns off the AUTOFAIL mechanism, allowing OS/2 to display a full-screen error message for a hard error or exception condition. This is the default setting.

boot [/dos | /os2 | /q]

Specifies the operating system (DOS or OS/2) your computer is to use the next time you restart it. You must have dual-boot installed on your computer before you can use the BOOT utility.

/dos   Specifies DOS as the operating system.

/os2   Specifies OS/2 as the operating system.

/q   Displays the current BOOT setting.

cache [/MaxAge:*time*] [/DiskIdle:*time*] [/BufferIdle:*time*] or cache [/lazy:on|/lazy:off]

Directs OS/2 to load the cache driver for the High-Performance File System (HPFS), turn lazy writing on or off, and set or display the lazy-writing parameters.

/MaxAge:*time*   Sets the maximum amount of time (in milliseconds) that a cache block can store information before OS/2 writes that information to the disk. The default time is 5000 milliseconds.

/DiskIdle:*time*   Sets the maximum amount of time (in milliseconds) that the disk can be idle before OS/2 writes unsaved information in the cache blocks to the disk. The default time is 1000 milliseconds.

/BufferIdle:*time*   Sets the maximum amount of time (in milliseconds) that a cache block can store information before it becomes subject to the effect of the /DiskIdle option. The default time is 500 milliseconds.

/lazy:on|/lazy:off   Turns lazy writing on or off for all disks or partitions that are formatted for HPFS. The default setting is on.

chcp [*nnn*]

Switches to the specified system code page, which must have been defined previously in your CONFIG.SYS file.

nnn   Specifies the code page to be used. This argument must be a three-digit number from the list under the CODEPAGE command.

chkdsk [*drive:*][*path*][*filename*] [/c] [/f[:*n*]] [/v]

Checks a disk or partition for errors and displays a summary of how space is used on that disk or partition.

drive: Specifies the disk drive to check.

filename   (FAT file system only) Specifies the file to check.

/c   (dHPFS only) Specifies that the CHKDSK utility is to correct errors only if the file system was in an inconsistent state when you restarted your computer; if the file system was in a consistent state, CHKDSK simply terminates, regardless of what other options you have specified.

/f [:*n*]   Specifies that the CHKDSK utility is to correct errors it finds on the disk. If you do not specify this option, CHKDSK does not correct any errors. The *n* argument is available only for HPFS. It specifies the level of data recovery and must be a number in the range 0 through 3; the default level is 2.

/v   Displays the name of each file in each directory as it is checked.

cmd [*drive:*][*path*] [/s] [/c *command* (s)|/k *command* (s)]

Starts a new OS/2 command interpreter.

drive:path   Specifies the location of CMD.EXE.

/s   Instructs the new command interpreter not to set up the signal handler.

/c *command* (s)   Instructs the new command interpreter to perform the command or commands specified and then return control to the command interpreter that called it. If you specify multiple commands, separate each pair with an ampersand (&).

/k *command(s)* Instructs the new command interpreter to perform the command or commands specified and then continue to run. If you specify multiple commands, separate each pair with an ampersand (&).

detach *command* [*options*]

Detaches a process to run in the background while you go on to another task.

command Specifies any OS/2 program or command that does not require you to type input from the keyboard.

options Specifies any valid options that the program or command can accept in the command line.

diskcache=*n*[,*m*]

Enables disk caching for the FAT file system and specifies the amount of memory to be set aside for the disk cache. To use this command, place it in your CONFIG.SYS file.

n Specifies the amount of memory, in kilobytes, to be set aside for the disk cache. This number must be in the range 64 through 7200.

m Specifies the disk-cache threshold value, in sectors. If the data exceeds *m* sectors, OS/2 does not store it in the disk cache. This value must be in the range 1 through 32; the default value is 7.

dpath [;|[*drive* :]*path*[;...]]

Specifies which directories besides the current directory an application should search to find data files (files with extensions other than EXE, COM, BAT, or CMD).

; When used alone (**dpath** ;), clears all data-path settings. Semicolons are also used to separate multiple data paths.

path Specifies the path of the directory that you want the application to search. You can specify more than one path, separating them with semicolons.

If you type **dpath** by itself, OS/2 displays the current data path.

eautil [/s [/r] [/p] | /j [/o | /m] [/p]] *filename* [*holdfile*]

Deletes or copies (splits) the extended attributes from a data file or directory and stores them in a separate file, or copies (joins) the extended attributes back to the original data file or directory. The EAUTIL utility enables applications that do not recognize extended attributes to manipulate files and directories without losing their extended attributes. The utility also enables you to send files over a network or copy them to systems that do not recognize extended attributes without losing their extended attributes.

filename Specifies the data file or directory to copy the extended attributes from or back to.

holdfile Specifies the file to store the extended attributes in or copy them back from. If you do not specify a filename for *holdfile* when splitting extended attributes, the EAUTIL utility creates a file with the same name as *filename* and stores it in a directory named EAS.

If you do not specify a filename for *holdfile* when joining extended attributes, EAUTIL looks in the EAS directory for a file with the same name as *filename*.

When you use the EAUTIL utility to split the extended attributes from a file or directory, you use the /s option. When you specify /s, you can also specify the /r and /p options.

/s Copies the extended attributes from *filename* to *holdfile*. This is the default option.

/r Replaces the contents of *holdfile* with the extended attributes currently attached to *filename*. This option is used with the /s option. If *holdfile* already exists, you must specify the /r option to copy the extended attributes from *filename*; otherwise, the operation will fail.

/p When used with the /s option, preserves the extended attributes attached to *filename*. If this option is not set, the EAUTIL utility deletes the extended attributes from *filename* after copying them to *holdfile*.

When you use the EAUTIL utility to join extended attributes to a file or directory, you use the /j option. When you specify /j, you can also specify the /o or the /m option and the /p option. If you specify the /j option and there are already extended attributes attached to *filename*, you must specify either the /o or the /m option, or the operation will fail.

/j   Copies the extended attributes from *holdfile* back to *filename.*

/o   Overwrites the extended attributes attached to *filename,* replacing them with the extended attributes in *holdfile.* This option is used with the /j option. You cannot specify the /o option with the /m option.

/m   Adds (merges) the extended attributes in *holdfile* to those in *filename.* This option is used with the /j option. You cannot specify the /m option with the /o option.

/p   When used with the /j option, preserves *holdfile* after the extended attributes in it have been copied to *filename.* If the /p option is not set, the EAUTIL utility deletes *holdfile* after joining the extended attributes to *filename.*

extproc [*drive*:][*path*]*filename* [*options*]
Defines an external batch processor for a batch file. You can use this command only in a batch file.

filename   Specifies the name of the file that contains the external batch processor. The filename must include the extension. You can also include a drive and a path, if necessary.

options   Specifies any valid options for the new batch processor.
    By putting this command as the first line of your batch file, you cause OS/2 to start a different batch processor and use that to run the batch file.
    You can use this command only in OS/2 batch files (files with the extension CMD).

fcbs=*x,y*
Specifies the number of file control blocks (FCBs) OS/2 can have open at one time and the number of those it cannot automatically close when too many FCBs are open. To use this command, place it in your CONFIG.SYS file.

x   Specifies the maximum number of file control blocks that can be open at one time. This number must be in the range 1 through 255; the default value is 16.

y   Specifies the number of file control blocks that OS/2 cannot close automatically.

This number must be in the range 0 through 255 and must be less than
or equal to *x*; the default value is 8.

help [on|off |*messageid* | [*document*] *topic*]

Displays Help information about OS/2 and about error or warning messages
displayed in an OS/2 session or in the DOS session, or starts a Presentation
Manager application that lets you view topics within an on-line reference
document.

on   Displays a Help line at the top of your screen. This line tells you how
to get Help and how to get back to Desktop Manager. The HELP ON
command replaces your current prompt setting with the Help line and the
current drive letter.

off   Removes the Help line from your screen. This is the default setting.

messageid   Identifies the particular Help message that you want more
information about. The message identification number consists of three
letters (for example, SYS) followed by a four-digit number. For system
messages, you can also specify the number without the letters and leading
zeros (for example, SYS0002 can be specified as 2).

document   Specifies the file that contains the reference document you want
to view. If you do not specify a document, the Help utility uses the OS/2
Command Reference. If you do not specify the filename extension, Help
uses the extension INF.

topic   Specifies the topic you want to view information about. For the OS/2
Command Reference, this can be the name of a command or utility or any
other topic listed in the table of contents. If you specify *document* but do
not specify *topic*, the Help utility displays the table of contents of *document*.
If you type only the first part of a topic name, Help displays the first topic
that matches the partial name.

If you type **help** by itself, the utility displays a list of Help options and
information.

The OS/2 installation program places the following line in your CON-
FIG.SYS file:

```
set bookshelf=c:\os2\book
```

The Help utility searches for the document file in the directory specified in the BOOKSHELF environment variable. If you do not explicitly name the document, Help searches each document in the directory for the topic. You can add other directories to the BOOKSHELF environment variable.

Help works the same way in a DOS session as it does in an OS/2 session.

ifs = [*drive* :][*path*]*filename* [/c[ache]:*nnnn*]

Installs the driver for an installable file system and specifies the amount of memory to be reserved for disk caching. To use this command, place it in your CONFIG.SYS file.

filename   Specifies the name of the file that contains the file-system driver. If this file is not in the root directory of the start-up drive, you must include the drive or path.

/c[ache]:*nnnn*   (dHPFS only) Specifies the amount of memory, in kilobytes, to be set aside for disk caching by the installable file system. You can abbreviate "/cache" as "/c". The value of *nnnn* must be a number in the range 64 through 2048 and should be a multiple of 2, since HPFS divides the cache into 2KB blocks. If you specify an odd number when you are installing the HPFS driver, OS/2 rounds it down to the next even number.

The default cache size is either 64KB or 10 percent of the total available memory, whichever is greater.

The IFS command should precede any device command in your CONFIG.SYS file except those that load device drivers required by the installable file system.

iopl = yes|no|*program*[,...]

Specifies whether OS/2 can give data-input/output privilege to a process that requests it in an OS/2 session. To use this command, place it in your CONFIG.SYS file.

yes   Allows OS/2 to give input/output privilege to a process.

no   Prevents OS/2 from giving input/output privilege to a process. This is the default setting.

program   Specifies the program that will be granted input/output privilege on request. You can specify more than one program, separating the names with commas.

libpath = [*drive*:]*path*[;[*drive*:]*path*][...]
Specifies the directories OS/2 is to search for dynamic-link libraries. To use this command, place it in your CONFIG.SYS file.

drive: Specifies the drive where dynamic-link libraries are located. If you do not specify a drive, OS/2 searches the disk in the current drive.

path   Specifies the directory to search for dynamic-link libraries. You can specify more than one directory, separating the names with semicolons.

maxwait = *x*
Sets the maximum time a process must wait before OS/2 increases its priority. To use this command, place it in your CONFIG.SYS file.

x   Specifies the number of seconds a process must wait before it is given a higher priority. This number must be in the range 1 through 255; the default value is 3.

When an active process has waited *x* seconds without running, the OS/2 scheduler increases the priority of the process for one execution cycle (time slice—for more information about time slices, see the TIMESLICE command).

The MAXWAIT command has no effect if the priority command is set to absolute.

memman = [swap|noswap][,][move|nomove][,][swapdos|no swapdos]
Specifies whether OS/2 can swap memory segments between memory and disk and whether it can temporarily move segments. To use this command, place it in your CONFIG.SYS file.

swap   Allows swapping of segments.

noswap   Prevents swapping of segments.

move   Allows moving of segments.

nomove   Prevents moving of segments.

swapdos   Allows swapping of memory segments from the DOS session. If you specify SWAPDOS, OS/2 automatically sets the swap and move options.

noswapdos   Prevents swapping of memory segments from the DOS session.

You can use a space instead of a comma to separate the arguments of a MEMMAN command.

The OS/2 installation program places a MEMMAN command in your CONFIG.SYS file.

If you start OS/2 from a hard disk, the default setting is MEMMAN = SWAP,MOVE,NOSWAPDOS; if you start from a floppy disk, the default setting is MEMMAN = NOSWAP,MOVE,NOSWAPDOS. If you have disabled the DOS session by specifying PROTECTONLY = YES in your CONFIG.SYS file, the installation program does not place the NOSWAPDOS argument in your CONFIG.SYS file.

move [*drive* :][*path1*]*source* [*path2*][*destination*]
Moves a file or directory from one directory to another on the same drive.

source   Specifies the file or directory to be moved. You can use wildcard characters to specify a group of files, but you can move only one directory at a time.

destination   Specifies where the file or directory is to be moved. If you are moving a file, the destination can be either a file or a directory.

You can change the name of a file or directory as you move it by specifying a new name in *destination*.

priority = absolute|dynamic
Specifies how a process receives enough priority over other processes to run. To use this command, place it in your CONFIG.SYS file.

absolute   Prevents the system from dynamically changing the priority of processes in the general-priority category.

dynamic   Instructs OS/2 to try to determine which process needs CPU resources most in any given interval of time (time slice).

protectonly = yes|no
Specifies whether OS/2 is to enable the DOS session. To use this command, place it in your CONFIG.SYS file.

protshell = [*drive:*][*path*]*filename* [*arguments*]
Specifies the user interface OS/2 is to use and the command interpreter to use in an OS/2 session. To use this command, place it in your CONFIG.SYS file.

filename Specifies the file that contains the user interface.

arguments Specifies the drive, path, and filename of the OS/2 initialization file and command interpreter.

replace [*drive:*][*path*]*filename* [[*drive:*]*path*] [[/a|/s]|[/a|/u]] [/p] [/r] [/w] [/f]
Selectively replaces files in the destination directory with new versions of those files from the source directory, or adds new files to the destination directory.

filename Specifies the source file that is to replace the file on the destination disk. You can use wildcard characters in the source-file name to replace groups of files that have similar names.

path Specifies the directory that contains the file to be replaced or to which you want to add the file. If you do not specify a directory, REPLACE uses the current directory on the current drive.

/a Adds only the files specified in *filename* that do not exist in the destination directory and does not replace existing files. You cannot use this option with the /s option.

/p Prompts you for confirmation before replacing or adding a file.

/r Replaces read-only files as well as unprotected files. If you do not use this option and you try to replace a read-only file, the replacement process stops and you see an error message.

/s   Replaces files in the subdirectories of the destination directory if the filenames match those specified in *filename*. The REPLACE utility never searches subdirectories of the source directory. You cannot use this option with the /a option.

/u   Replaces only the target files that are older than their corresponding source files. You cannot use this option with the /a option.

/w   Instructs the REPLACE utility to wait for you to insert a disk before beginning to search for source files. Otherwise, REPLACE starts replacing or adding files immediately.

/f   Specifies that the REPLACE utility should not discard the extended attributes of a file if the destination-file system does not support extended attributes. In this case, the utility does not replace the file.

rmsize=*x*

Specifies the amount of memory that OS/2 is to reserve for the DOS session. To use this command, place it in your CONFIG.SYS file.

x   Specifies the size, in KB, of the portion of memory reserved for the DOS session. This number must be in the range 256 through 640. The default value depends on the total amount of system memory.

run=[*drive*:][*path*]*filename* [*arguments*]

Starts a background program when you start your system. To use this command, place it in your CONFIG.SYS file.

filename   Specifies the program you want to start, which must be one that can run in the background. You must include the extension (COM or EXE), and you must give the drive and path if the file is not located in the root directory of your start-up drive. The file cannot be a batch file.

arguments   Specifies any valid options or other variables for the program.
      You can include more than one RUN command in your CONFIG.SYS file.
      OS/2 processes all the device commands in your CONFIG.SYS file before it starts processing RUN commands.

When processing a CONFIG.SYS file, OS/2 preserves the difference between uppercase and lowercase letters in arguments. This can be important for some programs that are case sensitive.

To run a program that requires input from you, use the CALL command.

In OS/2, you can use the SET command to define an environment variable by naming the variable and giving a value for it. You can use the SET command from the command line in CMD, or by placing it in your CONFIG.SYS file.

setcom40 COM*x* = on|off
Sets the address of the specified serial port so that a DOS application can find the port and use it.

x Specifies the number of the serial port for which you want to set the address. This number can be 1, 2, or 3.

on Sets the address of the serial port in memory.

off Removes the address of the serial port from memory.
If you used the device-configuration command in your CONFIG.SYS file to load the COM0*x*.SYS device driver, you must use the SETCOM40 utility before you run a DOS application. Most DOS applications send their output directly to the serial port rather than through the COM0*x*.SYS device driver; so, they must have the port address.

You must set the port address before you start the DOS application.

start ["*session*"] [/k |/c |/n] [/f] [/fs |/win |/pm] [/i] [/pgm] [*drive:*][*path*]*command*[*.ext*] [*options*] or start "*session*" [/k |/c] [/f] [/fs |/win |/pm] [/i] "[*drive:*][*path*]*command*[*.ext*] [*options*]" or start ["*session*"] [/k] [/f] [/fs |/win] [/i]
Starts an OS/2 command interpreter and tells it to carry out the command you specify.

session Specifies the name of the new session as it will appear in the Task List. The name can be up to 60 characters and can include spaces; it must be surrounded by double quotation marks. If you do not specify a name, OS/2 uses the filename you specify for the *command* argument. If you do not specify either *session* or *command*, OS/2 uses CMD.EXE.

/k   Instructs the new command interpreter to run the command you specify and then keep the session open when the command is completed. This is
the default option, unless *command* starts a Presentation Manager application, in which case the default option is /n. You cannot use /k with the /pm
option.

/c   Instructs the new command interpreter to carry out *command* and then
end the session and return to the program from which it was started. You
cannot use this option with the /pm option.

/n   Instructs OS/2 to run *command* without starting a new command
interpreter. This is the default option when *command* starts a Presentation
Manager application. You cannot use /n if you have enclosed the command
and its options in double quotation marks (see the following *options* description), nor can you use /n if *command* is a batch file or if it attempts to use a
batch file (batch files require CMD as their batch processor).

/f   Instructs OS/2 to run *command* in the foreground. Note that if you use
several START commands in a batch file, you can use only one /f option;
OS/2 ignores all but the first one.

/fs   Instructs OS/2 to run *command* as a full-screen application in the
foreground, in a session independent of Presentation Manager.

/win   Instructs OS/2 to run *command* in a foreground Presentation Manager window.

/pm   Instructs OS/2 to run *command* as a Presentation Manager application. You cannot use this option with the /k or /c option, nor can you use it if
command is a batch file.

/i   Instructs OS/2 to give the new session the environment set in your
CONFIG.SYS file. The environment includes environment variables, such as
path, dpath, and the drive and directory for a session.

/pgm   Specifies that the quoted string following this option in the command
line is the name of the program to be run.

threads=*x*

Specifies the number of threads OS/2 can run at one time. To use this command, place it in your CONFIG.SYS file.

x   Specifies the number of threads. This number must be in the range 64 through 512; the OS/2 installation program sets the number to 128.

timeslice=*x*[,*y*]

Sets the amount of time that OS/2 allocates to a thread before checking the priority of other threads. Time slices are the units of time that OS/2 uses to schedule its activities. To use this command, place it in your CONFIG.SYS file.

x   Specifies the minimum length of the time slice, in milliseconds; the default value is 32.

y   Specifies the maximum length of the time slice, in milliseconds. This number must be equal to or greater than *x*. If you do not specify *y*, OS/2 uses *x* as the maximum length. If you do not include the TIMESLICE command in your CONFIG.SYS file, the default value of *y* is 248.

unpack [*drive*:][*path*]*filename* [*drive2*:][*path2*] [/v]

Decompresses and copies a compressed file.

filename   Specifies the name of the compressed file. This filename has an @ symbol as the third character of its extension.

drive2:   Specifies the drive you want the files to be copied to. If you do not specify a drive, the UNPACK utility uses the current drive.

path2   Specifies the directory you want the files to be copied to. If you do not specify a directory, the UNPACK utility uses the current directory on the specified drive. The utility always uses the original filename and extension as the destination filename.

/v   Checks (verifies) whether the sectors that the files were written to can be read.

CHAPTER FOURTEEN

DOS and UNIX

In this chapter, we discuss the major features of UNIX and compare them with comparable DOS features. DOS and UNIX are surprisingly similar in many ways, even though they were developed for different purposes and distinct machines.

WHAT IS UNIX?

UNIX is a multiuser, multitasking operating system. It is designed to be used by many users at once, each of whom may run multiple programs, or *processes*. DOS is a single-user operating system and is incapable of true multitasking on its own.

Because the operating system is standardized, any UNIX machine can communicate with any other. Thus, UNIX is an ideal operating system to use for a network. Some of the largest and best-maintained networks, such as Internet, are connected to UNIX machines.

Different programs are blocked from interfering with each other and with the operating system. The operating system controls the memory allocated for each program. UNIX also uses *virtual memory management*. In virtual memory management, the memory state for one program may be saved to disk temporarily so that another program can have access to more memory. Once the memory log is done, the suspended program is loaded back from disk to its original memory space.

To prevent unauthorized users from accessing the system, the operating system requires you to log on each time you want to use the machine. You need to provide your name and a password, which you select when you first access the system.

UNIX uses the concepts of permissions, file ownership, and group membership to secure and protect files. This is indispensable in the UNIX world, where users might have access to each other's files. To define a group, you specify users who are able to read or execute files that belong to other members of the group. Once specified, this group affiliation helps determine who gets access to a file. For example, if one of your files has READ permission for the group, then any member of the specified group can read the file. (It's common to give a group READ permission but to deny it WRITE permission for files.)

UNIX is used on university campuses, where it runs mostly on large minicomputers. The schools are allowed to use it without paying a fee. UNIX is also popular on high-end workstations, such as Sun machines. Traditionally, these have been the environments in which UNIX is most strongly entrenched.

Over the past few years, UNIX has become more widely used on Intel-architecture machines that run DOS. Along with this migration have come programs to fulfill the needs of people with such machines.

THE ROOTS OF UNIX

UNIX was developed in 1969 and 1970 by a programming group at AT&T Bell Labs (then just Bell Labs). This group included Dennis Ritchie, Ken Thompson, and Rudd Canaday. These programmers had worked on an operating-systems project from which AT&T Bell Labs had withdrawn its support. They were looking for new challenges.

While they tried to accomplish an impossible task—to get equipment and money from management—these programmers began to design components of the operating system they would write once they were budgeted for the hardware. They sketched out the basic design of the UNIX file system.

Around the same time, Thompson worked to move a "Space Travel" game he had written to an available PDP-7 computer at the labs. In the process, he wrote the first components of the UNIX operating system. Ritchie and Thompson named their system UNIX, playing off the name of the operating system in the defunct project, Multics.

The earliest parts of the UNIX operating system included the file system, utilities to manipulate files (copy, delete, print, and so on), and a simple shell to serve as the command interpreter. (This primitive version had limited process control; current versions keep dozens of projects scheduled.)

In the next phase, the group asked for a PDP-11 to develop a text-processing system. J. F. Ossanna, another member of the group, was the driving force behind this proposal. When the request was granted, UNIX was transferred to the new machine. In the move, the system's process-scheduling facilities and several other features were improved. The first implementation on the PDP-11 ran in 24K, using 16K for the operating system and 8K for user programs. Files could be stored on a disk with a capacity of 512K, for which the machine had one drive.

The "roff text formatter" was one of the first major applications programs written in the UNIX system. This program could produce pages with numbered lines, something the Bell Labs patent department needed. As a result, three typists from this department were supported on the PDP-11 for about 6 months. The typists served as testers for the operating system and the text-formatting software. The software served as a tool for the patent department.

To manage all this in 24K of memory was impressive. And they did it with a single disk drive, which had a capacity of 512K! (Whenever the disk was full, the contents had to be transferred to tape.)

The original UNIX was written in assembly language. However, in its infancy, most of UNIX was rewritten in C. The development of C actually stems from the development of UNIX. C was developed from another language, called B, which was developed out of an abortive FORTRAN compiler project.

From its inception, the philosophy behind UNIX was to build a library of specialized functions for the computing environment. UNIX was also a community project. People added components to extend the operating system.

Over the years, many people have contributed to UNIX. Some of the more important contributions include pipes and redirection, sophisticated text-editing and formatting capabilities, compilers, and calculators. Several shells have been developed for UNIX. Three of these, the Bourne, C, and Korn shells, are in wide use in the UNIX community.

UNIX Takes Root

When the new operating system was developed and stabilized, Bell Labs made the operating system and source code freely available to universities and research institutions.

For the first time, an extendable operating system was available to a community of researchers and problem solvers. The universities began to modify and enhance UNIX. With UNIX in use on computers used for teaching, thousands of future computer scientists were educated with the operating system. This increased the demand for UNIX in the workplace.

By the late 1970s, the University of California at Berkeley had standardized many UNIX extensions and modifications. The university's version became known as the BSD version, to distinguish it from the AT&T versions. AT&T's System III and V versions of the operating system were developed and released by the early 1980s. AT&T also developed a System IV. This was used internally at AT&T but never distributed for general use. (System III and System V are for public use. System V is still the current version; however, several releases of this version have appeared. The most recent of these is Release 4.)

While there are considerable differences between the Berkeley and AT&T implementations, they have becomes more alike over the years. In particular, AT&T has incorporated many of the BSD features as it has prepared UNIX for the general market. For example, the C shell, popular among UNIX users, was created for the BSD version but was ported to System V and other versions.

A Graphics Standard for UNIX

For years, UNIX was a text-based operating system. Recently, various window-environment and graphics interfaces have been developed. The X Window system appears to be a good bet to become the de facto standard. This system was developed at MIT for its Project Athena, a large-scale computer project.

The hardware goal for Project Athena is to have about 10,000 terminals hooked up all over a college campus. The terminals and other hardware for the project have been donated by Athena's two major corporate sponsors: Digital Equipment Corporation and IBM. Both types of terminals would be scattered around campus. All students would have accounts. Any student would be able to log on at any terminal. Once logged on, the student could access any of the programs.

The programs need to be capable of running on either terminal type. The appropriate drivers should take care of any interface differences. Problem-free delivery should be possible even if the program relies heavily on graphics, as many of the Athena programs do.

Project Athena provides important experience in dealing with two major issues: connecting lots of machines and delivering graphics on different types of terminals. UNIX is an ideal way to resolve the first issue. The second, graphics, is difficult for UNIX.

Relatively little attention had been paid to graphics. To solve the graphics dilemma, MIT researchers resorted to an old UNIX technique: build it yourself. The X Window system was developed to make the programmers' lives easier. When the X Window system was distributed to other UNIX installations (a common practice in the world of UNIX), it was well received. A new tool was added to the UNIX collection.

The Flavors of UNIX

UNIX is *portable*, meaning that it can be transferred to different environments. This is partly because of the operating system's design philosophy and partly because it was coded in C (a high-level, but fast, language). Today, UNIX runs on computers that range from 8088 machines to supercomputers. In addition to the AT&T System V and the Berkeley BSD version, several other UNIX versions are available.

XENIX   XENIX was developed by Microsoft as a pared-down version that could run on 8088-based systems. (The early versions were painfully slow. It was improved once 80286 and 80386 machines became available.) Both XENIX and UNIX System V are available for PCs. XENIX and a version of System V are distributed by the Santa Cruz Operation (SCO); a System V version for the 80X86 architecture is also distributed by Intel.

XENIX and UNIX System V are solid packages and reliable operating systems. However, they are more expensive than DOS. The cost varies from hundreds of dollars to more than a thousand. The price is dependent on the additional packages, such as text processing or program development, that you want to include. (This will undoubtedly deter individual users.) As prices come down, the UNIX base will increase.

GNU   As an alternative to these commercial versions, the Free Software Foundation has developed GNU. This is functionally equivalent to UNIX, but it is distributed at cost (with the source code!). The FSF materials also include BASH, "Bourne Again SHell", which is similar to the Korn shell, and the spreadsheet program OLEO. (UNIX shells, such as the Bourne and

█ READ.ME █

Similarities Between DOS and UNIX

Some of the major similarities between DOS and UNIX are listed here.

Both are command-line oriented. Lines consist of a command, which may be followed by arguments for the command. A shell processes the command line, interprets the command, and takes the steps required to carry it out.

Both have a kernel, which contains the essential low-level functions needed to perform the operating system's tasks.

Both use shells to mediate between the kernel and the user or application programs. In DOS, this is usually COMMAND.COM, which you can replace by your choice of a shell. In UNIX, this is either the Bourne shell or the C shell. Most UNIX implementations include both these shells. Other shells exist, and you can substitute any of these for the current shell.

Both allow the creation and use of shells. Shell programs consist of commands and arguments and may include branch or loop instructions. In DOS, these programs are known as batch files; in UNIX, they are known as shell scripts. Shells interpret application programs.

Both have a hierarchical file structure, with a single, root directory at the top. This directory can contain files and subdirectories; these subdirectories can, in turn, have files and subdirectories.

Both support programs that call other programs.

Both support files and devices (such as screens, ports, and drives). Both allow redirection of output to files or devices.

Both come with documentation that is virtually impossible to use. The DOS documentation is minimal. What little documentation there is provides almost no detail about the operating system. The UNIX documentation, on the other hand, tells you more than you could possibly want to know. This information is scattered throughout half a dozen documentation volumes.

Korn shells, are discussed later in this chapter.) GNU is available from the FSF on a tape, and a floppy disk version is available from some user groups.

UNIX in the DOS Environment

There has been some discussion of UNIX as an alternative or successor to DOS as the PC and office-system operating system. As hardware becomes less expensive and memory becomes plentiful, UNIX offers several attractive features.

UNIX is a portable operating system. It has been implemented in a broad range of machines.

It is a true multiuser, multitasking operating system. Entire office staffs or work groups could work on the same machine. Because there is true multitasking, several people can run programs simultaneously, without interfering with each other's resources. (While you can't run more than one program at a time under DOS, you can under UNIX. In fact, you can actually run multiple DOS environments simultaneously under UNIX, provided you have the appropriate software.)

UNIX uses virtual memory management to juggle the memory needs of multiple programs. The operating system will, if necessary, save the memory state of a program to disk temporarily to give another program the additional memory it needs to carry out a particular task. Once the task is completed, the operating system will restore the saved program.

The UNIX community is hooked into an international communications network, which just about any UNIX user can access with the appropriate hardware. Much of this network is maintained by universities to allow communication between researchers at different locations. It's even possible for a researcher to use a machine in another city, state, or country. Think of it—if your machine can't perform a job you need, you may be able to find someone who will let you use a more powerful machine.

Despite such apparent advantages, UNIX's user base is less than 10 percent as large as DOS's. One reason for this is the higher cost of hardware and software to run UNIX. UNIX requires more powerful hardware than DOS, even for a minimal system. UNIX also demands more input from the user before he or she can get to work.

The Structure of UNIX

Figure 14-1 shows the structure of the UNIX operating system. This is a *layered architecture,* meaning the operating system is broken into distinct levels that create a chain of communication. Application and user programs

Figure 14-1

Layered architecture of the UNIX operating system

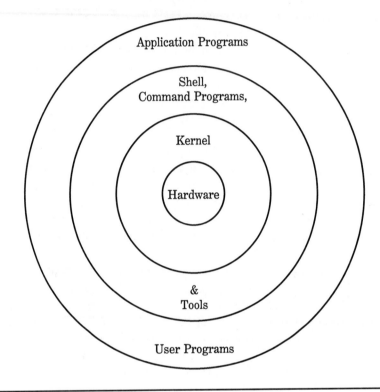

communicate with the shell, which communicates with the kernel. The kernel, in turn, communicates with the hardware.

The Kernel

At the core of the operating system is the kernel. Its function is to interact directly with the hardware. The kernel is responsible for the following tasks:

Security The kernel certifies that only authorized users are logged on. It also ensures that users deal only with files to which they have access. UNIX kernels are not always successful in the performance of their security functions, as the virus released by Robert Morris and the interloper caught by Clifford Stoll indicate. The viruses were able to circumvent the UNIX kernel security features.

Memory Management The kernel manages and allots memory. As a control to the memory allocation, the kernel can prevent programs from clobbering each other. The kernel is also responsible for virtual memory management.

File Management The kernel keeps track of the access restrictions for all files on the system and updates files as they are modified or accessed. This can be a formidable task, if you consider that the UNIX system itself has more than 2000 files, not including user files.

Process Management and Scheduling There are multiple processes in every UNIX session. Even the operating system gets into the act when the system is booted. The kernel administers these functions.

Hardware Requirements
The hardware for UNIX tends to be on the high (and therefore expensive) end of the machines capable of running DOS. However, once you have the hardware set up, you may be able to hook multiple users up to the machine. As far as the operating system is concerned, each of these users can work simultaneously and independently. If multiple users will share a machine, the per-user cost for a UNIX system can become competitive with the cost for several single-user DOS systems.

To run current versions of UNIX on a PC, you need at least 2MB of RAM (although you really should have 4MB or more). The amount of memory you need to have the system run comfortably depends on the number of users and on the kinds of program that will run. Considerable hard disk space is needed—about 40 MB.

Installation and Log-on Requirements
The general installation process for the available UNIX systems is automatic: You insert the diskettes when requested and answer a few questions in the installation process.

Once it's installed, you have abundant opportunity to fine-tune a UNIX system. A dozen parameters can be varied. For example, you can control such things as page size when swapping between memory and storage, memory-allocation strategies, and so on.

Someone must serve as the system administrator. This, presumably, is the person who answered the questions in the installation and who fine-tuned the parameters. This person has "superuser" status, meaning the person has access to all files on the system.

Once the operating system has been installed and a superuser has set up the environment, the users must be added. The superuser must create a user record and a subdirectory for each user's work environment. Once all this is done, the UNIX system is ready for use.

A UNIX Session

To illustrate the process of beginning a UNIX session, let's go through the steps from when the computer is first turned on and the operating system is started.

If you run UNIX on your own PC, turn the computer on. This starts up the operating system kernel. The kernel starts several programs, or processes, including a print process and a program named cron.

Once your machine is booted, you must log on as a user. The operating system kernel will require you to enter your name and password. It will check these and prompt you for a log-in name and password.

When the correct password is entered, the system will execute two shell-script files: /etc/profile and .profile. These files serve a function comparable to that of AUTOEXEC.BAT in DOS. They contain information about your environment, such as paths, characteristics of your terminal, and settings you want to specify. The /etc/profile script contains general settings that apply to all users. This file is always available. The .profile file applies only to you. You will generally need to write this file yourself.

Once you're logged onto the machine, you can perform your work. When you're done, you must log off the machine. When you do this, the kernel will update your environment and files. It will make sure all your files are in order, all your processes are finished, and your work environment is cleaned up.

If it's your machine and you're the system administrator, you have still more to do. After logging off as an ordinary user, you must shut down the system before turning the machine off. Without a shutdown process, the operating system will not update all the files and the records associated with the files.

Because shutdowns are essential to the proper maintenance of a UNIX system, power outages are disastrous for UNIX. To avoid such catastrophes, just about every UNIX system is connected to a generator or to an uninterrupted power supply. Such a power source will engage if a power outage occurs, keeping the system running long enough to allow proper shutdown.

Multitasking in a UNIX Session

In UNIX, you can take advantage of multitasking to run several programs at once. UNIX also allows you to run programs in the background. This involves more than simply spooling a repetitive task, as in DOS. A background program continues to execute the job but does not display any output. More importantly, a background process doesn't tie up the keyboard and screen.

To make the schedule of multiple tasks possible, the kernel executes a process named cron (for chronograph). Cron is a *daemon*, a program that can activate itself under the appropriate circumstances. Kernel monitors the system by checking periodically to see whether any processes, or jobs, await execution. If so, the kernel initiates the processes of cron and makes sure they are performed in the proper sequence and manner.

The UNIX shutdown process is elaborate. Among other things, the operating system must warn any logged-on users that the system will soon be shut down. Users must be given time to save files and end sessions. If a UNIX session is not ended properly, file structures may be corrupted, which could be disastrous.

Files in UNIX and DOS

Both DOS and UNIX use files for programs and data. These files are organized in a hierarchical directory structure. In DOS, files are identified by a name (up to eight letters) followed by a period and an extension (up to three letters). Certain types of files are distinguished by their extensions. For example, executable files have either EXE or COM as their extension. DOS batch files (text files with instructions for the command processor) have the extension BAT.

In UNIX, no distinction is made between a filename and an extension. Filenames can be as long as you want. They can include more than one period, if you wish. For example, you can use a name such as MYFILE-.EXE for a text file, and a name such as MYPROG.TEX.NOEXE for a program file.

To determine whether a particular file is executable, the UNIX kernel checks a record about the file. This record is known as an *inode*. An inode contains information about a file's size, its elements, and the permissions (DIRECTORY, READ, WRITE, EXECUTE) associated with the file. (Inodes are similar to file allocation tables in DOS.) If a file has EXECUTE permission and is not a directory, the operating system can execute the program.

The UNIX File Structure

In DOS, *you* are the file structure. The DOS file structure consists of a single root directory (designated by \), which can contain subdirectories and files. Each subdirectory can contain more subdirectories and files. Except for the operating system's two "hidden" files, you have complete control over the organization of the DOS file structure on your machine. You can decide where to put the command interpreter (COMMAND.COM), any required drivers, and the three dozen or so programs that represent the external commands for DOS. (These include ASSIGN, BACKUP, CHKDSK, DISKCOMP, DISKCOPY, and GRAPHICS.) Commonly, these files are put in a DOS or BIN directory.

In UNIX, things are different. In the UNIX file structure, you are neither the source of all nor the center of the universe. The general organization of this file structure is shown in Figure 14-2.

As in DOS, the top layer of this file structure is the root; however, this time it's not your directory. It belongs to a superuser, who administrates the system. The UNIX root directory is designated by a forward slash (/) in the UNIX file hierarchy. The backslash is the separator character when you specify path names in DOS; in UNIX, it's the forward slash.

Within the UNIX root directory, several other directories are predefined. These contain more than 2000 files stored in several directories. Keep in mind that these directories can have subdirectories and files. Some of these directories are:

bin   Bin contains several hundred command programs, including the default command shell (sh). The C shell (csh), if included with the UNIX implementation, is also in this directory.

etc   This has programs and files for system administration, including the cron program.

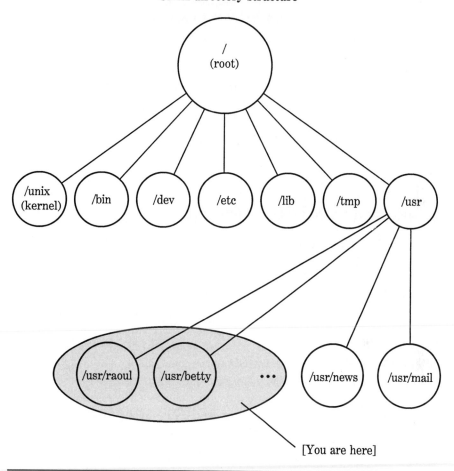

Figure 11-2

UNIX directory structure

[You are here]

dev Dev includes files that represent available devices (screens, terminals, printers, floppy drives, ports, and so on). If you add a new device (for example, a mouse) to your machine, the appropriate device file may already be included; if not, you may create your own file.

Peripheral devices are more important in UNIX than in DOS. Although there are dozens of brands of monitors and graphics cards for DOS, there are a small number of fundamental monitor and graphics adapter types. In contrast, UNIX machines must be prepared to deal with all sorts of odd monitors and machines. For this reason, the definition of devices is an important issue in UNIX.

388   Dvorak's Guide to DOS and PC Performance

lib   The lib directory contains libraries for programming languages.

tmp   The tmp directory can be used as a temporary storage area for certain tasks.

usr   This directory is used for the administration of mail and new services, among other things. When you are added to the system, your directory will be a subdirectory of /usr. As an ordinary user (as opposed to a superuser), you have access to the programs in /bin and to some of the programs in /etc. You can also use any programs you write yourself.

Interaction with UNIX: The Shell

Once you're logged on to UNIX, you're ready to begin. As in DOS, you communicate with the operating system through a shell. This shell interprets and processes your commands and makes the necessary requests of the operating system kernel.

DOS Shells

In the DOS world, COMMAND.COM is the most common shell, since this is included with DOS. However, other shells are available. Some shells take over the display to provide command menus. These shells use the "point-and-shoot" method to give commands. The following are some of the DOS shells that use this approach:

1DirPlus, by Bourbaki Inc.
PathMinder, by Westlake Data
PCTools Deluxe 6, by Central Point Software
XTreePro and XTreePro Gold, by XTree Company
Q-DOS II, by Gazelle Systems
Norton Commander, by Peter Norton Computing

DOS shells differ in their capabilities. Some are simply the standard shell with a menu-oriented interface; others include advanced features, such as command histories you can edit. Programs such as DESQview, by Quarterdeck, and Microsoft Windows are often mistaken for operating systems. These programs are really just powerful, graphics-oriented DOS shells.

Other DOS shells are designed to look more like a UNIX shell; these are command-line oriented. Such shells generally claim compatibility with one or more of the commonly used UNIX shells.

The following shells are available as alternatives to COMMAND.COM:

C-Shell, by GW Computing
MKS Toolkit 3.1, by MKS
PolyShell, by Sage/Polytron

DOS Shell Languages

The DOS shell is both an interpreter and a simple programming language. You can write DOS shell programs, which are batch files, to use the available operating system commands and to call programs. This command language provides some basic control. Unless you use a batch compiler (such as BAT.COM), the DOS batch language affords rather limited programming capabilities.

The DOS batch language has three constructs to control the flow of control in a batch file:

```
IF
```

```
GOTO
```

```
FOR ... IN ...
```

The IF command does not include an ELSE. Test conditions for an IF are limited to EXIST, NOT EXIST, and ERRORLEVEL. Thus, it's difficult to do any kind of complex branching using ordinary DOS batch commands.

UNIX Shells

There are several "standard" shells for UNIX systems: The Bourne shell, the C shell, the Korn shell, and graphics-based shells.

The Bourne Shell

UNIX implementations all include the Bourne shell (sh). This shell was created in the late 1970s by Steve Bourne at AT&T. The shell was designed to be small and efficient. Over the years, it has been extended in various ways. The Bourne shell lacks two features that make other shells attractive: command histories and alias capabilities.

A *command history* is a record of the commands that have been given in a session. In shells that keep such histories, users can recall an earlier command, edit it, and pass it to the shell as a new command.

In the context of command shells, *aliasing* is a mechanism by which you can provide a short name for a long command line that you need to use often. Aliasing allows you to define macros that the shell can understand. Because the Bourne shell lacks these two features, many UNIX users have switched to one of the other shells described here.

The C Shell

The C shell (csh) is also included with most implementations. This shell was developed at Berkeley for the BSD version of UNIX. The C shell is considerably more powerful than the Bourne shell. It includes command histories and aliasing.

The C shell has one drawback, however: it's slower than the Bourne shell. The C shell's greater power comes at the expense of speed.

The Korn Shell

The Korn shell (ksh) was developed by David Korn at AT&T. It is both powerful and fast. It was developed partly in response to the C shell and shares many of that shell's features, including the command history.

Graphics-Based Shells

Graphics-based environments in UNIX are recent developments. Looking Glass, by Visix Software, provides a desktop, icon-based environment that serves as a command interpreter and shell. Such a shell is still nonstandard in the UNIX world, however.

UNIX Shell Languages

For all practical purposes, UNIX shell languages are programming languages. In fact, it's not uncommon to use shell scripts (the UNIX counterpart to DOS batch files) to prototype programs in UNIX. There is even a bookkeeping package that uses Bourne shell scripts. UNIX shell languages support the full complement of if commands: if, if-else, and if-elif. Test conditions can be actual numerical expressions as well as checks on the values of any of several predefined variables. In addition to if, shell languages include for, while, and case constructs.

Shell scripts can invoke other shell scripts, and you can even create a shell script to create other shell scripts.

Shell Commands

DOS shells usually understand both internal and external commands. Internal commands (such as DIR or COPY) are built into the interpreter and cannot be changed or renamed. External commands (such as CHKDSK) are invoked by execution of a program that carries out the command. Such external commands are also known as *transient programs*.

In contrast, almost all the UNIX commands exist as separate programs. This means you can change or rename a command easily in UNIX— provided you have the appropriate access rights to the program. (The only internal commands are those that could not become separate programs for reasons that have to do with the way programs are executed.)

UNIX provides several hundred commands. However, you'll probably use only a few of these to do most of your work. Many of these commands are identical or similar to common DOS commands, but the UNIX names tend to be terser. For example, the UNIX equivalent to the DOS COPY command is cp. (Commands are case sensitive in UNIX, as are filenames.)

COMMANDS COMMON TO DOS AND UNIX

Several commonly used commands are the same in both operating systems. This is probably partly because revisions of DOS added features available in UNIX: to keep the names the same, the developers made it easier for people to move from one operating system to the other.

Some of the commands have the same name and roughly the same function in both operating systems:

backup   Backs up files or directories to floppies.

cd   Switches to the specified directory. You can also use CHDIR in DOS and in the C and Korn shells.

date   Sets the current date.

echo   Repeats to the screen.

fdisk   Specifies and checks the partition settings for your hard disk. (For example, with fdisk you can specify whether the computer will boot to a DOS partition or a UNIX partition on your hard disk.)
   Note: If you run both operating systems on your hard disk, you should use the fdisk program for the operating system that was on the hard disk first. For example, if you installed UNIX on a hard disk that already contained DOS and you use UNIX only occasionally, you should use the DOS FDISK.

format   Formats a floppy diskette under both operating systems. FOR-MAT may also be used to format a hard disk in DOS.

mkdir   Makes the specified directory. In DOS, MD can also be used as the command.

more   Displays the contents of a specified file one screen or one line at a time.

pwd   Shows the current working directory.

restore   Returns material from floppies to a hard disk. In DOS, only data backed up using BACKUP can be restored. In UNIX, material can also be restored from tape.

rmdir   Removes the specified directory. In DOS, the RD command will also work.

sort   Sorts the specified material in whatever way is specified. You can sort in ascending or descending order. You can also ignore characters at the beginning of each input line. For example, you can specify a sort starting at the third character on each line.

Same Command, Different Name

Table 14-1 shows the DOS and UNIX names for equivalent (or nearly equivalent) commands.

In cases where commands are not completely equivalent, the most appropriate commands are paired. For example, the chmod command in UNIX lets you specify file-access and -use privileges for three possible parties: yourself, members of your group, and other users. ATTR is the closest DOS equivalent. It lets the user establish access permission for the single user on a DOS system.

The commands cmp (UNIX) and COMP (DOS) compare the contents of two specified files and record any differences. UNIX also has diff and diff3 programs, which can be used to compare two or three files, respectively. These programs are more aggressive than cmp. They try to tell you what lines need to be changed to bring the files into conformance with each other.

The UNIX copy command does not accomplish the same thing as the DOS COPY command. Rather, the UNIX cp command is like the DOS

TABLE 14-1

UNIX and DOS names for equivalent commands or close relatives

UNIX	Command	DOS
chmod	change file access mode	ATTR
cmp	compare contents of two files	COMP
copy	copy files and subdirectories	
cp	copy files	COPY
cpio	copy file archives	BACKUP and RESTORE
du	check disk usage	CHKDSK
grep	search file for pattern	FIND
lp	send files to a printer	PRINT
ls	directory listing	DIR
mv	move file to new location	REN or RENAME
rm	delete a file	DEL or ERASE
tar	archive files	BACKUP and RESTORE

COPY command: Both copy files from one location to another. Neither the UNIX cp nor the DOS COPY command can copy a directory; the commands can, however, transport the entire contents of the directory.

The UNIX copy command is more powerful. With this command, you can copy entire directories—the directory itself along with any subdirectories. If the directories don't exist at the target location, they will be created before the copy takes place.

The UNIX commands cpio and tar are used for backing up to a tape or floppy. Both can also be used to restore this material from the tape or floppy to the hard disk. These commands combine the functions of the DOS commands BACKUP and RESTORE.

The UNIX du command reports the amount of storage in use in a specified directory (and, perhaps, in its subdirectories). The DOS CHKDSK command provides information about disk usage on an entire drive or logical partition. The DOS command also provides information about memory usage.

The commands grep (in UNIX) and FIND (in DOS) are used to search for a string pattern in a specified file. Of the two, FIND is more limited. For example, FIND is always case sensitive when it is used, whereas you can specify whether grep should be case sensitive or insensitive. With FIND, you can specify only string literals, which are matched exactly as they appear when the program is called. In contrast, with grep you can specify a string in which certain characters may have special meanings.

The UNIX ls command is equivalent to the DOS DIR command. Both commands provide a list of all files in a directory along with certain information about the files. The ls command includes more than 20 options you can specify. One option lets you see listings of any subdirectories in the directory you examine. Others sort files on the basis of name, date, or other features.

The following is a sample DOS directory, generated with a simple DIR command:

```
Volume in drive C has no label
Directory of  C:\QCB\PS

   .      <DIR>      5-01-90  12:43a
   ..     <DIR>      5-01-90  12:43a

ELEAVE   PS          202    5-02-90   2:16a
PROC     PS          2911   5-17-90   2:23a
NOTES    PS          1200   5-08-90   1:41a
```

```
2-4A      PS        5184    5-07-90    4:09a
GRID      PS         476    5-06-90    3:58a
IMAGE     PS         548    5-06-90    4:53a
EGS       PS        1142    5-17-90    2:37a
2-4B      PS        5582    5-08-90   12:31a
PROC      DOC       5639    5-18-90   12:59a
DONE             <DIR>      5-18-90    1:00a
        12 File(s)  17911808 bytes free
```

The following is part of a UNIX directory listing. It was obtained using the command ls −l, in which the −l indicates that the listing should be in long format. In this format, file size, type, and other information are displayed. In the short format, only the file or directory names are shown, as indicated:

```
total 322
rwxr-xr-x    1 wf       other       32108 Feb 28 00:07 bitand
rw-r--r--    1 wf       other        1883 Feb 28 00:06 bitand.c
rw-r--r--    1 wf       other        1854 Feb 27 18:17 bits.c
drwxr-xr-x  16 root     other         256 Jul 16 01:42 bk
rw-r--r--    1 root     other          30 Jul 16 02:00 bkdisk
rw-r--r--    1 wf       other         166 Feb 28 00:03 bmake
rw-r--r--    1 wf       other          83 Feb 28 00:13 cmake
rw-r--r--    1 wf       other          52 Feb 28 00:12 hello.c
drwxr-xr-x   5 wf       other         400 Mar  7 18:04 limbo
rw-r--r--    1 root     other          21 Jul 16 02:12 makedisk
rwxr-xr-x    1 wf       other       23694 Mar  9 00:27 p351
rw-r--r--    1 wf       other         591 Mar  9 00:27 p91out.d
rw-r--r--    1 wf       other         692 Jan 30 02:20 readme
rw-r--r--    1 root     other          27 Jul 16 02:06 seetar
rwxr-xr-x    1 wf       other       23296 Mar  7 00:54 st
rw-r--r--    1 wf       other          73 Mar  7 00:54 st.c
drwxr-xr-x   3 root     other          48 Jul 16 02:01 ttest
rw-r--r--    1 wf       other        1854 Feb 27 01:38 ub.c
```

The first part of this listing shows the file permissions (which were specified with chmod). The first element on the line is the directory flag. If the element is a directory, this flag is set to "d" (for directory); otherwise, a "-" is set for this flag. Each of three additional flags can be set for each of three contexts. A file can have READ ("r"), WRITE ("w"), and EXECUTE ("x") permissions for the user, for the user's group, and for other users.

The column with "wf" and "root" specifies the owner of each element. In the directory being examined, "wf" owns most of the files, which means that this directory is part of the directory structure for user wf. The next column specifies the group that each owner belongs to.

The remaining items specify the file size (in bytes), the last modification date for the file, and the filename.

Capturing a UNIX Listing

The preceding ls directory listing was created during a UNIX session. The listing was redirected to a file (using the redirection operator >, just as in DOS).

Next, DOS was started as a process under UNIX. This was done using the Merge 386 software (described later), by Locus Computing Corporation (and available through Intel). This program provides access to a DOS partition on the hard disk.

The contents of the listing file were simply copied to a DOS directory. Once this was done, the DOS process was terminated. After logging off from UNIX, the computer was booted to DOS, and the listing file was incorporated into this chapter using a DOS text editor.

Unique UNIX Commands

The following list summarizes a few UNIX commands that do not have counterparts in the command collection available with DOS. Most of these commands are available to DOS users as elements in function and program collections from third-party sources.

at   Schedules a task for later execution. With this command, you can specify a date and time (or an offset from the current time) and then specify a program to run or commands to execute. The following are two examples of at commands:

```
at 10:45am Mar 17
```

```
at now + 6 day
```

In the first example, the specified command would be executed at a particular time. (A system daemon will make sure this takes place as specified.) In the second example, the specified time is relative to another time. In each case, the command would be completed with material to be provided by the user.

cal Displays a calendar of the current month or of the period specified. You can specify a month or year. The following command requests a calendar for September 1752:

```
cal 9 1752
```

This calendar is shown in the next listing. The calendar is not defective; neither is the cal command. September 1752 was the month in which 11 days were dropped to make up for the fact that no leap year adjustments had been made up to that point. (George Washington was really born on February 11, not February 22. The following calendar shows where the discrepancy lies.)

```
September 1752
S  M Tu  W Th  F  S
         1  2 14 15 16
17 18 19 20 21 22 23
24 25 26 27 28 29 30
```

cat Concatenates, or links, two or more files. The following command links three files (file1, file2, file3) and saves the aggregate file as largefile:

```
cat file1 file2 file3 > largefile
```

dc Provides a desk calculator that uses reverse Polish notation. (*Reverse Polish*, or *postfix*, *notation* refers to the stack-oriented approach used in Hewlett-Packard calculators.) This calculator provides arbitrary-precision arithmetic functions.

A related program, bc, provides a preprocessor for the dc command. It allows you to enter your expressions using *infix* (that is, algebraic) *notation*, which it then converts to reverse Polish notation for dc. (Infix notation is what you use when you write expressions in everyday work.)

dd Converts a file according to instructions and copies the converted contents to a new file. The dd program can:

- Convert ASCII to EBCDIC or EBCDIC to ASCII. This can be useful if you need to move files between an IBM mainframe and a PC.
- Convert uppercase to lowercase or lowercase to uppercase.
- Swap every pair of bytes in the file. This can be useful if you need to move data from a big-endian to a little-endian machine. (*Big-endian* and *little-endian* refer to the high-order byte in a 16-bit value being stored first or second, respectively, in the architecture of a particular machine.)

dircmp   Compares two directories.

kill   Kills one or more specified processes.

line   Reads a single line from the standard input.

mvdir   Moves an entire directory (including its subdirectories) to a new location.

spell   Runs a specified file through the UNIX spelling checker, included with a UNIX package.

wc   Counts words and lines in a file. This command also determines the number of characters, the number of lines, and the amount of time it would take to print the file. The following is some sample output from this command:

```
lines     words     chars     pages     time at 100 cps
1143      7016      44376     18        7 min 23 sec          test.tex
```

who   Lets you check who is logged onto the system.

   While DOS has only about 70 shell commands, UNIX has about 400. This doesn't mean that DOS environments lack the abilities provided by those extra 330 commands; it just means that the abilities aren't built in. You need to get third-party programs that implement the additional commands. Thus, with UNIX you pay for these functions up front; with DOS, you pay for them only if and when you need them.

   Some of the alternative DOS shells (such as MKS Toolkit or PolyShell) include various subsets of the UNIX commands. There are also public domain and shareware implementations of "UNIX Utilities." Such collections are available from many user groups.

DOS users probably tend to use more third-party software than UNIX users, at least for conducting ordinary tasks. You could put together much of the utility of a UNIX system by combining DOS with appropriate add-on software. Once you had such a system, you might find the price to be comparable with the cost of a UNIX system.

Application Programs

Thousands of application programs are run in DOS. The number of programs for UNIX is considerably smaller, but it is growing.

Early UNIX users were usually hackers and programmers. These people often wrote their own applications and made use of the rich command set and shell languages. With all the UNIX machines and (by DOS standards) the small installed base, shrink-wrapped UNIX applications have not been practical.

As UNIX spreads through a more general user community, the demand for off-the-shelf application programs will increase. In particular, as people move from a DOS to a UNIX environment, they will want to see their favorite programs in the new environment.

Such ports (transfers across environments) are already being done. For example, WordPerfect 5.0 has been ported to UNIX, as has Lotus 1-2-3. PostScript interpreters have long been available for doing typesetting under UNIX. Other applications, including spreadsheets and desktop publishing programs, are being developed directly in UNIX.

UNIX Communications

In the DOS world, most electronic communication goes through a bulletin board system of some sort. This may be a commercial system, such as CompuServe, GEnie, or BIX, or a BBS system.

In UNIX, there are several ways to communicate with users. It just depends on where they are. If the person you want to talk to is on the same machine, you send e-mail (electronic mail). If the recipient's setup allows interruptions, he or she will be informed as soon as you've sent the message. Otherwise, the recipient will learn of your message the next time he or she checks the mail box in the current session or logs on for a new session.

Communicating with people on other machines can be just as simple if your machine is hooked up to a network. The UNIX uucp command (for "unix-unix copy") lets you send files from one location to another. The target location may be on the same machine or on a different machine.

If the target location is on a different machine, the operating system sends the files you want to copy on to the network. In a UNIX environment, no necessary distinction is made between files on your machine and files on other machines in the network (provided your machine knows about the other machine and you have access rights to those files). Most networks have sophisticated facilities for making sure such transmissions get to their destinations.

Such communications may not cost you anything, or they may simply cost the price of a phone call. At any rate, communicating with other machines can be quite easy in UNIX, since most of the details are handled by the operating system.

DOS Under UNIX

It's possible to run a DOS session as a process under UNIX if you have installed a special extender program. This enables UNIX to read files that are on a DOS partition and makes it possible to create DOS as a process.

So far, two extender programs have accounted for a large segment of the market: VP/ix is available for XENIX through SCO and for 386/ix through Interactive Systems; Merge 386 is available for System V through Intel.

To run a DOS process, an extender must create a memory space that looks like the memory space of an actual DOS program running under the DOS operating system. The extender will map all memory references to the memory space the extender has set aside for the DOS process. The DOS process, another UNIX process, should be able to access UNIX files. The DOS process, a DOS program, should access files on a DOS partition.

If the process can actually access DOS-based media, there must be some way of mapping between these locations and UNIX or XENIX. Extender programs make it possible to fulfill these criteria so that you can start a DOS session. Once the session has begun, you should be able to forget that UNIX is around and accomplish your work under DOS without any direct UNIX commands. (The extender program will give such commands to mediate between your process and the operating system.)

For this to work, the following restrictions must be met:

1. You run programs only (don't try any funny memory or hardware tricks). If you violate this rule, the program may work but may also cause difficulties. If you really get into trouble, you can always kill the DOS process. This will cause you to lose whatever program or file material was in memory before the process was terminated, but it will not cause the UNIX system to crash.

2. Your programs access files from only a single DOS partition. Extender programs can fool UNIX into seeing a DOS partition in UNIX terms. However, current versions can do this only for 32MB. As a result, if you have files on hard disk partitions C and D, you can access files only on C. (The partition will almost certainly not be called C in the program.)

The 32MB restriction actually arises because of DOS! The extender programs include a version of DOS in their environment. These versions happen to be too old to support partitions larger than this.

While much DOS software has yet to be tested in such an environment, quite a few of the most popular programs, including AutoCAD, Harvard Graphics, Lotus 1-2-3, Paradox, Ventura Publisher, and Windows, have been run. An application can run under Windows running as a DOS shell in a DOS process running under UNIX.

Starting a DOS Process

Once you've installed the appropriate extender, it's easy to begin a DOS session: Just type a simple command. The commands for VP/ix and Merge 386 are, respectively, vpix and dos.

You'll begin the DOS session almost immediately. The first thing that changes is the command-line prompt. From the UNIX-shell prompt (which will be #, $, or %, depending on what kind of user you are and what kind of shell you're using), the extender changes the prompt to a DOS format. The first line in the following listing is a prompt for VP/ix; the second is a prompt for Merge 386:

```
VP/ix Z:\USR\WF\DOSTEST>

C:\USR\WF\DOSTEST>
```

VP/ix refers to the UNIX partition as drive Z (and other names). The DOS partition is specified as drive C (or D) in VP/ix. Merge 386 refers to this partition as drive C (and other names). The DOS partition is specified as drive E in Merge 386.

To execute an accessible DOS program, just type the program name as you would in DOS. A program is accessible if it's in the current directory or in a directory specified in the PATH. Programs should execute normally. If the program crashes, don't worry: It won't affect the UNIX; the crash is just within the DOS memory space.

Transferring Files Between DOS and UNIX

Once you're running a DOS process, you can transfer files between DOS and UNIX partitions. To copy all files from c:\USR\WF\DOSTEST to e:\UXCHAP\TEST in Merge 386, for example, you would give the following command:

```
copy C:\USR\WF\DOSTEST\*.* E:\UXCHAP\TEST
```

The files would be transferred "as is."

If you're going from DOS to UNIX and you're transferring a text file, the UNIX file will have an extra carriage return (^M) character at the end of each line. This happens because, in text files, DOS changes each end-of-line character to line-feed and carriage-return characters. Both VP/ix and Merge 386 have programs to clean up such files.

Ending the DOS Process

When finished with your DOS work, you can terminate the process. The commands for doing this in VP/ix and Merge 386, respectively, are exitvpix and quit.

Extender programs make it possible to run two operating systems simultaneously. Actually, such programs make one operating system behave like two. Nevertheless, these programs give a UNIX user access to the large body of DOS programs.

Compatibility between the operating systems can be achieved in various ways. For example, suppose you need to print the product of a nice graphics program that runs only under DOS. If you can save this picture as a

PostScript file, the problem is solved almost immediately. Just save the file and then copy it to the UNIX partition. Since PostScript drivers exist for printers attached to UNIX systems, you can print the file from UNIX.

Extender programs will become even more important as more people install UNIX on their machines. Once the 32MB DOS partition barrier disappears, users will really have themselves a powerful combination, with UNIX and DOS on the same machine and able to talk to each other.

CHAPTER FIFTEEN

Using DESQview

DESQview is an essential piece of software for anyone who wants to do two jobs at once under MS-DOS. The newest version of Microsoft Windows claims to do this type of multitasking, but only for specially written Windows applications or on an 80386. DESQview multitasks DOS applications on all PC systems, with or without expanded memory. The more powerful your system, the more uses you can find for DESQview.

DESQview can manage both text and graphics. If a graphics adaptor is present, DESQview allows a graphical interface. DESQview works like an extra operating system under MS-DOS. Upon installation, it searches your hard disk for common commercial applications; then it automatically creates a menu. You may choose programs from the DESQ menu or record a script to open programs automatically.

USING DESQVIEW

DESQview allows as many open windows as you want (provided there's enough memory) to run many programs simultaneously. It goes beyond print spoolers, pop-up utilities, and task switchers. It works on all PC platforms and allows you to add more features as you upgrade your hardware.

Let's say that you first use DESQview with 640KB and a hard disk. DESQview lets you free up memory by swapping applications out of memory to disk files. Then, you upgrade to a machine with LIM 3.2 memory. DESQview lets you swap between large programs almost instantaneously. With EEMS or LIM 4.0, multiple programs exceeding 640KB are able to run simultaneously.

Here are a couple of typical PC scenarios where DESQview can be used to great advantage:

- There's a deadline, and you must print a document in a hurry. Meanwhile, an important client has dropped by and wants an ASCII disk file. With DESQview, you can open two copies of WordPerfect and a DOS command line window. One copy of WordPerfect sends your document to the printer, while the other sends the printer output to the ASCII file, including line and page numbering on your disk. At the same time, you use the DOS window to format a blank disk and copy the ASCII file for the client.

- You are printing a complicated newsletter with Xerox Ventura Publisher. While you wait, you would like to update a drawing. As Ventura prints your page, DESQview lets you open a copy of Corel Draw or PC Paintbrush. If you want to do text revision, you can open a copy of your word processor. You can even check your electronic mailbox or connect to an information service to check a fact.

Setup

The setup procedure for DESQview is typical: You make backups of the original program disks, place the first disk in a floppy drive, and type **install**. You may specify a drive and directory or accept the default. After the files are copied to your hard disk, the program scans for popular applications. DESQview presents a simple setup menu. You select options for your graphics adaptor and mouse, and you're ready to run.

The manual contains an advanced setup program for sophisticated users. The features include an automatic dialer for a modem, a hot key for the DESQ menu, and specifications for where windows should appear on the screen as they are opened.

If you have applications that were not recognized at installation, you may add them to the DESQ menu by running Add a Program. DESQview will recognize Program Information Files (PIFs) written for Microsoft Windows. You may add programs from scratch by typing in path information, memory requirements, and screen-display information.

You open a window by typing a two-key abbreviation from DESQview's Open Program menu. You can also execute a program by highlighting its name using the cursor keys or the mouse. The program will open in either a full-screen window or in a small window, depending on the setup. If the program runs in a small window, you can change its size or position on the screen. You can "zoom" the window up to full screen, make it small again, or hide it completely. A second program may be started the same way. If both programs are run in small windows, they will appear on the screen simultaneously.

You can cycle among opened programs, bringing one or another to the foreground, with the DESQ hot key or the mouse. If there is enough memory, the background programs will continue to run while the foreground program takes control of the keyboard. Background programs also can be "frozen," to resume their tasks only when they return to the foreground. For example, if you send a DOS command like DISKCOPY A: B: into the background, you can freeze it while you run another program and have it resume accurately when the program ends.

Mark and Transfer

A valuable DESQview tool is Mark and Transfer. With it, you can block out text in one application, copy it, store it in memory, and then transfer it to an application running in a different window. This is a way to transfer data from spreadsheet and data base programs to tables in a word processor. While on line with a telecommunications program, DESQview allows text to be marked and sent or to be captured and transferred to another window.

Learn

DESQview has a built-in macro feature called Learn. With it, any combination keystrokes may be recorded and assigned to a playback key within any window. This feature is similar to TSR utilities like SuperKey. It can be used to open or close program windows automatically and to switch between programs. Learn also enhances the macro feature in programs like WordPerfect. Learn makes it possible to program a single macro key to escape to the DOS shell, execute file-maintenance functions, run utility programs, and then return to the word processor.

DOSSERVICES

DESQview is equipped with its own DOS shell, called DOSSERVICES. DOSSERVICES allows you to run common DOS commands from a pull-down menu (see Figure 15-1). Directories can be sorted into two levels with seven categories.

Figure 15-1

DOSSERVICES pull-down menu

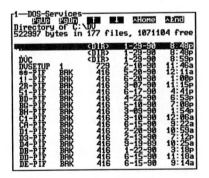

DESQview Companions and Others

Quarterdeck sells a number of utility programs specifically written to complement the DESQview operating environment. These include the following:

Notepad   Notepad is a small word processor with a WordStar-like interface.

Calculator Calculator is a pop-up calculator for standard mathematical functions, complete with a simulated paper tape. The tape scrolls on the screen as you do new calculations.

Mark and Transfer DESQview's Mark and Transfer feature works with Calculator. It can perform arithmetic functions on columns of numbers entered in Notepad or within another word processor in its own window.

Link Link (Figure 15-2) is a minicommunications program equipped with its own host mode and a scripting language. Nine prewritten scripts are supplied. You can automatically log onto the DESQview support BBS, as well as onto commercial information services, such as CompuServe. Link has a menu-driven interface and an on-line user tutorial. Link can upload and download ASCII files or send binary files by XMODEM. (Link's XMODEM is the older 128KB variation, which may be incompatible with recent versions.) Link can also connect with Checksum XMODEM as a transfer option.

Link's host mode will allow other people to call you and leave files or messages without interrupting your work in another application in the foreground. The manual documents the scripting language for developing sophisticated log-on and auto-download procedures.

Datebook Datebook (Figure 15-3) is a convenient pop-up clock, calendar, and appointment scheduler. It presents views by day, week, month, and year. Datebook can zoom down to a one-line clock and calendar at the top of the screen or expand to any size. Mark and Transfer lets you rearrange appointments or use Datebook's status line to date-stamp documents in other windows. You can also set an alarm to remind you of an appointment.

Figure 15-2

Link screen

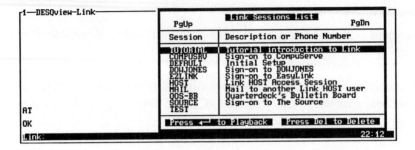

Shareware Enhancements

In addition to the Quarterdeck programs, DESQview enhancers are available from shareware authors. They are available on public bulletin board systems and on Quarterdeck's technical-support BBS.

Figure 15-3

Datebook screen

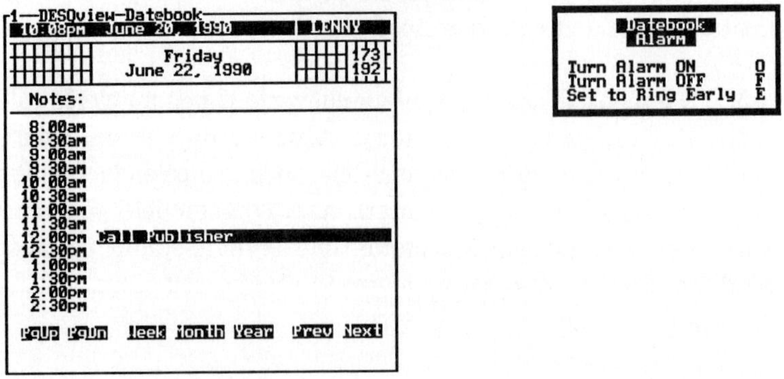

DV Commander, an all-purpose utility, allows most DESQview menu functions to be executed inside a window from the DOS command line. Windows can be opened, closed, rearranged, and sent to the background or foreground from DOS batch files. This is useful for setting up timed maintenance functions on your PC.

DV Commander also lets you construct DESQview submenus. This helps keep your list of DV applications from growing too long to fit on a single screen. For example, a submenu called PUBLISHING could list such programs as Ventura Publisher, Corel Draw, and Microsoft Word.

Memory Status

One way to recognize veteran DESQview users is by how they talk about available memory: There's no such thing as enough! Quarterdeck has addressed this issue with frequent revisions of DESQview that allow for larger and larger program windows.

DESQview's Memory Status utility serves as a multitasker's gas gauge. You open it by selecting MS from the menu. Memory Status displays three rows and three columns of information on the following:

- *Common Memory.*   This is a buffer used by DESQview to manage windows and video overhead.

- *Conventional Memory.*   This is the total in the 0 to 640KB area available to run programs. This includes "backfilled" memory from an EMS board and may include memory in the 64KB segment just above 640KB (if this memory is not used by a video-display adaptor).

- *Expanded Memory.*   This refers to RAM provided on EMS boards. Motherboard memory above 1MB can also be converted to EMS by special hardware or by software drivers. This excludes RAM on an EMS board used to backfill to the conventional area. It also excludes any EMS memory that was allocated to RAM disks, print spoolers, or disk caches before DESQview was started.

The following table indicates the total memory available on the system, the total memory available to all programs at the current moment, and the largest area of contiguous memory available to one program.

This information was taken from an 80286 machine equipped with an ALL Chargecard, 4MB on the motherboard, and an additional 512KB on an Everex expansion board. Several programs were loaded into conventional memory. Part of expanded memory was allocated for a disk cache and for a RAM disk prior to starting DESQview. After the 349KB of conventional memory has been used, a few 560KB windows can be opened by mapping expanded memory to DOS.

Memory	Total Memory	Total Available	Largest Available
Common	26624KB	19870KB	19788KB
Conventional	568KB	350KB	349KB
Expanded	3904KB	1488KB	560KB

When DESQview is told to open a program window, it finds the largest free block of contiguous conventional memory and compares it with the expanded memory available to run programs. If both numbers are too small, DESQview looks for a previously loaded program to swap out of memory. If previously loaded programs have been set not to swap, DESQview sends the following message: "A non-swappable window is in the way." You can't load your new application.

Tip: Pay attention to the order in which you load your programs. It's generally a good idea to load large programs first and smaller ones later. If you're running a non-swappable program, open it either first or last so that it doesn't get in the way of other programs.

More on Learn

DESQview's Learn feature (Figure 15-4) can record a series of keystrokes either within an application or globally from the DESQ menu. If the name for the macro begins with an exclamation point, the macro will execute automatically. (Don't confuse this with a physical key redefined on the keyboard. Use any key to run the macro manually.)

On the main screen, a macro named with an exclamation point will play back as soon as the DESQ menu appears. If the macro is recorded within a window, it will execute when the window is opened. Use the following procedure to configure an automatic start-up macro:

1. Press the Learn key (SHIFT-ALT).

2. Select Start Script.

3. Select a key to call the macro manually.

4. When you type in the script name, make the first character an exclamation point (!).

5. Record the macro.

6. Press the Learn key (SHIFT-ALT) and select Finish Script.

Figure 15-4

Learn screen

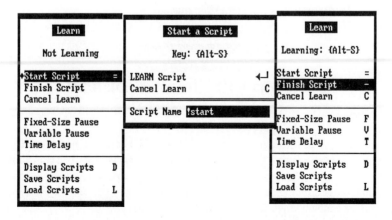

Deleting a Macro

To delete a previously recorded DESQview macro, call up the Learn menu with SHIFT-ALT. Start a script and use the key assigned to the macro you are canceling. (You can display the names of all recorded macros to get this information.) The name in the script box should be the name of the macro to be deleted. Press the equal-sign key to start recording. When the menu is gone, instead of recording any keystrokes, immediately call up the menu again by pressing SHIFT-ALT. Then, select Finish Script (not Cancel Script).

Tip: To quickly delete all macros in a DESQview window, delete the script file for that window. Script files are stored in the DESQview directory in the form *XX*-SCRIP.DVS, where *XX* is the two-letter code used to open the window. Global DESQview scripts are stored in the file DESQVIEW.DVS.

To start DESQview without summoning a start-up script, write a batch file to temporarily rename DESQVIEW.DVS, as in the following example:

```
Copy con NOSETP.BAT
cd \dv
Ren DESQVIEW.DVS START1.DVS
XDV
Ren START1.DVS DESQVIEW.DVS
   ^Z
```

Multiple start-up scripts may also be configured for DESQview. Save these as START2.DVS, START3.DVS, and so on.

READ.ME .

Problems with Graphics Display
on Hercules Systems

WordPerfect, WordStar, and Microsoft Word all allow the user to look at graphic page "previews." Consequently, these programs shift back and forth between text and graphics modes. With a Hercules card, DESQview is unable to follow these shifts accurately. Once a page has been previewed, the screen may get scrambled when it shifts back to text mode.

Problems with Graphics Display
on Hercules Systems (*continued*)

Quarterdeck has a program called DVHERC .COM that forces the Hercules card to return to text mode. Install DVHERC with a short batch file in the program that opens the word processing window. Here's an example for use with WordPerfect:

DVHERC.COM
WP.EXE

When DVHERC is installed, restore the text screen at any time by using the key combination of CTRL-ALT-1.

EGA and VGA displays give DESQview the option of running in higher resolutions (which allow more display lines on the screen). DESQview will support a dual-monitor (CGA/EGA/VGA and Hercules) configuration.

GETTING THE MOST FROM DESQVIEW

Most PC applications can be altered to coexist within DESQview. The diversity of PC programming standards may require some fine tuning. DESQview and QEMM may be modified with many user-adjustable performance settings. The Advanced Setup and Change a Program modules are the principal tools used to alter performance.

The Advanced Setup Program

The DESQview Advanced Setup Program has seven main entries, with menus nested under each. In the Performance category, an important key setting is Task Processing Time.

DESQview can be set to specify the number of CPU clock ticks allotted for both foreground and background windows. A PC cycles through 18 clock ticks in one second. DESQview allocates time to each program in round-robin fashion. The program in the foreground gets the specified number of foreground ticks, and each background program in turn gets the number of background ticks specified.

Tip: If you have a fast 386, DESQview is able to complete its cycle more frequently. Set a foreground-to-background ratio of around 5:3. On slower machines, you may want to allot more ticks for background applications. DESQview's default ratio is 9:3. Some users of fast 386s actually set the ratio to 1:1, to allow all programs equal weight. In general, extreme values should be avoided.

Background telecommunications programs like TELIX or QMODEM may suffer in accuracy during uploading or downloading. If errors are encountered in file transfers, increase the number of background clock ticks.

Optimize High Speed Communications is another Advanced Setup option. If this parameter is set to Yes, DESQview will give priority to DOS interrupts that address your serial ports. Quarterdeck recommends that you attach your modem to COM2, which is the port with DOS priority.

READ.ME

Ten Hot Tips

1. Older mouse software is a common cause of problems. Early mouse drivers were often written to address both serial ports at once. Newer mouse software is programmed not to interfere with a modem on another serial port. Check the mouse section of DESQview's Setup program to make sure the mouse and modem aren't configured for the same serial port.

2. If you have trouble uploading or downloading under DESQview, increase the background clock ratio to 7:5 or 9:6 or, on a fast 386, decrease it to 3:2 or 2:1.

3. Memory Usage in the Performance section of the Setup program controls the common memory DESQview allots for video and for keeping track of open windows. On Hercules and CGA systems, this can be set to as low as 14 or 15KB; on VGA systems, set it higher, from 20 to 30KB.

Ten Hot Tips (*continued*)

4. DOS buffers for EMS improve speed and performance on XT systems and systems that use add-on expanded-memory cards. On a 386, this setting can be changed to 0.

5. The Keyboard section of Advanced Setup allows you to specify a different hot key for DESQview and enable or disable the Learn (macro) feature. If you don't intend to set up DESQview macros, disable Learn to increase the size of your program windows.

6. On systems with a 101-extended keyboard, it may be convenient to redefine the DESQ key to the right or the left CTRL or ALT key or even to the SYS REQ key.

7. In version 2.26 and above, separate shift states can be maintained for each window. CAPSLOCK and NUMLOCK toggles can be set independently for each program. Otherwise, DESQview maintains the same keyboard status for all open windows.

8. The Logical Drives section controls where programs will be swapped to disk when DESQview runs out of memory. Logical Drives also simplifies operation for programs that can't handle directory path information. Say you have a word processor that won't accept the directory path to a file. You can assign that path to a drive letter. For example, C:\WS3\RECORDS\JUNE can be assigned to drive G. If you tell your word processor to load G:\JUNE1.DOC or G:\JUNE15.DOC, it will know where to find them.

9. When DESQview runs out of program memory, it looks first for expanded memory to make a background program swap. Its next priority is to bundle a background program into a file and write it to disk.

10. With an extended memory system on a system that can't be converted to EMS, configure an extended-memory RAM disk. Tell DESQview to use the RAM disk as your swap drive.

Changing a Program

To add a new application to the Program Menu, DESQview will look for a preconfigured information file. If none is supplied, DESQview will formulate a generic information file. This file stores information about individual application memory use, serial port usage, and window position. Each information file begins with the two-letter menu code to open the application, and ends with the extension DVP. You can modify the DESQview information for any program by editing its DVP file in Change a Program.

Change a Program includes two screens of program information. The first is used to name and locate a program, allocate memory, and describe video and serial-port usage. The Advanced Options screen allows for fine tuning and user control of each DESQview window.

The memory entry describes the size of the window that DESQview will open. If DESQview's available program memory is less than the number specified here, DESQview will inform you and refuse to open the window. (On the advanced user screen, the memory setting can be modified to span a range.)

To increase display speed, some programs bypass the standard BIOS routines that control screen display. If a program writes directly to the screen at a hardware register level, DESQview runs it in a full-sized window. If the program is well behaved and uses BIOS video calls, it can run in a small DESQview window. Set the "Writes text directly to screen" option accordingly.

DESQview must know whether the application is character based or uses the pixel-based graphics modes. DESQview can initiate an application in any graphics mode supported by your video card. On 8088 and 80286 machines, graphics programs must run in full-sized windows. The 386 provides an option to run graphics applications in small windows. This is called *virtualizing* text or graphics and is controlled by the third option on the first Change a Program screen.

The Advanced Options in Change a Program may be daring to a new user. But it is what allows for the "zing" in program performance.

Six Tricks

1. Under DESQview, programs can be run on two different monitors from one computer! If you install both a VGA and a Hercules card, DESQview can be brought up on the VGA monitor. If you want a

specific program to open up on the Hercules monitor, set "Writes text directly to screen" to "Y." Go to Advanced Options and enter 07 (for monochrome text) in the Initial Mode box. This application will now automatically open on the monochrome monitor when called from the menu.

2. To increase the performance speed of your applications, select "N" in the "Runs in background" box where appropriate.

   Some programs have no need to operate in the background. This is particularly true if you load a print spooler for background printing prior to starting DESQview. DOS command shells, graphics programs, and word processors will not do anything unless they are active in the foreground window. To increase the time available to other applications, freeze some programs when you switch away from them.

3. EGA graphics consume memory. Set "Share EGA when foreground/zoomed" to "N" to conserve memory.

4. Communications programs crash when swapped to disk. Set "Can be swapped out" to "N" for any telecommunications program.

5. You can set up applications to request a variable amount of memory by:

   a. filling in the Memory Size window on the first Change a Program screen, and

   b. filling in the Maximum Program Memory Size window on the Advanced Options screen.

   For instance, DESQview preconfigures "Big DOS" for a minimum of 128KB and a maximum of 640KB. This means that Big DOS will "settle" for a 128KB window size if that's all that's left on the system, but it will grow to 640KB as available memory permits. If the Maximum Program Memory Size window is left blank, DESQview will request the amount of memory specified on the first screen for an application.

6. Expanded-memory usage can be limited with the Maximum Expanded Memory Size box.

8088, 286, and 386 Compatibility

On a plain PC XT with 640KB, DESQview will let you divide about 475KB between concurrent applications. If you have more programs to run, the ones already loaded are frozen and swapped to disk files to make room for new ones. When you switch back to an earlier program, DESQview "scrapes" it off the disk and swaps out a newer one.

Add 1MB of LIM 4.0 memory to run a megabyte of programs concurrently. None of them will need to be frozen or swapped to disk. This requires PC hardware properly configured for memory.

On a 286 machine, DESQview can load part of itself into extended memory, leaving 550 to 600KB for applications. This is accomplished by loading the QEXT.SYS device driver into the CONFIG.SYS file.

Extended memory on a 286 can also be used for a "swapping" RAM disk. When DESQview uses a RAM disk to swap program files, it switches between applications very rapidly. This is similar to swapping programs into LIM 3.2 expanded memory.

To run programs concurrently beyond 640KB on a 286, memory-management units (MMUs), such as the ALL Chargecard and the SOTA Pop, can be installed. An MMU is a small card that plugs in between your motherboard and its 80286 chip. An MMU automatically converts all memory on a 286 from extended to LIM 4.0 Memory. When this is done, multiple large applications can run concurrently under DESQview.

For 386 machines, Quarterdeck (DESQview's manufacturer), makes QEMM 386. QEMM 386 is a software device driver that converts all memory on a 386 into usable LIM 4.0 memory. The 386's "virtual 8086" mode allows multiple DOS sessions of 600 to 640KB to run concurrently.

QEMM50/60 is a product for IBM PS/2 Model 50 and 60 machines. It converts extended memory on Model 50 and 60 machines into LIM 4.0 EMS.

READ.ME

Optimizing Hardware for DESQview

Here are a few general hints for obtaining the maximum benefits from DESQview:

Expanded-memory boards have become a less attractive option for owners of 80286 systems. If your motherboard can hold only 1MB of memory, consider an upgrade to a 386SX.

READ ME

Optimizing Hardware for DESQview
(*continued*)

In most 286 systems, it is difficult for DESQview to open an expanded-memory window larger than 128KB. If the motherboard can hold more than 1MB, adding an MMU card for $200 to $300 will overcome some 286 limitations. MMU cards can be used on 1MB-only machines with the addition of an inexpensive extended-memory board.

The ALL Chargecard and SOTA Pop can convert extended memory on a card to LIM 4.0, but performance will suffer. The card runs at the speed of the AT bus, rather than at the motherboard's higher speed. The advantage of an MMU card is that it automatically lets a 286 run programs larger than 500KB in expanded memory. With 2 or 3MB installed on the motherboard, an MMU makes a 286 a viable alternative to a 386SX. This option may be preferable to the replacement of a 286 motherboard with a 386SX; the costs, however, are about equal.

When IBM PS/2 Model 50 and 60 machines use Quarterdeck's QEMM 50/60, they must disable the first megabyte of memory on the motherboard to work properly. Fortunately, the ALL Chargecard for 286 clones may also be installed in PS/2 systems. The Chargecard converts all memory to LIM 4.0 without disabling any motherboard RAM. The LIM 4.0 driver provided with the Chargecard is also more powerful than what IBM includes with its XMA expansion boards.

If you own copies of DESQview and QEMM prior to purchasing a 386 machine, it's a smart move to audition your future hardware. 386s come in all speeds and flavors. Machines with older BIOS chips and certain combinations of BIOS and disk controller don't work optimally with QEMM. The best way to ensure compatibility is to buy a machine with a current BIOS and "test-drive" DESQview and QEMM on it before you sign the check. Quarterdeck's products are generally compatible with all 386 designs, but there are trivial adjustments to be made with some machines. Different combinations of motherboard and BIOS vary as to speed and maximal memory usage.

More Memory

In 1986, a Quarterdeck programmer made the discovery that Microsoft had left a hole in MS-DOS. Although DOS was written to address only memory between 0KB and 1KB, it turned out that the first 64KB of the second megabyte could be used to run programs. The 80286 device driver, QEXT-.SYS, was written to allow DESQview to load 64KB of its program code into this address range (10000:0000H to 11000:0000H). QEXT.SYS allowed users of 80286 machines to gain a precious additional 64KB of conventional memory for their DESQview windows.

Microsoft quickly developed a driver of its own, called HIMEM.SYS, and in 1987, users of Microsoft Windows also gained access to the first 64KB of extended memory. Microsoft published the code for HIMEM.SYS. Several third-party applications (specifically Xerox's Ventura Publisher) were rewritten to take advantage of HIMEM.SYS. In 1988, Quarterdeck revised QEXT.SYS and their 386 driver, QEMM.SYS, to be completely compatible with the published Microsoft standard.

Loadhi, QRAM, and Manifest

In 1990, Quarterdeck released some new products to provide users with even more conventional memory for DOS applications. These products proved to be so useful that a dozen memory-management imitators swiftly followed them into the marketplace.

Quarterdeck's 386 memory manager was bundled with an auxiliary utility called Loadhi for several years. Loadhi exploited the fact that DOS addresses not just the memory range up to 640KB, but also up to 1024KB (plus the small segment of extended memory discussed in the preceding section).

The region from 640KB to 1MB is referred to by Quarterdeck as high memory. The original IBM plan called for high memory to be used exclusively for ROM chips on peripheral devices: video cards and hard disk controllers. Quarterdeck reasoned that there were large blocks of high memory left over that could be made to map RAM from expanded memory as well.

Loadhi first made use of the 386's superior ability to map memory. A 386 can map expanded memory in 4KB increments to any DOS address in the first megabyte. Loadhi loans TSR utilities some RAM from expanded memory. QEMM tells DOS to "see" the memory used by TSRs in the 640KB to 1MB region. The space the TSRs formerly occupied, below 640KB, is freed up for other applications.

While DESQview also swaps large blocks of expanded memory in and out of conventional memory, it can use only what remains after the boot process. DOS needs to see mouse drivers, disk caches, and such independently of DESQview. PC users have learned the habit of loading special device drivers and pop-up utilities as DOS enhancers. When these are loaded in CONFIG .SYS and AUTOEXEC .BAT, they can gobble up from 20 to 200KB before the machine even gets to the DOS prompt.

In 1987 and 1988, Loadhi was available as a partial solution to this problem only on 386 machines. Discovering which areas of high memory were not claimed by controller ROM was a hit-or-miss operation. In early 1990, Quarterdeck developed Optimize, a utility that makes life easier.

Optimize automatically reads your boot files, tests high memory, and reboots your system several times. A report is passed to Loadhi to "shoehorn" whatever programs and drivers will fit above 640KB. This information is automatically written to new AUTOEXEC.BAT and CONFIG-.SYS files.

QRAM was developed to bring high-memory management to 8088 and 80286 machines. Both QRAM and QEMM use the Optimize program to configure a larger conventional memory size for most PCs. 8088 and 286 machines now share the 386's ability to map EMS into high memory.

Typically, Optimize reclaims 20 to 60KB of DOS memory by freeing up space formerly occupied by mouse drivers, buffers, and small TSR utilities. Sometimes, additional memory can be gained by configuring Loadhi manually. Manifest is the Quarterdeck utility written to help with this task.

Manifest takes a "snapshot" of a PC's inner workings and gives you an instant inventory of installed hardware and software. It will tell you your BIOS type and date, your video-display type, and what peripheral cards are installed. Manifest also provides extensive information on DOS-, extended-, and expanded-memory usage. It can be popped up over text-based applications to show a complete listing of DOS interrupt and address-space usage. A graphic map of conventional and expanded memory shows how each 4KB segment is used. A series of internal benchmarks can be called up to measure memory speed and to clock PC performance.

Manifest has seven information display sections (eight when QEMM 386 is active). They are arranged in columns down an attractive menu (see Figure 15-5). Each section displays one to five subsection headers across the screen.

Under the section labeled Expanded, the Overview tells you which version of LIM EMS is being used, the total EMS available, the address of the page frame, and the number of mappable EMS pages. The next subsection shows a map of what each 4KB memory segment can be used for. The third section lists which programs are already using EMS handles, and the fourth and fifth sections perform timing tests on memory.

Manifest's benchmarks are useful for evaluating EMS hardware to see if it will handle high-speed telecommunications. If the timing on Real Alternate Map Set registers 400 microseconds or less, a 9600-baud modem will usually function accurately in the background.

Tip: If your EMS software can increase the number of alternate memory maps used by the system, this generally will improve modem performance proportionately.

The Hints section of Manifest reports what Quarterdeck knows about optimizing your system configuration. It may suggest changes in your CONFIG.SYS or recommend settings for your expanded-memory manager. For instance, if you have the statement Files=100 in your CONFIG.SYS, Manifest will tell you that that may be more files than you need. The subsections under Hint explain any recommendations in detail.

The First Meg and DOS sections are the ones that help you fine-tune the Loadhi process. Manifest shows which programs are present in DOS memory by their address ranges, showing all drivers, files, buffers, and TSRs. If an area of memory between 640KB and 1MB is unused, Manifest marks it as available. Loadhi will optionally place a program at user-designated addresses. If Optimize has missed something in your setup, you can use Loadhi manually to squeeze in some extra programs.

Figure 15-5

Manifest screen

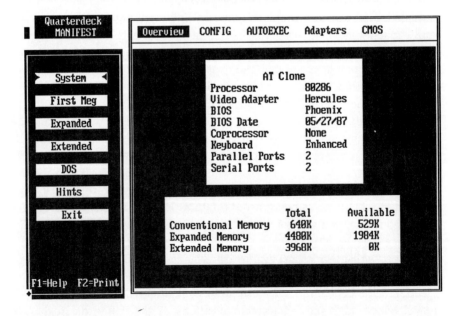

Tips for Running Specific Applications

DESQview and WordPerfect

WP 4.2   WordPerfect 4.2 will run in as little as 200KB, allowing users with no expanded memory to open two copies simultaneously. When Word-Perfect 4.2 is short on memory, it will swap documents out to disk. With a fast hard disk, this slows down performance only slightly.

You can speed up screen writing by installing Quarterdeck's NOFF-.SHP shared-memory utility under Advanced Setup in Change a Program.

WP5   WordPerfect 5.0 and 5.1 perform slower disk writes. Increase the amount of memory available to these programs to avoid disk writes and speed things up.

Some versions of WP 5.1 are incompatible with some versions of expanded memory. You can disable use of expanded memory by WP 5.1 by entering 0 for Maximum Expanded Memory Size in Change a Program under Advanced Setup. On most systems, adding NOFF.SHP under Shared Programs will increase performance speed dramatically.

DESQview and Microsoft Word Versions 4 and 5

Be sure that "Displays graphics information" under Change a Program is set to "Yes," even if you run Word in its character-based mode. If you experience odd problems with Word, use the /KB parameter with WORD-.COM.

DESQVIEW and Microsoft Windows

Windows 286 versions 2.11 and above won't run under DESQview unless DOS can open at least 10 files in conventional memory. Make sure the statement Files = 10 is included in your CONFIG.SYS. File allocation above 10 files can be placed in high memory with the Loadhi command.

Windows 386 version 2.11 can't be run under DESQview in its multi-tasking mode. You can open individual Windows applications by using WIN86.COM instead of WIN.COM.

Windows 3 can run in real mode only under QEMM v5.1 and DESQview. Add the parameter /r to WIN.COM under Change a Program.

If you're running Microsoft Windows in a high-resolution VGA mode, you may discover that the screen doesn't refresh properly after you switch windows. 1024x768 resolution takes a lot of video memory. Set the number of graphics pages under Change a Program to four or five.

DESQview and Communications Programs

The general tip is to load communications programs in the first DESQview window.

Quarterdeck's Manifest includes a benchmark that tests timing on the real alternate-map set of your expanded-memory card or motherboard. The manual says that a score of 400 or less on this test generally indicates that a 9600-baud modem can accurately exchange data in the background. If your EMS software can increase the number of alternate-map registers, modem performance is improved.

Many DESQview users have also reported overcoming telecommunications problems by changing the UART chip in their serial cards. Replacing the 8450 or 16450 UART chip with an NS16550 chip may dramatically improve high-speed telecommunications performance. The NS16550 provides a hardware buffer for the serial port. Many current telecommunications packages automatically recognize the NS26550's enhanced capacities. Public domain programs are available for older communications packages.

DESQview and Ventura Publisher

Ventura Publisher 2.0 is a memory hog, normally requiring at least 550KB to run without EMS, and 525KB with EMS installed. Users of VGA and EGA graphics on 286 machines may have difficulty configuring a DESQview window of that size. With Quarterdeck's or Microsoft's extended-memory management, Ventura Publisher can run outside of DESQview in as little as 490KB of conventional memory. Inside DESQview, Ventura Publisher 2.0 will still need a 525KB window with 92KB of EMS allocated. QRAM may allow some extra memory to be gained with the use of the Optimize and Loadhi commands.

Another solution is to install Ventura Publisher for Hercules monochrome graphics, if your monitor and card support it. Quarterdeck's VID-RAM utility will automatically add 64KB of memory to DOS from EGA/VGA cards used in Hercules mode. If you're within 5 to 10KB of enough memory, you can also decrease the amount of system memory allotted to DESQview or disable DESQview's Learn feature.

If you don't use Ventura Professional Extension, the Maximum Expanded Memory Size under Change a Program should be set to 92KB.

If your mouse stops working unexpectedly, it may help to change the mouse switch in Ventura's start-up batch file to /M = 32.

To run Ventura in a high-resolution VGA mode may also require an increased number of graphics pages allotted under Change a Program.

DESQview and Lotus Products

Lotus 1-2-3 Release 3 requires at least 700KB of conventional and extended memory combined. On a 386, QEMM will automatically allocate extended memory for Lotus.

On a 286, you need to reserve an amount of extended memory for Lotus that complements the available DOS memory. For instance, if CHKDSK shows you have 550KB available to DOS, be sure that at least 150KB of extended memory is reserved for Lotus by your EMS manager.

Lotus 1-2-3 also loads its graphics drivers at startup. This can cause conflicts if you've disabled the graphics modes of an EGA/VGA card to gain extra memory. You can either restore the EGA/VGA modes on your card or use Lotus's advanced setup outside of DESQview to disable its internal graphics.

To use Lotus Freelance 3.0 with DESQview version 2.25 or earlier, you must insert the complete path to the program into DV's program-information file. Users have reported that Freelance also can be launched from within a window running Lotus's Magellan with no difficulty.

The following is a captured Change a Program screen with settings that seem to work well for Lotus 1-2-3 Release 3 in most configurations:

```
Change a Program
Program Name...........: 1-2-3 Rel. 3
Keys to Use on Open Menu: L3 Memory Size (in KB): 360

Program...: 123.EXE
Parameters:
Directory.: {location of 1-2-3 files}

Options:          Writes text directly to screen.......: [Y]
                  Displays graphics information........: [Y]
                  Virtualize text/graphics (Y,N,T).....: [T]
                  Uses serial ports (Y,N,1,2)..........: [N]
                  Requires floppy diskette.............: [N]
```

```
Change a Program Advanced Options

System Memory (in K).....>>:    0
Maximum Program Memory Size (in K)..: 640
Script Buffer Size.......: 1000
Maximum Expanded Memory Size (in K): 1312
Text Pages: 1  Graphics Pages: 1
Initial Mode:        Interrupts: 00 to FF

Window Position:
     Maximum Height:  25     Starting Height:
     Starting Row...:        Maximum Width.:  80
     Starting Width.:        Starting Column:

Shared Program
     Pathname..:
     Data......:

Close on exit (Y,N,blank)........: [Y]
Uses its own colors..............: [Y]
Allow Close Window command.......: [N]
Runs in background (Y,N,blank)...: [ ]
Uses math coprocessor............: [Y]
Keyboard conflict (0-4)..........: [0]
Share CPU when foreground........: [Y]
Share EGA when foreground/zoomed.: [Y]
Can be swapped out (Y,N,blank)...: [ ]
Protection level (0-3)...........: [0]
```

Troubleshooting — Common Questions and Answers

Q: When I install my EMS card, the system refuses to boot up, or it displays a "Parity error" message.

A: Be certain that the chips are installed correctly on your motherboard and EMS card and that they are the right speed. See the instructions for your EMS card, and disable parity checking.

Q: I have 1MB of memory installed on my motherboard, but CHKDSK shows only 640KB. How do I access the rest of it?

A: The other 384KB may be configured as shadow RAM, as expanded memory, or as extended memory. Run the setup program that comes with your system, and determine how the 384KB is being used. Configure it as extended memory to use QEXT.SYS or as expanded memory if you have an appropriate software driver and would like DESQview to use it.

Q: Everything works fine when I run DV.EXE, but when I run XDV-.COM, the system locks up.

A: If you are using an AST memory board, load XDV.COM with the parameter switch /EE. For other systems, there is probably some memory conflict in the high-RAM area A000-EFFF. Run XDV with the /L switch, and note the addresses shown. Try excluding these memory areas from XDV.COM by using the /X= switch. For example,

XDV /X = C000-C7ff

will exclude this high-memory area from DESQview's control.

Q: I have plenty of expanded memory installed on my 286; yet the biggest window I can get under DESQVIEW is about 420KB.

A: Be sure to reserve about 128KB of your memory as extended, and place Quarterdeck's QEXT.SYS in your CONFIG.SYS file. This will add 64 to 128KB to your window size.

Q: My print spooler, disk cache, or RAM disk refuses to load with EMS 4.0.

A: Be sure that your EMS driver has a clearly indicated page frame setting. Although DESQview does not require a page frame to use the EMS 4.0 standard, most print spoolers do.

Q: My mouse acts oddly or intermittently stops working under DESQview.

A: The later mouse drivers from Microsoft and Logitech are more reliable than the earlier ones. If you have a serial mouse, installing it on COM1 is the preferred setup.

Q: When I hit the DESQ key in graphics mode with my Hercules card, the screen becomes unreadable.

A: Allocate more common memory from the DESQview setup program. If your application shifts in and out of graphics mode, install it from a batch file with DVHERC.COM.

CHAPTER SIXTEEN

VMS

The day may come when you, the DOS user, will be confronted by a minicomputer running Digital Equipment Corporation's VMS operating system. It, like DOS, evolved from the same root: TOPS. These minicomputer systems are more related to MS-DOS and PC-DOS than most people realize.

In this chapter, you will learn about the VMS operating system and its relationship with MS/PC-DOS. You'll learn about linking VMS to DOS with something as simple as a terminal emulator and a null-modem cable or with Digital's powerful PCSA program. You will also learn about key features and what the future holds for VMS.

VMS and DOS have many similarities, including several common commands. Over 50 percent of the eight million VMS users also operate PCs and run MS/PC-DOS. As far back as the 1960s, Digital decided to standardize user interfaces and created DCL (Digital Command Language). Many operating systems are based on these commands. In fact, most MS/PC-DOS commands conform to this convention. For example, DIRECTORY, COPY, and DELETE use the same commands in TOPS, RT11, VMS, CP/M, and MS/PC-DOS.

THE HISTORY OF THE VAX AND VMS

The VAX was developed in 1975. Development began for its operating system, VMS, in 1976. The first member of the VAX family, the model 11-780, was announced in October 1977, along with VMS. A base-level version, which some people call the "real" version 1, shipped in early 1978; version 1.00 officially shipped in August 1978. Since then, VMS has had an additional four major releases and is now at version 5.4.

Over time, VMS has grown in many ways. VMS supports all the members of the VAX family (more than 30 models), dozens of programming languages, hundreds of Digital products, thousands of customer applications, and several graphical user interfaces (GUIs).

The VAX and VMS supplanted the 16-bit PDP-11 minicomputer family, which used several techniques to overcome the limitations of 16-bit addressing. There are several operating systems for the PDP-11, and their importance has diminished over the years. Besides offering all the features of the PDP-11, the VAX, along with VMS, offers a wealth of powerful new features and options.

A 36-bit computer (Digital System 10 & 20) was popular in universities and other environments that used the TOPS operating system. When VMS was released, the intent was to have a single operating system that would run across the entire family of systems, from the desktop to the data center. That's exactly what happened. Over the last decade, the VAX/VMS system has become the primary platform sold by Digital.

WHAT IS VMS?

VMS is a general-purpose operating system for Digital Equipment's family of VAX computers. VMS's general purpose is to support all styles of computing. VMS's roots can be traced to program development for both technical and commercial shops. Since version 1.0 of VMS, there has also been a batch subsystem that resembles MS- and PC-DOS batch files. Over time, VMS has also supported various types of distributed processing, including client-server processing and, more recently, transaction processing. VMS supports three types of interfaces: VAX Command Language (DCL); DECwindows, a graphics-based interface similar to Microsoft Windows on the PC; and forms-oriented interfaces.

The base system of VMS consists of 5 million lines of code; Digital Windows has over 2 million lines of code. The development team for version 1.00 of VMS consisted of 20 people. More than 350 programmers are working on VMS. Besides the core operating system, which ships ready to install out of the box, VMS has extended systems, such as PCSA, and vendor services, such as All In One, FORTRAN, Ada, and DECwrite.

VMS is upwardly compatible and will run on any model of the VAX produced by Digital. VMS dynamically configures itself to fit the system on which it is being run. User programs written on early versions of VMS will run without any modification on current versions.

VMS is used worldwide. There are over 350,000 site licenses for VMS, and the user community exceeds 8 million. There are regional and district support centers for VMS, and Digital provides a substantial number of training and support services. VMS has a sophisticated on-line help system, and it can be modified to insulate users from some of the more onerous tasks, such as dealing with file-naming conventions.

VMS has some very sophisticated scheduler algorithms, which allow jobs to be specified with selected priorities for resource capabilities. With VMS, you can control how much of the CPU to make available to a particular task. VMS can also manage tasks dynamically and adjust their priorities for optimal work loads and system performance. Dynamic task management is most useful when there's a lot of time-sharing. VMS will support all flavors of systems, from single user to multiple-thousands of users.

By using VAX Clusters, VMS can run on one or more nodes. VAX Clusters will support up to 100 nodes and can be interconnected on either the CI (High Speed Computer Interconnect) or Ethernet. Participating nodes share a common computing environment with the same files, security, and system-management domain. Whether you take a small workstation on someone's desk or a large time-sharing node out of service, the overall system is able to remain fully functional, with little or no performance impact. Because VMS uses a software-library system called "binaries," if a node should fail, the application will resume execution on another node. VMS operates the same with one node as it does with hundreds of nodes. The system is always present even if one or more of the nodes are out of service.

The single-system architecture of VMS supports scaling, device sharing, and simplicity of management. Scaling is great: When adding more users to the system, you need to add only more processors or disk drives. Device sharing allows all users to share all devices, such as printers and disk drives. Simplicity of management is possible because VMS operates as one system. Although you can specify individual nodes, you can use one common node name to address all areas of the system for such functions as e-mail and file access. When a user logs onto a particular node, VMS will transparently pick the appropriate availability addressing. These features give users lots of flexibility in environment configuration.

VMS is a 32-bit-addressing, virtual-memory system. It uses working-set concepts that make optimal usage of physical memory. VMS can support large jobs that exceed available physical memory through use of a virtual scheme. Physical-memory availability ranges from 4MB to 512MB. VMS is a symmetric multi-processing system that supports up to six processors on an individual node. One or more processors can perform computations against a common set of memory. VMS's support for parallel processing is one of its most powerful features.

The physical characteristics of VAX machines may vary. But available memory, cache size, bus type, and I/O extensions all conform to the same VAX architecture; the same program binaries will run on every member of the VAX family. Binaries and images in VMS are part of shareable memory. This layer of generic services, called the *run-time library,* is available to applications.

One thing that makes VMS unique is its ability to support an entire range of computing styles. Batch, real-time, distributed, and transaction processing are all supported by the same general-purpose, self-configuring VMS operating system. VMS out of the box is a complete computing environment that can be easily tailored to individual needs.

VMS is a very stable operating system. Digital has found that most of the problems they are asked to help with center around users who push a particular system configuration to its limits. VAX users who "try to put ten pounds of sugar into a five-pound bag" end up needing help from Digital's support arm. Common VMS problems are not all that different from problems with DOS. For instance, users don't read the manual or don't have enough of the right hardware or software to get the job done properly.

Logon and logoff with VMS is simple. First, you capture the terminal's attention with the command key, also called the gold key. You are then prompted to enter your name and your password. Logoff is just as easy: A user need only enter the LOGOUT command.

There are several options for password protection. A system administrator can set user-access levels in many different ways, depending on just how secure a system is needed. Passwords can be a minimum length or expire automatically after a specified period of time, and VMS can force users to select passwords generated by the system. (Forced, system-generated passwords may sound harsh, but VMS handles this nicely. Users must choose passwords from a list that the system supplies. The passwords contain a manageable number of letters and are usually easy to pronounce and remember.) The system administrator can also make use of the Access Control List to control user access to individual files. The Access Control List can regulate file access for all operations, including read, write, and delete.

VMS offers varying levels of system security. In the beginning, VMS had an extensive number of privileges that could be assigned to individual users or groups of users. Eventually, Digital found that it would be easier to classify security or access levels. VMS's security has evolved to four primary levels of access:

- No privileges required

- Access to simple network operations

- System programmer

- System administrator

Like DOS, VMS allows user control of screen output. The CTRL-Y key combination will break out of an application that is running. Scrolling can be interrupted with CTRL-S and continued with CTRL-Q.

There are a growing number of VAX home users, including academics and telecommunicators. Although VAX prices are not unreasonable, VAX hardware usually exceeds the PC budget for the home user. Luckily, VMS users don't have to rely on an actual VAX to run VMS. Digital's PCSA package turns a PC into an Xterminal display device that works with a modem or null-modem connection and makes transferring files and running applications a simple process. Over 50 percent of VMS users use PCs to interact with VMS. A display terminal and modem will also do fine for most VMS tasks. There are even third-party packages that simulate the VMS operating system on the PC.

```
                              READ.ME
```

Transferring from a PC to the VAX

There are three different ways to transfer a file between a VAX system and a PC. If you are using a popular terminal emulator on your PC, you can send it as ASCII text. On the VMS terminal, you can simply enter the CREATE command at the DCL prompt. Whatever text is sent to the VAX will be recorded in the text file you are creating on the VAX. You would probably use a null-modem connection to transfer files this way.

Another method to effect file transfers with either null-modem or dial-up (using a modem connection) is by using a terminal program that supports the Kermit file-transfer protocol. Kermit is not supplied as a basic part of the VMS operating system, but it is a commonly available utility.

There's no question that the PCSA program is the best way to get PCs and VAXs to talk to one another. PCSA offers a seamless file transfer. A volume is created on your PC that will display the contents of a corresponding volume on the VAX. In this way, you can address a VAX volume as if it were on your own PC. You can use the standard DOS COPY command to move files between the PC and the VAX. The PCSA package offers a transparent link of VAX and PC that not only allows seamless file transfers but allows you to operate a VAX and VMS from an ordinary PC.

COMMON DOS COMMANDS AND THEIR EQUIVALENTS

All VMS commands can be used in their basic forms. You can also specify qualifiers similar to the command line options offered by DOS. DCL commands are structured to be straightforward for novice users, but they can be made very powerful by the simple addition of qualifiers. You don't need to learn additional commands to do some serious work. VMS also has shortcuts, such as batch files, and VMS needs only the first three or four letters of a command to recognize it. You can even specify a different name for a command or group of commands.

You can redirect the output of any VMS command to a text file, just as in DOS. A useful interactive-processing feature of VMS is command recall and editing. The VMS command buffer can hold the last 20 commands executed, which you can save to disk. You can also save a full log of your session's activity, including the commands you entered and the output to the screen. You'll find these features useful for creating batch files or studying what you did during a session.

DIR   Like DOS's DIR command, the VMS DIRECTORY command has options for displaying the file-creation or -revision date, the file size and type, and so forth. The VMS DIR command defaults to a multiple column listing, but you can use the column qualifier to specify the number of columns you want. VMS lacks the pause option found in DOS, but you can use CTRL-S to stop and CTRL-Q to resume the display. The WHOLE SCREEN key toggles the stop-and-resume state, and CTRL-Y cancels the entire operation.

TYPE   Like DOS, VMS supports the file-listing command TYPE and even has a one-screen-at-a-time qualifier. With DOS, you would need to combine TYPE with PIPE and MORE to accomplish the same thing.

CD   VMS's equivalent to DOS's CD (change directory) command uses a tree-structured, hierarchical directory. It allows eight levels of depth. The command SET DEFAULT allows you to traverse these directory levels in a variety of ways. As in DOS, you can address files located in other directory levels by being more descriptive in the filenames.

SEARCH LIST   Unlike MS-DOS, VMS lets you execute a command on a group of files in any number of drives and directory levels, which you specify. VMS's equivalent to the DOS PATH command is the SEARCH LIST command. SEARCH LIST allows you to create a logical structure with multiple branches that are dissimilar.

VMS supports file mapping with full use of wildcard characters. You'll find the familiar asterisk character, which is used for one or more characters, and the percent symbol, which is used like the DOS ? wildcard to substitute for any single character. If the user doesn't have privileges for one or more areas in the search list, VMS will ignore them, and the user will not "see" those areas.

LOGICAL NAMES   VMS allows you to associate directory and device pairs with LOGICAL NAMES. For instance, you can have SYSTALLIB, SYSTALLSYS, and SYSTALLPROG, which will help users identify what devices and files they can use. LOGICAL NAMES eliminate the need for the user to know the physical location of a file or device and insulate the user from the need to master the complexities of the VMS naming conventions.

COPY, DELETE, RENAME   VMS has a copy utility and a COPY command. DISKCOPY is one of several options of the VMS backup utility. The INITIALIZE command provides several functions, including a formatting ability. There is a DELETE command and a RENAME command, but, just like MS-DOS prior to version 5.0, VMS has no undelete command. VMS users will probably have a good chance of reclaiming any lost files, since full backups are made daily in nearly 99.9% of VMS installations. VMS also has a file-compare command, called DIFFERENCES.

RUN   One way to run a program with VMS is to execute a RUN command. In many cases, an application can be installed by the system administrator so that simply typing its name will invoke it, as in MS/PC-DOS. Another way is to create a synonym for any program or command. There is even a macro-type capability that makes it possible to turn a command into a single keystroke. VMS users can set up the LOGIN.COM defaults so that the VMS environment will be even more similar to MS/PC-DOS.

Other VMS Commands

These are only a sampling of the VMS commands. These commands tend to be fairly straightforward English. For example, to edit a file, you simply type **edit**. Users often associate a favorite editor with the EDIT command. If you want system information, there's a SHOW command. To establish parameters, there's the SET command. The PRINT command is used to send a job to the appropriate print queue.

The first thing VMS users are encouraged to access is the on-line help system. This offers a full display of all the commands available. The help system can also give more pointed help, such as frequently used commands or batch file commands. The Digital windows interface has an even more sophisticated help system; it is more like a book than an on-line documentation tool. All of the standard Digital reference manuals are available this way. Most of the VMS applications also have specific help built into them. Users can also access VMS system help from within an application.

In the time-sharing mode, VMS will allow you to execute multiple jobs and jump from one task to another. The command to jump to the DCL command line is SPAWN. You can also execute DCL by creating a new DCL thread. You can end a new thread with the LOGOUT command or use the ATTACH command to switch among multiple threads.

Besides all of the commands available in DCL, you can use the Fileview application while running Digital Windows. Fileview gives you a graphical display of all the files. You can use the mouse to point to files you want moved, copied, deleted, or even executed. Digital Windows sports pull-down windows containing frequently used commands and dialog boxes that prompt the user for command options. Digital Windows and Fileview are user-friendly ways to get started with VMS.

VMS's documentation includes a user's manual, which explains how you interact with VMS and describes the common utilities the average user needs to know about. The VMS user's manual covers such things as mail, editing, and file manipulation.

THE FUTURE OF VMS

Because a growing number of VAX and VMS users are using PCs, VMS will continue to improve the integration of VMS and DOS. VMS is already a very secure system, and plans are in place for significant additions to security features. These new features will meet government security requirements and offer new auditing features.

The long-term outlook for VMS is increased support for distributed computing. VMS will take applications and split them up in several pieces to speed program execution. Besides increasing execution speed, the distributed-computing model will allow VMS to interface with other computing environments, such as PCs.

VMS will continue to expand their role in network architecture with DECNET. There will be improved connectivity between VMS DECNET and systems like UNIX TCP/IP and IBM SNA. Although VMS has these capabilities now, expect to see substantial improvements in the future.

CONCLUSION

For many years, Digital Equipment's VAX has had the reputation of the ultimate affordable minicomputer. Even though new marvels like the 486 and machines like Sun and NeXT now offer blindingly fast computing power, the VAX will continue to be a major computing environment.

If you are part of the work force of a *Fortune*-1000 firm or your organization has some of these pups—and if you can get authorization—sit down at a terminal and check it out. Get yourself a user ID and password, and log in.

CHAPTER SEVENTEEN

DR-DOS 5.0 and Concurrent DOS

If you are looking for an operating system with DOS compatibility but a lot more power, Digital Research has two excellent operating systems that you should consider. DR-DOS 5.0 and Concurrent DOS 386 are both DOS-compatible, and both extend the power of DOS.

DR-DOS 5 preceded MS-DOS 5.0 with direct file transfers and exceptional memory-management capabilities. Like MS-DOS, DR-DOS 5.0 is a single-task operating system. DR-DOS grew out of Concurrent DOS, a multiuser, multitasking operating system that was released by Digital Research when Intel released the 386. Concurrent DOS Release 3 is a DOS-compatible, multitasking operating system. These operating systems are well worth a good look.

Digital Research, Inc. (DRI) was founded in 1976 and is a leader in operating system technology. DRI developed CP/M (Control Program for Microcomputers), the first disk operating system. They followed this with a multiuser version, called MP/M. For the early IBM PCs, DRI developed a version of CP/M called CP/M 86.

You have to give DRI credit for tenacity. They've stayed right in there—although always just a heartbeat behind the leader, it seemed. This time, however, they may have jumped out in front.

In 1990, Digital Research announced DR-DOS 5.0, a powerful and formidable alternative to MS/PC-DOS. It jumps way out in front in the critical area of memory management. Who ever heard of 620-plus KB of usable low-DOS memory? Or who ever heard of the operating system kernel being moved above the 1MB boundary? Well, now you have.

COMPATIBILITY

Let's start at the beginning. One of our first reactions to DR-DOS was "Why would anyone risk running an operating system whose functions might not stay abreast of the leader's?" There are three supercritical areas that could affect the software compatibility of any alternative to DOS:

- The BIOS
- IBMBIO.COM (IBM PC-DOS) or IO.SYS (MS-DOS)
- IBMDOS.COM (IBM PC-DOS) or MSDOS.SYS (MS-DOS)

READ.ME

GEM

No discussion of Digital Research would be complete without a mention of the first PC-based graphical user interface (GUI). Called GEM (Graphic Environment Manager), the interface is best exemplified by the Xerox Ventura Publisher desktop publishing package. Like other GUIs, GEM has icons, drop-down menus, scroll bars, and the other accoutrements that make the GUI easy to learn and use.

GEM was the first systems software that supported mice, windows, and bit-mapped graphics images, such as icons, drop-down menus, and raster fonts for IBM PCs and compatibles. DRI also develops and markets other presentation-graphics and illustration applications, such as Presentation Team and Artline, that run under the GEM environment. Many GEM features are incorporated in ViewMAX, the GUI supplied with DR-DOS 5.0.

The BIOS may be IBM, Phoenix, Award, American Megatrends, or some other. It *is* important to the system, but the BIOS either works or it doesn't. It doesn't bear on the compatibility of the operating system.

In plain view (unhidden) in the root directory are IBMBIO.COM and IBMDOS.COM, ensuring compatibility with DOS-based systems. While you might have differences in the shell, these differences are allowed. Every program written for MS/PC-DOS should run flawlessly with DR-DOS 5.0, because applications don't use the shell, anyway.

Okay, you don't get BASIC, but you probably can dig up a version of GW-BASIC around somewhere, and that will usually suffice. If you don't need it, you won't miss it. If you do, you can go out and buy QuickBASIC or Power BASIC cheap. On the other hand, why pay for functions you don't really need? Once past these issues, you have only the issues of features and personal preference, and DR-DOS 5.0 shines in these areas.

DR-DOS 5.0 FEATURES

Let's start by looking at some of the features that excel in DR-DOS 5.0. Chief among them are MemoryMAX, ViewMAX, BatteryMAX, FileLINK, a disk cache, and network support. DR-DOS can be put into executable ROM by manufacturers. *Executable* means that, unlike other implementations, the operating system does not need to be moved into RAM to execute. This has significant advantages, especially in laptops where you can save the power required to access a floppy drive by booting from ROM. It is also useful in diskless workstations and wherever "instant on" characteristics are useful.

MemoryMAX

MemoryMAX is a built-in memory-management facility that moves the operating system, terminate-and-stay-resident programs (TSRs), and device drivers (including network drivers and buffers) into high memory, thereby freeing up application software space (up to 620KB or more, depending on the configuration). When MemoryMAX is installed, it detects the type of CPU (80286, 80386, or 80486) you are using and optimizes operation for that CPU.

Programs like HILOAD, HIDOS, and HIINSTALL work directly or indirectly with other memory-management utilities. Their use is covered extensively in DRI documentation; there is simply not enough room to cover them here.

ViewMAX

ViewMAX is a so-called CUA (common-user-access) keystroke-compatible graphical user interface; it works equally well with the keyboard or a mouse. ViewMAX provides easy access to DOS commands through a point-and-click interface. It is very intuitive and eliminates the need to learn cryptic DOS commands. ViewMAX fully supports file and global password protection and will prompt you for the required passwords.

ViewMAX looks much like GEM, for those familiar with the GEM interface. Figure 17-1 shows the opening screen. Although the manual supplied by DRI is complete and augmented with help, some items are worth noting here.

Figure 17-1

ViewMAX opening screen

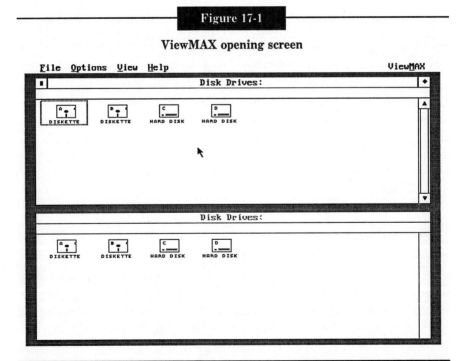

Across the top is a menu bar. On the desktop are two file areas with disk icons. You "open" the disk icons by double-clicking or by moving the bounding box over the appropriate icon with the arrow keys and pressing ENTER. The contents of the disk will then be displayed as icons. An icon can be selected with either the mouse or the keyboard, as above.

Figure 17-2 shows hard disk C opened in text mode. In Figure 17-3, the same disk is displayed in tree mode. Figures 17-4 through 17-6 show the File menu, the Options menu, and the View menu. Take a look at the available selections to get an idea of the wide range of choices available for file management.

BatteryMAX

BatteryMAX is a patent-pending technology designed to allow OEMs (original-equipment manufacturers) to incorporate battery-saving features into their laptops or other computers with batteries. It is not available off the shelf from your local dealer.

Figure 17-2

Text mode of hard disk C

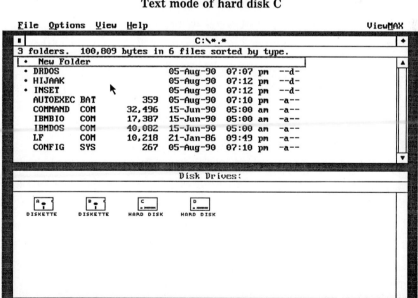

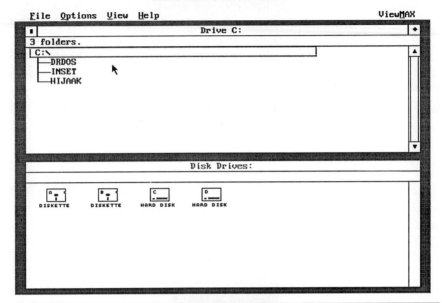

Figure 17-3

Hard disk C in tree mode

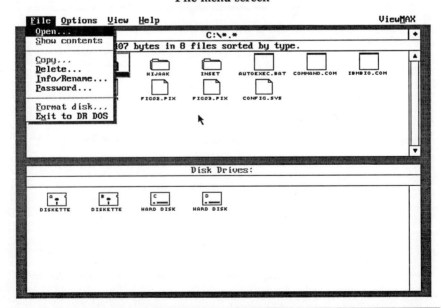

Figure 17-4

File menu screen

Figure 17-5

Options menu screen

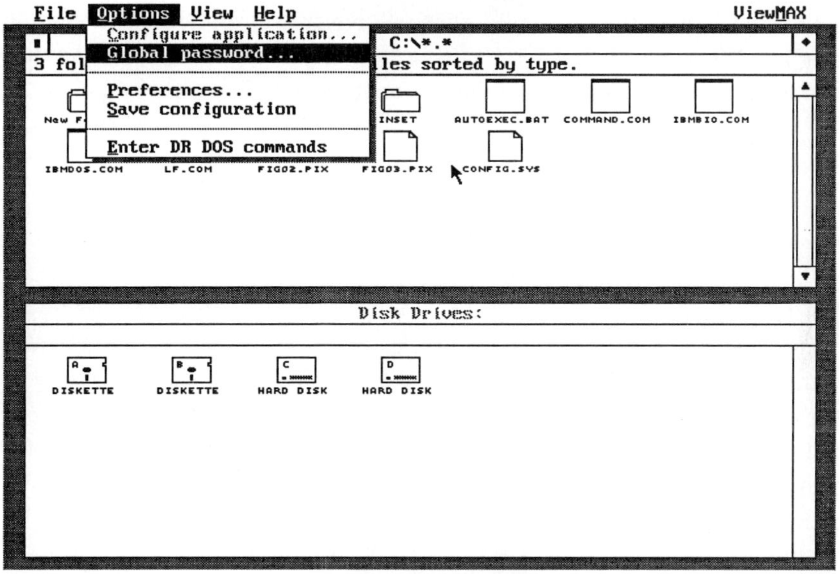

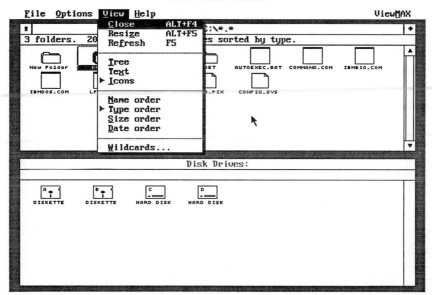

Figure 17-6

View menu screen

BatteryMAX can provide up to 2 or 3 times ordinary battery life, depending on implementation. It monitors both software and underlying hardware at the rate of 20 times per second, allowing BatteryMAX to control the use of circuitry and turn off hardware systems that are not being used. This activity, while invisible to users, provides significant reductions in battery use, resulting in longer operation between charges.

FileLINK

FileLINK is a file-transfer utility that provides high-speed transfers of files and programs over standard serial cables at up to 115 kilobaud, depending on the capabilities of the serial port being used. FileLINK will copy itself over the serial port to another computer to provide communication between the two computers. The second computer needs to be running some version of DOS, but, as with many similar utilities, you need not install FileLINK on the second computer. FileLINK does that for you over the communication line.

Disk Cache

CACHE.EXE is a disk-caching program. It allows disk reads to be cached to speed up disk access and improve throughput. You can set the cache size and assign it to extended or expanded memory. Note that it is a read cache with "write through." There is caching technology available that will allow "write behind," but the implementation is tricky.

Network Support

DR-DOS 5.0 provides network support for Novell Netware and other popular networks. The memory-management capabilities allow networking software to be loaded into high memory, thus freeing DOS memory for such memory-hungry applications as Xerox Ventura Publisher and Autodesk AutoCAD on these networks.

Editor

Although EDLIN is not provided, you won't miss it. DRI provides a full-screen editor, with commands similar to WordStar's, that will allow you complete freedom to edit your files as needed. The commands and operation of the editor are covered extensively in DRI's documentation. The editor also has a Help facility. To get information on starting and running the editor, you simply type **editor /h**.

Laptop Cursor

The cursor on laptop computers can be difficult to see. To help eliminate this problem, a CURSOR command is included. It allows the cursor to be converted to a slowly flashing block. The flash rate can be set from one-twentieth of a second to a full second in twentieths-of-a-second increments.

? Option and REM

REM is supported in CONFIG.SYS. This means that you can place explanatory remarks (comments) in this file, which can be a real advantage. In addition, *conditional* operations can be performed in CONFIG.SYS. For example,

```
?DEVICE=C:\DRDOS\ANSI.SYS
```

would prompt you with the following question each time the system booted:

```
DEVICE=C:\DRDOS\ANSI.SYS (Y/N) ?
```

You would then respond accordingly whether to load the device driver or not.

　　You can enter as many of these commands as you need in CONFIG.SYS. This means that you could have a single CONFIG.SYS file with all the drivers you might ever need. Each time the system boots, you can selectively load drivers appropriate to the applications you will be running.

For example, Windows needs HIMEM.SYS and SMARTDRV.SYS. It will not run in enhanced 386 mode if another expanded memory driver is installed. You could still have EMM386.SYS, HIMEM.SYS, and SMART-DRV.SYS in a single CONFIG.SYS, using the ? option for each one. You would simply answer **Y** for those drivers you needed during the session you were about to run.

HISTORY Command

DR-DOS 5.0 provides a HISTORY command. When enabled, this command allows the storage of commands you type. You can recall previous commands for execution by pressing the UP ARROW or DOWN ARROW key. When the appropriate command is displayed, you press ENTER to execute the command. You can also edit the command with the arrow keys, BACKSPACE, DEL, INS, and other appropriate editing keys. The HISTORY command can be included in your AUTOEXEC.BAT file or executed from the command line.

Installation

At one time, installing a new version of DOS was a tedious process. It involved backing up all files and reformatting your hard drive to ensure the proper location of the DOS files. With DR-DOS 5.0, this is not the case. You don't need to repartition or reformat your hard disk; you just follow some simple steps.

DR-DOS 5.0 is provided with an installation system. Simply insert the "Startup/Install" disk in the floppy disk drive of your choice, make that drive the default drive, and type **install**. You are presented with a series of screens that prompt you through the installation routine. Each screen has Help available for when you have questions about the options available. Once you have selected the appropriate options, the operating system and files will be transferred to the hard disk of your choice, with CONFIG.SYS and AUTOEXEC.BAT files installed.

Should you need to partition or format your hard disk, DR-DOS 5.0 will support partitions of up to 512MB. FDISK is used for partitioning and high-level formatting of hard disks. FDISK also provides information, through a menu system, about the way your hard disk is currently partitioned. The DR-DOS FORMAT command is only for floppy disks. This was by design to reduce accidental hard-disk formatting.

Once you've installed DR-DOS 5.0, you can use a program called Setup to reconfigure your system. Selecting new options will provide new CONFIG.SYS and AUTOEXEC.BAT files and new conditions when you reboot your system. It can save time over hand-editing these files, as is normally done. It can also prevent errors from creeping in—errors like the dreaded "Bad or missing COMMAND.COM."

MEM and TREE

Two unique commands rate special mention. The first of these is MEM, which allows you to look at the memory configuration of your system in great detail. The second command is TREE. You can find available options by typing **Tree /h** for Help.

Extended Commands

Several "extended" commands are available in DR-DOS 5.0, including XDIR, XDEL, DELQ, and ERAQ. A look at the command reference that follows will provide you with some additional detail.

COMMANDS EXCLUSIVE TO DR-DOS 5.0

This section is a complete reference for DR-DOS 5.0 commands. Each entry includes the command's full form, parameters, a description, and one or more examples, if appropriate.

CACHE

This is a disk-cache program that speeds up access to the hard drive. CACHE can be enabled during installation or in Setup.

Syntax: cache [/H] [/S=$nnnn$] [/X] [/E]

Options:

/H   Provides a Help screen.

/S=*nnnn*   *nnnn* is the buffer size in KB.

/X   Places the cache in expanded memory.

/E   Places the cache in extended memory.

Example: cache /s=256 /e

Enables caching with a 256KB buffer and places the buffer in extended memory.

CURSOR

This command will let you set a block cursor and set its blink rate. This is primarily for laptop screens.

Syntax: cursor [/H] [/S*nn*] [/C] [OFF]

Options:

/H   Provides a Help screen.

/S*nn*   Sets the flash interval in twentieth-of-a-second increments. The default is 4.

/C   Enables CGA compatibility.

OFF   Returns the cursor to the hardware cursor.

Example: cursor /s8

Sets a block cursor with a flash rate of 8/20 second.

DELQ and ERAQ

These commands are equivalent to DEL and ERASE, except that they ask for confirmation before deleting a file.

Syntax: delq [*drive:*][*path*] *filename*

Example: delq *.txt

Prompts on each TXT file. You confirm the deletion by typing **y** or leave the file by typing **n**.

EDITOR

This is the DR-DOS full-screen text editor, which includes an on-line help system and the ability to read and write to multiple files.

Syntax: editor [*filename*] [/H]

Option:

/H   Provides command line Help for the EDITOR command.

Example: editor

FILELINK

This command allows you to transfer files between computers.

Syntax: filelink [/H] *command* [@][*wildspec*] [*wildspec2*] [*comparm*] [*/switches*]

Options:

A wide range of options are provided under FILELINK. The /H (Help) switch will aid in expanding these options.

Example: filelink /h

HILOAD

This command will load a program, device driver, or TSRs into high memory. Before HILOAD can be used, a device driver supporting upper memory must be loaded. HILOAD is probably best used in AUTOEXEC.BAT, but it can be used from the command line.

You can load the following DR-DOS programs with HILOAD:

CURSOR.EXE
KEYB.COM
NLSFUNC.EXE
GRAPHICS.COM
GRAFTABL.COM
JOIN.EXE
SHARE.EXE

Syntax: hiload *filename*

Example: hiload cursor.exe

PASSWORD

This command assigns a password to a file or a path. The password can be up to eight characters long. Passwords can be assigned from the command line or from ViewMAX.

Syntax: password [/H] [*path*] *filename* [/R] [/W] [/D] [/P] [/G:*password*] [/N] [/NP] [/NG] [/S]

Options:

/R:*password*   Password required for reading, copying, writing, deleting, or renaming the file.

/W:*password* Password required for copying, deleting, or renaming the file.

/D:*password* Password required for deleting or renaming the file.

/P:*password* Password for a path rather than a file. Each time you try to access the path, you will be asked for the password.

/G:*password* Sets a global default password.

/N Removes all password protection.

/NP Removes password protection from a directory.

/NG Removes the global password.

/S Password for files and subdirectories associated with the current directory.

Example: password secret.doc /r:*password*

SETUP

This command brings up a menu-driven program that allows you to configure your system.

Syntax: setup

SHARE

The ability to share files is built into DR-DOS; so, you do not need to load SHARE to perform file-sharing operations. Some applications, however, look for certain things in SHARE. For this reason, SHARE is included with

DR-DOS for compatibility with packages that require it. This version of SHARE does not perform any functions; it simply makes itself known to applications that require its presence.

Syntax: share

SID

This is the Symbolic Instruction Debugger. It allows you to debug and test programs.

Syntax: sid

TOUCH

TOUCH changes the time and date stamps of a file or group of files.

Syntax:
touch [/H] [*path*] *filename* [*options*]

Options:

/H   Displays help information.

/T:*hh:mm:ss*   The time to set.

/D:*date*   The date to set.

/P   Prompts before touching each file.

/R   Includes read-only files.

/S   Includes subdirectories associated with the current directory.

Examples: touch *.doc /d:01-01-90 /s

touch *.txt /t:08:00:00 /p

TYPE

The TYPE command provides a /P option, for "pause." Using TYPE with the /P option will cause TYPE to display one screenful and wait for a keystroke before proceeding to the next screen.

XDEL

This is the extended delete function for files and subdirectories.

Syntax: xdel [/H] [*path*]*filename* [*options*]

Options:

/H   Displays Help information.

/D   Removes empty subdirectories.

/N   Deletes all specified files without prompting.

/P   Prompts before deleting.

/S   Deletes files in subdirectories.

Examples: xdel *.bak /s

xdel c:\work\letters*.bak /p

XDIR

This is the extended directory command.

Syntax: xdir [+|−ADHRS] [path][*filename*] [*options*]

Options:

+|− [A] [D] [H] [R] [S]   Includes (+) or excludes (−) files with certain attributes.

/B   Brief directory-display format.

/C   Computes hash code (checksum) for each file and display.

/H   Provides on-screen Help for command syntax.

/L   Long directory-display format. This is the default.

/P   Pauses after each screen.

/R   Reverses sort order.

/S   Displays subdirectories.

/T   Sorts by date and time.

/W   Wide directory-display format.

/Z   Sorts by file size.

Examples: xdir *.* /z

xdir a: *.* /s /p

DOS Commands Not Supported by DR-DOS

DEBUG
This command is replaced by the DR-DOS 5.0 command SID.

FC (COMP is the PC-DOS equivalent)

This command is replaced by the DR-DOS 5.0 command COMP. The MS and PC DOS command only supports file comparison. The DR-DOS COMP command compares both files and disks.

SELECT

This command is replaced by the DR-DOS 5.0 command SETUP.

CONCURRENT DOS 386

If you're looking for a DOS-compatible multitasking operating system, this may be the answer. Concurrent DOS 386 (CDOS) is the father of DR-DOS. As you would expect, it offers many similar features as well as DOS compatibility. Moreover, CDOS takes advantage of the 386 virtual mode and offers multitasking and multiuser capabilities. You can think of it as a low-cost, DOS-compatible, networking environment. Your server needs to be a 386 or above, but your workstations can be XTs. CDOS will support up to ten users in the network for only $495.

Concurrent DOS 386 will run DOS applications or applications developed to take advantage of the power of CDOS. A wide variety of vertical-market applications have been developed specifically for CDOS. Netware files may be transferred between the Netware server and a local hard disk drive on a CDOS system.

Other major features of CDOS include:

- DOS-3.3-compatible record locking

- Support for DOS 3.3 and DOS 4 disk-partition schemes

- A menu-driven File Manager

- On-line Help

- CP/M application support

- Support for the expanded-memory specification for applications that use expanded memory

COMMANDS EXCLUSIVE TO CONCURRENT DOS 386

This section is a complete reference for Concurrent DOS 386 version 3.0 commands. Each entry includes the command's full form, parameters, a description, and one or more examples, if appropriate.

8087

This command signals to CDOS 386 that the COM or EXE program about to be started is going to use the 80X87 math coprocessor.

Syntax: 8087 = [on|off]

Examples: 8087 = on

8087 = off

AUX

This command sets the auxiliary port. You can assign a different auxiliary port for each window.

Syntax: aux

aux = n

Option:

n The auxiliary port number.

Examples: aux

aux = 1

BACKUP

This menu-driven command is used to make backup copies of files from a hard disk to floppies or streaming tape. It is also used for restoring files.

Syntax: backup

BANK

This command controls how an application program will run in banked memory. The BANK command is overridden by PIFED information.

Note: bank = off can seriously degrade system performance by affecting the amount of memory available to other running applications.

Syntax: bank = [on|off]

Examples: bank = on

bank = off

CARDFILE

Just as the name implies, this is an index-card-like filing system. You can use it for storing names and addresses.

Syntax: cardfile [color]

Option:

color Used for color monitors; otherwise, cardfile comes up as a monochrome display.

Examples: cardfile

cardfile color

CDOS

This command invokes a copy of the Concurrent DOS 386 CDOS.COM command processor used to run terminate-and-stay-resident (TSR) programs, such as SideKick.

Syntax: cdos

cdos /c *command*

Examples: cdos

cdos /c wp

CHSET

This is the command-header SET program. It is used to change or display command-header information on programs with a CMD extension.

Syntax: chset [help]

chset [*path*]*filename*

chset [*path*]*filename* [*option = setting*[,*option = setting*. . .]]

Examples: chset [help]

chset myprog.com

chset myprog.com [8087 = on]

chset myprog.com [8087 = on, bank = on]

COPYMENU

This command allows you to copy one or more menus between existing menu files. COPYMENU has two complementary programs for use with menus: EDITMENU and RUNMENU.

Syntax: copymenu

copymenu *source target* —m

copymenu *source target* menulist (menu1, menu2, . . .)

Example: copymenu

Options:

—m   use in place of menu name to reference all of source.

CPM

This command allows you to read and write CP/M disks.

Syntax: cpm

CSPOOL

The Concurrent DOS 386 print spooler, CSPOOL, manages system printers and resolves printer-ownership conflicts by intercepting and scheduling print requests.

Syntax: CSPOOL *subcommand job#*

Options:

Priority *job# value#*

Stop Job: Completely removes a job.

Start   Initializes spooler.

Quit   Removes if from the system.

Status   Displays spooler and job status.

Status C   Continuously displays spooler status.

(For other options, see DRI documentation. Job numbers are not used with all subcommands.)

DELQ

This command is the same as ERASE, except that it asks if you want to delete each file.

Syntax: delq [*drive:*][*path*]*filename*

Example: delq *.txt

DREDIX

This is the CDOS 386 text editor. It allows you to read, write, and change text files.

Syntax: dredix

DSKMAINT

This is a disk-maintenance program. It combines FORMAT, DISKCOPY, and DISKCOMP into an easy-to-use, menu-driven utility.

Syntax: dskmaint

EDITMENU

This allows you to create, change, or delete menu files. Other menu programs include COPYMENU and RUNMENU.

Syntax: editmenu

editmenu [*path*]*filename*

Example: editmenu

ERAQ

This command is the same as ERASE, except that it asks if you want to delete each file.

Syntax: eraq [*drive:*][*path*]*filename*

Example: eraq *.txt

FM

This is the CDOS 386 File Manager system. It presents you with a menu of commands that you may select.

Syntax: fm

FUNCTION

This allows you to assign commands to function keys. The filename must have a PFK extension.

Syntax: function

function [*path*]*filename*.pfk

Examples: function

function mykeys.pfk

HELP

This command allows you to call up Help or create your own Help file.

Syntax: help

help [*topic*][*subtopics*]

help [*options*]

Options:

Extract   Creates a file called HELP.DAT from the HELP.HLP file. The HELP.DAT file can then be edited with a text editor.

Create   Takes the HELP.DAT file and creates a HELP.HLP file.

Examples: help

help dir example

help extract

IDLE

This command invokes CDOS's dynamic idle-detection feature for applications that waste CPU time.

Syntax:
Idle
Idle = on
Idle = off

Options:

On   Turns idle detection on

Off   Turns idle detection off

No option   Gives idle detection status. End is part of CCONFIG.SYS. This function is system wide.

LIMSIZE

This command lets you change the amount of expanded memory available to an application.

Syntax: limsize [*nnnn*]

Option:
nnnn

This is the amount of expanded memory, in KB. It is rounded up to the nearest 16KB. The default is 1008KB.

Example: limsize 800

LOADSYS

This command loads CDOS 386 if DOS is currently running.

Syntax: loadsys [*option*]

Options:

Ask Asks if you want to load CDOS 386.

Install Installs LOADSYS under CDOS 386 so that it will work under DOS.

Examples: loadsys

loadsys ask

loadsys install

MEMSIZE

This command lets you set the amount of conventional memory available to an application.

Syntax: memsize [*nnnn*]

Option:

nnnn The amount of conventional memory in KB. The default is 640KB.

Example: memsize 640

PASSWORD

This command assigns a password to a file or a path. The password can be up to eight characters long.

Syntax: password [/H] [*path*]*filename* [/R] [/W] [/D] [/P] [/G:*password*] [/N] [/NP] [/NG] [/S]

Options:

/R:*password*   Password required for reading, copying, writing, deleting, or renaming the file.

/W:*password*   Password required for copying, deleting, or renaming the file.

/D:*password*   Password required for deleting or renaming the file.

/P:*password*   Password operates on a path rather than a file. Each time you try to access the path, you will be asked for the password.

/G:*password*   Sets a global default password.

/N   Removes all password protection.

/NP   Removes password protection from a directory.

/NG   Removes the global password.

/S   Password operates on files and subdirectories associated with the current directory.

Example: password secret.doc /r:*password*

PIFED

This command allows you to change the program information imbedded in application programs. This information includes memory requirements, interrupts, and direct device access.

Syntax: pifed [*path*]*filename* [.com | .exe] [/t]

Option:

/T   Allows PIFED to work in Teletype mode, which allows you to use simple serial terminals.

Example: pifed myprog.exe /t

PRINTER

This command displays or sets a printer to the current window. CDOS 386 starts with all windows assigned to printer 0, which is analogous to LPT1.

Syntax: printer

printer *n*

Option:

n   A number from 0 to 4 for printer assignment:

0	First parallel interface (LPT1)
1	Second parallel interface (LPT2)
2	Third parallel interface (LPT3)
3	First serial interface (COM1)
4	Second serial interface (COM2)

Examples: printer

printer 1

PRINTMAP

This command allows the display or remapping of printers and auxiliary devices.

Syntax: printmap

printmap LPT n = PRNn

Options:

/**p**   lists available print devices

/**a**   lists available auxil devices

/*****   sets all consoles to same mapping

PRINTMGR

This command sets up a printer queue and prints files. The DR-DOS command CSPOOL offers these functions and more.

Syntax: printmgr [*path*]*filename* [*options*]

Options:

Reset   Stops and deletes a job.

Status   Displays current print jobs and their status.

Delete   Gives menu of print jobs you can delete.

Terminate   Suspends print manager while retaining jobs.

Start   Restarts a print job.

Printer numbers (0-12)

printer#	device
0	LPT1
1	LPT2
2	LPT3
3	COM1 or serial printer or terminal
4	COM2 or serial printer or second terminal
.	.
.	.
.	.

5—12 are successive serial devices

Examples: printmgr reset

printmgr status

printmgr delete

printmgr terminate

printmgr start 0

printmgr mytext.txt

printmgr mytext1.txt mytext2.txt

REBOOT

This command performs a system reset. It is the same as a press of CTRL-ALT-DEL.

Note: You may want to password-protect this command if you are running a multiuser system. This will prevent users from resetting the system without your permission.

Syntax: reboot

RUNMENU

This command runs a menu file. It is used with the commands COPYMENU and EDITMENU.

Syntax: runmenu

SCEPTER

This command initializes the banked memory routines for CDOS 386 XM.

Syntax: scepter

SETPORT

This command is a menu-driven program that configures your serial ports (COM1 and COM2) without having to restart the system.

Syntax: setport

SETUP

This command is a menu-driven program that configures the system and saves the start-up parameters.

Syntax: setup

SHOW

This command is used to show disk drive information and status.

Syntax: show [*drive*:][*option*]

Options:

Space   Displays the space remaining on a drive.

Drive   Displays drive characteristics.

Label   Displays the disk's label.

Help   Displays Help.

Examples: show c: drive

STOP

This command will stop a program that is currently running. It will also display running applications, memory use, and available memory.

Syntax: stop

stop *program window#*

Options:

Program The name of the program that is running.

window# The number of the window in which the application is running.

Examples: stop

stop myapp 1

SUSPEND

This allows a program to be suspended while it is in the background.

Syntax: suspend = [on|off]

Examples: suspend = on

suspend = off

TOUCH

TOUCH changes the time and date stamps of a file or group of files.

Syntax: touch [/H] [*path*]*filename* [*options*]

Options:

/H Displays Help information.

/T:*hh:mm:ss* The time to set.

/D:*date* The date to set.

/P Prompts before touching each file.

/R Includes read-only files.

/S Includes subdirectories associated with the current directory.

Examples: touch *.doc /d:01-01-90 /s

touch *.txt /t:08:00:00 /p

WINDOW

This command allows you to change and save window parameters.

Syntax: window [*command*]

Example: window view

WMENU

This is a menu-driven program that allows you to change window parameters.

Syntax: wmenu

XDEL

This is the extended delete function for files and subdirectories.

Syntax: xdel [/H] [*path*]*filename* [*options*]

Options:

/H Displays Help information.

/D Removes empty subdirectories.

/N Deletes all specified files without prompting.

/P Prompts before deleting.

/S Deletes files in subdirectories

Examples: xdel *.bak /s

xdel c:\work\letters*.bak /p

XDIR

This is the extended directory command.

Syntax: xdir [+|−ADHRS] [*path*]*filename* [*options*]

Options:

+|−[A] [D] [H] [R] [S] Includes (+) or excludes (−) files with certain attributes.

/B Brief directory-display format.

/C Computes hash code (checksum) for each file and display.

/L Long directory-display format. This is the default.

/P Pauses after each screen.

/R Reverses sort order.

/S Displays subdirectories.

/T Sorts by date and time.

/W   Wide directory-display format.

/Z   Sorts by file size.

Examples: xdir *.* /z

xdir a:*.* /s /p

DOS Commands Not Supported by Concurrent DOS 386

CHCP
This command is not needed by CDOS 386; the operating system takes care of the code-page switching itself.

CTTY
This command is replaced by the CDOS 386 command SETPORT.

COMP
This command is replaced by the CDOS 386 command FM.

EXE2BIN
This command is not needed by CDOS 386.

EXIT
This command is not needed by CDOS 386.

FASTOPEN
This command is not needed by CDOS 386.

FC
This command is replaced by the CDOS 386 command FM.

GRAFTABL
This command is not needed by CDOS 386.

GRAPHICS
This command is not needed by CDOS 386.

JOIN
This command is not needed by CDOS 386.

KEYB
This command is replaced by the CDOS 386 command SETUP, which lets you select the keyboard type.

MEM
This command is not needed by CDOS 386.

MODE
This command is replaced by the CDOS 386 commands SETPORT, WINDOW, and WMENU.

NLSFUNC
This command is replaced by the CDOS 386 command SETUP.

PRINT
This command is replaced by the CDOS 386 commands PRINTMGR and TYPE with I/O redirection.

RECOVER
This command is replaced by the CDOS 386 command CHKDSK with the /R parameter.

RESTORE
This command is replaced by the CDOS 386 command BACKUP.

SHARE
This command is not needed by CDOS 386.

QUICK REFERENCE

DR-DOS 5.0 Command Line Commands

APPEND
Specifies a search path for data and overlays.

ASSIGN
Reassigns a drive letter to a different drive.

ATTRIB
Displays and modifies a file's attributes.

BACKUP
Makes backup copies of hard disks and floppy disks.

BREAK (Built-in)
Allows you to break out of programs.

CACHE
The disk-cache program.

CHCP (Built-in)
Changes the specified code page.

CHDIR or CD (Built-in)
Changes the current directory path or displays the current subdirectory.

CHKDSK
Checks the integrity of data on disks and restores corrupted disks.

CLS (Built-in)
Clears the screen.

COMMAND
Loads a second copy of the DR-DOS default command processor.

COMP
Compares files character by character.

COPY (Built-in)
Copies files between directories and to devices.

CTTY (Built-in)
Redirects input and output.

CURSOR
Allows you to change the cursor characteristics.

DATE (Built-in)
Displays and changes the date.

DEL (Built-in)
Deletes files.

DELQ (Built-in)
Deletes files with query.

DIR (Built-in)
Displays the files in a directory.

DISKCOMP
Compares two disks of the same format.

DISKCOPY
Copies an entire disk to another of the same format.

EDITOR
The text-editing program.

ERAQ (Built-in)
Deletes files with query.

ERASE or ERA (Built-in)
Erases files.

EXE2BIN
Turns EXE files into binary files.

EXIT (Built-in)
Returns to a running application.

FASTOPEN
Increases the speed at which disk files are accessed.

FDISK
Sets and changes partitions on a hard disk.

FILELINK
The file-transfer program.

FIND
Locates a string of characters in a file.

FORMAT
Formats disks.

GRAFTABL
Displays extra characters on a color/graphics display.

GRAPHICS
Allows you to print graphics using the PRTSCR key.

HILOAD (Built-in)
Allows you to load an application into upper memory at startup.

JOIN
Joins a disk drive to an empty subdirectory on another disk drive.

KEYB
Allows use of non-USA keyboards.

LABEL
Sets the volume label on a floppy disk.

MEM
Displays how your system is using memory.

MKDIR or MD (Built-in)
Makes a directory.

MODE
Sets COM port parameters, printer type, and monitor type.

MORE (Built-in)
Causes output to the screen to be displayed one screen at a time.

NLSFUNC
Provides support of extended country information and allows CHCP to be used.

PASSWORD
Sets password protection to files or paths.

PATH (Built-in)
Sets or displays path information.

PRINT
Enables print spooling.

PROMPT (Built-in)
Sets the command prompt.

RECOVER
Recovers corrupted files from a disk.

RENAME or REN (Built-in)
Renames files.

REPLACE
Selectively copies files.

RESTORE
Restores files that were backed up using the BACKUP command.

RMDIR or RD (Built-in)
Removes subdirectories.

SET (Built-in)
Inserts strings into the command processor's environment.

SETUP
Changes system-configuration information.

SHARE
Installs file sharing.

SID
The debugging program.

SORT
Reads information from a standard input and writes it to a standard output.

SUBST (Built-in)
Allows you to replace a path with a drive letter.

SYS
Transfers the DR-DOS system files to a specified drive.

TIME (Built-in)
Displays and changes the time of day.

TOUCH
Sets the time and date stamps on groups of files.

TREE
Displays the path of directories and subdirectories.

TYPE (Built-in)
Displays the contents of a text file.

VER (Built-in)
Displays the version number.

VERIFY (Built-in)
Verifies that the data has been written correctly to disk.

VOL (Built-in)
Displays the volume label.

XCOPY
Selectively copies groups of files.

XDEL
Selectively deletes groups of files.

XDIR
The extended directory list.

Concurrent DOS 386 Command Line Commands

8087 (Built-in)
Indicates that a COM or EXE program uses an 8087 math coprocessor.

APPEND
Specifies a search path for data and overlays.

ATTRIB
Displays and modifies a file's attributes.

AUX (Built-in)
Selects auxiliary port.

BACKUP
Makes backup copies of hard disks to floppy disks and restores from floppy disks to hard disks.

BANK (Built-in)
Controls how a program works in banked memory.

BATCH
Executes a batch file.

BREAK
Allows you to break out of programs.

CARDFILE
Saves and loads index-card-like files.

CHDIR or CD (Built-in)
Changes the current directory path or displays the current subdirectory.

CHKDSK
Checks the integrity of data on disks, and restores corrupted disks.

CLS (Built-in)
Clears the screen.

COPY
Copies files between directories and to devices.

COPYMENU
Copies menus from one file to another.

CPM
Lets you read CP/M files.

DATE (Built-in)
Displays and changes the date.

DELQ (Built-in)
Deletes files with query.

DIR (Built-in)
Displays the files in a directory.

DISKCOMP
Compares two disks of the same format.

DISKCOPY
Copies an entire disk to another of the same format.

DREDIX
Lets you load, change, and save text files.

DSKMAINT
A menu-driven disk-format program.

EDITMENU
Creates, modifies, and deletes menus.

ERAQ (Built-in)
Deletes files with query.

ERASE or ERA or DEL (Built-in)
Erases files.

FDISK
Sets and changes partitions on a hard disk.

FIND
Locates a string of characters in a file.

FM
Allows you to select commands from a menu.

FORMAT
Formats disks.

FUNCTION
Allows you to set function key command assignments.

HELP
Brings up Help on CDOS 386 commands.

LABEL
Sets the volume label on a floppy disk.

LIMSIZE
Sets the amount of EMS memory available to an application.

LOADSYS
Starts CDOS 386 if DOS has control at startup.

MEMSIZE
Sets the amount of conventional memory available to an application.

MKDIR or MD (Built-in)
Makes a directory.

MORE (Built-in)
Causes output to screen to be displayed one screen at a time.

PASSWORD
Sets password protection to files or paths.

PATH (Built-in)
Sets or displays path information.

PIFED
Sets system parameters for an application so that Concurrent DOS 386 is configured correctly when the application is run.

PRINTER (Built-in)
Changes the current printer number.

PRINTMGR
Controls the printing of files.

PROMPT (Built-in)
Sets the command prompt.

REBOOT
Performs a system reset (same as CTRL-ALT-DEL).

RENAME or REN (Built-in)
Renames files.

REPLACE
Selectively copies files.

RMDIR or RD (Built-in)
Removes subdirectories.

RUNMENU
Runs a menu.

SCEPTER (Concurrent XM Only)
Initializes banked memory management.

SET (Built-in)
Inserts strings into the command processor's environment.

SETPORT
Configures the serial ports.

SETUP
Changes the default configuration.

SHOW
Displays status of current disk.

STOP
Displays memory allocation and terminates programs.

SUBST (Built-in)
Allows you to replace a path with a drive.

SUSPEND (Built-in)
Suspends execution of EXE and COM files when their windows are switched out.

TIME
Displays and changes the time of day.

TOUCH
Sets the time and date stamps on a group of files.

TREE
Displays the path of directories and subdirectories.

TYPE (Built-in)
Displays the contents of a text file.

VER
Displays the version number.

VOL (Built-in)
Displays the volume label.

WINDOW
Displays and modifies the window configuration.

WMENU
Changes the window configuration.

XCOPY
Selectively copies groups of files.

XDEL
Selectively deletes groups of files.

XDIR
The extended directory list.

CONCLUSION

For many years now, there have been two operating systems: PC-DOS and MS-DOS. (Okay, so that's really only one.) There are, however, fine alternatives. DR-DOS 5.0 and Concurrent DOS 386 are functional, full-featured operating systems that offer significant enhancements to DOS.

Your decision to use either of these programs should be based on taste and preference. Don't be concerned that they might not be quite what is offered elsewhere. Give them a try—you may find just what you need.

CHAPTER EIGHTEEN

Networks

Networks are important to DOS users, because they are going to encounter networks whether they want to or not. Most people have misconceptions about networks. This chapter will provide readers with information about networks that is different from anything they can read in any other book.

Networks, simply put, are a means for connecting many computers, allowing them to share resources. These resources include programs, files, printers, plotters, tape backups, modems, and fax cards. Networks allow computer users to work together more efficiently and effectively, lower hardware and software costs, improve reliability, and cut support costs.

Networks are one of the fastest-growing segments of the computer and office automation industries. As computer technology continues to improve, networks will become more and more prevalent.

"SNEAKERNET"

You are familiar with your own computer. It has its own processor, memory, screen, and disk drives. Perhaps you work in an office where 20 other people have computers similar to yours. Many of them have similar jobs and run similar software.

Now, suppose you need a file that is on someone else's computer. Perhaps it's a word processing file that you want so that you can send a letter similar to someone else's. So, you format a floppy disk and go over to the person at the other computer. You ask him if he wouldn't mind exiting his current program and copying a file for you.

Or perhaps someone is using the laser printer, and you have to print something that looks really nice. You go over to the person who has the laser printer and ask if you can borrow her computer long enough to print a couple of files.

What has happened here is that you have formed a computer network called "SneakerNet." This network is characterized by people running back and forth between computers with floppy disks in their hands. Under SneakerNet, you create a set of rules for transferring files from one machine to another, ensuring that everyone has the "latest and greatest." You create a set of rules about how resources will be shared, about who gets to borrow what, and about putting things back when you're done.

With SneakerNet, you create a system establishing who has priority access to the laser printer and what to do if someone is hogging it. A sophisticated print-share method might involve a system where users copy their print jobs onto floppies and stack them next to the laser printer in a "To be Printed" or "Print Queue" box. Then you establish rules for priority print jobs and for how conflicts over the printer are to be resolved.

Some SneakerNets are so big that they have dedicated print servers. This evolves when the person with the laser printer is being interrupted so much that he or she isn't getting any work done. You set up the dedicated print server by setting up your oldest, "clunker" PC to drive your laser printer and having someone shove the next disk in every time the PC beeps.

Perhaps everyone has a tape backup card in their computers and you have one or two external tape drives for doing backups. In a well-organized SneakerNet, you have a schedule as to who gets to use the tape backup when. And you have to make sure users put it back when it's done so that the next person doesn't have to hunt for it.

The interesting thing about SneakerNet is that the majority of Sneaker-Net users don't even realize that they are running on a network! It just kind of grew into one.

Although SneakerNet is easy to set up, it quickly runs into limitations. It's slow, and it requires a lot of effort on the part of the users. But what is a better way?

REAL NETWORKS

Imagine that instead of your hard disk being an internal drive, it is in a separate box a few feet away from your computer. A cable connection allows you to access it as if it were inside your computer. Now, suppose that someone else in your office has a cable connecting her computer to the hard disk box, too. She could access it as if it were in her computer. This is the basis of a network.

Common disk access is accomplished with a hard disk and a cable instead of carrying floppies back and forth. People in networks still have their own processors and memory, their own screens and keyboards, but they share a hard disk. It is as if the files on the hard disk are in each computer.

Now, let's expand this picture even further. You have a dedicated computer, called the *file server,* that has some big, fast disk drives and lots of memory. Connected to the file server are several printers. The file server has a *local area network (LAN)* card in it. The LAN card is a high-speed data-transfer card that connects the file server to all the other computers in the office over a coaxial cable. The other computers in the office also have LAN cards in them.

So, you have this file-server computer with a big disk and all the printers, and its LAN card is connected through coaxial cable to the LAN cards in all the other computers. OK, you're picturing this in your mind. Now, we are going to start calling the old computers *workstations.* The file server is where the hard disks are, and the workstations are where people do their computer work.

So now you're at your workstation. Your local hard disk is drive C, and now you have a drive F. Drive F is the network drive, but it looks like it's in your computer. It looks the same way from any other workstation on the network. Any file on drive F can be accessed by anyone on the network without people having to run around with floppies.

"Whoa," you say. "Wait a minute. I don't want everyone accessing my stuff!" Don't worry—networks have security that lets you share what you want to share and protect what you want to protect. This is done through *access rights.* (And don't forget that you can always use an encryption program, such as Secret Disk II from Lattice Software, to protect sensitive files.)

If everything is going to be on one great big hard drive, the first thing you are going to have to do is get organized. This means creating directories that allow people to find the files they need. Since the most popular network is the Novell network, we're going to write about this from Novell's perspective. Other networks are similar.

Under Novell, a directory structure might appear as shown in Figure 18-1.

Note the PUBLIC directory. With this system, shared programs are loaded from public directories, and data files are kept in private directories. So, if Dick wanted to copy a letter from Jane, he would merely copy from the F:\HOME\JANE\WORD directory to the F:\HOME\DICK\WORD directory (assuming he had access rights to do so).

Before we get too deeply into software, let's get back into the big picture on hardware. We want to work from the big picture down to specifics so that you can understand what networking is all about.

Since all the files and programs are out on the file server, you may ask at this point, "What do I do with my internal hard disk?" Quite frankly, get rid of it. One of the advantages of a network is that you no longer need an internal hard disk. This is an idea that is hard to grasp for a lot of people, but your internal hard disk drive becomes as useless as your appendix once you're on a network.

In many cases, there is an actual speed advantage to this. Novell keeps the entire directory structure and file allocation tables in RAM. Much of the rest of RAM is used for disk caching. This helps speed up reads over the local drive. Network writes are even faster. On a local drive, you have to wait until the write actually occurs until you can go on. Under the network, as soon as the LAN card sends the packet to the file server, the local workstation considers the job done and goes on. The physical disk write on the server takes place later.

After seeing the speed advantage and facing the hassle of keeping copies of files on both drives, many people remove the hard disks from their systems. The hard disk is not the only thing that you can eliminate with the network. A boot prompt can be installed on the LAN card, allowing workstations to boot up from the network. This eliminates the need for floppy drives. Also, the floppy controller and hard disk controller can be removed. This begins to sound like a terminal on a multiuser system now, doesn't it?

When a workstation attaches to the network, the workstation's clock is set from the server's clock. This eliminates the need for a clock chip at the workstation. With access to network printers, there is no need for local printers or printer ports. And, since tape backup is done for the entire network, no local tape drives or tape cards are necessary.

What this means for you is that a workstation can consist of as little as a motherboard, power supply, RAM, video card, LAN card, keyboard, and

Figure 18-1

A possible Novell network directory structure

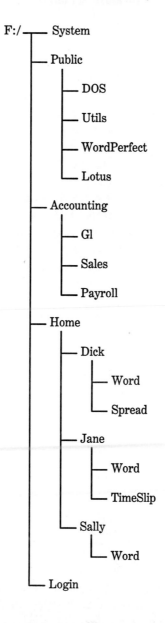

screen. Network workstations can be purchased for about $600 for monochrome XTs to about $1500 for 386s with VGA monitors. Once you need about six computers, a network can actually be less expensive.

NETWORK PRINTING

Since the printers are attached to the file server, any station can print to any printer. This is done by using some form of capture command, which redirects printer output from your workstation. When you print, output goes into a print queue on the server, which sends it to the printer. This frees up your workstation for other tasks. No longer do you have to wait for the printer to finish before going on to the next job.

If you are printing and another user prints to the same printer, the other user's print job is placed in the queue behind yours. The only limit to how many print jobs can be stacked is space on your file server. Print jobs are automatically deleted after they are printed.

NETWORK SOFTWARE

Here we attempt to answer the questions you must now have:

- "How will my present programs run on the network?"

- "Do I have to buy a network version of everything?"

- "What if two people get into the same file at the same time?"

First of all, all the workstations are running DOS. After booting up DOS, you load the network shell. This shell is a program that stays in memory and allows your workstation to talk to the file server as if the file server were a disk drive in your own computer.

Since the network shell stays in memory, you will have less memory available for your application software. How much less depends on which network you use. Novell takes up about 55KB. LANtastic can take up as little as 10KB. Some networks can take as much as 105KB! When you plan your network, be sure to take memory usage into account.

For the most part, running programs on the network is like running programs on a local hard drive. You install them to run on drive F rather that drive C. As long as you're not sharing the data files, most programs will work fine with several people running them at once.

Obviously, you wouldn't want to have two people editing the same word processing file at the same time or two people in the same spreadsheet at the same time. If this happened, one of two things would occur: Either the network wouldn't let the second person in, or "he who saves last, wins."

With data bases, it's a different story. You will want to choose a network version of your data base. This network-smart data base allows several people into the same file at once. The rules as to what they can do vary from program to program. Reading the manual, being careful, and using common sense are recommended here.

It is *not* OK to buy one single-user copy of a program and have several people using it at the same time. But, rather than having to buy a separate copy of a program for each workstation, as you do for each stand-alone computer, there are a couple of alternatives.

Several software companies sell network software for each file server. The license covers all users attached to a single server. This cuts the cost per user way down, allowing you to save big bucks on software. An example is a network menu shell called MarxMenu. Individual copies sell for $59.95 each, but the file-server version sells for $495. If you have 50 users on your network, your cost per user is only $10. Copies can be obtained from Mark Perkel at Computer Tyme, 417-866-1222.

Another way to save on software costs is with software metering. Suppose you own ten legal copies of Reflex and you have 50 users on the network. The software-meter system monitors how many people are using Reflex. When the eleventh person tries to run Reflex, the metering software won't let them in until someone else gets out. This way, you don't have to purchase a copy of every program for all users on the network.

Setting up software is often more involved on a network than on a single computer. Sometimes you put a copy of the software in each person's personal directory. Sometimes you put the software in a public directory and data files in personal directories. Sometimes you put it all in a public directory.

You may have situations where some people are running color monitors and some are running monochrome. Different users might have different preferences selected. Some software has to be configured specifically for the network it is running on.

When running a network, you should have access to a computer consultant—someone who really knows his or her stuff and can get you out of a jam. Networks are more complex than single-user systems; there is no shortage of people out there who can do dumb things on the network.

NETWORK SECURITY

Network security means keeping people out of files that they aren't supposed to be in. It also means keeping people from deliberately or accidentally deleting data. Different situations require different solutions. Sometimes you want everyone to access everything. Sometimes important, sensitive files are to be accessed only by the right people. For this section, we'll look at security as it works under Novell.

The first level of security is the LOGIN. Before it allows you to access the network, the file server wants to know who you are. After entering your name, you are required to type in a password. This helps ensure that you are who you say you are.

If you are a network user, don't tell anyone your password. If someone knew your password, they could access all the files you can access. If you suspect that someone knows your password, change it. It could cost you dearly if you don't.

Novell can be set to require users to change their passwords every 30 days. In a high-security area, this is a good idea. It also has an intruder-lockout feature. This means that if someone tries seven times to figure out your password, Novell won't let them in for 15 minutes, even if they get the password right.

Once Novell knows who you are, it knows what you have access rights to. It also can restrict you to access only during certain hours of the day or to login at only a certain workstation. It knows what directories you can access and what you can do in those directories.

Access rights are assigned on a per-directory basis. They can allow a user to open existing files, read from files, search for files, create new files, delete files, modify filenames, or write to files. Parental rights can be assigned to apply assigned rights to all subdirectories in the directory.

Users who have no access rights to a directory can still go to that directory. But when they try to do anything, it will look like there are no files there. There may actually be files there, but without access rights, it's the same as if there were none.

To make assigning rights easier, Novell lets you create groups, assign rights to the group, and make users members of that group. Users can be members of several groups and have the rights to all of those groups.

THE NETWORK MENU

Menus are a good idea for novice users on stand-alone systems. Menus allow users to select applications from a list on the screen.

On networks, menus are much more important. Menus help keep people out of trouble. If you are at the DOS prompt on a single-user system, and you do something dumb, you lose only what is on your computer. On a network, you can lose everything for everybody.

Besides keeping novice users out of trouble, the network menu adds to the security of the network. Menus can password-protect applications so that users can run the software only from the selections on the screen and only if they know the password.

Menus are handy for power users as well. Networks use many complex commands that are hard to remember and long to type. Even if you made batch files for everything, you could have so many batch files on a network that you can't remember them. And, if you're like me, in order to learn something new, you have to forget something else to make room for it. The menu allows you to put all these tasks into one menu program, thus freeing up space in your mind for other things.

When choosing a network menu system, there are several factors to consider. One factor is how much memory the menu system uses. Many menu systems stay in memory while your application is running. Some menus that stay resident take as little as 5KB, but some take as much as 100KB! With the network shell taking 55KB off the top and applications getting bigger and bigger, the less the menu takes, the better.

In fact, there is a new trend in menu systems towards the 0KB menu. An example of this is MarxMenu. MarxMenu is started with a batch file that brings up the menu. When the user selects an application, MarxMenu writes a batch file and then quits. The original batch file then calls the batch file that was just created, which loads your application. When your application finishes, the batch file brings you back to the menu.

Another advantage of 0KB menu systems is that they don't leave anything behind in memory that other applications won't like. If you are running a variety of software, you run the risk of having a conflict between your applications and the menu system. With a 0KB menu, you don't have this problem. When your application is running, the menu isn't there.

Another factor in choosing a menu is power. Because networks are more complex than single-user systems, you may find yourself wanting to program some "smarts" into the menu. You may, for instance, want to have everybody running the same basic menu but have the accounting group see only the payroll option. Under the payroll menu, you may want the print-checks option to show only on Friday.

Therefore, when looking at your network menu, look at its script language to make sure you have the flexibility your site requires. If you have a consultant helping you install your network, get him or her involved in choosing your network menu.

DATA INTEGRITY

"So," you ask, "how safe is my data on my network?" Different network vendors take different approaches to how they put data on the network drives. Some vendors use the same method as DOS, and some have their own methods.

DOS-Compatible Formats

LANtastic is a simple network. You install it by copying the network software onto an existing hard disk drive. After you have done some configuration, you start the network by running the server program. On the workstations, you run the workstation program, and you're running. In fact, you can run the server program on several computers to have multiple servers.

The advantages of using DOS-compatible formats are

- Ease of installation
- Low cost
- Availability of utility programs that do sector editing
- Simplicity

Proprietary Formats

On the other hand, Novell has its own disk format. Novell has duplicate directory structures, hash tables, hot-fix tables, and other structures that it stores on the drive. Because of this, it can do things that normal DOS-based disk formats can't. This allows for a much higher level of data security, better performance, and more network control.

The advantages of proprietary formats are

- High data integrity
- High performance
- Security

Under LANtastic, you can run disk optimizers, such as Norton Speed Disk or PC Tools Compress. (Be sure that no other users are on the net while you're doing it, though; the results could be unfortunate.) With Novell, these utilities will not work. On the other hand, they are not necessary: Novell keeps all the directory structures in RAM and uses hash indexes that let it access data quickly.

Novell supports such features as hot-fix redirection. That means that when data is written and verified, if the data doesn't match, Novell will write the data to a safe place and lock out the bad spot.

Which method is better depends on your needs. LANtastic does a good job and is simpler to install. Novell has performance and data-integrity advantages, but it takes a lot more know-how to set it up.

The more-advanced versions of Novell support *disk mirroring*. Disk mirroring is installing two identical hard disk drives and setting Novell up so that anything that is written to one drive will be written to the other. This way, if one drive fails, the other keeps on running. This minimizes downtime in critical situations.

With disk mirroring, if a file should fail to read, Novell will read the file from the other drive and fix it on the first drive. Disk mirroring provides an extra level for data correction. If your data is critical and you have the money, disk mirroring is something to seriously consider.

Backups

No network is properly installed or complete without a tape backup. This device is absolutely necessary; you should not consider purchasing a network without one. Mirrored drives help protect against loss due to hardware error, but tape backup protects you from human error. Not only should you have a tape backup, but you should use it properly.

Most network tape drives are installed, not in the file server, but in the workstations. You can even have several tape drives running at the same time. You might consider this if you have a large drive and want to back it up faster.

One thing to be aware of when doing a tape backup on a network is that you can't back up open files. If someone has, for example, the accounting files open while you are running the tape backup, those files will not be backed up.

It is best to do a backup when everyone is off the system. One way to do that is to have the last person out start the backup before leaving. Most tape backup software allows you to start the backup at a specified time.

There is another little-known trick for doing backups with the network running. When tape backup software runs, it flags files that it backs up by resetting their file archive bit. This marks files that have been successfully backed up. At the end of the day, when everybody is off the network, you can make another backup of only changed files. These are the ones that have the archive bit set. This way, you get them all without staying until midnight.

Another thing that is important is to have several generations of backups. The best way is to have a set of tapes for every day of the week. The idea here is that you could have a bad file and not know it until after you back up. You could also have a bad tape. Your network drive could fail in the middle of a backup. These things actually happen, and it could happen to you.

You should also keep a set of backup tapes off site. There is a story about a business that lost all its backup tapes in a fire. Hardware can be replaced, but you may find that your data is worth more than your network and is much harder to replace.

So, how often should you back up? That depends on how much you can stand to lose. Remember, if you lose your network drives, you go back to the last tape that you can successfully restore. If you have a paranoid-type person in your office, he or she may be best suited to be in charge of backups.

CHOOSING A NETWORK CONFIGURATION

This section deals with how to choose a network configuration. Here we see what the different options are in choosing file servers, disk drives, workstations, and LAN cards—how to get the most out of your network dollar.

The first thing you have to decide is whether you are going to use a dedicated or a nondedicated file server. A *nondedicated file server* is one that is also used as a workstation. Basically, unless your network is small, most experts recommend a dedicated file server.

There is a tendency to assume that you should use a fast machine for the file server. Actually, this would be a waste of a fast machine. Since the file server's duty is to pass out files, the processor speed of the server need not be the fastest of the machines you have. If I had a 286 machine and a 486 machine, I would use the 286 for the file server and the 486 for a workstation.

If you want to put some money into the file server, buy the biggest, fastest drives you can afford. File-server performance is strongly influenced by the speed that data can be accessed from the drives. If your data is critical and downtime is not acceptable, you should consider disk mirroring.

Another consideration is file-server memory. Here we recommend a minimum of 4MB of RAM; if you are using over 600MB of hard disk, increase it to 6 to 8MB of RAM. More than 8MB should not be necessary.

Workstations need be only a motherboard with memory, video, and a LAN card. Floppy drives can be added for those to whom you want to give floppy disk access. Not having floppies adds security when you want to make sure files do not leave the office.

Light-duty workstations can be 8088 XT machines, but the best thing to do is get 80386SX workstations. These can be purchased for under $1000. On the 80386, get at least 2MB of RAM. This can be configured as EMS memory and allows for compatibility with the growing number of 386 applications on the market.

As for LAN cards, our LAN consultant, Mark Perkel, likes the Arcnet card. The card allows for a 2.5Mb transfer rate and will beat most internal disk drives. They're inexpensive, easy to install, and reliable. Arcnet is expandable to 254 workstations. It is a *token-passing* network, meaning that each LAN card takes its turn. Arcnet holds its performance well under load.

Ethernet allows for a faster transfer rate—up to 10Mb. Ethernet is also reasonably priced. It is more trouble to get going than Arcnet, and it is collision dumb. Under load, Ethernet can bog down a lot faster than Arcnet.

Token Ring is also popular. Like Arcnet, it is a token-passing network and works well under load. Token Ring is available in 4Mb and 16Mb speeds. It is costly, but if you want speed, it's worth it.

When money is no object, there are several vendors of fiber optic networks. These allow speeds in excess of 100Mb! Fiber optics offer greater security, since coaxial signals can be received and decoded by enemy spies. If you're in a supersecret environment, you might consider fiber optics. If you don't feel that the CIA or the Russians are interested in your data, don't worry about it.

Under Novell, LAN cards can be mixed. You can put up to four LAN cards in your file server to divide up the load and improve performance. You could have an Arcnet, Ethernet, and Token Ring card all in the same server. Or you can use three Arcnet cards.

One thing that is important when buying a LAN is to have someone on your side whom you trust and who has a lot of knowledge about LANs. This could be a consultant or a local computer hacker who has a LAN at home or a respected computer dealer or VAR. There are a lot of people out there passing themselves off as experts who know less about LANs than you will know after reading this short chapter.

How do you tell if the person selling you a LAN knows what he or she is doing? There are several tests. First of all, don't buy a LAN from someone who doesn't own a computer. If you ask how many computers the dealer has at home and the answer is none, you have the wrong person. Don't be afraid to ask for references. Talk to at least one satisfied customer. A well-chosen LAN can be heaven; a poorly chosen LAN, hell.

SOME INTERESTING USES

Networks do more than allow you to share files; they help you save time in other ways. If you are the network support person and a user in a different part of a building is having a problem, you don't have to go over there to help. You just window into that workstation and fix the problem. This makes support much easier.

Another trick is to start a long job on someone else's computer. This frees up your computer for other things. You can window into the other station, start the job, and window in every now and then to see how it's running. You can also have a spare computer on your network that has no screen or keyboard. These computers are specifically for windowing into and starting jobs.

You can also run a "slave" computer on your network. The slave might run a job-control program that manages incoming and outgoing faxes. It can also run overnight processes, clean up backup files, and move old files into archives. These can all be done with MarxMenu. Having a slave computer is like having a full-time janitor on your net to do all the maintenance tasks.

If you can divide big jobs into several parts, you can run several computers on the same job. This adds the processing power of several computers together, allowing programs to run faster than they normally would on a single machine. It's amazing how fast things get done when you have four 386 machines working on it.

Large Networks

How large can your network get? A lot larger than you might think. There are networks that have more than 15,000 users linked in several states. How do they do that? This section presents an overview of wide-area networks.

As the load on a file server increases, several networks allow for multiple file servers. Each file server has its own LAN supporting its users. These file servers are connected through a backbone network, which consists of a second LAN card added to the servers to connect them. Under Novell, this is known as a *bridge*.

Users can access the other file servers over the backbone LAN. This makes all files available to all users. It is a good idea to design your LAN to minimize traffic between the servers, which can bog down the system. The backbone LAN cards should usually be the fastest LAN cards you can afford.

Under Novell, you attach to another server by mapping a drive letter that represents the other server's hard disk. That makes the second server look like another hard disk in your computer. To copy files from one server to another, all you do is copy files from one drive to another.

Networks can also be connected to mainframes. Instead of running a cable from the mainframe to dumb terminals for each user, the modern way uses PCs as terminals and links into the mainframe over the LAN. Most mainframe vendors support LAN ports, allowing PCs to access mainframe sessions. On large networks, you might have several mainframes of different types connected to several LANs. It is amazing that this all works together.

In the modern network environment, your PC can act as a DOS workstation, an IBM mainframe terminal, a DEC terminal, and a Prime terminal—all in one machine. You can even start a job on the VAX, switch over and start two IBM jobs, and run a Lotus spreadsheet on the same desktop computer.

The Home Network

Most people think that networks are for large businesses only. Not so. With low-cost computers and low-cost LAN cards, many people have a network at home as well as at the office. So what do you do with a home network?

First of all, let's see what it takes to put one up. We start with a basic 386SX clone and put 4MB of RAM on the motherboard. Now we add a hard disk. How big should the hard disk be? Well, 100MB to 330MB disks are reasonably priced these days. It all depends on the size of your family.

Let's say we pick up a copy of Novell ELS I, which is good for four users. You'll need five LAN cards. The extra LAN card is an internal bridge to connect to other servers.

The next thing to pick out is some workstations. You get a 386SX with about 2MB of RAM for the spouse. You fix up a couple of old XTs that are lying around the house for the kids. Then you add a couple of modems and a fax card.

Putting the kids on the network works out well, but you may want to restrict their access rights until they know how to keep out of trouble. It is important to make sure the kids understand never to tell their friends their passwords. And, of course, it's always best to keep good backups.

LANs offer a lot to the home user as well as the business user. In fact, some people think they are the wave of the future. Don't let this technology get past you.

Performance Computing — Making It Go Faster

CHAPTER NINETEEN

Diagnostic Utilities

In the early days of computer science, tracking down problems in a system was next to impossible without a tube tester, an oscilloscope, and a lot of knowledge.

The introduction of transistors made troubleshooting a more intimidating task. Transistors don't give off the friendly glow of vacuum tubes. In fact, unless you break out even more elaborate test equipment, it is nearly impossible to tell if a solid-state device is working. As computers got more complicated, it became more important for the system to report errors in a way that made sense to human operators and technicians.

Because of mainframe computers' modular construction, technicians use a number of diagnostic programs that test the integrity of subsystems and display a report on overall system reliability. Some diagnostics can even point out where a particular error is located. Programs of this type can be a blessing when a particular subunit on a computer system fails to operate. IBM's Personal Computer Diagnostics was one of the first of many such programs developed for PC-based systems.

Diagnostic programs all suffer from the same basic weakness: If a problem is serious enough to prevent any program from running, a diagnostic utility is useless, no matter how thorough it may be. It is also important to note that diagnostic programs will supply you with information about the problem, but not about how to fix it. This data can be very accurate or very misleading, depending upon the program used and the severity of the problem. It is up to the human element (you) to distill this information and come up with the appropriate corrective action.

Does this mean that software diagnostics are a waste of money? Not at all. Many troubles are not severe enough to completely disable a computer. The major-disaster type of problem is not what the diagnostic program was designed to detect. Where a system diagnostic can be of particular value is in spotting an intermittent problem or troubles that result from hardware-software conflicts. PC diagnostics can also provide you with the answers to questions that customer representatives ask during those embarrassing technical-support calls.

TYPES OF DIAGNOSTIC UTILITIES

CP/M (control program for microcomputers) is an operating system for microcomputers produced by Digital Research whose use has reduced over the years. Back when CP/M was king, system diagnostic software was the domain of the computer manufacturer. Because computers had such radically different design approaches, hardware functions could not be accessed on all machines in the same way, even though they shared the same disk operating system. System-specific diagnostic software is still available from manufacturers such as IBM, Compaq, DTK, and Tandy. While it is possible to run these programs on machines of different manufacture, some tests or functions may not be available or may return inaccurate results.

Since the introduction of MS-DOS, computer hardware has become more generic, allowing for the development of generic diagnostic utilities. A generic program will work reliably on most MS-DOS compatible equipment. While perhaps less thorough than the system-specific programs, generic utilities offer some degree of flexibility when used in different computer configurations.

Whether generic or system-specific, diagnostic utilities can be broadly divided into two categories: active and passive. An *active diagnostic* will perform a variety of dynamic tests on subsystems. Some of these tests, particularly memory and disk drive tests, can be potentially damaging to your data. The danger presented is usually well documented, and accidental erasure of data is difficult if you are paying attention to what you are doing. Unfortunately, destructive testing of memory and disk-drive-media surfaces is the only way to reliably detect an error. Tests must sometimes be repeated many times before anomalies pop up.

Technicians prefer active diagnostic programs for the variety of hardware-related tests they provide. These programs are a good choice for performing a "burn-in" of new equipment before delivery to a customer. The first 48 hours of operation on most electronic equipment is the most critical. Component failures after the 48-hour break-in period do occur, but much less frequently if the equipment is allowed to burn in.

A *passive diagnostic* takes a different approach. During passive testing, all functions are nondestructive in nature; that is, they are read-only tests on disk surfaces and tests that do not write to memory addresses in use. These programs will compensate for less rigorous testing processes by supplying you with a large amount of information about your system — usually more information than an active diagnostic program. A passive diagnostic is an appropriate choice for novice users or for testing unfamiliar equipment. The likelihood of inadvertent data loss is remote.

Programs written for the PC frequently stray over the line dividing these two program philosophies. A passive utility will sometimes provide destructive testing facilities, and active diagnostics will deliver a greater range of system information if their customers demand such services. The diagnostic services described in this chapter are not divided into destructive and nondestructive categories for this reason. What the test does to your system will be made clear by examination of the test descriptions.

TESTS PERFORMED BY DIAGNOSTIC UTILITIES

System-Configuration Tests

A system-specific diagnostic does not have to gather much in the way of configuration details, because it knows what to expect. When a program is written for a specific machine type, most details can be provided by the program. A generic utility, however, can be used on virtually any type of system. It must gather as many configuration details as possible in order to run properly on each system. Some typical details include:

- Microprocessor type (8088, 80286/386, etc.)
- Memory size (conventional, XMS/EMS)
- Number and types of disk drives
- ROM-BIOS maker, version, and date
- Numbers of serial and parallel ports
- Video adapter type
- CMOS RAM information (on AT-class machines)

Memory Tests

Tests performed on memory can be active or passive. Dynamic-RAM devices are the most failure-prone integrated-circuit devices on any computer. A RAM chip can operate flawlessly for hours or days on end and then, for no apparent reason, fail. As a result of this maddening tendency, RAM tests have been devised in great variety. It is possible to perform all of these tests sequentially, where memory locations are tested in ascending or descending order, or randomly, where locations are chosen in no particular progression.

Read/Write

Actually, this test should be called the write/read/verify test. The memory locations under test are written to and then read from. If the value read compares identically to the value written, the program proceeds to the next location. Oddly enough, the read/write test can be active or passive. In its destructive form, no consideration is given to values in memory before testing. In a nondestructive form, the data in memory is stored safely away, the location is tested, and the data is restored when the test is complete. The read/write test has evolved into several different flavors:

All Zero   0s are written to the test locations.

All Ones   1s are written to the test locations.

Complementary Bit Patterns   In digital logic, a complementary value has its bit values reversed; in other words, 1s become 0s and 0s become 1s. Common test values are 55 and AA hexadecimal (or 01010101 and 10101010 binary). The checkerboard test, as it is sometimes called, is designed to detect faults that occur when a bit cell in a RAM chip affects the cell adjacent to it.

Worse-Case Data Patterns   Arrangements of data patterns that systems seem to have difficulty storing reliably have been arrived at. A popular byte combination is DB5D hexadecimal.

Read-Only
The read-only test checks the same location several times and compares the values read at each pass with an originally read value. This test is really testing *parity,* or the RAM chip's ability to store data. If the chip "forgets," special circuitry on the PC will generate a nonmaskable interrupt (NMI), and you will see some kind of parity error message on the screen.

Addressability
Memory-addressability testing is a lot like the read/write test, but it is more concerned with extended memory (the memory space above 1MB). A block of extended memory is paged into the addressable space of the system, and data values are written to the locations. The block is then paged out and back in again. Memory contents are compared to the value written, and an error is registered if the two do not match. Addressability testing checks more than just a memory location's ability to hold data; it also checks the availability of the RAM to the system.

Other types of memory testing involve specific subsystems of the computer. Most IBM-compatible equipment will perform a *checksum* of data stored in the system's ROM BIOS chips. A checksum is a value arrived at by summing the data stored in specific locations, and passing the result through a special algorithm that generates a unique shorthand value representing the values being examined. Since the ROM is read-only memory, no tests that involve writes can be performed.

Video RAM can also be tested by some programs. The video adapter's ability to operate in graphics and text modes sometimes requires several test operations to be performed.

While not specifically a test, diagnostics will display the information contained in the CMOS RAM of AT- and 386-class machines. CMOS stands for complementary metal-oxide semiconductor, which is a type of extremely low power integrated circuit used in today's advanced computers. CMOS RAM is a special type of lower power memory which stores the configuration data for AT class systems. A small battery helps retain the information when the computer's power is turned off. You can verify that the memory size, disk drive types, and the time and date are correctly set. If the CMOS battery loses power (there is no indicator telling you that is doing so), the startup configuration of your machine will be lost. The system will no longer be aware of the existence of any hard disks, high-density disk drives, and other details about the machine setup. In fact, what appears to be a hard disk crash on an AT is often just the battery going belly-up. Make sure you check the battery before handing over several hundred dollars for a new hard drive.

Disk Drive Tests

Testing on disk drive media is similar to memory testing. A form of the write/read/verify test and the read-only test are used. Data is written to and read back one sector or track at a time. In addition to reading and writing, a disk drive must also be able to format a disk correctly. All of these tests check the read/write heads and the magnetic media (the disk surface) for integrity. Disk drives can also generate a form of parity error, called a CRC error on a floppy and an ECC error on a hard disk. (CRC stands for "cyclic redundancy check," and ECC is "error correction and compensation.") Both act pretty much the same way a parity error does during a RAM test.

Rotational speed on a disk drive is critical to proper operation. A good active diagnostic will provide a disk tachometer of some kind. The stepping motor that moves a drive head assembly across the disk surface can wear out, causing seek errors. The heads must be able to position over any track on the disk repeatedly and accurately. The seek test will put the stepping-motor controller into overdrive in an attempt to cause a seek error.

Hard disk drives can have other problems, as well. A hard-disk-controller card is a complex circuit combining a CPU, RAM, and ROM into a kind of dedicated computer system. The speed and performance of a hard disk demands that the controller circuits respond precisely. A program that tests hard drives should check the disk-controller circuits, as well.

I/O Port Tests

On some computer systems, each device plugged into the system has a unique *signature*, or address, that identifies it. This signature is sometimes based upon the physical position the card occupies in the computer. Apple systems have long used a method of giving each slot on the system board an address. Cards meant for use on these machines must be designed to reside in only one of these slots. If a card presents proper data to the system, it is possible to determine exactly what type of adapter cards are installed by taking an inventory of device signatures.

PC/XT/AT-class computers use a common bus approach. This means that any card can be plugged into any slot and work the way it is supposed to. Unfortunately, it also means that if you are looking to find out where a device is installed on the system, a diagnostic program has limited access to information. There is really no way to determine which card is installed in which slot.

Of course, DOS needs to know the resources it has to work with. During bootup, a table is created in memory that reflects the basic hardware setup of the machine. On AT-type systems, much information is taken from the CMOS RAM. On XT machines, the system-board switches provide information. A PC knows what is installed; it's just a little blind about where it's installed.

The address space above 640K (A0000-FFFFF) was designed as reserved space for input/output (I/O) cards, such as hard disk controllers and video cards. What many refer to as the 640KB DOS limitation is also a hardware limitation imposed upon the machine by its makers. In recent years, however, popular setups include 1MB of RAM installed on the system board.

Under normal circumstances, the 384KB of RAM above 640KB would not be available for use, because it shares the same address space as other devices installed in the A0000-FFFFF range. New memory-management techniques have made this *shadow-RAM*, or *high-DOS*, area usable by TSRs and device-driver programs. A good diagnostic should be able to report where in memory your TSR programs and device drivers are installed and how much memory they consume.

The problem arises when this space becomes loaded with memory managers, video cards, expanded memory boards, and the like. Remember that the PC knows *what*, not *where*. Many generic diagnostic programs map out the high-DOS area and allow you to see which areas are in use and which are not. If the card installed has a ROM device, copyright information and other details can be revealed.

The PC also has I/O space at the lower end of its address map (0000-FFFF). This is really the nuts-and-bolts I/O area of your system. Programmable integrated-circuit devices, such as video processors, disk controllers, and DMA (direct memory access) channels, used to transfer data between devices and memory bypassing the microprocessor, make their home here. Examination of these areas is a tricky proposition, as many devices will wrongly interpret a seemingly harmless read instruction. Extreme caution must be observed when working in this area to avoid an "unexpected event," as they say in the nuclear-power-plant business.

Serial and parallel ports are also part of the computer's input/output system. Active diagnostic utilities will have some method of testing this I/O as well. One method is called *loopback testing*. A special plug is included to provide paths for output signals to be returned, or looped back into the machine, through the same connector. Individual signal lines and data-transfer rates can be checked with loopback testing. It is necessary to unplug any external cables attached to the port under test and install the special loop-back connector. Many users feel this step is not worth the effort involved unless there is something seriously wrong with the I/O port.

Keyboard Tests

An engineering axiom says that if a device has moving parts, sooner or later one of those parts will break. If the keyboard on your system starts to act up, you will notice the problem long before you get around to running a diagnostic program. Keyboard testing is not provided in most newer diagnostic utilities for two reasons. First, a lot of different keyboards are available for the PC. Just keeping up with "new and improved" keyboard designs would be a programmer's nightmare. Second, most of these keyboards are very inexpensive and are usually thrown away before they are repaired.

If a diagnostic has keyboard testing available, a diagram of a keyboard layout (probably not your keyboard layout) will be displayed. The test is complex: Push a button and see what happens. If all keys pass, the test is complete.

Mouse and Joystick Tests

Mouse and joystick testing is conducted like keyboard testing. You move the unit around to check speed and response time. The buttons on the device are tested to determine if they are functional. Some programs will allow for calibration of joystick movement, although the joystick is not considered to be a "business" device and is usually not tested at all.

USING DIAGNOSTIC UTILITIES

A diagnostic program displays information about your system on the screen. If you enjoy reading from a video display, this is fine. Many users prefer to generate a hard-copy printout of system status to read more comfortably away from the machine. Hard-copy reports are also handy for record-keeping purposes when dealing with a large number of computers. Make sure the diagnostic program you choose can provide you with a printout of system information.

A discussion of the two most widely used diagnostic utilities, System Sleuth and CheckIt! will give you an idea of what diagnostics actually do.

System Sleuth Version 2.1
Dariana Technology Group, Inc.

System Sleuth is a passive diagnostic program. Its menu-driven user interface (see Figure 19-1) is first-letter sensitive. You can also scroll a highlight bar through the menu selections to choose options. You can display context-sensitive help screens by pressing F1. Help is also indexed and can be selected by subject.

True to the concept of generic utilities, System Sleuth gathers a great variety of hardware and software details. You can examine low-level details about your hard disk drive, view disk-file and memory data, and determine I/O-port- or hardware-interrupt availability without fear of destroying data in the process.

System Sleuth performs addressability testing on unallocated extended memory and provides you with a bad-track-mapping facility for the hard disk. In the areas that distinguish a passive diagnostic program, System Sleuth delivers in full. A particularly valuable feature is Sleuth's I/O port availability map (see Figure 19-2). High-DOS and low-I/O address space can be checked for use before you attempt to install a new piece of hardware or

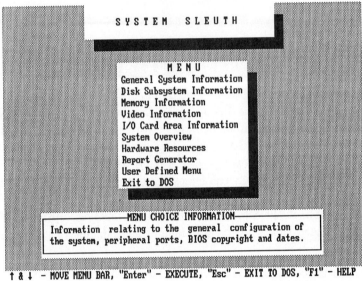

Figure 19-1

System Sleuth's main menu

software. This facility alone can greatly reduce your frustration level. In addition, Sleuth allows you to direct your system's configuration details to a disk file or hard-copy printout.

CheckIt! Version 2.10
TouchStone Software Corporation

TouchStone's CheckIt! is a program that crosses the line between passive and active diagnostic utilities. Its user interface features drop-down menus

Figure 19-2

System Sleuth's I/O card area map

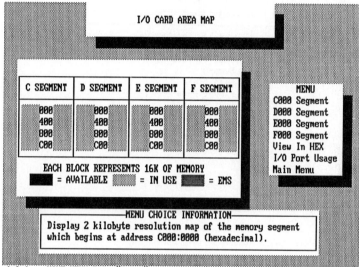

(see Figure 19-3). You select the options by highlighting your choice.

CheckIt! provides general system information like that provided by passive utilities. Also included are a series of active diagnostics that test memory, hard and floppy drives, the system board, the real-time clock, serial and parallel ports, and more. Hard disk facilities extend to low-level formatting on AT-class machines. You can also use the benchmark menu to compare the performance of your machine against selected baseline systems.

Because it is both active and passive, the information that CheckIt! provides is not so comprehensive as that of a purely passive utility, such as System Sleuth. On the other hand, passive programs do not allow you to "shake up" your system through testing to see if something falls apart.

Figure 19-3

An example of CheckIt!'s drop down menus

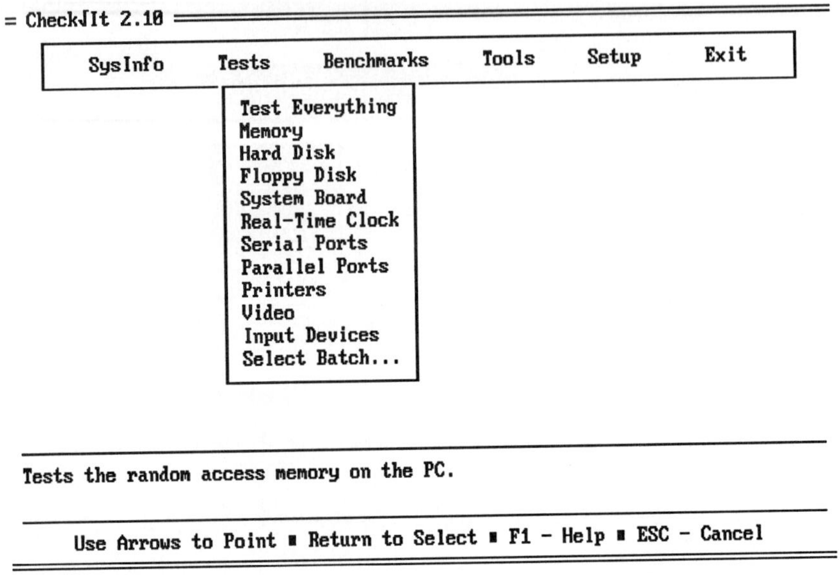

```
= CheckJIt 2.10 =================================================

    ┌──────────────────────────────────────────────────────────────┐
    │  SysInfo     Tests     Benchmarks     Tools    Setup    Exit   │
    └──────────────────────────────────────────────────────────────┘
                  ┌─────────────────────┐
                  │ Test Everything     │
                  │ Memory              │
                  │ Hard Disk           │
                  │ Floppy Disk         │
                  │ System Board        │
                  │ Real-Time Clock     │
                  │ Serial Ports        │
                  │ Parallel Ports      │
                  │ Printers            │
                  │ Video               │
                  │ Input Devices       │
                  │ Select Batch...     │
                  └─────────────────────┘


Tests the random access memory on the PC.


        Use Arrows to Point ▪ Return to Select ▪ F1 - Help ▪ ESC - Cancel
```

Programs dedicated to either active or passive functions will be more relentless in their scrutiny of your machine than will programs that combine the functions. Which diagnostic program you choose depends upon your personal needs. A well-stocked software library should contain examples of both active and passive utilities. In many cases, you will find them to be a handy alternative to a screwdriver.

CHAPTER TWENTY

Benchmarks

You might not realize how new computer technology is. Less than 30 years ago, the first true electronic computers were just being put into use.

Sometimes filling entire buildings, these enormous early computers were specially designed for specific jobs. The electronic components were designed and assembled only after an analyst had a thorough understanding of the job to be done. At more or less the same time, the analysts also defined the system programming. The hardware and software, as they came to be known, were then joined over the course of many months, if not years.

In those early days of computers, it was not reasonable or accurate to compare the performance of one system to another, since each was designed for a different task. It would be like comparing a 747 jumbo jet with an F-16 fighter. Still, some biased comparisons were made. The free market motto "caveat emptor" (let the buyer beware) began to mean something to the growing computer industry.

Analysts were faced with an interesting problem. How could they demonstrate improved performance without knowing what performance used to be? Programs called benchmarks were written to answer this question. The word *benchmark* has its origins in geographical surveying. It makes sense when you think about it. Surveyors had to answer the same basic question: "Where am I, and how do I know?" Surveyors used to find a point of known position, such as a big rock or a tree, and make a mark on it. They would then make their measurements relative to the known point.

Early computer-system benchmarks compared actual system performance against a calculated "ideal" performance. Usually, this was expressed in terms of the number of calculations or instructions executed in a given period. Sometimes it was expressed in terms of the amount of data that could be moved in a given period. In any case, the results of benchmark testing were used by the analyst to monitor and optimize the performance of a system. They were not used to make comparisons between systems.

As time went by, the cost of electronic technology declined. Computers became available to mass markets, and the personal computer was born. Highly specialized, custom systems were gradually replaced by general-purpose ones. Aided by "microchips," general-purpose systems could easily be applied to nearly any task. Still, most programs were custom designed to meet the requirements of specific tasks.

Most of these programs and computers were not compatible with each other. Making comparisons was more a matter of accepting trade-offs. Because system types were so different, comparisons could be made only within a genre.

Along came the personal computer and, with it, a standardization the mass market welcomed. After a brief battle, the standard promoted by IBM became the clear winner. The IBM standard promoted an existing disk-based operating system scheme and a layered architecture. For the first time, application programming was insulated from the hardware. The most significant outcome of this development was system compatibility. Hardware and software could now be designed to the standard, and you could interchange them among computers. Because of this standard, benchmarking became more important than ever.

There are more than a few benchmarks you may have heard of. In this chapter, you will become acquainted with the most significant benchmark programs.

THE NORTON SI

Among the first benchmark programs for the PC was the Norton SI (System Information). When the SI benchmark program is run, a specific set of instructions is executed. The execution time is measured, and the results are displayed on the screen as a comparison with the IBM PC running at 4.77 MHz. This benchmark measures the raw computational power of the computer without weighing I/O (input/output) processes or the speed of devices external to the CPU, such as memory. Personal computer designers have learned to optimize their hardware designs to get the highest raw computational speeds and, in turn, the best SI rating.

I want to make it clear that increasing processor speed is perfectly valid. In fact, some real gains can be made just by changing the clock speed from 10 MHz to 12 MHz. However, you would be wise not to consider the SI rating by itself. Many other factors can affect system speed, calling for additional testing.

THE DHRYSTONE

As systems have become more complex, more comprehensive benchmark programs than the Norton SI have been developed. One such benchmark is a popular program called the Dhrystone (pronounced "*dry* stone"). The Ada Dhrystone was created by Rheinhold P. Weicker. It has since been ported to C language by Rick Richardson, among others.

Known as a "synthetic" benchmark, the Dhrystone makes a reasonably good attempt at simulating "normal" system operation. In other words, the Dhrystone program runs a combination of operations over and over again in a process that simulates a statistically typical program. Basically, the Dhrystone program executes 100 passes, or *loops*, of a fixed pattern of instructions. Within the combination, or *mix*, are 53 assignment instructions, 32 control statements, and 15 procedure function calls.

An *assignment instruction* assigns some value to a variable, such as $x = 5$ or $A = B$.

A *control statement* is an instruction that gives a program some logical-decision-making ability. This includes simple jump statements as well as IF/THEN/ELSE instructions, which allow the system to choose between different conditions. We all use control statements in our daily lives. For example, when coming to a traffic light, the unconscious process might be "IF the light is red, THEN stop. Or ELSE, IF the light is not red, THEN don't stop."

A *procedure function call* is a fancy name for an instruction that calls another group of instructions. The second set of instructions performs a routine function, such as printing a line on the printer. Preprogrammed function calls save the programmer time and reduce the size of programs.

The mix is of critical importance. It gives you a way to relate the test results to a real application.

The Dhrystone performs no floating-point operations. Floating-point calculations are based on logarithms. They quickly yield very precise mathematical results. Floating-point operations were at one time reserved for the rarified air of scientific exploration. A 16-bit floating-point process was used to calculate the flight path of the first lunar orbiter. Only recently have they come into common use in graphics processors.

You might be familiar with the NPU, an optional numerical processing unit for personal computers. The NPU performs only floating-point operations and eliminates the need for programs that do the same. Because floating-point operations are of little value to the instruction mix of the Dhrystone, they are not run by this benchmark.

The looping process used by the Dhrystone worked well at first. Looping has always been a very simple and easy way to create time delays. Remember that each instruction requires a fixed amount of time to execute. If the instruction does nothing productive (for example, it jumps to a jump), then it is simply burning time. "Blind" timing loops have been used for many years to drive peripheral devices, such as printers. The earlier models did not have status lines or signals to tell the processor when to send data. So, the processor compensated by simply marking time while the printer finished its mechanical operation.

A lot of water has gone under the bridge since the Dhrystone was developed. Technology has advanced to the point where the simplicity of the Dhrystone is almost a detriment. Programmers have become more sophisticated. They have learned to write very compact and efficient programs that run faster and require less memory than larger programs. A powerful tool at their disposal is the *optimizing compiler.*

Basically, a *compiler* is a program that translates the programmer's *source code* into *object code* that will perform the specified task. The object code is the final executable program and is often called a *run-time program.* The individual instructions used by the computer are invisible to the user. Optimizing compilers simplify and reduce the size of the run-time program generated by a given object code. The optimized run-time program will execute faster and require less memory to run.

Optimizing compilers can significantly affect a benchmark program that was not written to counteract the optimizing effect. For example, they can eliminate calls to subroutines in memory and all of the overhead delays associated with them. The basic technique is to keep the subroutine local and "in line," rather than in some other part of memory.

Optimizing compilers will also remove redundant loops. Recall that every instruction takes time to execute. Any changes to the code will change the run time of the program and, consequently, the benchmark results.

In short, optimizing compilers do a lot of things that destroy the basic intent and usefulness of the benchmark. Note that the trouble does not lie with the optimizing compilers. For the most part, they perform a tremendous service. The problem is in old or poorly designed benchmarks that are susceptible to optimization—and in the unwitting user.

What optimizing does to the Dhrystone benchmark is circumvent the looping process in the program so that the test runs faster. This makes it difficult to use test results to compare system performance between machines that did not run the same compiled version. In fact, this is a problem with all benchmarks, since almost all of them involve loop delays. To eliminate this problem, a second version of the Dhrystone, called Dhrystone 2, has been developed. Dhrystone 2 is less susceptible to code optimizations than Dhrystone 1.

THE WHETSTONE

Another popular benchmark is the Whetstone (pronounced "*wet* stone"). In fact, the Whetstone was created before the Dhrystone, and the Dhrystone played on its name. The Whetstone is considered a classic benchmark developed to be representative of typical scientific programs. The Whetstone is based on the analysis of almost 1000 ALGOL 60 programs. (This was the usual method of establishing a statistical model of the "typical" program.)

Despite similarities in the name, the Whetstone performs fundamentally different processes than the Dhrystone. The main difference is that the Whetstone measures the computational performance of the system, including the math coprocessor if one is present. The Whetstone records the time it takes to perform a predefined set of floating-point operations. This result can then be compared with results from other computers. The Whetstone will run on a computer without a coprocessor installed, but it will run much faster with the help of an NPU.

The Whetstone is also highly susceptible to optimization. An optimizing compiler can appear to improve significantly the Whetstone's performance by in-line-coding its three small subroutines. This makes the Whetstones-per-second result of the test misleading and invalid. The performance is improved, not because the floating-point processes are executed faster, but because the optimizing compiler removed hundreds or even thousands of processor instructions from the code.

Some C language Whetstone programs contain redundant code, which an optimizing compiler may completely remove. It may also delete floating-point instructions, perhaps millions of them depending on the loop count, resulting in similarly misleading results.

The problem does not lie in optimizing compilers—the problem lies in the proper use of these compilers with benchmark programs that deliberately use inefficient code. And the solution does not lie in the hands of the typical user. Rather, it is up to the designers who port "canned" benchmark programs between different systems and languages to be sure the basic intent of the program remains intact.

As with all testing, you must make special efforts to be informed of the configuration of the system being tested. Because the Whetstone runs with or without an NPU installed in a PC, results can easily be misinterpreted by the uninformed user. A good benchmark program, such as CheckIt, from TouchStone Software, and Bench29, from PCLAB, will tell you if a coprocessor is present without your having to open the case.

THE SIEVE

Among the classics is the Sieve. The algorithm for this benchmark was first presented by Djikstra in his classic book on programming practice. It has since been revived numerous times, notably by Jim Gilbreath, who created his popular Sieve of Eratosthenes benchmark in 1982. Eratosthenes was an ancient Greek astronomer known for his work with numbers. He was the first to calculate the diameter of Earth accurately.

The Sieve of Eratosthenes is frequently used by programmers and developers to demonstrate compiler and system improvements. The benchmark has won wide acceptance because it is simple and easily coded in many different computer languages. Also, it computes something useful that is recognizable and verifiable: prime numbers. The speed at which the Sieve generates prime numbers is an indicator of the efficiency of the total system, including the compiler and the hardware. Performance improvements in the Sieve will also be reflected in other applications that do similar types of operations.

The Sieve was originally created to measure system efficiency relative to memory references, the most simple structured control statements, and integer operations. However, the Sieve is not immune to the effects of optimizing compilers. For example, certain looping structures used for timing delay may be removed by an optimizing compiler, resulting in misleading test results.

CONSIDERATIONS WHEN RUNNING BENCHMARKS

No matter how good a benchmark program is, your results will always reflect system conditions. A lack of controlled and appropriate test methods and procedures will cause you many problems with benchmark testing. For example, if you run PCLAB's Conventional Memory benchmark, you may find your system running slower than expected. It may even run slower than an apparently identical system sitting right next to it. If you look closer, you may find that the two systems are using different-speed RAMs or have different memory wait states selected.

As computer technology advances every day, new products become available that improve system performance remarkably. Cache memory and disk cache have finally found their way into the personal computer realm. A disk cache saves data pulled from the hard disk, expecting that you will want to use it again soon. For instance, if you were working on a 10-page document and switched from page 1 to page 8, the program would keep page 1 in RAM, ready and waiting for you to call again. The alternative, writing the data back out to the hard disk, takes up more time.

The actual amount of time depends on the system type. For a standard 8-MHz IBM PC AT, typical hard disk transfer rates run about 170K per second. You might think that's pretty good—until you learn that the same system can move 1.7MB of RAM data per second. Translated, this means you can access 10 times as much data in the same period if you don't have to go out to the hard disk. As CPU clock speeds increase and RAM chips become faster, the differences become even more substantial. An AT-type 286 system running at 20 MHz can access RAM data more than 16 times faster than data on the hard disk.

Real performance improvements are a big plus for users. They represent a big challenge for benchmark program writers. As you already saw, one of the dilemmas of benchmark programming is how to take into account the number of variables. Even small hardware differences can cause big differences in performance and apparent problems in benchmarks.

UNDERSTANDING BENCHMARK USE

When you run a benchmark, you must be sure you understand the configuration of the system under test. If you are comparing different systems, they should be configured as much alike as possible.

In a typical application, system performance depends upon the following factors:

- System architecture

- Operating system and compiler efficiency

- Configuration

- Application mix

- System loading

These factors also affect the results of a benchmark test.

Architecture

The 8086/8087 chip set used in the PC XT-type machine implements something called a BIU (bus interface unit). By using this scheme, the 8086 and 8087 can access the bus independently of each other. This parallelism provides an exponential increase in computing power when an 8087 is added to an 8086 system. Improvements of as much as 100 times are not uncommon.

The 80286/80287 chip set replaces the BIU with an MMU (memory management unit). This major structural change was needed to enable reaching out farther into memory. The functional trade-off is that the 80286 must implement the I/O arrangement of passing op codes and data between it and the 80287. Needless to say, the performance trade-off was significant. As a general rule, when you add an 8087 NPU to an 8086 system, you can expect an improvement in computational speed of as much as 100 times. Adding an 80287 to a 286 system improves performance by about one-third that of the 8086/8087 set.

You might be thinking by now that it's hardly fair to compare apples to oranges, and I agree. That's the point I'm trying to make. These two architectures are fundamentally different, and you cannot compare them on the basis of sheer processing power, even with matching clock rates.

Operating System

MS-DOS and OS/2 will run on the same type of machine with an 80386 processor at 25 MHz. All 80386 architectures have 32-bit CPU-to-memory pathways. However, because of the different bus width of the two machines, operations involving I/O are not comparable.

Most personal computers that run under the MS-DOS operating system are easy to compare. However, operations run under different operating systems are not necessarily comparable. For example, disk operations in a multiuser UNIX environment could not be compared to disk operations performed on a single-user system without taking into account all of the variables.

Benchmark results can also be controversial and unreliable if compiler efficiency is not considered. For example, if you are comparing the performance of two different processors using C language compilers, then you must be sure that the compilers generate the best code for each CPU.

Configuration

I have encountered many different personal computer configurations in my travels. It makes sense when you consider the general-purpose nature of PCs. To use a word processing application, you don't need the ultimate high-performance disk subsystem. However, if your main application is a data base manager, you will probably want the fastest hard disk drive subsystem you can afford.

As mentioned earlier, the Whetstone is a measure of how fast a processor can make computations. The results of this test can be radically different between a PC with an NPU installed and one without. Of course, benchmark comparisons are valid between differently configured systems. Most of the time, that's what we use benchmark programs for. But it would be a mistake for you to base your evaluation on the results of this test without knowing the NPU is installed.

Another consideration is the speed of the memory chips. As simple as it sounds, merely the different operating speeds of 150NS (nanosecond) and 200NS chips can result in a 25 percent difference in memory access time if the system has to install CPU *wait states.*

CPU wait states have an interesting origin. A memory cycle normally takes three CPU cycles. During the first cycle, an instruction is sent out to the memory in the form of an address. Then, during the second CPU cycle, the address is located. Finally, in the third cycle, the contents are fetched back to the CPU. When Intel, among others, began pushing CPU clock rates, they found that memory technology wasn't keeping up—at least not in speed. So, they gave the CPU the ability to "wait" for memory. The wait state is a forced condition in which the CPU can do nothing but wait for the memory to catch up. Adding one wait state will increase each memory access from three to four CPU cycles. The additional CPU cycle will reduce the system speed by a third. On the other hand, if the CPU is running at its maximum rate and no wait states are used, faster memory chips will not increase the throughput of the system.

As CPU speeds continue to climb, hierarchical memory systems will become more popular in the microcomputer environment. Hierarchical memory systems place small amounts of high-speed memory, usually SRAM, (Static Random Access Memory) the CPU. This high-speed memory is capable of running at the speed of the CPU and forms an associative cache from which the CPU references instructions and some commonly used data. Simple dynamic RAM (DRAM) comprises the main memory and can contain relatively slow and less expensive chips. DRAM stores data bits using a very small electrical charge. This charge needs to be "refreshed" every so often to keep it set. Each refresh cycle takes up valuable system time, and systems can use as much as 12 percent of their time just refreshing memory.

SRAM usually does not require a refresh cycle and therefore can match the CPU speed. The Motorola 68020 and the Intel 80486 both implement a small on-chip cache for instructions only, which improves system performance remarkably. Since the cache is selectable on the 486 but not on the 68020, the on-chip cache should be taken into consideration when running benchmark testing.

Another example of a difference in configurations is the number of buffers. We know that disk-buffer size can greatly affect the performance of disk I/O. Degraded performance is clear and conspicuous even to the user at the application level. But we seldom see the buffers taken into account in benchmark programs.

One very popular enhancement that can skew benchmark results is *disk cache*. Disk cache is a data-transfer management technique in which RAM is substituted for hard disk space. This is not the same as a *virtual disk,* where RAM is permanently allocated and configured to look like a disk drive. However, the net effect is similar. Some people refer to disk cache as a "grown-up" RAM disk. Disk cache saves a copy of the most recent files accessed from the hard disk. Then, if another request is made for one of these files, the system accesses it from RAM rather than going all the way out to the hard disk. This saves a lot of time, since memory access is about 1000 times faster than hard disk access. Applications don't have to be specially written to take advantage of disk cache, but they can be.

In general, the more disk I/O an application performs, the greater the benefit of disk cache. This applies to standard benchmark programs, such as IOBench 2. Like memory cache, disk cache has a nonlinear effect on system performance. Important considerations are the algorithm used, the size of the cache, and the application to be used. When running a benchmark, disk cache should be disabled and tested separately, because most benchmarks reread data in unrealistic proportions. Either the test data fits entirely into cache and you end up benchmarking a RAM disk, or the test data is too large and you have degraded overhead from cache code.

As a rule, benchmarks should approximate the actual running conditions as closely as possible. Application mix is one of the most difficult running conditions to get a handle on. As the following table shows, application mix can vary widely between different environments:

Business Environments

	WP	DB	SS	AC
General	50	25	25	0
Accounting	10	0	20	70
Data collection	20	70	10	0

Engineering Environments

	WP	DB	SS	AC	CAP	GPH	SCI	IF
Software development	40	0	0	0	60	0	0	0
CAD/CAM	0	0	0	0	35	40	0	25
Computation intensive	0	0	0	0	10	0	90	0

Note: These are averages; instantaneous values will differ.

Application mix is of critical importance when trying to approximate real-life situations. One application that can be demanding is a spreadsheet. Simple though it may seem, a large spreadsheet can bring a disk operating system to its knees. RAM can be almost completely filled by a single spreadsheet, and often each cell requires frequent recalculation. Slow video-redraw speed can frustrate the user who scrolls through a large spreadsheet. And disk access time will determine how quickly those last few columns or rows are retrieved.

The Jet Propulsion Lab (JPL) in Pasadena, California, is a computation-intensive environment. At JPL, scientists work with satellites, and astrophysicists measure distances between certain stars. In this environment, generally, raw NPU speed is what is important.

An environment quite different from JPL's is an application using a large data base. Conventional computers still haven't mastered parallel processing, as the human mind has. Under parallel processing, several things can be done at the same time. For us human beings, it might be as simple a combination as walking and chewing gum at the same time. For computers, multidimensional data bases present a special problem. In a world where computers can do only one thing at any given moment, searching through and sorting large data bases can take a great amount of time.

WHAT IS A "GOOD" BENCHMARK?

Opinions vary widely on what a benchmark should measure and how it should measure it. The dilemma stems from the lack of a standard. Benchmark testing is done for several reasons. One is to establish a basis for comparison. Systems may be different, or they may run different operating systems and applications. Benchmark testing should reduce and define all those variables so that a valid comparison can be made. Another purpose for benchmark testing is design evaluation. Benchmark testing provides feedback to the system designers about how well their design works. The dilemma of finding an ideal benchmark is made greater by the fact that computer technology is a moving target.

Meaningful Results

A good benchmark should present results that are meaningful in practical terms, since how you use the system for practical work is what's important.

Benchmark programmers have not given this much consideration since the Whetstone was developed. For example, programmers are just beginning to use popular applications as benchmarks. This technique is not new, but it has been neglected for a while. Actual applications reveal the sensitivity of a particular subsystem, such as the hard disk drive or the graphics display. In many cases, the performance of this subsystem is more important than the CPU speed.

Test results must also be reported in literal terms that are meaningful. For instance, we can talk about annual usage of Styrofoam cups in a couple of ways. We could say that the half-life of the total tonnage of nonbiodegradable plastics in current landfill is 500 years. We could also say that if the Styrofoam cups consumed by Americans in one year were stacked together end to end, they would reach to the moon and back four times. Both of those descriptions may be accurate, and they are certainly descriptive. But without a frame of reference, they have little meaning. There is an unfortunate tendency to report results under the authority of highly technical terms that are really quite meaningless.

An example of this "technobabble" is *MIPS*, or million instructions per second. MIPS has been referred to as "meaningless information on performance for salesman." Coined in the early days of computing to report assembler efficiency, MIPS literally refers to the actual number of instructions that can be executed in a second.

MIPS can be very useful in design environments, where engineers sit down with one another and compare the precise hardware performance between systems. Many times they decide that the best test is the simplest, even though it may have no practical purpose or yield any meaningful result. For example, a no-op (no operation) loop yields no result, and its main purpose is to inject delay time into a program. Whatever the case, the engineers know precisely what the hardware is doing under a no-op, and using MIPS to report the result is reasonable.

MIPS has the same basic problem as benchmarks: There has been no standard established for the set of instructions used. Different instructions take different times to execute, depending on the functions they perform. Simple instructions may perform only two or three operations local to the CPU. Other instructions may need to access RAM or disk memory or send data to execution registers. Each of these operations takes a machine cycle (or at least part of one) to perform. So, without declaring the exact nature and uniformity of the instruction set run in a benchmark, the results in MIPS is misleading. For the same reason, MIPS cannot be used across CPU architectures. This makes comparing the Intel 80286 with the Motorola 68000, for example, impossible in terms of MIPS.

Accuracy

The main issue in accuracy of benchmarking is how to clearly identify what is to be tested. This involves detailed knowledge not only of the programming aspects of the benchmark but also of the system under test. Scientific computing tends to give floating-point and memory performances greater weight. Word processing tends to consider integer computations and video speed more heavily. In theory, if you know the application mix and you can measure the performance of each subsystem independently of the others, you will be able to calculate the overall system performance — at least when it's running those applications.

A typical microcomputer system is composed of several different subsystems. These might be an ALU (arithmetic and logic unit, which is internal to the processor), memory, I/O interface, and a floating-point processor or numeric coprocessor. The overall performance of a computer system is the weighted sum of the performances of these subsystems. Weights must vary, depending on the application mix.

One way you can determine the performance of a subsystem is to run and time the execution of programs that use only that subsystem. These programs belong to a class of benchmarks called *microscopic benchmarks*. Micro benchmarks look at the performance of components in great detail, whereas *macroscopic benchmarks* look at the application-level performance of the entire system.

Some problems occur when trying to run micro benchmarks, and the results you get may not be comparable between two systems. When you set out to build an accurate micro benchmark, the particular subsystem needs to be isolated. At it turns out, this is practically impossible. For example, the primary intent of the Savage benchmark is to test the accuracy and speed of transcendental functions. However, analysis of the program shows that it uses the ALU to control the looping process and that it accesses memory for instruction fetches and data. For CPU/NPU subsystems that do not support transcendental functions, the net effect of these contributions is small. However, as floating-point units with direct transcendental function capability become more common, these effects can significantly alter program-execution time.

The ability or inability to isolate subsystems is one of the main considerations in micro benchmarking. Since it is usually impossible to totally isolate the performance of a single subsystem, the best you can hope for is to compensate for the contributions of the peripheral subsystems. Compensation is of paramount importance when making comparisons between systems.

Repeatable Results

A good benchmark must also provide repeatable results. You will notice benchmark results vary slightly from system to system and trial to trial. However, a good benchmark program will account for this variance and report it. Repeatability establishes the significance of a variance and validates a given test.

Repeatability is almost exclusively a function of *overhead*. Overhead is process time required to complete an operation without actually being part of the operating instruction. For example, some CPUs might need additional time to compute the effective address of the source or destination operands before they can actually do the operation. In this case, the execution time may vary between different CPUs and systems, but it would not vary much from trial to trial.

Overhead variations from trial to trial are typical in subsystems that have object-code-independent behavior, for example, the hard disk subsystem. Mechanical latency introduces some variance from trial to trial just by its nature. There are two forms of mechanical latency. Positioning is the time it takes for the hard disk's read and write head to move from one location to another. Rotational latency is the time it takes a piece of data to come under the read and write heads. Wider variances can be the result of the condition of the media and the degree to which the data is fragmented.

Sometimes, benchmarks are written to favor a particular brand of equipment. Needless to say, the authors of these programs are probably looking for ways to highlight the special advantages of their equipment. A good number of benchmarks have been written and sponsored by trade publications. In general, these programs are intended to give the reviewer a basis for comparison. And, in fact, this type of benchmark does a fairly comprehensive job. Most involve suites of tests for the important subsystems.

Another important type of benchmark program also is written by a third party. These programs don't promote any particular brand of equipment. They are intended more as a trending device, much like those little speedometer check signs along the highway out in the boonies. Your system's performance can begin to decline because of a number of factors. Third-party benchmarks can help spot those trends, and some even include utilities that correct them.

Whatever the type of program or its purpose, most experts agree that a good benchmark is one that contains a comprehensive suite of tests and provides consistent and repeatable results. At a minimum, a comprehensive benchmark should contain tests of the following:

- CPU speed
- Memory speed
- Video speed
- Hard disk speed

POPULAR BENCHMARK PROGRAMS

There are many popular benchmarks currently in use. In the following section, you will begin to get a sense of what some of them do, how they work, and what some of their limitations are. Keep in mind the application mix that you are going to be simulating.

The Norton SI

As mentioned before, Peter Norton developed this benchmark to a set standard. Although the subject of benchmarks has never been without controversy, the PC has been especially susceptible to misinformation. In the early days of the PC, we were just beginning to learn about the value of general-purpose computing with microcomputers. Those guys with the *big* machines knew about benchmarks, but remember: They used them to measure and analyze the performance of specific machines or applications.

Norton put together a test that attempted to simulate the typical application of the day. He used a specific set of instructions based on what the typical application might run. Whether these were really typical is not important. What is important is that Norton chose to give his results in terms of comparison. Instead of saying a system can execute, say, 1,870,000 instructions per second (which is rather like the Styrofoam-cup example), Norton gives his results in terms of an IBM PC running an 8088 CPU at 4.77 MHz. The IBM PC with an 8088 CPU running at 4.77 MHz has an SI rating of 1.0. So, an Intel 80386 CPU running at 33 MHz might have a Norton SI of 15.7, indicating it is 15.7 times faster than the standard IBM PC.

As I mentioned earlier, some clever designers caught on, and they began to optimize their systems for the highest SI rating. Some developed ways of optimizing their systems so that the Norton SI would run faster. This said nothing about the performance of actual applications and ultimately led to the decline of the validity of the "standard." However, like all benchmarks, the Norton SI is still a valid program if it is not used by itself. No single program can tell the whole story.

The LandMark CPU Speed Test

LandMark Software, in Sunnyvale, California, developed a spin-off of the Norton SI. LandMark continued to show the test results as comparisons with the standard IBM PC and the somewhat faster XT. However, it went that extra step and developed a comparison with the latest technology, the AT machine. LandMark also claims to have improved accuracy and repeatability of the test by changing the instruction mix of the program.

The display of LandMark is distinctly different from that of its fellows. While most benchmarks report a "snapshot" of the system performance, LandMark displays CPU speed dynamically. It even has a sound toggle so that you get the feeling that a motor is running. It's rather like a video game without any players. The speed is displayed digitally at the left of the screen above a horizontal-bar-and-grid system. Like the Norton SI, Land-Mark does not provide for a filed history of the test results.

MIPS

MIPS, written by Chips and Technologies Inc., is a single-function benchmark similar to the Norton SI and LandMark. It measures CPU speed by running a set of general, integer, and memory operations. The results of the test are displayed in an easy-to-read chart. Again, MIPS makes a comparison with the standard IBM PC. It also makes a comparison to the AT machine and the newer Compaq 386 technology. However, like LandMark, MIPS fails to indicate the configuration of these machines. The test results are given both in SI form, compared with an IBM PC, and in actual MIPS (million instructions per second). Also, results are distributed across the various instruction types, with a summary line at the bottom indicating overall performance.

CoreTest

CoreTest is among the class of benchmark tests written for specific equipment (in this case, not a specific brand so much as a specific subsystem).

CoreTest is a benchmark for disk subsystems. Written by CORE International Inc., the CORE Disk Performance Test Program (CoreTest) is used by CORE to highlight their disk drive performance for sales. As it turns out, CoreTest works as a fairly comprehensive test of other hard disk subsystems as well.

Early I/O testing did not consider the variable of random access. Rather than relying on a single indicator of performance, CoreTest measures track-to-track seek time, average seek time, and data-transfer rate. Seek time, an indicator of the mechanical responsiveness of the drive, is always an important consideration. Too often it is forgotten that the bandwidth of the controller ultimately determines the throughput of the subsystem. By measuring the data-transfer rate, CoreTest has developed a valuable tool for integrating hard disk subsystems.

Test results are displayed in two forms. First, they are displayed in a data box by drive number. This box also includes hardware configuration items, such as the size of the drive in megabytes, numbers of heads and cylinders, and so forth. Secondly, results are displayed in a comparison format. CORE provides tabular test results for seven different disk subsystems, including its own HC310. The results from testing the current system are "sandwiched" into the form in a kind of ranking style.

PC Magazine

PC Magazine maintains a lab, called *PC* Labs, for the purpose of developing benchmarks and testing hardware and software. *PC Magazine* uses these benchmarks to evaluate new systems being reviewed. *PC* Labs has developed a full battery of benchmark tests that cover a broad base of system functions. And, as new technology comes to market, *PC* Labs updates its test methods accordingly.

PC Labs' benchmarks are a suite of tests covering processor speed, disk drive speed, video speed, and operating system performance. Under each of these categories are several specific tests. In the processor-and-memory suite, there is a CPU-speed test, an instruction-mix test, a floating-point-calculation test, and a conventional-memory test. The Processor Speed Benchmark Test compares the system under test to the 4.77 MHz IBM PC and the 8.00 MHz AT. Results are reported in table form. This subtest contains a mix of CPU operations written in assembly language and sort routines written in Microsoft C. The instruction-mix test, which is written in assembly language, tests the overall speed of the computer by testing the CPU bus, system memory, and motherboard architecture.

In the floating-point and coprocessor test, *PC* Labs has done something different. In addition to a test of a physically installed coprocessor, *PC* Labs has developed a coprocessor-emulation library for estimating the potential improvement in performance if an NPU were installed. This library, loaded into RAM, exercises the processor and RAM access speeds during floating-point calculations. Test results are reported in table form, again, as comparisons with the IBM PC and AT.

The memory-access-speed test allocates 256K of conventional, Lotus/Intel/Microsoft expanded, and AT-type extended memory and treats it as a series of 64-byte records. Then, 16,384 random records are read into and written from local memory. Speed is reported in table format, with comparisons made with IBM PC and AT machines. Speeds for expanded and extended memory are reported as indices based on the Intel Above Board.

Disk-speed tests are handled in two different ways. First, the *PC* Labs benchmark tests file-access speed. It creates a 256K file, which it writes and reads both sequentially and randomly. The initial pass is run with a 512-byte buffer, and the second pass is run with a 4K buffer. Elapsed time is reported in a table format.

PC Labs recommends running this test on a nearly empty hard disk to minimize the hidden effects of fragmentation. *PC* Labs also recommends setting BUFFERS=3 in the CONFIG.SYS file to standardize the test condition. Under DOS, the buffers definition determines how much memory is dedicated to buffering disk accesses. While this is not at all the same as disk cache, the net effect is a similar but minor increase in disk-subsystem performance.

Second, *PC* Labs runs a disk-seek-time test using the hard disk BIOS. A thousand sequential and random seeks are performed using BIOS interrupt 13h. The result, a measure of the track-to-track access time, is reported in table form. No comparisons are given. This test works only on disks with BIOS that implement a seek call.

The video test suite includes direct-to-screen and video-BIOS-routine testing. The direct-to-screen test measures the speed of the memory on the video adapter. The BIOS test measures how quickly the BIOS on the video adapter can write text data to the screen.

PowerMeter

PowerMeter includes 23 different tests in 4 categories. These include overall system performance, CPU and memory tests, disk performance, and video performance. The authors used a VAX M.I.P. to standardize power. They do something different and simulate the environmental conditions of typical spreadsheet, word processing, data base, CAD/CAE (computer aided engineering), and program-development applications. This is considered one of the best commercial benchmark systems.

CheckIt

Written by TouchStone Software, CheckIt can be considered a third-party benchmark program. Unlike the other benchmark programs mentioned, CheckIt is a PC diagnostic program that contains a suite of benchmark tests. The CheckIt benchmark tests main system performance and hard disk performance. It's discussed in more detail in the diagnostics chapter.

In the main system test suite, CheckIt measures CPU speed, video speed, and NPU speed. The CPU-speed test is based on the Dhrystone program. The results are reported in a bar graph, which automatically scales to accommodate the speed of the system under test. This bar graph also displays the speeds of comparable models, and the number of Dhrystones is reported at the bottom of the screen. (Remember, a Dhrystone is a standard unit of measure that can be used on any system type.)

The video-speed test uses the standard video BIOS to transfer text characters. Test results are reported in an autoscaling bar graph on the same screen as the CPU speed. A line at the bottom of the screen reports the actual speed of the transfer, in cps (characters per second).

The NPU-speed test is based on the Whetstone. As you may recall, a Whetstone is a predefined set of floating-point operations used to test the speed of numeric operations on a given machine. The test results are also reported in an autoscaling bar graph on the same screen as the CPU-speed and video-speed tests. A line at the bottom of the screen reports the actual speed, in number of Whetstones.

There are other benchmarks available. The defunct *PC Tech Journal* had an excellent system, the public domain SSI system, which is still traded from person to person. Golden Bow has VBENCH, which comes with some of the company's software. *InfoWorld* has an elaborate benchmark program. And there are other competitors whose products, like SYSWIN, look very good. There are a lot of these programs, and more are coming out.

THE ART OF IT ALL

What we have been talking about is the art of benchmarking. I have heard it said that good judgment comes from experience, and experience comes from bad judgment. A benchmark is worthwhile only if you know what it is measuring. Blind comparisons are of little value and can be more misleading than anything else. You should make every effort to become informed, both about the configuration of the system under test and about the functions of the benchmark tests being used.

Since the purpose of benchmarks is to compare apples to apples, any differences in test conditions should be given special attention. For example, so-called "synthetic" benchmarks, such as Dhrystone and Whetstone, give almost no weight to I/O processes. They are therefore of limited value to interactive, multiuser, and multitasking environments.

Benchmarks that are written in high-level languages vicariously test the target-system compiler and associated utilities in addition to the actual system and hardware. Optimizing compilers may recognize and remove the empty loops used in many benchmarks. These compilers should have the optimizing feature disabled or turned off and tested separately.

Benchmark tests need to be flexible enough to measure performance in the actual operating environment. If your application uses programs and files large enough to exhaust disk cache, the benchmark should also.

Repeatability is also important. Standardization of the operating environment—including hardware and software configuration—is critical to repeatability. For instance, fragmentation (the dispersal of data within the disk subsystem) can degrade system performance by 20 percent or more. Establish conditions that can be easily duplicated, such as the use of a blank, newly formatted disk. Benchmark testing has created a kind of "pull system," in which designers strive to improve performance in critical areas. As technology changes, benchmarks will continue to improve and expand in usefulness.

CHAPTER TWENTY-ONE

Disk Caching

No computer system should be without a disk cache, period.

When it comes to computers, the instinctive desire is for more performance—that is, more speed. After all, the raw processing power of PCs has increased dramatically over the last ten years. But often, the performance of an application is limited by how quickly information on a disk can be accessed rather than by the processing speed of the microprocessor.

It is unfortunate that increases in the speed of disks have not kept pace with the speed of the processor. This is partly due to the mechanical nature of a disk drive. Microprocessors have no moving parts. In contrast, a disk drive moves a mechanical arm from place to place on a disk. Advances in this technology have produced some improvements in speed, but they are far short of the corresponding improvements in microprocessor speed. Disk caching is an important step in helping them catch up.

THE NEED FOR PERFORMANCE

When first introduced, personal computers were in limited use as a tool for individuals who did not have access to more powerful mainframes and minicomputers. As the machines became more powerful (and software became more sophisticated), their use grew, both in numbers and in scope. Our reliance on them to run our businesses has increased dramatically.

Instead of hobby machines, where users maintained simple, personal records, PCs are now business machines. The records of an entire department or even an entire company may be held on a hard disk. This increase in dependence on the PC and the data it can hold makes the computer's performance play a central role in productivity.

To many computer users, the need to increase performance seems obvious. Others may argue that their PC already has plenty of performance. You may have an opinion somewhere in between.

Probably the best measure of a PC's performance is its effect on productivity. PCs are usually justified as productivity-enhancement tools, after all. Let's consider a few perspectives on productivity.

Data-Entry Productivity

PCs are often used as repositories of information. Most likely, the information comes in from a keyboard, through data entry or word processing. The information may also be scanned in (with a data scanner and the related software) or come through telecommunications.

It may seem that the keyboard is unavoidably limited only by the speed of the typist. However, consider a writer stuck for a word or the spelling of a word. In such a case, the limiting factor may be how quickly a computerized thesaurus or dictionary can offer up a list of words.

Creative Productivity

When a computer holds information, the ability to retrieve it becomes key. Long delays dramatically reduce productivity. Whether we want to pull up some information, and alter or design it (as in CAD/CAM and desktop publishing), we want to see the results quickly. Any delays may destroy concentration and have an impact on productivity far greater than the bothersome delay itself.

INCREASING PRODUCTIVITY

The first response to a slow computer often is a desire to buy a faster computer. That might make some things faster. But most of the time spent languishing at computers is not spent in waiting for the processor to execute its instructions. The delay is in waiting for data to be found and retrieved from the disk. Disks are slow because of their spinning platters and mechanical arms. So, a faster processor can't really solve the problem. There needs to be a faster way to get the data off and back on the disk.

A Software Solution

The cost of random access memory (RAM) has, overall, dropped significantly. This has resulted in an increase in the availability of PCs with large reserves of memory and of low-cost memory upgrades.

Access to data through RAM is very fast, since it is not mechanical but electronic. Information in RAM is able to get to the processor much faster than information still on disk. There are three methods by which RAM can be used to shorten the time it takes to access disk information:

- Buffering

- Virtual disks

- Disk caching

Buffering

DOS provides a way to speed up disk access. This technique, called *buffering,* uses RAM to improve disk proficiency. DOS sets aside a section of RAM (512 bytes for each buffer you specify) and moves contiguous chunks of disk data into that section. In DOS 2.0 and later versions, you can specify the number of buffers to be used. The more buffers you specify, the more data is moved into memory and, theoretically, the fewer times you access the disk.

While buffering provides some performance improvement, it is primitive and counts on the data to be close together on the disk. This may be the situation only in the beginning, when you start using your computer. But as you erase and move and change your files, DOS splits them up to fit the data into the available segments of disk space.

Virtual Disks

Another technique is to create a completely separate *virtual disk* located in random access memory. The result is called a *RAM disk.* Typically, you copy frequently used programs to the RAM disk when you start working, and when it is time to run one of these programs, it is loaded from the RAM disk rather than from the physical disk. This means the program will begin to execute in a fraction of the normal time.

The main disadvantage of RAM disks is that they must use up a lot of memory if they are to be effective. In addition, if a power loss occurs while you are making changes in RAM disk data, those changes will be lost.

Disk Caching

The third way to dramatically reduce disk accesses is to use a *disk cache.* At its simplest, disk caching is a technique that keeps the most frequently used parts of a disk in RAM. A high percentage of the requests that would normally require the access of a relatively slow disk can be supplied through the faster semiconductor memory.

A disk cache works to amass copies of data at frequently used disk locations in RAM. The caching program figures out which data on the disk you are most likely to need next and moves those sectors into RAM. You decide how much of your PC's memory to use for the cache storage. When that space fills up, the disk-caching program throws out old data that hasn't been used recently. When data stored in the cache changes, it is usually written back to the disk; nothing is lost.

A disk cache reduces the number of times the application must access the disk drives. This decrease can dramatically speed up the response time for any application that must access the disk.

The memory used to store the collection of disk sectors held in RAM is often called the cache, from the nontechnical use of the word *cache* as a storage place. The software program responsible to set up the cache and provide copies of sectors from it is called a disk cache program; it also may be referred to as the cache. Context should make it clear whether we are referring to the program or to its storage area.

MEMORY IN ITS VARIOUS FORMS

The original PC architecture divided the 1MB (1024K) addressing capability of the 8088 microprocessor into two areas. The first is 640K of so-called *conventional memory*. The remainder of the 384K is normally reserved for BIOS ROMs and various input/output adapters. A common adapter is a video adapter that includes 16K or more of RAM and may include its own ROMs that take up part of the 384K.

At first, the 640K conventional memory area seemed adequate. In fact, most computers included only 64K to 256K of RAM in this area. As applications became more sophisticated, it became common for PCs to have 640K of conventional memory. The question then became how to supply a PC with more than 640K of memory. There were many answers. The industry standardized on two arrangements: extended memory and expanded memory.

Extended memory is memory that is placed above the 1MB addressing range of the 8088. (The 80286, 80386, and 80486 microprocessors can access more than the 1MB accessible by the 8088.) Unfortunately, DOS normally runs in the more primitive 8088 mode of these more advanced processors. Because of this restriction, most applications are limited to conventional memory even when a large amount of extended memory has been installed on a PC.

Expanded, or *LIM, memory* is memory that conforms to the Lotus/Intel/Microsoft Expanded Memory Specification (EMS). This is a method to access additional memory by way of a 64K area in the 384K area above conventional memory. Software applications written to either the 3.2 or 4.0 version of the LIM EMS take advantage of hardware boards that also comply with the specification.

Emulation-software packages are also available to convert extended memory to expanded memory. These emulators work particularly well on 80386-based computers, where they are able to take advantage of the mapping capability built into the microprocessor.

How to Select Memory for the Cache

Disk caching software utilizes memory to improve the performance of disks. The availability of extended or expanded memory can make a substantial difference in a software's effectiveness. While it may be possible to set up a small disk cache in conventional memory, such a cache will compete for the limited 640K with application programs.

It is more practical to configure the disk-caching software to use expanded or extended memory. This limits the cache's use of conventional memory to a minimum. Most commercial disk-caching programs furnish the user with an option of using either extended or expanded memory when available.

───────── **READ.ME** ─────────

Choosing a Cache Program

Five Practical Considerations

While the best disk cache programs take care of most of the details, there are a few things to consider:

A Cache Should Match Your Disk Drives   Not all disk cache programs are created equal. Check carefully to be sure that your disk drive and controller configuration are supported by the cache program.

Some Programs Can Cache Only Hard Disks   If, for instance, you have a hard disk (where most of your programs are) but you regularly run a program from a floppy disk, make sure that both disks can be cached. Otherwise, you'll lose the performance improvement while you run your program. Such cache programs as Multisoft's Super PC-Kwik can cache almost any mass-storage device, including HardCards, Bernoulli Boxes, and floppy disks.

Check What Kind of Controller You Have   Most PCs use either MFM or ESDI controllers. However, SCSI and RLL controllers are also available. Not all disk-caching programs can handle different kinds of controllers. In addition, if you have a very large hard disk or very large partitions, you may not be able to cache them effectively, or there may be restrictions. For instance, Super PC-Kwik caches large disks just fine, but the physical sector size must be 512 bytes, and it helps to have the disk partitioned into logical partitions of no more than 32K.

The Best Disk Cache is the One that Takes the Least Conventional Memory   A disk cache program will compete for memory space with your application programs. Fortunately, most of the space it needs is for buffers, which can be set up in expanded or extended memory. But there is still the matter of required space for the program itself.

Choosing a Cache Program (*continued*)

Many application programs require 512K or more of conventional memory. While most systems have 640K of conventional memory, some of the 640K is chewed up by DOS, drivers, and resident programs. There never seems to be much conventional memory over and above what is required for the application program.

Look for a Cache Program with a Variable Track-Buffer Size Most commercial disk cache programs use a technique called *track buffering*. Depending on requests from application programs, DOS will often request only a small portion of a disk track. A clever disk cache can accurately predict when DOS will need more of the same track. A disk cache that exploits the track-buffering technique reads more of the track than DOS actually requests. The extra data is stored in the cache. When DOS asks for the rest of the track later, it can be provided from the cache at electronic speeds rather than at the mechanical speed of the disk drive.

To implement this technique, the disk cache program must set aside some conventional memory as a track buffer. For subtle technical reasons, this buffer cannot be placed in expanded or extended memory. By default, the track buffer may be the size of the largest track in your system—34 sectors (or 17K) in the case of an ESDI drive.

Fortunately, many disk cache programs will allow a choice in the size of the track buffer. Nearly the same performance can be obtained with a smaller track buffer. If you are short on conventional memory, using a track buffer of 4 sectors rather than 34 could save you 15K of RAM. (To use this trick with Super PC-Kwik, add the /T:4 parameter to the command line that loads the cache program.)

Code Hiding

One way a good disk cache can conserve conventional memory is to hide some of its code and associated tables in other types of memory. These possibilities include expanded memory, Upper Memory Blocks (UMB), and DOS buffers.

If your system includes expanded memory, that's where the cache buffers will go. It turns out that a clever disk cache program can hide most of its code and tables in expanded memory. This can reduce the amount of conventional memory required by 48K or more.

The addresses between 640K and 1024K (1MB) are usually reserved for video RAM and BIOS ROM. But often not all this address space is taken. This provides an opportunity, particularly on 80386- and 80486-based systems, to set up *Upper Memory Blocks (UMBs)* where code can be hidden. These UMBs are set up by 386 memory managers, such as Qualitas's 386MAX and Quarterdeck's QEMM.

These programs use the 80386's memory-mapping feature to map extended memory so that it appears to other programs as if it exists in the unused address areas between 640K and 1024K. Some programs can request that the memory manager allocate some of the UMBs to them so that they can move code and data out of conventional memory. This technique can reduce the conventional memory used by the disk cache program to zero.

Another place where code can be hidden is in DOS buffers. DOS attempts to improve effective disk performance by providing a set of buffers to hold frequently accessed sectors of the disk. In the absence of a good disk cache, 20 to 30 buffers may be needed to obtain reasonable disk performance. But once a separate disk cache program is installed, the number of DOS buffers can be reduced to as few as 4. Most of the buffering function is efficiently provided by the cache program.

Each DOS buffer takes at least 512 bytes of conventional memory. By reducing the number of buffers to four, you can save 10K or more without sacrificing disk performance. You can add the following line to the CONFIG.SYS file in the root directory of your boot disk:

```
BUFFERS=4
```

Be sure and check the CONFIG.SYS for any other BUFFERS lines. Delete them so that the BUFFERS=4 command can take effect.

This trick, combined with using a disk cache program that uses one or both of the code-hiding techniques, can mean a net conventional memory cost of nil. Actually, you may gain memory! Consider the following examples.

Example 1   A disk cache is installed in expanded memory with a track-buffer size of four. The number of DOS buffers is reduced from 30 to 4.

Before installing cache:

DOS & drivers	64K
30 buffers	15K
Total	79K

After installing cache:

DOS & drivers	64K
4 buffers	2K
Super PC-Kwik	10K
Total	76K

The net cost of the cache is −3K.

Example 2   A cache program is installed in extended memory, and UMBs are available to hide its code, tables, and track buffer. The number of DOS buffers is reduced from 30 to 4.

Before installing cache:

DOS & drivers	64K
30 buffers	15K
Total	79K

After installing cache:

DOS & drivers	64K
4 buffers	2K
Super PC-Kwik	0K
Total	66K

The net cost of the cache is −13K.

Note: The above examples assume your DOS is using the standard 512-byte buffer size. Some disk-partitioning programs and optical disk drivers patch DOS to increase the buffer size to 1024K, 2048K, or 4096K. In these cases, reducing the number of DOS buffers can save you 20K, 80K, or more.

Cache Size

How much memory must be dedicated to a disk cache? The easy answer is: What you can afford. A well-written disk cache is able to put any amount of memory from 64K to 16MB (16,384K) to good use. Using more disk cache memory is advantageous, because it allows the cache program to keep more of the most frequently used sectors in memory.

With more memory available, more sectors can be available at electronic speeds rather than mechanical speeds. There is a slight overhead in locating a sector in the cache memory. This is essentially independent of the size of the cache. Keep in mind that it is certainly less than the time it takes to move the disk head and wait for the disk to rotate to the location of a particular sector.

A more precise answer to the cache-size question involves introducing the concept of working sets, a theory from computer science. In the case of disk caching, a working set consists of the sectors accessed by a program during a particular period of time.

If an application accesses between 500 and 750 sectors during, say, a five-minute period, we can say that it has a working set of no more than 750 sectors. A good disk cache size for such a program would be slightly more than 375K, assuming that the sectors are the standard 512 bytes each. On a 1MB system with 384K of extended memory, we might devote the 384K of extended memory to the disk cache.

If another program typically accesses 10,000 sectors over a short period, its working-set size is about 5000K or 5MB. A disk cache of 5MB or more would be appropriate for such a program. If you lacked the necessary memory to set up such a large cache size, you could examine the program's behavior in more detail. You might discover that while it accessed data records contained in about 9000 sectors, it made even more frequent access to a data base index in about 1000 sectors. In this case, you might receive nearly the benefit of the larger cache by setting up a cache large enough to hold the data base index—about 512K in this case. The disk cache automatically notices that the sectors holding the index are the most frequently used. These would tend to be the sectors held in the 512K cache area.

Sharing Memory

The role of a disk cache is to provide a performance increase to applications that run on your PC. The cache program exploits extra RAM in this role—the more the better. But some of your application programs may need to use this same memory on occasion. This could put you in the position of referee between the programs, to decide which program gets what memory. This is unfortunate in several ways:

1. The reason to use a disk cache is to save time. If the disk cache requires you to spend time to determine how much RAM to give it and your other programs, you may not receive the productivity gain desired.

2. The exact amount of memory needed by your programs may be difficult to predict. The need may be based on the size of documents or spreadsheets. To convert the size of documents and spreadsheets into the correct number of K of memory needed by your application programs may be difficult or impossible. It depends on how much, if any, guidance the application programs' manuals give you.

3. The amount of memory needed by the application programs may vary over time. You may not know at the beginning of the day which documents or spreadsheets you will be working on. To predict this in advance forces you to read a crystal ball as well as be a referee.

Fortunately, you don't have to predict the varying memory needs of your application programs. Some disk cache programs have the built-in intelligence to detect when an application program needs to allocate expanded or extended memory. The cache program lends some of its memory to the application. When the application is through with the memory, the cache takes it back and uses it to enhance the performance of disk accesses.

This solution is possible because the disk cache program does not insist on a particular amount of cache memory. Rather, it appreciates as much as it can get. When it must give up some memory to an application program, it can choose the parts of its cache memory that contain the less frequently used sectors, rearranging the memory as necessary. It can retain the most frequently used sectors in memory. In many cases, it will be able to maintain most of the performance benefit with a fraction of the memory it originally had at its disposal.

Some cache programs come bundled with other performance-enhancement programs. These may include a print spooler, a RAM disk, a keyboard accelerator, and a screen accelerator. These add-on programs need buffer memory to perform with the amount of memory varying over time.

For instance, the print spooler needs buffer memory only when an application generates printer output. The spooler can borrow the exact amount of memory necessary from the cache and then return it as the printing occurs. The RAM disk requires memory as files are copied to it or otherwise created. It can borrow memory from the cache. If some of the RAM disk files are deleted later, the freed-up memory is returned to the disk cache. The disk cache can then go back to its role of enhancing the performance of the system.

ADVANCED TECHNIQUES

A disk cache performs a variety of tricks that may speed up your applications. Many of these tricks are quite different from the basic concept of disk caching. Some of these tricks enhance the performance of writing data to the disk. This is possible because there may be ways to arrange for more data writing each time the disk rotates. Similarly, there may be ways to reduce the number of times the disk heads need to be moved to access the tracks where reading and writing is going on.

The question then becomes "Are these tricks safe, or do they expose your valuable data to some sort of increased risk?" The answer varies according to the type of trick used. Let's consider some of the techniques that might be included in an advanced disk cache program.

Overlapped Disk Activity

This technique amounts to a simple form of parallel processing. The disk controller that transfers data to and from your disk drives is essentially a separate microprocessor. Allow it to perform its function at the same time the main system processor is allowed to execute the instructions of your application, your programs, or the DOS operating system. This can allow almost twice as much work to be performed in any given period.

Delayed Writing

To delay writing to the disk has pluses and minuses. The main advantage is that, in some cases, more sectors can be written during each revolution of the disk. While this can provide a performance boost, you should consider the following:

1. By the time the cache begins writing to the disk, valuable time has gone by. Even if efficiency is improved after that, valuable time is lost by not beginning to write immediately. Thus, the performance gain must be large enough to make up for this lost time.

2. Normally, you may turn off the computer once the disks' lights have finished blinking. If the disk cache waits to start disk writing, you may turn off the computer before all your files are up to date. This may cause you to lose information.

Suppressed Obsolete Writes

There can be cases where the same sector of the disk is updated over and over again. Time can be saved by taking advantage of the fact that the only data that actually needs to reach the disk is the last version of the data destined for each sector. However, this technique can produce some unfortunate results if something goes wrong.

DOS updates its allocation tables and directories on the disk in a specific order. By doing so, it ensures that the effect of a hardware or software failure is minimal. If the disk cache suppresses certain writes and something goes wrong, DOS's careful plan doesn't work. A power failure can stop your computer in midstream. A far more common failure occurs when a DOS program contains a bug that stops the execution of your computer, requiring a reboot.

While either type of failure is possible with or without a disk cache, DOS takes care to order the way it updates your disk. If a failure occurs, some new data may be lost, but the basic structure of the disk is maintained.

If the disk cache program takes the liberty of changing the order of events on the disk and a failure occurs, some of your files may share the same space on the disk (known as *cross-linked files*). Unfortunately, the old rule that "two things can't be in the same place at the same time" holds true for disks. At least one of each pair of files that share the same space will be corrupted, because it will contain data of the other file.

Optimized Head Movement

To adjust the order of writing the data to the disk can reduce the number of times the disk's heads must be moved in a series of read-and-write operations. While this can save time, it also tends to violate DOS's fail-safe assumption. A small problem can turn into a major crisis if DOS's requests aren't carried out in the order they are requested.

CONCLUSION

Disk caching is a necessity, period. Disk caching can make a big difference in the performance of your system and the applications you run. By choosing the right disk cache, you can double or triple the performance of applications that make heavy use of the disk. We recommend you use the cache provided with this book and consider a more advanced one for your system at a later date.

CHAPTER TWENTY-TWO

Disk
Defragmenters

Your disk storage is, in many ways, the heart of your system. You can do very little without a reliable storage system. And accessing your disk is about the slowest thing your computer does.

In the previous chapter, we discussed how a disk-caching program makes getting to the data on your disks easier and faster. In this chapter, we'll talk about how a defragmenter can make those disk-storage systems more reliable and faster to access.

WHY DO YOU NEED A DEFRAGMENTER?

When you copy, delete, move, or rename files on your disk, DOS often splits up the file into pieces, called *clusters*, so that it can fit the file into the empty spaces on your disk. When you first start out and you haven't made many changes to the data on your disk, the pieces of each file are often right next to each other, that is, contiguous.

As you make more and more changes to your data, DOS splits the pieces up more, trying to fit the new clusters into the available spaces on your disk. The DOS *File Allocation Table (FAT)* keeps track of which clusters belong to which file so that when you access the file it looks as if the data is all in one place.

The more pieces your file is split into, the longer it takes DOS to find all the pieces and bring them to you—and the more fragmented your disk is. The more fragmented your disk is, the more mechanical and physical activity your disk has to do, increasing chances for problems.

A disk defragmenter finds all the pieces of each file, puts them together in one place, and changes the FAT so that DOS knows where everything is. A good defragmenter usually does more, including giving you reports on the state of your disk, checking the disk for bad clusters, and rescuing data in those bad clusters so that you won't lose any.

A good defragmenter should be able to test and defragment a wide variety of storage peripherals. It should offer several intelligent strategies for reorganizing your disk, allowing you to choose how much and how often to defragment.

Among the defragmenters on the market today are: Vopt, from Golden Bow, one of the originals and still a standard-bearer; PC Tools Compress, from Central Point Software; Multisoft's Power Disk; Fast Trax, from Bridgeway Publishing; Norton's defragmenting utility; Mace, from Fifth Generation Systems; and Gazelle Systems' OPtune.

What Kinds of Disks Can Be Defragmented?

Any type of disk storage can get fragmented, and they all need to be defragmented. Not all defragmenters can handle all kinds of disks, though. Some won't handle floppies, and some won't work on external drives or Bernoulli Boxes. Some can't handle large drives or exotic configurations. About the only one we've found that can successfully handle almost any configuration is Multisoft's Power Disk. Check the specifications carefully before you buy a defragmenter. Make sure that all the disk equipment you are running can be cleaned up with the program you want to buy.

Performance Versus Safety

Because a disk defragmenter moves data on your disk, there is always a risk of losing data when you defragment. Usually, the trade-off is between how fast the program runs and how safe it is, because the strategies for being careful with your data take extra time. I have to say, though, that I have used almost every defragmenter and have never experienced a problem in ten years of use. In any case, it's a very good idea to do a complete backup of the data on your disk before you defragment it.

Strategies for Organizing Your Disk

Another trade-off to make in defragmenting is in how you organize the data physically on your disk after it is defragmented. The fast ways frequently leave some fragmentation; to completely defragment takes more time. A good defragmenter should give you a number of options for reorganization strategies, including options that make it less necessary to defragment over time. You should be able to make different choices at different times, depending on the state of your disk and the kinds of applications you are running.

As an example, Power Disk from Mulitsoft offers four strategies, each of which can meet different needs at different times:

- Use the fast method, moving few files while closing up as much space as possible. This may lead to a need for more defragmenting over time, but it gets the job done quickly. This strategy is the default.

- Put fragmented files last, placing all fragmented files at the end of the disk. This tends to decrease the need for defragmenting later if you access the same files over and over (for instance, with a word processing package).

- Put your files on the disk in directory order. This strategy gives you the ability to specify placing certain files or directories first or last physically on the disk.

- Perform only partial reorganization, defragmenting without moving the files together on the disk. This is even faster than the first method, but it leaves you with more housekeeping to do later.

A defragmenter that doesn't offer at least three out of four of these or similar options may prove to be a problem. The more control you have over the way your data is organized, the more reliable your disk is going to be and the faster you will be able to get to that data. Only you know which programs and files you need to get to quickly; they should come first, towards the front of the disk. Only you know which programs and files change the most; they should go last, where there is more free space and they won't fragment as much.

Related Tasks

Disk housekeeping consists of more than just moving the pieces of files back together. In fact, most defragmenting utilities could more accurately be called "disk-cleanup utilities."

Related disk-housekeeping tasks include the following:

- Checking disk reliability
- Checking the level of fragmentation on your disk without running the defragmenter
- Remapping data in bad clusters
- Marking bad clusters so that they won't be used again
- Recovering from errors
- Protecting data while you defragment
- Producing reports of the cleanup activity for future reference
- Keeping you up-to-date on disk cleanup activity, by means of interactive graphics or status messages

The more of these auxiliary tasks you can perform with one software package, the better value you have for your money. Reliability testing and bad cluster remapping, in particular, are crucial for good disk health.

WHEN AND HOW OFTEN?

When should you defragment your disk and how often do you need to do it?

If you are constantly changing, deleting, and rearranging the information in your files, or if you work on many files in the course of a day, your disk is going to tend to fragment fast. If you usually work on only a few files or you make few changes, your disk will stay cleaner longer.

Most defragmenters have an option that checks your disk and sees whether it needs to be cleaned up or not. Some, like Power Disk, can be set up so that they check your disk and run only if a certain level of fragmentation is reached. You will certainly want to check your disk's fragmentation level at least once a week or so; some people may need to check daily.

Don't defragment unless the disk is more than slightly defragmented— say 15 percent fragmentation or more. Less than 15 percent is not enough fragmentation to warrant the time you spend waiting for the program to run, unless you have one of the very fast defragmenters, such as Power Disk or Fast Trax.

AUTOMATING THE PROCESS

It is often useful to set up your defragmentation program so that it runs automatically. You can invoke it in AUTOEXEC.BAT if you want it to run every time you reboot, although that can make bootup a time-consuming process. Some defragmenters (notably Power Disk) have conditional operation flags that can set it up to run only the first time the system is booted each day, only on a specific day of the week, or only when the disk reaches a specific level of fragmentation. It can even allow combinations of these conditions and change the organization and protection strategy depending on which conditions are met. This automation makes keeping your disks clean much easier. You don't have to remember whether you've run your weekly batch job or not.

If you don't want the defragger to run every time you boot (for instance, if your program can't check to see if it's already been run today), you may wish to set up batch files to run it. You can have one batch file specifying a fast reorganization to run every Friday. Another can pack everything in as tightly as possible by putting your fragmented files at the end of the disk once a month. You should check your disks' reliability as regularly as you defragment, either in the same batch file or separately.

CONCLUSION

Reliable, fast disk storage is crucial to good system performance. A flexible, safe, fast disk defragmenter is one key to maintaining performance.

CHAPTER TWENTY-THREE

Other Performance Software

Speeding up a disk and keeping it defragmented solves only some performance issues. There are a variety of utilities that you should consider adding to your system and using regularly.

PRINT SPOOLERS

Compared to most printers, your disk drives are speed demons. The process of converting bytes of information to printed form is a relatively slow mechanical process. To make matters worse, your computer usually speaks to you while printing is going on. Starting with DOS version 2.0, a partial solution to this problem became available in the form of the PRINT command, available from the DOS prompt. While this command allows you to request that a file be printed while you use your computer for other things, the command can be quite cumbersome to use. Consider the following situation:

You are in your favorite word processor when you decide to print a rough draft of your current document. You select the print function from a menu. If you move too quickly, your document is sent directly to the printer and you have to wait until it's completely printed before proceeding.

If you are careful, you figure out how to tell the word processor to divert the printer output to a file after it asks you for a name for the file. Then you exit the word processor (or, in some cases, "shell" to DOS) to get to the DOS prompt. You give the PRINT command with the filename you selected for the printer output (assuming you remember it). When DOS reports that the printing has begun, you re-invoke your word processor and reload the document you were working on.

While this involved process got the job done, the number of steps involved may make you wonder if you'd be better off directing the word processor to print directly to your printer and taking a break during printing.

Consider instead the scenario if a printer spooler is involved:

You request that your current document be printed on your standard printer. The printing begins and control is returned to you and your word processor. You continue editing the current document, switch to another document, or go on to some other activity.

As you can see, the role of a good print spooler is to make printing more efficient, not more complicated.

How a Spooler Works

The name *spooler* comes from an analogy of a spool of thread or cable. In this case, the spool can feed cable in at the same time it is feeding cable out. The amount of cable on the spool is the analog of the data waiting to be printed. In the case of a printer spooler, the spool in the analogy is actually RAM or disk space. As you might guess, RAM is the most efficient place for the data, assuming RAM is available. Most basic spoolers get the user involved by having the user select a particular number of kilobytes to be set aside as the spool space. This raises several questions:

- How much space is required to hold a particular document?

- How large will the documents be today?

- What do you do if the documents are larger tomorrow?

- Won't the spool space be going to waste when you're not printing?

Answering the first question involves estimating how many characters are in a document. You might use a certain rule of thumb, such as the number of words per line or lines per page. Or the size of your document files might provide a hint. In either case, it may not be clear how to account for control codes, fonts, graphics, and such. You may have very little idea in advance which documents you are going to print during a session, let alone exactly how big they will be at the time. Even if you guess correctly about the size of today's documents, what about tomorrow? Do you reconfigure the spooler each day?

If you set aside enough memory for printing your largest documents, chances are good that it will be going to waste most of the day, because you probably won't be printing all that often. If you guess wrong and set aside too little memory, you lose control of your word processor or other application while it waits for the printer to catch up with its ability to generate output for the printer.

Fortunately, there is a simple answer available: Use a print spooler that handles the allocation of the spool space for you. One way this is possible is for the spooler to work in collaboration with your disk cache, assuming they're both from the same manufacturer. For example, the PC-Kwik spooler comes with the PC-Kwik cache in Multisoft's PC-Kwik Power Pak, and Spool Master is an option to the Flash disk cache, available from Software Masters.

The spooler waits until you request something to be printed before it determines how much space it needs. It then borrows the needed space from the cache. As the printing occurs, it returns the space to the cache so that it can be used to speed up your disks again. As you can see, this technique ensures that your memory is being put to the best use. More importantly, it gets you out of the business of trying to estimate in advance how much space you will require.

RAM DISKS

Most application programs assume you have much more disk space available than you have RAM available. The designers of these programs put data on your disks when they it expect it to be too large to fit in RAM or when they assume you want a permanent copy of the data. This approach is good as far as it goes, but it may limit the performance of your applications if much reading and writing of the disk drives is required. As we saw in an earlier chapter, we can improve things dynamically by using a good disk cache.

But what if we want even greater performance? The answer may be a RAM disk. The idea here is to construct a virtual disk in RAM so that the application program will be fooled into using RAM instead of an actual disk. As long as the application can be told to use a drive other than the disk from which it was loaded, the trick should work. And you benefit from the greater speed of moving your data to and from the RAM disk at electronic speeds rather than to and from a real disk at mechanical speeds. There are three limitations of a RAM disk:

- Lack of permanent storage
- The need to copy or redirect data
- The need to predict the disk size required

Lack of Permanent Storage

Because the RAM disk is set up in RAM memory, any data in the RAM disk is lost when you turn the power off, or reboot. If a permanent copy of the data is kept on a regular disk, this restriction may not be of concern. But if you are creating new data on the RAM disk, you need to copy the data to a real disk before you shut the computer off. Meanwhile, you risk losing your data because of a power failure or software or hardware failure.

Because of these complexities and risks, many people either avoid using a RAM disk or restrict their use to copies of programs and reference files that do not change. Another good use for a RAM disk is for temporary files that are generated by some application programs and compilers in the process of producing reports or permanent files.

Copying or Redirecting Data

When you set up a RAM disk, you assign a unique drive letter to it, say, D. From there, it is up to you to exploit the RAM disk. For example, you could copy frequently used programs to "drive D" and invoke them from there.

You could set up a batch file to copy a set of programs from your hard disk to the RAM disk. If you have DOS 3.3 or 4.0, you can call this batch file from your AUTOEXEC.BAT file. If you have an earlier version of DOS, you can put an equivalent command line in your AUTOEXEC.BAT file. Let's consider an example:

You are using DOS 3.3 and you want to set up your RAM disk (assigned drive letter D) with copies of your frequently used DOS commands. Some of the DOS commands are included in the COMMAND.COM program, which stays resident most of the time but must occasionally be reloaded from disk. You can copy this program from the root directory of your hard disk to drive D. You can also copy a couple of other DOS commands from the DOS directory of the hard disk (where you placed them when you installed DOS). Here's how your SETUPRD.BAT file will look:

```
COPY \COMMAND.COM d:
COPY c:\DOS\XCOPY.* d:
COPY c:\DOS\CHKDSK.* d:
PATH d:\;%PATH%
SET COMSPEC = d:\COMMAND.COM /s ....
```

Note the last two lines of this batch file. The PATH command instructs DOS to check your RAM disk drive for programs you invoke before it checks the directories you had previously specified as its search path. The last line instructs DOS to reload COMMAND.COM from the RAM disk whenever it discovers it is no longer resident.

Redirecting Data

Some programs create temporary files in the process of performing their functions. A common example in the programming world is a compiler. Most compilers translate a source program into an intermediate form before creating the final object form. Some compilers allow you to specify which drive should be used for the temporary files. If you've set up a RAM disk of the right size, you may be able to tell your compiler to use the RAM disk to store its temporary files. That way, these files can be written and read at electronic speeds. You don't need a permanent disk copy, anyway.

Predicting the Size Required

The final challenge with using a RAM disk is predicting how big it will need to be. In some cases, this may be relatively easy. Consider the preceding example of the SETUPRD.BAT batch file. If the files listed in this file are the only ones you plan on copying to the RAM disk, you can check their sizes ahead of time by performing a DIR command on the root and DOS directories of the hard disk. This will give you the file sizes in bytes. If you know what the cluster size of the RAM disk will be (2K perhaps), you can round the sector sizes up to the cluster size, convert the total to kilobytes, and set up a RAM disk of at least that size. To make best use of a disk with limited space, the smaller the sector size is set, the easier it is to reduce, and the more likely you are to make best use of the space available. For instance, if the sector size is 8K, like on some high capacity hard disks, a one-byte file will occupy one byte and leave 8,191 bytes unusable. This wasted space is called slack. One advantage of RAM disks is the ability to control slack by using a cluster size setting that makes best use of available space.

In many cases, you may not be able to predict the size the RAM disk should be. For example:

- The files will be created on the fly by applications programs.
- The files may grow during a session.
- You will be using the RAM disk for a variety of purposes during the day.

In each of these cases, it is difficult or impossible to predict the exact amount of space you will need on the RAM disk. In the last case, you may be able to make a "worst-case" estimate of the amount of space you will need. But most of the time, less than this amount of space will be used, and the balance will go to waste.

If you read the preceding section on spoolers, you might be able to guess the solution to this problem. Some RAM disk programs dynamically borrow the memory they need from a companion disk cache. As files are created or enlarged, more memory is borrowed from the cache. When files are deleted, the space is returned to the disk cache. Flash RAM from Software Masters and the Multisoft's PC-Kwik Power Pak RAMDISK accomplish this.

The RAM-disk-size paradox can be solved so easily because a disk cache is comparatively flexible about its RAM needs. While it appreciates all the RAM it can get, it can do without RAM when necessary. The disadvantage of shortchanging a disk cache in memory space is that it will not be able to provide so much of a performance boost. But it is still usually able to increase the performance of your disk even with a minimal amount of RAM. In contrast, a RAM disk insists on getting exactly the amount of RAM it needs for your files. If it doesn't, it generates an error that is reported by DOS or your application.

SCREEN ACCELERATORS

This performance enhancer is a particular favorite of mine and one of the reasons we asked Multisoft to research this chapter with us. Multisoft makes a screen cache that literally makes my VGA scream on the screen. I said once (in *PC Magazine*) that it's as though it will blow off the top of the monitor.

Compared to an old-fashioned teletype or CRT, a PC displays text information at an amazing speed. But it's still not fast enough for the power hungry among us. There are cases where the delay in displaying is just long enough to cause you to lose your train of thought. The obvious cure is to buy a faster computer. Surprisingly, even top-of-the-line computers sometimes provide only limited screen-display speeds because of design limitations of the video adapters and the BIOSs that support them. Fortunately, there is a software cure for this performance disease.

A software screen accelerator takes over some of the functions of the BIOS and dramatically improves performance. On some systems, the improvements can be a factor of two, three, or four. Those who have one of these programs installed on their screens quickly get used to the increased responsiveness of their systems. When they try to use someone else's system, their instinctive reaction is "There must be something wrong with this computer—it seems awfully sluggish."

The screen accelerator provided by Multisoft in its PC-Kwik Power Pak—and the one I use—has a number of interesting features. For example, screen blanking prevents phosphor burn, and screen review lets you scroll backward and see all that occurred on the screen earlier. The key to the product, though, is based in its caching knowledge. The screen is cached in much the same way as a hard disk, and performance is increased accordingly.

KEYBOARD ACCELERATORS

At first, the idea of accelerating a keyboard sounds like a magical way of improving your typing speed. But that's not it. Rather, the idea is to make the cursor keys more responsive. Next time you're using a word processor, editor, or spreadsheet, notice how much time you spend waiting for the cursor to move from one side of the screen to the other (unless, of course, you're a mouse user, in which case you can skip the next paragraph).

A keyboard accelerator gives you control of the repeat rate of the cursor keys. You can choose any rate you want, depending on how quick your hand-eye coordination is. Suddenly, you can zip from one part of the screen to another.

CONCLUSION

As we have seen in this chapter, there are many ways that DOS can be enhanced to make your computer faster and make you more productive. When you add more productive printing, displaying, and keyboarding to the faster disk access we talked about earlier, it's amazing what a high-performance environment DOS can provide.

PART SIX

Programming DOS for Performance

CHAPTER TWENTY-FOUR

EDLIN and Other Line Editors

Line editors are a family of limited "word processors." EDLIN is the old DOS line editor. A line editor lets you create or alter text files; so will a word processor like WordPerfect. But an editor does not gracefully handle fancy fonts, proportional spacing, bold and underlining, automatic footnotes, pagination, and many other features we expect in a word processor.

So, if you have a word processor, why would you need a line editor? Editors exist for much the same reasons pocket calculators did not die out when personal computers came along. They are easier and faster to use for short, simple jobs. You are more likely to reach for a calculator to balance your checkbook than to load Lotus 1-2-3. When you need a short batch file or just want to knock out a grocery list, an editor is handier than Word-Perfect.

Despite requiring some arcane commands, editors are actually easier to learn than more sophisticated tools. Everyone "knows" how to use a borrowed calculator; editors are equally intuitive. You needn't learn WordStar to work on a friend's computer.

Editors are small programs. An editor neatly fits in a corner of a "travel kit" disk. WordPerfect 5, by contrast, occupies fourteen 5.25-inch disks! Many programs will let you "shell out" to use an external program, but not all free up enough memory to load a huge word processor.

Editors are preferable for work on "nonword" files, such as ANSI graphics screens or compiled programs. Such files contain CTRL-key and other nontext symbols that can make word processors choke and die. The humble editor is less finicky about its diet.

Editors do not make assumptions about the meaning of special characters. WordPerfect displays the CTRL-L character as a line of equal signs and interprets CTRL-L as a hard page break. The symbol might be intended to clear the screen in your program. An editor displays the character (^L); so, you can see exactly where it is in relation to other symbols. How a CTRL character is interpreted depends upon the program that is reading the file. For instance, if you load a WordStar file into a WordPerfect file you will find the WordStar formatting codes won't be interpreted correctly.

Finally, editors generate ASCII text, which can be imported directly into another editor or a word processor. This is a significant advantage if a document needs to be "passed around."

EDLIN, THE "UNIVERSAL" EDITOR

EDLIN.COM is the oldest MS/PC-DOS line editor. It is included with every copy of DOS. EDLIN is a living fossil, remarkably primitive compared to any other example of the species. Its sole virtue is omnipresence. If you know how to use EDLIN, you can create and edit files on any DOS machine you meet. This chapter covers EDLIN's commands and idiosyncrasies in all their painful detail. Then we will look at QEdit, a more civilized editor, and VDE, a chameleonlike editor that can imitate your favorite word processor, too.

Starting EDLIN

EDLIN came with your copy of DOS, on the second of the two floppies. If you copied these disks into a hard drive directory, look for EDLIN there.

Once you find EDLIN, make sure it will always be handy. You can do this by adding it to the PATH command in your AUTOEXEC.BAT file. The SET or PATH command will show you the current setting for your path. If your DOS command files are not one of the paths listed, you'll need to modify the DOS command in your AUTOEXEC.BAT file.

Type **edlin text.fil** to start EDLIN and open a file named TEXT.FIL. The phrase "New file" appears on the next line on the screen. Below it is an asterisk, the EDLIN "ready" prompt. (Don't expect menu bars, status lines, or help prompts.) If TEXT.FIL already existed, EDLIN would load the file and display "End of input file" instead of "New file".

EDLIN might not load all of a file. The MS-DOS manual says, "If the file is too large to be loaded into memory, EDLIN loads . . . until memory is 3/4 full." This passage must have been written when 64KB was considered "full memory." I have never gotten more than about 59,000 bytes into EDLIN at one time, using 440KB of free RAM. Fortunately, the WRITE and APPEND commands make it possible to edit a file larger than EDLIN's memory constraints.

An end-of-file character (^Z) in the middle of a file will also halt the loading process. This problem can be overcome by including the /b switch:

EDLIN TEXT.FIL /B

Then, you may use the SEARCH or REPLACE command (described below) to find the troublesome ^Z character and delete it.

Note: If you use DOS 3.3, be sure to use an uppercase *B*! For whatever reason, only DOS 3.3 cares about the case of EDLIN switches.

Inserting Text

Enter an **i** to INSERT text. EDLIN displays 1:* to show you are on line 1. Your display now looks like this:

```
New file
*i
    1:*_
```

The line number will not appear in the finished file. Line numbers are automatically adjusted when new lines are inserted in the middle of a file or when lines are deleted. Each line can hold up to 254 characters. (The manual says 253, but the manual is often wrong or incomplete with respect to EDLIN.)

Type the following lines (without the line numbers and asterisks). Press the ENTER key to end each line except line 3. For that line, just keep typing when you reach the right edge of the screen. Do not press ENTER when you reach the word *etc.*

```
1:*Line editors are simple programs.
2:*EDLIN is the built-in MS-DOS line editor.
3: It is possible to add text, search for strings of text,
replace specified characters with others, delete a line or range
of lines, etc.
```

Each time you press the ENTER key, a new line is started. When you reach the right edge of the screen on line 3, the cursor moves down and back to the far left. It looks like there are four lines, but no 4:* appeared: You are still on the third line as far as EDLIN is concerned. Because there is no word-wrap feature, a word may appear to be broken in the middle. If you try to enter more than 254 characters on a line, EDLIN balks and beeps.

Press the ENTER key to begin line 4. Enter a ^C character (hold down the CTRL key and press C). You should now see the following:

```
1:*Line editors are simple programs.
2:*EDLIN is the built-in MS-DOS line editor.
3:*It is possible to add text, search for strings of text, replace speci-
fied characters with others, delete a line or range of lines, etc.
4:*^C
*_
```

Enter l to LIST what you have typed:

```
1: Line editors are simple programs.
2: EDLIN is the built-in MS-DOS line editor.
3: It is possible to add text, search for strings of text, replace speci-
fied characters with others, delete a line or range of lines, etc.
```

Line 4, where you inserted ^C, is gone. The ^C character is a "break" command that gets you out of the text file and back to the ready state without saving anything entered on the current line. Always enter ^C on a new line, or you will lose whatever else was typed on that line!

Also notice that the asterisks are gone. The last asterisk on the screen indicates the current active line available for editing.

The INSERT command lets you add text to an existing file. Type a line number and **i** to insert new lines immediately before a line number other than the current line. If you type just the letter **i** from the ready state, a new line will be inserted immediately before the current line. This new line becomes the new current line, and you may enter text on it. Press ENTER at the end of the line, and EDLIN inserts another new line, renumbering all the following lines for you.

Character-Editing Commands

Now, let's edit the text. Enter **1** to edit line 1. EDLIN displays the following:

```
1:*Line editors are simple programs.
1:*_
```

The empty line 1 will hold the edited line. The line above it is called the *template*. If you wanted to edit the current line but couldn't recall the line number, you could simply press the ENTER key to jump from the ready state into edit mode at the current line. (Typing the plus, minus, or period character before pressing ENTER will accomplish the same as ENTER alone, but why bother?) You can jump in at the tail end of the file by typing the pound sign (#) before pressing ENTER.

READ.ME

UNDOCUMENTED FEATURE

Type **#i** to insert new lines at the end of the text held in memory. Others may tell you **#i** adds new lines to the end of the entire file, not just the part in memory. Don't believe it!

READ.ME

UNDOCUMENTED FEATURE

If you type a line number followed by a semicolon and press ENTER, EDLIN will let you edit two consecutive lines without exiting to the ready state. Press ENTER when finished with one line, and you will jump to the next in edit mode.

Press F1 four times, and you'll see the following:

```
1:*Line editors are simple programs.
1:*Line_
```

F1 copies one character at a time from the template to the edited line. Now, press F2 and S to copy everything from the cursor's current position in the template up to the first *s*.

```
1:* Line editors are simple programs.
1:* Line editor_
```

F3 will copy everything from the cursor's current position in the template to the end of the template line. Press F3 and then ENTER. You should now see the following:

```
1:*Line editors are simple programs.
1:*Line editors are simple programs.
*_
```

We are back to the "ready" state. Let's change our opinion as well as our text. Enter 1 to edit this line again. Press F2 and S, as you did above. Now press F2 and S again to get

```
1:*Line editors are simple programs.
1:*Line editors are _
```

Now, press the INS key, and type the word **not** followed by a space. Then press F3.

```
1:*Line editors are simple programs.
1:*Line editors are not simple programs._
```

The INS key "froze" the invisible cursor in the template while the editing cursor moved along. Had you not pressed INS, here's what you would have seen when you copied the rest of the template:

```
1:*Line editors are simple programs.
1:*Line editors are notple programs._
```

When you start EDLIN, the insert function is off. Anything typed on the editing line replaces whatever is in the corresponding position in the template. Pressing the INS key switches you back and forth between replace and insert modes.

Unfortunately, EDLIN doesn't tell you which mode is currently active. You must remember how many times you pressed INS. Perhaps we were right the first time; EDLIN is really too simple! Let's reverse our opinion again. Line 1 currently reads:

```
1:*Line editors are not simple programs._
```

Note that we are still in edit mode and the cursor is at the end of the line.

Press F5. The editing line will clear and become the new template. The "@" character appears at the end of the line to indicate this change, and the cursor moves down to a new line:

```
1:*Line editors are not simple programs.@
    _
```

Press F2 and N twice to copy the template up to the beginning of "not". Now, press the DEL key four times to skip the word *not* and the space that follows it. (Any "normal" word processor would delete the four characters and drag the remainder left to the cursor. EDLIN "skips" characters in the template when DEL is pressed.) Finally, press F3 to copy the rest of the template. We've changed our minds about EDLIN:

```
1:*Line editors are simple programs._
```

You didn't have to press DEL four times; the F4 key could have skipped the word *not* for you. F4 is the reverse of F2. It skips everything in the template up to the specified character. Press F5 to create yet another new template:

```
1:*Line editors are simple programs.@
    _
```

Press F2 and S twice to copy the template up to the beginning of "simple". Now, press F4 and P twice and then F3 once. Here's the result:

```
1:*Line editors are simple programs.@
    Line editors are programs._
```

The last template-editing function is ESC, an "undo" command. Press ESC-ENTER or CTRL-C, and the last change you made will be canceled:

```
1:*Line editors are simple programs.@
    Line editors are programs.\
    _
```

The backslash at the end of our "undone" line indicates that the line has been canceled. The cursor is now at the start of the editing line. Press F3, and the original template appears:

```
1:*Line editors are simple programs.@
    Line editors are programs.\
    Line editors are simple programs._
```

Now you know how to enter text, insert more text in the middle of a line, and delete portions of a line using EDLIN. The following is a summary of the character-editing keys and their functions, in pairs of action and opposite action:

F1	Copy the next character from the template
DEL	Do not copy (skip) the next character in the template
F2	Copy from the cursor position to the first occurrence of a character in the template

F4	Skip all characters in the template from the cursor position to the first occurrence of a character
F3	Copy the remainder of the current line from the template
INS	"Freeze" the cursor in the template, allowing new text to be inserted in the middle of the edited line (normally, the template cursor moves with the editing cursor, replacing old text with new)
F5	Make the edited line the new template
ESC	Undo the edited line, leaving the template as is

These commands operate within a single line of text. You must get from EDLIN's ready state into edit mode to use them. The next group of commands operate only from EDLIN's ready state. They allow you to operate on groups of lines or their contents. The commands are summarized below, grouped as logical pairs of complementary functions.

Line-Editing and File Commands

EDLIN can be rather picky about commas, even when the items the commas separate are optional. For example, 1,3D will delete lines 1 through 3. To delete all lines from the current line up to line n (assuming the current line is less than n) you would type a comma followed by nD (for example, ,3D).

READ.ME

UNDOCUMENTED FEATURE

You can "stack" more than one command in a line at the ready state, as long as each command is separated from the next by a semicolon. For example, 6W;6A will write six lines to disk and append six new lines to memory in one operation. 12,15D;13i will delete lines 12 through 15 and position you to insert new text at line 12 ("i" inserts text before the specified line, remember?).

APPEND

Syntax *n*W

Function Reads *n* lines from file into memory cleared by WRITE. Always use WRITE before using APPEND.

APPEND reads in lines from disk until it reaches the end of the file, *n* lines, or three-fourths of available memory (59,266 in practice), whichever comes first. You cannot append lines in the middle of the text held in memory, although WRITE will clear lines in the middle, as described above. Use the TRANSFER command to insert text from a disk file to a point in the file currently in memory.

COPY

Syntax *L1,L2,L3,[n]*C

Function Copies lines *L1* through *L2* and inserts the copy at a point beginning at line *L3*. If the number *n* is specified, the copy is replicated *n* times, beginning at line *L3*.

COPY leaves the originals in place. Use MOVE to delete the original lines after copying them to a new position in the file. This feature comes in handy when creating multiple IF ERRORLEVEL statements in a batch file.

DELETE

Syntax *L1, L2*D

Function Deletes lines *L1* through *L2*, inclusive. *L1*D deletes just one line, *L1* (see notes on commas at the beginning of this section).

EDIT

Syntax *L#*

Function Just enter 1 to edit line 1, 2 for line 2, and so on. Remember the undocumented semicolon feature, which lets you edit two consecutive lines at once (for example, 1;).

END

Syntax   E

Function   Ends editing, saves file, exits EDLIN.

END simply writes a new file and exits if you started with a new filename, for example, TEXT.FIL. If TEXT.FIL already existed, EDLIN would first copy the old TEXT.FIL to TEXT.BAK and then overwrite TEXT.FIL. This is a safety precaution. You always have the last revision of your file as backup.

INSERT

Syntax   *L1*I

Function   Inserts a blank line before line *L1* (see notes on inserting text earlier in this chapter).

LIST

Syntax   *L1,L2,*L

Function   Lists a range of lines from *L1* to *L2*, inclusive.

You should use LIST before every manipulation of lines. EDLIN renumbers lines moved, deleted, written, cleared, and so on. It can be difficult to keep track of where you are in a file and which line is now line 1200.

If you type **L** by itself, EDLIN will display 23 lines, with 11 before and after the current line. The current line should therefore appear somewhere in the middle of your screen—but don't count on it: A "line" can take up one to five screen lines, since an EDLIN line will hold 254 characters. Try to avoid entering lines wider than your screen.

Enter a line number followed by **L** to display that line number and the 22 lines following it. Again, extra-long lines may cause the starting line to scroll off the top of the screen.

Try typing a comma followed by a valid line number and then pressing ENTER. EDLIN will try to display the 11 lines preceding the "current" line and all the lines following the current line up to the line number specified.

MOVE

Syntax   *L1,L2,L3*M

Function   Moves lines *L1* through *L2* to a point beginning at line *L3*. Also renumbers all lines after deleting lines *L1* through *L2* at their original position.

The commas are mandatory, although *L1* and *L2* are optional. Thus, to move the current line to the top of the file, you would enter „1M. The pound sign can be used to move the block to the end of the text in memory: „#M.

To move everything from the current line through line 5 to the top of the file, use ,5,1M. The starting line of the range to be moved must be lower than the ending line of the range; if the current line in the example above were greater than 5, EDLIN would respond with "Entry error". Obviously you can't move a range of lines to a point within the range. For example, 1,12,7M just won't work.

PAGE

Syntax   *L1,L2*P

Function   Displays a page of length *L2* lines, beginning at line *L1*. *L2* equals 23 lines if not otherwise specified.

PAGE also changes the current line to *L1+L2*. (LIST doesn't change the current line.) *L2* (page length) can be #, in which case the scrolling won't stop until it reaches the end of the file. P by itself displays the 23 lines following the current line, but not the current line itself.

QUIT

Syntax   Q

Function   Ends editing and exits EDLIN, but does not save the file or create a new BAK file.

REPLACE

Syntax   *L1,L2*[?]R*findtext*^Z*replacement*

Function Looks for the string *findtext* beginning at line *L1* and stopping at line *L2*. If *findtext* is found, replaces it with the *replacement* text. *L1, L2* and the ? work the same as with SEARCH.

^Z marks the end of *findtext* and the beginning of *replacement*. Do not put spaces before or after ^Z unless *findtext* includes a trailing space or you want *replacement* to begin with a space.

REPLACE's "find" portion works just like SEARCH, with all the options and cautions discussed above except the stacking feature. REPLACE uses ^Z to separate the text to find from the replacement text.

SEARCH

Syntax *L1,L2[?]Stext*

READ.ME

UNDOCUMENTED FEATURE

You can stack commands by placing a ^Z character between them, without spaces (hold down the CTRL key and press z). The ^Z is used instead of the semicolon; otherwise, SEARCH would look for *text* plus a semicolon as its search string. One use of this stacking feature is to display the context in which *text* occurs; use *Stext* ^ZP to show the page on which *text* is found. You could also search for *text* and move its line to another location, and so on.

If *L1* is not specified, SEARCH begins with the line following the current line; it does not search the current line. If *L2* is not specified, SEARCH ends at the end of the file.

Control characters can be found, but they must be preceded by ^V. You can find any bothersome ^Z (end-of-file) markers in a file by entering S^V^Z. You can include nonkeyboard characters (graphics, language codes, the *pi* symbol, and so on) in a search string by holding down the ALT key and entering a character's ASCII code number (0-254) on the numeric keypad (*not* the top-row numbers).

Function   Looks for the string *text* beginning at line *L1* and stopping at line *L2*. Omit *L1* to start at the beginning of the line after the current line. Omit *L2* to search to the end of the file. Insert the ? to pause at each occurrence of the string *text* until you find the right one.

SEARCH is case sensitive; capital letters are not the same as small letters; so you must enter your search string exactly as you hope to find it in the file. Spaces count as characters; so, you can search for "complain" and find just that word, not "uncomplaining" and other variations.

If you use the ? option, EDLIN pauses each time it finds *text*. Press Y or y to stop the search at that point ("Yes, that's the one!"). Any other key will continue the search for the next occurrence of *text*.

TRANSFER

Syntax   *L1*T *file*

Function   Inserts the contents of another file into the current file. A new file is added at line *L1*.

File can include a drive letter and path. Note that you cannot select which lines to merge into the current file or how many lines. If *file* added to the current memory contents would overflow memory, *file* will be loaded up to the memory limit. But EDLIN will not warn you if there is insufficient memory!

WRITE

Syntax   *n*W

Function   Writes *n* lines from memory to file and clears the lines from memory. Use only to clear memory to make room for more lines using APPEND.

WRITE works in peculiar ways. If the whole file fits in memory, W alone does nothing; *n*W works, writing *n* lines to disk and clearing the memory the lines held. Be careful: *n*W starts writing and clearing memory from the current line, which may leave a gaping hole in the middle of your text file when you end the editing session.

QEdit: A "Kinder, Gentler" Editor

Learning EDLIN is like learning to start a fire using only two wet sticks. I advise you to carry matches or a cigarette lighter.

QEdit is an excellent shareware editor. It has the virtues of an editor described above and the human comforts EDLIN lacks. In fact, I am going to review QEdit using QEdit, something I would never attempt with EDLIN. Excuse me while I change programs . . . .

I started by typing **q edlin.art** to load the chapter. A status line shows the name of the file, the line being edited, and the position of the cursor on the line. The status line also tells you whether insert is on or off, but you don't have to look up to know; the cursor is thick when insert is on and thin when you are in "replace" mode.

QEdit supports full-screen cursor movement. The arrow keys, PGUP and PGDN move the cursor around in a file. The CTRL key used in combination with the cursor-movement keys enhances their movement. For example, CTRL-LEFT ARROW moves left one word, not just one character; CTRL-PGDN jumps to the end of the file, not just the end of the page. The DEL key works as it should. Life's simple pleasures are the best after EDLIN!

QEdit is far from simple. Its documentation takes up 250,000 bytes—five times more than the program itself! A "crib sheet" of commonly used keystrokes pops up at the touch of F1, but a screenful of notes doesn't begin to cover the features of QEdit.

The program can hold multiple documents in memory at once—as many as will fit in your available RAM. WordPerfect, by contrast, is limited to just two documents open at a time. You can move from one file to another in QEdit with a keystroke; view up to eight files at once through windows; adjust the size of windows; and cut, copy, and transfer parts of documents from one window to another.

You can customize default margins, toggles, tab lengths, screen colors, and many other features. QEdit can set the tab options for files grouped by their extensions. The tab options will be set to the configuration file with a matching extension. Then, whenever you load a document with the same extension as a default option file, QEdit configures itself for that document's particular style. You can change the one-page program help screen that you access by pressing F1. This is helpful if you change the command keys or want to adjust the wording of the Help screen.

If you don't want to learn QEdit's command keys, it will learn yours! Keyboard "map" files can be set up to translate any set of keystrokes into

QEdit commands. WordPerfect, for example, uses ALT-F4 to mark the beginning of a block of text; QEdit uses ALT-A. You could set up a keyboard map file so that when you press ALT-F4, QEdit executes ALT-A.

QEdit also supports macros, a powerful time-saving feature. One keystroke can execute a long series of commands or type a paragraph of boilerplate text. A complicated sequence of commands can be "recorded" until you get them all right and then saved to a macro for error-free future use.

All or part of a file can be printed. QEdit lets you set the margins and page length, tabs, and form-feed defaults. To print just part of a file, you mark it with the ALT-A command and select Print Block from the menu.

QEdit is a text editor, not a word processor. Its powerful features are optimized for programmers, who don't need proportional spacing, underlining, and bold highlights. These doodads can be inserted as CTRL-key codes with QEdit's Literal command. You won't see the effects on screen, but they will print.

Box drawing is a simple way to include charts, graphs, or paste-up markers in a text file. QEdit lets you draw single- or double-line boxes using just the cursor keys. You can use single or double lines all around the box or mix single and double lines for tops and sides. An eraser is included to make corrections easy and intuitive.

QEdit's Programmer Aids

Software engineers don't write like the rest of humanity. They must observe rigid syntax rules, match left and right parentheses nested twelve layers deep, and often repeat text with only minor variations. A typo in a C program may immediately crash the computer or, worse, generate a subtle error that can take months to notice and more months to find.

QEdit makes life much easier for programmers. Macros can store whole subroutines and enter them without error wherever needed. Other commands duplicate all or part of a line or block of code just written. Windows, with their cut-and-paste feature, let the programmer snip pieces of code from several programs and blend them in a new concoction.

Scratch buffers are another handy tool for programmers. A scratch buffer is a temporary macro. When you find a needed piece of code already written, QEdit lets you save the block to a scratch buffer and give it a name. You can save and name up to 99 scratch buffers. Now, when you need that code again, just enter the GETSCRBUFF command and the buffer's name. The alternative is to search for the desired code (perhaps several times in several windows), mark the block, copy it, go back to the place it's needed, and insert the copy.

Some programming languages, such as C, require specialized tab, margin, and line-width settings. QEdit can store a variety of default configurations and automatically load the right one with a given program file. QEdit's AutoIndent and SmartTab option settings line up tabs and new lines of code with the beginning of the line above, a handy feature for programmers who write nested loops and indent code for clarity.

The C language is so popular and so structured, QEdit includes a specific mode to handle C-program editing. When switched on, C-mode takes care of moving the cursor to the correct position relative to the brackets used to delineate procedures. Pressing the ENTER key on a line that contains a { character generates a line return followed by a TABRIGHT. When a } is entered, QEdit precedes it with a TABLEFT command. The programmer can concentrate on creation instead of format.

Programs often crash with an "Unmatched parentheses" error message, meaning the programmer lost track of how deeply nested some parentheses were. QEdit helps avoid this problem. It can be configured to start up in "enter-matching" mode, in which entering a left parenthesis automatically enters its mate. It is impossible to type unmatched parentheses! This mode also works on double quotes and square brackets. Of course, you might delete half of a pair somewhere along the way. Then, the ALT-F3 command can be used to locate the mate for each parenthesis, bracket, or double quote, one by one.

Programming is an empirical discipline: Programmers don't really know if their code will run until they try it. A program is usually test-run many times as it is written. QEdit's DOS Shell command lets the programmer compile and test his or her work, note the results, and return to editing without exiting the source file or QEdit.

Program lines can often be longer than a screen is wide. Programmers like to cram instructions into as few lines of code as possible to shorten run times. But a 200-character line is hard to follow on an 80-character screen. "Folding" a line (as EDLIN does) makes it hard to read. QEdit can be set to let long lines continue past the right margin. You can SCROLLRIGHT to jump to the "hidden" screen just as you would PGUP to jump to the preceding page.

QEdit's amenities go on forever. It is as fine an editor as any on the commercial market, and you can try it before you buy it! I suggest you do just that.

VDE: Almost a Word Processor

The Virtual Display Editor (VDE) might have been named the *Versatile Display Editor*. This chameleon can closely imitate any word processor you want. It lacks mail-merge features, but it can jazz up your text with highlights, italics, and even proportional spacing. VDE reads and writes files written in WordStar, WordPerfect, and XyWrite formats, and it can convert one format to another or to plain ASCII text. You can configure it to use these and other fancy features built into your printer.

VDE is versatile enough to work on "nearly compatible" PC/MS-DOS machines—a boon for people who bought certain computer brands during the "standard" wars of the early 1980s. Even today, we occasionally see near-compatibles—usually from European manufacturers—that won't always run software designed for 100-percent IBM-standard machines.

VDE can hold only 80KB of a given document in memory (unlike QEdit, which will hold as much text as your memory allows). To edit a larger file, you must use the "Split" function to divide it into several files. Why this seemingly arbitrary limitation? One of an editor's strengths is the ability to hold multiple files in memory and rapidly switch back and forth between them. QEdit will use up all memory for a large file if it has to, leaving no RAM for other files or for adding text to the only file in memory.

While it retains the editor features programmers cherish, VDE is intended for people familiar with at least one word processing program. VDE can run in menu-driven mode, but it starts up in WordStar command mode. Most CTRL-key commands work exactly as they do in WordStar. VDE adds several dozen ALT and ESC key combinations to activate its unique editor functions.

VDE, like other advanced text editors, can mimic other word processors to almost any degree. It comes with partial key-translation files for Word-Perfect and XyWrite. These files can be edited to "teach" VDE more translations. (I like a program that learns what I know instead of forcing me to learn its way of doing things!) Similar configuration files can be set up for several printers. "Style" files preset margins, page lengths, tabs, spacing, and other factors for a variety of writing tasks.

Configuration files may be assigned to a group of text files. When you load a file with the extension WPF, VDE will also load the WordPerfect key-translation file. You can give all your C-program files the same extension, and VDE will load the appropriate style file for such program listings without being asked.

Macros can be recorded or programmed—and we do mean "programmed." VDE includes commands that force macro execution to branch, loop, or jump to another macro. A macro can include a counter variable. Such "macro processors" are usually sold as separate utilities for more than the whole VDE program costs.

Printer-configuration files are included for IBM/Epson FX, HP DeskJet and LaserJet, and Toshiba P321SL printers. You may also create your own printer-configuration file. A table of character widths gives VDE proportional-spacing capability. VDE can store a set of 32 IBM graphic characters (useful for drawing boxes, charts, and such). All of these files may be modified.

Which Editor Is for You?

VDE is more versatile than QEdit. Versatility implies complexity, which in turn means a steeper learning curve. VDE assumes a higher level of first-time-user skill than QEdit. The former comes with half the documentation of the latter and is more "techie" in tone. If you already know WordStar, you can jump right in to VDE. But its advanced features will take a while to learn.

Availability

QEdit is distributed as shareware. SemWare, the publisher, maintains a public bulletin board system where you can download the latest version (2.1, issued February 1990). Set your modem to 8 data bits, no parity, and 1 stop bit, and dial 404-641-8968. QEdit can also be found on dozens of other boards, although they may carry only earlier versions.

Shareware is not free software. If you decide to keep QEdit after test-driving it, you must register your copy with SemWare. Registration costs only $44 for the latest licensed version and includes documentation on disk. A bound and illustrated manual is available for just $10 extra. Registration also entitles the licensee to discounts on future upgrades. To register or order QEdit, call or write SemWare.

SemWare
4343 Shallowford Road, Suite C-3
Marietta, GA 30062-5003
Voice: 404-641-9002, Monday through Friday, 9:00 A.M. to 5:00 P.M. EST
Fax: 404-640-6213, 24 hours a day, 7 days a week

The current version of VDE may be found on CompuServe in the file VDE154.VIP, in the Dvorak download library in the PC Magnet Editorial forum. It's in the IBMAPP forum, too, and may also be found on the Glendale (California) Littera QBBS (818-956-6164). VDE is also included in the disks included in this book.

VDE may be used by individuals without paying a registration fee, though the author gladly accepts donations. Businesses, government agencies, and other organizations are expected to buy a site license. The cost is just $50 for a license to use up to 20 copies of VDE in a given building. Contact the author of VDE for terms of larger-site licenses.

Eric Meyer
401 12th Avenue SE #139
Norman, OK 73071
CompuServe [74415,1305]

CHAPTER TWENTY-FIVE

Using DEBUG

DEBUG is one of the many free programs that come with most copies of DOS. It is one of the least used DOS programs—and probably also one of the most misunderstood. Most casual DOS users never use DEBUG at all. They often don't realize its power or even know it's there. Being more than just a casual user, of course, you will want to explore this useful and interesting utility.

As the name might imply, DEBUG is intended primarily to exorcise software "bugs" from programs. You can use it to fix programs that don't run properly. That doesn't mean, however, that you need to be a programmer to use it. On the contrary, you can use DEBUG to examine other people's programs and data files and even modify commercial programs. DEBUG is "the great equalizer," for it allows anyone with a moderate amount of understanding—and enough curiosity—to examine, disassemble, or even alter any DOS program.

Note: Although DEBUG will allow you to examine and alter any file, it does not directly support writing EXE or HEX files back to disk. It is possible to make modifications to these files and record them to disk by giving them a different file extension, such as DAT or TMP. Once the modifications have been made and recorded to disk, you can use the DOS RENAME command to change the file extension back to EXE. This prevents accidental changes to executable programs.

You can also use DEBUG to read and write to other devices and input/output (I/O) ports and to jump to the starting locations of programs stored in the PC's read-only memory (ROM) and execute the programs. The following is an example of code that will reboot your system by jumping to the power-on reset entry in the BIOS ROM:

```
CD\DOS
DEBUG
G=FFFF:0
```

In fact, you can create a one line batch file to do this:

```
Echo G=FFF:0 ¦ C:\DOS\DEBUG
```

Try it.

BACKGROUND

Like most things about DOS, DEBUG's roots can be traced to a similar utility, DDT. This utility was created for the DEC PDP-6/PDP-10 and is also an outgrowth of CP/M.

Before DOS, in 1980, there were no IBM PCs, although there were plenty of microcomputers. The operating system CP/M (Control Program for Microcomputers) dominated the world of business computing. CP/M was developed by Digital Research for the Intel 8080 and Zilog Z-80 microprocessors (the forerunners of the 8088, 80286, 80386, or 80486 chip in your PC). CP/M was distributed with a primitive program-debugging tool, Dynamic Debugging Tool (DDT), modeled after the DEC DDT program.

DDT allowed the experienced user or program developer to debug a program that was already compiled and running. It made it possible to implement quick fixes and changes without modifying the program source code and then having to recompile the program. This was especially attractive for end users, who seldom had access to the source code.

When CP/M moved over for DOS, DDT was one of the programs that got an overhaul—nothing major, just a lot of nice, little additions and alterations that made it somewhat more useful and less dangerous.

DEBUG is like a sharp butcher's knife: Left alone or used properly, it is harmless. Like the knife, though, it can be very dangerous in unskilled hands. If you use DEBUG, you must use it wisely. Don't attempt to experiment with it or try to fix something before you've mastered it. This is a prime example of the adage "a little knowledge is a dangerous thing." Many people know enough about DEBUG to be dangerous. In this section, you will learn how to use DEBUG confidently.

Note: Knowing DDT can actually get you into trouble, because some of the commands in DOS's DEBUG are different. For instance, S in DDT is used to substitute memory locations (enter data into memory). In DEBUG, S is the SEARCH command. There are quite a number of other differences, too. DEBUG is given away with DOS, and developers at Microsoft don't have a lot of incentive to improve on it much—after all, Microsoft does a brisk business selling stand-alone debugging tools. Therefore, DEBUG is still somewhat "raw." It has a lot of power and can be used for many things, but it requires careful attention.

USES FOR DEBUG

The DEBUG program is used for three major functions:

- To display and alter the memory inside your computer

- To display and alter the contents of a file on your hard disk or floppy disk

- To examine and modify the internal registers of your PC's CPU chip.

Between those three functions, there's almost nothing you can't do. Software can be altered, data files fixed up, strange behavior diagnosed, and secrets explored. By the same token, you can also corrupt data, destroy programs, and even damage your computer. Obviously, you won't do these things with malicious intent, but it is surprisingly easy to accidentally type the wrong command or leave out a parameter, causing irreversible damage. Therefore, throughout this section, we stress caution and patience.

Because DEBUG is used to modify programs, disk files, and CPU registers, some understanding of programming theory and computer architecture is assumed. However, you don't need to be an expert—just aware enough so that these concepts aren't completely foreign to you. If you haven't understood a thing in this section so far, perhaps you'd better skip over it until later; the remainder of this chapter becomes more technical, describing DEBUG's commands, and includes examples. Otherwise, here we go.

DEBUG BASICS

DEBUG has a "noninterface"—no windows or pull-down menus here. It carries only the most primitive of command line interfaces. It requires that you be familiar with the Intel 80X86 architecture to some degree and that you understand hexadecimal (base-sixteen) arithmetic. We'll cover some of the basics here.

Hexadecimal Numbers

People all over the world count in base ten. (Presumably, this is because we all have ten fingers.) You can see this by the way we write numbers. The numerals 0 to 9—digits—take up one place each when written down. (*Digit* is Latin for "finger.") When you write the number ten, you take up an additional space for the first multiple of ten; that is, 10 means "one set of ten and zero sets of ones." The next position over is for hundreds, of course. One hundred equals ten times ten, just as ten equals ten times one. Each position is worth ten times the position to its right.

If we were to count in, say, base eight (octal arithmetic), we would have no digits for eight or nine—only zero through seven. When we got to seven and wanted to add one, we'd write it like this: 10.

We've run out of unique digits, and it's time to "roll over" the units digit and add a new digit to the left. The figure 10 would mean "one set of eights and zero sets of ones." The next digit position over would be worth eight times eight (sixty-four to you and me).

That takes care of a number system with fewer than 10 digits. What about counting with more than 10 digits? For reasons too obscure to explain here, programmers almost universally prefer to count in hexadecimal (base sixteen). Therefore, DEBUG accepts only hexadecimal numbers as input and prints its answers in hexadecimal. If you're not accustomed to reading and writing hexadecimal numbers, you're going to have to form the habit if you want to get into low-level programming like Assembly Language and C.

In hexadecimal arithmetic (or just "hex"), there are sixteen different digits, from zero to fifteen. Rather than invent six new symbols for the digits ten through fifteen, everybody uses symbols already at hand: letters. For example, the digit for ten is A, eleven is B, twelve is C, and so on. Here's the complete hex symbol set:

HEX Symbol Set

0	zero
1	one
2	two
3	three
4	four
5	five
6	six
7	seven
8	eight
9	nine
A	ten
B	eleven
C	twelve
D	thirteen
E	fourteen
F	fifteen

Using this type of number set, you write the numbers zero to nine just as you do now. But when you add one to nine, you get A, not 10. Why? Because you haven't run out of digits yet: After 9 comes A. Fifteen plus one is written as 10.

That's "one set of sixteen and zero sets of one." The figure 100 represents "one set of sixteen times sixteen plus zero sets of sixteen plus zero sets of one," for a total of 256. What does 123 represent?

You can find out by running the following program, a little BASIC program (GW-BASIC, QuickBASIC, or QBI) that will convert hex to decimal and vice versa, depending on the input. It will handle quantities of up to about 24 bits. The H at the end of a hex number is required only if a number could be interpreted as either hex or decimal.

```
100  PRINT "Hex/Decimal Converter" : PRINT
110  INPUT "Enter a number, end with 'H' if hex:"; A$
120  L = LEN(A$) : IF L = 0 THEN SYSTEM
```

```
130  HF=0 : X=0 : Y=0
140  FOR I=1 TO LEN(A$)
150     J=ASC( MID$(A$,I,1))
160     IF (J >= 97) AND (J <= 102) THEN J=J-32
170     IF J >= 48 AND J <= 57 THEN X=X*16+(J-48) : Y=Y*10+(J-48) : GOTO 210
180     IF J = 72 THEN HF=1 : GOTO 220
190     IF (J >= 65) AND (J <= 70) THEN X=X*16+(J-55) : HF=1 : GOTO 210
200     PRINT CHR$(7);"Error!" : GOTO 110
210 NEXT I
220 IF HF <> 0 THEN 250
230 PRINT HEX$(Y/4096);
240 PRINT RIGHT$(HEX$(4096+(Y-INT(Y/4096)*4096)),3);" (hex)" : GOTO 110
250 PRINT USING "#,###,###,### (decimal)" ;X : GOTO 110
```

Since DEBUG is limited to 4 hex bit numbers, this program's 24-bit limit will be more than you need. If you entered the program correctly (or resorted to an appendix in the back of this book, or happened to have a pocket calculator that supports hex), you should have 291 as your answer.

If you plan to be doing a lot of this in the future, you may want to invest in a new calculator that can perform hexadecimal arithmetic. Very good ones are available from Hewlett Packard, Texas Instruments, Sharp, Casio, and other companies. Even a $15, solar-powered, Radio Shack calculator is suitable for working with hex. Some keyboards even have a built-in calculator with decimal and hex functions. While hex support isn't a given, you'll find that almost all calculators support "normal" decimal calculations.

Addresses

After having mastered hex notation, the next two concepts you need to understand are those of addresses and data. These concepts baffle some newcomers, but they are really quite simple.

All computers manage data. The data in a digital computer is stored in binary form (base two) and can represent anything from financial reports to graphic images on your screen or the notes of a song. This data is stored in your computer's random-access memory (RAM). The CPU chip inside your PC reads, writes, and manipulates the data stored in memory to perform the work you want done.

The memory inside your computer is compartmented, like a row of post office boxes. Each compartment is exactly the same size, just big enough to hold one byte of information. All PCs have enough memory to hold several thousand (usually several hundred thousand) bytes of data.

Like the long row of boxes at the post office, each memory location in your PC has an address that uniquely identifies it. Addresses start at 0 and count up; the more memory your PC has in it, the higher the addresses will go. The CPU chip inside your PC uses the address to specify what byte of data it wants to read or write to at any given moment. You will, too, when you start to use DEBUG to examine and modify your computer's memory.

So, remember: Data is what your computer stores and manipulates, and an address is where a particular item of data is stored in memory.

The CPU chip inside your PC can "reach" 1,048,576 different addresses. (If you have an 80386 or 80486, it can go to 4,096 times that many, but not in native DOS.) This is generally called one *megabyte*. The prefix *mega* usually means "one million" or just plain "large," but in computer parlance it means exactly 1,048,576. Why not 1,000,000 even? Because 1,048,576 is an even power of two, and that number is significant to computer engineers.

Similarly, 1024 bytes is called one *kilobyte*. As you might have guessed, 1024 is also a special power of two. You will hear the term *kilobyte* used quite often when describing the amount of memory in one's computer. Even more common, though, is the abbreviation KB for kilobyte. A computer with 512KB of memory has exactly 524,288 bytes of memory (512 times 1024), while a 640KB machine has 655,360 bytes. Table 25-1 will give you an idea of the maximum memory your system can address.

Segmented Addresses

To make things more interesting, the Intel CPU in your PC uses a particularly perverse scheme to specify memory addresses. As we just saw, your

---

TABLE 25-1

Maximum Addressable Memory

Address	System Processor	Maximum Address	Bits
PCs & XTs	8088/8086	1,048,576	20
ATs	80286	16,777,216	24
386/486	80386/80486	4,294,967,296	324

PC can address 1,048,576 different memory locations (assuming your PC *has* that much memory). But rather than simply start at 0 and count up to that number, the CPU uses a two-step process known as *segmentation.* Each address is made up of a *segment address* and an *offset address.* The two of them are added together, producing an *effective address.* You'll have to master this scheme before you can really use DEBUG.

Here's how it works. The segment address is a kind of "coarse tuning." The offset address is the "fine tuning." Between the two of them, you can zero in on any particular address you want. The segment address specifies memory in 16-byte chunks called *paragraphs.* Using only the segment address, you can get to within 16 bytes of the particular address you want. The offset address, on the other hand, specifies memory in 1-byte increments.

Both the segment address and the offset address can count up only to 65,535, or FFFF in hex. But since the segment address is really counting 16-byte paragraphs, that allows you to create addresses up to 1,048,560 (65,535 times 16). After adding the value of the offset address, you can create any valid address. In fact, it is easy to create an address larger than the maximum. In that case, the CPU just starts over at zero (for example, 1,048,600 becomes 25).

A simple procedure for calculating addresses is shown here:

```
DS        1  2  3  4  0
SI    +      1  2  3  4
         ─────────────────
          1  3  5  7  4
```

As you can see, the segment address is shifted left, and a 0 is appended to it. In hexadecimal, this is the same as multiplying by 16.

For simplicity, most people try to use segment addresses like 8000 or C000, because they make the math easier. If the last three digits of the segment address are 0, adding the segment and offset in your head becomes trivial.

Segment Registers

Your CPU has four registers that can hold segment addresses for you. This relieves you from having to type in and remember different values. There are some rules about what you can and cannot use the segment registers for. The list below summarizes the recommended usage of the four segment registers:

CS	Code segment
SS	Stack segment
DS	Data segment
ES	Data segment (Intel calls this the extra statement)

For example, when you are debugging a program, the CS register should hold the segment address you are using to address the code or program instructions. The SS register should be used for addressing the program's stack space. DS and ES can be used for addressing miscellaneous data items.

Later in this chapter, you will see how to use the segment registers as a shorthand way of specifying segment addresses.

USING DEBUG

DEBUG has a terse, unfriendly user interface. Its commands are sometimes obscure, and the syntax can be difficult. A carelessly typed command can destroy valuable data. Altogether, this is not a place where your fingers will fly. Be patient and cautious.

Nearly all of the DEBUG commands take (or require) additional parameters. If parameters are missing, DEBUG will not prompt you for them. It will simply print a brief error message, and you can try again. In some cases, missing parameters will result in a command that is syntactically correct but that does not do what you want. Watch out for these.

Commands and parameters can be typed in either uppercase or lowercase. For clarity, the commands here are in uppercase, while parameters are in lowercase. DEBUG is also fairly forgiving of spacing. Added or missing spaces are usually ignored. Leaving out all the spaces produces terrifically obscure command lines—great for confounding innocent bystanders. All of the examples in this section follow a reasonable and readable pattern.

Table 25-2 is a summary of DEBUG commands and syntax. Parameters in brackets are optional; for example, the A (ASSEMBLE) command will work either with or without an *address* parameter. If the parameters are not in brackets, they are required.

TABLE 25-2

TABLE 25-2

DEBUG Command Summary

A [*address*]	ASSEMBLE a program
C *range address*	COMPARE memory
D [*range*]	DISPLAY memory
E *address* [*list*]	EDIT memory
F *range list*	FILL memory
G [=*address*] [*address...*]	GO
H *value*	HEXADECIMAL calculator
I *port*	INPUT from I/O port
L [*address* [*drive sector count*]]	LOAD a file from disk
M *range address*	MOVE memory
N *filename* [*filename*]	NAME a file
O *port value*	OUTPUT to I/O port
Q	QUIT
R [*register*]	REGISTER display/modify
S *range list*	SEARCH memory
T [=*address*] [*count*]	TRACE a program
U [*range*]	UNASSEMBLE a program
W [*address* [*drive sector count*]]	WRITE to a file

You *can* specify the breakpoint addresses even if the start address isn't specified.   '

Although these commands are usually all the commands DEBUG supports, your version may have additional commands not covered here. For instance, some versions of DEBUG have some "X" commands that support EMS and even some two-letter commands. If you're using DOS 4.0 or higher, take a few minutes to review your DOS manual and make note of any "extended" commands that may be supported.

Here is a description of the special parameters for the commands listed in the table:

Address This means a memory address. You can type this as a four-character segment address and a four-character offset address or as a two-character segment register and an offset address. Either way, you must separate the two with a colon—for example:

1000:FFFF

or

CS:FFFF

In most cases, you can get away without a segment address at all. In those cases, DEBUG will assume you mean the value in either register DS or register CS. It depends on the command. Your best bet is to play it safe and always specify a segment register or value.

Range   This means a range of memory addresses. You can specify either a beginning address and an end address or a beginning address and a length. Either way, you must put a space between them. The two-address method should be entered like this:

6000:1200 1280

If you want to specify a length instead, use the following form:

6000:1200 L 80

If you use the L form, you can omit the space after the L:

6000:1200 L80

List   This is a series of 1-byte values, with spaces between them. For example:

12 F0 94 CD 00 00 34

Value   This is a hexadecimal number. All values from 00 through FF are legal here.

Port   This is the address of an I/O port in your PC. The port address is specified in hex (of course). Keep in mind that this is not a memory address; it is an I/O address. So, there should be no segment address—just one to four hexadecimal digits.

Drive   This is a disk drive identifier, from 0 on up. A value of 0 means drive A, 1 is drive B, 2 is drive C, and so on.

Sector   This is a logical disk sector number. It's also DOS's relative sector. Therefore, 0 is the boot, 1 is the first sector of the file allocation table, and so on. Pay careful attention to this: it's not the DOS sector number used in most disk-maintenance utilities. DEBUG writes directly to the disk, bypassing DOS.

Count   This simply specifies the number of disk sectors you want to read or write to.

Filename   This is the name of a DOS file on disk, including its three-letter extension.

Register   This represents a one- or two-character register name. For a list of valid register names, refer to the REGISTER command (described later in this chapter) or an 80X86 programming manual.

Starting DEBUG

Starting DEBUG is really quite simple. Just type

```
DEBUG
```

and press the RETURN key. You can also tell DEBUG that you want to debug a particular file. In that case, type

```
DEBUG filename
```

and DEBUG will load the file for you. It can be either a program file or a data file. Either way, you must specify the entire filename—for example,

MYFILE.COM or DATAFILE.DBF. It is perfectly okay to include a DOS path along with the filename. For example, specifying D:\USR\WORK\ MYFILE.COM is allowed.

If you are debugging a program file and the program requires command line arguments to work, you can specify those at the same time. The syntax is

```
DEBUG filename arglist
```

where *arglist* is a list of arguments. Specify them just the way you would if you were running the program normally. Remember, these are arguments to the program being debugged, not to DEBUG itself. DEBUG will look at only the first argument, the name of the file to be debugged. Any arguments following the filename will be passed to the program file being debugged as though you had typed them at the DOS prompt.

Whether or not you start DEBUG with parameters that precede the filename, you will be greeted with the following DEBUG prompt:

```
-
```

This is your cue. You can now enter any of the 18 valid DEBUG commands. If this prompt is not displayed, DEBUG will ignore you.

Initial Setup

If you have DEBUG load a file for you, it will do a small amount of setup and housekeeping for you. Exactly what steps DEBUG performs depends on the type of file you have it load.

A set of virtual CPU registers is maintained by DEBUG when a file is loaded. When files are first loaded, DEBUG sets these registers to default values; however, you can use DEBUG's commands to examine and modify them. Table 25-3 is a list of the default values of the CPU registers for COM and EXE programs.

The AX register will contain information about the second and third command line parameters used when DEBUG was invoked on the command line. Table 25-4 lists codes that may appear in the AX register and gives explanations of these codes.

Besides the CPU registers and AX registers, DEBUG also maintains a set of virtual flags that can have the value of "set" or "cleared." Table 25-5 lists flag names along with their cleared and set values.

TABLE 25-3

Default Values for Registers

Register	COM Program	EXE Program
AX	Drive error status	Drive error status
BP	Zero	Zero
BX	Top half program size	Top half program size
CS	PSP	Program's base code segment
CX	Bottom half program size	Bottom half program size
DI	Zero	Zero
DS	PSP	PSP
DX	Zero	Zero
ES	PSP	PSP
IP	100H	Entry-point offset of the program's code segment
SI	Null	Zero
SP	FFFFEH or top half of available segment memory less 2	Stack-segment size
SS	PSP	Program's base stack segment

TABLE 25-4

Values for AX Registers

Code	Explanation
0000H	The drives specified in the second and third command line parameters are valid, or only a single filename was specified on the command line.
00FFH	The drive specified in the second command line parameter is invalid.
FF00H	The drive specified in the third command line parameter is invalid.
FFFFH	Both drives specified in the second and third command line parameters are valid.

TABLE 25-5

Virtual Flags

Flag Name	Cleared Value	Set Value
Carry	CY [carry]	NC [no carry]
Direction	DN [down]	UP [up]
Interrupt	EI [enabled]	DI [disabled]
Sign	NG [minus]	PL [plus]
Overflow	OV [overflow true]	NV [overflow false]
Parity	PE [even]	PO [odd]
Zero	ZG [zero]	NZ [not zero]

Whenever DEBUG loads a file, it records the exact length of the file in two CPU registers. Register CX holds the least significant 16 bits of the file's length, while register BX holds the most significant 16 bits. Taken together, they give you a 32-bit file-size tally. If your file is smaller than 64KB, BX will be zero. This little feature will become important when you discover the W command.

DEBUG will load a file into whatever memory is available at the time. It is impossible to predict exactly where your file will go, but this is not normally an issue. With one exception, DEBUG will always load your file beginning at offset address 0100 (256 decimal) into whatever segment it chooses. This is important to remember when you begin displaying or editing data: Your data begins at offset 0100—not at offset 0.

The exception is a file with an EXE extension. Program files with the EXE extension are somewhat more complex than other executable files. DOS performs some relatively fancy memory-allocation games whenever it loads one. One of the side effects is that EXE files don't load into DEBUG quite the same way other files do.

DEBUG is particular about writing to COM and EXE files. You can fool DEBUG and DOS's file handler by renaming your EXE file to anything but a COM file before you load it with DEBUG. Using a file extension such as DAT or TMP will prevent the DOS file handler from knowing you're loading an executable file. Don't change the extension to COM, because DEBUG checks that EXE and COM files are constructed the way they are supposed to before writing to them. DEBUG doesn't have any restrictions on other file extensions. When you complete your debugging session, you can change the name back after you exit DEBUG.

Special Keys

If you want to interrupt DEBUG while it is doing something, you can press CTRL-C. A CTRL-C press will abort most operations. CTRL-SCROLL LOCK will also work.

If DEBUG is displaying a lot of information and it starts to scroll off the top of your screen, you can temporarily stop the display by pressing CTRL-S. Pressing any other key will start the display scrolling again. CTRL-NUMLOCK or PAUSE will also work.

If you want to keep a hard copy of your DEBUG session, you can press CTRL-P at any time. From that point on, everything displayed by DEBUG will be copied to your printer. Pressing CTRL-P will not print anything that's already on the screen; only new output will be copied there. Pressing CTRL-P again will turn off the printer output.

Pressing PRTSC will copy whatever is on your screen to your printer. This is different from CTRL-P in two ways. First, "old" output (text already displayed on your screen) will be printed. Second, it turns itself off automatically after the screen has been printed. Pressing PRTSC is like taking a snapshot of your current display screen. PRTSC may vary from one system to another: Other key combinations may be SHIFT-PRTSC, PRTSC twice in rapid succession, and CTRL-PRTSC.

Editing a Command

DEBUG also responds to the same editing keys that are available at the DOS prompt. In other words, you can use BACKSPACE, INS, and DEL to edit your command line before your press RETURN. After pressing RETURN, of course, it's too late to make changes.

The F1 key repeats your last command to DEBUG, one character at a time. Every time you press F1, another character is repeated. This is handy for retyping your last line when you've accidentally struck the wrong key. Pressing F1 allows you to reuse as much or as little of your last command as you like.

The F3 key repeats your entire last line. This works the same as holding down F1. This is handy if your mistake is at the end of the line.

Pressing ESC and then ENTER tosses out your entire command line and lets you start over.

Pressing INS allows you to insert new characters in the middle of a command line. For example, after pressing F1 a few times, you can press INS, add a word or two, and then press F1 some more to finish off the command.

Pressing DEL has the opposite effect of INS. This allows you to remove characters from the command line while keeping the rest of the line intact.

You will probably use F1, F3, INS, and DEL most of the time. Of course, you're not compelled to use any of them if you don't want to. There are some other command-editing keys that DEBUG will accept. Table 25-6 is a complete rundown of DEBUG's command-editing keys.

The F2 and F4 keys are odd. After pressing F2, you must press another key. This keystroke will not be echoed. Instead, your last command line, up to but not including the character you just pressed, will be repeated. For example, if your last command was

```
D cs:0100 L 200
```

you could press F2 and the L key, and DEBUG would display

```
D cs:0100
```

DEBUG has repeated everything up to but not including the L in your last command. The F4 key operates in a similar manner but in reverse: It will begin repeating from the character you specify.

TABLE 25-6

DEBUG Function Keys

F1	Repeat the last command, one character at a time (the RIGHT ARROW key does the same thing)
F2	Repeat the last command up to the next keystroke
F3	Repeat the entire last command
F4	Repeat the last command starting from the next keystroke
F5	Copy the current command line into the recall buffer

The F5 key allows you to create a "dummy" last command. You can type anything you like and press F5, and the line will be copied into DEBUG's command-recall buffer, where it will be available for future editing.

Error Messages

If you still type a command incorrectly, DEBUG prints a brief error message. In fact, that's all it prints: "Error". The DEBUG error message looks like this:

```
D cs:0100 L 23 GO
                ^ Error
```

Whenever possible, DEBUG will point to the offending part of the command line. In this case, DEBUG is complaining that G is not a hexadecimal character. It has suggested this by placing the arrow under the G. In other cases, it will simply point to the first character on the line; for example:

```
D cs:0100 ss:0FFF
^ Error
```

Here, the D command itself is okay, but the parameters passed to it (specifically, the ss:0FFF at the end) were invalid. This gives you an opportunity to use the editing keys described above.

There are four other things that DEBUG will complain about. Three of them are related to the REGISTER command, and the fourth might occur after a GO command. They are identified by the following error codes:

BF This stands for "Bad Flag." DEBUG doesn't understand which CPU flag you're trying to change. It is probably a typing error.

BR When the "Bad Register" error occurs, DEBUG doesn't understand which CPU register you want to modify. Check your typing.

DF Like the BF error, the "Duplicate Flag" error occurs when you're modifying the CPU flag register. Specifically, DEBUG is complaining that you've changed one flag bit twice.

BP   This is the "Breakpoint" error code. DEBUG can handle only up to 10 breakpoints at a time. This error will be displayed if you specify 11 or more breakpoints with a GO command.

DEBUG COMMANDS

In this section, we'll look at each of the DEBUG commands in a logical sequence. You'll be given examples and a thorough explanation of what each command does and what it can be used for. By the time you reach the end, you will have assembled your own program and modified somebody else's. No experience necessary!

Q (QUIT)   This is certainly a valuable command. On the theory that you should know how to get out of something before getting into it, this command is presented first. It is also the only command that never needs parameters; so, you can never do it wrong. While you'll have no trouble entering this command correctly, you may enter it at the wrong time — such as after spending an hour typing a program script and quitting before writing it to disk.

You can type the QUIT command anytime the DEBUG prompt is displayed. If you don't see the prompt, try pressing CTRL-C.

H (HEXADECIMAL Calculator)   This command isn't nearly so interesting as you might think. For one thing, it's only a two-function calculator: It adds and subtracts and displays the results — period. Second, you can use it only while you're using DEBUG; so, it's not very convenient. The one thing it does have going for it is its price.

This calculator is so simple, you don't even have to tell it what to do. Just give it two numbers, and it performs all the functions it knows on them. For example,

```
H D077 0143
```

produces the following response:

```
D1BA CF34
```

The first result is the sum of your two numbers. The second is the second number subtracted from the first. That's it.

The calculation is limited to a 16-bit, unsigned calculation. If either of the two values is greater than four hex digits, DEBUG will return its familiar error indicator, the ^ symbol.

Like an odometer that passes 999,999 miles, DEBUG will truncate results greater than 4 hex digits, or 16 bits; for instance, FFFF+2=1, not 10001. (In this example, the leftmost hex digit is truncated.)

D (DISPLAY)   The DISPLAY command is used to display the contents of memory. You can display as many or as few bytes as you wish, from any valid address in your PC. Since the DISPLAY command cannot alter anything, it is pretty harmless.

DISPLAY shows you the data in two different ways: first, bytes are displayed in hexadecimal notation; then, the same data are displayed in ASCII form. While this is usually meaningless for program files, the ASCII display is wonderful for browsing through text or data files.

Not all 256 binary data values have ASCII representations. For those data items that are out of range, DEBUG displays a period for an ASCII value.

When you enter the DISPLAY command with only one parameter, DEBUG displays 256 bytes of data. Entering **D** again without any parameters will pick up where you left off.

Here's a DEBUG display of a COMMAND.COM file:

```
C:\> DEBUG COMMAND.COM

-D
27A5:0100  E9 2D 0D BA DA 0A 3D 05-00 74 1B BA BF 0A 3D 02   .-....=..t....=.
27A5:0110  00 74 13 BA 85 0A 3D 08-00 74 0B BA 71 0A 3D 0B   .t....=..t..q.=.
27A5:0120  00 74 03 BA 62 0A 0E 1F-E8 6A 06 EB 0C CD 21 72   .t..b....j....!r
27A5:0130  D2 B4 4D CD 21 2E A3 EA-0B E9 76 01 2E F6 06 59   ..M.!.....v....Y
27A5:0140  0C 01 74 0C 2E F6 06 59-0C 02 74 03 E9 08 13 CF   ..t....Y..t.....
27A5:0150  2E F6 06 59 0C 04 74 11-80 FC 01 72 F2 80 FC 0C   ...Y..t....r....
27A5:0160  77 ED 83 C4 06 F9 CA 02-00 2E 80 0E 59 0C 04 FB   w...........Y...
27A5:0170  0E 1F A1 F3 0B 0B C0 75-06 50 B4 0D CD 21 58 F7   .......u.P...!X.
-q

C:\>
```

It is also possible to display only a single byte, as in the following:

```
C:\>DEBUG COMMAND.COM
-D ds:0123 L 1
27A5:0120              BA

-Q

C\>
```

Look at the byte at address ds:0123 from the previous display to verify that DEBUG is, in fact, displaying the same data. Use the following command:

```
D 123
```

or

```
D123
```

Either will work fine. The space is optional, and the colon is necessary only if you explicitly specify a segment register. The S in DS represents "segment"; if you omit it, you will be referencing the absolute address instead of the segment address in the DS register.

You can use ES (extra segment) in place of DS for programs that use more than 64KB of data. These are called "huge-model programs." All COM files are "tiny models."

The DISPLAY-command output always starts the line at an address that is an even multiple of 16 bytes. (Since the address is hexadecimal, that means starting with a last digit of 0.) If you specify a start address that isn't an even multiple, the first byte shown will not be at the left edge of the displayed output. The output from the "D ds:0123 L 1" command shows this.

If you leave out the segment part of the address, the DISPLAY command will use the current value in the DS register.

S (SEARCH) The SEARCH command is a useful and powerful time-saver. With as many as 1,048,576 different possible memory locations, you'd have a tough time finding a particular section of a program or a specific data item if you didn't know where it was. Fortunately, DEBUG can find these for you.

SEARCH can find a single byte, or it can locate a long sequence of bytes whose sum is now greater than 65535 (FFFF). The patterns can be anything—ASCII text, program instructions, data structures. As long as you know what it looks like, DEBUG will find it.

The following command will search 256 consecutive bytes, looking for a byte of zeros:

```
S ds:0100 0200 00
```

Every time it finds a byte of zeros, DEBUG will print its full address.

To find a longer sequence, simply enter the list of bytes you are looking for, as in the following example:

```
S ds:0100 0200 01 02 03 04 05
```

This will look for the five-byte sequence specified above. If it exists, DEBUG will print the address of the first byte of the pattern. In this example, DEBUG will print the address where the 01 is stored.

Note that the pattern "01 02 03 04 05" must be stored in memory in exactly the order in which you typed it. DEBUG won't find just *any* combination of those five values.

Often, you might be looking for an ASCII string, rather than for certain hexadecimal values. For example, you might be looking for a misspelled word in a program. Fortunately, DEBUG will search for ASCII values as well as for hex ones. The following command will search the entire 64KB code segment looking for the word *progrdm*.

```
S cs:0000 FFFF "progrdm"
```

Note that the uppercase and lowercase letters must match exactly. DEBUG isn't smart enough to know the difference between capital and lowercase letters.

If you leave out the segment part of the address, the SEARCH command will use the current value in the DS register.

F (FILL)   The FILL command allows you to fill an area of memory with a constant value, or a pattern. For example,

```
F 4000:0000 1000 99
```

will fill 4096 consecutive bytes (1000 hex) with the value 99. You can also specify a sequence of bytes, if you like, as in the following command:

```
F ds:5080 7000 34 35 36 37 38
```

This will fill the specified range of memory with a repeating pattern of five bytes. Just as with the SEARCH command, you can specify your pattern as an ASCII string:

```
F 3000:0400 04FF "Hello there!"
```

This will repeat your greeting as many times as it will fit. If your pattern is longer than the range you're filling, DEBUG will use only as much as will fit.

As with most memory-related commands, you can specify a starting address and a length, instead of a starting address and an ending address. The following command performs exactly the same function as the preceding one:

```
F 3000:0400 L FF "Hello there!"
```

If you leave out the segment part of the address, the FILL command will use the current value in the DS register.

M (MOVE) The MOVE command allows you to copy a chunk of data to another area of memory. The name is a misnomer: DEBUG actually *copies* the data. With one exception, the original data is never altered or deleted.

To see how this works, let's first fill an area of memory with a recognizable pattern, using the following command:

```
F ds:0000 0100 "This is a test "
```

Now, let's copy that to another area of memory with the following command:

```
M ds:0000 0100 4000
```

This copies the memory between DS:0000 and DS:0100 (256 bytes) to memory between DS:4000 and DS:4100.

Notice that you didn't need to specify an ending address for the copy. DEBUG can figure out that you want to copy 256 bytes, and so it writes over 256 bytes at the destination address. To verify that your data got there correctly, use the following DISPLAY command:

```
D ds:4000
```

The source address and the destination address don't have to be in the same segment. For example, the command

```
M ds:0000 100 es:0350
```

is perfectly legal, and in fact, not unusual.

What happens if your source block and your destination block overlap? Consider the following example:

```
M ds:0000 2000 ds:1000
```

This will copy 2000 (hex) bytes starting at address 0000 to a 2000-byte area starting at address 1000. Clearly, the first half of the destination block overlaps the second half of the source block. What will happen?

Fortunately, DEBUG is smart enough to detect these situations and always handles them properly. Sometimes, that means it copies data in reverse order (from high addresses down), but it will never corrupt the source data area before it has been copied.

You may also specify a starting address and a length, instead of a starting address and an ending address.

If you leave out the segment part of the address, the MOVE command will use the current value in the DS register.

C (COMPARE)   After moving a block of memory, you may want to compare the two areas to ensure that they really are the same. This is what the COMPARE command is for.

COMPARE takes three addresses as parameters, as in the following example:

```
C cs:0200 1200 7000
```

This will compare the memory between CS:0200 and CS:1200 with the memory between CS:7000 and CS:8000.

With DEBUG, no news is good news; that is, if the two blocks are exactly the same, DEBUG will say nothing and simply display another prompt. If any differences are found, DEBUG will provide a display like the following:

```
0234:1200 67 68 0234:7000
```

This means that the memory at address 0234:1200 held a value of 67, while 0234:7000 held a value of 68. A line like this would be displayed for every difference found within the specified range of addresses.

You may also specify a starting address and a length, instead of a starting address and an ending address.

If you leave out the segment part of the address, the COMPARE command will use the current value in the DS register.

E (EDIT)   The EDIT command is used to alter individual bytes of memory. Often, this is used to patch a program file or to modify data records. It can also be used to alter the behavior of your computer, depending on what addresses you edit.

The EDIT command is like a one-byte fill command. Rather than making you specify a single value or a string of values to be written into memory, the EDIT command prompts you for new data a byte at a time. For this reason, it is one of the most commonly used commands for modifying programs.

Let's look at the following simple example:

```
E ds:1234
0650:1234 00.
```

DEBUG waits for you to enter a new value to replace the 00 currently written there. Type **99** and press RETURN. You should see the DEBUG prompt again.

Now, type the command line again. This time, you should see a 99 displayed. DEBUG prompts you to change it again. This time, though, you can just press RETURN. By pressing RETURN without typing a new value first, you can leave the current address unmodified.

Type the command line again. After DEBUG displays the address and the value 99, press the SPACEBAR once. As you can see, DEBUG advances to the next address, shows you its contents, and prompts you to change it.

```
E ds:1234
0650:1234 99.  23.
```

You can go on pressing the SPACEBAR as long as you like. Each time, DEBUG will advance one byte and allow you to alter the data there or leave it alone. When you come to the end of a line, DEBUG will start a new line automatically. When you're done, press RETURN.

You can go backward, too. Once again, enter the edit command:

```
E ds:1234
```

This time, press the HYPHEN key (near the P key), and watch what happens: DEBUG backs up one byte and displays it. Continue pressing HYPHEN. Just as with a press of the SPACEBAR, DEBUG will back up as long as you like. You can alternate between the two, if you want, to move forward and backward through memory.

Now, let's modify something interesting. Enter the following command:

```
E 0000:0417
```

You should see something like this:

```
0040:0017 80.
```

Press RETURN to leave the current value unchanged. Now, use the hexadecimal calculator to see what the value would be if you added 40 to it:

```
H 80 40
C0 40
```

The first value returned is the sum of the original value (80 in this example) and 40. Now, type in the EDIT command again, and enter the total as the new value:

```
E 0000:0417
```

```
0040:0017 80.C0
```

If you have an AT class machine, press RETURN and watch your Caps Lock indicator.

Although the keyboard interfaces vary from PC to XT to AT, your PC has several interesting, special memory locations down in the low addresses that are used by DOS and the BIOS to keep your computer running smoothly. One of these stores the current state of your keyboard. By adding 40 to the current value, you can make your PC believe the Caps Lock toggle is on. Adding 80 turns on Insert; 20, Num Lock; and 10, Scroll Lock.

If you leave out the segment part of the address, the EDIT command will use the current value in the DS register.

Port I/O Commands

The next two commands are used to read to and write from your PC's I/O ports, rather than to and from memory. The Intel CPU family, unlike some other processors, makes a distinction between memory and I/O. Your PC has an I/O address range of 64KB; so, I/O addresses can range from 0000 through FFFF. Not all I/O addresses are used, and there are many "holes," or unused addresses, throughout that 64KB space.

Your PC will have I/O devices for serial (COM) ports, parallel (LPT) ports, video, and disk drives. You can find the addresses for these devices elsewhere in this book. Particular care should be taken when writing to I/O addresses. It's not hard to change vital parameters, such as floppy disk step rate or video sync. Even reading from an I/O address can sometimes alter the operation of your computer. So, please, be careful where you're poking.

I (INPUT) The INPUT command reads a byte from the specified I/O address. Unlike with the memory-related commands, there is no way to display a range of I/O addresses. The following command:

```
I 02F8
```

will read a byte from I/O address 02F8, which is your COM1 port. There are seven separate port addresses for a single COM adapter. Because this is I/O space now, no segment addresses are required or allowed.

O (OUTPUT)   The OUTPUT command is the complement to the INPUT command. You use it to write a byte to an I/O address. The command sends data; it doesn't change an address. Unlike with the memory-related commands, there is no way to alter a range of I/O addresses or to move or compare I/O ranges. The following command:

```
O 02F8 99
```

will write the value 99 at I/O address 02F8. Because this is I/O space and not memory space, segment addresses are not required or allowed.

Program-Debug Commands

These five commands are the real workhorses for program debugging. They allow you to run a program, step through a program one machine instruction at a time, examine program flow, and assemble new instructions on the fly. Most of them require (or at least benefit from) some familiarity with 80X86 programming, but the examples that follow will provide you with everything you need.

G (GO)   The GO command allows you to run a program that has already been loaded into memory. Normally, you get a program into memory using the following command syntax:

```
DEBUG MYFILE.COM
```

The DEBUG program loads MYFILE.COM into memory for you before printing the DEBUG prompt. Entering the GO command now will begin execution of MYFILE.COM just as if you had run it normally, outside of DEBUG. If MYFILE.COM requires command line arguments, you can include them, too. Here's an example:

```
DEBUG MYFILE.COM arg1 arg2
```

Either way, MYFILE.COM is loaded and ready to go. If you want to start executing the loaded program at someplace other than the normal starting point, you can specify a starting address by inserting an equal sign in front of it. For example,

```
G =0700
```

will start executing from address CS:0700. Hopefully, this contains a valid 80X86 instruction.

You can also stop the program execution at a specified address. The syntax is just like in the preceding example, but without the equal sign:

```
G 3450
```

This will start executing the currently loaded program at its normal starting point but will stop it when execution reaches address CS:3450. This address, too, must hold a valid 80X86 instruction. More specifically, it must hold the first byte of an instruction if the instruction is more than one byte long.

This effectively sets a breakpoint in your program. That is, program execution will take a break at that point, and DEBUG will display the instruction it was about to execute and the contents of the CPU registers. You can set more than one breakpoint at a time, if you wish.

The following command sets four distinct breakpoints:

```
G 3450 29A5 C08C 0104
```

The order in which you specify them is completely irrelevant. DEBUG will stop execution whenever any one of them is reached. At that time, all of the breakpoints will be cleared.

This raises an interesting point: DEBUG implements its breakpoints by carefully overwriting portions of the program being debugged. The instructions at the breakpoint addresses you specify will be replaced with a special breakpoint instruction (opcode CC), which will cause the CPU to stop. This implies, however, that the memory can be written to.

What all this means for you is that you cannot set breakpoints in a program that is stored in ROM (such as your BIOS). Because ROM cannot be altered, DEBUG cannot write its breakpoints, and setting them will have no effect.

There is one other concern: Since DEBUG modifies your program every time you set breakpoints, you must be careful to remove them all before you save it back to disk. DEBUG replaces all breakpoint instructions with your original instruction every time it stops because of a breakpoint; in other words, breakpoints are self-removing. But if your program stops executing for some other reason, DEBUG will not remove them. Therefore, it's a good idea to set a breakpoint deliberately and then "hit" it before saving a program file.

You can specify both a starting address and a stopping (breakpoint) address at the same time. For example,

```
G cs:0460 125D 320E 0F38
```

will begin execution at the specified address and stop when any one of the three specified breakpoints is reached.

Unlike with the memory-related commands, if you leave out the segment part of the address, the GO command will use the current value in the CS register.

R (REGISTER)   The REGISTER command allows you to look at and even change the internal registers of your CPU chip. The microprocessor's registers are its own internal "scratch pad" where it carries out calculations, stores intermediate results, and controls the flow of programs.

Very rarely does a single instruction change most of the registers. However, at least one register changes every time an instruction is executed. Even while your PC is running DEBUG, the registers are constantly getting updated. For this reason, DEBUG maintains a second copy of the CPU registers in memory. It is this copy that you actually examine and modify. Whenever you run a program under DEBUG, DEBUG loads the side copy into the real registers. Whenever your program stops running, the real registers are copied into memory.

Type **R** by itself to show the current contents of the registers, as in the following example:

```
-R
AX=0000  BX=0000  CX=0000  DX=0000  SP=FFFC  BP=0000 SI=0000  DI=0000
DS=0000  ES=0000  SS=0000  CS=0245  IP=0100   NV UP EI PL NZ NA PO NC
0245:0100 E92D0D  JMP 0E30
```

Without covering all of the finer points of 80X86 architecture and programming, here is what this register dump means:

Across the top line, DEBUG displays the eight "general-purpose" registers. (Actually, any seasoned Intel programmer will tell you that the 80X86

CPU has no truly general-purpose registers—they're all used for something specific.) Registers are all identified by two-letter names, recognized by all assemblers, debuggers, and programmers. Registers have no addresses, because they reside inside the silicon of the CPU itself. Each of the registers is 16 bits wide; so, each value displayed is four hexadecimal digits.

The second line displays five more registers. The first four of these are your segment registers, mentioned earlier. They hold the segment addresses of your two data segments, stack segment, and code segment, respectively. The fifth register is your instruction pointer, IP. Register IP points to the next instruction that the processor will execute. (Remember, this really means the next instruction to execute if you were to run your program—the CPU is really executing DEBUG now.)

After the segment register and the instruction pointer. DEBUG displays eight cryptic, two-letter "flags." All eight of these actually represent a single register, the FLAGS register. Like the other registers, FLAGS is 16 bits wide, but each bit has a particular significance. Of these, eight of them are either meaningless or merely uninteresting. The other eight are displayed by DEBUG as abbreviations.

Each of the bits in the FLAGS register controls some particular aspect of CPU operation. One bit, for example, controls whether or not the CPU will respond to interrupts. Another indicates whether a previous arithmetic instruction has caused an overflow. Rather than display FLAGS as a hex number like the other registers, DEBUG displays a helpful two-letter mnemonic for each one. The meanings of the flag bits are shown in Table 25-7.

If all the bits were set, DEBUG would display

```
OV DN EI NG ZR AC PE CY
```

The third and final line displayed by DEBUG shows what the next instruction to be executed is. Note that the four-digit segment address will always match the contents of CS, and the four-digit offset address will match IP. Following the address are some hex numbers, which are followed by the mnemonic for the yet-to-be-executed instruction.

The hex numbers displayed in the last line are the actual value of the next opcode. It may be only one byte, or it may be several—not all 80X86 instructions are the same length. DEBUG displays the entire opcode, whatever its size. The mnemonic following it represents exactly the same data, but displayed in a form that is more readable for people.

TABLE 25-7

DEBUG Flag Bits

Bit Position	Value if 0	Value if 1	Meaning
0	NC	CY	Carry
2	PO	PE	Parity
4	NA	AC	Auxiliary Carry
6	NZ	ZR	Zero
7	PL	NG	Sign (+/-)
9	DI	EI	Interrupt
10	UP	DN	Direction
11	NV	OV	Overflow

Rather than displaying all of the registers at once, you can display only one, if you like. For example,

```
R AX
```

will display just the AX register. DEBUG will accept and understand only those register names shown and F for the FLAGS register. Intel programmers should note that DEBUG will not accept byte-sized register names, such as AL or AH. It will, however, accept PC as an equivalent for IP. Any other register name will result in a BR error.

The REGISTER command operates like the EDIT command in that it allows you to alter values as well as display them. To alter the contents of a register, just type a register name after the **R**, as in the following example.

```
-R BX
BX 0000
:
```

DEBUG starts off by displaying the current contents of the specified register (in this case, BX). Then, it drops down one line and waits for you to type a new value. If you wish to leave the current value unchanged, just press RETURN; otherwise, type a new hex number:

```
-R BX
BX 0000
:1234
```

To check your work, enter the REGISTER command again:

```
-R
AX=0000  BX=1234  CX=0000  DX=0000  SP=FFFC  BP=0000  SI=0000  DI=0000
DS=0000  ES=0000  SS=0000  CS=0245  IP=0100    NV UP EI PL NZ NA PO NC
0245:0000 E92D0D    JMP 0E30
```

As you can see, the contents of BX have been changed. (In reality, only DEBUG's copy has changed. Changing actual CPU registers on the fly like this would almost certainly crash your machine.)

You can edit the FLAGS register, too, but the method is a little different: Instead of typing a new hex value, DEBUG wants you to use its system of two-letter abbreviations. Therefore, when you type

```
R F
```

DEBUG produces

```
R F

OV DN EI PL ZR AC PE NC  -
```

DEBUG is now waiting for you to type one or more of the flag-bit mnemonics listed. If you don't want to change anything, just press RETURN; otherwise, type the abbreviations corresponding to the way you'd like the flags to be. You can specify more than one flag at the same time. For example, the following command:

```
R F
OV DN EI PL ZR AC PE NC  -  NV NG CY
```

is perfectly legal. It will change three flags: overflow, sign, and carry.

You can change all the flags at once, if you want. The only thing you can't do is specify the same flag twice. The following command:

```
R F
OV DN EI PL NZ AC PE NC  -  NV ZR NV
```

will produce a DF (duplicate flag) error, because the overflow flag is specified twice. Besides the DF error, there is also a BF (bad flag) error
condition, caused by the ZR.

You can't change the instruction displayed on the third line with the
REGISTER command. You can change CS or IP to make them point to a
different instruction. In fact, this is a pretty common debugging technique.
To change the instruction itself, you need to use either the EDIT command,
described earlier, or the ASSEMBLE command, coming later.

T (TRACE)   The TRACE command is like the GO command, except that
DEBUG will execute only one instruction of your program. Once that
instruction has executed, DEBUG will display all of the processor registers
for you and disassemble the next instruction, just as if you had typed the
REGISTER command.

Because TRACE executes only one instruction at a time, and because
single machine language instructions don't do very much, using TRACE can
be an extremely tedious procedure. You need to use trace only when you've
got a tough, hard-to-find bug somewhere in a small, well-defined area of
your program. It doesn't make sense to trace through an entire program on
the first pass. It's better to use the GO command first and then use TRACE
as a microscope when you've located the problem area.

To trace a program instruction, simply type **T** at the DEBUG prompt:

```
-T
AX=0000  BX=1234  CX=0000  DX=0000  SP=FFFC  BP=0000  SI=0000  DI=0000
DS=0000  ES=0000  SS=0000  CS=0245  IP=0100    NV UP EI PL NZ NA PO NC
0245:0000 E92D0D     JMP 0E30
```

This will execute the instruction that CS:IP was pointing to and then stop.
The IP register now points to the next, upcoming instruction. The instruction mnemonic displayed by TRACE has not been executed yet. Rather,
DEBUG displays the instruction that it will execute if you enter another
TRACE, PROCEED, or GO instruction. Register IP may point only a few
bytes away from where it did before the TRACE, or it may point someplace
completely different. This can happen after tracing a flow-control instruction like JMP, CALL, LOOP, or RET.

Like GO, TRACE can start from any arbitrary address. Simply enter the address you want to start tracing from, and include an equal sign:

```
T =C504
```

You can even jump code segments this way:

```
T =0300:4F60
```

If you know you want to trace several instructions, you can save yourself the tedium of typing **T** after every one by including an instruction-count parameter. For example,

```
T 20
```

will begin tracing from the current instruction (according to CS:IP) and continue for 32 (20 hex) instructions. DEBUG is not silent when you do this. It will still produce a full register dump and instruction disassembly after every single instruction. It simply continues automatically until the count is exhausted. This may be good or bad, depending on your point of view. Some people don't like their screens filled with unnecessary clutter, while others like to study the effect of each and every instruction.

If you trace more than six instructions, DEBUG will display more information than will fit on one screen, and some of it will begin to scroll off the top. As mentioned earlier, you can use CTRL-S to halt the scrolling temporarily until you've read it all. Press any other key to resume scrolling.

Using the TRACE command will show you each and every instruction the CPU executes while running your program. It will trace into and out of all loops, subroutines, and functions. About the only thing you won't see are asynchronous hardware interrupts (such as keyboard, disk, and timer interrupts). If your program makes use of several large functions (especially if you're calling DOS or BIOS services), this can get boring fast.

The TRACE command doesn't work well on instructions that talk directly to the BIOS or DOS and that are also being used by DEBUG as it communicates with you.

P (PROCEED) The PROCEED command is an alternative to the TRACE command. PROCEED works just like TRACE except that PROCEED only covers "top-level" code, skipping over subroutines. PROCEED will not follow the processor into subroutine calls, functions, or traps. It does follow the CPU back "up" through function returns (RET instructions), however. Other than that, it operates just the same way as TRACE. To tell DEBUG to trace an instruction but skip over any subroutines, just type **P**. Here's a sample output.

```
-P
AX=0000  BX=1234  CX=0000  DX=0000  SP=FFFC  BP=0000  SI=0000  DI=0000
DS=0000  ES=0000  SS=0000  CS=0245  IP=0100   NV UP EI PL NZ NA PO NC
0245:0000 E92D0D     JMP 0E30
```

You can tell DEBUG to proceed from a particular address, like this:

```
P =5680
```

or you can use PROCEED to trace a number of instructions at once, like this:

```
P 1C
```

You can even use both kinds of arguments together, like this:

```
P =23C0 3E
```

For most debugging tasks, you will probably use the PROCEED command mixed in with some TRACE commands. You might want to use TRACE through your own subroutines but use PROCEED to skip over DOS and BIOS calls.

U (UNASSEMBLE) The UNASSEMBLE command disassembles machine instructions into the corresponding assembly language mnemonics. You can specify the starting address and the number of bytes of the machine language source file you want dissembled.

If a starting address isn't specified, DEBUG defaults to the value of the CS register. Relying on this default for the starting address can cause you trouble. The address in the CS register may not be within the 8086 instruction boundary; although the file will disassemble, it may not be an accurate representation.

If the length or ending address isn't included, the first 32 (20 hex) bytes of memory will be disassembled. The range that will be used will be the last instruction encountered by any subsequent UNASSEMBLE commands. If the range is omitted and there haven't been any other UNASSEMBLE commands performed, DEBUG will use the starting address of the CS:IP registers of the program being disassembled.

DEBUG's UNASSEMBLE command cannot be used for instructions that are not native to the 8086 (80186-, 80286-, 80386-, and 80486-specific instructions). It will display these instructions as DBs.

Here is an example of disassembling 16 bytes of machine instructions at CS:0100H, the default address for most COM programs:

U 100 110 (*This method uses starting and ending address.*)

or

U 100 L10 (*This method uses starting address and length.*)

A (ASSEMBLE)   The ASSEMBLE command assembles each line of Intel 8086/8088 (microprocessor) and 8087 (math coprocessor) assembly language instructions into executable machine code (machine language). ASSEMBLE works with machine instructions only and does not work with hexadecimal values. You can specify the starting address of the machine language source file at which you want the assembly to begin. If a starting address isn't specified, DEBUG defaults to the value of the CS:IP registers.

Both COM and EXE programs have standard starting addresses, although they can vary. It is possible for a user to enter a starting address not within the 8086 instruction boundary; this will cause the assembled file to be unuseable.

DEBUG's ASSEMBLE command cannot be used for instructions that are not native to the 8086 80186-, 80286-, 80386-, and 80486-specific instructions).

After you enter the ASSEMBLE command, DEBUG displays the address or segment offset where the assembled instruction will be saved. Each time you press the ENTER key, the contents of this segment offset are overwritten with this new value. DEBUG conveniently displays the next address that follows the previous segment offset, which makes it easier to enter succeeding instructions. To terminate DEBUG's ASSEMBLE command, press ENTER without any other instructions at the address prompt.

DEBUG's ASSEMBLE command uses a syntax different from that of other assemblers (such as Microsoft's Macro Assembler). In DEBUG, the letter *H* is omitted after hex numbers. There are also differences in the use of segment overrides and file-control directives. You can learn about other differences in the DOS technical reference manual and the documentation of your assembler.

Here is an example of assembling some code at starting address CS:0100H:

```
A 100
```

Here's the instruction sequence we want to assemble:

```
LODS  WORD PTR[SI]
XCHG  BX,AX
JMP   [BX]
```

And here is the what the DEBUG session looks like:

```
-A 100
1983:0100  LODSW
1983:0101  XCHG BX,AX
1983:0103  JMP [BX]
1983:0105
```

If we didn't intend to stop here, we could resume by simply entering **A**. Don't forget **Q** for QUIT here.

The following UNASSEMBLE command uses starting and ending addresses:

```
U 100 110
```

The following one uses starting address and length:

```
U 100 L10
```

Mnemonics and DB and DW

Debuggers like DEBUG have their own language, which consists of a series of symbols called *mnemonics*. The DB (define byte) and DW (define word) mnemonics define a specific amount of storage to be used by a program. They are nothing more than place holders. The DW, however, is a two-byte storage area, while the DB is only a single byte.

The value of these two may vary. They can be predefined values (for example, decimal 1, hex 23H, or binary 10101010B) or literals (for example, H and HI). A question mark is used to indicate that the variable is undefined.

Once you become an "ace" assembly language programmer you can do other things with the variables, such as define different data types.

JMP NEAR, JMP FAR, JMP SHORT, PUSH, POP, and CMP

While DB and DW are used to tell DEBUG's assembler how the program is put together (compiler directives), instructions like JMP NEAR, JMP FAR, JMP SHORT, PUSH, POP, and CMP are the actual instructions.

Labels

Like DB and DW, labels are compiler directives and are targets for your jump instructions. By themselves they take up no space in the program.

File Commands

The next three DEBUG commands have to do with reading and writing files. DEBUG can't actually modify disk files directly. You have to load them into memory and then save the modified contents back into the file. Or, if you wish, you can save your modified file as a brand new file.

N (NAME) The NAME command is used to give your work a DOS filename. DEBUG needs to know the name of a file before you can read it from disk or write it to disk. If you are debugging an existing file, you would normally specify it when you first start DEBUG, like this:

```
DEBUG FILE1.COM
```

You can also name the file after the fact. This allows you to start DEBUG without a filename, edit memory, and then save memory as a new file. For example,

```
DEBUG
N FILE1.COM
```

gives the file the same name as in the preceding example, but it doesn't load the file.

DEBUG isn't very flexible about filenames when you're using the NAME command. You can't specify path names (for example, \USR\TOOLS \FILE1.COM), nor can you specify a drive letter as part of the filename (as in C:FOO.BAR). Only an eight-character primary filename and three-character extension are allowed. DEBUG will, however, let you type the name in either uppercase or lowercase letters.

If you want to create a new file with DEBUG, you can use the syntax shown in the preceding example. The NAME command places the filename you specify in a special buffer that DEBUG will use for all subsequent LOAD and WRITE commands (which are described later).

Another way to create a new file is to just pretend that it already exists:

```
DEBUG NEWFILE.COM
File not found
```

DEBUG complains that the specified file does not exist, but it still places the name (NEWFILE.COM) in its special filename buffer, just as with the NAME command.

The NAME command has a second use. After a program file has been loaded, you can use NAME to "stuff" arguments into the program's command stream. Recall from an earlier example that you can start DEBUG with the name of a program file followed by one or more arguments. The arguments are passed to the program being debugged. Just as you can specify the program file after DEBUG has started, you can specify arguments after the program has been loaded. For example, the following command sequence:

```
DEBUG MYFILE.COM
-N arg1 arg2
```

will pass two arguments to the program MYFILE.COM just as if you had typed them on the command line after the name of the program.

Using the NAME command in this way has a funny side effect, though: it clobbers the name of the program you're debugging. Every time you use the NAME command, DEBUG copies the subsequent string of characters into its special filename buffer. It has no way of knowing whether you're specifying a filename or arguments to a program; either way, they go into the buffer. Therefore, if you use the NAME command to pass command line arguments to a program, be very careful before saving anything with the WRITE command, or you'll wind up creating a new file with a funny name. For example, the preceding command would replace the name MYFILE-.COM with ARG1. If you were to save the file now, DEBUG would use that name rather than MYFILE.COM.

L (LOAD)   The LOAD command is used to read a file from disk and copy it into memory. Once it is in memory, you can examine it or edit it in any way you like. The LOAD command has two very different formats. One simply loads a specified file from disk, and the other reads absolute disk sectors and copies them into specified memory addresses.

The simplest form of the LOAD command is the letter *L*.

```
N ANYFILE.USA
L
```

DEBUG loads the file specified and places a copy of it at CS:0100. It also sets the registers BX and CX equal to the length of the file, in bytes. In short, using the NAME command followed by the LOAD command has the same result as loading a file with

```
DEBUG ANYFILE.USA
```

The advantage it gives you is flexibility. You can load a file into a particular range of memory, by specifying the beginning address, as in the following:

```
N ANYFILE.USA
L DS:0480
```

The entire file will be loaded and the registers updated just as before, but this time the file will be loaded into a different place in memory. Using the NAME command with the LOAD command, you can load more than one file into memory at a time.

The other form of the LOAD command allows you to read any arbitrary disk sectors and copy them into memory. The syntax looks like this:

```
L DS:0100 0 6C 10
```

The first parameter (DS:0100) is a memory address, just like in the preceding example. This can be almost anything, with or without a segment address. The second parameter (0) is a disk drive identifier; a value of 0 specifies drive A. Next comes the beginning sector (6C). The last parameter (10) is a length, in sectors. Therefore, this command will load 16 sectors (10 hex) from drive A, starting at sector 108 (6C hex), and load the data beginning at offset 256 (100 hex) into the current data segment.

The address parameter is an optional part of the LOAD command. If it is omitted, DEBUG will load your file at offset 100 into the current code segment (CS:0100), with two exceptions. First, if you're loading an EXE file, DOS will relocate the file before loading it, and so it may not (and probably won't) wind up at CS:0100. In this case, DEBUG will ignore an address parameter even if you specify one.

Second, if you're loading a HEX file created by a linker, DEBUG will load the file into whatever address is specified in the header of the HEX file. In this case, if you specify an address parameter, it will be added to the address in the HEX file's header.

W (WRITE)   The WRITE command performs the opposite function of the LOAD command: it writes a portion of memory to a disk. The WRITE command is probably the single most dangerous command DEBUG has. Use this one with extreme caution. If you accidentally write to the wrong part of a disk, you stand a good chance of losing valuable data. Not even Mace or Norton utilities can rescue you now. DEBUG is a powerful, unforgiving tool, and the WRITE command is the most potentially hazardous part of that tool.

DEBUG needs to know two things to perform a disk write: what part of memory you want to write and where on disk you want to write it. There are easy ways to supply this information, and there are difficult ways. First, the easy way.

When you have DEBUG load a file (either with the LOAD command or from the DOS command line), it remembers the name of the file you've loaded and the length of the file. It also remembers where in memory it loaded the file. The name is kept in DEBUG's filename buffer; the length, in registers BX and CX; and the starting memory address, in another buffer. All of these will be used again when you use the WRITE command to write

READ.ME

COM and EXE Files

DOS treats and loads COM and EXE files differently. First, DOS needs to distinguish the two. This is not too difficult, because the header for EXE files is always the same: Unless the program was written for Windows or OS/2, you'll find the letters *MZ*, which are the initials of its designer, Mark Zbiko-ski.

The EXE file header does some real magic. It lets DOS load portions of the program as they are needed, making it possible to write programs that exceed the system's capacity. PageMaker's main EXE file, for example, is so large it won't fit on a standard 360KB floppy. EXE files also have improved memory-management capabilities.

COM files are allocated all of DOS's available memory when loaded. When programming a COM file, you must make sure your program deallocates this memory if any other programs need to be run. When both COM and EXE program execution is completed, all memory is returned to DOS.

COM files are almost always less than 64KB. EXE files can be as large as your available disk space (and sanity) permits. Because COM files are memory images loaded into a fixed memory address and have no headers, they load faster than EXE files, which can be relocated and aren't loaded at a fixed address.

EXE files have a feature that, although common in other operating systems, is unique in DOS. This feature, called the *relocation table*, is what gives EXE programs the ability to be relocated in DOS. More advanced operating systems such as OS/2, have improved memory management, and all programs can be relocated.

the file back to disk; so long as none of these three parameters changes, you're all set. For example, the following command sequence:

```
C:\> DEBUG MYFILE.COM
-E cs:023C
0282:023C 45.00
-W
Writing 094E bytes
-Q
```

will load the specified file (MYFILE.COM), edit one byte of the file, write it back to disk, and quit the DEBUG session. This kind of quick "patch" is common and easy to do with DEBUG.

The following are relevant points to remember here:

- The name of the file has not changed

- The length of the file has not changed

- The placement of the file in memory has not changed

Given all three of these requirements, you can simply use the WRITE command without any parameters. This allows you essentially to edit a file in place on the disk.

Even in these simple cases, however, it is always a good idea to keep a backup copy of your file before you start editing it. Fingers can be funny things, and you never know when you might accidentally type something wrong and destroy your only copy of a good file. DEBUG doesn't have an undo command!

Now, let's look at instances where one or more of the vital DEBUG parameters might be changed—first, the filename.

If you haven't loaded an existing file, DEBUG will have no idea what to call the file it is about to write. In that case, you can use the NAME command to give your file a name. You can also use the NAME command to change the name of a file you have already loaded. For example, the following works just fine:

```
C:\> DEBUG MYFILE.COM
-E cs:023C
0282:023C 45.00
-N NEWFILE.COM
-W
Writing 094E bytes
-Q
```

This example is just like the preceding one, except that the name of the file is changed before it's written to disk. If a file by that name already appears on your disk, it will be overwritten with the edited copy of MYFILE-.COM; otherwise, a new file will be created.

If the length of your edited file has changed, you'll have to specify the correct length before saving the file. DEBUG has no way of telling whether you've shortened or lengthened a file or left it alone. You need to be sure that registers BX and CX hold the correct length. One good idea is to write down their respective values right at the beginning of your DEBUG session.

Let's look at the following example:

```
C:\> DEBUG MYFILE.COM
-R
AX=0000  BX=0000  CX=094E DX=0000  SP=FFFC  BP=0000  SI=0000  DI=0000
DS=0000  ES=0000  SS=0000 CS=0245  IP=0100  NV UP EI PL NZ NA PO NC
```

Here, register BX is 0, and register CX holds 094E. If you add or subtract bytes from your file, be sure to add or subtract the same amount from CX before writing it back. For larger files, be certain to carry the addition or subtraction over into BX, as well.

These two registers won't necessarily stay still, either. If you ever execute your program (with a GO, TRACE, or PROCEED command), all of the CPU registers will probably change. That's why it's a good idea to write down the values of the BX and CX registers first.

Now, let's say you move your file in memory. Normally, DEBUG loads files at CS:0100 (with the exception noted above — under the LOAD command). That's also where DEBUG expects to find it when it starts writing. If you move your file, be sure to tell DEBUG where it is, or you'll wind up writing random data to your disk.

You'll most likely move your file around in memory with the MOVE command. Or you might be composing a brand new file somewhere in memory. Either way, if you need to specify a nonstandard starting address, simply type it on the command line, as in the following example:

```
-W DS:1120
Writing 094E bytes
-Q
```

This writes to disk using the default filename (in DEBUG's buffer) and the default length (in registers BX and CX). Only the starting address has changed.

That takes care of the "normal" forms of the WRITE command. Now let's look at the complete — and riskier — form.

DEBUG lets you write to absolute disk sectors if you want to. This gives you a surprising amount of power in a little package. There is absolutely no place on the disk—hard disk or floppy disk—to which you can't write. And there's no data you can't write. In short, you can do anything anywhere.

The complete form of the WRITE command requires that you specify four parameters:

- The starting memory address to write from

- The disk drive to write to

- The first sector on that disk to write to

- The number of sectors to write

The length parameter is no longer required in registers BX and CX, because DEBUG will write out as many disk sectors as you tell it to. In all current versions of DOS, each sector holds 512 (200 hex) bytes of data.

Absolute-sector writes ignore any filenames and write to a specified location on disk. Don't experiment with this sample until you've read the warning below.

An absolute-sector WRITE command sequence might look like this:

```
C:\> DEBUG
-F DS:0000 07FF "Hello there! "
-N HELLO.FIL
-W DS:0000 0 12 4
Writing 800 bytes
-Q
```

This set of commands starts DEBUG with a "blank slate"—no file is loaded or named. Then, it fills 2048 bytes (800 hex) with a string pattern.

Next, the filled memory is written to the disk in drive A, starting at sector 18 (12 hex). Since we've written a 2048-byte pattern, we need to write 4 sectors' worth of data.

Warning: This program illustrates one of the ways DEBUG can nail you. Although we have given this program a new filename, HELLO.FIL, before writing memory to disk, DEBUG's WRITE command writes absolute disk sectors to disk. The data is simply stored at the specified locations on the disk and can possibly wipe out your files, file allocation table, directory, or other data. The filename in this example would be ignored. To use the filename correctly, you must pass the name on the command line, like this:

```
C:\> COPY MYFILE.COM NEWFILE.COM
C:\> DEBUG NEWFILE.COM
-E cs:023C
0282:023C 45.00
-W
Writing 094E bytes
-Q
```

DEBUG Scripts

A DEBUG *script* is one of the best ways to use DEBUG. A script is a series of DEBUG commands. When it is put in an ASCII file (say, REBOOT.SCR) with a text editor and passed as input to DEBUG with the following command:

```
DEBUG <REBOOT.SCR
```

it causes DEBUG to read the commands as if they had been typed from the keyboard. DEBUG executes them, creating the file REBOOT.COM. Here's the script:

```
n reboot.com                ;set filename
a 100                       ;assemble at address 100
CLI                         ;This program reboots the
XOR AX,AX                   ;  computer.  Storing 1234
MOV DS,AX                   ;  at location 0:472 makes
MOV WORD PTR [0472],1234    ;  it a warm boot instead of
JMP FFFF:0000               ;  a cold boot
                                ; blank line to stop assembly
r cx                        ;set CX value
11                          ;program is 11 (hex) bytes long
w                           ;write it out
q                           ;and quit debug
```

Source-Level Debuggers

Source-level debuggers let you work on the program and set breakpoints at the beginning of the source statement instead of the machine code. Instead of debugging machine language, you debug the source representation. Your compiler must be capable of supporting this kind of debugger; it will need to supply the debugger with tables, source code, and other information. For instance, you can't use a source-level debugger on the programs that come with DOS, because they don't include these tables—or the source file, for that matter.

There are several leading source-level-debugger programs. These include CV, or CodeView, from Microsoft; TD, or Turbo Debug, from Borland; and Periscope, from The Periscope Company.

Changing the Names of Intrinsic Commands

Here's a way to exercise DEBUG and give yourself a more secure COMMAND.COM at the same time. You'll create a copy of COMMAND.COM, find an internal command (ERASE), and rename it. If you run that copy on top of (or, using SHELL, instead of) COMMAND.COM, ERASE will be effectively disabled. You'll rename it ERAS!, although you could rename it #!@@^ or whatever, as long as it was exactly five characters.

First, copy COMMAND.COM:

```
copy command.com comcopy.com
```

Now run DEBUG on this program:

```
debug comcopy.com
```

Use the SEARCH command to find ERASE. Since all versions of COMMAND.COM maintain the internal command list less than 32KB into the program, the following command line will work for SEARCH (eternal commands are uppercase):

```
s 0 8000 'ERASE'
```

DEBUG returns the following address, where ERASE can be found:

```
3225:54AC
```

Back up a byte, and dump that section:

```
- d 54AB

3225:54A0                               05 45 52 41 53           .ERAS
3225:54B0  45 01 BD 11 03 44 45 4C-01 BD 11 04 54 59 50 45   E....DEL....TYPE
3225:54C0  01 9E 12 03 52 45 4D 02-04 01 04 43 4F 50 59 03   ....REM....COPY.
3225:54D0  35 2A 05 50 41 55 53 45-02 B0 11 04 44 41 54 45   5*.PAUSE....DATE
3225:54E0  02 41 21 04 54 49 4D 45-00 59 22 03 56 45 52 00   .A!.TIME.Y".VER.
3225:54F0  94 13 03 56 4F 4C 01 3E-13 02 43 44 01 DD 18 05   ...VOL.>..CD....
3225:5500  43 48 44 49 52 01 DD 18-02 4D 44 01 20 19 05 4D   CHDIR....MD. ..M
3225:5510  4B 44 49 52 01 20 19 02-52 44 01 64 19 05 52 4D   KDIR. ..RD.d..RM
3225:5520  44 49 52 01 64 19 05 42-52 45 41                  DIR.d..BREA
```

Note that a length byte precedes each command. There's a 5 before the ERASE at offset 54AB, a 3 before DEL at 54B4, and so on. So, your alterations can't add or subtract characters; they can only change them.

To change the command, find the letters you want to change. For example, to change ERASE to ERAS!, you'll need to add the position of the character you want to change. In this case, the ! is the fifth character. To do the addition, which can be tricky in hex, use the HEX command:

```
h 54AB 5
```

This shows two values: the first value is the sum of the two numbers, and the second is the difference:

```
54B0   54A6
```

So, the ! should be placed at 54B0. Use the DISPLAY command to convince yourself that it's there:

```
-d 54B0
3225:54B0  45 01 BD 11 03 44 45 4C-01 BD 11 04 54 59 50 45   E....DEL....TYPE
3225:54C0  01 9E 12 03 52 45 4D 02-04 01 04 43 4F 50 59 03   ....REM....COPY.
3225:54D0  35 2A 05 50 41 55 53 45-02 B0 11 04 44 41 54 45   5*.PAUSE....DATE
3225:54E0  02 41 21 04 54 49 4D 45-00 59 22 03 56 45 52 00   .A!.TIME.Y".VER.
3225:54F0  94 13 03 56 4F 4C 01 3E-13 02 43 44 01 DD 18 05   ...VOL.>..CD....
3225:5500  43 48 44 49 52 01 DD 18-02 4D 44 01 20 19 05 4D   CHDIR....MD. ..M
3225:5510  4B 44 49 52 01 20 19 02-52 44 01 64 19 05 52 4D   KDIR. ..RD.d..RM
3225:5520  44 49 52 01 64 19 05 42-52 45 41 4B 00 15 29 06   DIR.d..BREAK..).
```

Sure enough, the last letter in ERASE, *E*, is shown. To change it, use the ASSEMBLE command:

```
a 54B0
```

The address at which your assembly will start is displayed, and the cursor awaits instructions:

```
3225:54B0
```

Use DB to replace the character. DB lets you insert literal values either as numbers or as ASCII characters. To enter ASCII values, enclose them in single or double quotes. It's much easier done than said:

```
3225:54B0 db "!"
```

That's it. To save the new file, press ENTER to stop assembly, and then use the WRITE command:

```
3225:54B1
-W
Writing 62DC bytes
```

The 62DC figure may differ; it depends on the version of COMMAND.COM used.

Type **Q** to exit DEBUG. Now run the copy of COMMAND.COM, and it will become the new command processor until you type **EXIT**. Here's the simple command:

```
comcopy
```

MS-DOS will sign on as usual:

```
Microsoft(R) MS-DOS(R)  Version 3.30
          (C)Copyright Microsoft Corp 1981-1987
```

Everything will work fine until you try to use ERASE. For example, let's copy this copy and attempt to erase it:

```
copy comcopy.com test.com
erase test.com
```

When you type **ERASE**, the notorious "Bad command or filename" message pops up. But type **ERAS!**, and it works:

```
eras! test.com
```

When you use this trick, don't replace characters with * or ?, since they'll be read as wildcard characters.

A program called SafetyShell (Hyperkinetix, Inc., 666 Baker #405, Costa Mesa, CA 92626) lets you selectively disable, password-protect, or rename internal DOS commands using a similar technique.

Displaying the ROM Release Date

To display the ROM release date, display the absolute address F000:FFF5. It's eight characters in, surprisingly, ASCII:

```
-d f000:fff5
F000:FFF0              30 31 2F-31 35 2F 38 38 FF FC 00        01/15/88...
```

Viewing a Disk Directory

The use of the LOAD command to load a disk sector into memory can easily be demonstrated with a bootable 360KB disk. The root directory information starts at sector 5. To load one sector from drive A (drive specifications start at 0, for drive A) into the data segment starting at offset 100, enter the following command:

```
L 100 0 5 1
```

To see it, just display memory starting at offset 100:

```
-D 100

320A:0100  49 42 4D 42 49 4F 20 20-43 4F 4D 27 00 00 00 00   IBMBIO  COM'....
320A:0110  00 00 00 00 00 00 00 60-54 07 02 00 80 12 00 00   .......'T.......
320A:0120  49 42 4D 44 4F 53 20 20-43 4F 4D 27 00 00 00 00   IBMDOS  COM'....
320A:0130  00 00 00 00 00 00 00 60-54 07 07 00 80 42 00 00   .......'T....B..
```

```
320A:0140  56 49 44 32 20 20 20 20-41 53 4D 20 00 00 00 00   VID2   ASM ....
320A:0150  00 00 00 00 00 00 B9 A0-87 13 18 00 B9 47 00 00   .............G..
320A:0160  52 45 4E 44 49 52 20 20-41 53 4D 20 00 00 00 00   RENDIR ASM ....
320A:0170  00 00 00 00 00 00 2C BA-81 14 2A 00 63 10 00 00   .......,...*.c...
```

The directory structure is rigidly laid out. You can see how the filename and extension start at bytes 1 and 9, padded out with spaces (hex 20). Most other parts of the entry are encoded, but the file size appears at byte 29. For example, the file RENDIR.ASM is 4195 bytes long. That's 1063 hex, and you can see the bytes 63 and 10 at the bottom of the listing.

WRITING YOUR OWN PROGRAM WITH DEBUG

You can write a useful program that's just seven bytes long using DEBUG. The program, FF.COM, sends a form feed to the printer, ejecting a page. Since some programs forget to do this after printing, it's a handy program to have.

First, issue the following command at the DOS prompt:

```
debug ff.com
```

The following message appears—as it should (the program hasn't been written yet):

```
File not found
```

Issue the assemble command:

```
A
```

Since COM files always start at hex 100, that's the default. You could also issue type **a 100** to make it explicit.

Now, assemble the following lines, typing them in exactly as shown:

```
0100 mov ah, 5   ; DOS subroutine 5 sends a character to LPT1.
0102 mov dl, C   ; Hex C is decimal 12--the form feed character.
0104 int 21h     ; Call subroutine 5.  This prints the character.
0106 ret         ; Return to DOS.
0107
```

At offset 107, just press ENTER to quit assembly.

Now, set CX to 7, since the WRITE command writes CX bytes out:

```
rcx
```

CX's current value is displayed:

```
CX 0000
```

Enter **7**

Finally, issue the WRITE command to save the program you just created as file FF.COM:

```
-W
Writing 0007 bytes
```

Type **Q** to quit. To run the program, make sure your printer is connected to LPT1 and is ready, and enter **FF** at the DOS command line. Your printer should eject a sheet of paper.

Writing to the Screen with the ENTER Command

The ENTER command writes values to memory. A vivid example of writing to memory is writing directly to the screen. Screen memory starts at hex B800 on color machines and hex B000 on monochrome systems.

There are 4000 bytes for the 2,000 characters on an 80X25 screen (80 times 25 is 2000). That's because the characters displayed on the screen alternate with attribute bytes. The normal attribute is 7. To display *Dvorak* at the upper left corner of the screen, you fire up DEBUG and type in a command. On a color system, use the following command:

```
e b800:0000 'D' 7 'v' 7 'o' 7 'r' 7 'a' 7 'k' 7
```

On a mono system, use the following:

```
e b000:0000 'D' 7 'v' 7 'o' 7 'r' 7 'a' 7 'k' 7
```

CONCLUSION

Now you can update your resume and apply for all those senior development positions at the leading software houses. Or maybe you'll simply have gained some new understanding of how DEBUG can be used to examine and manipulate things and even write programs.

As you can see, DEBUG is a powerful tool. When used correctly, it can really allow you to get into the innards of your machine.

By now you may have tired from our warnings of its potential for damaging your data. However, an additional note is in order here. While DEBUG is useful in reading and writing to your disk and can perform file and absolute-sector writes, your needs will be much better served with a menu-driven utility, such as Norton, PC Tools, or Mace, that has appropriate error trapping. In fact, that's why we've avoided giving examples of fiddling with your disk's file allocation table and critical hard disk areas, such as the DOS partition.

As a practical matter, you won't be using DEBUG too often. When you do, it will probably be to start the program stored in your hard drive controller's ROM or execute a DEBUG script. In fact, along with being careful, using scripts with DEBUG is the best way to use DEBUG.

CHAPTER TWENTY-SIX

Batch File Basics and Commands

Batch files are important and useful tools for both occasional and experienced PC users. At their simplest, they do nothing more than enter a series of keystrokes for you. This lets you reduce a complex command to a single word that you choose yourself. At their most complex, batch files are equivalent to a medium-power programming language. Programmers sometimes speak of "Batch," as if it were an actual language.

There is no need to become an expert in batch file programming to benefit from batch files. The more you learn, though, the more you can do. This chapter will explain some ins and outs of "batching it." It will try to remove some of the mystique that many users associate with programming and with "learning a new language." You'll also learn about batch file compilers, some of which use ordinary language. The most important thing to remember is if you understand DOS commands, you already speak batch.

You will do best with this chapter if you try out the examples for yourself. It is intended to be, in part, a tutorial. If you try variations on the examples, you will come to understand the inner workings of batch much more completely.

WHY CALL IT A BATCH FILE?

Let's start with a little bit of batch history. Its very name hints at the origin of the language. In computers predating the PC, commands were often issued, not by a keyboard, but by cards with holes in them. These "punch cards" were the kind that used to arrive with bills and were labeled, "Do not fold, spindle, or mutilate." When used to program a computer, these cards were collected into big trays and loaded into the computer all at once, one after another, in batches.

A batch file works much the same way. It contains a list of commands you want DOS to execute, one per line. Instead of typing each command separately, you just type the name of the batch file. DOS reads the commands in the file sequentially, one after another. As DOS reads each line, it tries to execute the command it contains, just as if you had typed it at the keyboard and pressed ENTER.

Every batch file ends with the extension BAT, short for "BATch." DOS knows that in a file with a BAT extension, each line represents an independent command. DOS reads a line, tries to execute the command, and then goes on to the next line. It treats the lines in the file just like an early computer treated a batch of punch cards.

WHAT BATCH FILES CAN DO FOR YOU

Batch files save lots of typing. They can automate routine tasks, such as formatting diskettes, switching directories, starting programs, and cleaning up the clutter that accumulates on a hard disk drive. A batch file won't make a spelling error in the middle of a long command, and it won't forget to set or reset environment variables for different application programs. This attention to detail allows the advanced user to concentrate on more creative tasks. The less experienced user won't need to spend time looking up command options.

Batch files are programs, just like BASIC or C program files. They can branch to perform different actions depending on initial conditions and input. They can loop through a subset of actions several times. They can create environment variables and change them. They can even call subroutines outside themselves. Most batch commands are not complicated, and they give you enormous control over your PC.

The following batch file simply displays the message "Strike a key when ready . . ." and waits for the user to press any key:

```
REM Await a keystroke
PAUSE
```

Both REM and PAUSE are batch commands. The batch interpreter has specific instructions to deal with them.

One important difference between batch file programs and programs in other languages is that a statement not recognized by the batch interpreter is still considered correct. It's merely passed to DOS to run as a program. The following batch file changes to the C:\123 directory, runs Lotus 1-2-3, and returns to the root directory:

```
CD \123
123
CD \
```

Neither CD nor 123 is an intrinsic batch command. The batch interpreter handles this by passing the buck to DOS. DOS recognizes CD as an internal command and changes directories accordingly. However, it doesn't know 123 from Adam. It passes the buck in turn to its EXEC (execute) routine, which loads and runs programs. If no program named 123.COM or 123.EXE is available, the infamous "Bad command or file name" message is issued. This behavior is markedly different from that of other languages, such as BASIC or C, which halt execution immediately upon encountering an unknown command.

There are some limitations. Generally, batch files can't perform tasks that require input from the user, make calculations, or make use of the PC's color capabilities. Here are some things batch files can't do:

- Accept keyboard input and act on it

- Prevent a user from altering the batch program

- Display colors (without ANSI.SYS present)

- Tell whether a diskette drive is ready

- Set ERRORLEVEL (Batch files can only read it.)

Batch language, however, is uniquely extendable because you can write programs that interact with the batch interpreter. A number of programs included on the disk accompanying this book help you get around these limitations.

Here's an overview of the Dvorak utilities. They can give your batch files colors without ANSI.SYS, create slick-looking menus, and process keystrokes in a way that's just not possible with batch alone.

Program Name	What It's For
ASK	Displays a message and accepts keys from list
BEEP	Beeps
BOX	Draws a single- or double-filled, colored box anywhere onscreen
FREADY	Sets error level to 1 if drive is ready
GETKEY, GETKEYNL	Accepts a keystroke and converts it to an ERRORLEVEL value
GETYN	Accepts only the Y or N keys and sets ERRORLEVEL accordingly
RESTPATH	Retrieves a disk and directory from a file created by SAVEPATH and changes to that directory
ROWCOL	Positions the cursor onscreen and optionally displays text in any foreground or background color
SAVEPATH	"Remembers" the current drive and directory so that RESTPATH can return to it later
SHOWTIME	Displays the time, "am" or "pm", the day, the date, and the year
TESTANSI	Sets ERRORLEVEL to 1 if the ANSI.SYS driver is present and to 0 if it's not

THE AUTOEXEC.BAT BATCH FILE

When you start your computer, the command sequence you execute will set the system up for the rest of your computing session. The start-up command sequence is usually the same every time:

- If your computer doesn't have a battery-powered clock (most do), the DATE and TIME commands will tell your computer to set the correct date and time stamp on your files.

- The PATH command tells your computer where it can find program files in other subdirectories.

- PROMPT sets up your prompt to give you just the information you want.

As you learn the value of disk caching, you may want to automate a disk caching program that loads each time you start your computer. You may also want a printer spooler if your printer continually ties up your computer. Keyboard-accelerator programs and keyboard-macro programs are handy, too. There are programs that set a path for data files, (for example, DOS's APPEND command). And terminate-and-stay-resident (TSR) programs are available for just about everything.

You can have your computer install these programs and perform these functions automatically each time you start it up. You do this by creating a start-up batch file and naming it AUTOEXEC.BAT. Power users find AUTOEXEC.BAT an essential part of their systems. Many people consider AUTOEXEC.BAT the most important batch file in any system.

NONBRANCHING BATCH FILES

In a branching batch file, the logic flows from line to line until it reaches a go-to command. From there it will branch to other branch files or programs. In a nonbranching batch file, the logic flow of the program proceeds line to line until it reaches the end of the program.

Once you've seen a few straightforward examples to give you a feel for batch files, you can move on to the more powerful programming techniques.

For example, suppose you keep your word processing program in a subdirectory named C:\PROGS\WP and the word processor's filename is WP.EXE. To start the program, you would normally type

CD C:\PROGS\WP

to switch to the right directory and

WP

to run the program.

That's a lot of keystrokes to start one program—especially if you are prone to typing errors. A batch file called WP.BAT can accomplish these chores with only two keystrokes on your part. This section will help you create your own WP.BAT file.

WRITING BATCH FILES

You can use any of three techniques to write batch files. Many people like to write them with their word processors. But be careful: many word processors insert invisible control characters for tabs, margins, and other special features. These characters will cause batch files to behave oddly. If you use a word processor, be sure to save WP.BAT in plain ASCII format (variously called "nondocument," "DOS text," or some other generic term in word processor manuals). The VDE text editor included in the disks in this book is also useful for creating and modifying batch files.

You can also use the line editor included with DOS, EDLIN.COM, to write short batch files. Despite its limitations for major text projects, EDLIN is quite good for batch files.

Finally, you can always use the DOS COPY command. To create a file named WP.BAT, type

```
COPY CON WP.BAT
```

at the DOS prompt, and press ENTER. This tells DOS to copy everything you type at the CONsole (keyboard) into a file called WP.BAT as well as to the screen. The cursor drops down one line. Type

```
CD C:\PROGS\WP
```

and press ENTER. Now type

```
WP
```

but do *not* press ENTER just yet. Instead, press the F6 function key, and watch the ^Z symbol appear. This is the end-of-file character DOS needs in every batch file. EDLIN and most other editors will add ^Z for you, but you must remember to insert it yourself when you use the COPY CON technique.

If you notice that you typed a line incorrectly, press CTRL-C and start over. If everything's correct, press ENTER. Now you'll see "1 File(s) copied". This tells you DOS got the message to end the file and save it to disk.

Now, type **wp** and press ENTER. You will see

```
CD C:\PROGS\WP        <-- The batch file changing directories

C:\PROGS\WP           <-- The DOS indication of the new current directory

WP                    <-- The batch file starting up your word processor
```

Batch File Management

Perhaps you didn't see the directory change (shown in the first two lines above). Instead, all that happened is that your word processor started up. DOS executed WP.EXE instead of WP.BAT.

DOS has some simple rules for dealing with files that share the same name. When you enter WP, DOS first looks for an internal command by that name. If it finds one, DOS executes the command. A batch file named COPY.BAT would never be executed, since COPY is an internal DOS command.

If it does not find an internal command, DOS looks next in the current directory for a file with the extension COM. If it finds one, it executes it. If no COM file is found, DOS looks for a filename with the extension EXE, again in the current directory. DOS executes WP.BAT only if it fails to find an internal command named WP, a WP.COM file, or a WP.EXE file in the current directory.

To summarize, DOS looks for files in the following order:

COM
EXE
BAT

If you have two or more files with the same name and any of the above extensions in the same directory, your computer will search for the extensions in the above order and implement the first one it finds. This is important to keep in mind when naming your files.

If you collect all your batch files in a single directory, you could incorporate the directory into your path. Put your C:\BAT (or whatever name you choose) directory near the front of the PATH statement.

Notice that WP.BAT will leave you in the C:\PROGS\WP directory when you exit your word processor. This is fine if you like to keep everything you write in that directory. However, if you want to return to the directory in which you started, WP.BAT should read

```
C:\PROGS\WP\WP
```

Some programs will allow you to work on files in other directories, but other programs won't. Suppose you want to use a data base program, DATAB.EXE, that requires you to work on files in the same directory with the program. Your DB.BAT file might look like the following:

```
CD C:\PROGS\DB
DATAB
```

This batch file will leave you in the C:\PROGS\DB directory when you exit DATAB. There is no simple way to return to your starting directory from a batch file, especially if the batch file switches drives. So, you should put SAVEPATH.COM and RESTPATH.COM in your path. These programs are included in the program disks bundled with this book and work with any version of DOS starting with 2.0. They give you the ability to "remember" the current directory by writing it to a file with SAVEPATH, and then restore it from the file with RESTPATH.

The format for SAVEPATH is

```
SAVEPATH [d:][path]filename.ext
```

The format for RESTPATH is similar:

```
RESTPATH [d:][path]filename.ext
```

The drive and path specifications are optional, but you should always use them.

Here's an example of SAVEPATH in action:

```
REM Save current location on disk in the file SAVEPATH.TXT
SAVEPATH C:\SAVEPATH.TXT
CD C:\PROGS\DB
DATAB
REM Return to the starting location listed in C:\SAVEPATH.TXT
RESTPATH C:\SAVEPATH.TXT
```

You might want to tidy up your disk by adding a line to remove the SAVEPATH.TXT file:

```
DEL C:\SAVEPATH.TXT
```

Replaceable Parameters

If a program or DOS command you want in a batch file makes use of filenames or options on the command line, you will need to use *parameters*. A parameter is any program option or variable that makes a program take a specific action. If that seems abstract, consider the following command:

```
edit
```

The command, with no parameters, will probably cause the program named Edit to report that you failed to tell it *what* to edit. Edit might instead offer some sort of window where you can enter a filename or other information. On the other hand, if you add a parameter, Edit will immediately allow you to edit the file you name.

In the command

```
edit this.fil
```

the name of the file you want to edit—THIS.FIL—is the parameter. You can, of course, replace it with the name of any other file you want to edit. For this reason, it's called a *replaceable parameter*.

To make a place for the replaceable parameter in your batch file, you use the symbol, %1. Wherever DOS sees %1, it inserts your replaceable parameter. If you have a batch file, ED.BAT, consisting of

```
REM Run Edit program on any specified file
edit %1
```

and you enter the following command:

```
ed this.fil
```

DOS will substitute THIS.FIL for the replaceable parameter %1. The result will be the same as if you had entered

```
edit this.fil
```

from the keyboard. This may not be very impressive in this simple example, but wait until you start setting up a series of complex options. You might use /e to keep the program from asking if you want an automatic backup file, /co to display color instead of monochrome, and /43 to display 43 lines instead of 25 on your EGA screen. Your simple batch file now looks like this:

```
REM Edit any file, no backup, color display, 43 lines high
edit %1 /e /co /43
```

   Now, when you enter

```
ed this.fil
```

what DOS transmits to your edit program is

```
edit this.fil /e /co /43
```

You've saved a lot of keystrokes. Better yet, you don't have to remember to add /e /co /43 every time you use the edit program. That's the essence of using a batch file to save work.

   Another use is to avoid having to type unfamiliar keys, such as the backslash (\) or pipe (l) symbol. Many people have to hunt and peck for these keys no matter how fast they normally type. The following batch file, DS.BAT, that lets you view your directory with file names sorted in alphabetical order. Note the use of the pipe symbol.

```
REM DS.BAT -- Displays directory in sorted order.
dir | sort
```

This batch file can't limit the display to a file specification, such as *.COM. If you entered

```
DS *.COM
```

you'd still get a list of all the files in the directory. By making a simple change to the command line in DS.BAT, you can get the flexibility you need.

```
REM Son of DS.BAT -- Displays directory in sorted order.
dir %1 | sort
```

Now any file specification will work. In the command

```
DS *.COM
```

the batch language will obligingly replace the %1 with the command line parameter, *.COM.

Batch files look for multiple words (groups of characters separated by spaces or tabs) on the DOS command line when they are invoked. The batch language assigns the words to parameters in the order they appear on the command line. Since the first word is always the name of the batch file, it is assigned to parameter %0. The second word (if any) is assigned to %1, the third to %2, and so on.

DOS batch files will assign up to ten command-line words to parameters %0 through %9, but since %0 is always the name of the batch file, only nine parameters can be added at the command line without using the SHIFT command (described later).

The equivalence operator (= =) lets you compare a parameter to another value. The other value can be another parameter, an environment variable, or normal text. Here are some examples:

```
IF %1 == t ECHO Tom is logging on
```

```
IF %1 == %TMP% ECHO TMP directory in param 1
```

```
IF %1 == %2 ECHO Params 1 and 2 are the same
```

Parameters replace the % signs literally. This makes testing for occurrence of no parameters more guesswork than intuition.

The secret is to "paste" the replaceable parameter to a literal character. If only the literal character survives, you know the parameter is not there. To understand how this works, consider this simple program:

```
REM TEST.BAT -- Try running with and without something after TEST.
ECHO off
IF %1x == x ECHO Missing Parameter.
```

If you run it by entering TEST and nothing else at the command line, it will display the "Missing parameter" message. If you enter TEST and something else, as in

```
TEST BEAT ME
```

the "Missing Parameter" message will not display, because there is indeed a parameter to replace %1.

Parameters give you tremendous control over how a batch file behaves. They are used extensively in the branching batch file programs explored later in this chapter.

The ECHO Command

DOS insists on showing you each line of a batch file before executing it unless you tell it not to. This on-screen display is similar to the phenomenon of an echo, when sound comes back to you. The screen "echoes" what you type or what the computer intends to do. You can control screen echo with the ECHO command.

ECHO comes in three varieties:

```
ECHO ON
ECHO OFF
ECHO [Any text you specify]
```

ON forces each line of the batch file to display what its intentions are before it executes them. OFF suppresses that behavior. [Any text you specify] is a message you want printed. The message can be up to 122 characters long.

If you ran the batch files in this chapter, you were no doubt distracted by the display of each line before it was executed. To disable this display in any batch file, start with ECHO OFF and follow it with CLS. Here's an example:

```
REM Son of DS.BAT redux    Displays directory in sorted order.
ECHO OFF
CLS
dir %1 | sort
```

One irritating problem with this approach is that ECHO OFF itself is displayed until the screen is cleared. If you are using DOS 3.3 or a later version, you can suppress the echo by starting the line with an @ sign, as shown here.

```
REM Son of DS.BAT II    Needs DOS 3.3 or later for the @
@ECHO OFF
CLS
dir %1 | sort
```

When ECHO is OFF, commands will not appear on the screen, but messages from DOS will still be displayed. For example, a batch file containing these lines

```
@ECHO OFF
LLCOOLJ
```

will still display the message "File not found" if you don't have a program named LLCOOLJ.COM, LLCOOLJ.EXE, or LLCOOLJ.BAT in the path.

If the file name of a program you want to execute from a batch file begins with an @ character, you need to precede the filename with an extra @ character. For example, if the filename is @GAME.EXE, the line in the batch file must read

@@GAME

You can still use ECHO when ECHO is off, but it won't echo the line before printing it. The following batch file displays "hello, world" once:

```
ECHO OFF
CLS
ECHO hello, world
```

If the batch file did not include ECHO OFF, the line "ECHO hello, world" would be displayed above "hello, world".

DOS uses the comma, semicolon, and equal sign characters as *delimiters*, or separators between commands and parameters. ECHO treats these three characters as blank spaces. However, percent signs are used by batch files to indicate variable names. You must enter two percent signs in an ECHO command to get one printed. For example,

```
ECHO %%
```

displays

```
%
```

The DOS pipe and redirection symbols (|, <, and >) can be echoed only if they are surrounded by double quotes, as in the following:

```
ECHO "|" is the piping symbol
```

```
ECHO 55 is ">" 54
```

The quotes tell ECHO to print the character instead of performing the operation.

Unquoted redirection symbols can send ECHO output to a file instead of to the screen. For example,

```
ECHO Here I go to a file > FILE.EXT
```

creates a file named FILE.EXT and stores "Here I go to a file" in it. If FILE.EXT already existed, a single > symbol would cause it to be overwritten. Use a double > to add lines to an existing file without overwriting previous entries:

```
ECHO Here I go again >> FILE.EXT
```

Some commands, such as COPY, always display some sort of message. You can suppress display by redirecting the messages from the screen to the NUL device, DOS's never-never land, as in the following example:

```
COPY C:\*.* C:\DOS > NUL
```

If you want to eliminate *all* screen-cluttering messages with one statement, you can redirect everything intended for display to never-never land. Place the line

```
CTTY NUL
```

at the beginning of a batch file and

```
CTTY CON
```

at the end.

Never run a batch file that contains CTTY NUL without also including CTTY CON. The CTTY NUL command effectively disconnects the display *and* the console (keyboard). If a batch file terminates without restoring the console, you'll be sitting there with a blank screen and a dead keyboard. At this point, cold restart is the only solution. Don't use CTTY if you're going to distribute the batch file to users who are running DOS1.X, which only supports CTTY externally and also requires the file CTTY.EXE to run to work correctly.

If you enter ECHO followed by nothing, DOS reports whether ECHO is currently on or off. Since ECHO treats delimiter characters as blanks, any ECHO command followed only by one or more commas, semicolons, or equal signs will report only the on/off status.

You can cause blank lines to be echoed to the screen by echoing certain characters. Unfortunately, the blank-producing characters vary from one version of DOS to another. Version 3.0 and above uses the following characters, with no space between ECHO and the character:

```
ECHO"
ECHO+
ECHO.
ECHO/
```

```
ECHO:
ECHO[
ECHO]
```

With DOS 3.3 or greater, you can also display a blank line by following ECHO with a space and ASCII character 0, 8, or 255. You generate these nonprinting characters by holding down the ALT key and entering 0, 8, or 255 on the numeric keypad. Do not use the row of numbers across the top of the keyboard.

Earlier versions of DOS require the blank-producing characters to immediately follow ECHO, with no space between ECHO and the character. The line must also end with a space, for no discernible reason. DOS 2.X versions will echo blank lines with any of the following ASCII characters followed by a space:

0, 1, 2, 3, 4, 5, 6, 7, 8, 9, 10, 11, 12, 14, 15, 16, 17, 18, 19, 20, 21, 22, 23, 24, 25, 27, 28, 29, 30, 31, 32, 34, 43, 44, 47, 58, 59, 61, 91, 92, 93.

One simple technique works in both DOS 2.X and 3.X: ECHO, the ASCII character 0, and a space, in any order. ASCII 0 is generated by pressing the F7 function key. It appears at the DOS prompt as an @ symbol. Don't use SHIFT-2 to put an @ in a batch file—it's not the same.

ECHO is fine for displaying short prompts or paragraphs, but it is better to use the DOS TYPE command to present a dozen or more lines of information. Since batch files are read one line at a time, a long series of ECHO lines will involve a lot of disk accesses and unnecessary wear and tear on your drive mechanism.

If you have a screenful or more of text to display, save it in an ASCII file. Then use the TYPE command in your batch file to display it. Supplement it with the MORE command to pause the display if the file is more than a screenful long. The following batch file segment turns off ECHO, clears the screen, and displays a file of instructions for DATAB.EXE:

```
@ECHO OFF
CLS
TYPE DATAB.HLP | MORE
```

Omit the @ in versions of DOS prior to 3.3. CLS clears the screen. Only the contents of DATAB.HLP will appear on the screen, and it will start at the top left corner. The first page of text will not scroll up the screen, as it would if it started displaying lower on the screen. The MORE command will temporarily halt the display when it reaches the bottom of the screen. Press ENTER to display more text.

The PAUSE Command

PAUSE can be found one a line either by itself, or with an optional message:

```
PAUSE
```

```
PAUSE Your message here
```

Each causes the message "Strike a key when ready..." to appear. If ECHO is ON and the second form is used, that message is preceded by your own.

Often a batch file should pause to let the user read instructions or take some action. For instance, in the earlier example that uses the MORE command, the last page of DATAB.HLP will not stay on the screen long enough to be read. Another instance is when a user must swap diskettes in the middle of a batch file or decide whether to continue or abort the batch file processing.

The PAUSE command suspends processing until the user signals readiness to continue by pressing any key. Our example display of instructions might read:

```
@ECHO OFF
CLS
TYPE DATAB.HLP | MORE
PAUSE
```

When the last line of DATAB.HLP has been displayed, the user will see

```
Strike a key when ready . . .
```

This DOS prompt is slightly incomplete. If the key struck is CTRL-C or CTRL-BREAK, the batch file will ask, "Terminate batch file (Y/N)?" A more helpful last line of DATAB.HLP would read

```
PAUSE Press Ctrl-C or Ctrl-Break to abort loading of DATAB.
Otherwise,
```

Then, when DB.BAT reaches the PAUSE command, the user will see

```
PAUSE Press Ctrl-C or Ctrl-Break to abort loading of DATAB.  Otherwise,
Strike a key when ready . . .
```

The batch file could also prompt the user to insert a new disk in drive A, turn on the printer, change paper, or perform some other task before the batch file proceeds.

The batch language doesn't offer any other keyboard handling. There's no way, for example, to tell which key the user pressed. A problem is solved by GETKEY.COM on one of the program disks supplied with this book and explained later in this section.

The REM Command

You can insert comments in a batch file to help you remember what the program does when you read it. Preface each comment line with REM, as shown here:

```
SUBST E: .
REM Assigns current directory to virtual drive E:
```

REM comments will not display when ECHO is off. If ECHO is on, the word REM shows on your monitor along with your comments. This is a handy tool if you are a new user or if you want to remind some other user of a particular instruction.

You can also include nonprinting comments by pretending they're labels (which are explained later in this chapter). Interestingly, they are suppressed even with ECHO ON. The following batch file would never print anything:

```
: Even with ECHO ON,
: these lines aren't
: displayed.
```

THE SET COMMAND

SET lets your batch file use the DOS environment as a scratch pad to store variable values created by the batch file. While SET commands are not technically a part of the batch language, they are commonly used in batch files. The SET command has three general forms:

```
SET
SET ENVAR=VALUE
SET ENVAR=
```

If you want to display the contents of the environment, enter SET by itself at the command line. You can create or reassign an environment variable by using the second syntax, SET ENVAR = VALUE. If the specified value doesn't exist, it will be created. You can remove an environment variable and thus free up the space it occupies by using the third syntax, SET ENVAR = .

The DOS path, COMSPEC, and PROMPT environment variables can be set at the DOS command line or in a batch file with or without using the word SET. All other environment variables require the use of the DOS SET command or a special utility. When using the command SET = variable = value, it is critical that no spaces are used before or after the equal sign. SET does not trim leading or trailing spaces, it treats them as characters. The following program will display "Beat me", not "%A%", which you might expect:

```
ECHO OFF
SET A=Beat me
ECHO %A%
```

ENVAR can be any sequence of nonblank characters. For clarity and simplicity, restrict them to letters and numbers. Avoid spaces around the equal sign. They may appear after the first character of VALUE, however. Anywhere ENVAR appears between % signs in the batch file, it will be replaced with VALUE. For example, the following line displays your path:

```
ECHO %PATH%
```

Here's an example of environment variables in action. You may want to return to a particular directory often during a computer session—call it your "home" directory. You could write a batch file called HOME.BAT:

```
REM HOME.BAT -- returns to the most often-used directory.
CD C:\PROGS\DB\DATA
```

This works fine—until you change gears and want the home directory to be C:\PROGS\SS\LOTUS. Then you'll have to edit HOME.BAT. The SET command provides a shortcut that will work wherever you are in DOS. Rewrite HOME.BAT as follows:

```
CD %HOME%
```

Now, from the DOS command line type

```
SET HOME=C:\PROGS\DB\DATA
```

Type the word SET by itself; you may see several other environment variables, but look for HOME = C:\PROGS\DB\DATA.

Now, whenever you invoke HOME.BAT, the % signs surrounding the word HOME tell DOS to look for an environment variable by that name and substitute its value in the batch file. The advantage here is that you can SET HOME without having to load an editor, load a batch file, edit it, save it, and exit the editor.

If you forget the % signs, HOME will be printed literally. The following line would actually try to change to a subdirectory HOME in the current directory:

```
REM Missing the "%" signs
CD HOME
```

Many systems are critically short of environment space, with an average of 33 bytes available. That's because PATH, PROMPT, and COMSPEC often consume most of it right away. You can increase the amount of environment space by tweaking shell parameters, but the procedure requires a reboot and can't be done under batch control. If you plan to distribute your batch file to someone with a system that you can't control, be stingy about environment usage.

The SHIFT Command

You can use up to ten replaceable parameters, %0 through %9. DOS can actually accept many more command-line parameters. Up to ten parameters can be assigned on the DOS command-line, and even more by using the SHIFT command. Ten parameters to %0 through %9 can be assigned at any given moment by a tricky use of the SHIFT and SET commands.

SHIFT deletes %0, the lowest parameter, and moves all higher parameters down one notch—%1 becomes %0, %2 becomes %1, and so on. This makes room for DOS to read more "words" from the command line into the recently vacated parameters. The following is an example of a batch file that reads more than ten command-line parameters:

```
: DELM.BAT -- Deletes all files listed on the command line
:
: Usage:
:
:   DELM file1 file2 ... filen
:
@ECHO OFF
:REPEAT
IF EXIST %1 DEL %1
SHIFT
IF NOT %1. == . GOTO REPEAT
```

The batch file reads in %1 (a filename) and deletes any file by that name. The IF EXIST test avoids having "Invalid number of parameters" appear when no files are listed on the command line. SHIFT clears %1 and bumps the next filename to the right into its place. The last line tests to see if another filename is available to read from the command line. Let's say there is one, called FILE4.TXT. Then the statement

```
IF NOT %1. == .
```

would expand to

```
IF NOT FILE4.TXT. == .
```

This statement is true—FILE4.TXT plus a period is not equal to a period by itself. So, the command GOTO REPEAT is executed, and you loop back to the top of the batch file.

When no more filenames are available from the command line, %1 is nothing after the SHIFT. The IF NOT statement becomes false, and the loop ends.

THE CALL COMMAND

The CALL command executes another batch file. Without it, your program would not continue after running the file in question. Its format is

```
CALL filename
```

A true programming language lets you leave a program, run another and return to the original program. The first program calls the second to perform a task. When the second program ends, control returns to the line following the CALL command in the calling program.

Batch files "implicitly" call other programs all the time. The DB.BAT program, for instance, calls DATAB.EXE, which returns to DB.BAT when you exit DATAB.EXE. Every time a batch file uses a DOS command such as CHKDSK, SUBST, or TYPE, it is calling a program. After that program runs, control returns to the batch file, and the next line executes—unless the called program is a batch file. For example, suppose you have a batch file called CURLY.BAT that looks like this:

```
REM CURLY.BAT
MOE
SHEMP
```

Because of this rule, if MOE and SHEMP are batch files, SHEMP will never run.

The CALL command is used to call other batch files. To solve the problem with CURLY.BAT, use CALL, as follows:

```
REM Son of CURLY.BAT
CALL MOE
SHEMP
```

SHEMP will now run when MOE is finished.

CALL became available beginning with DOS 3.3. An alternative method that works with all versions of DOS starting with 2.0 is COMMAND /C.

```
REM Son of CURLY.BAT revisited -- DOS 2 to 3.2 version
COMMAND /C MOE
SHEMP
```

One shortcoming of this technique is that COMMAND /C costs an additional 3K of memory.

CALL is necessary only if you plan to return to the original batch file after the called program runs. Otherwise, just invoke the called batch file as you normally would at the command line:

```
REM READ.BAT
SUBST E: C:\PROGS\DB
SUBST F: .
E:
SET DBDIR=%1
DATAB %DBDIR%
C:
SUBST E: /D
SUBST F: /D
SET DBDIR=
READ16
```

Be careful about calling batch files this way. If you moved the batch file up just a couple of lines:

```
READ16
C:
SUBST E: /D
SUBST F: /D
SET DBDIR=
```

only the batch file READ16 would execute. Because you didn't use CALL or COMMAND /C or strategically place the command in the batch file, you'd never get back to drive C, virtual drives E and F would not be cleared, and there would be a useless environment variable named DBDIR.

Passing Parameters Between Programs

You can save disk space by using one batch file as a called subroutine in other batch files. The subroutine need not be duplicated in every batch file that uses it. The batch file can just call it when needed and return to the main program. The main program can generate parameters (actual values, not variable names) and pass them to the subroutine for processing. The subroutine can store its results in an environment variable that the main program can use.

It's easy to pass parameters to a subroutine batch file: just include the parameters on the line that calls the subroutine, as in the following example:

```
CALL SUBROUT GREEN RED BL26-UE
```

The subroutine stores parameters passed in this way in its replaceable parameter variable names (%1, %2, %3, and so on), following the same rules for parameters entered on the DOS command line. You can use SHIFT in the subroutine to pass more than nine parameters.

With the initial parameters now in the subroutine, how can you get the results back to the main batch file? You can't just call the program that called the subroutine—that would load a new copy of the main program instead of picking up where you left off. What to do?

Suppose SUBROUT.BAT compares the passed parameters to a table of light-wave frequencies and determines GREEN's wavelength is 1000, RED's is 900, and BL26-UE's is 1500. It could store these results in environment variables before returning to the main program. Environment variables are independent of batch files and can be read by any batch file. SUBROUT.BAT could read like this:

```
SET COLOR1=1000
SET COLOR2=900
SET COLOR3=1500
```

When you return to the main program, you will see the values calculated by SUBROUT.BAT from the environment variables:

```
ECHO The wavelength of GREEN is %COLOR1%
ECHO The wavelength of RED is %COLOR2%
ECHO The wavelength of BL26-UE is %COLOR3%
```

CONDITIONAL PROCESSING

So far, you've seen only *linear processing* in your practice batch files. In linear processing, each batch file steps through every line from start to finish. But real programs often must decide which of their parts should be executed and which ignored. The programs base their decisions on user input or calculated conditions. A program should also be able to execute a command or set of commands several times and know when to stop looping. This "intelligence" is the most useful aspect of a well-designed program. Now you will see how batch files implement it.

The GOTO Command and Labels

The GOTO statement skips to a specific line in a batch file. That line must have a label corresponding to the destination given in the GOTO statement. A batch file recognizes labels by the colons that start them. Labels are not case sensitive; that is, :END would work just as well as :end. DOS 3.X does not mind if the label is indented, which makes reading the batch file a bit easier for the programmer. However, earlier versions of DOS require the label to start at the far-left column.

The following example prints the same message until you press CTRL-BREAK:

```
REM TEST.BAT     Loops endlessly until the user presses Ctrl-Break.
:Top
PAUSE Press Ctrl-Break, then Y to stop.  To redisplay this message,
GOTO TOP
```

In a more realistic example, BU.BAT copies selected files (*.DOC and *.TXT) to another drive, which must be specified on the command line. It displays an error message if the user omits the drive specification.

```
: BU.BAT    Backs up *.DOC and *.TXT to the drive specified in %1.
:           If %1 isn't given or is not a valid drive, it prints
:           an error message and quits.
ECHO OFF
CLS

REM If no parameter, issue error message and quit.
IF %1. == . GOTO BadParam

IF NOT EXIST %1\*.* GOTO BadParam
```

```
REM If here, there was at least one file param
COPY *.DOC %1
COPY *.TXT %1

REM Skip error message & go to end of file.
GOTO END

:BadParam
ECHO Missing or bad drive specification.
ECHO Example:  BU A:

:end
```

One little-known aspect of GOTO is that the batch interpreter always begins at line 1 when it searches for a target label. It has no "memory" of where a previously encountered label appeared. In the following example, when the label L3 is encountered, the batch file begins searching from line 1, even though it already encountered the label L1 on line 3. Likewise, the line following label L4 has no recollection that L3 is just three lines above.

```
:Top
GOTO L4
:L1
PAUSE Got here, finally!
GOTO Top
:L3
GOTO L1
:L4
GOTO L3
```

If speed is a consideration, put frequently used labels as close to the top of the file as possible.

A label can be any length you want, though DOS will read only the first eight characters. This has two consequences. First, if you use labels longer than eight characters, be careful not to use the same first eight characters in two labels. If you do, DOS will always read only the first label and stop there. For example, DOS would consider the following two labels equivalent because it would read only ":ThisIsLa":

```
:ThisIsLabel1

:ThisIsLabel2
```

If you used both labels in the same batch file, DOS would never find the second one.

Second, you can use long labels to put comments inside your batch file. Since DOS never displays or processes a label, you have a "free" line—so long as the first eight characters aren't the same as those in another label in the batch file. One way to make sure you don't confuse DOS is to begin each "label comment" with a "tag character," such as a hyphen, following the colon.

The FOR Command

FOR is one of DOS's most powerful and underutilized commands. It lets you perform a command or a set of commands on a set of files. Its format is

```
FOR %%c IN (<set>) DO <command>
```

where c is any printable character except numbers; letters are traditionally used. <set> is a list that may contain one or more sequences of nonblank characters (usually filenames or wildcard specifications) separated by spaces, commas, or semicolons. Examples are

```
*.txt
*.txt *.doc
%1 %2 ??.EXE pokey and gumby
```

FOR steps through each of the items in <set>, replaces %%c with the text of the item, and performs <command>. If %%c appears anywhere in <command> it too is replaced with the current item in the file list.

One of FOR's most useful applications is to give commands that don't natively process wildcard specifications the ability to do just that. For example, you can't use the TYPE command with a wildcard specification, because TYPE works only with a single, unambiguous filename.

```
REM Doesn't work:
TYPE *.BAT
```

The following short batch program T.BAT, lets you do it:

```
REM T.BAT -- Lets you apply wildcard specifications to the TYPE command
FOR %%a IN (%1) DO type %%a
```

DOS commands can also be used as variables in FOR statements. One of the worst chores in DOS is moving files from one directory to another. Normally, you must do double work: copy a file, delete the file, copy a file, delete the file, ... The following batch file makes such moves easy:

```
FOR %%A IN (COPY DEL) DO %%A %1
```

Name the batch file MOVE.BAT. To use this batch file, at the command line, type the following: MOVE C:*.BAK. MOVE.BAT first copies a file to a new location and then deletes it from its original location. (You could do the same thing at the DOS command line, using %A instead of %%A.)

You can't nest FOR loops. A statement such as

```
FOR %%A IN (D:\ D:\DOS) DO FOR %%B IN (*.COM) DO COPY %%A %%B
```

will result in the error message "FOR cannot be nested." But you can fool DOS by loading a second copy of COMMAND.COM just before executing the nested FOR statement. The following command will copy and delete all BAK files in D:\ and then do the same in D:\DOS.

```
FOR %%A IN (D:\ D:\DOS) DO COMMAND/C FOR %%B IN (*.BAK) DO COPY
%%A %%B
```

This is one of the rare occasions when it is better to use COMMAND /C instead of CALL.

Here's a program written using TEMPLATE.BAT, a template batch program presented later in the chapter. Called RUNALL, it lets you apply wildcards to programs that ordinarily wouldn't allow them.

For example, you can't issue the following command to Microsoft Word:

```
WORD *.DOC
```

Word won't accept a wildcard in a file specification. However, you can use RUNALL to make it do just that:

```
RUNALL WORD *.DOC
```

You can also use RUNALL with the TYPE command:

```
RUNALL TYPE *.TXT
```

or with any other program.

```
ECHO OFF
CLS
REM RUNALL.BAT     Runs %1, which is a program name, on each file
REM                     in the specification %2.
REM
REM If %1 is missing, none of the required parameters is available.
IF %1. == . GOTO NoParam1

REM If %2 is missing, it means there's only one of the two
REM required parameters.
IF %2. == . GOTO NoParam2

GOTO Okay

REM This message displays when the filename is entered at the DOS
REM command line with no parameters.
:NoParam1
ECHO Missing both parameters (2 are required).
REM Print the rest of the help screen.
GOTO Help

REM This message displays when the filename entered at the DOS
command line is missing its second parameter.
:NoParam2
ECHO Missing the second parameter (2 are required), which must be
ECHO an existing directory.
REM Print the rest of the help screen.
GOTO Help

:NoDir
ECHO No file matches the specification "%2".
GOTO Help

:Okay
REM There are indeed 2 parameters.
```

```
REM Check for Param 2, which is probably a filespec
REM (it could be a single file).
IF EXIST %2 GOTO Success

REM The target filespec doesn't exist.
GOTO NoDir

:Success
REM This is where the action is.  Put your code here.
FOR %%r IN (%2 %3 %4 %5 %6 %7 %8 %9) DO %1 %%r
GOTO End

:Help
ECHO.
ECHO Correct usage:
ECHO.
ECHO    RUNALL program filespec.ext
ECHO.
ECHO Where program is an .EXE or .COM program and filespec.ext
ECHO represents a wildcard specification such as *.DOC.
ECHO.
ECHO Example 1:
ECHO.
ECHO    RUNALL WORD *.DOC
ECHO.
ECHO Example 2. You can even use several wildcards:
ECHO.
ECHO    RUNALL WORD *.DOC  *.ACT  *.DVO  *.RAK
ECHO.
ECHO RUNALL lets you run a program using a filespec such as *.DOC for the
ECHO second parameter, even if the program doesn't support such behavior.
ECHO.

:End
REM End of RUNALL.BAT listing.
```

IF Tests

The IF statement tests a condition and continues execution only if the condition is true. It has the following formats:

```
IF [NOT] EXIST <filename> <command>
```

```
IF [NOT] <string1> == <string2> <command>

IF [NOT] ERRORLEVEL <number> <command>
```

where [NOT] is an optional NOT, <number> is a number from 0 to 255, and <command> is any DOS statement or batch command. To determine whether a file is on the disk, use EXIST. For example, the following program runs DATAB.EXE only if WORK.DBF is in the current directory. If not, it prints an error message.

```
IF EXIST WORK.DBF DATAB WORK.DBF
IF NOT EXIST WORK.DBF ECHO Database WORK.DBF not found!
```

Using EXIST to determine whether a directory is available is a bit more opaque. If you know that the directory contains at least one file, the test *.* in that directory will succeed. This test would fail in empty subdirectories. You must do an explicit check for any files in the subdirectory. Failing that, you must try to create a dummy file in the directory and then test for that file's existence. If it's there, the directory is valid.

Why not just use MD to create the directory? First of all, in rare cases there may be no disk space available, and even an empty directory hogs 2048 bytes. Second, the MD may be performed on a network volume where the disk-write privileges required to create a directory may not be available.

Keep in mind that the file you create via redirection should be given a name that would not otherwise be used.

```
:TESTDIR.BAT     Demo batch program to test if %1 is a valid
:                directory.  Try creating the directory
:                \dos\tmp and running this program by
:                entering:
:
:                testdir \dos\tmp
:
:                then remove the directory and run it again
ECHO off
CLS

REM Test command line has a parameter
IF %1.==. GOTO END              [Terminate if no parameter given]

REM First, let's check if the drive is ready
```

```
c:\dvorak\fready c:
IF NOT ERRORLEVEL 1 GOTO bad_drive

REM Now let's check if the root directory for files to
REM determine if the drive is empty.

IF NOT EXIST C:\*.* GOTO empty_drive

REM Now let's check if the directory \dos\tmp exists
REM (This test only works if the directory isn't empty)

IF EXISTS C:%1\*.* GOTO valid_dir

REM To see if the directory is valid but empty
REM try the following

ECHO Checking for %1 Directory >%1\test.$$$
IF EXISTS C:\%1\test.$$$ goto empty_dir
goto invalid_dir

:empty_drive
ECHO Drive C: doesn't have any files or subdirectories
goto end

:valid_dir
ECHO %1 is a valid subdirectory with files in it
goto end

:empty_dir
DEL %1\test.$$$
ECHO %1 is a valid subdirectory but is empty
goto end

:bad_drive

ECHO Drive C: is invalid or not ready
goto end
:end
```

Use IF <string1> = = <string2> for comparisons inside batch files. Its use has been illustrated many times in this chapter already, but one aspect of its use bears mention: If either string contains DOS variables, such as replaceable parameters (for example, %1 and %2), or environment variables, they will be replaced with the expected values. In the following example, VIEW runs only if ACCOUNT.WK1 is in the current directory:

```
SET WKS=WK1
IF EXIST ACCOUNT.%WKS% VIEW ACCOUNT.%WKS%
```

There is one more very powerful variation on IF: IF ERRORLEVEL. DOS commands such as FORMAT, RESTORE, BACKUP, KEYB, and RE-PLACE perform their tasks and pass a number back to DOS indicating whether the task was completely successful, partially successful, or interrupted. These numbers are called *exit* (or *return*) *codes.* The IF ERROR-LEVEL test can read exit codes and execute appropriate commands.

The ERRORLEVEL test takes the form:

```
IF ERRORLEVEL <number> <command>
```

where < number > is an exit code from 0 to 255 and < command > is the action to be taken if the exit code tested is equal to or greater than < number >.

You can pinpoint a particular value by using IF NOT ERRORLEVEL for the number plus 1. For example:

```
IF ERRORLEVEL 27 IF NOT ERRORLEVEL 28 <command>
```

will execute the command only if the exit code tested is exactly 27. If the exit code is less than 27, the first IF statement is false; the batch file skips the second IF statement and the command and moves on to the next line. If the exit code is 27 or greater, it passes on to the second IF statement. The word NOT in the second IF statement reverses the test. The batch file skips the rest of the line if the exit code is equal to or greater than 28. What's left to trigger the command? Only 27!

Batch files can't set ERRORLEVEL; they can only act on it. COM and EXE files can set ERRORLEVEL. This opens the door to user-written programs that set ERRORLEVEL—a seemingly minor ability that can make a world of difference in your batch programs.

GETKEY.COM on your program disk translates keystrokes into exit codes. GETKEY simply reads a character from the keyboard and returns its ASCII code to DOS, allowing it to be read by IF ERRORLEVEL. You can use GETKEY.COM and IF ERRORLEVEL in a batch file to see which single-digit number the user has pressed and execute a corresponding action. Create a batch file named MENU.BAT.

The batch file calls could be replaced with the actual commands to execute each program (for example, C:\PROGS\DB\DATAB), eliminating the need for lots of little batch files. You could combine all those little files into this MENU.BAT file, label each segment, and use GOTO statements in place of calls. Here is how it would look:

```
@ECHO OFF
:TOP
CLS
ECHO Press a number to run a program
REM Insert a blank line
ECHO.
ECHO 1.   Word Processor
ECHO 2.   Data Base
ECHO 3.   Spreadsheet
ECHO 4.   Communications
ECHO 5.   Graphics
ECHO 6.   Quit this Menu
GETKEY
IF ERRORLEVEL 55 GOTO TOP
IF ERRORLEVEL 54 GOTO WP
IF ERRORLEVEL 53 GOTO DB
IF ERRORLEVEL 52 GOTO SS
IF ERRORLEVEL 51 GOTO CM
IF ERRORLEVEL 50 GOTO GR
IF ERRORLEVEL 49 GOTO END
IF ERRORLEVEL 0  GOTO TOP
:WP_run_word_processor
    SUBST E: C:\PROGS\WP
    REM "Save" our current path setting (see SUBST stunt above)
    CD E:
    WP.EXE
    CD C:
    SUBST E: /D
    GOTO TOP
:DB_run_data_base
    SUBST E: C:\PROGS\DB
    CD E:
    DATAB.EXE
    CD C:
```

```
    SUBST E: /D
    GOTO TOP
    .
    .
    .
    (Similar routines for SS, CM, & GR)
:END
```

When you run this batch file, you will always return to a fresh screen and menu when you exit any of the five programs. When you select 6 to exit the MENU.BAT program, you will return to the DOS prompt.

Such all-in-one batch files save disk space. Each of the subroutines in MENU.BAT takes up only 60 or so bytes, but DOS allocates an entire 4,096-byte block to each file anyway! (Your actual mileage may vary. The number depends on whether it's a hard disk, which version of DOS it was formatted under, and other factors. The number is typically 2 to 4K and is never less than 512 bytes.) You can verify this absurdity by running DIR and noting the free space on your disk. Now, delete a small batch file and run DIR again. See the difference?

BATCH FILE FORMATTING

If you keep the following basic formatting guidelines in mind, you'll find that you have neater, more easily understood batch files. You can pat yourself on the back as you find yourself making changes to the programs you're writing now.

1. Don't use all uppercase letters when you write your batch files. Text in all capitals is hard to read. If you uppercase keywords (ECHO, for example) and use mixed or lowercase for everything else, it will be easier to correct typing errors or edit a file later. Compare these examples:

Example 1—Good usage

```
echo off
if %1. == . goto bad_item
type %1
goto end
:bad_item
echo Please tell me what file you want to see.^G^G
:end
```

Example 2—Better usage

```
ECHO off
IF %1. == . GOTO bad_item
TYPE %1
GOTO end
:bad_item
ECHO Please tell me what file you want to see.^G^G
:end
```

Example 3—Bad usage

```
ECHO OFF
IF %1. == . GOTO BAD_ITEM
TYPE %1
GOTO END
:BAD_ITEM
ECHO PLEASE TELL ME WHAT FILE YOU WANT TO SEE.^G^G
:END
```

2. Indentation and blank lines help emphasize your program's structure. Example 1a is OK, but you can make it more understandable by including either indentation or blank lines. Here are some examples:

Example 2a.

```
echo off
if %1. == . goto bad_item
type %1
goto end

 :bad_item
echo Please tell me what file you want to see.^G^G

 :end
```

Example 2b.

```
    echo off
    if %1. == . goto bad_item
    type %1
    goto end
:bad_item
    echo Please tell me what file you want to see.^G^G
:end
```

In example 2a, the batch file commands are separated from the error message by blank lines. This helps you quickly identify different parts of the program. The indentation used in the second example has the same effect. It's all a matter of preference. If you place all your labels in the left hand margin and indent each command, you can easily locate all program labels. Since each label usually indicates the beginning of a new part of the program, you can easily see the program's structure. The point is to be consistent.

3. Use descriptive labels for GOTO statements. They help to explain the flow of the program. Examples 1 and 2 use proper labels. However, consider how difficult it would be to understand a long program if it used abbreviated labels. Here's a short example:

```
    echo off
    if %1. == . goto bi
    type %1
    goto e

    :bi
    echo Please tell me what file you want to see.^G^G
    :e
```

The labels "bi" and "e" don't describe what that part of the program does. It's much better to use "bad_item" and "end" instead. Remember that GOTO labels are significant only to eight characters. Disk_Missing_A and Disk_Missing_B would be considered identical.

BATCH FILE STRUCTURE

The following simple procedures will help ensure that all your batch files will be structured the same way:

1. Begin all batch files with ECHO OFF. If you see each command before it's executed, your screen will be cluttered. You can use @ECHO OFF with newer versions of DOS (3.3 and later). If you are unsure which version will be used, stick with the ECHO OFF command. It's also common to follow ECHO OFF with CLS to be sure you start with a clean screen.

2. Test to be sure you have entered enough parameters for the batch file. This is important if you were not the originator of the batch file. Be sure every parameter that requires a value has one. If your batch file is supposed to have three parameters passed to it, it should look like this:

```
echo off
if %1. == . goto MissingPram
if %2. == . goto MissingPram
if %3. == . goto MissingPram
 ...
:MissingPram
echo Parameters missing.  The correct format is:
 ...
```

3. Test all parameters for validity, if possible. To test a filename's validity, use a statement such as "if not exist %1 goto bad_name". If the parameter is not valid, the program will branch to the label ":bad_name". Instructions following this label should tell you that you didn't enter the correct name of a file. If it does find a file with that name, the batch file continues.

To test the validity of an unnamed path, you need to follow three steps:

1. Check using the test "*.*", as in the following example from TEM-PLATE.BAT (a procedure that requires at least one file in the directory):

```
IF EXIST %2\*.* GOTO Success
```

2. Check for the root directory in a separate test:

```
IF %2 == \ GOTO Success
```

3. Finally, try copying a dummy file into the directory. This is necessary if you're not sure there's at least one file in the target directory.

```
REM Program fragment from TEMPLATE.BAT to check for the
REM existence of a directory with 0 files in it.
ECHO Checking for directory > %2\TMP.$$$
REM See if the junk file was copied successfully.
IF EXIST %2\TMP.$$$ GOTO DirExists
REM The target directory doesn't exist.  Remove the junk
REM file, which got created in the current directory.
DEL TMP.$$$
GOTO NoDir
```

It is not possible to test for every possible valid or invalid response in batch files. However, you should trap as many errors for the user as possible. Batch file compilers and language extenders are the only way to get airtight error checking.

4. Include all the "meat" of the batch file.

5. Follow the main command with any error messages and terminating messages the batch file generates or might generate.

6. Finally, include a label such as :end for the end of the batch file. That way, you can stop the batch file at any point in your program by including a GOTO END command line.

READ.ME

A Model Batch File: TEMPLATE.BAT

The text covers six basic points for building a good batch file. The following batch file includes examples of all six points. It is heavily "remindered," meaning it includes many REM lines to help you track your way through the program. Note that power users often use a colon rather than REM. In a line that begins with a colon, DOS reads the first eight characters as a label and does not process the line. This can be marginally faster than using REM lines the whole way.

———— █ **READ.ME** █ ————

A Model Batch File: TEMPLATE.BAT (*continued*)

This batch file, called TEMPLATE.BAT, assumes the first parameter is a file,and the second parameter is a directory.

```
ECHO OFF
CLS
REM TEMPLATE.BAT    Template batch file that does the following:
REM                 1. Checks for missing command line parameters
REM                 2. Ensures that the first parameter (%1) is
REM                    an existing file
REM                 3. Ensures that the second parameter (%2) is
REM                    an existing directory
REM                 4. Displays a help screen if the command line
REM                    is in error
REM
REM                 Each possible error condition displays a unique
REM                 error message, then a common help screen listing
REM                 a formal syntax diagram, an explanation of the
REM                 program's purpose, and examples of correct syntax.
REM If %1 is missing, none of the required parameters is available.
 IF %1. == . GOTO NoParam1

REM If %2 is missing, it means there's only one of the two
REM required parameters.
 IF %2. == . GOTO NoParam2

REM More than 2 parameters also constitutes an error.
 IF NOT %3. == . GOTO TooMany

REM At this point, we know that there are exactly 2 command line
REM parameters.  Now check for validity.
 GOTO Okay

REM This message displays when the filename is entered at the DOS
REM command line with no parameters.
 :NoParam1
ECHO Missing both parameters (2 are required).
REM Print the rest of the help screen.
 GOTO Help
```

READ.ME

A Model Batch File: TEMPLATE.BAT (*continued*)

```
REM This message displays when the filename entered at the DOS
REM command line is missing its second parameter.
:NoParam2
ECHO Missing the second parameter (2 are required), which must be
ECHO an existing directory.
REM Print the rest of the help screen.
GOTO Help


:TooMany
ECHO Too many parameters (only 2 are required).
REM Print the rest of the help screen.
GOTO Help


:NoFile
ECHO The file named "%1" does not exist.
REM Print the rest of the help screen.
GOTO Help


:NoDir
ECHO The directory "%2" does not exist.
GOTO Help


:Okay
REM There are indeed 2 parameters.  Ensure they both exist.  Param 1
REM is a filename, and that's easy--just use IF EXIST.  Param 2 is
REM a directory, however, and we have to employ two methods to make
REM sure it's done correctly.
IF NOT EXIST %1 GOTO NoFile


REM The check for Param 2, which must be a directory, is a bit trickier.
REM If we know there's at least 1 file in the directory (if it's there
REM at all), the first test will suffice.  If not, resort to the
REM trickery of redirecting to a dummy file in the target directory and
REM checking for that file's existence.
IF EXIST %2\*.* GOTO Success
```

A Model Batch File: TEMPLATE.BAT (*continued*)

```
REM Just in case the check was for the root directory, use a
REM special case.
IF %2 == \ GOTO Success

REM The first two tests for the directory didn't work.  Try
REM shenanigans this time by creating a junk file.
ECHO Checking for directory > %2\TMP.$$$

REM See if the junk file was copied successfully.
IF EXIST %2\TMP.$$$ GOTO DirExists
REM The target directory doesn't exist.  Remove the junk file,
REM which got created in the current directory.
DEL TMP.$$$
GOTO NoDir

:DirExists
REM We found the target directory.  Now remove the junk file
REM before proceeding.
DEL %2\TMP.$$$
GOTO Success

:Success
REM This is where the action is.  Put your code here.
PAUSE All tests are positive.  Plug in your own program here.
GOTO End

:Help
ECHO.
ECHO Correct usage:
ECHO.
ECHO    TEMPLATE filename.ext dir
ECHO.
ECHO Where filename.ext is valid and dir is an existing directory.
ECHO.
ECHO Example:
ECHO.
```

READ.ME

A Model Batch File: TEMPLATE.BAT (*continued*)

```
ECHO    TEMPLATE autoexec.bat  c:\dos
ECHO.
ECHO TEMPLATE is a shell batch file you can cannibalize for your
ECHO own use.  It contains parameter checks, a check for a valid
ECHO directory, and this help screen.
ECHO.

:End
```

BATCH FILE TECHNIQUES

Here are some general rules for designing batch files:

- Try to catch errors before the batch file interpreter does. Use TEM-PLATE.BAT or something similar as a starting point—there's no need to reinvent the wheel. Your help screen should explain, at a minimum, what the program does, what the correct syntax is, and what it will do.

- Explain what's happening while a program is running. If it entails a two-hour print job, the user should know it. The message "Now printing . . ." isn't enough.

- Comment your programs thoroughly. No matter how obvious it seems when you write it, the purpose of a complex batch file will elude you when you look at it a week later. It's a rule of nature.

- Erase any temporary environment variables the batch file created. Environment space is usually scarce.

BATCH FILE PITFALLS

Here are some common batch file pitfalls to watch out for:

1. Don't change disks while a batch file is running. Suppose you start a batch file on a disk in drive A and then, while the batch file is running, you replace the disk. You'll get the ominous "Batch file missing" message, and the batch program will quit unceremoniously.

You have two choices. One, you can copy the batch file to every disk you plan to use. That way, no matter what disk you use, the computer can find the batch file it needs. However, for this to work, every copy of the batch file must be identical.

Two, if you know the computer you'll be working on has a hard disk, you can use the "double-layered" batch file technique. Make a batch file you want to use, and then make a copy of it with another filename. Set up this second file to do two things: copy the batch file you want to use to the hard disk, and run it from the hard disk. Here's an example:

```
copy resume.bat c:\resume.bat
c:\resume
```

This way, you can change disks in your floppy drive without problems. Be certain the target drive is available, however, or this procedure won't work.

2. Multiple batch files can cause problems. For instance, you would expect the following batch file to run the programs named TEST1, TEST2, and TEST3 in that order:

```
TEST1
TEST2
TEST3
```

However, problems can arise if TEST2 is a batch file rather than a COM or EXE program file. TEST1 will run as usual. The computer will then execute TEST2 as expected, but it will stop after TEST2. TEST3 will never be executed. This is an example of what can happen when running batch files within batch files. This is an annoying distraction in dealing with batch files. When one batch file executes another batch file, the first batch file aborts execution at that point so that the second batch file can run.

Again you have two choices. The first is a bug fix introduced into DOS that allows you to work around this problem. If you use CALL TEST2 on a line rather than TEST2, the original batch file will not abort execution. Instead, it will execute TEST2.BAT and then return to execute TEST3. This is exactly what you want to happen.

This CALL statement is available only in DOS 3.3 and higher. If you have an older version, you will need to use the "interrupt-and-resume" method. In this method, your main batch file calls the secondary batch file with a single parameter. Before the second batch file finishes, you include a statement to restart the main batch file along with the parameter that was passed to the secondary batch file. Next, you return to the beginning of the main batch file and test for the secondary parameters. If you find any of them, you go to the statement in your program just following the one that started the secondary batch file with that same parameter.

This is confusing to explain, but it's a lot easier to visualize with the following example, MAIN.BAT:

```
ECHO off
IF %1 == call1 GOTO call1
IF %1 == call2 GOTO call2
ECHO This is line 1.
second call1

:call1
ECHO This is line 3.
third call2

:call2
ECHO This is line 5.

This is second.bat:

ECHO This is line 2.
main %1

This is third.bat:

ECHO This is line 3.
main %1
```

Here's what happens:
When you execute MAIN.BAT, it runs down to the line containing

"second". This executes SECOND.BAT, which interrupts MAIN.BAT. SEC-OND.BAT displays line 2 and then restarts MAIN.BAT with parameter call1, which MAIN.BAT passed to it.

When MAIN.BAT is restarted (interrupting SECOND.BAT), the batch file goes to the label call1 and displays line 3. The interrupt-and-resume process is repeated for the batch file named THIRD.BAT. This displays lines 1 through 5 on your screen in the proper order.

3. AUTOEXEC.BAT does not have any parameters. As hard as you may try, you can't configure AUTOEXEC.BAT for more than one setup at a time. A rather tricky fix to this is described later, but it's a shame DOS assumes all programs use exactly the same setup. It isn't always the case, and there's no way to pass AUTOEXEC.BAT a parameter that tells it how to configure the computer. For example, one program might work best with a disk cache, and another might not. It would be simple if you could write

```
IF %1 == 1 cache
```

to load the disk cache if you chose setup configuration number one. Unfortunately, it can't happen this way. However, auxiliary programs can help with reading keyboard input. A batch file compiler can also help here.

4. Running batch files from floppy disks can be slow. Floppy disks are ordinarily slower than hard disks, but running a batch file from a floppy disk seems to magnify how slow they are. This is especially true if you are using GOTO statements and your batch file is long.

Why? Each statement in your batch file must be read from disk before being executed. To execute a GOTO statement, the computer searches the batch file from the beginning until it finds the proper label. If your batch file is long and you use a lot of GOTO statements, the batch files can be slow, *slow*, ***slow***.

You can take measures to make your life easier if you must use floppy disks when running your batch files:

- Put frequently used labels near the beginning of the file.

- Replace REMs with colons, making them dummy labels. (Labels are never echoed.)

- Shorten your PATH statement and specify a program's full path in a batch file, as in the following example.

```
REM Only works under DOS 3 and beyond.
C:\ACCOUNT\GL
```

ECHO Quirks

1. You want your batch files to be neat and uncluttered, meaning you want blank lines. To display a blank line in DOS versions 3.0 and higher, you need to use "ECHO.". However, for earlier versions you need to use "echo" without the period. This is quite a nuisance, since you may not know ahead of time what version of DOS a computer will be using.

If your word processor or editor will let you include low-level ASCII characters in a file, you can include a control-L character (or the ASCII ^L line-feed value of 12) at the end of the line in an ECHO statement where you want a blank line. This will place a blank line in the output for all versions of DOS. Be sure to include a line-feed character *only:* If you also include the carriage return, DOS will consider the combination to be a blank line in your batch file and will ignore it.

2. If you end up with displayed text in your ECHO statement longer than 127 bytes, your computer will stop dead. This can occur if you are using command line parameters or environment variables. Once this happens, all you can do is restart your computer.

3. Depending on what version of DOS you have, leading spaces before the text in an ECHO statement are either displayed or ignored. For example, consider the following simple program:

```
echo Line 1.
echo  Line 2.
echo   Line 3.
```

This will display on your screen either as

```
Line 1.
Line 2.
Line 3.
```

or as

```
   Line 1.
Line 2.
Line 3.
```

Early versions of DOS ignore the leading spaces, while later versions of DOS include them. This can make it hard to format your screen if you rely on leading spaces to place things where you want them.

More Pitfalls

1. When you run a program in DOS, DOS automatically moves the cursor down an extra line when the program is done. In DOS terms, it displays an extra carriage return and line feed. DOS does not do this when a batch file is finished running. While this is ordinarily not a problem, it can ruin a carefully planned screen display. It can also be a problem when you run a program from a batch file that does not end its last displayed line with a carriage return and line feed.

For example, many users have made batch files like

```
format a:
```

In DOS 4.0, the FORMAT command does not end the final line it displays with a carriage return and line feed. When running FORMAT from DOS, you don't notice this error because DOS adds an extra line. However, when you run FORMAT.BAT, the DOS prompt is placed on the same line as the last line of text displayed by the FORMAT command. This makes the screen display confusing. Here is what you see if you use the DOS FORMAT command:

```
Format another (Y/N)? n
C:\> _
```

Here is what you see if you use FORMAT.BAT:

```
C:\> _ another (Y/N)? n
```

This is terrible screen formatting and quite confusing. You can avoid this problem by adding "ECHO." to your batch files after running troublesome programs such as FORMAT.

2. Sometimes you need to read keyboard input for something other than selecting menu choices. Batch language doesn't have any native ability to accept keyboard input, but you can fake it. Here is a technique that allows you to read keyboard input.

First, you need to create a text file called SETTEMP.TXT, consisting of only the following text with no line feed after it:

```
SET TEMP=
```

Create it by entering the following at the DOS prompt:

```
copy con settemp.txt
SET TEMP=^Z
```

Don't press ENTER at the end of the second line until you have pressed F6 to insert the ^Z character. Ensure this file is in the same directory as the batch file. If it isn't, move it.

In the batch file, you use the command COPY CON TEMP to read keyboard input into a file named TEMP. Since COPY CON terminates input with F6, you need to be sure the batch file user knows this.

You now have what you want in a file named TEMP. This is important information that belongs in your batch file. To do this, create the file SETTEMP.BAT by pasting TEMP onto the end of SETTEMP.TXT and copying the result to SETTEMP.BAT. The batch program can then run the file with call (available only in DOS 3.3 and later versions). Here is the whole picture:

```
ECHO off
REM SETNAME.BAT     Accepts the user's name from the keyboard
REM                 and sets the environment variable TEMP to
REM                 that name.
REM
```

```
REM Make sure you've created a file called SETTEMP.TXT containing
REM only the text
REM    SET TEMP=
REM with no line feed after it.

ECHO Please type your name, then press F6, and then press ENTER.
REM Get the user's name from the keyboard.
copy con temp

REM Concatenate files to produce SETTEMP.BAT.
copy settemp.txt + temp SETTEMP.BAT
del temp
ECHO Thank you.  The environment variable TEMP has been set to
ECHO your name.  Here it is:
call settemp
ECHO %temp%
```

Keyboard Redirection

Batch files can't intercept keyboard input and replace keystrokes that you would ordinarily have to type in. But you can fake it using redirection as the program uses DOS for keyboard input. Here, for example, is the skeleton of a program that deletes a subdirectory on drive A. Whereas deleting a subdirectory normally requires three steps (enter DEL *directory name**.* at the DOS prompt, enter a confirming y and a return, enter RD *directory name*) you can reduce it to one keystroke using this batch file.

First, create a file called YES.TXT containing the letter y and at least one blank line following it. Your screen should look like this:

```
C:\>copy con yes.txt
y
^Z
```

The ^Z means you pressed F6.

Now create the following file named RMDEL.BAT in the same directory:

```
REM RMDEL.BAT -- Removes a directory and all its files in one fell swoop.
```

```
REM
ECHO OFF
PAUSE About to wipe out the directory A:\%1.  Press Ctrl-Break to stop.
DEL A:\%1 < yes.txt
rd A:\%1
```

RMDEL is limited in that it can work only on drive A. This ensures that casual readers can't access this program and wipe out a huge subdirectory on their hard disks. You can, however, alter it easily enough.

BATCH FILE ENHANCERS

A batch file enhancer is a program used only within batch files. Its primary purpose is to add to batch file programs capabilities that are inconvenient or impossible with DOS. These programs can be simple or elaborate. They are available both from public domain sources and as commercial software.

The simplest batch file enhancement program would be one such as BEEP.COM. Its only function is to beep once. It was made to allow programmers to include beeps in their batch files if their editors do not support adding ^G. Here is how it would be used:

```
echo That file does not exist.  Please use a file that exists.
 beep
 beep
```

This is equivalent to the following:

```
echo That file does not exist.  Please use a file that exists.^G^G
```

BEEP is a simple program. Many other enhancement programs allow you to add keyboard input, screen colors, and menus to your batch files. Among the more popular batch file extenders are some of the programs included with the Norton Utilities. For example, Norton's ASK command allows batch file programs to wait for keyboard input.

The only problem with batch file enhancers is you need to have a copy for each computer that has batch files using these enhancers. If you use commercial software, that can add up to a big price tag. And you may need to distribute dozens of little enhancement programs from the public domain to get the capabilities you need. This can clutter disk space. Nevertheless, these programs add new life and capabilities to DOS.

The Norton Utilities

While originally designed to recover accidentally deleted data, the Norton Utilities have added some utility programs designed to enhance batch files. While this package is not worth buying for the batch-enhancement features alone, they are a valuable addition to anyone who also wants the file-recovery tools.

Symantec ($99.95)
Published by: Peter Norton Computing
10201 Torre Avenue
Cupertino, CA 95014
(800) 441-7234

The Dvorak Utilities

A suite of programs to create menus, process keystrokes, and provide system information has been included on this book's program disks. You can use these utilities to make your batch files easier to use for novices and better at handling erroneous input.

Program:	**ASK**
Format:	ASK *Message* <KeyList> <TextColor> <BackColor>
What it does:	Displays the text of *message* at the current cursor position and awaits a keystroke. The foreground (text) color is set using <TextColor>, and the background color is set using <BackColor>. <KeyList> is a list of letters with no tabs or spaces between them.

If the key the user presses matches any of the letters in <KeyList>, ERRORLEVEL is set according to the key's placement in the list: if the key is first, ERROR-LEVEL is set to 1; if it's fourth, ERRORLEVEL is set to 4; and so on. It's a case-insensitive match—A and **a** have the same value.

If the user presses ESC, ERRORLEVEL is set to 0.

<TextColor> is a number from 1 to 16, and <BackColor> is a number from 1 to 8.

Number	Color	Number	Color
1	Black	9	Gray
2	Blue	10	Bright blue
3	Green	11	Bright green
4	Cyan	12	Bright cyan
5	Red	13	Bright red
6	Magenta	14	Bright magenta
7	Brown	15	Yellow
8	White	16	Bright white

What it's for:	Creating menus
See also:	**BOX**
Example:	

```
Ask "Please choose from A-C" abc 8 1
REM If user presses A, ERRORLEVEL is set to 1.
REM If user presses B, ERRORLEVEL is set to 2.
REM If user presses C, ERRORLEVEL is set to 3.
REM 8 is the text color (white) and 1 is the
REM background color (black).
```

Program:	**BEEP**
Format:	Beep
What it does:	Sounds the computer's bell
What it's for:	Getting the user's attention
Example:	

```
goto Error
...
:Error
beep
echo You pressed the wrong key!
```

Program:	**BOX**
Format:	BOX \<Type\> \<Row\> \<Col\> \<Width\> \<Height\> \<Frame\> \<Box\>
What it does:	Displays a box starting at \<Row\>, \<Col\> on the screen. The upper left corner is (1,1). The box is \<Width\> characters wide and \<Height\> characters tall. If \<Type\> is 1, a single box (four lines) is created. If \<Type\> is 2, a double box (eight lines) is created. The frame of the box is displayed in the color \<Frame\>, a number from 1 to 16. The interior of the box is displayed in the color \<Box\>, a number from 1 to 8.
What it's for:	Creating menus
See also:	**ASK**
Example:	

```
: Put up a single box (the first "1")
:    at row 1, column 1.
:    Make it 80 characters wide, and
:    24 characters deep.
:    Use an interior color of white (8)
:      and a frame color of blue (2).
box 1 1 1 80 24 8 2
```

Program:	**FREADY**
Format:	FREADY Drive
What it does:	Checks the specified drive and tests if it is ready. Sets ERRORLEVEL to 1 if ready. Any other value indicates the drive tested isn't ready.

Program:	**GETKEY**
	GETKEYNL
Format:	GetKey
	GetKeyNL
What it does:	GETKEY awaits a keystroke and sets ERRORLEVEL to the value of that keystroke. GETKEYNL does the same thing but prints a blank line after accepting the keystroke.

What it's for: It's quite convenient in place of PAUSE. First of all, GETKEY doesn't print a line feed. Second, it allows you to determine which key the user presses, information that is not available from PAUSE.

It also gives you fine-tuning for those rare occasions when you need case sensitivity, which ASK doesn't provide for.

Notes: Keys set ERRORLEVEL to these values:

Key	ERRORLEVEL
A-Z	65-90
a-z	97-122
0-9	48-57
ESC	27

Example:
```
echo off
echo Please press the {A} key.
GetKey
if errorlevel 97 echo Lowercase "a" was pressed.
if errorlevel 65 echo Caps Lock is on.
```

Program: **GETYN**

Format: GetYN

What it does: Awaits a keystroke and accepts only Y or N (case insensitive). Any other key results in a beep. Displays the key only if it's Y or N, and then prints a blank line. Sets ERRORLEVEL to 1 if Y is pressed, 0 if N.

What it's for: Makes life simple if your batch files require specific input from the user. You have to test for only two values. Handy for confirmation before a dangerous path is about to be taken.

Example:
```
echo Would you like to review help on this subject?
GetYN
if errorlevel 1 type help.txt
```

Program: **RESTPATH**

Format: RESTPATH [d:][path]filename.ext

What it does: Changes to the directory stored by SAVEPATH and to the specified filename.

What it's for: There's no easy way to "remember" both the current drive and the current directory, and return to that location after running other programs. Use SAVEPATH to preserve the current directory in a file, and return to it with RESTPATH.

While the drive and path specifications are optional, you should always specify them. Otherwise, you can easily confuse yourself by saving the directory location in several directories using identical filenames. REST-PATH won't know the difference.

This also means you can save multiple directories, one per file, and return to any of them as starting points in the same batch program.

Note: The directory is saved in a special format. You'd best use SAVEPATH to preserve the current directory.

See also: **SAVEPATH**

Example:
```
REM Use SAVEPATH to save the current directory
REM in the file C:\DIR.TXT.  Change to the
REM directory named in the environment variable
REM NEWDIR, then return to the current directory via
REM the RESTPATH utility.

REM Remember what directory we're in.
savepath c:\dir.txt

REM Change to a different directory.
cd %newdir%
REM In a real program, other stuff would happen here.

REM Return to start.
restpath
```

Program: **ROWCOL**

Format: ROWCOL <Row> <Col> *message* [<TextColor> <BackColor>]

What it does: Positions the cursor at <Row>, <Col> (both are numbers) and displays the text within the double quotes. The upper left corner of the screen is row 1, column 1.

<TextColor> and <BackColor> are optional numbers specifying colors for the foreground and background text. <TextColor> can be from 1 to 16, and <BackColor> can be from 1 to 8. The default colors are white (8) text on a black (1) background.

What it's for: Designing slick-looking menus

Number	Color	Number	Color
1	Black	9	Gray
2	Blue	10	Bright blue
3	Green	11	Bright green
4	Cyan	12	Bright cyan
5	Red	13	Bright red
6	Magenta	14	Bright magenta
7	Brown	15	Yellow
8	White	16	Bright white

See also: **ASK, BOX**

Example:
```
REM Displays white text on black on row 12,
REM column 20.
ROWCOL 12 20 "Journey to the center of the screen"
REM Display the word "Quit" at row 14, column
REM 30 using a cyan (4) background.  Print the
REM "Q" in red (5) and the rest of the word in
REM dark blue (2).
ROWCOL 14 30 "Q" 5 4
ROWCOL 14 31 "uit" 2 4
```

Program: **SAVEPATH**

Format: SAVEPATH [d:][path]filename.ext

What it does: Saves the current directory to a file, which you can later retrieve using the RESTPATH utility.

There's no easy way to "remember" both the current drive and the current directory and return to that location after running other programs. Use SAVEPATH to preserve the current directory in a file, and return to it with RESTPATH.

While the drive and path specifications are optional, you should always specify them. Otherwise, you can easily confuse yourself by saving the directory location in several directories using identical filenames. REST-PATH won't know the difference.

This also means you can save multiple directories, one per file, and return to any of them as starting points in the same batch program.

Note: The directory is saved in a special format. You'd best use SAVEPATH to preserve the current directory.

See also: **RESTPATH**

Example:
```
REM Use SAVEPATH to save the current directory
REM in the file C:\DIR.TXT.  Change to the
REM directory named in the environment variable
REM NEWDIR, then return to the current directory via the
REM RESTPATH utility.

REM Remember what directory we're in.
savepath c:\dir.txt

REM Change to a different directory.
cd %newdir%
REM In a real program, other stuff would happen here.

REM Return to start.
restpath
```

Program: **SHOWTIME**
Format: SHOWTIME

What it does: Displays the time, day, date, and year. For example: 5:23 pm, Tuesday, November 13, 1990

What it's for: Useful for logging utilities or displaying the time in a menu program

Example 1:

```
echo off
cls

: In the center of the screen, put up a double
: box (the 2) at row 7, column 20.
:   Make it 40 characters wide and
:   12 characters deep.
:   Use a frame color of yellow (15) and an
:   interior color of cyan (4).
box 2 7 20 40 12 15 4

: Display the time inside the box and wait for a keypress.
: Position the cursor at the center of the box.
rowcol 12 25 ""

: Display the time.
showtime

: Await a keypress.
getkey
```

Example 2:

```
REM To log time on the word processor Word,
REM redirect SHOWTIME's output to a new file.
echo Beginning work on "%1" at: > log.txt
showtime >> log.txt
word %1
showtime >> log.txt
```

Program: **TESTANSI**

Format: TESTANSI

IF ERRORLEVEL 1 REM (Has ANSI.SYS driver)

What it does: Checks for presence of the ANSI.SYS driver. If it's running, sets ERRORLEVEL to 1; if not, sets ERRORLEVEL to 0.

What it's for: Sometimes you need the features of ANSI.SYS in your programs. This lets you check to ensure the user has ANSI before spraying the screen with useless codes such as ^[43^[22.

Example:

```
: This shell program tests for ANSI.SYS and
: quits if it's not available.
ECHO OFF
CLS
testansi
IF ERRORLEVEL 1 GOTO HasIt

REM ANSI not found.
ECHO ANSI driver isn't installed.  Please add
ECHO it to your CONFIG.SYS and reboot.
GOTO End

:HasIt
ECHO ANSI driver present.
PAUSE Your code goes here...

:End
```

COMMAND.COM ENHANCERS AND REPLACEMENTS

Command enhancers are functionally equivalent to other batch-enhancement programs, but they are much more comprehensive. Rather than adding a single additional capability, they add dozens. They also work a little differently than other batch enhancer programs.

Command enhancers are very powerful, but the same caveats apply to them as to batch enhancers. You need a copy for every computer running a batch file that needs it. This runs up costs fast if you have many computers. In addition, since they are memory resident, they use some of your computer's main memory.

EBL

EBL was created in 1982. It is a memory-resident program that "hooks into" DOS's own command interpreter, COMMAND.COM. Its main function is to add commands to DOS's batch-processing capabilities. This it does with a vengeance. But EBL is showing its age and will soon be superseded by the next generation of DOS batch programming tools: batch file compilers.

EBL ($49.95)
Published by: Seaware Corp.
P.O. Box 1656
Delray Beach, FL 33444
407-738-1712

BATCH FILE COMPILERS

A batch file compiler offers the following advantages:

1. Compiled programs are faster than regular batch files. Each command is interpreted in advance. So, the program doesn't need to interpret each command while it's running. In addition, compiled batch files load from disk once and go. Regular batch files must keep accessing the disk to read in each instruction.

2. Batch file compilers offer many more commands than DOS does.

3. A compiler protects your source code. Because the compiler translates what you have into the computer's own primitive internal instructions, it is less obvious to others how you made the batch file. A compiler prevents others from modifying your batch files.

4. Compilers solve the "Batch file missing" problem. Since the computer loads the entire compiled program into memory before executing it, there is no need for the computer to find that program on the disk again while the program is running. This allows you to change disks easily without getting the "Batch file missing" message.

5. Compiled batch files eliminate the need for DOS's call statement.

6. One big advantage of compiling your batch files rather than using DOS extenders is you don't need to buy a copy of the DOS extenders for each computer using batch files. You can create your programs on one computer and then copy the compiled batch files to as many computers as you want. This gives compilers a huge cost advantage.

7. Compiled batch files give your programs a slick, professional look.
   Compilers are not perfect, however. First, you need to recompile your batch file whenever you make changes to it, even if the changes are minor. Second, a compiler will not execute commands exactly the same as DOS. Of course, neither of these is a major problem.

BATCOM

BATCOM is the original batch file compiler. It has been greatly expanded since its introduction in 1987. It currently sports more than 60 commands and enhancements in addition to DOS, and it compiles and executes quickly. BATCOM has an external language interface, an interface that allows you to use an optional $25 library to create your own TSR programs, and commands for string, arithmetic, file, disk, and keyboard functions. I like BATCOM. It's a solid buy.
   BATCOM was the brainchild of Lee Pelletier, an electrical engineer and graduate of M.I.T. It was conceived years before its introduction in 1987, when Mr. Pelletier decided it was time we finally had a compiler for batch files. The compiler was an instant success.
   Compiling a batch file is actually a simple process, even if it sounds complicated. For example, with BATCOM you would just type something like

```
BATCOM test.bat
```

This command would compile the batch file TEST.BAT into an executable file named TEST.EXE. That's all that's needed.

BATCOM ($59.95)
Published by: Wenham Software Company
5 Burley St.
Wenham, MA 01984
508-774-7036

User-Defined Variables

One of the most valuable features a batch file compiler can add to your batch files is *user-defined variables*. These variables allow you to read keyboard input, perform arithmetic and string functions, and do much more with ease. In addition, they can be used just like command line parameters to replace anything in your batch file.

In BATCOM, you name a user-defined variable by starting with %! and then adding a letter. Any place where you would normally include a command line parameter (for example, %1), you can use a user defined variable such as %!f, instead. For example,

```
echo I'm now copying A:%1 to C:%1.
copy A:%1 C:%1
```

can be replaced by:

```
echo I'm now copying A:%!f to C:%!f.
copy A:%!f C:%!f
```

This assumes the variable %!f has been assigned an appropriate value earlier in the program.

There are numerous ways to create and modify user-defined variables. To create a user-defined variable, just use a statement like the following:

```
let %!f = %1
```

This example doesn't show the power of user-defined variables, but it does show how to make variable %!f equal to whatever is in %1. Remember, you could also have used variable %!a, %!g, or %!w. What's important is that the variable you use starts with %! and ends with a single letter.

Let's see how user-defined variables are helpful. If you wanted to allow the user to copy EXE files by typing the name of the batch file and then the name of the file to be copied *without* having to type the extension, you could use:

```
let %!f = %1.exe
```

In the rest of the file, you could use %!f without having to worry about adding .exe to %1 every time.

User-defined variables also allow us to use default values more easily. For example, if the user doesn't type in a value for %1, you may just want to use the default of TEST.EXE. This is also easy to do with user-defined variables. Here is the completed example:

```
if %1. == . let %!f = test.exe
if not %1. == . let %!f = %1.exe
echo I'm now copying A:%!f to C:%!f.
copy A:%!f C:%!f
```

The first line assigns the default value TEST.EXE to %!f if %1 has no value. If %1 does have a value, then line 2 adds the extension EXE to %1 and assigns it to variable %!f. The next two lines work as before.

If that was all you could do with user-defined variables, they would be pretty ho-hum. But batch file compilers add much more. For example, if the user forgets to enter a value for %1, you can have the program prompt the user for the program name rather than assume a default value. This is probably a better idea. In BATCOM, you just type **READ** followed by a user-defined variable. The program will wait for the user to enter a value, which will be stored in the user-defined variable. Now your program gets even better:

```
if %1. == . echo What file do you want me to copy?
if %1. == . read %!f
if not %1. == . let %!f = %1
let %!f = %!f.exe
echo I'm now copying A:%!f to C:%!f.
copy A:%!f C:%!f
```

In this program, if the user doesn't enter a value for %1 on the command line, the first two lines in the program prompt the user for a filename and let him or her type it in. That makes user-defined variables quite powerful.

There are still more enhancements that can improve your programs. For instance, BATCOM adds the ECHONOLF command in addition to ECHO. This new command does the same thing as ECHO except that it doesn't add a carriage return and line feed at the end of the message. This causes the cursor to stay at the end of the message rather than drop to the next line. That would make this program look even better. In addition, BATCOM has string functions that can check to see if the user already added EXE to the end of the file. This keeps your batch file from mistakenly creating such filenames like TEST.EXE.EXE. While this can be done in numerous ways, the simplest is the following:

```
if %1. == . echonolf What file do you want me to copy?
if %1. == . read %!f
if not %1. == . let %!f = %1
let %!t = %!f
upper %!t
findstring %!t .EXE
if FALSE let %!f = %!f.exe
echo I'm now copying A:%!f to C:%!f.
copy A:%!f C:%!f
```

Your simple program has now become much more elaborate. However, it has also made life much, much easier for the user. Here's what happens. The first two lines prompt the user for a filename if the user didn't type one in on the command line. The third line uses the command line parameter if one was typed in. Next, variable %!f is transferred to temporary variable %!t. Line 5 converts %!t to all uppercase, and line 6 searches %!t for EXE. If EXE is not found, line 7 adds it to %!f. The next two lines then tell the user the file is being copied.

However, the program is still not complete. It should test the filename given to be sure it exists. If the file doesn't exist, the program should warn the user. Since BATCOM allows keyboard input from batch files, the user should be allowed to reenter the file name or quit the batch file.

You should include a few blank lines to separate functional parts of the program. Some program comments are also in order. BATCOM's BEEP command is helpful for people who don't have editors that support including ^G in their programs. And since BATCOM allows you to see if we have enough room for copying the file, you can add that error check also. Here is the finished program:

```
REM Prompt the user if no file was typed on command line.
if %1. == . echonolf What file do you want me to copy?
if %1. == . read %!f

REM Use the filename typed on the command line if one was typed in.
if not %1. == . let %!f = %1

REM Now check if .EXE needs to be added.  Add it if necessary.
:restart
let %!t = %!f
upper %!t
findstring %!t .EXE
if %!t == 0 let %!f = %!f.exe

REM Make sure this file exists on drive A:
if not exist A:%!f goto bad_name

REM Now make sure we have enough room on drive C: to copy the file.
let %!t = A:%!f
filesize %!t
let %!d = C:
freedisk %!d
GT %!t %!d
if TRUE goto no_room
REM Here is the "meat" of the program.  It actually copies the file.
echo I'm now copying A:%!f to C:%!f.
copy A:%!f C:%!f
goto end

REM If the file didn't exist, ask the user for another filename.
:bad_name
echo The file you typed in does not exist.  Please type the name of
echonolf another file (or just press <Enter> to quit):
beep
beep
read %!f
if %!f. == . goto end
goto restart

REM Tell the user there wasn't enough room for copying the file.
:no_room
echo There wasn't enough room on C: to copy the file.  You will
```

```
echo need to make enough room on C: or choose another file to copy.
beep
beep

:end
```

Now you have a bulletproof batch file you can be proud of. Many of the error checks and convenient additions would not have been possible with normal DOS.

Batman

The public domain Batman compiler is not a true compiler. It simply creates an EXE file that sends every command to DOS's own COMMAND.COM, which actually executes the commands. While Batman is slower than a normal batch file, it does compile about three additional commands as well as solve the "Batch file missing" problem. It will prevent others from changing your source code, too.

Builder

Builder is a fully integrated development system consisting of a compiler, a multiwindow screen editor with hypertext help, and a DOS-compatible linker. Builder has a uniquely English-like syntax and menus (drop-down, light-bar, and free-form) built directly into the language.

The language that Builder compiles is slightly different from the batch language. Its Smart Import feature detects batch (as opposed to Builder) files and automatically translates them into Builder syntax. For example, a FOR statement converts from

```
FOR %%c IN (*.txt *.doc) DO CLEANUP %%c
```

to

```
FOR %%c IN "*.txt *.doc" DO RUN CLEANUP %%c
```

By tweaking the batch language slightly, Builder can integrate its extensions in a much more natural fashion. Whereas BATCOM has a syntax that looks like batch language, Builder's draws more from English, Hypertalk, and BASIC. For example, the following lines from the BATCOM example cited earlier:

```
findstring %!t .EXE
if %!t == 0 let %!f = %!f.exe
```

are translated to the following line in Builder:

```
if the Target contains ".EXE" then put File2 + ".EXE" into File2
```

or, more tersely; the following one:

```
if Target contains ".EXE" File2 := File2 + ".EXE"
```

Builder handles many details that ordinarily fall into the laps of system programmers and makes them simple for a beginner. For example, the IBM handles function keys differently from the way it handles other keys. Builder, on the other hand, covers up the system details. Compare the following two programs, which do exactly the same thing: wait for the user to press a key, and print a message if the key is F1. Here's the C version:

```
#include <stdio.h>
#include <conio.h>
main()
{
  int Key;
  Key = getch();
  if (Key == 0) {
    Key = getch();
    if (Key == 59) printf("F1 was pressed.\n");
  }
}
```

Here's the Builder version:

```
if GetKey is {F1} say "F1 was pressed."
```

Other constructs look like the following program fragments (the apostrophe (') can be used instead of REM in Builder scripts):

```
' Hide the cursor.
Don't use the cursor

' Display numbers with commas.
Use commas

' Draw a bright white box in the center of the screen.
' Make the interior blue.  The box is located at
' row 6, column 20.  It's 40 characters wide and 10 high.
double box 6, 20, 40, 10 bright white on blue

' Clear the screen to bright white text on a blue background.
CLS Bright white on blue

' Let the user type in text.  If {Esc} was pressed, handle
' that condition separately.
string Name
Input Name
if Canceled then say "You pressed Escape."

' Get handy system information:
Put EMSInstalled into EMSMem
Put DiskFree "C:" into D
Put PrinterReady 2 into PrtTest
Put DiskSpace "%1" into FreeSpace
Put DOSRAM into D
if the AdaptorType is "Mono" then UseMonoColors

' Display the text "hello, world" in reverse video
say "<reverse>hello, world."

' Display the contents of a file:
File Auto
String Next
Open "c:autoexec.bat" for reading as Auto
While not eof Auto
  ReadLine Next from Auto
  say Next
end ' While
```

Builder's nicest feature is menus. DropDown is typical: Just give it a name, names for each of the items, code to execute when items are chosen, and an optional starting screen location. (The default is the upper left corner of the screen). Unlike the hundreds of lines of code required by C or BASIC to build a menu, Builder can do it in fewer than ten—and integrate the menu into the language as a control structure. Here's an example:

```
Dropdown "Install" @ 6,30

  Item "Full Installation"
    say @ 24, 1 "FullInstallation"

  Item "Minimum Installation"
    say @ 24, 1 "Mini Installation"

  Item "Quit"
    say @ 24, 1 "Thank you for using Install."
    exit 0

end
```

Builder automatically uses a mouse if one is present. It allows you to select items instantly by pressing the first letter, or it waits for you to press ENTER. You can also change an item's hot key from the first letter to any other and change any aspect of a menu's colors, from its hot key color to the highlight. When an item is selected, the code executes until the next item is encountered. Control then transfers to the bottom of the menu. It's just like having a CASE statement (also supported in Builder) combined with a menu generator.

Builder ($149.95)
Published by: Hyperkinetix, Inc.
666 Baker St. Suite 405
Costa Mesa, CA 92626
714-668-9234

The Case for Batch File Compilers

Every computer user needs to know how to use batch files. Many people who use batch files don't realize they are programmers. Batch files are the mainstay programming language of IBM PCs. Batch file mastery is important for efficient use of your IBM PC. Understanding this area of computing fully will help you get the most out of your computer.

Batch file compilers are the state of the art in batch files. They are fast, powerful, easy to use, and cost effective. Anyone serious about batch files should have a batch file compiler.

CHAPTER TWENTY-SEVEN

Device Drivers

Device drivers and their importance is one of the least understood aspects of PC computing for the average user. The introduction of device drivers in DOS 2.0 added substantial power and flexibility to DOS. In this chapter, we'll show you how to create and edit CONFIG.SYS to make use of DOS device drivers. We'll also discuss many device drivers, device driver substitutes, and support programs. Several of these are included on the disks bound with this book.

Unlike many computers, PC compatibles are "open" systems: They can be connected to many types of peripherals, whether designed by IBM or not. Browse through any computer magazine and you'll find peripherals from the commonplace (display screens and keyboards) to the exotic (robot arms and security systems). Literally thousands of third-party peripherals are available.

The "openness" of compatibles is an advantage. It has inspired competition among manufacturers, which has, in turn, kept prices down and PC technology on the cutting edge. But connecting these peripherals to a PC presents a certain problem. Even though a PC and peripheral may be physically connected (through an expansion card or port), it does not mean that they inherently know how to talk with one another.

Fortunately, a solution—device drivers—was created. A device driver is simply a program that allows DOS to communicate with a particular peripheral device. Beginning with version 2.0, DOS has included several device drivers (each with a SYS or DEV extension). Also, third-party peripheral developers usually write their own device drivers to control the peripherals they sell and manufacture. No doubt, the advent of device drivers has made DOS infinitely more flexible. Here's how they work.

Imagine that you purchase a mouse and connect it to your PC through a cable. The device is connected, but until you tell your PC about it, it has no way to communicate with the mouse. This is where a device driver comes into play. Through the DEVICE directive in your CONFIG.SYS file, you load the appropriate device driver, and it becomes the link between your PC and the mouse. It regulates communication and ensures that everything runs properly. You might say the device driver is the "interpreter" that enables your system and the mouse to communicate. This is an example of an installable device driver. The driver is installed as a program, like a terminate-and-stay-resident (TSR) program.

Another type of device driver is resident. Most of us take the resident device drivers for granted, but we use them every time we turn on our computer. Resident drivers are built into DOS and are referenced by reserved device names (CON, AUX, COM, LPT, and NUL). They handle basic communication between your PC and the keyboard, display screen, and serial and parallel ports.

As PC software has matured, software developers have realized that device drivers can be used for purposes beyond just controlling physical devices. For example, two popular 386 memory managers, 386MAX (Qualitas) and QEMM (Quarterdeck), are implemented as device drivers. Yet, they control a "device"—memory—that is integral to the system, not an add-on.

Let's make this clear. Installable device drivers are used to regulate communication between add-on hardware peripherals and I/O ports. Not built into DOS, they are installable programs that come in the form of SYS or DEV files. When you buy a new piece of hardware, it is likely to come with its own device driver. Resident device drivers are built into DOS to handle the standard I/O between your PC and common peripherals, such as a keyboard or display screen.

In this chapter, we describe the common device drivers included with DOS, as well as generalized instructions for loading any device driver.

CONFIG.SYS

CONFIG.SYS is a special text file used to configure your system each time you boot your computer. The way your system is configured depends on the directives you enter in the CONFIG.SYS file. In this chapter, we are concerned with only one CONFIG.SYS directive: DEVICE. The DEVICE directive is used to load installable device drivers.

THE DEVICE DIRECTIVE

Resident device drivers are always in use; you don't need to do anything to activate them. However, installable device drivers must be loaded or installed.

To install an installable device driver, you must place the appropriate DEVICE directive in your CONFIG.SYS file. For DOS to use CONFIG-.SYS, the file must be located in the root directory of the boot disk. DOS searches for CONFIG.SYS each time you boot your computer. If DOS locates the CONFIG.SYS file, it acts upon the directives within, loading each device driver specified.

Your DEVICE directive should follow this format:

DEVICE=*filename parameters*

where *filename* is the name of the file containing the device driver, including the drive and path if necessary (the default drive and path are the root directory of the boot disk). Most drivers have the extension SYS. The optional *parameters* specify any additional information needed by the driver; its format varies and can be found in the documentation for the specified driver. For example, to load the ANSI.SYS device driver from the DOS subdirectory on the C drive, you would enter:

```
DEVICE=C:\DOS\ANSI.SYS
```

We recommend that you store device drivers somewhere other than in the root directory of your boot disk (as in the example). Typically, PC users spend a lot of time in the root directory, making it easy to inadvertently delete or destroy a crucial driver file—and you won't notice it until the next time you boot the system. Since DOS allows you to specify a path in the DEVICE statement, there's no reason not to keep driver files with the software they came with or in a directory all their own.

Loading High

Recent software improvements have added a new capability for device drivers: the "loadhi" option. This allows drivers to be loaded into the area between 640KB and 1MB, conserving precious low-memory resources. The major programs that provide this capability are Qualitas's 386MAX and Quarterdeck's QEMM for 386s and Qualitas's MOVE-EM and Quarterdeck's QRAM for other systems. Newer versions of DOS and DR-DOS also have this capability.

Loading drivers high requires a line like the following in the CONFIG-.SYS file:

DEVICE = D:\QEMM\LOADHI.SYS *filename parameters*

In this case, as far as DOS can tell, the driver being loaded is LOADHI-.SYS. But what this driver does is load the real driver, whose name is specified by *filename* and whose parameters are *parameters*, and store it in high memory.

Loading drivers into high memory is a bit of an art. Some drivers require considerably more memory to load than they do to run, and some won't work at all if loaded high. Couple that with the need to load certain drivers in the right order and the characteristics of a typical system where "high memory" is really two or more pieces of noncontiguous memory space, and it can be quite tricky to find a load order that meets everyone's needs. Quarterdeck's new OPTIMIZE program for use with QEMM attempts to automate the loadhi process and determine the best loading order, and Qualitas is reported to be preparing a similar program for use with 386MAX. But these software approaches aren't perfect. If you want the benefits of loading drivers into high memory, you should plan to spend some time getting it done right.

CREATING AND MODIFYING CONFIG.SYS

To add the DEVICE directive to your CONFIG.SYS file, you must edit the file editor or create a new CONFIG.SYS file. This is a simple process.

CONFIG.SYS is a standard text file and can be edited or (if it doesn't already exist) created with any text editor that allows you to edit standard ASCII files. When editing your CONFIG.SYS file, be careful not to make any changes to existing lines.

If you don't have a text editor on hand, you can create your CONFIG-.SYS file from the DOS command line. However, if CONFIG.SYS already exists on your system, you should first print its contents by entering the following:

```
COPY CONFIG.SYS PRN:
```

You can then use this printout as a guide to retype each line as it appeared in the original CONFIG.SYS file, adding your new commands where you need them. Follow these steps to create your CONFIG.SYS file:

1. Move to the boot disk by entering the appropriate drive designator (commonly, C for hard disks and A for floppies).

2. Move to the root directory by entering **CD \\.**

3. Enter the following command:

    COPY CON:CONFIG.SYS

4. Enter the exact contents of the previous CONFIG.SYS file, if any.

5. Enter your device directives, such as

    DEVICE = MOUSE.SYS

6. Press F6 to close the file with the end-of-file character (^Z), and press ENTER.

Throughout the rest of this chapter, we describe the three most common and useful DOS device drivers: ANSI.SYS, DRIVER.SYS, and VDISK-.SYS.

ANSI.SYS

In the days before CGA, EGA, VGA, and monochrome monitors, the computer world was made of mainframes, miniframes, and dumb terminals.

READ.ME

Warning

Before you create or edit CONFIG.SYS, be aware of two things:

1. If CONFIG.SYS already exists, *don't* alter or delete any commands unless you know exactly what you are doing and have made a printed copy of the file.

2. If CONFIG.SYS already contains a DEVICE command or you are entering multiple DEVICE commands, make sure they are in the proper order (see VDISK.SYS and DRIVER.SYS).

Dumb terminals did nothing more than allow users to converse with computers in plain ASCII or text mode. No fancy graphics or windows were possible on these dumb terminals. Plain text scrolled off the screen as it was being displayed. There was nothing elegant to the output shown on the screen. This mode of conversing with computers was normally called *CTTY*, or *console teletype.*

Eventually, terminals evolved with special features that could clear the screen, move the cursor to a different position on the screen, change the intensity of screen text from normal to bright, and even reverse the video display. Special computer codes were required to perform this action, and thus was born the ANSI (American National Standards Institute) escape control sequences.

DEC was among the first to implement a standard set of escape control sequences around their VT100 terminals, which worked with their VAX minicomputers. In the world of IBM PCs, IBM (and Microsoft) chose the ANSI standard because it was widely used in many terminals and computers. ANSI was a limited, but standard, version of the VT100 escape control language.

As usual, IBM added some features to the ANSI standard and renamed it IBM Extended ANSI. With the IBM extended definition of ANSI, you can:

- Set the foreground and background colors of the screen

- Control the cursor position on the screen

- Clear the entire screen, a single line, or part of a line
- Change the definition of keys on the keyboard
- Program keys to perform a group of commands

IBM puts all these features in a device driver called ANSI.SYS, which normally comes with your DOS disks. The ANSI.SYS device driver captures strings of data that were sent through DOS to the monitor by a software program. Once captured, the string is examined for special-character sequences. If a special-character sequence is found, ANSI.SYS removes it from the string sent to the monitor, interprets it, and translates it to a predefined screen or keyboard command.

When you create a program with ANSI escape sequences to handle the monitor display, your program will have compatibility or portability with many terminals. All MS-DOS operating systems and clones support ANSI-.SYS. However, not all terminals support the IBM extended definition of ANSI. Using ANSI.SYS escape sequences will give you the widest compatibility possible.

ANSI has become popular in batch files and programs, as its usage ensures compatibility with any MS-DOS system. In the world of telecommunications and bulletin boards, ANSI is the standard method of displaying special screen attributes. If there were museums for ANSI screens, many bulletin boards would make it into the ANSI gallery of great art.

Is ANSI.SYS Loaded?

If you call bulletin boards or run batch files and software that use ANSI escape sequences, you must load the ANSI.SYS device driver to take advantage of them. To see if ANSI is currently loaded on your system, you can run one of the Dvorak utilities, TESTANSI.COM, which is included with this book. If TESTANSI.COM determines that ANSI.SYS is installed, it will set the DOS ERRORLEVEL to 1; if it's not installed, the ERROR-LEVEL will be set to 0. Here's a sample batch file that uses TESTANSI-.COM:

```
@echo off
cls
rem Batch program to test for existence of ANSY.SYS:
```

```
testansi
if errorlevel 1 goto hasans
echo No ANSI driver
goto end
:hasans
  echo HAS ANSI driver!
  goto end
:end
```

How Do I Load ANSI.SYS?

If ANSI.SYS is not already loaded, you may instruct your computer to do so by placing the following DEVICE command in your CONFIG.SYS file:

```
DEVICE=ANSI.SYS
```

Or, if you follow our advice about keeping your device drivers in a subdirectory on your hard disk, use the following:

```
DEVICE=C:\DOS\ANSI.SYS
```

With one of these commands in the CONFIG.SYS file, ANSI.SYS will be loaded every time you start or reboot your computer.

The ANSI.SYS driver does not take up very much memory (about 4KB), and it doesn't conflict with any other device or software on your system. If other software conflicts with ANSI.SYS (a rare occurrence), don't give up using ANSI.SYS too quickly: You may find the misbehaved program is more expendable than ANSI.SYS. You can also try one of the fine ANSI.SYS substitutes discussed later in this chapter.

Several versions of ANSI.SYS support three command line switches for the DEVICE = ANSI.SYS command: /X enables ANSI's ability to handle extended keyboards, and /K disables it; /L tells ANSI to retain screen size after a mode change. These commands would be entered like this:

```
DEVICE=ANSI.SYS /X
DEVICE=ANSI.SYS /K
DEVICE=ANSI.SYS /L
```

Warning: If you enter this command as the last line in your CONFIG-.SYS file and you use version 2.X of DOS, be sure to press the RETURN key after entering the command. A bug in DOS 2.X will cause errors if there is no RETURN character at the end of a CONFIG.SYS file.

Loading ANSI is only the start. Throughout the rest of this chapter, we'll give you detailed instructions on using ANSI.SYS escape sequences in your own batch files and programs.

READ.ME

Summary of IBM Extended ANSI Escape Commands

The following is basic syntax of the ANSI screen and keyboard control sequences:

<ESC> [*parameters COMMAND*

where ESC is the 1-byte ASCII code for escape (1BH), [is the [(left bracket) character, and *parameters* are numeric values you specify for the different commands of ANSI. Some commands have default values; so specifying 0 or no value results in the default value being used.

The following are the IBM extended screen and keyboard control sequences:

ESC[2J	Clears the screen; retains the cursor position.
ESC[#;#H	Moves the cursor to *row;column* position; the default is the home position.
ESC[H	Moves the cursor to the home position (top left corner).
ESC[K	Erases from the current cursor position to the end of the line.
ESC[#A	Moves the cursor up # rows; the default is 1.
ESC[#B	Moves the cursor down # rows; the default is 1.

─────── **READ.ME** ───────

Summary of IBM Extended ANSI
Escape Commands (*continued*)

ESC[#C	Moves the cursor forward # columns; the default is 1.
ESC[#D	Moves the cursor backward # columns; the default is 1.
ESC[#;#f	Same as ESC[#;#H.
ESC[s	Saves the current cursor position.
ESC[u	Restores the cursor position saved with ESC[s.
ESC[#;#p	Keyboard redefinition.
ESC#;...;#m	Sets the character color attributes specified by the # parameters. This is an IBM PC-specific command. The color parameters are:

0	All attributes off (normal light gray on black)
1	Bold on (high intensity)
4	Underscore on (mono-compatible mode)
5	Blink on
7	Reverse video
8	Cancel on (invisible)
30	Black foreground
31	Red foreground
32	Green foreground
33	Yellow foreground
34	Blue foreground
35	Magenta foreground
36	Cyan foreground
37	White foreground
38	Reserved
39	Reserved
40	Black background
41	Red background
42	Green background
43	Yellow background
44	Blue background

READ.ME

Summary of IBM Extended ANSI
Escape Commands (*continued*)

45	Magenta background
46	Cyan background
47	White background
	For example, ESC[33;44m will turn on yellow on a blue background.
ESC[= #h	Changes the screen width or monitor video type. The following parameters are understood:
0	40x25 black and white
1	40x25 color
2	80x25 black and white
3	80x25 color
4	320x200 color
5	320x200 black and white
6	640x200 black and white
7	Wrap at end of line

ANSI Escape Sequences

Using ANSI escape sequences in your own programs and batch files may seem a bit difficult at first. But once you get some practice, it is very easy. To create an ANSI command, you must first enter two signature characters that identify the text as a command rather than normal text. The first character is an escape ESC (ASCII 27) character, and the second is a left bracket ([, ASCII 91).

For these escape sequences to take effect, you must print them to the screen. This is where things get a little confusing. To print ANSI escape sequences to the screen, you can use batch files, programs, or the DOS PROMPT command. Using the DOS PROMPT command is fairly simple, as you will see. Entering the commands into batch files and program source code can be a little more difficult.

The difficulty arises when you attempt to enter an ESC code into a text editor. Sure you can press ESC whenever you want, but this doesn't mean that the computer will recognize it as an ESC character. For example, when you use DOS and you press the ESC key, DOS takes this as an "Abort this operation" command instead of as "Insert an ESC character." For this reason, it is impossible to create ANSI escape sequences with COPY CON or EDLIN.

Even some commercial text editors won't let you enter an ESC character. To place ANSI escape sequences in your batch files and programs, you must find an editor that allows you to enter a true ESC character. The method used to enter ESC will be different for each editor.

Some editors allow what is called the alternate-keypad mode of input. The ASCII value for ESC is 027. To place the escape character in your text file, hold down the ALT key, type **027** on the keypad, and release the ALT key.

READ.ME

Using ANSI with The DOS PROMPT Command

If you want a certain ANSI effect to take place immediately, straight from the DOS prompt, you can use programs such as COLOR.COM and ESC.COM (included with this book and described later), or the DOS PROMPT command.

The PROMPT command is normally used to set the system prompt (the A> or C> you see in DOS), but because the prompt is echoed to the screen, it can also be used to send ANSI codes.

When you enter PROMPT commands, the characters $E[represent an ESC character. This makes it very easy to enter ANSI escape sequences. To clear the screen, for example, you enter:

```
PROMPT $E[[2J
```

The $E[is the ESC character, and the [2J is the ANSI code for "Clear the screen."

Remember, since the PROMPT command's purpose is to change the system prompt, you just told DOS you want a prompt that clears the screen. To change the prompt back to the A> or C>, simply type **PROMPT** without any command line options.

WordStar requires you to enter a special keycode combination: CTRL-P, CTRL-ESC. Others may simply let you press ESC. If you cannot find an editor that will allow you to enter the ESC character, you can use the ESC.COM program (provided with this book) to generate the appropriate text and load it into your batch files and source code files.

ESC.COM

This program is used to execute any ANSI escape sequence from the DOS command line. It can also be used with DOS redirection to place ANSI escape sequences in a text file. You can then include this text file in your own batch file and program source files to create ANSI escape sequences.

First, decide what ANSI characters you wish to use. Once you've decided, enter the command ESC followed by the ANSI codes. For example: **ESC 2J** would clear your screen, and **ESC 37;44m** would set the screen colors to white on blue.

This program's redirection feature may come in handy if you can't find an editor that allows you to enter escape sequences in your batch files. To use redirection, simply enter your commands like this:

```
ESC 2J>MYFILE
ESC 37;44m>MYFILE
```

This would copy both ANSI escape sequences to the file MYFILE. You could then load the text from MYFILE into your AUTOEXEC.BAT file and move the characters to the appropriate location.

COLOR.COM

Included in the utility disks accompanying this book is a DOS utility program called COLOR.COM, which can be used to change the color of your monitor through ANSI codes. If you don't like the standard white-on-black setup of your color monitor, use COLOR.COM to set different colors, such as

```
COLOR YELLOW ON BLUE
```

Assuming that an ANSI.SYS-compatible device driver is loaded, this command will change the color of your monitor to a blue background with a yellow foreground (meaning the text color is yellow).

You can get a complete list of the command line options simply by typing **COLOR** at the command line. COLOR.COM has the same syntax as the popular Norton Utilities' BE SA (Screen Attributes) program. COLOR-.COM also has additional options not found in other screen-attribute utilities. You can use the /F option to create a DOS batch file with the ANSI string sequences of the command line text you enter.

For instance, you can enter my favorite screen colors with the following command:

```
C:\ DVORAK>COLOR /F BRIGHT WHITE ON BLUE
```

Besides a change of the screen colors, you'll end up with the following file, named ANSI.OUT:

```
REM
REM     ANSI Color sequence generated by COLOR (C)
REM     Copyrighted by Thumper Technologies, 1989
REM
REM     BRIGHT WHITE ON BLUE
REM
ECHO [;44;1;37m
```

You can use this file with ANSI escape sequences to change the screen's foreground and background colors each time you run the batch file or even type it to the screen.

ANSI Screen Control

Now that you have the ESC problem out of the way, you can learn to use the ANSI codes themselves. In ANSI, the command

```
ESC[x;yH
```

can be used to relocate the cursor position. The following example clears the screen and writes a character string to the center of the screen:

```
PROMPT $E[2J;$E[10;30HJOHN DVORAK
```

This method uses the DOS PROMPT command. If you program in a common language such as BASIC, C, or Pascal, you can achieve the same results with the language's unique commands. Here are more screen-control sequences in common programming languages, including DOS batch file commands:

BASIC

```
PRINT CHR$(27);"[2J";              : clear the screen
PRINT CHR$(27);"[33;44m";          : set yellow on blue
PRINT CHR$(27);"[20;10H";          : move cursor to position 20,10
```

Pascal

```
write(output,chr(27),'[2J');       (* clear the screen *)
write(output,chr(27),'[33;44m');   (* set yellow on blue *)
write(output,chr(27),'[20;10H');   (* move cursor to position 20,10 *)
```

C

```
printf("\027[2J");                 /* clear the screen */
printf("\027[33;44m");             /* set yellow on blue */
printf("\027[20;10H");             /* move cursor to position 20,10 */
```

DOS Batch File

```
: clear the screen
   ECHO ^[[2J
: set yellow on blue
   ECHO ^[[33;44m
: move cursor to position 20,10
   ECHO ^[[20;10H
```

ANSI Keyboard Control

Keyboard control is a large IBM extension to ANSI. ANSI's keyboard control lets you redefine keyboard keys. For instance, the letter *A* can be changed to the letter *P*, for example, or to a group of characters. Keyboard redefinition can have some useful applications and give some utility to keys not normally used, such as function keys at the DOS level.

ANSI Screen Creation, the Easy Way: THEDraw

THEDraw, from TheSoft Programming Services, is an ANSI program used to design full-color ANSI text screens. A computer screen is traditionally made of up of 25 rows and 80 columns. THEDraw gives you a 25 by 80 canvas to draw text characters, lines, and boxes with color. THEDraw can also be used to create animated ANSI screens.

Many bulletin boards and DOS batch files use full-screen ANSI art to make their menus and graphical displays interesting. In the past, users had to issue a number of hard-to-read ANSI commands to make such screens.

The program offers on-line help and full mouse support. Unlike most ANSI drawing programs, THEDraw saves files in many formats, including the following:

    ANSI color text
    ASCII text
    Binary files
    BSAVE, for use with BASIC programs
    COM files
    Assembly language
    Turbo Pascal source code
    Turbo C format
    OBJECT, suitable for linking
    THEDRAW, a custom storage format

These make possible ANSI screens that can be used in assembler language and BASIC programs, batch files, editors, word processors, C, and Turbo Pascal.

    TheSoft Programming Services
    1929 Whitecliff Court
    Walnut Creek, CA 94596
    Registration: $15
    CompuServe ID: 70047,744

Many people are unaware of what function keys can do at the DOS prompt. For instance, F3 can be used to repeat a command. This is neither a keyboard redefinition nor an ANSI command; it is a feature of the operating system. With ANSI, you can extend this concept through keyboard redefinition. For example, you can program the F1 key to provide a directory listing.

To change one key to have the meaning of another, enter the following:

```
ESC[#;#p
```

where the first # is the ASCII value of the key being changed and the second # is the ASCII value of the new definition. For example, the letter *A* has the ASCII value of 65, and the letter *Q* has the value of 81; so, the following command:

```
ESC[65;91p
```

will result in the A key being redefined as the Q key.

With function keys or extended keys, you must first enter a 0 and the extended key's ASCII value. The following table shows the ASCII values for function keys:

Key	Normal	SHIFT	CONTROL	ALT
F1	59	84	94	104
F2	60	85	95	105
F3	61	86	96	106
F4	62	87	97	107
F5	63	88	98	108
F6	64	89	99	109
F7	65	90	100	110
F8	66	91	101	111
F9	67	92	102	112
F10	68	93	103	113

Each function key is assigned an "extended function code," which DOS uses to recognize that a function key has been pressed and in what shift mode. Each number is expressed as a 0 followed by a semicolon and then the number from the chart. For example, the following command will redefine the F1 key as the string DIR followed by a carriage return (ASCII value 13):

```
ESC[0;59;"DIR";13p
```

Now, imagine someone or some software redefining one of your keys, say, the D, to "ECHO Y | ERASE *.*?." If this were to occur, when you hit the D, your current disk directory would be erased. This is an ANSI virus. You have to watch out for these. No cause for major alarm—ethical software developers are keen to ANSI viruses and do not allow them to occur. Popular programs like PKZIP (data-compression software) strip out ANSI commands that are often used for colorful comments and left in a "zipped" file. Bulletin board systems, which often use ANSI commands to control screens and display colorful pictures, strip out and disarm the keyboard-redefinition command. (Rest assured, a bulletin board system will not redefine your keyboard.)

Of course, this is not the only way to redefine your keyboard. There are macro programs, such as Borland's SuperKey, and specialty programs like SWITCH.COM, which comes with WordStar, and the shareware program KFIX101.COM, that are designed just to switch the CTRL and CAPS LOCK keys. These programs are compatible only with the 101-extended keyboard on AT-class systems. If you want to switch other keys or use an XT-class system, you'll need to use ANSI.SYS or a keyboard macro program. One clear advantage of ANSI.SYS over the other programs (which are TSRs) is compatibility. In terms of memory usage, CAPS LOCK/CTRL switchers take 400 bytes, while ANSI.SYS uses about 4KB, and keyboard macros use 16KB or more.

ANSI.SYS Replacements

Although ANSI.SYS is a vast improvement over the old-style CTTY interfaces, it has its own set of inadequacies. ANSI.SYS is a good idea that was poorly executed.

ANSI is, by nature, inherently slow compared with other methods of displaying information on the screen. Modern programs take advantage of video hardware speed either by displaying directly to the screen or by using DOS or BIOS. By the same token, these fast screen programs are compatible only with the PC world of computers.

To get around some of the inadequacies of ANSI.SYS, programmers have written a fairly numerous assortment of replacement programs. The main advantage of an ANSI.SYS replacement is the improved speed of output display. Some allow users to disable keyboard redefinition (to be safe from ANSI viruses). In general, these programs enhance the basic functions of ANSI.SYS. Some go further than others. Let's take a look at some of the better ANSI.SYS replacement programs.

ZANSI.SYS, designed by Thomas Hanlin III, directly replaces the ANSI.SYS provided by DOS. ZANSI speeds up the interpretation of escape sequences (but not by much compared with ANSI.COM, which is described next). It also completely disables the keyboard-redefinition feature. The author claims there was a bug in his keyboard redefinition, which, owing to lack of complaints, he made a permanent feature—the old "It's not a bug, it's a feature" method of programming.

ANSI.COM is a public domain program designed by M. J. Melford for *PC Magazine.* Not a device driver like ANSI.SYS or ZANSI.SYS, ANSI.COM is a program executed as a TSR. ANSI.COM is faster in character output than ZANSI.SYS and allows you to use the ANSI escape sequence codes dynamically. This is a nice feature for when you don't want to allow a program to issue escape codes. For example, the following command sequence:

```
ANSI ON
RUN_A_PROGRAM
ANSI OFF
```

keeps the malicious RUN_A_PROGRAM from ever having the opportunity to use ANSI escape sequences to perform keyboard redefinition.

NANSI.SYS is another ANSI replacement that directly replaces the ANSI.SYS file. The first version of NANSI appeared around 1986. It gives complete support to the ANSI standard and also allows for faster screen writing. Over the years, NANSI has been revised several times to compete with the new graphics interfaces. It has been altered by the original author, Dan Kegel, as well as by other programmers (Kegel released the source code with NANSI).

Dan Kegel
2648 169th Avenue S.E.
Bellevue, WA 98008

Chris Dunford, author of CED, PCED, and several other programs, created a revised version of NANSI.SYS for VGA systems. When first introduced, FANSI-CONSOLE did little more than provide enhanced ANSI functions. Over the past several years, the program has been improved; it is now much more than just a simple replacement to ANSI.SYS. In addition to improved screen display, FANSI-CONSOLE offers the following features:

Keyboard macros
Screen blanking
Scroll-back buffer
One-finger typing
43-line mode
50-line mode
Alteration of the "locking" keys
Enlarged keyboard buffer
Enhanced typematic rate
Rearrangement of the keyboard
And *more*

FANSI-CONSOLE uses more RAM than other ANSI replacements. It does, however, provide more features. On the average, FANSI-CONSOLE uses between 32 and 42KB of DOS RAM. That may seem astronomical, but consider this: Alone, FANSI-CONSOLE can replace a keyboard macro program, a screen blanker, a keyboard-buffer expander, a keyboard enhancer, and other enhancements. If you currently use any of these, consider the RAM they employ. FANSI-CONSOLE will have more appeal and look like less of a RAM hog.

FANSI-CONSOLE is compatible with most IBM-compatible computers, and it has a large number of users. The shareware version comes with a manual. The program is updated regularly and includes many utility programs for various computers.

FANSI-CONSOLE
Hersey Micro Consulting, Inc.
P.O. Box 8276
Ann Arbor, MI 48107
313-994-3259

DRIVER.SYS

The DRIVER.SYS device driver serves two purposes: First, it allows your computer and a previously unrecognized disk drive to communicate; second, it enables you to treat one physical disk drive as two logical drives. DRIV-ER.SYS works with all common disk formats.

You can load DRIVER.SYS to provide better control over an existing drive, especially in the case where you have an older PC whose BIOS cannot recognize the capabilities of a newer drive. It is even possible (though not recommended) to use DRIVER.SYS with hard disks. DRIVER-.SYS is distributed with DOS 3.3 and above. It was also available in some versions of DOS 3.2.

As with all device drivers, you must enter a DEVICE command in your CONFIG.SYS file to activate DRIVER.SYS. The format for the DRIVER-.SYS DEVICE command is as follows:

```
DEVICE=d:path\ DRIVER.SYS /D:ddd /F:f /T:ttt /S:ss /H:hh /C /N
```

Options

d:path   d: is the drive that holds DRIVER.SYS, and *path* is the directory path to DRIVER.SYS. If your DRIVER.SYS file resides with CONFIG .SYS in the root directory, you won't need to specify this information.

/D:ddd   /D:*ddd* specifies the drive number (from 0 to 127 for floppies or 128 to 255 for hard disks). This is the only required DRIVER.SYS command line option. 0 specifies disk drive A; 1 specifies drive B. If you enter 2, your drive letter will depend on whether you have any hard disks installed: DRIVER.SYS will always take the lowest available drive designator. If you had one hard disk installed (C), your external floppy disk would be referred to as drive D. If you had two hard disks (or a hard disk with two partitions, C and D), your external floppy disk would be referred to as drive E. If you used DRIVER.SYS with a hard disk, you would enter enter 128 for C, 129 for D, and so on.

/F:f   /F:*f* specifies the disk's form factor, or the type of disk DRIVER.SYS uses. Here you must enter the special code number for the type of disk, which is one of the following:

0	160/180/320/360KB 5.25" floppy
1	1.2MB 5.25" floppy
2	720KB 3.5" microfloppy
7	1.44MB 3.5" microfloppy

This command line switch is optional; if you enter no value, it defaults to 2.

/T:*ttt*   /T:*ttt* specifies the number of tracks on each side of the disk. You may enter a number from 1 to 999. The default setting is 80. 80 tracks are used by 720KB, 1.2MB, and 1.44MB disk drives; 40 tracks are used by 160/180/320/360KB drives.

/S:*ss*   /S:*ss* specifies the number of sectors per track. The default setting is 9, but you may choose anything from 1 to 99. 160/180/320/360KB and 720KB drives usually use 9 sectors; 1.2MB drives use 15, and 1.4MB drives use 18.

/H:*hh*   /H:*hh* specifies the number of read/write heads per drive. The default setting is 2. You may choose anything from 1 to 99. Almost all drives have two heads, except for hard disks (which have more) and single-sided 160/180KB floppy drives (which have only one).

/C   /C turns on change-line support. This option is used with disk drives that are capable of sensing when a disk has been inserted or ejected. These include 720KB, 1.2MB, and 1.44MB drives.

/N   This option tells DOS the disk is nonremovable. This flag should be used if you use DRIVER.SYS with a hard disk.

The following are some examples of common DRIVER.SYS DEVICE directives. If you attached a standard 720KB 3.5-inch disk drive to your two-drive floppy system, you would enter:

```
DEVICE=DRIVER.SYS /D:2
```

No command line options (besides the required drive number, 2) are needed, because a 720KB 3.5-inch drive uses all of DRIVER.SYS's default settings.

If you were installing DRIVER.SYS for some other type of drive, you would need to enter the appropriate command line options. For example, if you wanted to install a 1.44MB drive on a two-drive floppy system, you would enter the following:

```
DEVICE=DRIVER.SYS /D:2 /F:7 /S:18 /C
```

This example specifies the drive number (2), the form factor (7), the number of sectors (18), and change-line support (/C). The tracks (/T) and heads (/H) options need not be specified, because the 1.44MB drive uses the default settings.

DRIVER.SYS also lets you refer to one disk drive with two drive designators. In effect, it creates two logical disk drives out of one physical drive. DOS does this automatically for a single-drive system: It lets you refer to the disk drive as both A and B. This makes it possible to copy files from one floppy disk to another. DRIVER.SYS lets you do this for any disk drive, regardless of its format or how many other drives you have installed in your system.

To refer to a single disk drive with two drive designators, you must enter the same DEVICE command twice. The process is the same for both internal and external drives. For example, if you wanted to refer to the 1.44MB drive in the preceding example as two logical drives, you would enter duplicate commands:

```
DEVICE=DRIVER.SYS /D:2 /F:7 /S:18 /C
DEVICE=DRIVER.SYS /D:2 /F:7 /S:18 /C
```

This tells CONFIG.SYS that you'll be referring to the drive as both C and D.

You can also refer to an internal disk drive as two logical drives. For example, if you had a system with a 720KB 3.5-inch floppy (A) and a 360KB 5.25-inch floppy (B), you could enter the following command:

```
DEVICE=DRIVER.SYS /D:1 /F:0 /T:40
```

to let you refer to the B drive as both B and C. If the system used C for its hard disk, you would refer to the drive as B and D. You can also use DRIVER.SYS to provide better control of an existing drive, especially in the case where you have an older PC whose BIOS cannot recognize the capabilities of a newer drive.

For example, suppose you have a 3.5-inch, 1.44MB floppy drive installed as drive B, but your system's BIOS can handle only the older 3.5-inch 720KB drives. Let's assume you have a hard disk partitioned into two logical drives, C and D. You can install DRIVER.SYS to create a new drive, E, which will allow you to access the full capacity of your 1.44MB drive. You would use the following command to do so:

```
DEVICE=C:\DRIVER.SYS /D:1 /C /F:7
```

With DRIVER.SYS installed in this way, the drive would be accessible as a 720KB drive under the letter B and as a 1.44MB drive under the letter E. Since 1.44MB drives can read and write 720KB disk, you could refer to the drive as E for any disk, if you wished.

READ.ME

Order of DEVICE Commands

Unlike the order of configuration commands in CONFIG.SYS, the order of DEVICE commands is important. DEVICE commands used with DRIVER-.SYS and VDISK.SYS (described next) will yield different results depending on their order of appearance.

The first internal floppy disk drive in your system is always referred to as A; the second, B. Beyond that, the directives in your CONFIG.SYS file will determine which drives have which letters. Basically, whatever DOS finds first gets the next drive letter. DRIVER.SYS commands should come before VDISK.SYS commands.

In short, make sure when you use DRIVER.SYS and VDISK.SYS—or multiple copies of either—that you plan which drive names each logical disk should have. Add your directives in the order you want to refer to them: The first directive takes the lowest drive letter available, the second takes the next, and so on.

One tip for solving compatibility problems with device drivers is to try rearranging the DEVICE statements to load the drivers in a different order. Sometimes drivers that appear to conflict with each other will get along fine when a different load order is used. Unfortunately, the number of possible combinations of drivers is so large that the only tip we can give you is to try for yourself and see what works. It isn't hard to do so long as you are systematic and thorough and change only one thing at a time.

If you do have compatibility problems (drivers that don't work or don't work correctly), it's often best to remove all the drivers you can and reload them one by one until the problem occurs. That approach can often identify the culprit much faster than random rearrangements or guesswork.

VDISK.SYS

Not long after the PC was introduced, many third-party software companies introduced utilities known as *RAM disks*. A RAM disk is what you might call an "imaginary" disk drive. The RAM disk is used like any other drive and is referred to with standard drive designators, but no physical disk drive actually exists. Instead, the program sets aside a portion of the PC's memory and uses the memory as if it were a disk drive.

RAM disks are advantageous because of their speed: they are often 10 to 50 times faster than a floppy disk. The disadvantage is that since a RAM disk is not a physical disk, all data will be lost once the computer is turned off (or worse, if there is a system crash or power failure). Of course, you can copy data to a RAM disk, work as normal, and copy it to a real disk when you are finished. But it is possible to forget or have your system lock up and lose all your work.

DOS 3.0 introduced VDISK.SYS, a device driver that acts as a RAM disk. VDISK (which stands for "virtual disk") can be used to create a virtual RAM disk in conventional or extended memory. With DOS 4.0 and above, you can also create a VDISK in expanded memory. (*Note*: Some versions of DOS call it RAMDRIVE.SYS instead of VDISK.SYS.)

To install a virtual disk, place the VDISK DEVICE command in your CONFIG.SYS file. The format is as follows:

DEVICE = *d:path*\VDISK.SYS *disksize secsize dirsize* /E:*n* /X:*n*

Options

d:path   *d*: specifies the disk drive that contains the VDISK.SYS file, and *path* specifies the directory path to VDISK.SYS.

disksize   First—and most important—is the size of the RAM disk. If you do not enter this value, the RAM disk defaults to 64KB. If you entered **128** here, you would have a 128KB RAM disk. Keep in mind that you cannot specify a RAM disk that is larger than your system's available memory less 64KB; that is, you must have 64KB of memory left over after VDISK takes its chunk of memory. Also, note that the size of the RAM disk you specify will not be the actual useable size: A RAM disk works just like a real disk; thus, space is needed for the directory entries, file allocation tables, and boot sectors.

secsize   Next, you may specify the sector size, which may be 128, 256, or 512KB; the default is 128. If you will be working with several small files on the RAM disk, choose 128 or 256; if you normally work with large files, use 512.

dirsize   Here you may specify the number of directory entries, from 2 to 512; the default is 64. This number specifies how many files you can store on the RAM disk (including one for the volume label). Each file uses one directory entry. DOS may automatically adjust your directory entries according to the amount of available memory. If you don't have enough memory, DOS will decrease the number of directory entries. If you have enough memory but the number of directory entries doesn't fill up an entire sector, DOS will increase the number of directory entries until the entire sector is full.

/E:*n*/   /E instructs DOS to install the RAM disk in extended memory. In most cases, a RAM disk won't be large enough to be useful if you have to squeeze it into main memory; so, you'll probably use this parameter most of the times you use VDISK.

/E can be followed by a number (/E:*n*) to limit the number of sectors VDISK will transfer to extended memory at one time. This capability is available only in PC-DOS 3.1 and later. The *n* must be between 1 and 8; the default is 8. The value of *n* should be reduced below 8 only if you have trouble with I/O devices while using VDISK (for example, characters lost by a printer or communications port). Reducing *n* limits the amount of time VDISK will disable processing of interrupts from these devices while it is transferring data to and from extended memory.

/X:*n*/   /X works like /E but uses expanded memory instead of extended (available only in DOS 4.0 and above).

Examples of VDISK DEVICE Commands

```
DEVICE=VDISK.SYS
```

This tells DOS to install a 64KB RAM disk with the default specifications. You will refer to this disk by a drive letter like other disks, but the drive letter you will use depends on what is currently installed in your system and where the driver is loaded in the DEVICE command.

```
DEVICE=VDISK.SYS 360 512 112
```

This RAM drive specification mimics the standard 360KB 5.25-inch IBM drive.

```
DEVICE=VDISK.SYS 1024 512 512 /E
```

This places a 1MB RAM disk with 512-byte sectors and 512 directory entries in extended memory.

READ.ME

A RAM-Disk Tip

The installation of a RAM disk is only a start. How you use the RAM disk is what can really increase your efficiency and computing power. What follows are some tips for RAM disk usage that we have found to be invaluable:

1. In general, the best way to use a RAM drive is to store files that are frequently accessed but are never or rarely modified. A data file for a spelling checker is a good example.

2. Copy small utility programs or applications that you access regularly to the RAM disk.

3. Use the RAM disk as a work disk for programs that are frequently accessed from disk (for example, SideKick, Shez, and PKZIP).

4. Copy COMMAND.COM to your RAM disk. For floppy users, no longer will you have to insert a DOS disk every time a program finishes and requests a copy of COMMAND.COM in drive A. For hard disk users, things will run faster.

If you do load COMMAND.COM into a VDISK RAM drive, make sure you include a line in CONFIG.SYS that tells your system to look for COMMAND-.COM in the appropriate drive. By default, your system will check the root directory of your hard disk and then your A floppy's root directory for COMMAND.COM. If you placed the command

```
SET COMSPEC=D:\COMMAND.COM
```

READ.ME

A RAM-Disk Tip (*continued*)

in CONFIG.SYS, DOS would know to look in the RAM disk for COMMAND-.COM.

When entering this command, make sure you don't put a space before or after the equal sign. Also, make sure the COMSPEC command appears after the VDISK command and that you enter the correct drive designator. If DOS can't find your COMMAND.COM where you told it to look, you will receive an error message and will be unable to boot your system. (The SET command is described in detail elsewhere in this book.)

CONCLUSION

After reading this chapter, you should be familiar with key DOS device drivers and how to create and modify CONFIG.SYS to make use of them. You should also have a working knowledge of the ANSI.SYS device driver, which gives DOS increased screen and keyboard control with a minimum amount of memory usage and substantial compatibility. Along the way, we've pointed out some traps and given you some shortcuts.

Besides the means to increase the capabilities of your screen and keyboard, you now have the basics to configure your system to recognize other disk drives and even create a simulated disk drive with some of your system's RAM. These features of DOS are not well documented and have been underutilized for years.

As in other chapters of this book, the information presented here gives you a general overview of some of the things you can do with these tools. As you continue to work with DOS, you'll discover even more ways to increase your system's speed and performance. The DOS commands and programs discussed here will get you off to a good start.

CHAPTER TWENTY-EIGHT

Upgrading Hardware

In this chapter, we cover the basics of hardware upgrades. This includes opening the computer case, removing cards, installing cards, and closing the case. We will also cover upgrading drives, CPU type, motherboards, and other cards that will enhance the performance of your computer. This chapter will help you decide on what type of upgrades to perform on your computer and help you get all the parts together.

WHY UPGRADE?

New and faster components are being shipped every day. This does not mean that a 4.77 MHz PC is not a good machine—just that it takes a little longer to get things done.

Hard drives have also gotten better, bigger, and faster. When the PC was first introduced, a 10MB hard drive was considered large. Now you can get a 1.2GB drive that takes the same amount of space.

CPU Speeds

CPU speeds are always given in megahertz (MHz). This is the number of cycles per second at which the chip will run with no problems. This speed is controlled by a crystal on the motherboard.

You might think that switching to a faster crystal would boost your speed. The problem is that the CPU and other components must be able to run at the higher speed. To avoid problems, you should run the CPU at the speed for which it is rated or slower.

Note: Some manufacturers are selling systems with "pushed chips"; that is, they are supplying chips that are being run faster than the recommended speed. Pushing a chip (for example, running an 80286-20 at 23 MHz) will normally void any warranty that comes with that chip. Also it will heat up the chip to a point where it might fail.

8088, 8086, or 80186

The first PCs and XTs had a clock speed of 4.77 MHz. Most PC/XT computers have this chip. Intel subsequently created faster versions of this chip. To tell the difference, look at the chip number:

Number	Speed
8088	4.77 or 5 MHz
8088-3	4.77 or 5 MHz
8088-2	8 MHz
8088-1	10 MHz

80286

The first ATs had a clock speed of 6 MHz or 8 MHz. Most early AT computers have this chip. Intel has created faster versions of this chip:

Number	Speed
80286-6	6 MHz
80286-8	8 MHz
80286-10	10 MHz

80286-12	12 MHz
80286-16	16 MHz
80286-20	20 MHz

80386, or i386

This was the first of Intel's 32-bit CPUs. The first AT/386 had a clock speed of 16 MHz. Intel has created faster versions of this chip:

Number	Speed
80386-16	16 MHz
80386-20	20 MHz
80386-25	25 MHz
80386-33	33 MHz

80386SX

The first 80386SX had a clock speed of 16 MHz. Intel has created faster versions of this chip:

Number	Speed
80386SX-16	16 MHz
80386SX-20	20 MHz

80486, or i486

The first 80486 had a clock speed of 25 MHz. Intel has created faster versions of this chip:

Number	Speed
80486-25	25 MHz
80486-33	33 MHz

Drive Types

There are currently four major hard drive interfaces available: the ST-506/412, the ESDI, the SCSI, and the IDE.

ST-506/412

The ST-506/412 interface was popularized by Seagate Technology and was adopted by other drive manufacturers as a standard. It is broken down into categories by the encoding method used for storing data:

MFM MFM stands for "modified frequency modulation," the standard recording method for most hard drives.

RLL RLL stands for "run length limited," a recording method that uses data encoding. This recording method allows up to 50 percent more data to be written to a drive. So, a 40MB hard drive will hold 60MB.

ARLL ARLL stands for "advanced run length limited," another recording method using encoding.

ESDI

ESDI stands for "enhanced small device interface." These hard drives have some controller circuitry built into them. This means the controller is fairly simple to set up.

SCSI

SCSI stands for "small computer system interface." This interface is becoming increasingly popular, especially on machines other than the PC. One interface card will support up to seven devices, including optical drives, CD-ROM drives, tape drives, and other drives. Configuring this interface correctly can sometimes be difficult.

IDE

IDE stands for "intelligent drive electronics." This type of interface is the simplest, with only a single connector on the drive. There is no setup required, as the drive tells the computer how large it is. When you see a controller built into the motherboard, it's usually of this type.

Case and Power Supply

When upgrading a system, you must be aware of power requirements and motherboard sizes.

Motherboards come in two basic sizes: PC (or "Baby AT") and AT. If you have a PC and want to upgrade to an 80286 or 80386 motherboard, you must get a Baby AT motherboard if you are staying with the PC case. A PC or Baby AT motherboard will fit in either a PC case or an AT case. An AT motherboard will fit only in an AT case.

Case Styles

There are two case choices that can be made: a horizontal case or a vertical (tower) case. Good sources for cases are JDR Microdevices, 2233 Branham Lane, San Jose, CA 95124, 408-559-1200, and JAMECO Electronics, 1355 Shoreway Road, Belmont, CA 94002, 415-592-8097. You can find many other sources in *Computer Shopper*.

Horizontal Case   Horizontal, or desktop, cases have been around for a long time and have been the standard for most computer manufacturers. Horizontal cases have either a slide-off top or a "flip top" to provide access to the motherboard and expansion-card slots.

Note: The flip-top case is not FCC approved. Personal computer devices must meet FCC class B radio frequency noise standards. If you are using one of these computers and it interferes with your neighbor's radio or television reception, you may find the FCC knocking at your door. The FCC has the authority to levy fines and confiscate equipment.

There are drawbacks to this case style. The first is the number of drives that can be mounted in the case. A PC/XT case has room for four half-height drives, all accessible through the front of the case. An AT case has room for five half-height drives. Only three positions are accessible through the front of the case; the other two require removal of the cover. Another drawback is that they take up desk space, unless you get a floor stand.

Vertical Case   Vertical cases are becoming increasingly popular. They do not take up desk space and are normally set on the floor next to the desk. They also have a swing-out door on the side to provide access to the motherboard and expansion-card slots. Depending on the case, you can mount up to ten half-height drives.

Power Supply

Many original PCs had a 60-watt power supply. The XT had a 135-watt power supply, and the AT had a 192-watt (most times rounded up to

200-watt) power supply. There are several choices that can be made concerning size, wattage, noise, and temperature.

Wattage Requirements   The wattage requirement varies, depending on the number of drives, CPU, and adapter boards. A good rule of thumb is to match wattage with the type of computer you are upgrading to. Try to get the largest power supply possible the first time, as this will give your system room to grow.

From	To	Watts
PC	AT	200
XT	AT	200
PC	AT/386	250
XT	AT/386	250
AT	AT/386	250

Standard Power Supplies   Standard power supplies come in a variety of wattage outputs, depending on the cases they are being installed in. Good sources for standard power supplies are JDR Microdevices and JAMECO Electronics.

PC/XT Case
135 watt
150 watt
200 watt

AT Case
200 watt
250 watt

Deluxe Power Supplies   You may want to get a special power supply if your computer overheats or if you want a quieter-running system. A good source for deluxe power supplies is PC Power & Cooling, Inc., 31510 Mountain Way, Bonsall, CA 92003, 619-723-9513.

PC/XT Case
150-watt Standard
150-watt Silencer
150-watt Turbo-Cool
200-watt Turbo-Cool

AT Case
200-watt Standard
200-watt Silencer
250-watt Turbo-Cool
375-watt Turbo
450-watt Turbo

Compaq
270-watt Compaq Deskpro

Memory

Systems may come with two banks of 256KB and two banks of 0KB, for a total of 512KB. When upgrading memory, rather than adding two banks of 64KB for a total of 640KB, it is better to install two banks of 256KB, for a total of 1024KB (1MB). This way, if you upgraded to 1024KB, you would not have to throw away the 64KB chips that you removed when you added the 256KB chips.

Memory Speeds

The speed at which memory runs is measured in nanoseconds (ns). The larger the number, the slower the chip. The following is a list of speeds and the types of computers that use them:

Speed	Computer
200ns	None (If you have a chip this speed, switch to a faster chip.)
150ns	PC/XT
120ns	Turbo XT
100ns	AT
80ns	80386
60ns	80486

Memory Types

Memory comes in three different styles:

- Dual Inline Pin, or DIP
- Single Inline Memory Module, or SIMM
- Single Inline Pin, or SIP

DIP Memory The standard DIP memory used is called DRAM (dynamic random-access memory). It is available in several different sizes and speeds. SRAM (static random-access memory) memory is used primarily for cache memory on the motherboard.

Normally, nine memory ICs (integrated circuits) make one bank of memory. A four-bank motherboard normally has 36 sockets for memory.

Note: When upgrading, make sure each bank has the same manufacturer and batch stamp. There are sometimes minute differences in speed between batches. This could cause timing problems.

SIMM Memory SIMMs are memory ICs mounted on a small circuit board. They have a notch cut on the circuit board for orientation.

SIP Memory SIPs are memory ICs mounted on a small circuit board with pins on the bottom. They have a notch cut on the circuit board for orientation.

PREPARATION

We will now cover the actual steps involved in upgrading your system. You should read this chapter thoroughly and refer to the appropriate sections when doing the upgrade. You should have all the required tools and a clear spot on your desk for laying out parts before you begin. You should also label and keep notes of all parts that you disconnect and their orientation.

Precautions

- Turn off your computer and unplug it from the wall.
- Unplug any peripherals from the wall socket.
- Remove all cables attached to the computer.
- Ground yourself before handling any static-sensitive devices (for example, CPUs, memory, and math coprocessor). This can be done by touching a grounding strap or the little screw in the middle of the wall outlet plate. If there is a lot of static in the air, you should keep yourself grounded at all times and keep motion to a minimum.
- Lay a blanket or towel on the work surface. This will prevent scratching of the work surface. It will also prevent parts from rolling away.

Gaining Access

Tools Required
You will need screwdrivers (both Philips head and flat blade) or nut drivers, and a chip puller. On Compaq systems, you will need to use the TORX drivers supplied.

Good sources for computer tool kits are JDR Microdevices, JAMECO Electronics, and Specialized Products Co., 3131 Premier Drive, Irving, TX 75063, 214-550-1923. Also look for the Curtis toolkits, available at most computer stores.

Opening The Case

Horizontal Case   Unscrew the five screws on the back of the computer. Then, slide the case forward and lift it off.

Vertical Case   Unscrew the three screws holding the door closed. Then, slide the door back. When the catches are free, swing the door open.

If your system is different, you should check the system manual for information on opening the case.

Removal of Components

We will now explain how to remove the components that make up the system. If you are swapping a motherboard, you will need to remove all the components that are attached to the motherboard. If you are adding an accelerator card, you just need to remove a slot cover (unless you have no slots left—then you need to remove a card and install the accelerator).

Removing Cards
To remove a card, you need to

1. Remove the hold-down screw that holds the adapter bracket to the case.

2. Rock the card gently along the long access while pulling up to disengage it from the connector.

3. Remove any cables attached to the card. (Make sure to note the connections so that you connect the right cables when you reinstall the card.)

4. Lift the card from the case.

Removing Drives
Removing a drive will depend on the type of case you have. In most PC/XT cases, the drives are screwed into place. In AT cases, the drives are mounted on rails that slide into the case.

Removing the Power Supply
To remove a power supply, undo any power connectors that are attached (such as the motherboard and drives). Undo the screws holding the power supply to the chassis (these are located at the back of the chassis). Slide the power supply to the front of the chassis to disengage the hold-down bracket. Lift the power supply out of the chassis and set it aside.

Removing the Motherboard
The only thing that should be left in your computer is the motherboard. To remove the motherboard, locate all the hold-down screws and remove them. There can be up to nine screws holding the motherboard down, or there may be some screws and standoffs. Once the motherboard is loose, slide it to the left (as viewed from the front of the case), and lift it out.

Note: On ATs, there is normally a separate battery to power the clock. Remove the battery plug from the motherboard before removing the motherboard. Note the way the plug is oriented on the motherboard so that you can connect it right when reinstalling the battery.

Removing Integrated Circuits
To remove integrated circuits (ICs), you should use a chip puller. There are different styles to handle the different types of ICs. For PC/XT computers, you will need an IC puller designed for dual inline pin (DIP) ICs. For ATs, you will also need a PLCC (plastic leaded chip carrier) puller.

If you do not have IC pullers, you can use a flat-blade screwdriver or a chip lifter. To use these, work very carefully and slowly so that you do not bend pins. Start at one end, and alternate lifting the chip at each end a little at a time.

Dust and Performance

No matter what environment you work in, your system will collect dust and other airborne debris. In the long run, this can reduce cooling power and cause premature failure of components. You should clean the system thoroughly about every three months.

The components most susceptible to dust are the floppy drives and the power supply. Since the drives are at the front of the system and air is drawn in through them by the cooling fan, dust tends to settle on the read-write heads, the write-protect sensor, and the sector sensor. To clean a drive, use a paint brush, a vacuum cleaner, or a compressed air can to remove dust.

The power supply will collect dust in the air vents. Use a paint brush or a toothbrush and a vacuum cleaner to remove the dust from the air vents.

Installation of Components

In most cases, installation is just the reverse of removal.

Installing ICs

When reinstalling ICs, pay attention to the Pin 1 orientation marks on the chip. Also, the motherboard or adapter card will have a silk-screened pattern on the component side of the board. To identify Pin 1 on the silk-screened pattern, look for a little U-shaped indent. The most common Pin 1 orientation marks are

- A little indent next to Pin 1.

- A U-shaped indent or notch in one end of the IC.

- A missing corner on the chip. This is seen primarily on PLCC and Pin Grid Array (PGA) ICs, such as the 80286, 80386, 80387, and 80486.

Place the IC in the socket, making sure of the orientation, and press down. The IC should seat firmly in the socket.

Note: When inserting ICs, make sure the leads are all straight. If a lead is crooked, it could bend during insertion and cause problems. If in doubt, remove the chip and check it.

——————————————— **READ.ME** ———————————————

Chip Creep

The heating and cooling cycle that a computer goes through when it is turned on and off will cause a socketed IC to expand and contract in the socket. Eventually, the chip may slowly creep out of its socket.

To prevent this, any time you have a board out of the computer, you should press down on the socketed ICs to seat them. This serves two purposes: (1) The ICs are reseated, and (2) any corrosion on the leads of the ICs is rubbed away, making for better connections.

Installing the Motherboard
Installing a new motherboard comprises the following steps:

1. Remove the standoffs from the old motherboard.

2. Install memory on the new motherboard.

3. Install the math coprocessor, if one is being installed.

4. Install any other components.

5. Install the standoffs on the new motherboard.

6. Lower the new motherboard into the chassis and set the standoffs into their slots.

7. Slide the motherboard to the right to engage the standoffs.

8. Install and tighten the hold-down screws.

9. Install the battery connector.

Refer to your notes to make sure the connections are correct.

Note: Most standard AT batteries last from 12 to 18 months. Several companies supply rechargeable battery systems for ATs. One of the best, called LAST*BAT, is made by Accumation, Inc., 8817 Southwest 129 Terrace, Miami, FL 33176, 305-238-1034.

Installing the Power Supply

To install the power supply, follow these steps:

1. Lower the power supply into the chassis. Make sure that it is not back all the way, or the hold-down clamps will not engage.

2. Slide the power supply back, making sure the hold-down clamp engages.

3. Install the four hold-down screws, and tighten them.

4. Install the motherboard power connectors. These are normally keyed so that they go on only one way. Make sure the black wires are in the center of the two connectors.

Refer to your notes to make sure the connections are correct.

Installing Drives

If you are reinstalling drives, reverse the order in which you removed them. If you are installing a new drive, either attach the rails (AT system), or screw it in (PC/XT system). Connect the power cables and drive cables as appropriate. Refer to your notes for correct orientation.

Installing Cards

To install a card:

1. Make sure the adapter bracket cover is removed.

2. Line the card up in the slot and insert it. If it is a full-length card, make sure the card is in the card guide at the front of the system.

3. Attach any cables to the card.

4. Press on the card so that it seats into the connector on the motherboard.

5. Install the hold-down screw, and tighten it to anchor the drive.

Closing the Case

You should go through the following steps when you finish upgrading anything in your system:

1. When all the cards and drives are installed, check your notes and doublecheck all connections to make sure they are right.

2. Close the case, installing only one screw at this point. This will hold the case together but allow easy access if you need to reset switches or jumper settings.

3. Make all the external connections.

4. Plug in the power.

5. Turn on the system.

6. If everything is working fine, install the rest of the case screws.

You have now upgraded your system.

PC/XT UPGRADES

What can I upgrade in my PC/XT system? You probably have asked this question before and gotten a variety of answers. The correct answer is: Everything. You may already have the tools required to do the job but no idea where to start.

CPU Upgrades

Upgrading the CPU in a PC/XT system can range from a CPU swap, installation of an accelerator card, or a full motherboard replacement.

Adding an accelerator card is the easiest way to increase the performance of your computer. All that is required is for you to open the case, add the card, and close the case, and your work is basically done.

A motherboard swap is a little harder than the accelerator card installation, but the benefits are fantastic.

The CPU swap is a little more technical than the motherboard swap. You will have to remove the old CPU and install the new CPU in its place.

CPU Swap

One of the ways of improving the speed in your PC/XT computer is to replace the 8088 or 8086 CPU with a SOTA Express/286, NEC V-20, or NEC V-30 CPU. The advantage of a CPU swap is that it does not take up an expansion slot.

SOTA Express/286   This is a small circuit board that plugs into the socket where your 8088 or 8086 CPU is located. The circuit board has an 80286 mounted on the board and is available in 10 MHz and 12.5 MHz versions. (SOTA Technology, Inc. 559 Weddell Drive, Sunnyvale, CA 94089, 408-745-1111)

NEC V-20   This chip is a replacement for the 8088 chip on your motherboard. The V-20 is available in 5 MHz, 8 MHz, and 10 MHz versions.

NEC V-30   This chip is a replacement for the 8086 chip on your motherboard. The V-30 runs at 8 MHz. Note that only a few machines use an 8086.

Accelerator Cards

One of the simplest ways of improving the speed in your PC/XT computer is to install an accelerator card. An accelerator card is a plug-in card that has its own processor and memory. There are a number of accelerator cards on the market, including the following:

Intel Inboard 386/PC   The Inboard 386/PC is a full-length card providing a 16 MHz 80386 system with 1MB of memory. You can expand the memory to 5MB by adding a 4MB option card. A 2MB option card is also available. There is space for an 80387-16 math coprocessor on the card. (Intel Corp., Personal Computer Enhancement, 5200 N.E. Elam Young Parkway, Hillsboro, OR 97124-6497, 800-538-3373)

SOTA 286i   The SOTA 286i is a half-length card providing a 12.5 MHz 80286 system. You can expand the memory to 4MB or 8MB by adding a SOTA Memory 16/i and optional daughter card. There is space for an 80287 math coprocessor on the card.

SOTA 386si   The SOTA 386si is a half-length card providing a 16 MHz 80386SX system. You can expand the memory to 4MB or 8MB by adding a SOTA Memory 16/i and optional daughter card. There is space for an 80387SX math coprocessor on the card.

READ.ME

PC/XT Motherboards

Currently, many companies are making motherboards that will fit into a PC/XT case. These are the so-called "Baby AT" motherboards—"AT" because of the 16-bit slots available, and "Baby" because of the size (most are 8.5 by 13 inches). These motherboards will also fit in mini-AT and full-AT cases.

There are many choices for motherboards, whether a faster 8088 or 8086 to replace a 4.77 MHz motherboard, an 80286, an 80386SX, an 80386, or an 80486. Choosing the right motherboard depends on the type of applications you are running. Word processing can be done on a 4.77 MHz PC, but a faster speed is better. CAD packages are best run at the highest speed possible.

Another thing to look for in a motherboard is the use of Single Inline Memory Modules, or SIMMs. This is the easiest way to expand the memory on your motherboard.

Motherboard Swaps

Western Digital 286 The Western Digital 286 motherboard has got almost everything built right into it: hard and floppy drive controllers, EGA, two serial ports, one parallel port, and a PS/2 mouse port. It can have up to 4MB of memory using SIMMs. The hard and floppy controller will handle two MFM hard drives and two floppy drives (360KB, 1.2MB, 720KB, or 1.44MB). Designed for reduced power consumption, it has a 12.5 MHz 80286 processor and a socket for the 80287.

Drive and Controller Upgrades

After upgrading the CPU, the next upgrade possibilities are the controller and the drives. Most systems will have either two floppy drives or one floppy drive and a hard drive. If you have two floppy drives, you should consider getting a hard drive.

The size of the hard drive will depend on the amount of work you do on your computer. If you run just a single application (such as a word processor or spreadsheet), then a 10MB or 20MB drive is sufficient. If you will be running multiple applications with various data files, you will need a larger drive. How large depends on the space available in the machine, the controller, and, of course, the price.

If you already have a hard drive, switching to an RLL controller can increase your hard disk size by about 50 percent: A 20MB drive will handle 30MB, a 40MB drive will handle 60MB, and so on. Below are descriptions of controllers and drives that you may want to upgrade to.

Floppy Drives

There are four basic sizes for floppy drives on the market today:

- 360KB 5.25-inch

- 1.2MB 5.25-inch

- 720KB 3.5-inch

- 1.44MB 3.5-inch

Most PC/XT systems have either one or two 360KB, 5.25-inch floppy drives. Upgrading the floppy drives to a 1.2MB, 5.25-inch floppy drive will still allow you to read from and write to 360KB disks. The optimum setup is to have a 1.2MB, 5.25-inch floppy drive and a 1.44MB, 3.25-inch floppy drive. This will allow you the most flexibility.

There are several floppy drive controllers that allow you to have up to four drives in your system. Cumulus Stepping Stone and MicroSolutions CompatiCard allow you to have four floppy drives, including two external ones.

Controllers

The controller is a major consideration in the system. It is tied directly to the type of hard drive you have or that you are considering upgrading to. The best controller upgrade is from an MFM controller to an RLL or ARLL controller.

Hard Drives

The standard hard drives in most PC/XT systems are MFM-type hard drives. There are a number of sources for hard and floppy drives that will work in PC/XT systems.

AT UPGRADES

The same reasons for upgrading apply to ATs.

CPU Upgrades

Upgrading the CPU in a AT system can range from a CPU swap, installation of an accelerator card, or a motherboard replacement.

Adding an accelerator card is the easiest way to increase the performance of your computer.

The motherboard swap is a little harder than the accelerator card installation, but the benefits are fantastic.

The CPU swap is a little more technical than the motherboard swap. You will have to remove the old CPU and install the new CPU in its place.

CPU Swap

Cu386SX   The Cu386SX is an 80386SX mounted on a small circuit board. It plugs into the 80286 socket on your AT motherboard. This card is manufactured by Cumulus Corporation.

SOTA Express/386   The SOTA Express/386 is an 80386SX mounted on a small circuit board. It plugs into the 80286 socket on your AT motherboard and is available in 16 MHz and 20 MHz versions. This card is manufactured by SOTA Technology.

Accelerator Cards

One of the simplest ways of improving the speed in your AT computer is to install an accelerator card. An accelerator card is a plug-in card that has its own processor and memory.

Motherboards

Currently, many companies are making motherboards that will fit into an AT case.

Drive and Controller Upgrades

After upgrading the CPU, the next upgrade possibilities are the controller and the drives. Most systems will have either two floppy drives or one floppy drive and a hard drive. If you have two floppy drives, you should consider getting a hard drive. If you already have a hard drive, switching to an RLL controller can increase your hard disk size by about 50 percent.

Floppy Drives
Most AT systems have either one or two 1.2MB, 5.25-inch floppy drives. The optimum setup is to have a 1.2MB, 5.25-inch floppy drive and a 1.44MB, 3.5-inch floppy drive. This will allow you the most flexibility.

Controllers
The controller is a major consideration in the system. It is tied directly to the type of hard drive you have or are considering upgrading to.

Hard Drives
The standard hard drives in most AT systems are MFM-type hard drives. A number of manufacturers supply drives that will work in AT systems.

GENERIC SYSTEM UPGRADES

Some performance upgrades do not target the CPU or other portions of the system. Instead, these upgrades speed up how you do your work.

Specialty Cards

Some adapter boards replace some of your office equipment just as the computer and printer replace the typewriter and adding machine.

Fax Cards
A card can replace your fax machine. Instead of printing a letter, taking it to the fax machine, dialing the number, and sending it, you can have the

computer dial the number and send the text file to a fax machine or another computer with a fax card.

FRECOM FAX 96   The FRECOM FAX 96 is a full-featured fax card for a little under $200. (FRECOM 46309 Warm Springs Boulevard, Fremont, CA 94539, 415-438-5000)

Intel Connection Coprocessor   The Intel Connection Coprocessor is a full-featured fax board that can also send files to another Connection Coprocessor. (Intel Corporation, Personal Computer Enhancement, 5200 N.E. Elam Young Parkway, Hillsboro, OR 97124-6497, 800-538-3373)

CHAPTER TWENTY-NINE

The Future of DOS

In this chapter, you'll learn about new commands and features offered by a version of DOS to be released in early 1991. This chapter will introduce you to DOS 5.0's new and improved memory-management tools, on-line Help system, command line editor, and data-recovery commands.

We'll also discuss some of the powerful additions to DOS that are useful in editing text files, performing DOS commands, and running QuickBASIC programs.

BUY IT!

An estimated 80,000 PC-based software applications are run by over 35 million DOS users. In the past, most revisions of DOS coincided with the introduction of new IBM models that had new features requiring additional DOS support. For example, when double-sided floppies were introduced, DOS 1.1 was issued to keep pace, and the same thing happened when hard disks began to appear: DOS 2.0 arrived with paths and subdirectories and new hard-disk-specific commands. File sharing, record locking, 3.5-inch floppies (of varying storage capacities), and many other features of DOS updates have been driven by the requirements of the hardware available at the time.

There has been an explosive growth of new technology: CD ROMs, high-capacity hard disk drives, and multitasking-systems software (such as DESQview, Windows 3, and local area networks) are now very common.

The DOS 640KB memory barrier, always an obstacle, is becoming intolerable as precious memory is gobbled up by the DOS kernel, files, buffers, disk caches, RAM disks, and huge RAM-hungry applications (Paradox, dBASE IV, PageMaker, Ventura and so on). Networks, notorious for their memory requirements, can leave a user who once had 575KB of available conventional memory with a scant 420KB.

In many cases, users aren't able to run their software without first removing most of their TSRs and device drivers from RAM. Often, this can mean that network users must do without their network connections if they want to run certain applications.

Third-party developers, of course, have wasted no time in marketing new products that would offer some relief. Memory-manager programs were developed to shift many of the device drivers and resident programs from conventional memory to extended and expanded memory.

Other programs even found new and creative ways to squeeze extra memory from the 1MB most versions of DOS can directly address. They manage to reallocate memory addresses reserved for noncritical or unused system ROMs, page frames, and display adapters. All of these tricks have helped keep things going as long as they have.

And now, *everything* has changed. With the introduction of DOS 5.0, users can get *more* for *less*. Microsoft DOS 5.0 gives users more commands and features while using less conventional memory. Microsoft got the DOS 5.0 development effort started on the right track by first conducting a detailed analysis of what users and developers want in an operating system. They also took a good look at DR-DOS 5.0!

Microsoft also took care to ensure that the updated DOS would be compatible with earlier versions of DOS and the huge number of programs on the market. DOS 5.0's beta testing included *Fortune* 1000 firms, developers, and journalists. And through it all, the company maintained close contact with users for feedback.

MS DOS 5.0's improved support for loading files, buffers, and TSRs has reduced, if not eliminated, the need for many of these utilities. The MS DOS 5.0 kernel takes less memory than DOS 4.X and earlier versions. What's more, it can be almost totally loaded into high RAM, a feature not possible with commercial memory managers. In fact, when used on a system with extended or expanded RAM, DOS 5.0 will give you more available conventional memory than any other version from 2.X to 4.X.

DOS 5.0 has facilities to undelete files and unformat disks. Many of the commands you have come to know and love now have more options, and many new commands have been added. Cryptic or nonexistent messages have been replaced with messages that tell you when a command is working and whether it is successful.

Even the purveyors of TSR DOS "help" programs now have competition. DOS 5.0 supports a complete on-line Help system for its commands. Invoking Help is as simple as entering a command followed by "/?" on the command line. For example, to get Help on the XCOPY command, you would enter the following:

```
XCOPY /?
```

This displays information on the command syntax.

The shell, first introduced with DOS 4.0, has been updated and expanded in DOS 5.0. DOSSHELL uses a graphical user interface (GUI) that works in ordinary text mode and offers full mouse support.

Throughout DOSSHELL, you'll find title bars that display names of menus and menu bars that list the names of available menu choices. DOSSHELL also has other features commonly found in GUI programs, including scroll bars, a status line, and a mouse pointer. This shell takes considerably less memory than the one in DOS 4.0, and its interface closely resembles Microsoft Works and Windows 3.

Starting with DOS 4.0, disk volumes have 8-digit hex serial numbers that DOS can use to tell if a floppy disk is switched at the wrong time.

The directory command has been revised. Now you can use DIR to get a quick handle on both the size of a group of files and the remaining disk space available. There are several new options for the DIR command, which can be used with or without the familiar /P and /W options. You invoke the options by typing /O and one or more of the following:

/D	Date
/E	Extension
/N	Name
/S	Size
—	Reverse order

RECOVERING DELETED FILES

DOS 5.0's new UNDELETE command can recover files that have been deleted with the DEL or ERASE command. For example, to undelete the text file we used to create this chapter, we would enter

```
UNDELETE C:\JCD-DOS\CHAP29.TXT
```

The file would be restored if the data on the disk were still intact.

The data in a file isn't erased when you delete the file. Instead, DOS simply marks the file as deleted, and it will reuse the sectors of the disk that the file occupies only when the space is needed. If the space has been reused or written to, DOS's UNDELETE (or any utility, for that matter) will not be able to recover the file. UNDELETE even supports the use of a delete-tracking file, which is an advanced feature of similar commercial utilities. When a tracking file is used, the chances are greater that the information can be recovered.

UNDELETE will not work on deleted directories. If a directory has been deleted, the files inside it cannot be undeleted unless the directory is undeleted first. The new program REBUILD will restore both removed directories and deleted files. Like UNDELETE, REBUILD will be successful only if the data on the disk is still intact. (UNDELETE and REBUILD will *not* work if you squeeze directories after deleting.)

The DOS FORMAT command is now not so deadly as it used to be. The FORMAT warning message has been improved, and hard disk partitions accidentally formatted can be unformatted with the new UNFORMAT or REBUILD command. To restore a hard disk that has been formatted with the safe-format program, use the following command:

```
rebuild c:
```

Unless you used the /u switch when you formatted the disk, the original format would be recovered.

The command MIRROR is used to create a delete-tracking file called PCTRACKR.DEL. MIRROR is also a TSR that monitors the system and detects and records file deletions. MIRROR can be loaded into high RAM and can be set to track multiple drives. To have MIRROR track drives C and D, you would enter

```
mirror /tc /td
```

Each time you deleted a file or removed a directory, MIRROR would create or update the file PCTRACKR.DEL, which it places in the root directory of each drive.

If you have assorted-size disks, you'll find the improved formatting options that were introduced in DOS 4.0 useful. The /F switch can be used to specify the size of the disk you wish to format. The options are /F:160, /F:180, /F:320, /F:360, /F:720, /F:1200, and /F:1440. Since many DOS 3.30 users are expected to upgrade directly to DOS 5.0, bypassing DOS 4.X altogether, this feature and others will be new to these users.

You can also use the options of other DOS versions to specify how you want to format disks. If your version of DOS doesn't support the /F option, the more complex /N, /T, and /4 options can be used. If you are using DOS 4.0 or higher, you'll find the /F option the easiest to work with. Although the /T and /N options can be used wherever the /F option can, they are harder to remember. Since they require more keystrokes, they are more prone to error. Table 29-1 compares DOS FORMAT command line options.

WORKING WITH DOS 5.0'S DOSKEY

DOSKEY is a TSR command that lets you display, edit, and run commands you previously entered. DOSKEY uses the keys native to DOS (F1, F2, F2, INS,

---

TABLE 29-1

DOS Format Command Line Switches

Form	DOS 4.0 and above	DOS 3.2 and above
5.25″	f:160	/t:40 /n:8 /1
5.25″	f:180	/t:40 /n:8 /1
5.25″	f:320	/t:40 /n:9 /1
5.25″	f:360	/t:40 /n:9 /1
5.25″	f:360	/4 (for 80-track drives)
3.5″	f:720	/t:80 /n:9
5.25″	f:1200	/t:80 /n:15
3.5″	f:1440	/t:80 /n:18

DEL, RIGHT ARROW, and LEFT ARROW) and supports additional keys. DOSKEY also offers command macros, which are series of DOS commands similar to batch files but are stored in RAM. You can also use DOSKEY to enter multiple DOS commands on one command line.

Using DOSKEY will increase the capabilities of DOS command line editing, but it will also use a small amount of RAM. If you need more conventional 640KB memory, you can load DOSKEY into high memory, or you can unload it and stick with DOS's standard editing keys.

To load DOSKEY, simply enter the following:

```
doskey
```

Unless you specify /bufsize = *nnn*, DOSKEY will reserve 512 bytes of memory for commands and recording of macros. The default of 512 bytes will store about 35 commands averaging 15 characters in length. In addition to the bufsize, DOSKEY occupies about 3KB of memory.

To load DOSKEY with a bufsize of 1024 bytes, enter the following:

```
doskey /bufsize=1024
```

As you enter commands, the oldest ones will be removed to make room for the new ones.

If you have already installed DOSKEY, you can reinstall it by entering the following:

```
doskey /reinstall
```

DOSKEY will then work fine with command prompts in environments like Microsoft Windows.

Using DOSKEY to Enter Multiple Commands

Since its release in 1981, DOS has supported only a single command on the DOS command line. The closest DOS came to supporting multiple commands was its use of the pipe command (|) to process the output of the primary command. For instance, you could combine MORE and DIR by entering the following:

```
DIR | MORE
```

This command displays as much of the current directory listing as it can fit on one screen and waits for a keypress before displaying the next screenful. Now, you can enter multiple commands on the DOS command line by separating them with the ^T character. When you press CTRL-T, DOS will echo the paragraph mark on the screen. For example, if you wanted to move the XTREE files in the \DVORAK directory, you would ordinarily need to enter the following commands:

```
md \xtree
cd \dvorak
copy xt*.* \xtree
del xt*.*
cd \xtree
```

With DOSKEY loaded, you can combine the commands on a single command line by entering

```
md \xtree ¶ cd \dvorak ¶ copy xt*.* \xtree ¶ del xt*.* ¶ cd \xtree
```

The only limit on the number of commands you can enter is that they cannot exceed 128 characters combined.

Displaying and Editing Previous Commands

Once DOSKEY is loaded, a command buffer records commands as they are entered. Early commands will be released as space is needed to record new ones. You can reexecute any command in the buffer by displaying it and pressing ENTER. When you reuse a command, DOSKEY will place it at the end of the buffer again. The following keys act on commands in the DOSKEY buffer:

ESC	Clears the command line
F7	Displays the entire command list in DOSKEY's buffer
F8	Searches DOSKEY's buffer and displays commands that match the string you enter
F9	Selects the number of commands for DOSKEY to display
DOWN ARROW	Displays the next command in DOSKEY's buffer
UP ARROW	Displays the last command in DOSKEY's buffer
PAGE UP	Displays the oldest command in DOSKEY's buffer
PAGE DOWN	Displays the newest command in DOSKEY's buffer

Let's take a look at how the DOSKEY command buffer would work with the preceding example. If DOSKEY were loaded and you entered the following commands:

```
md \xtree
cd \dvorak
copy xt*.* \xtree
del xt*.*
cd \xtree
```

the commands would be saved in DOSKEY's buffer. You could press F7 to
cause DOSKEY to display the commands like this:

```
1: md \xtree
2: cd \dvorak
3: copy xt*.* \xtree
4: del xt*.*
5:>cd \xtree
```

The current command is marked with a "greater than" sign (>). The
current-command indicator will change as you move through the command
list.

Changing and Reusing Commands

In addition to the standard editing keys supported by native DOS, DOS-
KEY supports the following keys:

BACKSPACE	Deletes the character to the left of the cursor
CTRL-END	Deletes all the characters from the cursor to the end of the line
CTRL-HOME	Deletes all the characters from the cursor to the beginning of the line
CTRL-LEFT ARROW	Moves the cursor left one word on the command line
CTRL-RIGHT ARROW	Moves the cursor right one word on the command line
DEL	Deletes the character at the cursor
END	Moves the cursor to the end of the command line
ESC	Erases the command displayed
HOME	Moves the cursor to the beginning of the command line
INS	Inserts characters at the cursor
LEFT ARROW	Moves the cursor left one character on the command line
RIGHT ARROW	Moves the cursor right one character on the command line

DOSKEY Macros

DOSKEY macros are similar to the command synonyms supported by Chris Dunford's CED and PCED, Steve Calwas's Anarkey, and JP Software's 4DOS.

The DOSKEY command must include the name and commands of the macro. For example, to create a DOSKEY macro that gives a wide directory, you would enter the following:

```
doskey wdir-dir /w
```

For the remainder of your DOS session, you could execute the command

```
DIR /W
```

by entering

```
WDIR
```

Macros with multiple commands are slightly different. While multiple commands on command lines require the ^T character, in macros the $t character is used, instead. If you wanted a directory listing of all BAK, TMP, and $?$ files, you would enter the following:

```
doskey jdir-dir *.bak $t dir *.tmp $t dir $?$
```

When you entered **JDIR** on the command line, you'd get a listing of the files with those extensions. In case you're wondering, the **J** in **JDIR** stands for "junk," but you can use any macro name you like.

Displaying, Changing, Saving, and Deleting Commands and Macros

The F10 key is used to display the DOSKEY macros. The other keys listed earlier allow you to make changes to the macros. To save the macros you created, you would enter the following:

```
doskey /dmacs >macrolst.txt
```

The macros would be recorded to disk. You could then edit the file to rearrange, change, or delete commands. You could also store them in a DOS batch file, such as AUTOEXEC.BAT.

You can also save commands in DOSKEY's buffer by entering the following:

```
doskey /dhist >cmdslst.txt
```

You can delete macros by entering the following:

```
doskey wdir-
```

Following the macro name with a dash causes DOSKEY to delete the macro from memory.

What About Parameters?

DOS command macros are more useful when they support a variable number of command line parameters. DOSKEY has a special parameter, $0, which is a replaceable parameter. It allows a single parameter to be assigned to all the text that follows the command in a macro. For example, if you entered

```
doskey d-dir $0
```

the SDIR macro would support the following commands:

```
d *.txt
d *.wks *.bak
d /w /p *.txt
d >prn
```

In fact, the commands D and DIR would now work the same.

THE DOS 5.0 SHELL

The DOS 5.0 shell offers many new features. For example, task switching allows you to load several programs and toggle between them. This feature may well eliminate the need for some of the commercial task switchers on the market and satisfy users who don't quite need a true multitasker. For our purposes, we'll limit this discussion to the DOS shell's configuration and command options.

Microsoft has made customizing the shell easier than ever. You can change the shell's default values for monitor type and colors by creating or modifying the DOSSHELL.INI file, which is normally found in the directory with your DOS command files.

The DOS shell's most powerful option, program grouping, can also be customized. Groups of programs can be displayed in a file list in the order you specify—even with custom Help files you've created. You can create and change these groups and control the way they are displayed.

Program shortcut keys and even program-memory allocation can also be assigned.

MOVE OVER, EDLIN—HERE COMES EDIT!

EDIT is the new text editor that comes with DOS. EDIT can be used to create, edit, modify, save, and print ASCII text files, such as CONFIG.SYS, AUTOEXEC.BAT, any other batch files, and even memos and letters. EDIT has a well-designed user interface that supports the keyboard and a mouse.

Once you become familiar with EDIT, you will probably want to use EDLIN (still included with DOS) only for special purposes. Since some publications or programs may refer to or use EDLIN, it makes sense to have it available. You'll find a detailed discussion of EDLIN in Chapter 24.

To use EDIT with a file named DEARJOHN.TXT, type

```
EDIT dearjohn.txt
```

You will see a screen similar to the one used with the editors found in Microsoft QuickBASIC and Microsoft Works. Many of EDIT's keyboard commands should already be familiar to you.

Help Commands

ALT-F1	Displays Help window of previously viewed topics (up to 20 topics)
CHARACTER	Moves the cursor to the next Help topic that begins with that character
CTRL-F1	Displays the next help topic
SHIFT-CHARACTER	Moves the cursor to the previous Help topic that begins with that character
SHIFT-CTRL	Displays the previous Help topic
SHIFT-TAB	Moves the cursor to the previous Help topic
TAB	Moves the cursor to the next Help topic

Edit and Delete Commands

BACKSPACE or CTRL-H	Deletes one character to the left of the cursor
DEL or CTRL-G	Deletes the character at the cursor position
CTRL-T	Deletes the word at the cursor position
CTRL-V	Toggles the Overwrite mode
INS	Inserts characters on the line (default mode)

Cursor-Movement Commands

Arrow Keys	Move the cursor up, down, left, and right
Mouse	Moves the cursor; uses the left button to anchor
CTRL-LEFT ARROW	Moves the cursor left one word
CTRL-RIGHT ARROW	Moves the cursor right one word
HOME	Moves the cursor to the beginning of the file
END	Moves the cursor to the end of the file
CTRL-ENTER	Moves the cursor to the beginning of the next line
CTRL-Q E	Moves the cursor to the top of the screen
CTRL-Q X	Moves the cursor to the bottom of the screen
CTRL-UP ARROW or CTRL-W	Scrolls up one line
CTRL-DOWN ARROW or CTRL-Z	Scrolls down one line
PAGE UP	Scrolls up one screen
PAGE DOWN	Scrolls down one screen

CTRL-HOME or CTRL-Q R	Moves the cursor to the beginning of the file
CTRL-END or CTRL-Q C	Moves the cursor to the end of the file
CTRL-PAGE UP	Scrolls left one screen
CTRL-PAGE DOWN	Scrolls right one screen

OTHER NEW FEATURES

Another convenient feature in DOS 5.0 is the INSTALL command, which can be used to load TSR programs directly from the CONFIG.SYS file.

DOS's extended-memory manager, HIMEM.SYS, has also been updated. You'll need to load a device driver for your extended memory before you can use the SMARTDRV.SYS disk cache, which is included with DOS, too. Extended memory is also the best choice if you're running Microsoft Windows 3. DOS 5.0's HIMEM.SYS is fully compatible with Windows 3.

The most critical reason to use an extended-memory manager is that running DOS 5.0 in extended memory will give you more conventional memory for your applications.

Caches, Buffers, and Secondary Caches

DOS 5.0 has it all. Buffers can be set to the size of your disk's sectors (usually 512 bytes), and a disk cache, SMARTDRV.SYS, speeds up disk activity by using conventional, extended, or expanded memory. The CONFIG.SYS option BUFFERS=nn has been changed to BUFFERS=nn,nn, where the second number is a secondary cache. If you're not using SMARTDRV.SYS or other disk-caching software, you'll find this option useful.

Note: Don't run SMARTDRV.SYS version 2.0 with Windows / 386 or other disk-caching software.

You'll also need to have a memory manager like HIMEM.SYS loaded before loading SMARTDRV.SYS. To load the HIMEM.SYS memory manager, enter the following line in your CONFIG.SYS file:

```
device=c:\dos\himem.sys
```

If you're one of the growing number of 386 or 486 system owners, DOS 5.0 has a new memory manager for you, too. Adding the EMM386.EXE device driver to your CONFIG.SYS simulates expanded memory and allows you to load your devices and TSRs high. To load the EMM386.EXE memory manager, enter the following line in your CONFIG.SYS file:

```
device=c:\dos\emm386.exe
```

If you want to reserve some of your system's RAM for extended memory, you can use the line

```
device=c:\dos\emm386.exe 640
```

to reserve 640KB of extended memory. The remaining memory would be allocated to expanded memory.

Once the EMM386.EXE memory manager is loaded, the two DOS 5.0 commands DEVICEHI and LOADHI can be used to load device drivers and TSRs into available upper memory blocks (UMBs).

One DOS 5.0 CONFIG.SYS option supported by HIMEM.SYS and EMM386.EXE is the DOS=HI command, which loads the DOS kernel into high memory. To use this feature, enter the following in your CONFIG-.SYS:

```
device=c:\dos\himem.sys
dos=hi
```

If you have a 386 or 486 system, enter

```
device=c:\dos\emm386.exe
dos=hi
```

GOODBYE BASIC, BASICA, AND GW-BASIC—HELLO, QUICKBASIC INTERPRETER

Updates for GW-BASIC have been few and far between. Since the majority of new BASIC programs are written in QuickBASIC, it made little sense to

continue shipping an older, less powerful product. Most GW-BASIC programs will run unchanged in QuickBASIC. Older versions of DOS that
include GW-BASIC will still be available in the market—and at substantial
discount.

Including QuickBASIC Interpreter (QBI) with DOS should help bring to
market many more graphical user interface programs with menus that rival
what we've seen over the years. Developers with the complete QuickBASIC
package can compile their programs, and now users can run them with the
interpreter included with DOS. QBI will save disk space for programmers,
who will no longer need to ship a QuickBASIC run-time program.

SETVER

All of us have things we just can't seem to do without: an old sweater or
hat, a vehicle that has more miles on it than Lindbergh's *Spirit of St. Louis,*
or an outdated version of an application program that requires an earlier
version of DOS. DOS 5.0's SETVER command lets you control the version
number that DOS is "seen" as when you execute a program. You can give
SETVER a list of programs and the version numbers you wish DOS to be
set to when they are executed.

I thought this was a clever idea when I first came across Mark Perkel's
shareware program VERSION, and I still do. If you're like me, you've got
all kinds of stuff, and who knows which one of the programs is version
specific?

CONCLUSION

After reading this chapter, you should have a basic understanding of some
of DOS 5.0's new memory-management tools HIMEM.SYS, EMM386.EXE,
LOADHI, DEVICEHI, DOS=HI, and INSTALL.

If you need help with DOS 5.0, you now have an extensive on-line Help
system to guide you.

You can save your keystrokes with the new DOSKEY command and
create your own DOS command macros.

Your data is safer than it's ever been now that you can track deleted files and use such commands as MIRROR, UNDELETE, and REBUILD.

And, finally, your DOS environment has a state-of-the-art editor with the unclever name EDIT, a DOS shell, and a programming language interpreter, QBI. All you need now is a keyboard.

PART SEVEN

Appendixes

Introduction to BASIC

BASIC (*B*eginner's *A*ll-Purpose *S*ymbolic *I*nstruction *C*ode) started life in the early '60s at Dartmouth College as Dartmouth BASIC. It was rapidly adopted by many companies, since it was designed to make programming as easy as possible. It is considered the most popular programming language in the world. A full ANSI standard for BASIC was adopted in 1988. Literally hundreds of BASIC interpreters and compilers are available today. We will cover those that you are most likely to find in the PC and DOS world: BASIC, BASICA, GW-BASIC, QuickBASIC 2.0 through 4.5, the full Microsoft BASIC Compiler now at Version 7.0 (called the Professional Development System, or PDS), or DOS QBasic. BASIC and BASICA come with IBM PCs and depend on ROM code. For this reason, they will not run on compatibles.

GW-BASIC comes as part of MS-DOS through 4.01 and will run on compatibles and true IBM PCs, XTs, and ATs. QuickBASIC was developed by Microsoft as a stand-alone product. It is a low-cost alternative to the PDS and offers full compilation. The BASIC Compiler Version 7.0 combines a QuickBASIC (QBX) environment running under DOS or OS/2 with a robust and powerful full compiler. (In fact, you can obtain a kit from Microsoft that allows the development of Presentation Manager programs under BASIC.) And, in a move to the new QB environment, MS-DOS 5.0 provides DOS QBasic in the package. (It will not generate COM or EXE files.)

In the material that follows, we will try to give you enough information about the various BASICs to allow you to decide which is for you. We will also give you a fairly complete guide to the statements and functions available.

BASIC AS A COMPUTER LANGUAGE

The following material will explain commands, statements, functions, and variables. Many commands and statements will be part of the list of keywords, which is included at the end of this appendix.

Keywords

PRINT, GOTO, GOSUB, and LET are some examples of the two hundred or so keywords in BASIC. These words cannot be used as variable names or line labels, but they could be used in combination with them:

print.line.five
goto.next

Commands

Loading, saving, and editing programs and other program-maintenance operations are carried out using commands. When BASIC is started, the BASIC prompt, Ok, indicates that the system is at the command level. In QuickBASIC, most of the commands are displayed in the menu bar at the top of the screen. All commands are keywords.

Statements

Statements, such as PRINT, GOTO, and GOSUB, are used in BASIC program lines as part of a program. Running the program executes these statements as they occur in the BASIC lines. Essentially, a statement tells the program what to do next. All statements are keywords.

Functions

Functions are used in BASIC to return values. Functions are either numeric, string, or user-defined. All built-in functions and the DEF FN statement, used to build user-defined functions, are keywords.

Numeric Functions

BASIC can perform arithmetic or algebraic calculations. Examples are returning the sine (sin), cosine (cos), or tangent (tan) of the angle x. Integer or single-precision results are normally returned by numeric functions, but other results can be requested by the programmer.

String Functions

TIME$ and DATE$ are string functions that return strings representing the time and the date, respectively. If the current time and date are entered during system startup or were in CMOS RAM at startup, the values returned will be the time and date from the system's internal clock. There are other string functions.

User-Defined Functions

The DEF FN statement can be used to write string or numeric functions of the programmer's choice.

Constants and Variables

The values used during the operation of a program take three forms. They may be direct values that you use only once; they may be *named constants,* which simply means that a value is assigned and never changes; or they may be *named variables*, which are assigned new values during the execution of the program.

Numeric Constants or Variables

There are five types of numeric constants: integer, fixed-point, floating-point, hexadecimal, and octal. Numeric constants should be entered without commas.

Variable Names and Declarations

BASIC and QuickBASIC variable names may be any length up to 40 characters. Letters, numbers, and the decimal point are allowed in a variable name. The first character must be a letter.

The BASIC and QuickBASIC statements DEFINT (define integer), DEFSTR (define string), DEFSNG (define single), and DEFDBL (define double) may be included in a program to declare the types of values for certain variable names.

Array Variables

Array variables may be assigned with a name followed by the array dimensions enclosed in parentheses. The dimensions are separated by commas. An array-variable name has as many subscripts as there are dimensions in the array.

EXPRESSIONS AND OPERATORS

An *expression* may be simply a string, a numeric constant, or a variable, or it may combine constants and variables with operators to produce a single value.

Operators perform mathematical or logical operations on values. The operators provided by BASIC and QuickBASIC are divided into four categories: arithmetic, relational, logical, and functional.

Arithmetic Operators

The following are the arithmetic operators recognized by BASIC and Quick-BASIC, in order of precedence:

Operator	Operation
^	Exponentiation
−	Negation
*	Multiplication
/	Division
+	Addition
-	Subtraction

Operations within parentheses are performed first. Inside the parentheses, the usual order of precedence is maintained.

Relational Operators

The following are the relational operators recognized by BASIC and Quick-BASIC:

Operator	Operation
=	Equality
< >	Inequality
<	Less than
>	Greater than
< =	Less than or equal to
> =	Greater than or equal to

All BASIC commands, statements, functions, and variables are individually described in the BASIC or QuickBASIC User's Reference.

LOADING BASIC

Both GW-BASIC and BASICA are *interpretive* BASICs and must be loaded to use the language.

Use the following procedure for floppy disk systems:

1. Turn on your computer.

2. Insert your working copy of the MS-DOS disk into drive A of your computer, and press RETURN.

3. Type **gwbasic** (or **basica**) after the A> prompt, and press RETURN.

Use the following procedure for hard disk systems:

1. Turn on your computer.

2. If you have not copied BASIC to your hard drive, do so now.

3. Type **gwbasic** (or **basica**) after the C> prompt, and press RETURN.

The BASIC prompt Ok will appear below the line "*XXXXX* Bytes free," which indicates how many bytes of memory are available to BASIC. Function key assignments appear at the bottom of the screen.

Modes of Operation

The Ok prompt means that BASIC is at command level, ready to accept commands, and may be used in either of two modes, direct or indirect.

Direct Mode

In *direct mode*, BASIC statements and commands are executed as they are entered. The results of arithmetic and logical operations can be displayed immediately and stored for later use, but the instructions themselves are lost after execution. This mode is useful for debugging and for using BASIC as a calculator for quick computations that do not require a complete program. Commands, statements, and other executables entered at this level must not be preceded by a line number or label.

Indirect Mode

The *indirect mode* is used to enter programs. Program lines are always preceded by line numbers in BASIC, BASICA, or GW-BASIC and are stored in memory. The program stored in memory is executed by the RUN command.

LOADING QuickBASIC

To use QuickBASIC, you must have it installed on your hard disk. Use the following procedure:

1. Turn on your computer.

2. Type one of the following commands after the C> prompt, and press RETURN:

qb (QuickBASIC 2.0 through 4.5)

or

qbx (BASIC 7.0 or QuickBASIC)

or

qbasic (DOS QBasic)

BASIC LINES AND PROGRAMS

A BASIC program is made up of lines of code containing commands, statements, functions, and variables. In BASIC, BASICA or GW-BASIC, each line must be preceded by a line number to indicate the sequence of operation of the program.

Note: You can have multiple statements per line, but each one after the first must be preceded by a colon (:). A BASIC program line always begins with a line number and must contain at least 1 character but no more than 255 characters. Line numbers indicate the order of execution. They are also used as references when branching and editing. The program line ends when you press ENTER.

An existing line is deleted if the line number matches the line number of an existing line and the entered line contains only a line number.

QUICKBASIC LINE FORMAT

A QuickBASIC program line may begin with a line label. Line labels are used in flow control to indicate where the program should proceed. Line labels are not required unless the line must be referred to from elsewhere in the program.

BASIC, BASICA, and GW-BASIC programs with existing line numbers will run under QuickBASIC.

THE QUICKBASIC ENVIRONMENT

QuickBASIC 2.0 through 4.5, QBX, and DOS QBasic (MS-DOS 5.0) are run and executed from a windowed environment. When you start these programs, you are taken to a full-screen editor with pull-down menus that allows you to enter and run programs.

The screen is initially divided into two windows, a menu bar, and a reference bar. The two windows are the View window and the Immediate window.

The View window is where you type lines of your program. Also, when you read a program from disk, the program is displayed in the View window. The title at the top of the window shows you which program is currently in the View window.

The Immediate window is similar to BASIC direct mode. You can type statements to see how they work or to use them for debugging calculations. The Immediate window's title says "Immediate." Normally located below the View window, the Immediate window may be sized to full screen.

QuickBASIC Menu Selections

Most of your actions will take place in the menu bar area. Following some of the menu items are three dots (...), denoting that a dialog box is associated with that selection. The menu bar has the following menu selections:

File

New Program	Same as BASIC NEW command
Open Program	Same as BASIC LOAD command
Merge...	Same as BASIC MERGE command
Save	Saves the file in the View window
Save As...	Same as BASIC SAVE command
Save All	Saves all currently open files
Create File...	Begins a new program module
Load File...	Loads a program module into memory
Unload File...	Removes a file from memory
Print...	Same as BASIC LLIST command
DOS Shell	Returns temporarily to the DOS command level
Exit	Returns to DOS

Edit

Undo	Undoes the last command or action
Cut	Deletes selected text to the clipboard
Copy	Copies selected text to the clipboard
Paste	Copies the clipboard to the cursor location
Clear	Deletes selected text permanently
New SUB...	Starts a new SUB in its own window
New FUNCTION...	Starts a new FUNCTION in its own window

View

SUBs...	Moves modules and files among windows
Next SUB	Places the next alphabetical procedure in the window
Split	Splits the View window
Next Statement	Moves cursor to the next statement
Output Screen	Switches you to the output screen
Included File	Loads include files
Included Lines	Displays include files

Search

Find...	Searches for text
Selected Text	Searches for a match to the currently highlighted text
Repeat Last Find	Searches for text again
Change...	Searches and replaces
Label...	Searches for the specified line label

Run

Start	Same as BASIC RUN command
Restart	Restarts the program
Continue	Same as BASIC CONT command
Modify COMMAND$...	Modifies the command line argument
Make EXE File...	Makes an executable file
Make Library...	Makes a Quick library
Set Main Module...	Sets the selected module to the main module

Debug

Add Watch...	Displays the values of variables in the Watch window
Instant Watch...	Displays the value of a variable
Watchpoint...	Halts the program when a condition becomes true
Delete Watch...	Deletes an item from the Watch window
Delete All Watch	Deletes all items from the Watch window and closes it
Trace On	Same as BASIC TRON command
History On	Records the last 20 lines of execution
Toggle Breakpoint	Turns breakpoints off and on
Clear All Break	Clears all previously set breakpoints
Break on Errors	Sets a breakpoint at the most recent error-handling statement
Set Next Statement	Sets the statement at the cursor as the next one to be executed

Calls

The BASIC call statement is used to add Assembly Language subroutines to your program. Shows current calls, modules, and programs.

Options

Display...	Changes the QuickBASIC environment
Set Paths...	Sets search paths
Right Mouse...	Changes what the right mouse button does
Syntax Checking	Toggles syntax checking
Full Menus	Toggles Full menus off and on

Note: QuickBASIC loads with Full menus off.

Help

Index	Displays QuickBASIC keywords
Contents	Shows a visual outline of the Help contents
Topic:	Displays syntax and usage information on Quick-BASIC keywords and variables
Help on Help	Provides information on using Help

QuickBASIC Function Key Assignments

Key	Action (Menu command, if any)
F1	Shows Help information on the keyword closest to the cursor (Topic on Help menu)
SHIFT+F1	Shows general Help information (Help on Help command on Help menu)
ALT+F1	Shows up to 20 previous Help screens
F2	Shows a list of files, SUBs, and FUNCTIONs (SUBs command on View menu)
SHIFT+F2	Shows the next procedure in the active window (Next SUB command on View menu)

Key	Action (Menu command, if any)
CTRL+F2	Shows the previous procedure in the active window
F3	Searches for the next occurrence of previously specified text (Repeat Last Find command on Search menu)
F4	Switches between QuickBASIC and Output screen (Output Screen command on View menu)
F5	Resumes program execution from the current statement (Continue command from Run menu)
SHIFT+F5	Starts the program (Start command on Run menu)
F6	Causes the next window to become the active window
SHIFT+F6	Causes the previous window to become the active window
F7	Runs the program to the current position of the cursor
F8	Runs the program's next statement; traces the procedure
SHIFT+F8	Runs back through the last 20 statements recorded by either the Trace On command or the History On command
F9	Toggles breakpoints (Toggle Breakpoints command on Debug menu)
SHIFT+F9	Shows Instant Watch dialog box (Instant Watch command on Debug menu)
F10	Runs next statement
SHIFT+F10	Runs through the last 20 program statements recorded by either the Trace On command or the History On command
CTRL+F10	Switches between full screen and multiple windows for active window

BASIC COMMAND SUMMARY

ABS Function

Syntax: abs(x)

Use: Returns the absolute value of x

ASC Function

Syntax: asc(*x*$)

Use: Returns the ASCII code for the first character of the string

ATN Function

Syntax: atn(*x*)

Use: Returns the arctangent of *x*, where *x* is in radians

AUTO Command

Syntax: auto *line, increment*

Use: Enables auto line numbering as you enter a program

BEEP Statement

Syntax: beep

Use: Sounds the speaker; same as PRINT CHR$(07)

BLOAD Command

Syntax: bload *filename, offset*

Use: Loads a memory image from disk into memory

BSAVE Command

Syntax: bsave *filename,offset,length*

Use: Saves a specified portion of memory to a specified device

CALL Statement

Syntax: call *subroutine,args*

Use: Calls machine language code

CDBL Function

Syntax: cdbl(*x*)

Use: Converts an expression to a double-precision number

CHAIN Statement

Syntax: chain merge *filename,line*,all,delete,*range*

Use: Runs a new program and passes the variables to it

CHDIR Command

Syntax: chdir *path*

Use: Changes the current directory

CHR$ Function

Syntax: chr$(x)

Use: Converts a number into the ascii character of the value "x"

CINT Function

Syntax: cint(x)

Use: Converts an expression to an integer

CIRCLE Statement

Syntax: circle (x, y),radius,color,start,end,aspect

Use: Draws a circle on a graphics screen

CLEAR Command

Syntax: clear ,x,y

Use: Clears all variables; the second parameter is stack space

CLOSE Statement

Syntax: close #x,#y

Use: Closes disk files; must be between 1 and 255; CLOSE by itself will close all

CLS Statement

Syntax: cls

Use: Clears the screen

COLOR Statement

Syntax: color x,y,z

Use: Allows the selection of foreground, background, and border colors

COM Statement

Syntax: com(n) on
           com(n) off
           com(n) stop

Use: Allows monitoring of communication activity

COMMON Statement

Syntax: common x,y

Use: Allows the passing of variables between programs

CONT Command

Syntax: cont

Use: Continues program execution after a break

COS Function

Syntax: cos(x)

Use: Returns the cosine of x, where x is in radians

CSNG Function

Syntax: csng(x)

Use: Converts an expression to a single-precision number

CSRLIN Variable

Syntax: x = csrlin

Use: Returns the current line position of the cursor

CVD, CVI, CVS Function

Syntax: $y\#$ = cvd($x\$$)
$y\%$ = cvi($x\$$)
$y!$ = cvs($x\$$)

Use: Converts the strings to numbers for random-access file handling

DATA Statement

Syntax: data $x,y,z\ldots$

Use: Acts as data-storage line for the READ statement

DATE$ Statement and Variable

Syntax: date$ = x$
             x$ = date$

Use: Allows retrieval and changing of the system dates

DEF FN Statement

Syntax: def fn *name paramlist* = *funcdef*

Use: Defines a user-written function

DEF SEG Statement

Syntax: def seg = *address*

Use: Sets the current segment address for a CALL statement

DEF*type* Statement

Syntax: defdbl
             defint
             defsng
             defstr

Use: Defines the variables as double, integer, single, or string

DEF USR Statement

Syntax: def usr*x* = *intexp*

Use: Sets the starting address of an Assembly Language subroutine

DELETE Command

Syntax: delete *line1-line2*

Use: Deletes lines in a program

DIM Statement

Syntax: dim *var(sub),var(sub)*

Use: Dimensions subscripted variables

DRAW Statement

Syntax: draw *x$*

Use: Allows drawing of objects

EDIT Command

Syntax: edit *line*
            edit .

Use: Allows editing of program lines; the period means the current line

END Statement

Syntax: end

Use: Ends the execution of a program

ENVIRON Statement

Syntax: environ *x*$

Use: Allows changing of the system environment string

ENVIRON$ Function

Syntax: environ$(*x*)
         environ$(*x*$)

Use: Reads the system environment string

EOF Function

Syntax: eof (*filenum*)

Use: Returns a −1 if the end of the file is reached

ERASE Statement

Syntax: erase *arraylist*

Use: Allows the undimensioning of variables

ERDEV$ and ERDEV Functions

Syntax: erdev$ erdev

Use: Returns the error code and identifies the device that had the error

ERL and ERR Variables

Syntax: erl err

Use: Returns the error code and indicates on what line the error occurred

ERROR Statement

Syntax: error x

Use: Simulates error conditions

EXP Function

Syntax: exp(x)

Use: Returns the exponent of the expression

FIELD Statement

Syntax: field *filenum,width* as *x$,y$*. . .
field# *filenum,width* as *x$,y$*. . .

Use: Allocates space in the random-file buffer for variables

FILES Statement

Syntax: files *filename*

Use: Prints the directory of the drive

FIX Function

Syntax: fix(*x*)

Use: Returns the absolute integer portion of an expression

FOR-NEXT Statement

Syntax: for *var* = *x* to *y* next *var* for *var* = *x* to *y* step *z* next *var*

Use: Allows a program to loop a specific number of times

FRE Function

Syntax: fre(*x*) fre(*x*$)

Use: Returns the amount of memory not used by BASIC

GET Statements

Syntax: get #*filenum, recordnum*
get #*filenum, numbytes*
get *x1, y1 − x2, y2, arrayname*

Use: Reads a record into the random-access buffer from a random-access file; allows fixed-length I/O for COM; reads pixels from an area on the screen

GOSUB-RETURN Statement

Syntax: gosub *line* return

Use: Branches to a user-defined subroutine; RETURN returns control to the main program

GOTO Statement

Syntax: goto *line*

Use: Branches unconditionally to a specified line number

HEX$ Function

Syntax: hex$(*x*)

Use: Returns the hexadecimal equivalent of the expression

IF-THEN-ELSE Statements

Syntax: if *exp* then *line* # else *line* #
             if *exp* goto *line* else *stmt line*

Use: Makes a decision regarding program flow based on the result of an expression

INKEY$ Variable

Syntax: inkey$

Use: Returns either a one-character string containing a character read from the computer or a null string

INP Function

Syntax: inp(*x*)

Use: Returns the byte read from port *x*; valid machine ports are 1 to 65535

INPUT Statements

Syntax: input ; *"string"* ;, *x,y,z*...
input# *filenum, varlist*
input$(*x,#y*)

Use: Allows keyboard input during program execution; reads data from a sequential disk file; returns a string of characters from the keyboard or from file number *y*

INSTR Function

Syntax: instr(*x, x$,y$*)

Use: Searches for the first occurrence of *y$* in *x$* and returns the position

INT Function

Syntax: int(*x*)

Use: Returns the integer portion of an expression

IOCTL Statement

Syntax: ioctl #*filenum,x$*

Use: Transmits a control string to a device driver

IOCTL$ Function

Syntax: ioctl$(#*filenum*)

Use: Receives a control string from a device driver

KEY Statements

Syntax: key *keynum,x$*
key list
key on
key off

Use: Allows resetting of the soft keys at the bottom of the screen; turns them on or off

KEY(*X*) Statements

Syntax: key(*x*) on
key(*x*) off
key(*x*) stop

Use: Activates or deactivates trapping of a specific key

KILL Command

Syntax: kill *filename*

Use: Deletes a file from disk

LEFT$ Function

Syntax: left$(*x$,y*)

Use: Returns the leftmost *y* characters of *x$*

LEN Function

Syntax: len(*x$*)

Use: Returns the number of characters in the string expression

LET Statement

Syntax: let $x = y$

Use: Assign values to variables; the "LET" is optional

LINE Statement

Syntax: line $(x,y) - (x1,y1),color,bf,style$

Use: Draws and removes straight-line objects; the b makes a box; the f means fill; the *style* is a bit pattern

LINE INPUT Statements

Syntax: line input ; *"string"*;$x\$$
          line input# *filenum*,$x\$$

Use: Allows entry of string variables up to 254 characters long; reads characters from a sequential file until it reaches a carriage return

LIST Command

Syntax: list *line1-line2,file*

Use: Lists the program to the screen or other devices

LLIST Command

Syntax: llist *line1-line2-line3*

Use: Lists the program to the line printer

LOAD Command

Syntax: load *filename*,r

Use: Loads a program into memory; the optional *r* runs it

LOC Function

Syntax: loc *filenum*

Use: In a random-access file, returns the record number within the file; in a sequential file, returns the current position divided by 128

LOCATE Statement

Syntax: locate *row,col,cur,*start,stop

Use: Moves the cursor to a specified position on the screen

LOF Function

Syntax: lof *filenum*

Use: Returns the number of bytes allocated to a file

LOG Function

Syntax: log(*x*)

Use: Returns the natural logarithm of *x*

LPOS Function

Syntax: lpos(x)

Use: Returns the current position of the pointer in the printer buffer

LPRINT and LPRINT USING Statements

Syntax: lprint *explist*
          lprint using *string;explist*

Use: Directs unformatted printing to a line printer; directs formatted printing to a line printer

LSET Statement

Syntax: lset $x\$ = y\$$

Use: Moves and left-justifies data into a random-file buffer

MERGE Command

Syntax: merge *filename*

Use: Merges a program from disk into one already in memory

MID$ Function and Statement

Syntax: mid$ $(x\$,x,y) = y\$$
          $x\$ = $ mid$(y\$,w,y)$

Use: Returns a portion of a string or replaces a portion of a string with another string

MKD$, MKI$, MKS$ Functions

Syntax: mkd$(*x*)
         mki$(*x*)
         mks$(*x*)

Use: Converts numbers to strings in preparation for random-access file handling

MKDIR Command

Syntax: mkdir *pathname*

Use: Makes a new subdirectory

NAME Command

Syntax: name *oldfilename* as *newfilename*

Use: Renames files

NEW Command

Syntax: new

Use: Removes a program from memory

OCT$ Function

Syntax: oct$(*x*)

Use: Returns the octal equivalent of an expression

ON Statements

Syntax: on com(*n*) gosub *line*
         on error goto *line*
         on exp gosub *linelist*
         on exp goto *linelist*
         on key(*x*) gosub *line*
         on play(*x*) gosub *line*
         on timer(*x*) gosub *line*

Use: Enables branching in programs to selected subroutines by values

OPEN Statements

The BASIC open statement is used to control access to sequential data files.

Syntax: open *device*,
         filename for *mode* as #*filenum*
         len = *recl* open com
         dev:speed,parity,data,stop,rs,cs,ds,cd,lf,pe,asc,bin as
         #*filenum*

Use: Opens a file on disk for access; opens a communications port for access

OPTION BASE Statement

Syntax: option base *x*

Use: Declares the minimum value for subscripted arrays; *x* is 0 or 1

OUT Statement

Syntax: out *x,y*

Use: Sends a byte of information to the selected output port; both must be in the range of 0 to 65535

PAINT Statement

Syntax: paint *(x1,y1),paint,border*

Use: Fills an area on the screen with the selected color

PEEK Statement

Syntax: peek *x*

Use: Allows viewing of a particular byte in memory

PLAY Statements and Functions

Syntax: play *x$*
play*(x)*
play on
play off
play stop

Use: Plays music as specified by the string expression

PMAP Function

Syntax: pmap *cxp,func*

Use: Maps world coordinates to physical locations or maps physical expressions to a world-coordinate location for graphics mode

POINT Functions

Syntax: point *(x,y)*
point *(func)*

Use: Allows reading of the pixel color from the screen

POKE Statement

Syntax: poke *x,y*

Use: Allows changing of a particular byte in memory

POS Function

Syntax: pos(*x*)

Use: Returns the current cursor position

PRESET Statements

Syntax: preset (*x,y*), *attrib*
preset step (*x,y*), *attrib*

Use: Turns one pixel on or off on the screen

PRINT and PRINT USING Statements

Syntax: print *explist*
print using *strexp,explist*
print# *filenum explist*
print# *filenum* using *strexp,explist*

Use: Directs unformatted printing to a line printer; directs formatted printing to a line printer; directs unformatted printing to a file; directs formatted printing to a file

PSET Statements

Syntax: pset *(x,y),attrib*
      pset step *(x,y),attrib*

Use: Turns one pixel on or off on the screen

PUT Statements

Syntax: put *#filenum,recordnum*
      put *#filenum,numbytes*
      put *x1,y1,array,action*

Use: Writes a record into the random-access buffer from a random-access file; allows fixed-length I/O for COM; writes pixels to an area on the screen

RANDOMIZE Statements

Syntax: randomize *x*

Use: Seeds the random-number generator

READ Statement

Syntax: read *varlist*

Use: Reads information stored in the DATA lines

REM Statement

Syntax: rem *remark*

Use: Allows the user to include remarks or notes within the program

RENUM Command

Syntax: renum *newnum, oldnum, increment*

Use: Renumbers the lines of code

RESET Command

Syntax: reset

Use: Closes all currently open files

RESTORE Statement

Syntax: restore *line*

Use: Restores DATA items

RESUME Statements

Syntax: resume
resume 0
resume next
resume *line*

Use: Resumes execution of a program

RETURN Statement

Syntax: return *line*

Use: Returns control to the main program following a GOSUB statement

RIGHT$ Function

Syntax: right$(*x$,y*)

Use: Returns the rightmost *y* characters of *x$*

RMDIR Command

Syntax: rmdir *pathname*

Use: Removes a subdirectory

RND Function

Syntax: rnd(*x*)

Use: Generates random number

RSET Statement

Syntax: rset *x$* = *y$*

Use: Moves and right-justifies data into a random-file buffer

RUN Command

Syntax: run *line*
   run *filename*,r

Use: Runs a program; the *r* keeps all data files open

SAVE Command

Syntax: save *filename,*a,p

Use: Saves a program to a disk file; the *a* keeps it in ASCII format; the *p* puts it in binary protected format

SCREEN Statement and Function

Syntax: screen *mode,burst,apage,vpage*
             x = screen (*x,y,oper*)

Use: Used to set the screen format; 0 is alpha mode; 1 and 2 are graphics modes

SGN Function

Syntax: sgn(*x*)

Use: Indicates the sign (positive or negative) of a number in relation to 0

SHELL Statement

Syntax: shell *commandstring*

Use: Runs DOS commands

SIN Function

Syntax: sin(*x*)

Use: Returns the sine of *x*, where *x* is in radians

SOUND Statement

Syntax: sound *freq,dur*

Use: Generates a sound from the speaker; the frequency (*freq*) is between 37 to 32767; the duration (*dur*) is the number of clock ticks (18.2 = 1 second)

SPACE$ Function

Syntax: space$(*x*)

Use: Returns a blank string *x* blanks long

SPC Function

Syntax: spc(*x*)

Use: Allows spacing on print lines

SQR Function

Syntax: sqr(*x*)

Use: Returns the square of *x*

STOP Statement

Syntax: stop

Use: Stops program execution; CONT will continue it

STR$ Function

Syntax: str$(*x*)

Use: Returns a string representation of *x*

STRING$ Functions

Syntax: string$(*x,y*)
string$(*x,y*$)

Use: Returns a string *x* characters long of ASCII character *y*, returns a string *x* characters long of the first character of *y*$

SWAP Statement

Syntax: swap *x,x1*

Use: Swaps one variable for another

SYSTEM Command

Syntax: system

Use: Returns to DOS

TAB Function

Syntax: tab(*x*)

Use: Move the cursor *x* number of spaces on the current print line

TAN Function

Syntax: tan(x)

Use: Returns the tangent of x, where x is in radians

TIME$ Statement and Function

Syntax: time$ = $x$$
          $x$$ = *time*$

Use: Displays and resets the clock

TIMER Statements

Syntax: timer on
          timer off
          timer stop

Use: Enables and disables real-time clock trapping

TRON-TROFF Commands

Syntax: tron
          troff

Use: Turns trace mode on or off

USR Function

Syntax: usr *digit(arg)*

Use: Calls an Assembly Language subroutine

VAL Function

Syntax: val($x\$$)

Use: Returns the numeric value of $x\$$

VARPTR Functions

Syntax: x = varptr(z)
          y = varptr(#*filenum*)

Use: Returns the location of variables in memory; returns the first byte of the file control block for the opened file

VARPTR$ Function

Syntax: varptr$ ($x\$$)

Use: Returns a string expression of the variable's memory address

VIEW Statements

Syntax: view (vx1,vy1) –(vx2,vy2),*color,border*
          view screen (vx1,vy1) –(vx2,vy2),*color,border*
          view print *topline* to *bottomline*

Use: Defines the screen limits for graphics activity; defines the screen limits for graphics activity; defines the screen limits for text activity

WAIT Statement

Syntax: wait *port,andbyte,xorbyte*

Use: Waits while monitoring the status of a machine port; port number should be between 0 to 65535; andbyte and xorbyte should be between 0 and 255

WHILE-WEND Statements

Syntax: while *exp* wend

Use: Executes a series of statements until a given condition is true

WIDTH Statements

Syntax: width *size*
width *filenum,size*
width *dev,size*

Use: Sets the printed-line width

WINDOW Statements

Syntax: window (w*x1*,w*y1*) − (w*x2*,w*y2*)
window screen (w*x1*,w*y1*) − (w*x2*,w*y2*)

Use: Defines the size of a viewport

WRITE Statements

Syntax: write *explist*
write# *filenum,explist*

Use: Writes information to a file

ASCII Codes

Decimal Value	Hexadecimal Value	Control Character	Character
0	00	NUL	Null
1	01	SOH	☺
2	02	STX	☻
3	03	ETX	♥
4	04	EOT	♦
5	05	ENQ	♣
6	06	ACK	♠
7	07	BEL	Beep
8	08	BS	◘
9	09	HT	Tab
10	0A	LF	Line-feed
11	0B	VT	Cursor home
12	0C	FF	Form-feed
13	0D	CR	Enter
14	0E	SO	♫
15	0F	SI	☼
16	10	DLE	►
17	11	DC1	◄
18	12	DC2	↕
19	13	DC3	‼
20	14	DC4	¶
21	15	NAK	§

Decimal Value	Hexadecimal Value	Control Character	Character
22	16	SYN	▬
23	17	ETB	↨
24	18	CAN	↑
25	19	EM	↓
26	1A	SUB	→
27	1B	ESC	←
28	1C	FS	Cursor right
29	1D	GS	Cursor left
30	1E	RS	Cursor up
31	1F	US	Cursor down
32	20	SP	Space
33	21		!
34	22		"
35	23		#
36	24		$
37	25		%
38	26		&
39	27		'
40	28		(
41	29		)
42	2A		*
43	2B		+
44	2C		,
45	2D		-
46	2E		.
47	2F		/
48	30		0
49	31		1
50	32		2

Decimal Value	Hexadecimal Value	Control Character	Character
51	33		3
52	34		4
53	35		5
54	36		6
55	37		7
56	38		8
57	39		9
58	3A		:
59	3B		;
60	3C		<
61	3D		=
62	3E		>
63	3F		?
64	40		@
65	41		A
66	42		B
67	43		C
68	44		D
69	45		E
70	46		F
71	47		G
72	48		H
73	49		I
74	4A		J
75	4B		K
76	4C		L
77	4D		M
78	4E		N
79	4F		O

Decimal Value	Hexadecimal Value	Control Character	Character
80	50		P
81	51		Q
82	52		R
83	53		S
84	54		T
85	55		U
86	56		V
87	57		W
88	58		X
89	59		Y
90	5A		Z
91	5B		[
92	5C		\
93	5D		]
94	5E		^
95	5F		—
96	60		`
97	61		a
98	62		b
99	63		c
100	64		d
101	65		e
102	66		f
103	67		g
104	68		h
105	69		i
106	6A		j
107	6B		k
108	6C		l

Decimal Value	Hexadecimal Value	Control Character	Character
109	6D		m
110	6E		n
111	6F		o
112	70		p
113	71		q
114	72		r
115	73		s
116	74		t
117	75		u
118	76		v
119	77		w
120	78		x
121	79		y
122	7A		z
123	7B		{
124	7C		¦
125	7D		}
126	7E		~
127	7F	DEL	⌂
128	80		Ç
129	81		ü
130	82		é
131	83		â
132	84		ä
133	85		à
134	86		å
135	87		ç
136	88		ê
137	89		ë

Decimal Value	Hexadecimal Value	Control Character	Character
138	8A		è
139	8B		ï
140	8C		î
141	8D		ì
142	8E		Ä
143	8F		Å
144	90		É
145	91		æ
146	92		Æ
147	93		ô
148	94		ö
149	95		ò
150	96		û
151	97		ù
152	98		ÿ
153	99		Ö
154	9A		Ü
155	9B		¢
156	9C		£
157	9D		¥
158	9E		Pt
159	9F		ƒ
160	A0		á
161	A1		í
162	A2		ó
163	A3		ú
164	A4		ñ
165	A5		Ñ
166	A6		ª

Decimal Value	Hexadecimal Value	Control Character	Character
167	A7		º
168	A8		¿
169	A9		⌐
170	AA		¬
171	AB		½
172	AC		¼
173	AD		¡
174	AE		«
175	AF		»
176	B0		░
177	B1		▒
178	B2		▓
179	B3		│
180	B4		┤
181	B5		╡
182	B6		╢
183	B7		╖
184	B8		╕
185	B9		╣
186	BA		║
187	BB		╗
188	BC		╝
189	BD		╜
190	BE		╛
191	BF		┐
192	C0		└
193	C1		┴
194	C2		┬
195	C3		├

Decimal Value	Hexadecimal Value	Control Character	Character
196	C4		─
197	C5		┼
198	C6		╟
199	C7		╟
200	C8		╚
201	C9		╔
202	CA		╩
203	CB		╦
204	CC		╠
205	CD		═
206	CE		╬
207	CF		╧
208	D0		╨
209	D1		╤
210	D2		╥
211	D3		╙
212	D4		╘
213	D5		╒
214	D6		╓
215	D7		╫
216	D8		╪
217	D9		┘
218	DA		┌
219	DB		█
220	DC		▄
221	DD		▌
222	DE		▐
223	DF		▀
224	E0		α
225	E1		β

Decimal Value	Hexadecimal Value	Control Character	Character
226	E2		Γ
227	E3		π
228	E4		Σ
229	E5		σ
230	E6		μ
231	E7		τ
232	E8		ϕ
233	E9		Θ
234	EA		Ω
235	EB		δ
236	EC		∞
237	ED		$\varnothing$
238	EE		ϵ
239	EF		$\cap$
240	F0		$\equiv$
241	F1		$\pm$
242	F2		$\geq$
243	F3		$\leq$
244	F4		$\lceil$
245	F5		$\rfloor$
246	F6		$\div$
247	F7		$\approx$
248	F8		$\circ$
249	F9		$\bullet$
250	FA		$\cdot$
251	FB		$\sqrt{}$
252	FC		η
253	FD		^{2}
254	FE		$\blacksquare$
255	FF		(blank)

Bound-In
Software

At the back of this book, you will find two 5.25-inch disks packed with programs that every DOS user should have. (If you need a 3.5-inch disk, we'll tell you how to get one in a moment.) The documentation for these files can be found in Appendix D. You'll also find references to some of these programs in the text.

The programs offered are a special collection of shareware, custom-written utilities, and special versions of commercial programs.

QUICK PROGRAM SUMMARY

In this appendix, we will show you how to install the supplied disks, how to obtain the programs on 3.5-inch media, and how to get up and running as quickly as possible.

If you are loading the files on a hard disk or on 1.2MB or 1.44MB floppies, all the files will fit. If, however, you load them onto 360KB floppies, you will need three disks. In that case, put DV1A and DV1B or. disk one, DV2 on disk two, and DV3A and DV3B on disk three. If you load on 720KB floppies, you will need only two disks; put DV2 and DV3B on the second disk.

Here is a quick summary of the programs supplied with this book. The programs are in self-extracting, compressed files.

AUTOPARK	Automatically parks a hard drive (positions the drive heads over a nondata area on the disk) after a specified period of inactivity.
COLOR	Allows you to set the screen's attributes using real words instead of numbers.
DESKCONNECT	Connects two PCs by their serial ports and allows seamless disk and file sharing.
DOG	DiskOrganizer, a lightning-fast disk defragmenter that offers advanced options, such as directory squeezing.
DOSCACHE	From Multisoft, makers of the PC-Kwik cache; dramatically speeds up disk reads and writes.
FREE	Provides a detailed report of your system's RAM and each of its hard drives.
GLOM	A very small terminate-and-stay resident program that captures all DOS console output. Useful for writing batch files, it's sort of a macro recorder.
INFOPLUS	Information Plus System Diagnostic Reporter.
LS	Lists files and sizes in KB, rounded to three decimal places, in a four-column display with totals.
MV	Moves files and subdirectories; can also be used to rename subdirectories.
PKLITE	An executable-file compressor that compresses programs but leaves them executable—*great!*
PKUNZIP, PKZIP	Creates archive files to conserve storage space and manages files that have been compressed.

REBOOT	Does a warm system boot by default. The /C option will cause the system to do a cold boot.
TOGGLE	Turns CAPS LOCK, NUM LOCK, and SCROLL LOCK on or off, by resetting the keyboard-status byte at location 417 hex.
VDE	A full-featured text editor that is tiny, fast, and powerful. Supports popular file formats and printers.
VIEW	A tiny, but powerful, program for viewing files.
WPD	Write-protects your disks.
XT4	XTree 4.0, a best-selling DOS shell /file manager.
XTREEDOC1.EXE XTREEDOC2.EXE	Self-displayed documentation for XTree, parts 1 and 2.
XTREEPATH.EXE	Use this to configure XTree.

The Dvorak Utilities

ASK	Displays a message and accepts keys from list.
BEEP	Beeps.
BOX	Draws a single or double, filled, colored box anywhere on the screen.
ESC	Takes whatever is on the command line, prefixes it with the ASCII ESC/left-bracket combination, and outputs the entire string to the console. Requires an ANSI-compatible driver to be loaded.
FREADY	For use in batch files, returns ERROR-LEVEL 1 if a floppy drive specified on the command line is ready. Usage: **FREADY d[:]**, where *d* is a drive letter followed by an optional colon.
GETKEY,GETKEYNL	Accepts a keystroke and converts it to an ERRORLEVEL value.

GETYN	Accepts only the Y or N key and sets ERRORLEVEL accordingly.
MKREBOOT.BAT	A batch file used by one of the Dvorak Utilities.
RESTPATH	Retrieves a disk and directory from a file created by SAVEPATH, and changes to that directory.
ROWCOL	Positions the cursor on the screen and optionally displays text in any foreground or background color.
SAVEPATH	"Remembers" the current drive and directory so that RESTPATH can return to it later.
SHOWTIME	Displays the time, "am" or "pm," the day, the date, and the year.
SOURCE.ZIP	The source code for the Dvorak Utilities.
SUBTEST.BAT	A batch file used by one of the Dvorak Utilities.
TESTANSI	Sets ERRORLEVEL to 1 if the ANSI.SYS driver is present, and to 0 if it's not.
TESTIT.BAT	A batch file used by one of the Dvorak Utilities.

Mace Utilities, Special Edition

PARK	Parks your hard disk (by moving the read / write heads to the safety zone of the disk) to help protect your data and drive from damage.
RXBAK	Makes an image backup of your drive's partition, file allocation table, and directory information.
SORTD	Sorts directories in various orders.
SQZD	Squeezes or removes deleted directory entries. This speeds up disk operations and, if followed by disk defragmentation, makes future file recovery more reliable. When you use SQZD, you cannot recover any previously deleted files, but you can recover any deletions made after SQZD was last run.

| UNDELETE | Restores an erased file if it hasn't been overwritten. |
| UNFORMAT | Recovers from an accidental disk FORMAT (can use the RXBAK image for greater accuracy). |

TSR Utilities

DISABLE	Disables or reactivates TSRs, leaving them in memory.
EATMEM	Uses up memory for controlled program testing.
FMARK	Performs the same function as MARK, but uses less memory.
MAPMEM	Shows what memory resident programs are loaded.
MARK	Marks a position in memory above which TSRs can be released.
RELEASE	Removes TSRs from memory.
RAMFREE	Shows how much RAM is available.
WATCH	Keeps records of other TSRs.

SHAREWARE AND "BOOKWARE"

Some of the programs supplied with this book are *shareware*—software marketed on the honor system. Programmers allow their work to be distributed to others free of charge. If a user finds a shareware program of value, he is expected to remit a specified registration fee to the program's author. Registration fees are usually a fraction of what the commercial software equivalent would cost.

Shareware is a system under which everyone benefits. The user benefits by getting high-quality software at a very low price. Programmers benefit by having their products marketed economically. Shareware distribution saves the author a fortune on marketing and advertising—costs usually passed on to the consumer. Shareware can also allow authors to retain their product rights and market their programs themselves.

Registering the Programs

Shareware programs obtained from shareware disk vendors, computer-user-group libraries, or on-line services often include certain special files.

These spell out the author's copyright, registration, and site-licensing policies, the availability of technical support, and other details. Many programmers even include a handy, ready-to-print order form to make it as easy as possible for you to register the product.

Most shareware packages include on-disk manuals. Because of space limitations on the disks accompanying this book, the documentation files have been removed from the disks. A condensed version of the documentation is printed in Appendix D, and the XTREE program has special self-displaying documentation on the disk. That's why you'll find this book a handy reference for all these programs. You can get additional documentation, more-advanced versions, technical support, and more by registering these programs or taking advantage of the publisher's offers.

The version we have provided of the shareware programs bound with this book might best be described as "bookware." These programs are special editions of the shareware products, which we are distributing by special arrangement.

Since these programs may not represent the program authors' complete packages, please do *not* distribute them to others. If these versions are distributed without all the documentation and registration information, people may assume none exists. We hope you will honor this request, and we certainly encourage you to register these products. We have made this as easy for you as possible. The registration and licensing information is included in the back of the book.

The programs that have been custom-written for this book don't require registration.

3.5-INCH MEDIA, BONUS DISKS, AND DISK REPLACEMENT

If you need the supplied programs on a 3.5-inch disk, simply mail the 5.25-inch disks at the back of this book to Computer Business Services (the addresss is given shortly), and we will send you a 3.5-inch disk free of charge.

We will also be happy to replace the 5.25-inch disks. We have no reason to believe that you'll have any problems at all, but accidents do happen. We want to make sure that every reader has working copies of this important software. You can contact PCSIG (coupon in back of the book), Osborne/

McGraw-Hill or Computer Business Services for replacement disks. Do not go back to where you purchased the book because they won't have replacement disks. If either of your 5.25-inch disks proves defective, mail it to Computer Business Services for a free replacement. If the disk is missing, replacements are available for $2. Similarly, if you'd like to order the programs on a 3.5-inch disk, the cost is $2.

The software is supplied in large archive files, which must be extracted (uncompressed) onto a hard disk or three floppy disks. If your system has only a single floppy and no hard disk, you will need to borrow a friend's system to install the software or order three uncompressed disks from us. We can send you three 5.25-inch floppies for $6 or two 3.5-inch disks for $4.

Finally, we are pleased to offer some additional disks, each of which costs $10 in either 5.25-inch or 3.5-inch format. Here is a list of the disks we are offering:

Disks 3 and 4	"The Modem Tutor," by John C. Dvorak and Nick Anis (2 disks, $10)
Disk 5	"The Hard Disk Tutor," by Alfred Glossbrenner and Nick Anis
Disk 6	"The CompuServe Tutor," by Brad Schepp and Deb Schepp

You can use the order form in the back of the book to order any of the disks, or you can send your order to the address below. Please print your name and address clearly, and don't forget to include your telephone number and specific instructions on what you want. Make checks or money orders payable to Computer Business Services (U.S. funds drawn on a U.S. bank only, please). For overseas shipment, please add $5 per order. Write to:

Dvorak's Guide to DOS Disks Offer
Computer Business Services
1125 Bramford Court
Diamond Bar, CA 91765
714-860-6914 (Please write if possible!)
Remember to make your checks payable to Computer Business Services.

INSTALLING THE SUPPLIED SOFTWARE

Installing the software supplied with this book is easy. Simply put the disk in any drive and type **install**. This activates a special installation program, INSTALL.EXE, that will guide you through the process. The program assumes that the source drive is drive A and that the target drive is drive C, but you can specify any drives you like (if you are installing to floppies the program will not allow your source and destination to be the same). You will also have to specify if you're doing a floppy or hard disk installation. When your drive selections are correct, you can confirm them by entering a Y in the appropriate prompt box.

Note: You can abort the installation process at any time by pressing CTRL-C. Hit your ESC key then to return instantly to the DOS prompt.

Warning: If you have trouble running XTREE, type **XTREE *path*** to reconfigure the program for your drive and directory.

The INSTALL program will create a subdirectory called DVORAK on the target hard drive. Installation to a floppy will use the root directory and will prompt you when to switch diskettes. Next, INSTALL will begin extracting files from the source drive to the target drive.

When all the files have been extracted, if your target is a hard disk, INSTALL will analyze your CONFIG.SYS and AUTOEXEC.BAT files. If CONFIG.SYS does not exist, INSTALL will create one with the following lines:

```
FILES = 20
BUFFERS = 25
DEVICE=C:\ANSI.SYS
```

These settings are not required to run most of the supplied programs, but they will make your computer run better. You will need an ANSI.SYS compatible driver loaded to use some of these programs, like COLOR and ESCAPE. If you are using a substitute program like ANSI.COM, you can remove ANSI.SYS from your CONFIG.SYS file. The new CONFIG.SYS settings will not take effect until you reboot your computer. If AUTO-EXEC.BAT does not exist, INSTALL will create a file with that name containing the following:

```
ECHO OFF
PATH C:\;C:\DVORAK
SET MACE=C:\DVORAK
```

If, as is more likely, you already have these files on your hard disk, INSTALL will make sure that the files and buffer settings are equal to or greater than those given here. Only at your option will it add C:\DVORAK to the PATH statement in your AUTOEXEC.BAT and set a DOS environment variable used by Mace Utilities SE. If you already have a PROMPT statement, INSTALL will not change it; if you do not have one, the program will add one to your AUTOEXEC.BAT file. The program will ask your permission before changing either CONFIG.SYS or AUTOEXEC.BAT.

If your system path is too large, INSTALL will not make any changes to it. If INSTALL modifies your CONFIG.SYS or AUTOEXEC.BAT file, it will make a backup copy of the original with a .DB extension. If your system doesn't have enough environment space, INSTALL's modifications to CONFIG.SYS and AUTOEXEC may trigger an "out of environment space" error. You can increase the environment size by adding the following line in your CONFIG.SYS file: SHELL=C:/COMMAND.

INSTALL Features and Files

INSTALL is a menu-driven program that supports color, monochrome, and LCD screens. It will not override your DOS setting. The program can be run from any floppy drive. You can install the programs to your floppy or hard disk; a hard disk is recommended. You'll need about 1100KB of free space for the programs. If you need the software in its uncompressed state, contact Computer Business Services, as discussed earlier in this appendix. The supplied disks contain the following files:

INSTALL.EXE	Installation program
DV1A.EXE	Self-extracting archive, part 1A
DV1B.EXE	Self-extracting archive, part 1B
DV2.EXE	Self-extracting archive, part 2
DV3A.EXE	Self-extracting archive, part 3A
DV3B.EXE	Self-extracting archive, part 3B

Selecting a Subdirectory Name

Program and disk-space requirements make it necessary for INSTALL to default to creating a subdirectory called DVORAK for the programs. Each of the programs will work fine this way. If you prefer, however, you can use the MV program to move files to other directories.

If you move the Mace files, you'll need to change the SET file. If you move the XTree files, you'll need to modify XTREE.COM and XT4.EXE so that they have the correct drive and directory with the XTree overlay files. The program XTPATH.EXE, which we've provided, will update these files automatically when you execute it. All you need to do is log onto the drive and directory where the XTree files are located and type **xtpath**. XTPATH will verify the presence of the XTree overlay files and the files XTREE-.COM and XT4.EXE and update them to the current drive and directory.

Once the programs are installed, you can rename the DVORAK subdirectory like this:

```
mv \dvorak \utils
```

Don't forget that you'll need to make adjustments to your AUTOEXEC-.BAT and run XTREEPATH.EXE.

To move only some of the files, do the following:

1. Make a new subdirectory with the MD (Make Directory) command.

2. Log onto the DVORAK subdirectory.

3. Enter

```
MV INFOPLUS.EXE *.* \[new directory name]
```

Alternatively, you can reinstall the software. If INSTALL detects a subdirectory called DVORAK on your disk, it will notify you that DVORAK already exists and prompt you to abort, overwrite, or specify a different subdirectory name. The Abort option will cancel this operation and return you to DOS. The Overwrite option will install the files in DVORAK and overwrite any files in the target path.

Do-It-Yourself Installation

If you are an old hand at DOS and have a hard disk, you can skip the installation program altogether. Simply make a subdirectory of your choosing on your hard disk, and copy all of the files on the supplied disk into it.

Then, key in **DV1A** to start the first self-extracting file. When it finishes, do the same for DV1B, DV2, DV3A, and DV3B. If you already have PKUN-ZIP.EXE (version 1.0 or later), you can use it to decompress these files by entering **PKUNZIP DV*.EXE**. Once you've extracted them, you can delete the compressed files by typing **DEl DV*.EXE**.

Finally, you may want to use your word processor or the VDE program to modify your CONFIG.SYS and AUTOEXEC.BAT files as appropriate.

IF YOU HAVE PROBLEMS . . .

Most readers will have no difficulty installing the supplied software, but problems can arise. We want you to begin using and enjoying this software as quickly as possible, and PC SIG and Computer Business Services stand ready to help you overcome any serious installation problems. Before writing to us, however, please read the following troubleshooting guide.

Problem Reading the Floppy Disks

Some disks may not spin freely inside their jackets because of variables in manufacturing, temperature, or handling. Many times, you can solve the problem by loosening the disk by hand. Try inserting two fingers into the disk hub and exerting enough pressure so that the disk remains stationary while you revolve the jacket. If the disk turns freely, put it in the drive and try again.

If this does not solve the problem, try removing and inserting the disk and trying again. You may have to make several attempts. You may also wish to try the disk on a different computer: some disk drives supply more torque (spinning power) than others.

Problem Reading the Screen Prompts

The supplied INSTALL program has been tested on a wide variety of systems without problems. However, if you find that you're having difficulty reading the program prompts, exit the program by hitting your ESC key. Then, use the DOS MODE.COM utility to convert to an 80-column black and white display. (MODE.COM is supplied with your DOS package.) Make sure MODE.COM is accessible, and type **mode bw80** at the DOS prompt.

If you still cannot easily read the INSTALL screen, follow the instructions for a do-it-yourself installation, as outlined earlier.

Why Is My Prompt C:\DVORAK> Instead of C>?

If you type **prompt pg** at the standard DOS prompt, the system shows you the current path, followed by a greater-than sign (>) as the prompt. This makes it easy to know where you are on the disk. At your option, the INSTALL program adds that PROMPT line to your AUTOEXEC.BAT file before it finishes its work. The new prompt becomes effective the next time AUTOEXEC.BAT is run. To return to the standard DOS prompt, simply key in **prompt**; to return to it forever, use your word processor to remove the PROMPT line from AUTOEXEC.BAT.

Compatibility

Support for the programs supplied with this book is available only from the programmers who created them, and only to registered users. All of the programs are "well-behaved" and should work on any DOS system. If you are having difficulty, however, the problem may be due to one or more of the following conditions:

- Less than 640KB of RAM
- A version of DOS earlier than 3.10
- A system BIOS dated 1987 or earlier
- A non-Hercules-compatible monochrome video adapter
- An LCD screen (some systems)
- A system motherboard dated 1987 or earlier
- A computer known to be somewhat less than 100-percent compatible (Leading Edge, PC Unlimited, Unisys, Burroughs, and possibly Tandy)

If your system falls into one or more of these catagories, don't panic yet—the programs may still work fine. But these systems are known to have compatibility problems with some software.

If All Else Fails

If all of your own efforts fail, consider calling on a friend or the computer guru at your place of business. It may be that you are overlooking something obvious, and sometimes a second pair of eyes can solve the problem in a flash.

If you have tried everything and still can't get the software installed, you can write to PC SIG or Computer Business Services at the addresses given below. Please include a clearly readable description of your system components and your problem. It would also help if you included your phone number. Computer Business Services cannot promise to call you, but it is committed to making sure you have the benefit of these programs and promises to respond to every query. Write to:

PC SIG
ATTN: Dvorak's DOS Installation Problems
1030 East Duane Avenue
Sunnyvale, CA 94086
408-730-9291

Installation Problems
Computer Business Services
1125 Bramford Court
Diamond Bar, CA 91765

Documentation for Supplied Programs

Several programs bound with this book can affect the data on your disks. If we were a commercial software publisher, this package could cost hundreds of dollars or more, and you'd receive a large box with multiple volumes of documentation, tutorials, and a technical-support hotline. There would also be a substantial reduction in the number of programs included, to keep the cost of support under control.

You're not just a user—you're a reader, too. And we need you to read the instructions and use due care. If you require technical support for these programs, you will need to contact their respective publishers. In the case of shareware publishers, you may need to register their products first. For technical support from the commercial publishers (Mace, Traveling Software, Multisoft, XTree Systems, and so forth), you'll need to respond to their offers for the latest versions of their products.

Making Backup Copies
One strict rule of working with floppies is *always back up your program disks!*

Even the most patient people will be distressed if they are faced with the delay of having replacement disks sent to them. You can avoid this problem—take two minutes to make a backup set of your disks.

Hard Disk or Floppy

The programs bound with this book can be run from floppy or hard disk. Hard disk operation is more convenient and faster. If you run these programs from floppies, you should make sure you have each of the files each program needs.

Interrupting Programs

To avoid possible data loss, you *must* properly exit or interrupt the programs that write to your disk before you reboot or shut down your system.

SOFTWARE DOCUMENTATION

AUTOPARK Hard Disk(s), Chuck Guzis, Sydex Software

```
AUTOPARK   COM        1222     7-29-90      9:16p
```

AUTOPARK.COM version 2.0 is a terminate-and-stay resident program that requires DOS 2.0 or later, 1KB of memory, and at least one hard disk drive.

AUTOPARK automatically parks a hard drive after a specified period of inactivity. After parking, the drive may be used normally, as any new requests for data will cause the drive heads to move from the parking zone.

Autopark can also be used to force an immediate park of the hard disk heads. Parking can also come in handy for disk drives having "stiction" problems—that is, difficulty starting when heads are positioned over outer tracks.

Using AUTOPARK

To use the program, at the DOS prompt, type

AUTOPARK *time*

where *time* is the number of minutes of inactivity before a hard drive is parked. *Time* must be in the range of 1 to 60 minutes. If *time* is omitted or incorrectly specified, 5 minutes is assumed.

The command

AUTOPARK NOW

forces an immediate park of all hard disk heads. The NOW option may be used even when a "delayed" AUTOPARK is already resident in memory.

The command

AUTOPARK R

causes an installed copy of AUTOPARK to be removed from memory.

Restrictions
This program and its documentation remain the property of Sydex and may not be copied and distributed. In no case does Sydex assume any responsibility for the performance or fitness of this product. All rights reserved. Write or call for a free brochure describing other quality software products.

Sydex
P.O. Box 5700
Eugene, OR 97405
Copyright 1989, 1990 Sydex
Voice: 503-683-6033
Fax: 503-683-1622
Data: 503-683-1385

COLOR, ANSI.SYS Screen-Color-Attribute Control

COLOR allows you to set the screen's color attributes using ANSI commands. Using real words instead of numbers, COLOR makes it easy to set your screen colors. Here's the syntax:

854   Dvorak's Guide to DOS and PC Performance

COLOR [HELP] [/C] [/F] [BLINK] [BRIGHT] [*foreground*] **[[ON]** *background*]   The foreground and background colors are

Black
Blue
Green
Cyan
Red
Magenta
Yellow
White

Options

HELP   This option gives you the Help screen.

/C   This option clears the screen, using ANSI commands.

/F   This option writes the ANSI command to the file ANSI.OUT. You can copy this file into batch files to change colors.

foreground   This sets the foreground color. You can use the BRIGHT option to use high-intensity foreground colors. Using the BLINK option will cause the screen to blink.

COLOR [*foreground*] [*background*] and **COLOR** [*foreground*] **ON** [*background*]   These two commands set both the foreground and background colors. You can use the options BLINK and BRIGHT, also.

COLOR ON [*background*]   This command sets only the background color.

Examples

COLOR /C BRIGHT WHITE ON BLUE   This sets COLOR to bright white on a blue background and clears the screen.

COLOR /F BRIGHT YELLOW   This writes the ANSI sequence for yellow to the file ANSI.OUT.

COLOR ON GREEN   This sets the background color to green. Copyright 1989 by Thumper Technologies, Eric Cockrell. (Custom written for John C. Dvorak and Nick Anis.)

DeskConnect, Traveling Software

```
DC        BIN    15653   7-12-90   9:49a
DC        EXE    21359   7-12-90   9:32a
DCINSTAL  EXE    49093   7-12-90   9:55a
```

DeskConnect is a special-edition program written for this book by Traveling Software, makers of LapLink and DeskLink. DeskConnect connects two PCs by their serial ports. You'll need DOS version 2.X or later and a null modem cable.

Your system may have a 25-pin serial port connector or the newer, 9-pin type. Most of the time, the connector on the computer end is male; that means you'll need a female-to-female cable with a DB9 or DB25 connector. Traveling Software offers a special two-headed cable with 9- and 25-pin connectors that will work in just about any configuration. They offer cables that use ordinary four-conductor RJ11 telephone wire in lengths of 25, 50, and even 100 feet.

The DCINSTAL program allows you to specify the hot-key for the program setup screen, printer, serial port, program path, baud rate, and server sector size. You can move between each of the configuration items with the UP ARROW and DOWN ARROW keys. Pressing the SPACEBAR switches between options (H)elp, (S)ave, (R)estore, and (Q)uit and, in DCINSTAL, the added option (U)ninstall. Once one of these choices is highlighted, you press H, S, R, U, or Q to proceed.

To install the DeskConnect device driver and set program defaults, enter

DCINSTALL

You will see the installation screen, and you can use the cursor keys to advance.

To start DeskConnect, enter

dc

and you'll see the Server Program screen.

The program DC.EXE is the server program, and the DC.BIN device driver is the client. A computer can be both a client and a server at the same time. The client system can access server drives by using the first available drive letter designator. Up to five drives are supported. The server program allows you to assign whichever drives you like, but they must be valid and they can't be duplicated.

From the DOS prompt, things work just like they always did, but you now have additional drives available. You have to get used to the new designators. You'll find that most of your applications will support the new server drives. The XTree program supplied with this book works just fine, too.

Large Disk Partitions

This version of DeskConnect can be used on computers with hard disks that were partitioned into volumes greater than 32MB when the partitions were created with MS/PC-DOS 4.01.

Partitions larger than 32MB with a sector size of 1KB or larger that have been created with Disk Manager or SpeedStor are not supported by this version of DeskConnect.

CHKDSK

Do not attempt to conduct a CHKDSK on a drive that is performing a background print through DeskConnect. Wait until the printing operation has finished.

Video Compatibility

High-Resolution Graphics   If you use a program that requires a high-resolution EGA or VGA graphics mode (such as some desktop publishing programs) and you call up the Device Window, the graphics screen for your application may not be restored correctly when you exit the window. You may have to redraw the screen or exit the high-resolution graphics program before you call up the Device Window.

Video Compatibility Between the Two Computers   If the computer you are using as the lead does not have the same video capability as the server computer, you may not be able to call up some programs from the server until they are reconfigured for the video capability of the lead computer.

Printer Support

The printer you select for installation (lead or server) is the one to which printer output will be directed every time you boot your computer, unless you call up the Device Window and change your selection. If you select the server printer and that printer is not turned on or the server program is not running when you give the print command, the lead computer may appear to lock up. If you have printers connected to both computers, it is recommended that you select the lead printer during installation.

Printer Redirection When the user selects the lead printer, DeskConnect always directs printer output to LPT1. If the printer on the lead is connected to LPT2, redirect the output to LPT2 using the DOS PRINT or MODE command. See your DOS manual for additional information on these commands, since all versions of DOS may not handle this the same way.

Printer-Error Handling DeskConnect manages the DOS operation on the lead computer, the server computer, and the peripherals connected to each computer. To the extent that DOS provides error messages, DeskConnect will pass them on to the user. In cases where, for example, the selected printer is out of paper or not on line, DOS does not return an error message, and so DeskConnect has no message to pass on to the user.

If you are printing inside an application program, the error messages from that application may not be returned. If you give the instruction to print a file on the lead computer and the server printer is selected but not available for some reason, the lead will not give an error message. The server will be locked, and a "lead computer accessing server" message will appear on the screen.

Additional Technical Information

Custom Versions of DOS Some hardware manufacturers have customized the MS-DOS operating system that they provide for their machines. Most DOS versions use a sector size of 512 bytes, but some use a sector size of 1024 bytes. DOS 4.X cannot use any sector size except 512 bytes. So, if your lead computer is running DOS 4.X, you will not be able to communicate with a server computer using a larger sector size.

Maximum Number of Drives Supported This version of the server program can accommodate a maximum of five physical or logical drives in the system. This means that drives A, B, C, D, and E are supported. If additional physical or logical drives (F, G, H, . . .) are present in the system that the server program is running on, the server program may not operate correctly.

Changing Server Computers   After you have accessed one computer as a server, if you move the DeskConnect cable to another server computer, type CTRL-C on the lead and do a directory of the drives on the new server computer before you use any other DeskConnect capabilities.

Using DeskConnect with Disk-Caching Programs   When you install the cache, do not install it so that it tries to cache the disks shown by DeskConnect.

Using DeskConnect with Multitasking Programs   The server program should not be used with multitasking software (such as DESQview or Concurrent DOS 386) where two copies of the server might be running at the same time.

Copying Graphics Screens   If you want to print a graphics screen that has been saved to disk on the server, use the command

COPY *filename* /b *port*

The DOS PRINT command is not used for printing graphics.

Path Size for DeskConnect   During installation, you will be prompted to type in the path where the DeskConnect file will be found. You may indicate a drive and a directory path, or you may simply type in the path if the DeskConnect file is on the disk the system boots from. Because the filename is DC.BIN, the maximum length of the path that may be used is 57 characters (*not* 64 characters, as indicated in the manual).

Memory Requirements   The current version of DeskConnect requires a minimum of 49KB. Depending on the DOS version and the server sector-size parameter, that can increase to as much as 350KB.

   For technical assistance, please fill out the coupon in the back of this book.

Traveling Software, Inc.
18702 North Creek Parkway
Bothell, Washington 98011
206-483-8088

DOSCACHE, Multisoft

```
DOSCACHE  COM     43840    8-07-90    9:47a
DOSCACHE  DAT      6256    8-07-90    9:53a
```

Multisoft's DOSCACHE is a special miniversion of the award-winning Super PC-Kwik disk-caching utility. DOSCACHE substantially improves the speed of your system by storing frequently accessed data in RAM. Because getting the data from RAM is much faster than getting it from the disk, your programs and applications can run much faster than they used to.

When you run the INSTALL.EXE program, the DOSCACHE is extracted to the target drive and directory you specify (usually C:\DVORAK); however, you can install the program on any drive or directory you wish.

To load and run the cache, change to the directory containing the cache program file, or be certain that the directory is listed in your PATH variable. Then type

DOSCACHE

and press the ENTER key. The disk-cache program loads into memory and automatically configures itself for your system hardware, memory type, and disk type. The start-up screen gives you more instructions about using the cache. A cache "hit" indicator (an asterisk) flashes in the upper right corner of your screen each time data is retrieved from the cache instead of from the disk.

This version of the cache includes an information viewer and a measurement utility, which you access by pressing both SHIFT keys simultaneously. When you press this hot-key combination, a window pops up on your screen, from which you can choose Measurements or Information. Move the highlight bar to the one you want, and press ENTER.

If you choose Measurements, another screen shows you how many disk accesses you've made and how many of those disk accesses came from the cache instead of the disk. You should see a substantial percentage of your accesses coming from the cache. If you choose Information, information about DOSCACHE and Multisoft's other products is displayed. To exit any of the screens and return to the DOS prompt, press ESC.

DOSCACHE remains resident until you reboot your system, improving your program performance for the entire time you work. You can use the programs MARK and RELEASE if you would like to be able to remove the program from memory without having to reboot your system. To load DOSCACHE each time you boot, put the DOSCACHE command in your AUTOEXEC.BAT file.

DOG Disk OrGanizer, Soft GAMS Software, G. Allen Morris III

```
DOG      EXE     42460    3-27-90    1:06p
```

Disk OrGanizer Version 2.05, by G. Allen Morris III of Soft GAMS Software, is an excellent disk defragmentor.

A disk that has been in use for a while will have fragmented files and directories. This increases the time required to access data, puts more wear on your disk drive's head actuator, and increases the noise generated by the disk.

Disk OrGanizer speeds up your disk-access times by defragmenting files and removing deleted entries from directories. It also allows you to determine the order of files and subdirectories, and can free some disk space by truncating subdirectories.

Running Disk OrGanizer the First Time

Disk OrGanizer has been tested with MS-DOS 2.10, 3.01, 3.10, and 3.30 on logical drives as large as 32MB. It is believed that Disk OrGanizer will operate on any MS/PC-DOS disk, except for DOS version 4.0 disks with 32-bit file allocation tables (FATs), which are not supported at this time.

Disk OrGanizer performs extensive tests before it starts to move data, making sure that the FATs, and directories are in good repair, and verifies all data written to the disk.

You can test Disk OrGanizer by typing the command

DOG [*d:*] /TEST

where [*d:*] is an optional drive specifier. The current drive is the default. If you do not receive any error messages from this command, you will be able to run Disk OrGanizer on the tested drive. Be sure that you have a backup of your data before you continue.

You can now run Disk OrGanizer and defragment all of the files on a drive by typing

DOG [*d:*] /FAST

If you would also like to recover some disk space by truncating your subdirectories, type

DOG [*d:*] /FAST /TRUNCATE

Please note that you may not have any directories with enough deleted files to allow truncation.

Disk OrGanizer reads and tests the FATs and directories, gives you a report, tells you what it is going to do, and asks you if you wish it to organize the disk. Nothing will be written to the disk unless you answer Yes to this question.

You may abort from Disk OrGanizer at any time by pressing ESC or CTRL-C. (There may be a slight delay.) Under no circumstances should you reboot, reset, or power down your system while Disk OrGanizer is moving clusters: Aborting from Disk OrGanizer while it is moving clusters may cause extreme fragmentation. Rerun Disk OrGanizer as soon as possible if you abort while it is moving clusters.

If you think that Disk OrGanizer has stopped running, press the SPACE-BAR; you should hear a beep within a minute.

If you get an error while running Disk OrGanizer, run CHKDSK with the /F switch (see your DOS manual). If you get an "Out of memory" error message try running Disk OrGanizer after removing any terminate-and-stay resident (TSR) programs. If this does not solve the problem, try decreasing the number of files and buffers in your CONFIG.SYS file. (Disk OrGanizer will run with FILES=6 and BUFFERS=1.) If you still get the "Out of memory" error message, decrease the total number of files on the drive. The easiest way to do so is to reboot from a DOS disk that has no CONFIG.SYS or AUTOEXEC.BAT files.

Running Disk Organizer from the Command Line
For most applications, DOG can be run from the command line or a batch file. The general syntax for running Disk OrGanizer from the DOS prompt is

DOG [*d:*] /*mode* [/TRUNCATE][/BATCH][/NOVERIFY]

where *mode* is one of the following:

FAST   This mode will defragment all files and attempt to put them in one area of disk space. FAST mode may leave gaps of free space between files. This is the mode that should be used by most people.

FILL   This mode will defragment files and put them as close to the FAT as possible. FILL will not leave any free space between files and may leave files fragmented around bad disk sectors and unmovable files.

DATE   This mode will put the files on the disk with the oldest files first (closest to the FAT). This mode used once in a while can take a long time to run and may decrease the number of clusters that Disk OrGanizer will need to move with the FAST or FILL mode.

DIRE   Directory mode will put the files on the disk in the order it finds them in the directories; that is, the first file or subdirectory in the root directory will be closest to the FAT, followed by the second file in the root, and so on.

TRUNCATE   This switch tells Disk OrGanizer to truncate all sub-directories. /BATCH is a switch telling Disk OrGanizer to suppress all prompts. If this switch is set, any error will cause Disk OrGanizer to return an error code (see Appendix A) and terminate. This is useful for running Disk OrGanizer from a batch file.

NOVERIFY   This switch tells Disk OrGanizer not to verify data written to the disk. This increases the speed of Disk OrGanizer but allows data to be lost. This switch is for people to whom speed is more important than data integrity.

Running Disk OrGanizer with an ORDER File
If you would like to have more control over the location of files on your disk (a subdirectory is a special "file"), you can create an ORDER file. This file allows you to move named files close to the FAT or away from the FAT. Any files that are not named in this file are then placed between the two areas.

The area of the disk close to the FAT is called the "low" area, and the area away from the FAT is called the "HIGH" area. Any file that is not named anywhere in the ORDER file is said to "float." In making this file, you should name as few files as possible.

The command to run Disk OrGanizer with an ORDER file is

DOG [*d:*] [*orderfile*] [*/mode*] [*/switch*]

where *orderfile* is the path and file specification of the ORDER file. If this is not included, Disk OrGanizer will look for a file called ORDER.DOG in the root directory of the drive being organized. If it does not find that, it will look in the environment for DOG=*d:\path\filename* and use that file.

Modes You must include a mode. The mode affects only files not included in the ORDER file. A mode given on the command line will override the mode in the ORDER file. The modes are FAST, FILL, DIRE, and DATE.

Switches You may also set some of the following switches from the command line: TRUNCATE ALL, BATCH, and NOVERIFY.

Commands

LOW This tells Disk OrGanizer to place the file close to the FAT. This also affects the FREE command, described below.

HIGH This tells Disk OrGanizer to place the specified files away from the FAT. This also affects the FREE command.

FORCE This tells Disk OrGanizer not to move the specified files.

FLOAT This tells Disk OrGanizer to ignore the specified files. This is used if you wish to TRUNCATE a subdirectory but don't want to specify LOW, HIGH, or FORCE.

TRUNCATE Subdirectories named between TRUNCATE and END-TRUNCATE will have their sizes changed so that they will use as little space as possible.

FREE *nn* This tells Disk OrGanizer to leave *nn* clusters of free space after the last file named in the ORDER file if files are being placed low, or before the file if files are being placed high. Disk OrGanizer ignores this command if there isn't enough free disk space. The *nn* may be replaced with an asterisk if you want all available free clusters in a location.

Comments
A comment starts with a semicolon and ends with a carriage return.

Sample ORDER File
The following is a simple ORDER file:

```
[FAST]              ; This sets the mode.
[TRUNCATE]
\DIR_A\             ; Truncate subdirectory DIR_A, but let
                    ; it FLOAT.
                    ;
[LOW]               ; Set move files LOW.
\DOS\               ; Truncate subdirectory DOS, and put it
                    ; next to the FAT.
[ENDTRUNCATE]
\COMMAND.COM        ; COMMAND.COM will be placed after \DOS.
[HIGH]              ; Set move files HIGH.
\AUTOEXEC.BAT       ; As this file is used only once, on reboot
                    ; we can move it away from the FAT.
\ORDER.DOG          ; This file will be place just in front
                    ; of AUTOEXEC.BAT.
```

License Agreements
This is a shareware program; it is not free. You may use the program for a 30-day trial period. If you wish to continue using this program after that time, you must purchase a license agreement. The cost of a license agreement for noncommercial use is on a sliding scale of $5 to $30. For commercial use, the cost is $30 for the first unit and $15 for each additional unit. Site licenses and commercial-distribution licenses are available.

Please make checks payable in U.S. dollars to:

Soft GAMS Software
P.O. Box 1311
Mendocino, CA 95460
Copyright 1988
CompuServe: #73210,3374
Source: BFH700
BIX: gam3
UUCP: gam3@well
Voice: 707-961-1470

The Dvorak Utilities, Tom Campbell

ASK	COM	1836	6-11-90	3:59a
BEEP	COM	10	6-11-90	3:59a
BOX	COM	1382	6-11-90	3:59a
FREADY	COM	882	7-06-90	2:08p
GETKEY	COM	8	6-11-90	3:59a
GETKEYNL	COM	20	6-11-90	4:00a
GETYN	COM	56	6-11-90	4:00a
RESTPATH	COM	490	6-11-90	4:00a
ROWCOL	COM	1599	6-11-90	4:00a
SAVEPATH	COM	426	6-11-90	4:00a
SHOWTIME	COM	532	6-11-90	4:00a
SUBTEST	BAT	273	5-26-90	10:31a
TESTANSI	COM	64	6-11-90	4:00a
TESTIT	BAT	322	7-06-90	2:07p

The Dvorak Utilities are a series of useful batch-file-related assembly language utilities. You'll find instructions for most of these utilities in Chapter 26. The source code for each of the Dvorak Utilities (compressed with PKZIP) may be found on the disks bound with this book in the file SOURCE.ZIP.

Here is a brief rundown of the Dvorak Utilities:

Program Name	What It's For
ASK	Displays a message and accepts keys from list.
BEEP	Beeps.
BOX	Draws a single or double, filled, colored box anywhere on the screen.
FREADY	Returns ERRORLEVEL 1 if a floppy drive specified on the command line is ready (for use in batch files). Usage: FREADY d[:] (where d is a drive letter followed by an optional colon).
GETKEY, GETKEYNL	Accepts a keystroke and converts it to an ERRORLEVEL value.
GETYN	Accepts only the Y or N key and sets ERRORLEVEL accordingly.
RESTPATH	Retrieves a disk and directory from a file created by SAVEPATH, and changes to that directory.
ROWCOL	Positions the cursor on the screen and optionally displays text in any foreground or background color.
SAVEPATH	"Remembers" the current drive and directory so that RESTPATH can return to it later.
SHOWTIME	Displays the time, "am" or "pm", the day, the date, and the year.
TESTANSI	Sets ERRORLEVEL to 1 if the ANSI.SYS driver is present and to 0 if it's not.

ESC.COM, Chuck Guzis, Sydex Software

This is a useful ANSI.SYS utility for sending ANSI.SYS sequences to the console. You can produce this file yourself by using the source code file ESC.IN, which is also included with DOS's DEBUG.

You can redirect the ESC.IN file into DEBUG with the following command:

DEBUG <ESC.IN

or enter its contents manually from the keyboard.

ESC.COM is another one of those useful oddities we created to help you work with ANSI.SYS-compatible screen drivers. ESC.COM takes whatever is on the command line, prefixes it with an ASCII ESC left-bracket combination, and outputs the entire string to the console.

If you have an ANSI.SYS-compatible device driver installed, you can clear the screen with

ESC 2J

You can set the screen colors to white-on-blue

ESC 37;44m

Or you can reassign the F2 key to provide a wide directory listing

ESC 0;60;"DIR *.* /W";13p

(13 is the ENTER key.)

In addition, you can build a file full of setup information (such as the commands above) and output it to the console later

ESC 37;44m > myfile
ESC 0;60;"DIR *.* /W";13p > > myfile
ESC 2J > > myfile

Then, you can simply put the following command in your AUTOEXEC.BAT file to set things up

TYPE MYFILE

If you have any questions or would like to learn more about ANSI-string command sequences, you'll find Chapter 27's extensive coverage just what you need.

FREE RAM and Disk Report,
Chuck Guzis, Sydex Software

```
FREE    COM      2164    4-02-90    2:19p
```

FREE is a program that was designed by Nick Anis and supercoder Chuck Guzis, of Sydex Software. FREE provides a detailed report of your system's RAM and disk storage. The listing gives amounts and percentages for total, used, and available memory and storage and reports on each drive unit, including sectors per track, tracks per cylinder, total cylinders, and bytes.

When you run FREE, the report is directed to the screen by default. You can redirect the report to disk with the DOS redirection command, like this:

```
FREE >FREE.RPT
```

FREE detects when the output is not to the console and automatically proceeds without pausing.

FREE does a nice job of laying out the information and providing totals. The program works with systems with a single hard disk or hard disk partition as well as with multiple drives and partitions.

FREE is brought to you by Sydex, creators of quality shareware. For a free brochure describing the product line, call or write:

Sydex
P.O. Box 5700
Eugene, OR 97405
Voice: 503-683-6033
Fax: 503-683-1622
Data: 503-683-1385

GLOM.COM Tiny Console Capture,
Chuck Guzis, Sydex Software

```
GLOM    COM      1447    8-18-90    12:12a
```

GLOM is a terminate-and-stay resident program that captures all console output produced by means of DOS calls. It is very small—about 2KB—but we've found it to be very useful. GLOM will not capture console output produced by means of direct display-memory writing (such as a word processor) or by ROM BIOS calls.

If the command

GLOM

is entered, a short summary of GLOM command syntax is displayed. If the command

GLOM *filename*

is entered, the file specified by *filename* is created to hold console output. GLOM has an internal buffer of about 1KB; when this buffer is filled, the data is written to the specified file. If the disk containing the file has no more space, GLOM will cease to write any more display output to the file, even if more disk space becomes available.

If the command

GLOM UNLOAD

is entered, GLOM is removed from memory and the space occupied by it is freed.

Special Notes

This program, like several others packaged with this book, is provided courtesy of Sydex. Write or call Sydex for a free brochure, or send $5 for a three-disk sampler (overseas orders, please add $3 for airmail).

Corporate site licenses are available, as is a sample disk. See the back of this book for a Sydex coupon, or send $5 to the address below (specify disk size):

Sydex
P.O. Box 5700
Eugene, OR 97405
Voice: 503-683-6033
FAX: 503-683-1622
Data: 503-683-1385

Licensing Information

GLOM is provided by Sydex free of charge and may be distributed for noncommercial use only. GLOM may not be sold, nor may a fee be charged for its use. For commercial distribution, please contact Sydex at the above address.

InfoPlus, Diagnostics, and Benchmarks, Andrew Rossmann

```
INFOPLUS   EXE     34568    7-08-90          1:01a
```

This is a special version released for *Dvorak's Guide to DOS and PC Performance,* by Andrew Rossmann, based on Steve Grant's public domain SYSID 4.4.

INFOPLUS is a utility that provides a technical description of DOS-based PC/XT/AT- and PS/2-class machines. It generates 18 screens of information. INFOPLUS runs under DOS 3.0 and later versions and may also support earlier versions of DOS.

INFOPLUS uses techniques that may not be documented or supported officially by IBM or Microsoft. Since INFOPLUS is only a diagnostic reporting tool, this shouldn't get you into any trouble. If you're using a multitasker like DESQview or Windows 3, you may want to be in native DOS first.

INFOPLUS is easy to use. Simply type **infoplus** on the DOS command line. Once it's running, the PGUP and PGDN keys will move you from one page to another. The HOME and END keys move you to page 1 and page 17, respectively. A press of the ENTER key prompts you to enter a number from 1 to 17, allowing you to jump to any page. Pressing the ESC key ends the program. Some of the 17 pages take more than one screen. You can use the DOWN ARROW and UP ARROW keys to see remaining portions of the screens.

Mail your comments, suggestions, and questions to the program's original author at

BIXMail: sjgrant
CompuServe: 71101,706

or contact

Andrew Rossmann
Wheeling, IL

Central Command:	708-359-9346 (1200/2400)
	708-359-9396 (HST 14.4)
DDSW1 BBS:	708-808-7300 (6 lines)
	708-808-7306 (Telebit PEP only!)
Igloo BBS:	708-272-5912 or 708-272-5917 (Telebit PEP)
RCS Defender BBS:	708-390-6603
UNIX Mail:	andyross@ddsw1.MCS.COM
	a <well-connected>!ddsw1!andyross
	andyross@igloo.UUCP

INSTALL

```
INSTALL.EXE    2338      10-01-90      5:00p
```

The programs included in this book are in compressed format. They need to be converted to their original format before you will be able to use them. Once you've made a few selections, the program INSTALL will do this for you automatically. You can run INSTALL from any drive, usually Drive A or B. First logon to the drive with the distribution disk. Then type **IN-STALL**.

Note: This version of the INSTALL program requires a dual floppy or hard disk system. Other versions are available. For more information, refer to the installation instruction in Appendix C.

LIST Size for Group of Files, Chuck Guzis, Sydex Software

```
LS      COM      2047      1-24-90      11:29a
```

LIST is a useful program by Sydex Software that lists the files and size in KB rounded to three decimal places in a four-column display with totals. You can use DOS's wildcards with LIST to quickly get the size of a group of files. Typing **LS** without any parameters will give you the size of all the files in the default directory.

For instance, type

LS D:\UTIL2\D*.COM

to get the filenames and sizes of all COM files.

MACE Utilities Special Edition, Fifth Generation Systems

Fifth Generation Systems (FGS) has made a special edition of the popular Mace Utilities 1990, a set of easy-to-use data-recovery programs. Because the possibilities of losing data are endless, FGS provided a program that maximizes data recovery.

Files Included

Here is an overview of what the special edition can do. FGS has included six easy-to-use utilities that you can put to work right away:

```
PARK      EXE      20004     12-15-89    12:00p
RXBAK     EXE      42826     4-23-90     11:00p
SORTD     EXE      45308     12-15-89    12:00p
SQZD      EXE      43318     12-15-89    12:00p
UNDELETE  EXE      64434     5-21-90     4:58p
UNFORMAT  EXE      56546     12-15-89    12:00p
```

PARK   This parks your hard disk by moving the read/write heads to the safety zone. It helps protect your data and drive from damage.

RXBAK   This makes an image backup of your drive's partition, FAT, and directory.

SORTD   This sorts directories in various orders.

SQZD   This squeezes or removes deleted directory entries, speeding up disk operations. If followed by disk defragmentation, it makes future file recovery more reliable. When you use SQZD, you cannot recover any previously deleted files, but you can recover any deletions made after SQZD was last run.

UNDELETE   This lets you unerase a file if it hasn't been overwritten.

UNFORMAT   This lets you recover from an accidental disk format. You can use the RXBAK image for greater accuracy.

Warnings

The following are precautionary steps we advise you to take. Read the warnings carefully before using any of the Mace Utilities.

- Do not experiment with any Mace utility on your hard drive. If you want to experiment, we strongly advise that you use a floppy containing data you do not need.

- Do not reboot your computer during a run of any Mace utility! You may cause serious damage to your hard drive.

- The Mace Utilities Special Edition will work on floppy or hard drives. If you use floppies, you'll have to insert the correct floppy each time you want to run one of the programs.

- If your drive is part of a network, *do not run unformat!*

- The instructions following RXBAK assume you have installed Mace on your hard drive and have included Mace in your AUTOEXEC.BAT file. If you do not put Mace on your hard drive, you will have to insert the disk with the Mace Utilities Special Edition files each time you want to use one of the utilities. In this case, type the name of the utility to use at the A> prompt.

- SORTD, SQZD, UNDELETE, and UNFORMAT will work on Bernoulli system.

Program Instructions

To familiarize you with the practice of disk maintenance, we are presenting the Mace Utilities in the order we recommend they be used:

RXBAK
SORTD
UNDELETE
UNFORMAT
SQZD
PARK

The following sections provide brief explanations of how the utilities work and step-by-step instructions for using them. To maximize your ability to recover data, please read each section before using Mace.

RXBAK

RXBAK allows you to make a backup copy of the information in the system area of the disk; that is, RXBAK copies the boot sector, the file allocation table, and the root directory. It is very important to use RXBAK every time you boot up, because it makes a duplicate copy of your disk's system area. Backup copies of this information are the key to data recovery.

Note: We strongly urge you to include RXBAK in your AUTOEXEC-.BAT file. By doing so, you automatically back up every time you boot your computer. You should use RXBAK daily when booting up and periodically after making changes to files.

Using RXBAK When You Boot Up   To automatically run RXBAK every time you boot up, Mace must be installed or copied on to your hard drive, and RXBAK must be part of your AUTOEXEC.BAT file. If you already have an AUTOEXEC.BAT file, we recommend that you add Mace to the PATH statement. Follow the instructions in the following pages that apply to your situation.

Creating an AUTOEXEC.BAT File   If you don't have an AUTOEXEC-.BAT file, the installation program supplied with the distribution disks will create one for you. If you give INSTALL permission, it will include the two lines that follow shortly in your AUTOEXEC.BAT file. You'll find more help in Chapter 24.

Here is how you can create or modify AUTOEXEC.BAT on your own if you want to run RXBAK automatically each time you boot up. First, you'll need Mace on your hard drive, and you'll need to address it in your PATH statement. For instance if your path is

PATH = C:\;C:\DOS;C:\BATCH

you'll need to add the subdirectory on which these files are located (the default is \DVORAK):

PATH = C:\;C:\DOS;C:\BATCH;C:\DVORAK

Here are the two lines you need to add to your AUTOEXEC.BAT file:

SET MACE = C:\MACE
C:\MACE\RXBAK C:

If you have partitioned drives or multiple drives, you can enter those drives on the second line:

C:\MACE\RXBAK C: D: E:

When to Use RXBAK   You should use RXBAK whenever there have been significant changes made to your files. If you've made the recommended changes to your AUTOEXEC.BAT, you can use RXBAK easily when the need arises. You should always run RXBAK after defragmenting your disk with programs like DOG (included with this book).
    To run RXBAK at the DOS prompt, enter

RXBAK C:

Using RXBAK from a Floppy   You can use RXBAK without Mace being part of your AUTOEXEC.BAT file and without Mace being installed on your hard drive. It's a little tedious, but possible.
    To run RXBAK from a floppy, at the A> prompt enter

RXBAK C:

What RXBAK Does   RXBAK copies files and names them BACK-UP.M_U and OLDBACK.M_U. The first time you use RXBAK, BACKUP.M_U is created. The next time, the information in BACKUP is transferred to OLDBACK, and the updated information is placed in BACKUP. Each time you use RXBAK, information is transferred from

BACKUP to OLDBACK. With FGS Mace, you have two backup files: the most recent updates and the preceding update.

SORTD

SORTD allows you to reorder the directory entries on your hard drive or floppy disk. You can command Mace to sort them by filename, extension, date and time, or length. SORTD always moves subdirectories in a directory to the top of the listing.

Using SORTD   To rearrange the directory on your hard drive, follow these steps:

1. Enter **SORTD** at the DOS prompt. A listing of the ways you can sort appears.

2. At the next DOS prompt, enter the drive letter and the letter of the desired sort.

3. To sort directories in more than one way, you can list two sort options on the SORTD command line; for example, **SORTD *drive*: EN** *or* **SORTD *drive*: NE**.

To sort a subdirectory, follow these steps:

1. Go to the subdirectory you want to sort by typing

    ```
    CD \subdirectory
    ```

2. At the subdirectory prompt, enter

    ```
    SORTD
    ```

3. The next prompt lists the options available. Enter the desired option.

Note: SORTD does not remove references to deleted files; it sorts them along with all active files. To remove deleted entries, see SQZD on page 880.

UNDELETE

UNDELETE allows you to recover files and directories that have been deleted. When you use DOS to delete or erase a file or to remove a directory, it does not completely destroy the data. The DEL command changes the first letter of the deleted file's entry to a sigma character. This "renaming" takes place in the root directory, which DOS relies on to locate the file. Since the data is still there, UNDELETE allows you to retrieve the information.

There are certain times when UNDELETE may not retrieve the entire file. Suppose you are working on Document A. You delete it and begin working on Document B. You suddenly realize that you need Document A again. UNDELETE will search the root directory for A's entry. If you saved Document B and did not use RXBAK first, UNDELETE may not find Document A—when you saved Document B, DOS may have used Document A's entry in the root directory. If this happened, the entry for Document A is gone; it is now the entry for Document B. You cannot retrieve Document A unless you use Mace Muse (available in the upgrade).

To use UNDELETE to recover a single file, enter the following at the DOS prompt:

```
UNDELETE filename
```

Mace may ask you to be more specific. If so, enter

```
UNDELETE drive:filename
```

To undelete multiple files, follow these steps:

1. At the DOS prompt, enter

   ```
   UNDELETE drive: *.*
   ```

2. Mace may ask you to enter the correct first letter for each file it finds:

   ```
   Correct first letter-> ilename.exe Apr.23, 1990 11:00pm
   ```

   At each prompt, enter the correct first letter of the filename, or, to leave the file undeleted, press the SPACEBAR.

3. When the process is complete, Mace prompts you to press any key to exit to DOS.

4. At the DOS prompt, go to the subdirectory the deleted files were originally in. Once you are in that subdirectory, enter DIR for a directory listing. The deleted files should appear in the listing. They are now undeleted.

To undelete multiple files within subdirectories, follow these steps:

1. Go to the subdirectory the deleted files were in:

```
CD \subdirectory
```

2. At the subdirectory prompt, enter

```
UNDELETE drive:*.*
```

3. Follow the instructions above for undeleting multiple files.

UNFORMAT

UNFORMAT allows you to recover information on your hard drive or a floppy disk that was accidentally formatted. UNFORMAT works the same way as UNDELETE. When a disk is reformatted (formatted), the information in the root directory is altered.

When information in the root directory is altered, it is temporarily unretrievable. UNFORMAT is able to recover this information; however, UNFORMAT works differently depending on your use of RXBAK:

- If you ran RXBAK before your hard drive was formatted, all the information in the root directory that DOS looks for is still available. UNFORMAT searches for this information and restores it.

- If you did not run RXBAK before your disk was formatted, UNFORMAT renames any subdirectories that it finds as SUB_000, SUB_001, and so on. The files in the subdirectories keep their original names; however, your root directory will be lost.

UNFORMAT can work with 100-percent success if you formatted your hard drive with Mace FORMATH or your floppy with FORMATF. These format versions do not overwrite the data required to unformat the disk, they deal only with system information. However, if you used a DOS format on your floppy, the information is unrecoverable. It is good practice to use FORMATH or FORMATF when formatting disks. (They are available in the Mace upgrade.)

Note: We strongly urge you to establish the practice of running RX-BAK. When you use RXBAK, UNFORMAT can recover data; if you do not use RXBAK, UNFORMAT will not work with 100-percent success all of the time.

Warning: The following DOS systems have a "lethal" format command. This means that when you format your hard drive with any of these systems, your data is unrecoverable.

- Compaq MS-DOS through version 3.2
- AT&T MS-DOS prior to version 3.1
- Burroughs MS-DOS through version 3.1

Using UNFORMAT

1. At the DOS prompt, enter

   ```
   UNFORMAT
   ```

2. The next prompt lists the options you have with UNFORMAT. Enter

   ```
   drive: desired option
   ```

3. If you do not want Mace to search for backup information, or if RXBAK was never run against the drive, enter

   ```
   UNFORMAT drive:/N backup options display option
   ```

   Choose the option that best suits your situation. Follow the Mace prompts as they instruct you. When you see the DOS prompt, UN-FORMAT is done.

4. Go to the drive you unformatted, and call up the directory listing. You may notice the listing

   ```
   SUB000 <DIR>
   ```

in your directory. Mace placed the files from the disk in that subdirectory.

SQZD

"SQUEEZE D," as it is pronounced, examines a directory and removes all references to deleted files. As mentioned before, when a file has been deleted, DOS replaces the first character of the entry with a sigma character. The file is still on your hard disk but is not recoverable.

SQZD allows you to use this space for another file. It does this by gathering all nondeleted entries and placing them at the top of the directory. The deleted entries are marked as unused, and their space becomes available.

Note: We recommend using SQZD once a week. If there are any files you need to undelete or if you need to unformat your hard drive, do so before using SQZD. Once a directory has been squeezed, deleted files cannot be retrieved.

Using SQZD on Your Hard Drive   To squeeze all the directories on your hard drive, enter

SQZD *drive*:

at the DOS prompt. When the squeeze is complete, press any key to return to the DOS prompt for the current drive.

To squeeze a particular directory on your hard drive, go to that directory, and enter **SQZD** at the prompt. Mace will prompt you to press any key when SQZD is complete.

PARK

PARK allows you to protect your hard disk when you leave your computer idle or when it is shut down.

When your computer is turned off, the read/write heads fall directly above the system area of your hard drive. This is dangerous, because if your computer is moved, the heads will also move. Such movement could cause them to drop on your system information. If this happens, the system information may be destroyed by the crash and may be unrecoverable. PARK moves the read/write heads to an area of the hard disk where system data is not stored.

Parking Your Read/Write Heads   At the DOS prompt, enter

PARK

Mace lets you know when your read/write heads are parked with the following message:

HEAD PARKED ON 1 PHYSICAL FIXED DISK(S).
TURN OFF THE POWER OR PRESS A KEY.

To resume using your computer, press any key; this will take you to the DOS prompt. Otherwise, turn the computer off.

Technical Support
Before calling the FGS Technical Support Department, please have the following information available:

- Type of computer (XT, AT, PS/2, and so on)
- DOS version (type **VER** and press ENTER)
- Contents of your CONFIG.SYS and AUTOEXEC.BAT files

Fifth Generation Systems
10049 N. Reiger Road
Baton Rouge, LA 70809-4559
Technical Support Hours: 7:00 A.M. to 7:00 P.M. CST, Monday through Friday
FGS BBS (2400-baud modem): 504-295-3344

Move Files and Rename Directories, Chuck Guzis, Sydex Software

```
MV      COM     2749    3-14-90    8:51p
```

MV, written by Chuck Guzis of Sydex Software, moves or renames files and subdirectories. MV can also be used to rename subdirectories. The format is

MV *options sources . . . destination*

Options   Options may be omitted. If used, it takes the form of one or more of the following characters:

/o   If a destination file of the same name as the source is present, MV overwrites it with the source file; otherwise, MV prompts for approval.

/k   This option keeps a copy of the old source file. (MV usually removes the old source file after a new copy is made at the destination.)

/e   This option tells MV that under no circumstances should it allow a destination file of the same name to be overwritten with a source file. MV usually prompts for approval before doing so; this option assumes that the answer to the prompt will be "N" (don't move the file).

/q   This option causes MV to always question and prompt for approval when moving any file. Normally, MV doesn't bother to ask about moves unless a destination file of the same name already exists.

Sources   Sources may be files or subdirectories. At least one must be specified.

Destination   Destination specifies a directory to which the sources are to be moved.
    There are a few rules:

• If MV is used to move files from one disk to another, the original source file is left after the move.

• If there is exactly one *source* name and it is the name of a directory, and the *destination* name is not the name of an existing file or directory, MV assumes that the *source* directory is to be renamed to the *destination* name.

• A "many-to-one" move is disallowed by MV; in other words, you can't move ten files to one filename.

The following are examples of MV commands:

MV THISFILE THATFILE	Renames THISFILE to THAT-FILE. THISFILE no longer exists at the conclusion of the move.
MV /K THISFILE THATFILE	Copies THISFILE to THATFILE. THISFILE remains at the conclusion of the move.
MV *.* \MYDIR	Moves all files in the current directory to the directory MYDIR. At the conclusion of the move, the current directory will be empty.
MV \THISDIR \THATDIR	Renames the directory THISDIR to THATDIR.
MV A:THISFILE C:THATFILE	Copies A:THISFILE to C:THAT-FILE. A:THISFILE remains at the conclusion of the move.

Sydex
P.O. Box 5700
Eugene, OR 97405
Copyright 1985, 1990
Voice: 503-683-6033
Fax: 503-683-1622
Data: 503-683-1385

PKLITE Executable File Compressor, PKware

```
PKLITE    EXE       13326    5-29-90    3:34p
```

PKLITE is made by PKware, Inc., makers of the popular PKZIP data-compression utility. PKLITE makes compressed executable files and saves you lots of drive space. By special arrangement, PKware and Phil Katz made this product available in this book prior to releasing it to the general public. Please note: Do not use earlier BETA versions because the file formats are incompatible.

PKLITE is very convenient since you don't need to extract the files to use them. When you execute a file that has been compressed with PKLITE, there will only be a few seconds delay while it uncompresses directly into your system's RAM.

One of the nice features of PKLITE is the ability to restore files back to their original sizes with the −x option. You can get additional compression with the −t option, but then the file cannot be converted back to its original format.

The syntax is

PKLITE [*options*] [*d:*][*path*]*Infile* [[*d:*][*path*]*Outfile*]

Options

    −b   Makes a backup BAK file of original
    −l   Makes a load-high EXE file
    −o   Overwrites output file if it exists
    −t   Trashes extra EXE data
    −u   Updates file time/date to current time/date
    −x   Expands a compressed file

Using PKLITE

If you enter

PKLITE C:\DVORAK*.*

all the files in the \DVORAK subdirectory will be compressed, freeing up about 400KB of disk space. If you do this, you'll need to use the −x option to convert back any files that are *self-modifying*. (A self-modifying file is one that is read into memory and saved back to disk. This usually occurs with files that have a built-in install or configuration option that saves the settings to the program file instead of to a configuration file.)

PKWARE disclaims all warranties as to this software, whether express or implied, including without limitation any implied warranties of merchantability, fitness for a particular purpose, functionality, or data integrity or protection. Contact PKware for further disclaimers and information.

If you find PKLITE easy and convenient to use, a registration of the program would be appreciated. Send $47 for registration to:

PKWARE, Inc.
7545 N. Port Washington Road
Suite 205
Glendale, WI 53217-3422
Voice (9:00 A.M. to 5:00 P.M. CST): 414-352-3670
PKware Support BBS (available 24 hours): 414-352-7176
Fax: 414-352-3815

PKZIP and UNZIP Data-Compression Utilities, PKware

| PKUNZIP | EXE | 23528 | 3-15-90 | 1:10a |
| PKZIP | EXE | 34296 | 3-15-90 | 1:10a |

PKZIP, by Phil Katz of PKware, lets you compress one or more files into an archive called a ZIP file. PKUNZIP lets you extract one or more of the files in such an archive, creating an exact, full-size copy of each original file.

This package can save you a great deal of hard disk space. In some cases the compressed version of a file will be 50 to 80 percent smaller than the original. The package also allows you to back up files or entire subdirectories faster and with fewer floppy disks.

Using PKZIP on One or More Files
The syntax is

PKZIP ZIPFILE [*options*] [*files*]

PKZIP is the name of the program and ZIPFILE is the name of the archive file you want to create. The ZIP FILE will have the ZIP extension, unless you specify another.

The *options* can include a variety of letters, each preceeded by a hyphen. The *options* tell the program what you want it to do.

The *files* are the actual files you want PKZIP to compress into the archive. The simplest way to put all of your TXT files into an archive called, say, SAVE.ZIP, is to use the following command:

PKZIP SAVE *.TXT

By default, the program assumes that you want to create and add files to an archive. There is no need to use the −a option in this command if you don't want to. Also, in most cases when you use an option, you can place it anywhere on the command line.

Options
All command options for the software must be preceded by a hyphen character or the MS-DOS switch character (usually /). Except where noted, most options can be combined (for example, −x −y or −xy).

−a	Adds files to a ZIP file.
−b[*path*]	Creates a temporary ZIP file at the specified alternate location. This temporary file is used only in the creation of the ZIP file and is deleted when the process is complete.
−c −C	Adds file comments to individual files within the ZIP file.
−d	Deletes the specified files from the ZIP file.
−e[x,s,a,b]	Specifies the compression method.
−f	Freshens the files in the ZIP file.
−h	Calls up a Help screen.
−i	Adds to the ZIP file only those files that were changed since the ZIP file was last updated.
−j −J<h,r,s>	Specifies masking or unmasking of file attributes.
−k	Retains the original date of the ZIP file that is being updated.

−l	Displays the license screen.
−m[u,f]	Adds files to the ZIP file and automatically deletes the original or source files.
−o	Sets the time and date of the ZIP file to the time and date of the latest file contained in the ZIP file.
−p −P	Stores paths that are recursed along with the filenames in the ZIP file. The −p option should be used with the −r option.
−q	Enables ANSI comments.
−r	Recurses subdirectories from the specified directories.
−s <*password*>	Scrambles files in the ZIP file with password protection.
−u	Updates the ZIP file.
−v[b,r,t,c,d,e,n,o,p,s]	Views technical information about files in the ZIP file.
−w −W <h,s>	Specifies whether hidden or system files will be included in the ZIP file.
−x	Excludes files from a ZIP file operation.
−z	Creates a comment for a ZIP file.

Examples

There are many things you can do with PKZIP. Here are a few examples:

PKZIP −a A:NEWFILE *.*

This creates a file named NEWFILE.ZIP. The extension is added automatically. In this example, all of the files in the current directory are compressed into NEWFILE.ZIP.

PKZIP −a B:BUDGET \LOTUS\CHECKS.WKS \LOTUS\MONEY.WKS

This creates a ZIP file named BUDGET.ZIP on the B drive. BUDGET.ZIP will contain two files, both currently located in the C:\LOTUS directory.

PKZIP −f FILES *.TXT

This updates an existing ZIP file named FILES.ZIP. Files that have a TXT extension and that are dated later then those already in the ZIP file will be updated.

PKUNZIP

When you want to extract a copy of a file from an archive or extract all of the files an archive contains, use PKUNZIP. The program operates like PKZIP, but some of the available command line switches are different. Here is the syntax:

PKUNZIP [*options*] *zipfile* [*d:\path*] [*file. . .*]

Options

Unlike PKZIP options, unrelated options for PKUNZIP cannot be combined. Also, if no options are entered, the program assumes you want to extract files.

−c[m]	Extracts files to the console (with MORE).
−d	Uses the path stored in the ZIP file, and creates the paths on extraction if they do not already exist.
−h	Displays a Help screen.
−j −J<h,r,s>	Specifies masking or unmasking of file attributes.
−l	Displays the license agreement.
−n	Extracts files from the ZIP file only if they are newer than the ones already on the disk.
−o	Overwrites existing files without asking for confirmation.
−p[a/b][c][n]	Extracts files to a printer.
−s<password>	Unscrambles the files with password protection.
−t	Tests the ZIP file for corruption.
−q	Enables ANSI comments.
−v[b,r,c,d,e,n,p,s]	Views technical information about files in the ZIP file.
−x	Extracts files from the ZIP file

PKUNZIP Examples

Here are examples of how you might use PKUNZIP to extract files from an archive (ZIP) file:

PKUNZIP ANYFILE.ZIP A:

This command will extract all the files in the ZIP file ANYFILE.ZIP and place extracted files on the A drive.

PKUNZIP A:ANYFILE.ZIP *.C

In this example, the ZIP file located on the A drive will be extracted on the C drive (the default destination). Only the *.C files will be extracted.

PKUNZIP \COLLECT\ANYFILE.ZIP A: −o

In this example, the path location of the ZIP file is specified. The files will be extracted on the A drive. With the −o option, any file with the same name as one existing on the A drive will overwrite the existing file, without asking for confirmation.

Registration

The manual that accompanies the full PKZIP/PKUNZIP package is more than 65 pages; we have been able to present only a brief summary here. The full PKZIP/PKUNZIP package also includes files to fix corrupted archives and a file to make a ZIP file *self-extracting*. (A self-extracting file is an EXE file; it does not require PKUNZIP.)

The basic shareware registration fee for PKZIP is $25. For $47 PKware will send you the program's next version and a manual when they become available. For more information, contact:

PKware, Inc.
7545 North Port Washington Road
Suite 205
Glendale, WI 53217-3422
Voice (9:00 A.M. to 5:00 P.M., CST): 414-352-3670
PKware Support BBS (available 24 hours): 414-352-7176
Fax: 414-352-3815

REBOOT

REBOOT   COM   56   6-25-90   8:41p

REBOOT does a warm boot (no memory test) by default; if /C is specified, it does a cold boot instead. The switch is not case sensitive. The syntax is

reboot [/c]

Note that initiating a cold boot with software is *not* the same as pressing the reset button or cycling the power, but it does more than a CTRL-ALT-DEL warm boot. Specifically, it tests memory, and it may perform other tests as well, depending on your BIOS.

The cold-boot option does not work under 386MAX, which converts all cold-boot requests of this type to warm boots. Assemble and link as follows:

masm reboot;
link reboot;
exe2bin reboot.exe reboot.com

Tom Rawson
J.P. Software
P.O. Box 1470
E. Arlington, MA 02174

TOGGLE

TOGGLE   COM   673   4-30-88   1:32a

This program will turn some of your PC's keys on and off. Operation is pretty simple: To turn on Caps Lock, Num Lock, or Scroll Lock, type **TOGGLE** followed by C, N, or S. To turn them off, type **TOGGLE** followed by **c**, **n**, or **s**. Use uppercase to turn them on and lowercase to turn them off.

When you run TOGGLE, a message is displayed confirming which keys were toggled (for example, "Num Lock ON"). If you want to use TOGGLE in a batch file and don't want to see these messages, place >nul after the last parameter. If you type TOGGLE without any parameters or give incorrect parameters, Help is displayed.

Here's the program's syntax:

[d:][path]TOGGLE param[param...]

where param is one or more of the following:

C	Turns Caps Lock on
c	Turns Caps Lock off
N	Turns Num Lock on
n	Turns Num Lock off
S	Turns Scroll Lock on
s	Turns Scroll Lock off

For example,

TOGGLE Cn

Turns Caps Lock ON and Num Lock OFF.

This program is in the public domain, but it cannot be sold without permission from its author. You can contact

Jeff R. Fontanesi
CompuServe: 74017,1650
GEnie: FONTJR

and lots of Orange County California BBSs (area code 714).

TSR Utilities, Terminate-and-Stay-Resident Program Manager

```
DISABLE   COM    10292   6-02-87    2:15p
EATMEM    COM      239   3-12-89    1:34p
FMARK     COM      586   5-04-89    8:38p
```

MAPMEM	EXE	14320	5-04-89	8:43p
MARK	COM	218	5-04-89	8:38p
RAMFREE	COM	96	3-12-89	1:34p
RELEASE	EXE	12464	5-04-89	8:38p
WATCH	COM	540	5-04-89	8:38p

The TSR Utilities, by Kim Kokkonen of TurboPower Software, are probably the most widely used tools to manage terminate-and-stay-resident programs. The version included with this book is 2.9. The following programs, which overlap with other programs on the disks, have not been included because of space limitations:

MARKNET   Like MARK, but saves a more complete picture of
               system status.
RELNET   Removes TSRs marked with MARKNET.
DEVICE   Shows what device drivers are loaded.

The included programs are described in detail here. If you haven't used them before, be sure to read this documentation. All of the programs are command line driven, and unexpected events may occur if you just start typing the program names at the DOS command line.

If you're familiar with previous versions of the TSR Utilities, the most important change in version 2.9 is the addition of MARKNET and REL-NET. These new programs allow marking and releasing of the Novell NetWare shell as well as of other "problem TSRs" that could not be released successfully in previous versions.

MARK and RELEASE

MARK.COM and RELEASE.EXE are used to remove TSRs from memory without a system reboot. Here's how to use MARK and RELEASE in their simplest form:

- Run MARK before installing your TSRs. This marks the current position in memory and stores information that RELEASE will need to restore the system later. A good practice is to place MARK in your AUTOEXEC.BAT file.

- Install whatever TSRs you want, using the normal method for each one.

- To remove those TSRs from memory, run RELEASE. This releases all of the memory above and including the last MARK, and restores the system to the state at the time the MARK was made.

There are a number of variations of this simple method. First, marks can be stacked in memory, as shown in the following hypothetical batch file:

```
MARK
TSR1
MARK
TSR2
MARK
TSR3
```

Each call to RELEASE releases memory above and including the last mark. In this example, the first call to RELEASE would remove TSR3 and the last mark from memory, the second call would remove TSR2 and its mark, and so on.

MARK and RELEASE may be called using a command line parameter. The parameter specifies a "mark name" and allows releasing TSRs to a specific point in memory. Consider the following example:

```
MARK TSR1
TSR1
MARK TSR2
TSR2
MARK TSR3
TSR3
```

This loads the three TSRs just as in the previous example. However, if RELEASE were called like this:

```
RELEASE TSR2
```

then both TSR2 and TSR3 would be removed from memory. Note that the use of such a name does not allow just a single layer of TSRs to be removed (just TSR2, for example). RELEASE always removes all TSRs beyond and including the one named.

A mark name is any string up to 126 characters long. The name may not include white space (blanks or tabs). Case (upper or lower) is not significant when matching mark names.

When named marks are used, calling RELEASE without specifying a mark name will still remove the last TSR from memory. Assuming that TSR1, TSR2, and TSR3 are still in memory, typing **RELEASE** would remove only TSR3 and the last mark. It is possible to change this behavior by using "protected marks," which can be released only by explicitly specifying their names. A protected mark is placed by giving it a name that starts with an exclamation point. Consider the following:

MARK TSR1
TSR1
MARK TSR2
TSR2
MARK !TSR3
TSR3

Here, !TSR3 specifies a protected mark. Typing **RELEASE** would produce an error message:

```
No matching marker found, or protected marker encountered
```

The same error would occur after entering the command

RELEASE TSR2

When this error occurs, RELEASE does not remove any TSRs from memory. The only way to remove TSR3 in this case is to enter

RELEASE !TSR3

Each time a mark is placed in memory, it consumes about 1600 bytes of RAM. This space is used to store a copy of the system interrupt-vector table and other information with which RELEASE can later restore the system. In the complete version of these utilities, you can use the FMARK program to save this 1600 bytes to disk instead of to memory.

RELEASE has several command line options to modify its behavior. None of the options is required for normal use of RELEASE.

/? (or −?) writes a help screen.

/E (or −E) is made available for systems running early, buggy EMS (expanded memory) drivers that don't correctly implement all of the EMS 3.2 system calls. Don't use it unless you have an EMS-related problem during or after running RELEASE.

/K (or −K) is useful when you will be releasing and reloading a TSR repeatedly. With it, you avoid the need to replace the mark each time the TSR is released. Using /K in combination with a file mark also prevents RELEASE from deleting the mark file.

/S (or −S) followed by at least one space and a short string of 15 characters tells RELEASE to stuff the string into the keyboard buffer just before exiting. RELEASE automatically adds a carriage return to the end of the string.

To explain why the /S option is important, we must digress a moment. Let's assume that you normally keep SideKick loaded but that you must unload it to have enough memory free to run Lotus 1-2-3. It would seem reasonable to write a little batch file, like this:

```
RELEASE SK
LOTUS
MARK SK
SK
```

to remove the previously loaded SideKick from memory, run Lotus, and then load SideKick again. Unfortunately, this won't work!

The reason is complicated. Suffice to say that DOS batch files trap memory, and the memory freed by a call to RELEASE does not truly become available until the current batch file ends.

Now, perhaps the need for the /S option becomes clear. We can split the previous batch file into two batch files:

```
RELEASE SK /S BATCH2
```

and

```
LOTUS
MARK SK
SK
```

The first batch file releases the memory and stuffs the characters BATCH2 <enter> into the keyboard buffer. When the batch file ends, the released memory becomes available. DOS automatically reads the keystrokes waiting in the buffer and starts up the second batch file, which runs Lotus and later reloads SideKick.

To keep things simple, the /S option pokes the specified keystrokes directly into the system keyboard buffer. As a result, the number of keystrokes is limited to 15 (not counting the ENTER key, which RELEASE adds automatically). This always allows enough keys to start another batch file, and the new batch file can take over from there.

RELEASE detects when it is releasing memory within a batch file. It writes a warning message to that effect but continues processing anyway, under the assumption that the batch file is about to end. You can ignore the warning if you've already taken into account DOS's memory-management behavior within batch files.

MARK and RELEASE are capable of removing many, but not all, TSRs from memory. The TSRs that cannot be released fall into two categories: those that cannot be released without specific internal knowledge of the TSR, and those that can be released by storing additional general information about the system.

The most common examples of TSRs that can't be released without internal knowledge are those that cooperate with other TSRs in memory. Examples include Microsoft's mouse driver and its associated menu program, and the program CED with its "user-installed commands," such as KEYIN, HS, and RAW. These programs can be released, but only if all the cooperating partners are released at the same time. CED is well behaved in that it provides a built-in command (KILL) to release its partners. The mouse driver is not so flexible, though.

Other TSRs modify well-defined areas of DOS memory that MARK simply doesn't record. Examples of such TSRs include the Novell NetWare workstation shell and certain DOS utilities, such as MODE and SHARE. To deal with these programs, the programs MARKNET and RELNET have been created. These programs store just about every imaginable DOS data area, including some that are undocumented by Microsoft. These programs are available in the regular version of the TSR Utilities.

Warning: (1) You should not use RELEASE to try to release most disk-caching programs. If you do, part of the information that should be stored on disk will never make it, and you may end up with a corrupted disk as a result. If you know that the disk cache uses a "write-through" algorithm (which guarantees that all writes immediately go to disk), or if the disk cache has a "Flush the cache" command, then it may be safe to release the cache. (2) You cannot release the DOS 3.3 FASTOPEN and APPEND TSRs. These TSRs patch internal DOS data areas that cannot be located reliably even by MARKNET and RELNET.

WATCH and DISABLE

WATCH.COM is a memory-resident program that keeps track of other memory-resident programs. As a TSR goes resident, WATCH updates a data area in memory that contains information about what interrupt vectors were taken over. This information can later be used by MAPMEM and DISABLE to show more details about interrupts than are normally available.

Installation of WATCH.COM is optional. All of the TSR Utilities except DISABLE can be used whether or not WATCH is installed.

If you want to use it, install WATCH.COM as the first TSR in your AUTOEXEC.BAT file. WATCH uses about 4000 bytes of memory when it is installed. Most of this memory holds various information about the TSRs installed in the system, including two copies of the interrupt-vector table and a data area containing a list of the interrupt vectors taken over by each TSR. This information is used by DISABLE to deactivate and reactivate TSRs without removing them from memory.

With DISABLE.EXE, you can disable and reenable specified memory-resident programs without removing them from memory. Its function is analogous to that performed by REFEREE, from Persoft, although DISABLE has neither a fancy user interface nor an option to work from within other programs. DISABLE can allow conflicting TSRs to coexist, and it can let you run applications whose keystrokes conflict with those of TSRs already loaded. DISABLE also provides a small bonus in that it can be used to detect the presence of a particular TSR in memory, thus allowing the design of semi-intelligent batch files.

To use DISABLE, you must install WATCH.COM as the first memory-resident program in your system. WATCH keeps detailed information about each memory-resident program that DISABLE uses to later control them.

Like the other TSR Utilities, DISABLE is operated from the command line. You specify a single TSR by its name (if you are running DOS 3.0 or later) or by its address, as determined from a MAPMEM report (described below). If you specify an address, immediately precede the address with a dollar sign, and specify the address in hexadecimal.

The name specified for a TSR is the one reported by MAPMEM in the "owner" column. If the owner column reports "N/A," then you must instead specify the address from the "PSP" column.

DISABLE uses the following syntax:

DISABLE TSR*name*|$PSP*address* [*options*]

Options   Options may be preceded by either / or −. Valid options are:

/A or −A   Reactivates the specified TSR.
/C or −C   Checks for the presence of the specified TSR.
/? or − ?   Writes a help screen.

If no option is specified, DISABLE will disable the named TSR.
Here are some examples:

DISABLE SK   Disables SideKick.
DISABLE SK /A   Reenables SideKick.
DISABLE SK /C   Checks for the presence of SideKick.
DISABLE $2F2E   Disables the TSR at address 2F2E (hex).

DISABLE sets the DOS ERRORLEVEL to return status information to a batch file. It uses the following values of ERRORLEVEL:

0   Success-TSR is present, was disabled, or was reenabled.
1   TSR is present, but no action was required to enable or
        disable it.
2   TSR is not present in memory.
        Invalid command line.
255   Severe error.

Note: You cannot use DISABLE to deactivate SideKick Plus, whose swapping technique is incompatible with DISABLE.

MAPMEM and RAMFREE
These utilities provide status information about DOS memory usage. They don't make active changes to the system like RELEASE and DISABLE do.

MAPMEM.EXE displays a map of DOS memory. It shows the resident programs, how much memory they use, and what interrupt vectors each one controls. MAPMEM also shows information about expanded and extended memory, when available.

MAPMEM writes to the standard output; hence, the output can be printed or stored to a file with DOS redirection.

Here is an example of MAPMEM output:

PSP	blks	bytes	owner	command line	chained vectors
0008	1	34240	config		
1228	2	3536	command		
1315	2	3888	WATCH	TSR WATCHER	16 21 27
140A	2	22128	CED	N/A	1B 21 64
1973	1	144	N/A	C:\MARK\PS.MRK	
197D	2	736	PSKEY	S3	09 15
19AD	2	68400	PS	/B:0 /E:1 /R:0 /...	01 03 06 0D
2A62	2	1504	MARK	test	00 3F
2AC2	2	10384	EATMEM	10	
2D4D	2	469808	free		

block	bytes	(Expanded Memory)
1	1048576	
free	1048576	
total	2097152	
		(Extended Memory)
total	379240	

"PSP" stands for Program Segment Prefix. This is the physical address, specified in hexadecimal, where the program was loaded. If you're running DOS 2.X, you'll need to use an address from this column to pass to DISABLE.

"Blks" is the number of memory blocks DOS is using to manage the program. This will typically be two: One for the program itself and another for the environment that stores the program name, the DOS path, and other environment variables.

"Bytes" is the number of bytes of memory, specified in decimal, allocated to the program.

The "owner" column shows the name of the program that allocated the block. "N/A" in this column means either that the program deallocated its environment to reduce memory usage or that the system is running DOS 2.X, where the owner names are not available.

"Command line" shows the command line entered when the TSR was originally loaded. Some TSRs overwrite their command lines with other code or data to save memory space. MAPMEM can usually detect this behavior; it displays "N/A" in the command line column when it does.

The last column is titled either "chained vectors" or "hooked vectors." When WATCH is loaded, "chained" appears; otherwise, "hooked" does. The numbers in this column indicate what interrupt vectors the TSR has grabbed. Without WATCH, MAPMEM must use a heuristic technique to identify the owner of each vector; don't be surprised if you see some ridiculous looking vector numbers. With WATCH, MAPMEM should report an accurate list for each TSR and show the complete chain of control for each interrupt.

MAPMEM indicates disabled TSRs by displaying "disabled" in the interrupt-vector column of the report.

The expanded-memory report shows each allocated block of expanded memory as well as the free and total EMS space. MAPMEM shows just the total amount of extended memory available, if any. The extended-memory report is not highly reliable, because of the lack of a standardized method for allocating extended-memory space. Some applications that use extended memory allocate the space by making it appear that the memory is no longer in the system.

MAPMEM shows the various types of marks so that you can examine them prior to releasing them. As shown in the example, MAPMEM reports a call to MARK with the owner name "MARK" and the mark name, if any, in the command line area. The result of a call to FMARK or MARKNET will show "N/A" in the owner column (because of the minimal memory kept by an FMARK) and the name of the mark file in the command line area.

MAPMEM offers the following command line options:

/V   Verbose report
/?   Write a Help screen

The verbose report shows each individual memory block rather than just one for each program. It also adds two new columns of information. "Mcb," stands for "memory control block," is a physical address, expressed in hexadecimal, of the DOS data structure used for managing each block of memory. The MCB address is typically one less than the address of the program. "Files" reports the number of files kept open by the TSR. In most cases, this will be zero. When it is nonzero, the maximum number of files opened by the rest of the programs (including the foreground application) is reduced accordingly.

RAMFREE.COM is a tiny program with a single purpose: to tell you how many bytes of memory are free for the next application. The number it reports is the same as that reported by the DOS CHKDSK utility. RAMFREE's advantage is that you don't need to wait for your hard disk to be analyzed before you find out how much memory is free.

EATMEM

EATMEM is a small program that is useful to software developers. It is a TSR that consumes a specified amount of memory. Developers can use it to simulate a system with less memory or to create a buffer zone between an application and programs preceding it.

The memory used by EATMEM can be freed only by using MARK and RELEASE. Call EATMEM with a single command line parameter, specifying the (decimal) number of kilobytes to eat up:

EATMEM *KiloBytesToEat*

EATMEM will allow you to eat up all available memory, leading to a system crash when COMMAND.COM cannot be reloaded. Be sure to calculate how much memory to use before calling EATMEM.

Copyright and License Information

The TSR Utilities are copyright 1986, 1987, 1989 by Kim Kokkonen. All rights reserved.

License is granted to distribute these copyrighted programs for personal, noncommercial use. You may use them yourself, give them to your friends or co-workers, or distribute them for a cost-based fee ($10 or less) as part of a users' group or bulletin board service. If you wish to distribute these programs as part of a commercial package, please contact Turbo-Power Software for a license agreement.

These programs are not shareware; no donation is required. However, if you request a new version, a $20 fee is necessary to cover costs. The disk will include the latest version of the TSR Utilities, including the complete source code.

New versions of the TSR Utilities may be found in the BPROGA forum on CompuServe, in the latest Turbo Pascal library, which at this time is LIB 2. The executable programs are stored in a file called TSRCOM.ARC, and the source code is stored in a file called TSRSRC.ARC. From CompuServe, the programs fan out to public domain bulletin boards around the world.

You can reach Kim Kokkonen at:

TurboPower Software
P.O. Box 66747
Scotts Valley, CA 95066-0747
408-438-8608 (voice only, Monday through Friday, 9:00 A.M. to 5:00 P.M.)
CompuServe: 72457,2131

VIEW File, John Bean, JB Technology Inc.

```
VIEW    COM    1010    6-01-88    12:00p
```

VIEW is a tiny but powerful program by John Bean of JB Technology, who also wrote our Install program. Use VIEW to display a file on your disk, by typing

VIEW *filename*

and the file will be displayed on your screen. You can use the cursor keys to scroll through the file. HOME and END take you to the beginning and the end of the file, respectively. The left and right arrow keys will scroll the text on the screen horizontally, and the up and down arrow keys will scroll vertically one line a time. PGUP and PGDN will scroll one page at a time.

To exit the program, hit the ESC key. VIEW does an effective job of overcoming the limitations of the DOS TYPE command and is useful for reviewing shareware documentation.

VIEW comes with two outstanding utilities that will help you find duplicate and unnecessary files: FD (Find Duplicate) and BO (Back Off) programs are published by:

JB Technology Inc.
28701 N. Main Street
Ridgefield, WA 98642
206-887-3442

VDE Text Editor, Eric Meyer

VDE	COM	47278	9-04-90	8:23p
VINST	COM	22758	9-04-90	8:08p
EXAMPLES	VDK	1024	5-17-90	10:41p
WS4	VDF	1024	9-06-89	5:53p
WP	VDF	1024	5-17-89	10:41p

VDE 1.54, written by Eric Meyer, is a full-featured text editor that is small, fast, and powerful. VDE offers

- Easy menu-bar operation or WordStar command set
- Multiple files, windows, cut, and paste
- Block copy, move, delete, read, write, and zoom
- Find/replace, undo, and automatic save
- Keystroke macros with full programming ability
- Utilities to browse disk files, split files, compare files, count words, and number lists automatically
- Full DOS access to subdirectories, DOS commands, and a shell
- Programmable function keys and many other user-configurable options
- Ability to run on non-IBM compatibles and in limited space

It is also an efficient small word processor, with

- Word wrap, reformat, left and right margins, and variable tabs
- Center, flush right, and proportional spacing
- Customizable printer drivers for special effects (such as bold and underline)
- Printing options: headers, pagination, selective print, and print to file
- Multiple file formats and text exchange (plain ASCII, WordStar, WordPerfect, XyWrite, and Microsoft Word)

VDE requires an IBM-compatible system with DOS 2.X or above. VDE's versatility is due to its combination of the most important word processing features with the simplicity of an editor designed to work with plain text files. VDE's ASCII mode makes it an ideal choice for a DOS file editor or a practical editor to run from a shell within telecommunications, data base, file-maintenance, programming, and other applications software. Its full formatting and printing features also make VDE a highly WordStar-compatible word processor.

VDE is very fast. It edits files entirely in memory and displays text directly to video RAM (on IBM PCs). Speed is a factor that commercial programs often overlook: Finding a string near the end of a 60KB nondocument file takes WordStar 4 about 20 seconds (on an 8-MHz 8088), while VDE does it in half a second.

VDE is also very small; taking only about 45KB of disk space and running in as little as 90 to 140KB of RAM, it is well suited to portable computers and other applications with limited memory or disk space.

VDE Usage Policy
Please note that copies of VDE on disk cannot be ordered directly from the author, except for purchasers of site licenses. Primary distribution points for VDE are:

- Glendale Littera QBBS, Glendale, CA, 818-956-6164
- CompuServe, on PCMAGNET Editorial Forum Dvorak Library

VDE is updated regularly, and users with access to a modem can always find the most recent release on these systems.

The VDE editor and its documentation are copyright 1987, 90 by Eric Meyer. All rights reserved. They may not be circulated in any incomplete or modified form or sold for profit without written permission of the author. The use or sale of VDE is subject to the following terms:

Individual Use VDE may be freely used and shared with others; no registration fee is required. (If you like VDE and find it useful, please do consider sending a contribution!)

Institutional Use A corporation or institution must purchase a site license. A standard license, allowing the use of VDE on up to 20 different computers, can be ordered for $50; write for terms concerning larger quantities. A disk containing the latest release of VDE will be included at no additional charge. (Specify 5.25- inch or 3.5-inch disk.)

Commercial Sale   Any software dealer or library may offer VDE for sale, as long as the price charged for the disk containing VDE does not exceed $5. With this single exception, the sale of VDE for profit, either alone or together with other software or hardware, requires a licensing agreement providing for royalty payments. Please write for terms:

Eric Meyer
3541 Smuggler Way
Boulder, CO 80303
CompuServe: 74415,1305

Disclaimer   You use VDE at your own risk. The author assumes no liability for damages that result from your use of VDE.

Configuring VDE

Before running VDE, you should first run VINST, the install program that customizes VDE to your specifications. To run VINST, type **VINST** on the DOS command line.

Starting VDE

To run VDE, you can just type **VDE** with no arguments, or you may specify a list of up to eight filenames. Any filename may include a DOS directory or be followed by a mode option. A key definition-file may also be specified at the end of the command line, following a semicolon. All spaces are ignored. The syntax is

VDE [*filename*] [/*m*] [, *filename2* [/*m*]] [,. . .] [;*name*.VDK] [;*name*.VDF]

Here are some examples:

vde
vde sample.fil

vde a:summary,\recs\sep85
vde article.doc/w;ws4.vdf
vde b:myfile,myfile.bak
vde prog.doc/a,prog.asm/n,errors

Filename is the file to edit. If no name is given, you begin a new (untitled) file. Multiple filenames are separated by commas. A path specified for one file carries over to the next file, unless the latter begins with a drive or root designation. (In the example above, MYFILE.BAK is on drive B.)

The optional /m refers to the choice of file modes; *m* can be (A)SCII, (W)ordstar, WordStar (5), Word(P)erfect, (X)yWrite, (M)icrosoft Word, or (N)ondocument. Normally, VDE defaults to /A.

The optional *name*.VDK or *name*.VDF represents a macro- or function-key-definition file to load.

Universal Keys

Once you are in the editor, the following universal keys are always available to you (asterisks mark features unique to VDE):

* SHIF-[TAB]	Backward variable tab—moves to previous stop.
* CTRL-DEL	Deletes character in the opposite direction from DEL.
INS	Toggles Insert mode.
CTRL->	Moves to the start of the next word to the right.
CTRL-<	Moves to the start of the word to the left.
—	Scrolls back one line.
+	Scrolls forward one line.
PGUP	Scrolls back one screen.
PGDN	Scrolls forward one screen.
* CTRL-PGUP	In Split-Screen mode, scrolls both files back one screen.
* CTRL-PGDN	In Split-Screen mode, scrolls both files forward one screen.
HOME	Moves to the top of the screen.
END	Moves to the bottom of the screen.
CTRL-HOME	Moves to the top of the file.
CTRL-END	Moves to the end of the file

Operating Modes

VDE has two distinct modes of operation: MenuBar mode and Command mode.

If you see the message "ESC=MenuBar" at the right end of the header line, you are in MenuBar mode. If this area is blank, you are in Command mode.

To switch into MenuBar mode from Command mode, press ESC; to switch to Command mode from MenuBar mode, select Misc:Command mode (ESC-MC)

MenuBar   If you are new to word processing, you may find MenuBar mode to be easier: Just press the ESC key, and a series of menu bars will guide you to the function you need. Type a highlighted letter to select from each menu. Most (though not all) of VDE's features are available in this mode. Menu-bar commands are referred to in the following manner: stYle-:Underline. This designates selecting "stYle" and then "Underline" from the menu-bar sequence (you actually press ESC, Y, and U).

Command Mode   Control-key commands (WordStar compatible) are more concise, although they do need to be memorized. They give access to the full range of VDE features, including powerful macros. If you're familiar with the popular WordStar command set, you can probably start right in editing files with VDE. It uses simple one- or two-key combinations, such as CTRL-Q F.

Most of these commands in VDE are identical to those in WordStar. But VDE also has a number of extra ALT-key and ESC-key commands to invoke additional features, such as multifile editing.

Using the Menu Bar

To use the menu bar, press ESC and select an option by typing the capitalized, highlighted letter. For example, the main menu bar reads:

Delete moVe Text stYle Set sCreen Misc Print Block File Exit

If you wanted to underline text, you would type **Y**, for "stYle." You would then see a new menu bar, listing Underline, Bold, and so on. You could press ESC again to back up one menu or exit. The entire menu-bar set appears in Table D-1 for your reference.

VDE Command Mode Menu-Bar Equivalents

{Delete: del Line}	CTRL-Y		{Misc: insert Time}	ALT-T
to line Start}	CTRL-Q[DEL]		Date}	ALT-D
End}	CTRL-QY		file Info}	CTRL-KI
del to Char}	CTRL-QT		about VDE}	ALT-I
del Block}	CTRL-KY		Command mode}	ESC-?
Undelete}	CTRL-U			
			{Print: overstrike Char}	CTRL-PH
{moVe: Find}	CTRL-QF		Line}	CTRL-PM
Replace}	CTRL-QA		Formfeed}	CTRL-PL
rEpeat f/r}	CTRL-L		Tab}	CTRL-PI
Overview bar}	ALT-O		Graphic}	ALT-G
place Set}	CTRL-PZ		Driver}	ALT-V
Go}	CTRL-QZ		Print file}	CTRL-KP
{Text: rUler}	CTRL-OT		{Block: Begin}	CTRL-KB
set mrgn L}	CTRL-OL		End}	CTRL-KK
R}	CTRL-OR		Unmark}	CTRL-KH
Mrgn rel}	CTRL-OX		Copy}	CTRL-KC
Center}	CTRL-OC		Move}	CTRL-KV
Flush}	CTRL-OF		cuT}	ALT-C
rEform}	CTRL-B		Paste}	ALT-P
Autoindent}	CTRL-OA		Write}	CTRL-KW
			Zoom}	CTRL-KZ
{stYle: Underline}	CTRL-PS			
Bold}	CTRL-PB		{File: rEname work}	CTRL-KN
Doublestrike}	CTRL-PD		Dir}	CTRL-KF
Italic}	CTRL-PY		Read in}	CTRL-KR
Subscript}	CTRL-PV		Load new}	CTRL-KL
suPerscript}	CTRL-PT		Add file}	ALT-L
			Next file}	ALT-N
{Set: tab Set}	CTRL-OI		Prev}	ALT-B
Clr}	CTRL-ON			
Varitab}	CTRL-OV		{Exit: Save to disk}	CTRL-KS
Double spc}	CTRL-OS		eXit w/save}	CTRL-KX
Prop spc}	CTRL-OJ		Quit w/o save}	CTRL-KQ
Hyphens}	CTRL-OH		Run DOS command}	ALT-R
pg Length}	CTRL-OP			
{sCreen: make Top}	CTRL-OE			
Window}	ALT-W			
Other win}	ALT-F			
Header}	CTRL-OQ			
Blank}	CTRL-OZ			
Preview}	CTRL-OD			
50/43 Ln}	ALT-E			
132 Col}	ALT-A			

Using Command Mode

When in Command mode, you enter commands by entering a series of CTRL-
or ALT-key combinations. This method is quicker and more efficient than
choosing options from the menu bar. A table of all the available Command
mode key combinations follows.

On-Line Help   CTRL-J displays basic help menu (for ALT-, ESC, CTRL-K, CTRL-O,
CTRL-P, CTRL-Q commands, press A, E, K, O, P, or Q next).

Control Keys: Single-Keystroke Commands

Wordstar Key Commands

CTRL-E	Up		CTRL-_	Inserts a space
CTRL-X	Down		CTRL-P#	Inserts a numbering marker
CTRL-D	Moves right		CTRL-B	Reformats the paragraph
CTRL-S	Moves left		CTRL-R	Scrolls back one screen
CTRL-F	Moves to the start of the next word		CTRL-C	Scrolls forward one screen
CTRL-A	Moves to the start of the preceding word		CTRL-Y	Deletes the current line
CTRL-W	Scrolls back one line		CTRL-U	Undoes the last deletion (character, word, line, or block)
CTRL-Z	Scrolls forward one line		CTRL-N	Inserts a line break
CTRL-G	Deletes the character to the right		CTRL-P	Inserts a printer code
CTRL-T	Deletes the word to the right		CTRL-PZ	Inserts a place marker
CTRL-V	Toggles Insert mode		CTRL-CTRL	Toggles case (upper or lower) of the character at the cursor
CTRL-]	Toggles Word Insert the		CTRL-L	Repeats the last find or replace

File and Block Commands   First press CTRL-K and then the key shown.

CTRL-KI	File/memory information		CTRL-KP	Prints the text
CTRL-KF	Disk file browser		CTRL-KR	Reads a file into text
CTRL-KL	Loads a new file to edit		CTRL-KJ	Deletes a disk file

CTRL-KN	Renames the current file	CTRL-KS	Saves the current file to disk and continues
CTRL-KD	Done — saves and loads a new file	CTRL-KX	Exit — saves the current file and quits to DOS
CTRL-KA	Sets Autosave interval	CTRL-KQ	Quits to DOS — abandons current file
CTRL-KB	Marks the start of a block	CTRL-KK	Marks the end of a block
CTRL-KH	Unmarks the block	CTRL-KY	Deletes a marked block
CTRL-KC	Copies the block at the cursor location	CTRL-KV	Moves the block to the cursor location
CTRL-KZ	Zooms into the marked block	CTRL-KW	Writes the block to a disk file
CTRL-K#	Automatically numbers items in the block	CTRL-K",',^	Changes to uppercase (") or lowercase (') or switches the case (^) of a block of text

Quick Commands   First press CTRL-Q and then the key shown.

CTRL-QS or <	Moves to the start of the line	CTRL-QA	Finds and replaces a string
CTRL-QD or >	Moves to the end of the line	CTRL-Q or CTRL-QT	Deletes up to the specified character
CTRL-QR	Moves to the top of the file	CTRL-QE or ^	Moves to the top of the screen
CTRL-QC	Moves to the end of the file	CTRL-QX or V	Moves to the bottom of the screen
CTRL-QL	Moves to the last page	CTRL-QB	Moves to the block's start marker
CTRL-QN	Moves to the next page	CTRL-QK	Moves to the block's end marker
CTRL-QZ	Moves to the next place marker	CTRL-QI	Moves to the specified page or line
CTRL-QP	Moves to the previous position in the file (before the last sizable move)	CTRL-QY	Deletes from the cursor to the end of the line
CTRL-QF	Finds a string		

Screen Commands   First press CTRL-O and then the key shown.

CTRL-OR	Sets the right margin	CTRL-OX	Toggles margin release
CTRL-OL	Sets the left margin	CTRL-OC	Centers the line
CTRL-OF	Sets the line flush with the right margin	CTRL-OT	Toggles the ruler-line display
CTRL-OQ	Toggles the header display	CTRL-OB	Toggles the hard return display
CTRL-OD	Previews text with no control codes or hard returns	CTRL-OV	Toggles tab mode (hard or variable)
CTRL-OH	Toggles hyphenation	CTRL-OJ	Toggles proportional spacing
CTRL-OS	Toggles double-spacing	CTRL-OA	Toggles auto indent
CTRL-OI	Sets variable tab stops	CTRL-ON	Clears variable tab stops
CTRL-OP	Sets page length (0 turns off pagination)	CTRL-OE or ^	Makes the current line the top of the screen
CTRL-OW	Splits the window to show two different portions of the file	CTRL-OZ	Temporarily blanks the screen

VDE ALT-Key Commands   Press ALT and the key shown. (*Note*: These commands will also work with an ESC, ESC prefix.)

ALT-I	Shows VDE version information	ALT-S	Splits a large file
ALT-B	Moves back to the previous file	ALT-W	Splits a window with two files
ALT-N	Moves forward to the next file	ALT-F	Moves to the other file window
ALT-C or P	Cuts or pastes a block from one place or file to another	ALT-M	Compares the two files on the screen, showing differences
ALT-X	Exits from all files	ALT-Q	Quits from all files
ALT-R	Runs a DOS command (or shell)	ALT-L	Loads an additional file
ALT-T or D	Enters the current system time or date in the file	ALT-G	Enters an IBM graphics character into the text
ALT-E	Sets EGA screen (43 or 50 lines)	ALT-U	Uses (loads or saves) macro or function-key-definition file
ALT-O	Moves with overview bar	ALT-V	Changes printer drivers
ALT-A	Sets wide screen (132 columns)		

VDE ESC-Key Commands   First press ESC and then the key shown.

ESC, TAB	Inserts a variable tab forward (even in hard tab mode)
ESC < or >	Shifts the screen horizontally 32 columns
ESC^ or v	Shifts the screen vertically one-quarter screen.
ESC?	Switches to MenuBar mode (in Macro mode; calls up menu bar)
ESC[	Defines a macro string of commands
ESC″	Records a macro from keystrokes
ESC]	Stores a macro on an alphanumeric key for later recall
ESC,0...Z	Uses a stored key (in Macro mode, jumps to a label)
ESC!, =, ~	Jumps and loops (used in macro programming)
ESC( ), +, −	Counter (used in macro programming)
ESC;	Pauses briefly during macro execution only
ESC&	Chains to another macro

Detailed Command Descriptions

Whether you use the program in MenuBar mode or in Command mode, this section provides a reference to the many features of VDE. The descriptions appear in alphabetical order. Refer to the preceding tables to find the feature you are interested in learning about.

Auto Indent (CTRL-OA)   This command toggles Auto Indent mode. When it is on, word wrap or the RETURN key will cause the cursor to advance to any existing indentation on the line (if Insert mode is off) or to the same indentation as the previous line (if Insert is on). Thus, once you set the indentation level, VDE will automatically maintain it. (Indentation must *not* be done with hard tabs; it can be changed with a space, a backspace, or variable tabs, which insert spaces.) Auto Indent is useful for paragraph indents, outlines, structured program source code, and so on.

AUTO NUMBER (CTRL-P#, CTRL-K#)   The CTRL-P# command inserts a marker (a highlighted #) in the text to stand for a sequential number in a list; for example:

#.   First item
#.   Second item

You can then mark the list off as a block (see Block Commands), and use the CTRL-K# command: VDE will insert (1, 2, and so on) in place of the markers. You will be asked for the starting number; the default is, of course, 1. (Once this is done, the markers disappear. For frequently revised lists, leave the # markers in the file on disk; use CTRL-K# just before printing, and do not save afterward.)

Auto Save (CTRL-KA)   You can instruct VDE to save any changes you have made to disk automatically at regular intervals. The CTRL-KA command lets you set the interval (1 to 255 minutes) or turn this feature off entirely (0). Just press RETURN to restore the default, normally 0. (This can be changed with VINST.)

Block Commands (CTRL-K-B, K, H, Z, Y, C, V, W, PB)

CTRL-QB and K	A block of text is delimited by two markers, which remain in memory until reset or deleted. The block-operation commands all require a block to be marked.
CTRL-KB	Marks the beginning of the block.
CTRL-KK	Marks the end of the block.
CTRL-KH	Unmarks the block, removing any markers set.
CTRL-KY	Goes to and deletes the block (including markers).
CTRL-KV	Moves the block (including markers) to the present cursor location.
CTRL-KC	Copies the block, leaving the original marked. Any place markers present are not transferred. (The cursor cannot be in the block.)
CTRL-KZ	Zooms into a block. The rest of the text is hidden, and the block is temporarily treated as the entire file. This can serve a number of purposes, from simply concentrating attention on one portion of a text to limiting the scope of many VDE commands to that portion. Use CTRL-KZ again to zoom back out. In Zoom mode, pagination is off. You can use block operations, although any block markers will disappear when you zoom back out. If you save with CTRL-KS, VDE will automatically zoom back out of the block first. CTRL-KW writes the block text to a disk file; you will be asked for the filename (and optional mode). Normally this will overwrite any preexisting file; however, you can choose instead to append the text at the end of the file by typing a + before the filename.
CTRL-QB	Moves to the block start.
CTRL-QK	Moves to the block end.
CTRL-KPB	CTRL-KP with B option; prints the block text only (see Printing).

Deleting (CTRL-G, DEL, CTRL-DEL, CTRL-T, CTRL-Y; CTRL-Q-Y, DEL, T)

CTRL-G or CTRL-DEL	Deletes the character to the right of the cursor. Normally, as in WordStar, DEL deletes the one to the left, and BACKSPACE (CTRL-H) moves left without deleting. (These can be changed.)
CTRL-T	Deletes the word to the right (up to 255 characters).
CTRL-Y	Deletes the current line.
CTRL-QY	Deletes the part of the line to the right of the cursor
CTRL-Q[DEL]	Deletes the part of the line to the left of the cursor.
CTRL-QT	Deletes to the next occurrence of a specified character (up to 4095 characters). For example, CTRL-QT. (period) deletes to the end of the sentence. *Special case*: CTRL-QT CTRL-M (RETURN) deletes to the next hard return that is the end of the paragraph. Accidentally deleted text can be recovered (see Undeleting).

Files (CTRL-K-L, R, J, F)

CTRL-KL	Loads one or more new files to edit, replacing the current one. (If the file has been modified, you will be prompted to confirm this.) You may enter either a single filename or a list delimited with commas (see Syntax). If you want to load files in *addition* to the current one, use ALT-L instead (see Multiple Files).
CTRL-KR	Reads in the contents of a disk file, inserting the text at the current cursor position.
CTRL-KJ	Deletes any disk file you specify. (If you need more complex file utilities, remember that you can run any DOS command with ALT-R.)

All these commands prompt for a specific filename. If you are unsure or would rather see a directory first, you can call up the file browser by pressing RETURN alone (for *.*), or typing a filename with wildcards (for example, \WORK*.BAK).

Note: If you want to begin an untitled file, press CTRL-J or CTRL-RETURN instead of RETURN, at the CTRL-KL prompt.

The file browser can also be called directly with the CTRL-KF command. You may specify a directory or filename mask, and the files will be alphabetically listed. (The default, if you just press RETURN, is the current file's directory and *.*.) Files display in uppercase, directories in lowercase. If all items will not fit on the screen, you will see "..." at the end to indicate that there were more. Display of COM/EXE files can be suppressed.

To remove the display, press ESC or SPACEBAR. While it is on the screen, you may also select one of the files shown by moving the cursor to it with the arrow keys. Then, you can press:

RETURN	To load this file instead (see CTRL-KL);
CTRL-L	To load it as an additional file (see ALT-L);
CTRL-R	To read it into the current file (see CTRL-KR); or
CTRL-Y	To delete this file.

If the file you want to load or read requires a different file mode, you can first press / and the correct mode-designator (A, N, W, 5, P, X, or SPACEBAR).

You can also select a directory, in which case you may press:

RETURN	To view its contents; or
CTRL-Y	To remove it (if it is empty).

Find/Replace (CTRL-QF, A; CTRL-L)   CTRL-QF is the command to Find a string. The search normally proceeds from the cursor position forward and is case sensitive. The character CTRL-_ (CTRL-underline) functions as a wildcard. Control codes like CTRL-M (for newline) can be included with the CTRL-P prefix, where needed. Graphics characters can be included using ALT-G. Examples:

Find: CTRL-MLABEL	Matches "LABEL" at start of line only
Find: 4^_^_01	Matches "42201", "47401", and so on
Find: ^_ank	Matches "tank", "Bank", and so on

CTRL-QA is the replace command. It asks for a string to find, as above, and then asks what to change it to. The cursor will move to each successive occurrence of the string, starting at the cursor location, and you will see the prompt "Chg?" in the header. To change the string, press Y; anything else skips to the next. To change all further instances without being asked, press *. ESC cancels the replace at any time.

There are several options for find and replace. After you enter the text strings, you will be prompted to enter any of the following:

B	Search backward through the file
U	Case-insensitive search (ignore upper/lower distinction)
G	Search globally (from start or end of file)
A	Align (reform) paragraphs again after each replacement
N	No query (replace all instances without asking)

If you don't want to be prompted for options, finish entry of the find or replace string with CTRL-J or CTRL-RETURN instead of RETURN.

Foreign Characters   Characters in the upper ASCII range (128-255), such as the foreign letters and accents, can be entered directly into text using either standard DOS method: one of the DOS keyboard map utilities or the ALT key used with the numeric keypad.

VDE treats these characters as "graphics." You are limited to 32 such codes at a time, and any that you have used may be found in the menu brought up by the ALT-G command (see Graphics, next).

Graphics (ALT-G)   You can enter an IBM graphic (or foreign) character into the file text with the ALT-G command. You will be presented with a menu of up to 32 characters (labeled A-Z and 1-6) to choose from.

Any unused menu entry can be defined on the spot. Type = and the code (A-5) to change. You can then select the desired character from the complete graphics set by moving the cursor to it and pressing RETURN. Alternatively, if you press any other key, you may enter the extended ASCII code in either hex (two digits 80-FF) or decimal (three digits 128-255) format. For example, a Greek alpha can be entered either as E0 hex or 224 decimal. Once defined in the menu, the graphic can be entered into the file; its definition cannot be changed again during editing.

Caution: If you load a file containing many graphics (or binary data that will be interpreted as graphics), VDE will try to add each character to its table. If the graphics table fills up, any further graphics will be replaced by fuzzy blocks (graphic #6)! You will see an error message, and the file will become "untitled," to guard against saving to disk and corrupting the file. If you frequently work with graphics characters, you will want to keep your default table relatively empty to avoid this. Graphics are stored in disk files in accordance with the current file mode. Printing of graphics depends on whether your printer is installed as an IBM graphics printer (see VINST.DOC). If so, they will print directly; if not, VDE will "emulate" them, choosing standard ASCII-character overstrikes that come as close as possible.

Header (CTRL-OQ)   VDE gives you an informative "header" at the top of the screen. If you like, you can toggle this display on and off with the CTRL-OQ (Quiet) command.

```
------------------------------------------------------------------
+ VDE.DOC  /A      Pg 14  Ln 11  Cl 48  Ins  vt hy AI DS MR  CTRL-K_
                   (OP/BZ)                    (WIn)           (PS)
------------------------------------------------------------------
```

+	Multifile flag; present if other files are being edited.
VDE.DOC /A	Current filename and mode. The full drive and path information, along with other files being edited, can be displayed with the CTRL-KI command (see Information).
Pg 14 Ln11 Cl 48	Current position in file by page (in document modes), line, column.
INS, WIn	Insert mode (CTRL-V) or Word Insert (CTRL-]) on.
vt	Variable Tab mode on (CTRL-OV).
hy	Hyphenation enabled (CTRL-OH); it doesn't display in "N" mode.
AI	Auto Indent Mode on (CTRL-OA).
DS	Double-spacing (CTRL-OS).
MR	Margins released (CTRL-OX); it doesn't display in "N" mode.
PS	Proportional spacing (CTRL-OJ); overridden by MR.
''	Quote mark; appears during macro recording (ESC).
CTRL-K_	WordStar key prefixes and some prompts.

Hyphenation (CTRL-OH)   VDE can't hyphenate automatically, but it can recognize hyphens in the text, treating them as a legitimate place to break a line. If you have a long word running over the margin, you can type a hyphen, and word wrap or reformat will break the word there.

VDE can't dehyphenate automatically. If VDE is trying to reformat and finds a hyphen at the end of a line, it will have to ask you what to do; you will see the prompt "Remove?" in the header.

You can toggle hyphenation on and off with CTRL-OH. If hyphenation is off, hyphens are not recognized. (The CTRL-OH default can be changed.)

Information (CTRL-KI; ALT-I)   CTRL-KI displays an Information message telling you:

- The full directory, name, and time stamp of the current file

- Whether (Y/N) the file has been changed since last saved

- Any print toggles that seem to be mispaired

- A word count for documents (useful for professional writing)

- The current size of the file in bytes or KB

- The number of bytes of memory used and free in this text segment

- The size (in KB) of the largest block of RAM still free

- The names of all other files being edited

For large files, all this may take a moment to calculate. Note that words are not counted in nondocuments.

The ALT-I command displays the VDE version, date, and usage policy. (An uninstalled copy of VDE displays this automatically on startup.)

Inserting (CTRL-V, INS, CTRL-], CTRL-_, CTRL-N)   CTRL-V or INS toggles Insert mode on and off, and CTRL-] toggles Word Insert. When both are off, VDE is in Overwrite mode: Any text to the right of the cursor is replaced as you type. With Insert mode on, what you type is inserted, and any existing text is moved to the right.

With Word Insert on, you can type over the letters of a word, but anything you add at the end of the word (when the next character is a space) is inserted. This is a handy feature for revising text.

The CTRL-_ or (CTRL-hyphen) and CTRL-N commands (insert a space and RETURN) are most useful when Insert is off. (The default insert status can be changed.)

Line Spacing (CTRL-OS)   The CTRL-OS command toggles between single and double line spacing. In double-space mode, Return (CTRL-M), Insert Return (CTRL-N), Reform (CTRL-B), and word wrap generate double carriage returns. You can easily mix single- and double-spacing; the CTRL-B command can convert between the two.

Note: A single-spaced file can also be printed out double-spaced with the D option of the CTRL-KP command (see Printing).

Margins (CTRL-O-R, L, X, C, F) CTRL-OR sets the right margin and enables word wrap, reformatting, and centering. At the "Column:" prompt, enter the column number (2-255), or just press RETURN for the current cursor column. If the value entered conflicts with the current left margin, the left margin is removed. There are two special values for the right margin:

1 All formatting disabled (as in Nondocument-mode files)
0 Unlimited right margin: text can be reformatted to undo word wrap

CTRL-OL sets the left margin in an identical fashion. Of course, the value must be less than the current right margin; you may need to set the right margin first.

Note: Margins cannot be set in Nondocument mode; a left margin cannot be set in /X and /M modes. CTRL-OX temporarily releases the margins (resets them to 1), allowing you to type outside them. Use CTRL-OX again to restore the margins.

CTRL-OC centers the current line with respect to the margins, if they are set. CTRL-OF sets the current line flush right, if the right margin is set.

Matching Up Files (ALT-M) This command is used to locate small differences between two largely similar files (perhaps an earlier and a later revision of a text). To use it, you must first load these two files (ALT-L), split the screen between them (ALT-W), and position the cursors on corresponding lines in both files (for example, the top lines). Then press ALT-M.

Starting from the cursor positions, VDE searches for any differences between the files. If it finds one, VDE stops showing the differing passages side by side. If you want to continue, reposition the cursors to corresponding lines, if necessary, and press ALT-M again. If no further differences are found, VDE reports "Not Found".

Moving Around (arrow keys; CTRL-F, CTRL-A; CTRL-Q-R, C, I, L, N, P; ALT-O)
VDE supports two sets of arrow keys, which function interchangeably. The first is the actual IBM cursor keypad (the four arrow keys); the second is the WordStar "arrow key diamond" CTRL-E, CTRL-X, CTRL-D, CTRL-S.

Preceded by CTRL-Q, any arrow key moves more quickly to the top or bottom of the screen or to the left or right end of the line.

There are also two word-movement commands: CTRL-F moves right, to the start of the next word; CTRL-A moves left, to the start of the preceding or current word. Both have a maximum travel distance of 255 characters.

For quickly covering large distances, CTRL-QR and CTRL-QC move all the way to the beginning and the end of the file, respectively; CTRL-QI moves directly to a given page (for documents) or line (for nondocuments). In documents, CTRL-QL and CTRL-QN move to the start of the last page and the next page, respectively.

CTRL-QP returns the cursor to its position before the last command causing a large movement was executed. (CTRL-QP can be used again to cycle between these two positions in the file.)

Finally, the ALT-O command displays an "overview" bar at the top of the screen. The length of the bar corresponds to the file size, and the current position is marked so that you can see where you are. You can move the place marker to the left or the right with the arrow keys; the cursor remains in the original (current) position. To move to the selected position, press RETURN; press ESC to cancel. (If the file is empty or too small, ALT-O does not function.)

Multiple File (ALT-L, B, N, X, Q, C, P)   VDE allows you to edit several different files simultaneously, if you have enough memory. This can be initiated from the command line by specifying the filenames separated by commas.

To load additional files, press ALT-L. You may specify a single filename or a list delimited with commas (see Syntax); for an untitled file, press CTRL-J or CTRL-RETURN. You can also access the file browser with RETURN or wildcards (see Files). (This command will fail if you run out of memory, if you are already editing the maximum number, or if another file by that name is in use.)

Once multiple files are in use, ALT-B and ALT-N can be used to cycle back and forth through the files being edited. If you quit or exit (CTRL-KQ, CTRL-KX) from one file, you will be returned to the preceding one.

ALT-X exits *all* files immediately, saving any changes made. ALT-Q quits *all* files immediately, without saving; if any of them have been modified, you will be prompted once to confirm the quit.

ALT-C cuts a marked block of text, placing it in a buffer for later recovery. (The original remains, unless you delete it with CTRL-KY.) ALT-P pastes in the previously cut text at the cursor position. The text in the buffer remains available for further pasting. (Cut and paste thus allow copying and moving blocks between files.)

Pagination (CTRL-OP; CTRL-PL)   The CTRL-OP command sets the page length. Enter a value from 0 through 255 lines, or just press RETURN to restore the default. (normally 56.)

When the value is nonzero, it determines the page and line shown in the document header ("Pg *xx* Ln *xx*"), and all page functions in the Print routine (pagination, headers, start/stop at page) are enabled. A form feed will be sent after printing. (VDE does not send a form feed before printing; install one in your printer initialization if you want.)

When the value is zero, pagination is off. The header will say "Pg 0 Ln xxxx", showing you the absolute line number in the file. Also, printing occurs with no page breaks. (This is useful for printing small blocks of text right after each other on the same sheet or, in conjunction with the * option, printing out multiple copies of index cards, labels, and so on.)

The CTRL-PL command embeds a form feed (CTRL-L) in the text. This code functions as a page break: you can type CTRL-PL at the start of a line to begin a new page. In document-file modes, this will be reflected in the header page/line count, use of CTRL-QI and other page-related commands, and so on; it does not affect line count in nondocuments or when pagination is off (CTRL-OP 0).

Place Markers (CTRL-PZ; CTRL-QZ)   You can set any number of temporary place markers in the text with CTRL-PZ (they display as highlighted Z). The CTRL-QZ command moves the cursor to the next place marker in the file, cycling back to the top of the file as needed. (Place markers are *not* saved to disk.)

Printer Codes (CTRL-P)   This command prefix is used to enter "control codes" in the ASCII range 00-1F or 7F into the text, usually for purposes of printer control. Most codes are entered in a standard fashion: CTRL-P@ embeds ^@, CTRL-PA embeds ^A, and so on; and in documents they display as highlighted letters—@, A, and so on (in nondocuments, they display as graphics). There are exceptions 1A: (CTRL-Z) can be entered as a graphic only with ALT-G (see Graphics), not with CTRL-PZ (see Place Markers above). Many programs treat this code as an end-of-file marker—use caution. 06 (CTRL-F) displays as the # marker (see Auto Numbering). 1C-1F,7F (CTRL-\ ,CTRL-] ,CTRL-^, CTRL-_, DEL) always display as graphics.

The IBM extended codes 80-FF also must be entered with ALT-G. Several common control codes produce special effects:

CTRL-P or CTRL-I	Hard (ASCII) tab; printers respond variously to this.
CTRL-L	Form feed; will cause a page break.
CTRL-H	Backspace; will overstrike previous character.
CTRL-M	Carriage return; enters a return without a line feed to overstrike line (do not hit another RETURN after this; just continue typing).

The codes below do not operate in nondocuments. CTRL-P CTRL-G causes printing to pause, with ^PG in the display, until you press RETURN to continue. This allows you to adjust the platen for printing various forms.

Note: On many dot matrix printers, codes can be used only at the start of a line.

In addition, in place of complex "escape sequences" for effects such as underlining in document files, VDE lets you enter a single marker, which is translated into the proper code during printing. VDE supports a set of 13 codes for this purpose—seven toggles and six switches. (See VINST.DOC on how to install the proper commands for your printer. Without such installation, only CTRL-PS and CTRL-PX will work.) The conventional WordStar meanings of these codes are

CTRL-P CTRL-B	Boldface
CTRL-P CTRL-Q	User definition 1
CTRL-D	Doublestrike
CTRL-W	User definition 2
CTRL-S	Underline
CTRL-E	User 3
CTRL-Y	Italic ("ribbon")
CTRL-R	User definition 4
CTRL-T	Superscript
CTRL-A	Alternate pitch
CTRL-V	Subscript
CTRL-N	Standard pitch
CTRL-X	Strikeout

Toggles are good for features like underlining that are turned on and off; enter them at the beginning and the end of the desired text. Switches are better for multivalued parameters like character pitch; enter them once. For example, using CTRL-PS for underlining, you could type: **This is how you get** CTRL-PS **underlined text** CTRL-PS **in VDE.** If toggles are not properly paired, you will find print effects continuing throughout the rest of your document. To save time and effort, use the CTRL-KI command to check for this before printing. If an S appears under the "^Check" heading, there is an unpaired CTRL-S somewhere.)

Printer Drivers (ALT-V) Since many people use more than one kind of printer, VDE accommodates two different printer drivers: a primary and an alternate. (You can change the two drivers with VINST.) Before printing a file, you can select one to be active using the ALT-V command.

Printing (CTRL-KP) The CTRL-KP command prints the file from memory. You will be prompted for options, at which point you may enter one or more of the following, in any order:

'...'	Sends a string of escape commands to the printer before printing. These must be entered in ASCII format: Type in the actual characters or control codes. (For control codes, 01 = ^A, 02 = ^B, and so on. Some will require the ^P prefix: 00 (^@) = ^P@, and so on. You may find an ASCII table in your printer manual.)
Tnn	Sets the top margin to nn lines; the default can be set with VINST.
Lnn	Sets the left margin to nn columns; the default can be set with VINST.
D	Double-spaces the printout.
^	Filters control characters so that they print out as text; for example, CTRL-X prints as ^X.
*nn	Prints the entire job out nn times (up to 255).
P	Pauses for your keystroke before each page (sheet feed).
B	Prints only the currently marked Block.

(filename)	Redirects printer output to a disk file. All print control codes will go into the file just as they would have been sent to your printer. If you want to append the output to an existing file, type a + before the name: (+filename).
N	Numbers pages sequentially at the top right.
C	Numbers pages at bottom center.
"..."	Uses the quoted string as a header. The string will print in the top right corner of each page, followed by the page number if N is selected. Maximum length is 50 characters. *Note:* you can include the current time or date in the header by entering CTRL-T or CTRL-D, respectively.
S	Suppresses the header or page number on the first page of output.
@*nn*	Begins printing at page *nn*.
#*nn*	Prints only (up to) a total of *nn* pages.
O,E	Prints only odd or only even pages. (For double-sided printing, print one, and then run the paper back through and print the other.)
=*nn*	Makes the first page number show as *nn*.

The paging options (N/C, @, #, O/E, =,) are not allowed if the page length is set to 0 (CTRL-OP), or if block print was chosen. C cannot be used with N or . . . .

EXAMPLE 1:   Options: L12P

will print the file with a left margin of 12, pausing before each page until you press a key (other than ESC).

EXAMPLE 2:   Options: @6#2=21(CTRL-T) Instructions, pageN

will print the sixth and seventh pages, numbering them 21 and 22, with a header like this: (3:41 PM) Instructions, page 21.

EXAMPLE 3:   Options: BD(+SCRATCH)

will append the print output of the current marked Block, double-spaced, to the disk file SCRATCH.

The left margin setting (set with L*nn* or VINST) is in columns, and its width will vary according to the font in use. If you need a fixed margin, it is better to find your printer's ESC command for a left margin setting in inches or dot columns and add this to your printer initialization string.

If you are in W or 5 file mode, any dot commands in the file (lines beginning with .) will not be printed. You can abort printing at any time by pressing ESC.

Proportional Spacing (CTRL-OJ)   If your printer has a proportionally spaced font, you can get VDE to use it and to format text so that it will print with more appropriate margins. With CTRL-OJ on, your printer will be put in proportional mode when printing (CTRL-KP). All word wrap and reformatting (CTRL-B, CTRL-OC, CTRL-OF) will take advantage of a built-in table of character widths, resulting in a better-justified printout.

Run Command/Shell (ALT-R)   Typing ALT-R causes VDE to produce a replica of the DOS prompt (for example, C:\WORK>). At this point, you are still in VDE, and all its input rules apply (for example, you can press CTRL-U to cancel) but you can execute any command just as you would under MS-DOS. You can copy or rename files or run any other program you like; when you are finished, VDE prompts you to press ESC (or the SPACEBAR) to return to your intact VDE editing session. VDE leaves no disk files open, so you can do anything you like with an ALT-R command. (*Exception*: Don't load new memory-resident utilities, as this fouls up the DOS memory allocation.)

In addition, there is a special VDE command that can be typed at this "fake DOS" prompt: SHELL. This lets you out into what is known as a command shell. You are actually back in MS-DOS, and can use any number of commands or move around as you like. When you are through, type **exit** to leave the shell. At that point, you will be back in VDE and will see the "Press ESC" prompt to return to editing.

VDE must be able to find your command interpreter (usually COM-MAND.COM), and there must be enough free memory to load it and run the chosen program. VDE reads the COMSPEC environment variable; if your CONFIG.SYS file doesn't include a line similar to SET COMSPEC=C:\COMMAND.COM, you should add one.

Using the ALT-R command in macros is tricky. Any keyboard input expected by the program or shell must be typed by you; it will not be taken from the macro. And you must remember to include in your macro the ESC keystroke needed to return to editing in VDE after it finishes.

Save/Exit (CTRL-K-N, S, X, D, Q)   CTRL-KN renames your work. This allows you to change the filename in the header before saving. It accepts mode options; you can also specify a mode alone (for example, /W) simply to change the current mode. *Caution*: If you give the name of a file that already exists, it will be overwritten.

CTRL-KS saves your work; what's in memory is written to disk under the filename in the header. (You must have a filename; one will be requested if necessary.) If the file has not been modified, you will be prompted to confirm whether you meant to resave it.

A copy of the existing file is preserved as a backup file (with extension BAK) each time you save changes. (If you prefer not to use BAK files, you can suppress their use with VINST.)

There are several different commands for finishing up:

CTRL-KX   Saves your work (if modified) and then exits to DOS.
CTRL-KD   (Done) Saves your work, and then loads a new file to edit.
CTRL-KQ   Quits without saving to disk. If the file has been modified, you will be prompted to confirm that you meant to do this.

Screen Controls (CTRL-W, CTRL-Z; ESC^, v, <, >; CTRL-O-E, D, Z; ALT-E, A)   VDE provides a number of commands affecting the screen display.

The CTRL-W and CTRL-Z commands scroll the screen up and down a line at a time, without moving the cursor in the text (unless necessary).

Preceded by ESC, any arrow key shifts the screen, leaving the cursor in place. The text view moves up or down one-quarter screen or right or left 32 columns. (The cursor must be past column 32 to allow horizontal shifts.)

Preceded by CTRL-O, either the UP ARROW key or CTRL-OE makes the current text line the top of the screen.

The CTRL-OD command shows you a preview of the screen with all non-printing codes (markers, CTRL-P codes, and so on) hidden. This is handy for making sure that text is aligned properly. Press ESC to continue editing.

The CTRL-OZ command temporarily "zaps" (blanks) the entire screen. This is good for avoiding CRT burn-in or just protecting work from prying eyes or fingers. Restore the screen by pressing ESC. This is also useful if some other software (such as a resident utility) has messed up the screen: Press CTRL-OZ and ESC, and VDE will completely restore it.

The ALT-E command lets you see more lines of text on the screen. It toggles between normal, 25-line mode and a compressed mode of 43 (EGA) or 50 (VGA) lines.

The ALT-A command toggles between normal, 80-column mode and wide, 132-column mode. It can be used alone or in combination with ALT-E to provide a 43- or 50-by-132 screen. (This command works *only* on certain VGA or EGA cards; see Installation in VINST.DOC to specify what kind you have.)

Splitting Files (ALT-S) If you encounter a text file that is too large for VDE to load and edit, you can divide it into manageable chunks with the Split command. Suppose you have a big file, HUGE.DOC. Type ALT-S, and then answer at the prompt:

```
Split file, output name (w/#): HUGE.DOC, PIECE.#
```

VDE will go through the file HUGE.DOC and write out a series of smaller files named PIECE.1, PIECE.2 and so on, which can then be edited. (You can tidy up the transitions between them with Cut and Paste, if you like.)

Note that the output name must be separated from the input name by a comma, and it must contain one # sign. This sign will be replaced by 1, 2, and so on, in sequence. (The example above could have used HUGE-#.DOC as the output name.) Make sure you have enough disk space for the output files.

Tabs (TAB, SHIFT-TAB, ESC-TAB; CTRL-O-V, I, N) There are two tab modes, Variable and Hard; the CTRL-OV command toggles between them. In Hard Tab mode, the TAB key produces an actual CTRL-I (ASCII tab). Whether this overwrites any existing text depends on the Insert toggle. Hard tabs display at fixed intervals of eight screen columns.

In Variable Tab mode, the TAB key moves the cursor to the next variable tab stop. Existing text is not overwritten; spaces are added at the end of a line as needed. Up to eight tab stops may be set with CTRL-OI and cleared with CTRL-ON. The defaults are in columns 5, 15, 35, and 55; these are reconfigurable. The SHIFT-TAB command tabs backward (left); it is useful for moving around in tables.

You can always get a hard tab with CTRL-PI, or a variable tab with ESC-TAB, no matter what tab mode you are in.

The set and clear commands prompt you for a column number; or you can press RETURN for the current cursor column. In addition, the Set command CTRL-OI accepts two further options, both of which replace all earlier tab settings:

@*nn*   Sets tabs every *nn* columns
#*n*1, *n*2,. . .   Sets tabs to columns *n*1, *n*2, . . .

You can clear all variable tabs by typing @ or # alone.

Time/Date (ALT-T, D)   If your MS-DOS maintains the system clock properly, VDE can read it and insert the current time and date in your file automatically. Just press ALT-T for the time, or ALT-D for the date. The string will appear at the current cursor location, as though you had typed it in yourself. For example,

> 1:21 PM   (or 13:21 — the format can be selected)
> January 15, 1988 (or 1/15/88, 15 January 1988, or 15.1.88)

Undeleting (CTRL-U)   The Undelete function can be used to recover any amount of text lost by the last deletion operation (whether a character, word, line, or block). This includes an overstruck character. The text is inserted at the current cursor location.

Uppercase/Lowercase (CTRL-^; CTRL-K,',^)   The CTRL-^ (or CTRL-6) command reverses the case of the letter character at the cursor and moves to the next character.

The CTRL-^ command reverses all text in a marked block (see Block Commands); CTRL-K makes all block text uppercase; CTRL-K' makes it lowercase.

Windows (CTRL-OW; ALT-W,F; CTRL-PGUP, PGDN)   VDE can split the screen into two windows, showing you either two parts of the same file or two different files. ALT-F moves the cursor back and forth between the two windows. The CTRL-PGUP and CTRL-PGDN key combinations can scroll through both windows in synchronization.

The CTRL-OW command is used in a single file, creating a window in the bottom half of the screen and duplicating the current file text in it. You can move to a different place in the file within this window and continue editing, with the original text still in view in the top window. (*Note:* Any modifications made to the file will not be reflected in the inactive window until you return to it.) Pressing CTRL-OW again removes the window.

The ALT-W command splits the screen window between the two different files being edited, showing you both at once. (If the file you get in the window isn't the one you want, find it by cycling through the files with ALT-B/ALT-N.) Pressing ALT-W again restores full-screen editing.

Word Wrap and Reformat (CTRL-B, CTRL-OB)   Word wrap is automatic in all document modes whenever the right margin is set; any text entered is kept within the current margin settings. The end of a paragraph is marked by a hard return when you press the RETURN key. (This is a carriage return immediately following a nonspace.) In contrast, when word wrap occurs, you get a soft return that is actually a return with a space before it).

You can change a hard return into a soft one or vice versa by deleting or adding a space at the end of the line; hitting RETURN also hardens a soft return. The distinction between hard and soft returns is important only when reformatting.

General Information/Tips

Multitasking   VDE should be compatible with multitasking environments, including DESQview. In order for VDE to run properly in a DESQview window, you must identify it as a "program that writes directly to the screen."

Compatibility   VDE is compatible, to varying degrees, with several other word processors, including WordStar, WordPerfect, XyWrite, and Microsoft Word. It can be a handy accessory for users of these programs. (See File Modes.)

WordStar is highly compatible. /W file mode supports all WS version 3 and 4 features except right justification, which it removes. /5 file mode also removes all the additional WS 5 embedded codes (formatting, fonts and so on) that are not supported in VDE. With these exceptions, document files can be exchanged freely between VDE and WS.

Aside from the absence of a "No-File" menu, VDE operates very much like WS, although it does lack some WS commands and has some new ones of its own. VDE's macro commands are completely different. (They were developed before WS had macros!)

Note also that, VDE does not obey WS "dot commands" in text, although in /W or /5 mode it will avoid printing them. You can get a page break (WordStar .PA) in VDE with the CTRL-PL command.

WordPerfect has limited compatibility. /P file mode reads files created by WP versions 4.X or 5.X, recognizing margin changes and print codes for bold, underline, superscript, subscript, and overstrike. No other formatting features are supported; if any are present in the file, the results will be unpredictable. /P mode writes text that can be read by WP.

You can also edit in VDE using a command set much like Word-Perfect's, by loading the WP.VDF key-definition file (see VINST.DOC). It causes the function keys to call up the menu bar in a manner similar to WP's commands.

XyWrite has limited compatibility, too. /X mode reads files created by XW and recognizes margin changes and print codes for bold, underline, and italics. No other formatting features are supported; if any are present in the file, the results will be unpredictable. /X mode writes text that can be read by XW.

Microsoft Word also has limited compatibility. /M mode reads files created by version 5; it does not support any print effects or formatting features. /M mode writes text that can be read by Word.

Note: /P, /X, and /M modes are intended for exchange of text only, with a limited set of print effects. They do not offer full compatibility with the respective word processors.

Directories   During editing with VDE, the default directory assumed by the file commands (CTRL-KL, R, N, F, J; ALT-L) is that of the current file; with multiple files, this can differ from one to the next. The directory is not displayed in the header, but it can be seen with CTRL-KI or at the CTRL-KF prompt. The current DOS directory remains unchanged, and it is the default when you use the ALT-R command. (You can change it with CHDIR under ALT-R.)

Error Messages   Press ESC or SPACEBAR to continue. "Error" alone means the command used just won't work in this situation. (For example, a block command was used with no block marked.) More specific error messages are

Out of Memory	The file, block, or key string won't fit in RAM.
Invalid Key	An illegal command key sequence was pressed.
Invalid Name/Path	The file was not read or written because the path does not exist or the filename is a duplicate or an "illegal" name.
No File	The file was not found.
I/O Error	Read or write error, disk full, invalid drive, and so on.

Cannot Reformat A word is too long, or the margins are invalid.
Not Found The object of a search was not found.
Graphics Overflow The file has too many graphics to fit in the table.
Macro Error A programming command was misused, or there was a recording overflow.

Important Note: On DOS 2.X systems, an attempt to access an empty disk drive or to print when the printer is not online can produce a critical error message directly from DOS—something like "Device not ready; Ignore, Retry, or Abort?" If this happens, correct the situation and press R for "Retry." Pressing I usually has no effect. Do *not* press A, as this will exit from VDE back to DOS, losing any text in memory!

If, after you recover from such an error, the message is still on screen, you can press CTRL-OZ, ESC to redisplay your text.

File Modes VDE has seven file modes: (A)SCII, (W)ordStar, WordStar (5), Word(P)erfect, (X)yWrite, (M)icrosoft Word, and (N)ondocument. In general, the document modes all have word wrap, pagination, and variable tabs; nondocuments do not have word wrap or pagination, and they have hard tabs.

The file-mode option can be specified along with the filename at any VDE file-function prompt (such as "Read in file:"), allowing you to read or write text in whatever format needed. (The default mode is /A, but this can be changed, and exceptions declared, with VINST.)

Most VDE users will select /A mode for documents (word processing) or /N mode for programming and other special applications. Both modes use plain ASCII text files, which are produced or accepted by virtually all software (DOS, compilers, data base, telcom, and so on).

The /W, /5, /P, and /M modes allow VDE to read and write WordStar, WordPerfect, or Microsoft Word files (see Compatibility).

The /X mode uses plain ASCII text but without returns at the ends of lines—returns occur only at the ends of paragraphs. These files can be exchanged with XyWrite and most other word processors that use this text-stream format (again, see Compatibility).

You can easily use VDE to mix text from several different formats or to convert a file from one format into another. Just specify the appropriate mode with each file loaded or read in, or change to the appropriate mode with CTRL-KN before saving. (Note the limits on supported features in each format, described earlier.)

Memory   VDE allocates memory for a file according to need, up to a maximum of 64KB (1KB = 1024 bytes). If you check the usage of memory (CTRL-KI) you will find that VDE compresses text: A file typically occupies 20 to 25 percent less memory than its actual size. Thus, the largest file that can be edited with VDE in 64KB is roughly 80KB.

VDE runs well with anywhere from 128KB to 640KB of RAM; the number and size of files you can edit depends on the amount of memory you have. If you are running short of memory while editing, try exiting files you no longer need or cutting (with ALT-C) an empty block to empty the cut buffer.

Running a DOS command requires enough free memory (beyond VDE's usage) to load a copy of COMMAND.COM and any programs you intend to run under it. You may not have enough memory to do this if you are editing many files with VDE or if you have lots of memory-resident software installed.

Prompts   First, VDE has several simple prompts requiring you to confirm an action by typing **Y** or **N**. The following warning messages appear on line 1 (though they are *not* given when a macro is running):

Abandon changes?	A file you want to quit has been changed.
Unchanged; save?	The file you want to save hasn't been changed.
File exists; overwrite?	Such a file already exists and will be lost.
Not recoverable; delete?	The block to delete is too big for undeletion.

The following confirmation prompts appear at the right edge of the header:

Chg?	Change this instance of a string? (Y/N/*)
Remove?	Remove this hyphen? (Y/N/ESC)
Rdy	Press a key to print next page. (ESC quits)

There are a number of standard prompts for either numeric or string input; for example, "Column:" or "Find string:". You are expected to type in a string (up to 65 characters). The following control keys operate this way:

BACKSPACE (CTRL-H)	Correct error.
RETURN (CTRL-M or CTRL-J)	Finish entry.

CTRL-R	Replay last filename (except in macro strings).
CTRL-X	Erase entire entry.
CTRL-U	Abort operation.

Note that to get any of these codes, including CTRL-P into the string itself, you must precede it with CTRL-P. For example, to find a line beginning with an asterisk, type ^QF^P RETURN * RETURN. Graphics can also be entered into strings using ALT-G.

For further information, see VINST.DOC for information on MACROS and the use of VINST or VDE.UPD for version history, including recent changes.

Write Protect Disks, Barry Emerson, Golden Bow Systems

WPD   COM   800   4-12-90   1:00a

WPD is a compact utility that lets you write-protect or write-enable any drive (floppy, hard, or virtual). WPD can help reduce the possibility of accidentally formatting a disk, and prevent new programs or users from making undesired disk writes. The format for WPD is

WPD [+/− *drive*]

You can have multiple drives on the command line, but each one must have a plus or minus sign preceding it. If you enable and disable the same drive, WPD will honor the last request received.

The minus sign and a drive letter will not write-protect the disk (or will enable it.) The plus sign will write-protect the disk or disable it. Up to 36 drives can be specified on the same command line.

A system reboot returns all drives to their original, write-enabled state. WPD will not conflict with most well-behaved programs. If you have problems, reboot the system.

WPD monitors DOS interrupt 13H. When a program tries to write to a write-protected drive, the standard DOS write-protect error message appears. Where logical drives are mapped to the same physical drive, they will be enabled or disabled as a group. When you execute WPD, the status of each of the drives in your command line will be displayed.

Running WPD—or any program that intercepts DOS INT 13H—may trigger warnings from TSR antivirus programs. You may want to disable any TSR antivirus program or load it after WPD.

WPD is a TSR program that occupies only 400 bytes of RAM and 800 bytes of disk space. Call for a free catalog and a special offer for their VCACHE and VFEATURE products.

Golden Bow Systems
P.O. Box 3039
San Diego, CA 92103
619-483-0901

XTREE4, DOS Shell, and File Manager

The documentation for XTree is included in the program disk. The files XTDOC1.COM and XTDOC2.COM are self-displaying DOC files with wordprocessor-like functions. These display programs allow you to view them, convert them to text files, or output them to your printer.

To start the program, simply type **XTREE** at the DOS prompt. If the program doesn't run, it may need to first be configured. You can do this by typing **XTREEPATH**. Refer to the installation instructions and the documentation on disk for further instructions.

The manuscript for this book was prepared and submitted to
Osborne/McGraw-Hill in electronic form. The acquisitions editor
for this project was Jeffrey Pepper, the technical reviewer was
Jeff Nelson, and the project editor was Madhu Prasher.

Text design by Stefany Otis and Cheryl Tucker, using Century
Expanded for text body and for display.

Cover art by Bay Graphics Design Associates. Color separation
and cover supplier, Phoenix Color Corporation. Screens
produced with InSet, from InSet Systems, Inc. Book printed
and bound by R.R. Donnelley & Sons Company,
Crawfordsville, Indiana.

4DOS—Power at the DOS Prompt

4DOS helps you get the most out of your PC. It replaces COMMAND.COM, the command interpreter that comes with all versions of DOS. You'll find **4DOS** provides many capabilities COMMAND.COM can't, including

- On-line help for all **4DOS** and DOS commands

- Command line editing with full cursor key support

- Recall, editing, and reexecution of previous commands

- Shorthand names (*aliases*) for commonly used sequences of commands

- Enhanced internal commands, including vastly more powerful COPY and DIR commands

- Over 40 new internal commands, including COLOR, LIST, MOVE, TIMER, and many more

- Descriptions of up to 40 characters for any file

- A rich batch file language, including IF / THEN / ELSE capability, box and line drawing, and prompted user input

- Batch file processing up to five times faster than COMMAND.COM

- Point-and-shoot file selection for any command

- Swapping to XMS, EMS, or disk to reduce resident memory requirements

4DOS is compatible with COMMAND.COM, and requires less than 3K of DOS memory while your applications are running—as little as 256 bytes if your system has "load high" capability!

4DOS is a trademark of J.P. Software.

4DOS ORDER FORM

See for yourself—try the shareware product that won finalist honors in *PC Magazine*'s 1989 Technical Excellence Awards! *4DOS* is just $45 with this coupon—a 10% discount off the regular price of $50. Shipping and handling: $4 U.S., $5 Canada, $10 others.

Name _____

Company _____

Address _____

City _____ State ____ Zip/Postal Code _____

Phone (____) _____ Disks: ____ 5.25" ____ 3.5"

____ Check or money order enclosed   ____ VISA   ____ MasterCard
____ American Express

Acct. no. _____ Exp. date _____

Signature _____

Print name on card _____

To order by phone, call 617-646-3975

J.P. Software
P.O. Box 1470
East Arlington, MA 02174

✂ Clip Here ✂

❏ Send Me Check✓It© & Basic PC Maintenance Hands-On Video™for $129.95 ($179.95 Value) Save $50 With This Coupon.

Here is how to order your copy of Check✓It & Basic PC Maintenance:

1. Fill out order form completely.
2. Include method of payment.
3. Mail to: TouchStone Software Corp.
   "Special Order Desk"
   2130 Main Street, Suite 250
   Huntington Beach, CA 92648
4. Or Call NOW
   ☎ (800) 531-0450
   (714) 969-7746 inside CA

Ship To:

Name _____

Phone _____

Address _____
_____

City _____ State _____ Zip Code

Please Calculate Your Total

Check✓It & Basic PC Maintenance Video

$ _____ = _____ x$129.95 each
              # of units

+ $ _____ $5.00 Shipping & Handling

= $ _____   Subtotal

+ $ _____   Sales Tax
             (California Residents
             ONLY add 6.25%)

= $ _____   **TOTAL**

Payment Information:
   ❏ Check Enclosed
(Make check payable to: TouchStone Software Corp.) NO C.O.D.
   ❏ Visa   ❏ Mastercard

Account Number _____

Expiration Date _____

Print Name _____

Signature (as on card) _____

FIFTH GENERATION SYSTEMS

SPECIAL OFFER

Direct Access v 5.0

This Menu Generator makes DOS easier for everyone. This top rated menu program is *PC Magazines* Editor's Choice. Through this offer, any book owner may get the complete Direct Access for only $49.50

Please Print

Company _____

Name _____

Title _____

Address _____

City _____ State _____ Zip _____

Day Phone ( ) _____

Disk Size Required: ❑ 5 1⁄4 ❑ 3 1⁄2

PAYMENT METHOD
❑ Check ❑ Money order
❑ VISA ❑ Mastercard ❑ American Express

Check # _____

Card # _____

Expires _____/_____

Signature _____

NOTE: Please make sure the order form is filled out correctly. Quantities limited to one unit only on our Special Offers. Then, enclose this order card in an envelope and mail to:

FIFTH GENERATION SYSTEMS
ATTN: BOOKWARE SPECIAL OFFER
P. O. Box 83260
Baton Rouge, LA 70884-0359 U.S.A.

ITEM #	PC Special Offer	Special PRICE	AMOUNT
100	Direct Access v 5.0	$49.50	
	Sales Tax (Residents of LA, GA, TX, CA, NY and the District of Columbia must add applicable tax.)		
	Shipping & Handling (only if destination is outside Continental U.S.A. & Canada)	$15.00	
		TOTAL	

Please allow 4 weeks delivery.
Sorry, no PO's or COD's accepted.
For a limited time only — Act Now!

you can also place your order by phone:
1-800-873-4384

BACK OFF!

To order a registered version of **BACK OFF!**, return this form with a CHECK or MONEY ORDER for $12 (U.S.) to:

JB TECHNOLOGY INC.
28701 N. MAIN ST.
RIDGEFIELD, WA. 98642

Complete and return this order form to be granted a single user license.

After receiving **BACK OFF!**, you may make copies for backup purposes and operate the program on any computer, provided only one user and one copy of the program are in use at any one time.

FIND DUPLICATES

To order a registered version of **FIND DUPLICATES**, return this form with a CHECK or MONEY ORDER for $12 (U.S.) to:

JB TECHNOLOGY INC.
28701 N. MAIN ST.
RIDGEFIELD, WA. 98642

Complete and return this order form to be granted a single user license.

After receiving **FIND DUPLICATES**, you may make copies for backup purposes and operate the program on any computer, provided only one user and one copy of the program are in use at any one time.

Single User Order Form

I am enclosing my fee of $12.00, for the latest version of **BACK OFF!**.

Name _____

Company _____

Street address _____

City _____

State _____ Zip _____

Check disk format 3.5″ 720K _____ 5.25″ 360K _____

Osborne **McGraw-Hill** assumes NO responsibility for the fulfillment of this offer.

Single User Order Form

I am enclosing my fee of $12.00, for the latest version of **FIND DUPLICATES**.

Name _____

Company _____

Street address _____

City _____

State _____ Zip _____

Check disk format 3.5″ 720K _____ 5.25″ 360K _____

Osborne **McGraw-Hill** assumes NO responsibility for the fulfillment of this offer.

DR DOS. 5.0. SPECIAL OFFER. $64.95.

- MemoryMAX. – Provides 620K or more for applications.
- ViewMAX. – Graphical user interface, use with keyboard or mouse.
- Menu-Driven – easy to load and change system configuration without reformatting hard disk.
- Large Disk Support – Allows partitions larger than 32MB.
- FileLINK. – Easy data transfer between two computers.
- Disk Cache – Faster file access with full security.

For more information, call Digital Research Inc. (800) 443-4200.

DR DOS 5.0
 Digital Research®
WE MAKE COMPUTERS WORK

Protect Your Data From A Computer Virus

You never know when a hard disk catastrophe might strike. Or when you could pick up a computer virus from an electronic bulletin board or public domain software.

You Need Protection

That's why you need the protection of our Jumbo Tape Backup System. Jumbo stores as much as 120 MB of data on a cartridge about the size of a deck of playing cards.

It works with almost all IBM computers and compatibles, including 386 and 486 based machines. Jumbo installs easily and can backup an entire 40MB drive in less than 20 minutes.

Jumbo comes complete, too, with the drive and all software, along with installation and operation manuals. Find out how easily you could protect your vital data. Just fill out the other side of this coupon, and mail it for a free demo diskette and complete details.

DR DOS 5.0. ORDER INFORMATION.

Name: _____

Company: _____

Address: _____

City: _____ State: _____ Zip: _____

Phone: _____

☐ Check enclosed   Charge to: ☐ MasterCard   ☐ VISA   ☐ American Express

Card Number: _____ Expiration Date: _____

Signature: _____

SEND TO: Digital Research
          DR DOS Dvorak Guide Offer
          Box DRI
          Monterey, CA 93942

Please allow 4–6 weeks for order processing. On orders from the following states, please add the indicated sales tax:

CA – 6.75%   NY – 8.25%   TX – 7.5%   VT – 4%

Payment must be made in U.S. currency. Limit one order per customer.

AMOUNT ENCLOSED:

DR DOS 5.0 _____ $64.95
(Price subject to change without notice)

Tax (if applicable): _____

Shipping/Handling _____ $5.00

Total: _____

SEND FOR YOUR FREE JUMBO DEMO DISK TODAY

To receive your free Jumbo Tape Backup demonstration diskette simply fill out and mail this coupon.

Name _____
Title _____
Company _____
Address _____
City _____
State/Zip _____
Phone Number _____

Mail Coupon To:
Colorado Memory Systems, Inc.
Dept. OS-002
800 South Taft Avenue
Loveland, Colorado 80537

SPOT 2.13 Registration Form

Please fill out the order form and send it with your payment to:

USA: Santronics Software
1451 Plymouth Ave.
Irwin, PA 15642

Check Option

☐ Single User Copy $15

☐ Network Users . . . . $10 per Copy   # of Copies _____ X $10 = _____

Full Name _____

Address _____

_____

_____

_____

Voice Phone Number (_____) _____ Hours _____

Order Form

Qty	Product	√ Send Info	5-$\frac{1}{4}$	3-$\frac{1}{2}$	Price Each	Totals
	DESQview 386 v2.3 Multitasking windowing environment	❏			$109.95	
	DESQview v2.3 Multitasking windowing environment	❏			$64.95	
	QEMM-386 version 5.1	❏			$49.95	
	QEMM-50/60 version 5.0	❏			$49.95	
	QRAM Memory optimizing utility	❏			$39.95	
	Quarterdeck Manifest Memory analyzer	❏			$29.95	

Shipping & Handling $5 in USA/varies outside USA

Mail coupon to: Quarterdeck
150 Pico Blvd, Santa Monica, CA 90405

California Residents add 6.75%

Grand Total

Payment ❏ Visa ❏ MasterCard Expires ____/____ Acct # ☐☐☐☐☐☐☐☐☐☐☐☐☐☐☐

Name _____ Title _____

Address _____

City _____ State _____ Zip _____

This coupon entitles the purchaser to a maximum of one each of the product(s) above at the listed prices when purchased direct from Quarterdeck under the following conditions: Check the product you wish to buy and return this coupon (no copies) to Quarterdeck Office Systems, 150 Pico Boulevard, Santa Monica, CA 90405.

Fill out credit card information or enclose a check made out to Quarterdeck for the price of the selected product plus $5 shipping and handling within the United States (call for shipping charges to other countries). Add 6.75% state sales tax to price of product shipped to California address. Offer good through December 31, 1991.

METHOD OF PAYMENT

☐ Cash ☐ Check ☐ Money Order ☐ MasterCard ☐ VISA

MasterCard/VISA Card Number _____

Expiration Date _____ 4 digits above name _____

Signature _____

Subtotal _____

(foreign checks) add $5.00 _____

Total _____

Put System Sleuth™ On The Case

With System Sleuth you can resolve hardware and software conflicts on your system quickly and easily. Standard features of System Sleuth include:

I/O Port Availability Map

Extended and Expanded Memory information

Terminate and Stay Resident (TSR) Program Reporting

Hardware Interrupt (IRQ) Status

Hardcopy Report Generator

On-Line Help and Tutorial Facilities

And Much More!

Free Utility Toolkit:

Findfile - Locates files across multiple drives

Findupes - Finds duplicate files

SSDiskcache - A hard disk caching program

SSEMS286 - Expanded and Extended memory management

GetCMOS/PutCMOS - Save and recover CMOS setup information

SSBackup - A high speed hard disk backup utility

SSEMS386 - Memory mangement for 80386 systems.

For more information about System Sleuth, WinSleuth - diagnostics for Windows 3.0, MacSleuth - diagnostics for the Apple Macintosh and the other fine products published by Dariana Technology Group, fill out the form on the reverse side of this card and mail in today

Special: System Sleuth PLUS the Utility Toolkit, for $99.00 (a $150.00) value.

Sydex

Diskette "Disk-Set"

Format - quick copy - analyze - repair - transmit! Our special package of proven software prepares, clones, and even repairs your diskette collection! Unbeatable performance!

ConFormat	This "background" diskette formatter lets you format diskettes while you're working on more important tasks.
FormatQM	Just made for back-up time. Fastest diskette formatter around; features "hands off" operation. Supports all DOS formats.
CopyQM	A diskette duplicating machine. Formats, copies and verifies in one pass from a master, with "hands off" convenience.
Anadisk	The "compleat" diskette utility. Scan, edit, copy or repair *any* diskette--even non-DOS ones!
Teledisk	Our diskette "FAX machine". Turn *any* diskette into a DOS file and then reconstruct the exact diskette from the file!

Regular registration price: $85.   **WITH THIS COUPON: $55.00**

Name _____

Address _____

_____

City _____ State _____ Zip _____

Phone _____

Intended Use: If Business, please include company name and address

Personal   ☐

Business   ☐

Dariana Technology Group, Inc.

6945 Hermosa Circle

Buena Park, CA 90620-2698

(714) 994-7400 (714) 994-7401 Fax

Order Form

☐ Sydex Diskette "Disk-Set" with documentation, **$55.00.**
Add **$5.00** shipping+handling inside U.S., **$10.00** outside.   _____

☐ The Sydex Shareware Sampler. Evaluation versions of
the "Disk Set" programs--and more! **$5.00** (S/H incl.)   _____

                                        TOTAL   _____

Name_____ Company _____

Street Address _____

City_____ State_____ Zip_____

☐ Check or money order enclosed   ☐ Charge my VISA or MASTERCARD:

Acct. No._____   Exp. Date _____

Signature_____

Send your order to: **Sydex**
P.O. Box 5700
Eugene, OR 97405
Allow 15 days for delivery.

I want the whole works!
The POWER TOOLBOX includes
MarxMenu
The DOS Toolbox
and *new* Directory Master 3 (DM3)

DM3 is our new highpowered file manager FOR POWER USERS.

SYSTEM REQUIREMENTS
All Computer Tyme products require a DOS compatible PC, running DOS 3.0 or later.
384K RAM and a hard disk drive.

ORDER FORM

Name _____

Company _____

Address _____

City _____ State _____ Zip _____

Country _____ Phone (_____) _____

❏ 5.25" disk   ❏ 3.5" disk

❏ Check   ❏ MasterCard   ❏ VISA   ❏ American Express   ❏ Discover

Card # _____ Expires _____

Signature _____

Support Group, Inc. • P.O. Box 130 • McHenry, MD 21541
(800) USA-GROUP • (301) 387-4500 • (301) 387-7322 (Fax)

"SUCH A DEAL" COUPON
ORDER FORM

Please send me _____ copies of the Power Toolbox, single user version at $99.95 each, regularly $150.00.

Please send me _____ copies of the Power Toolbox, network version, at $750.00 each, regularly $1,000.00.

(Add $3.00 shipping, $10.00 overseas, Missouri residents add 6.175% sales tax.)

❏ I need 3½ inch disk.

Computer Tyme

Name _____

Company _____

Address _____

City _____

State _____ Zip _____

Country _____

❏ Check enclosed

❏ Charge to my (circle one):   MasterCard   Visa

    Card No. _____

    Exp. Date _____

    Signature _____

Mail to: 216 S. Glenstone
        Springfield, MO 65802
        1-800-548-5353

Osborne **McGraw-Hill** assumes NO responsibility for the fulfillment of this offer.

AVAILABLE FROM DIGITAL PRESS
The VAX Users Series

THE VMS USER'S GUIDE
James F. Peters III and Patrick J. Holmay

Teaches, step-by-step, the major features of the VMS operating system. It covers in detail – files and directories, command procedures, two text editors, and the MAIL and PHONE utilities. Review quizzes, hands-on experiments, exercises, and summary tables reinforce newly acquired skills and serve as reference aids for the commands and utilities in the text.

1990/softcover/305 pages/$28.95, ISBN 0-13-502808-6, Part Number EY-6739E-DP-EAP

UNIX FOR VMS USERS
Philip E. Bourne

Intended for VAX users who are making the transition from the VMS to the UNIX operating system, this book follows a logical sequence from discussion of fundamental concepts and basic command procedures through the use of high-level languages, programming the operating system, text processing, and the networked communications.

1990/softcover/368 pages/$28.95, ISBN 0-13-947433-1, Part Number EY-C177E-DP-EAP

VAX/VMS : Writing Real Programs in DCL
Paul C. Anagnostopoulos

This book explains how to use the Digital Command Language (DCL) more effectively. The book begins where the VAX/VMS documentation leaves off and explains how to write large applications, describes pitfalls and how to avoid them, and presents paradigms to assist the serious user.

1989/softcover/409 pages/$29.95, ISBN 0-13-940256-X, Part Number EY-C168E-DP-EAP

A BEGINNER'S GUIDE TO VAX/VMS UTILITIES AND APPLICATIONS
Ronald M. Sawey and Troy T. Stokes

This is a book for the first-time user of the VMS operating system and contains information on thirteen popular applications. Students and other beginners will appreciate its concise and practical approach to such basic topics as: file maintenance, text editing and formatting, electronic communication, PC-to-VAX file transfers, spreadsheet calculations, simple databases, and programming.

1989/softcover/278 pages/$26.95, ISBN 0-13-072349-5, Part Number EY-6738E-DP-EAP

WORKING WITH WPS-PLUS
Charlotte Temple and Dolores Cordeiro

This is a user-level guide containing tips and tricks for anyone who has a basic understanding of word processing, using either the VAX or MS-DOS versions of WPS-PLUS. It is a reference book—intended for WPS-PLUS users while at the screen. It stresses the how rather than the why and shows how to implement time-saving and advanced techniques.

1990/softcover/235 pages/$24.95, ISBN 0-13-963141-0, Part Number EY-C198E-DP-EAP

Available directly from Digital Press or through your local technical/reference bookstore.

d|i|g|i|t|a|l ™
Digital Press
12 Crosby Drive
Bedford, MA 01730

digital™
Digital Press
ORDER FORM

Purchaser's Name: _____

Phone Number: _____ Date: _____

Method of Payment: ☐ Invoice upon Receipt   ☐ Check/Money Order

☐ VISA/MasterCard   ☐ DECPlan # _____

Charge Card Account No: _____ Expiration Date: _____

Card Owner's Name (printed): _____

Billing Address: Customer Code: _____

Company: _____

Dept/Attn: _____

Street: _____

City: _____ State _____ ZIP _____

Ship to Address: Ship to Code: _____

Company: _____

Department/Attention: _____

Street: _____

City: _____ State _____ ZIP _____ Purchase Order #: _____

Taxable: ☐ Yes   ☐ No   Tax Bond or Exempt #: _____

Tax Exempt Reason: _____

Shipping Method: ☐ Best Way Surface   ☐ Other _____

Transit Insurance: ($.60 per $100 order value) ☐ Yes   ☐ No

Ship:

_____ THE VMS USER'S GUIDE, $28.95, EY-6739E-DP-EAP   _____

_____ UNIX FOR VMS USERS, $28.95, EY-C177E-DP-EAP   _____

_____ WRITING REAL PROGRAMS IN DCL, $29.95, EY-C168E-DP-EAP   _____

_____ A BEGINNER'S GUIDE TO VAX/VMS, $26.95, EY-6738E-DP-EAP   _____

_____ WORKING WITH WPS-PLUS, $24.95, EY-C198E-DP-EAP   _____

Sales Tax: _____

Transit Insurance: _____

Total Due: _____

Prices are for U.S only and subject to change without notice.

Order from Digital Press, 12 Crosby Drive, BUO/E94, Bedford, MA 01730
or call 800-DIGITAL (800-344-4825)

Registration Forms and Coupons for Software on Disks

WHY YOU WANT BATCOM!

Wenham Software's *Batcom* is a batch file compiler that transforms your normal DOS batch files into ".exe" files. Compiled programs execute much **faster** than normal batch files, **protect your source code, add additional capabilities** to DOS, and give your batch programs a touch of professionalism never before possible!

Batcom speeds your DOS batch files by interpretting each command before it needs to be executed. DOS must read each statement from disk as it is executed; compiled batch programs load once and go. The result is batch file programs that execute up to **4 times faster** (and more) than normal batch files.

Batcom extends DOS with over 60 new commands:

- User defined variables.
- Powerful string functions.
- Read keyboard input.
- **AND MUCH MORE!**
- Arithmetic functions.
- 'While' looping.
- Subroutines.

Batcom compiles your batch files to small programs. A four choice menu program compiles to under 4000 bytes of memory. Try that with any other programming language!

In addition, compiled batch files are your property, and you may distribute them without restrictions and without paying royalties.

If you need more performance from your batch files, you need Wenham Software's *Batcom*. Only **$59.95**!

---

hyperkinetix, inc. is proud to offer you :

BUILDER
What batch should have been in the first place.

BUILDER is the upwardly compatible batch file compiler that transforms your vulnerable .BAT files into fast and secure .COM or .EXE files. It also extends the batch language with over 90 new commands and keywords.

- * Slick color PopUp, LightBar, and DropDown Menus
- * Full file I/O
- * Security for your batch files that DOS never had

BUILDER also includes a powerful editor to provide an integrated development environment a la Turbo Pascal. Hyper text on-line help and a linker are also included.

It's the perfect tool for creating intelligent installation scripts. It has DOS dexterity that BASIC and C can't match. And its small compiled code size won't hog memory or disk space.

(See reverse for special offer.)

YES! Send me Batcom NOW!

Name: _____ Company: _____
Address: _____
City: _____ State: _____ Zip: _____

Send me _____ at $59.95 each.   Total: _____

☐ Check or money order enclosed   ☐ Visa   ☐ MasterCard
Account # _____
Expiration Date _____ – _____
Name of Card Holder: _____

Send to:

Wenham Software Co.

5 Burley St.

Wenham, Ma. 01984

Or call: (508) 774–7036

Retail price: $149.95. **With this coupon: $99.95**

hyperkinetix, inc.
Builder Mail Order Form

Name: _____

Company: _____

Address: _____

City: _____ State: _____ Zip: _____

Country: _____ Phone: (   )_____

Please send me _____ copies of **Builder**™!

Payment type: _____ Check Enclosed   _____ COD

_____ Visa/Mastercard   Card #: _____

Name on card: _____ Exp Date: _____

Signature of card holder: _____

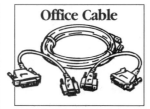

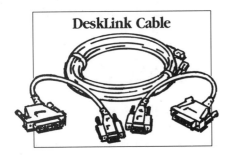

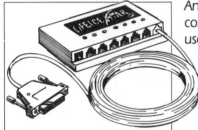

Tutor Software -- Offer & Registration

Modem Tutor ☐   Hard Disk Tutor ☐   CompuServe Tutor ☐

Name:

Company:

Address:

City: State: ZIP:

Day Phone: (   )   Eve. Phone: (   )

Computer Type: PC XT 286 386 486 PS/2 (circle one) Disk Size: 5.25" 3.5"

Brand: IBM   Compaq Other: _____   Video: MGA   CGA   EGA

Hard Disk: YES   NO (circle one) Comments:

Use this form for n/c registrations and orders. Enclose a check or money order made payable to **Computer Business Services** *for programs ordered. The cost is **$10 each or $25 for all three.** (California residents please add 6.75% sales tax.) Fill out both sides of this form. Please specify disk size, and include your street address – not just a post office box. Make sure you give us a phone number where we can reach you, too. Allow 2 - 3 weeks for delivery. Mail a copy of both sides of this and your payment to:*

Computer Business Services -- Special Tutor Software Offer,
1125 Bramford Court, Diamond Bar, CA 91765 (714) 860-6914

SUPER PC-KWIK (suggested retail price $79.95)

Super PC-Kwik uses advanced cache technology to improve read and write throughput from diskette, hard, and Bernoulli drives. Runs in conventional, expanded, or extended memory; caches up to 16 Mb.

PC-KWIK POWER PAK (suggested retail price $129.95)

PC-Kwik Power Pak is a performance enhancement package for PCs running DOS. It includes the Super PC-Kwik Disk Accelerator, RAM Disks, Print Spoolers, a Screen Accelerator with ReView and screen blanking, and a Keyboard Accelerator with ReDOS, a command-line editor.

PC-KWIK POWER DISK (suggested retail price $79.95)

PC-Kwik Power Disk is a high-performance file reorganizer and disk defragmenter, a data reliability test and repair utility, and a tool for viewing file structures on a disk.

Software Digest
Rated #1
(Vol. 6, No. 10)

PC MAGAZINE
EDITORS' CHOICE
February 14, 1989
Super PC Kwik, Version 3.08

Multisoft CORPORATION

PC MAGAZINE "BEST OF 1988"

PC WORLD
BEST BUY

Tutor LICENSE and REGISTRATION

These tutors are commercial products, NOT shareware, and may not be distributed in any form without express written consent from Computer Business Services.

Circle "register" on this form for any programs you received with one of our books. A $10 payment is required for any additional tutors ordered. Return your payment with a copy of both sides of this form.

After signing and returning a copy of both sides of this registration form along with any required payment, you may make copies of the registrated programs for backup purposes. You may operate the program(s) on any computer, provided only one user and one copy of the program(s) are in use at any one time.

We support our software. Many of the tutor's features are the result of user input. If you have any suggestions or comments, feel free to write us.

	Modem Tutor	$10	register	order	
	Hard Disk Tutor	$10	register	order	
	CompuServe Tutor	$10	register	order	
	All three programs	$25	register	order	
	Total for programs ordered				
	(California residents, please add 6.75% sales tax)				
	Disk Size: 5.25" 3.5"	Shipping and handling $4			
	(There is no charge to register the tutor programs you receive with one of our books.)			Total	

Computer Business Services -- Special Tutor Software Offer,
1125 Bramford Court, Diamond Bar, CA 91765 (714) 860-6914

Signature: _____   Date: _____

- -

MULTISOFT SPECIAL PRICING ORDER FORM

☐ SUPER PC-KWIK $45.00

☐ POWER PAK $75.00

☐ POWER DISK $45.00

☐ POWER PAK *and*

  POWER DISK $110.00

FAX Orders to: (503) 646-8267

Call Orders to: (503) 644-5644

Mail Orders to: **Multisoft Corporation**
15100 S.W. Koll Parkway
Dept. D5
Beaverton, OR 97006

Payment Information

☐ C.O.D. (add $3.30)   ☐ Check enclosed

☐ VISA ☐ MasterCard   ☐ American Express

Card number _____

Expiration date _____

Signature _____

Shipping Address

Name _____

Company _____

Address _____

City, ST, Zip _____

Day Phone _____

XTreePro Gold...

"the undisputed marathon winner among file managers"

—PC Magazine

Attention XTree users! You have a chance to upgrade to the most comprehensive file and hard disk management utility in the industry. XTreePro Gold creates an environment that helps you manage your files, directories and disks faster, yet just as easily as before. Now you can log up to 26 drives and 13,000 files, 7 times faster! No need to leave XTree to edit your files, XTreePro Gold has a built-in text editor.

XTreePro Gold now lets you easily view, extract, transfer, archive and encrypt files. Search multiple files by contents. Execute applications by selecting associated data files created by most popular word processing, dBASE and Lotus applications.

Additional features include Keystroke History, Prune and Graft, Split Screen displays and EGA/VGA support. "There is no better value than XTreePro Gold." (InfoWorld) Retail: $129

To upgrade your copy of XTree for only $40, simply fill out the coupon on the reverse side and send with your payment to:

XTREE COMPANY

Attn. Gold Upgrade
14 Inverness Dr.
Bldg. E Suite 104
Englewood, CO 80112

Or call 1-800-282-5003 to place your order over the phone 24 hours a day!

Here is your XTree registration card.

Completely fill out the form on the reverse side and send to:

XTREE COMPANY

Attn: Registration
4330 Santa Fe Road
San Luis Obispo, CA 93401

Special Offer for XTree Users

Here is your chance to participate in one of our special Upgrade offers. In order to take advantage of this offer, please send us your proof of purchase, (original diskette) with the coupon below and your payment. Then, we will send you your upgraded version within 3-4 weeks. Please fill out entire form.

UPGRADE FROM	UPGRADE TO	DISCOUNT PRICE
XTree	XTreePro Gold	$40 U.S.* ($42.50 for CA residents)

Name _____ Title _____

Company _____

Address _____

City _____ State _____ ZIP _____ Phone _____

Serial # MH100466 Country _____

Disk Size: 5.25" _____ 3.5" _____

Payment Method: (No P.O.'s please)

Check Enclosed: _____

Credit Card (circle one)   MC   VISA   American Express

Credit Card # _____ Exp date _____

(*International orders add $10.00 shipping charge)

Send your payment to:

X T R E E
C O M P A N Y

Attention: XTreePro Gold Upgrades
14 Inverness Drive East
Building E, Ste. 104
Englewood, CO 80112

XTree Registration Form

Thank you for registering your copy of XTree. To receive technical support, update information, and new product announcements, you must return this card. Your signature on this card indicates that you have read and agree to the terms of the license agreement.

PLEASE print clearly

Name _____

Address _____

City _____ State _____ ZIP _____

Company _____ Title _____

Home Ph (_____) _____ Work Ph (_____) _____

Computer Name _____ Model Number _____

Operating System _____

Date Purchased _____ XTree Serial # MH100466

How would you rate XTree's ability to help you manage your disk?
☐ Excellent   ☐ Good   ☐ Fair   ☐ Poor

What is your level of computer expertise?
☐ Novice   ☐ Intermediate   ☐ Expert

Was XTree purchased for use at
☐ Home   ☐ Business   ☐ Both

What computer peripherals do you use or own?
☐ Printer   ☐ Modem   ☐ Network (type) _____
☐ Other   ☐ Backup program   ☐ Mouse

Number of PC's in company?
☐ 0-5   ☐ 6-20   ☐ 21-100   ☐ 101 plus

Comments _____

Signature _____ Date _____

SITE LICENSE ORDER - VDE EDITOR

*"This may be the finest piece of word processing
code* **ever written**. *I have never been as* **impressed**
with anything as I have with VDE 1.5."
- John Dvorak, *PC Magazine* (24 April 1990)

Complete this card to order a commercial site license for
VDE. Along with the license your company will receive the latest
version of VDE, including utilities, examples, and manual, on
disk. Return this card with a check or money order to:

*Eric Meyer
3541 Smuggler Way
Boulder, Colorado 80303*

The license fee depends on the number of computers on which VDE
will be used; see reverse. (Personal use of VDE on an individual's
home computer does <u>not</u> require a site license.) Payment must be
in US dollars. Checks must be drawn through a US bank. Company
or government purchase orders are accepted. Sorry, no credit cards.

SITE LICENSE ORDER - VDE EDITOR

Check
box: Copies   Fee   <--- *Check box for quantity required.*

Check box	Copies	Fee	
|__|	Up to 20	$ 50	Payment is enclosed for a **site license**
|__|	" " 50	$100	**for commercial use** of the VDE editor on
|__|	" " 100	$150	the number of computers shown. The fee
|__|	" " 200	$200	includes disk, postage, and handling.

Date: _____   Ship to attention of: _____

Company name: _____

Street address: _____

_____

City, State: _____

Country, Postal code: _____

DVORAK'S PC-SIG FREE DISKS
ORDER FORM

Please send me:

Disk #3 (including Point and Shoot Backup and HDTEST programs
at no charge)   _____

All three disks decompressed at $10.00   _____

For 3 1/2-inch disks, check here   _____

If your **Disk #1** and/or **Disk #2** are defective or you need your **Disk #1** or **Disk #2** in
3 1/2-inch format, we will replace your disk free.

Yes. My **Disk #1** is defective. Please send me a free replacement.   _____

Yes. My **Disk #2** is defective. Please send me a free replacement.   _____

Yes. I need 3 1/2-inch format for my **Disk #1** and I am enclosing $2.00
for a replacement.   _____

Yes. I need 3 1/2-inch format for my **Disk #2** and I am enclosing $2.00
for a replacement.   _____

Shipping and handling $ 4.00

Total   _____

Payment by: ☐ Check   ☐ VISA   ☐ MC   ☐ Not Applicable

Card No. _____

Exp. Date _____

Name _____

Address _____

1030 D East Duane Ave., Sunnyvale, CA 94086. FAX: 408-730-2107

VISA/MasterCard Phone Orders: 800-245-6717 Ask for Operator #2222

Software Order Form

The preceding coupons are solely the responsibility of the manufacturers. Osborne **McGraw-Hill** takes NO responsibility for the fulfillment of these offers.